MATHPOWER™ 11

WESTERN EDITION

Teacher's Resource

Carryl Koe, B.Sc., M.A., Ed.D.
Delta, British Columbia

**McGraw-Hill
Ryerson**

Toronto Montréal New York Burr Ridge Bangkok Bogotá Caracas Lisbon London Madrid
Mexico City Milan New Delhi Seoul Singapore Sydney Taipei

McGraw-Hill
Ryerson Limited
A Subsidiary of The McGraw·Hill Companies

MATHPOWER™ *11, Western Edition*
Teacher's Resource

ISBN 0-07-552599-2

http//www.mcgrawhill.ca

1 2 3 4 5 6 7 8 9 0   JFM   99

Printed and bound in Canada

Care has been taken to trace ownership of copyright material contained in this text. The publishers will gladly take any information that will enable them to rectify any reference or credit in subsequent printings.

Claris and ClarisWorks are registered trademarks of Claris Corporation.
Microsoft® is a registered trademark of Microsoft Corporation.

Canadian Cataloguing in Publication Data

Koe, Carryl
  MATHPOWER™ 11, Western Edition, Teacher's Resource

ISBN 0-07-552599-2

1. Mathematics — Study and teaching (Secondary).   I. Title.   II. Title: Mathpower eleven, Western edition

QA107.M37649   1999   Suppl. 2   510   C99-931524-2

PUBLISHERS: Diane Wyman, Carol Altilia
DEVELOPMENTAL EDITOR: Sheila Bassett
ASSOCIATE EDITOR: Janice Nixon
SUPERVISING EDITOR: Crystal Shortt
COPY EDITOR: Debbie Davies
SENIOR PRODUCTION COORDINATOR: Yolanda Pigden
PRODUCTION COORDINATOR: Madeleine Harrington
ELECTRONIC PAGE MAKE-UP: Heather Brunton/ArtPlus Limited
INTERIOR DESIGN: ArtPlus Limited
COVER DESIGN: Dianna Little
COVER IMAGE: Kaz Mori/The Image Bank

Contents

The *MATHPOWER*™ *11, Western Edition,* Program

The *MATHPOWER*™ *11, Western Edition,* Texts

- Each *MATHPOWER*™ *11, Western Edition,* text provides a real-life program connecting topics within mathematics as well as between mathematics and other subjects, different areas of mathematics, and the real world.
- The content and approach of the *MATHPOWER*™ *11, Western Edition,* program are planned to accomplish the aims of the NCTM *Curriculum and Evaluation Standards* and of the *Western Canadian Protocol, Common Curriculum Framework for K–12 Mathematics.*
- Cooperative learning assignments in pairs, small groups, and large groups are suggested, as are individual assignments.
- Communication is an integral part of the program as students share their ideas in discussions, record explanations of their solutions, and create their own problems.
- Problem solving is emphasized in all stages of the development of concepts and skills, as well as in problem solving sections. Questions are designed to lead students to generate their own learning.
- Technology includes calculators, graphing calculators, computers, the Internet, and other technological advances in homes, entertainment, and careers.
- Manipulatives are recommended at any stage students find them helpful.

The *MATHPOWER*™ *11, Western Edition,* Teacher's Resource

- Each *MATHPOWER*™ *11, Western Edition, Teacher's Resource* contains teaching suggestions to introduce concepts, extension, enrichment, and assessment.
- Each *MATHPOWER*™ *11, Western Edition, Teacher's Resource* provides the answers to the Explore/Inquire sections and the power problems, and provides some sample solutions to the student problems given in the student text.
- Assessments for groups and individuals reflect the learning outcomes of the program.
- Additional technology tips are also provided for use with scientific calculators, graphing calculators, computers, and the Internet.
- Teacher's Resource Masters provide materials such as grid paper, number lines, algebra tiles, graphing grids, and budget sheets.
- Assessment Masters give variations for evaluation and assessment.

The *MATHPOWER*™ *11, Western Edition,* Blackline Masters

- *MATHPOWER*™ *11, Western Edition, Blackline Masters* includes Tips for Learning Math, Practice, Graphing Calculator, and Testing masters, answers for all questions, and Rich Assessment Tasks.
- The Tips for Learning Math are 10 masters designed to help the student gain some insight into how to succeed in Math.
- The Practice masters include a practice sheet for every numbered section in each chapter. These masters provide additional practice with the skills and concepts new to the section.
- The Graphing Calculator masters provide practice in using a graphing calculator. They are geared to the most commonly used calculators— TI-83/TI-83 Plus, Sharp EL-9600, and Casio *CFX-9850GB PLUS*— enabling the teacher to use the masters appropriate to the calculators used by the students.

- The Self-Check is designed to help students identify their own areas of weakness, and suggests how to review the problem areas. Test 1 tests the chapter content at an average level. Test 2 provides a more challenging test of the material. In addition, there are three Cumulative Reviews: the first reviews the content of Chapters 1 to 4, the second reviews the content of Chapters 5 to 8, and the third reviews the content of Chapters 1 to 9.
- The Answers for each chapter are found at the end of the chapter, and include numeric, word, diagram, and graphing solutions, where appropriate, for each question.
- The Rich Assessment Tasks provide suggestions for assessing student performance through challenging problems and projects related to the math curriculum. They include a detailed assessment guide by mathematical processes, samples of real student work with comments, and other problems with teaching suggestions and assessment rubrics.

The *MATHPOWER*™ *11, Western Edition, Computerized Assessment Banks*

- Each *MATHPOWER*™ *11, Western Edition, Computerized Assessment Bank* is a Windows-based program.
- The software generates and prints tests, quizzes, or practice assignments, complete with graphics, charts, and diagrams. An answer key is automatically generated for each text, quiz, or practice assignment. You can easily and quickly generate daily quizzes, chapter tests, or cumulative tests, giving you the ability to provide ongoing assessment while saving you time in the preparation of the necessary tests.
- The algorithm technology generates unique permutations for each question every time it is used, providing you with the ability to easily generate unique tests, quizzes, and practice assignments for each student.
- You can choose multiple choice, true/false, or free response questions. The Question Editor in the program allows you to edit existing questions or add your own questions and save them for future use.
- The *MATHPOWER*™ *11, Western Edition, Computerized Assessment Bank* is written to the specific outcomes of *The Common Curriculum Framework*, grade 11 and the *MATHPOWER*™ *11, Western Edition*, text. Questions can be selected by either *The Common Curriculum Framework* outcome code or by the *MATHPOWER*™ *11, Western Edition*, chapter/section. You determine which outcomes, chapter, or section you are testing or assigning. This provides you with a solid source of information about what the students can do and is tied directly to the curriculum you are teaching.

The *MATHPOWER*™ *11, Western Edition, Computer Data Banks*

Database Applications
ClarisWorks 4.0 and 5.0, Windows® 95
Microsoft Works 4.0, Windows® 95
ClarisWorks 4.0 and 5.0, Macintosh OS 7.0
Microsoft Access 97, Windows® 95

Data Banks
A data bank of several databases is provided in each database application. For each database application, the data bank is on CD-ROM, except for Microsoft Access, which cannot be read-only and is on floppy disk. The databases provide excellent opportunities for cross-curricular applications.

Teacher's Resource

For each database application, there are

- *Getting Started* **BLMs** providing step-by-step instruction in using the database application to organize, sort, find, calculate, summarize, and graph data
- *Applications* **BLMs**, identical to the *Computer Data Bank* pages in the student text, providing explorations to assign as special interest projects, cross-curricular projects, rich problem solving projects, and assignments that apply understanding of math concepts in the real world
- detailed **teaching notes** and answers for each *Applications* BLM (Computer Data Bank page in the student text)

The *MATHPOWER*™ *11, Western Edition, Solutions*

- Solutions are provided for the odd-numbered questions in the practice sections of the odd-numbered chapters and for the even-numbered questions in the practice sections of the even-numbered chapters.
- Complete solutions to the Problems and Applications sections, the Chapter Reviews and Chapter Checks, the Exploring Math sections, and the Problem Solving sections are provided.
- All tables and graphics related to the solutions are provided.

The *MATHPOWER*™ *11, Western Edition, Outcome Tracker*™

- Each *MATHPOWER*™ *11, Western Edition, Outcome Tracker*™ is a Windows-based program.
- The *MATHPOWER*™ *11, Western Edition, Outcome Tracker*™ is a classroom assessment and management system that tracks and manages students' mastery of the specific outcomes of *The Common Curriculum Framework* and the outcomes taught in *MATHPOWER*™ *11, Western Edition*, text.
- The *MATHPOWER*™ *11, Western Edition, Outcome Tracker*™ facilitates outcome-based methodology by taking over assessment and record-keeping tasks.
- With the *MATHPOWER*™ *11, Western Edition, Outcome Tracker*™, you assign the outcomes of your choice and set the level of mastery of each assigned outcome for each student, small group, or whole class. The program will then automatically track the mastery of assigned outcomes by individual students, small groups, or the whole class. The *MATHPOWER*™ *11, Western Edition, Outcome Tracker*™ will also allow you to generate practice sheets that are directly based on the outcomes not mastered. This will assist you in addressing the wide range of ability levels in today's classrooms.
- The *MATHPOWER*™ *11, Western Edition, Outcome Tracker*™ generates a variety of reports that provide you, administrators, parents, and students with a clear indication of what the student can do. The diagnostic reports generated allow you to identify and correct problem areas before they become frustrations for the student.
- Tests can be scored either online or by scanner technology, thus saving you time in the marking of tests.

The Common Curriculum Framework

The Common Curriculum Framework for K–12 Mathematics was developed through the cooperative efforts of the provinces of Alberta, British Columbia, Manitoba, and Saskatchewan, and the Northwest Territories and Yukon Territory. Their ministers of education initiated The Western Canadian Protocol in Basic Education K–12 in 1993, and had the goal of establishing agreed-upon general and specific student outcomes of the school mathematics curriculum.

The *MATHPOWER™ 11, Western Edition*, program supports the belief that students learn in different ways and must construct their own meaning of mathematics, by promoting the learning of mathematics in a variety of ways. Investigating Math sections encourage students to work in small groups to explore new ideas; manipulatives, such as algebra tiles, are used for understanding abstract concepts; and appropriate technology usage is integrated throughout the text.

The Common Curriculum Framework specifies that the main goals of mathematics education are to prepare students to:
• use mathematics confidently to solve problems
• communicate and reason mathematically
• appreciate and value mathematics
• commit themselves to lifelong learning
• become mathematically literate adults, using mathematics to contribute to society.

The Common Curriculum Framework is based upon the following conceptual framework.

STRAND (Suggested Time Allotment)	Organization of Outcomes by Grade Level (K–12)	*Integrated Concepts*
• Number (25–35%) • Patterns and Relations (20–30%) • Shape and Space (20–30%) • Statistics and Probability (15–25%)	General Outcomes, Specific Outcomes, and Illustrative Examples to outline knowledge, skills, and attitudes about Mathematics	NATURE OF MATHEMATICS Change, Constancy, Dimension (size and scale), Number, Pattern, Quantity, Relationships, Shape, Uncertainty, ...
Integrated Mathematical Processes	Communication, Connections, Estimation and Mental Mathematics, Problem Solving, Reasoning, Technology, Visualization	

The seven interrelated mathematical processes are intended to permeate teaching and learning. This approach is derived from and consistent with the NCTM Standards (see pages MS 1 to MS 15 of this teacher's resource). The introductory section of the curriculum document provides detailed explanation of the meaning of each of the concepts listed under the Nature of Mathematics and suggestions as to how they may be integrated. *MATHPOWER™ 11, Western Edition*, presents the topics in the same order

The components of the Conceptual Framework for K–12 mathematics, as described, dictate what should be happening in mathematics education. The components are not meant to stand alone, but are to be interrelated to enhance one another.
*Assignments that take place in the classroom should stem from a problem solving approach built on the **mathematical processes** and lead students to an understanding of the **nature of mathematics** through specific knowledge, skills and attitudes related to each of the strands.*

from The Common Curriculum Framework for K–12 Mathematics

as in *The Common Curriculum Framework*, and within that sequence, students are encouraged and challenged to use interrelated concepts and skills. Both in the presentation of examples and in the nature of the exercises, *MATHPOWER™ 11, Western Edition*, fully integrates the mathematical processes of communication, connections, estimation and mental mathematics, problem solving, technology, and visualization. As well as special sections focussing on Mental Math, Connecting Math, Problem Solving, and Technology, *MATHPOWER™ 11, Western Edition*, uses icons to identify exercises in which students are specifically called upon to work together, to use their problem solving skills, to carry out independent research, and to write about mathematics.

Each of the four strands in the curriculum is split into substrands with general outcomes as shown in the following chart. The corresponding chapters and page references in *MATHPOWER™ 11, Western Edition*, are indicated. The specific student outcomes with illustrative examples are presented in the latter part of *The Common Curriculum Framework* and are reflected in the Learning Outcomes listed at the beginning of each section in *MATHPOWER™ 11, Western Edition, Teacher's Resource*.

STRAND	Substrand	*Students will:*	*MATHPOWER™ 11, Western Edition*
Number	Number Concepts	• use numbers to describe quantities • represent numbers in multiple ways	Chapter 4 Quadratic and Polynomial Equations, pp. 181–186, 233
	Number Operations	• demonstrate an understanding of and proficiency with calculations • decide which arithmetic operation or operations can be used to solve a problem and then solve the problem	Chapter 9 Personal Finance
Patterns and Relations	Patterns	• use patterns to describe the world and to solve problems	Chapter 3 Quadratic Functions Chapter 4 Quadratic and Polynomial Equations Chapter 6 Reasoning
	Variables and Equations	• represent algebraic expressions in multiple ways	Chapter 1 Systems of Equations Chapter 2 Linear Inequalities Chapter 4 Quadratic and Polynomial Equations Chapter 5 Functions
	Relations and Functions	• use algebraic and graphical models to generalize patterns, make predictions and solve problems	Chapter 3 Quadratic Functions Chapter 4 Quadratic and Polynomial Equations Chapter 5 Functions
Shape and Space	Measurement	• describe and compare everyday phenomena, using either direct or indirect measurement	Chapter 8 Coordinate Geometry and Trigonometry pp. 500–513
	3-D Objects and 2-D Shapes	• describe the characteristics of 3-D objects and 2-D shapes, and analyze the relationships among them	Chapter 7 The Circle Chapter 8 Coordinate Geometry and Trigonometry
Statistics and Probability	Data Analysis	• collect, display, and analyze data to make predictions about a population	
	Chance and Uncertainty	• use experimental or theoretical probability to represent and solve problems involving uncertainty	

National Council of Teachers of Mathematics

The McGraw-Hill Ryerson series, *MATHPOWER™*, *Western Edition*, provides a comprehensive program for grades 10, 11, and 12 that addresses the mathematics standards in the documents NCTM *Curriculum and Evaluation Standards for School Mathematics 1989* and NCTM *Professional Standards for Teaching Mathematics 1991*.

The *MATHPOWER™ 11*, *Western Edition*, begins with a Math Standards section consisting of fourteen one-page sections. Each section is based on one of the following fourteen standards from NCTM *Curriculum and Evaluation Standards for School Mathematics*, Grades 9 to 12. The teacher's resource for each section starts with a quote from the NCTM *Curriculum and Evaluation Standards* explaining the aim for the mathematics on the page.

Standard 1	Mathematics as Problem Solving
Standard 2	Mathematics as Communication
Standard 3	Mathematics as Reasoning
Standard 4	Mathematical Connections
Standard 5	Algebra
Standard 6	Functions
Standard 7	Geometry From a Synthetic Perspective
Standard 8	Geometry From an Algebraic Perspective
Standard 9	Trigonometry
Standard 10	Statistics
Standard 11	Probability
Standard 12	Discrete Mathematics
Standard 13	Investigating Limits
Standard 14	Mathematical Structure

These fourteen standards form the basis of *MATHPOWER™ 11*, *Western Edition*, text and teacher's resource. Assignments and topics are designed to meet the needs of students as they develop an understanding of mathematics and an approach to studying mathematics as described by the standards.

The NCTM *Curriculum and Evaluation Standards* states the following assumptions behind the fourteen standards. The *MATHPOWER™ 11*, *Western Edition*, text addresses these assumptions with a wide variety of experiences.

- Number and operations sense, estimation skills, and the ability to determine whether results are reasonable should be developed in the context of applications and problem solving.
- Conceptual understanding, multiple representations and connections, mathematical modelling, and problem solving should be emphasized.
- A variety of instruction methods should be used for investigation situations, preparing arguments for conjectures, and applying problem solving strategies.
- Students should have opportunities for small-group and individual exploration, as well as for class discussions.
- All students should have access to scientific calculators with graphing capabilities. Computers should be available for group work and for individual work.
- Assessment should be part of instruction.

The *MATHPOWER™ 11, Western Edition*, program is structured to accommodate the increased emphasis on assignments and open-ended problem solving with the reduced emphasis on drill advocated by the NCTM *Curriculum and Evaluation Standards*. In the text, concepts and skills are presented in assignments that are based on problem situations for students to solve, usually in pairs or small groups. Learning and communication are continued with Inquire questions designed to lead the students to think and communicate about the assignments. Teaching suggestions in the teacher's resource are also assignment oriented. Students are encouraged to relate mathematics to their lives and to express their ideas about mathematics orally and in writing.

The NCTM *Curriculum and Evaluation Standards* emphasizes that it is important for the students to be able to connect ideas within mathematics and to be able to recognize the relevance of mathematics in other curriculum areas and in their own lives. The organization of topics in the *MATHPOWER™ 11, Western Edition*, text demonstrates connections among strands of mathematics. For example, in Chapter 1, Systems of Equations, knowledge of the intercepts of linear equations is used to develop methods of solving systems of linear equations. In Chapter 3, Quadratic Functions, previous experience with writing perfect square trinomials as square binomials is used to learn skills with writing quadratic equations in general form as quadratic equations in standard form. In Chapter 8, Coordinate Geometry and Trigonometry, previously learned algebra skills are used in developing the law of sines and the law of cosines for the ambiguous case. Throughout the text, Logic Power, Number Power, and Pattern Power questions interweave skills from different areas of math as students solve challenging problems. Word Power problems connect math and language.

Reading mathematics and reading about mathematics are both important assignments to improve students' understanding of mathematical language and to help students appreciate the role of mathematics in everyday life. The *MATHPOWER™ 11, Western Edition*, program emphasizes the importance of reading pictures, graphs, words, and symbols. Assignments in the text and in the teacher's resource use newspapers, magazines, and other reference books as sources of math information.

Writing about mathematics helps students to create their own knowledge by reflecting, clarifying, and explaining their thinking. A pencil logo in the text indicates questions where students are required to write about mathematics.

The *MATHPOWER™ 11, Western Edition*, program contains the content for grade 11 mathematics, accommodating differences from school to school and from teacher to teacher. Chapters, and sections within chapters, can be selected to fulfil the requirements of provincial or district guidelines. The order of the content of the *MATHPOWER™ 11, Western Edition*, text is planned to enhance learning processes and maintain skills. The topics, however, are not necessarily sequential and could be reorganized according to the discretion of the teacher and the needs of the students, with an understanding that some sections require skills introduced previously in the program.

Students should have many opportunities to observe the interaction of mathematics with other school subjects and with everyday society. To accomplish this, mathematics teachers must seek and gain the active participation of teachers of other disciplines in exploring mathematical ideas through problems that arise in their classes.

from NCTM Curriculum and Evaluation
Standards for School Mathematics

Using *MATHPOWER*™ *11, Western Edition, Teacher's Resource*

The teacher's resource provides notes about each text page, with a choice of assignments, according to the needs and interests of the students and the time available.

1 **Chapter Introduction** provides a table of contents of the student text pages of the chapter.

2 **Chapter Materials** section provides a list of all the Teacher's Resource Masters and manipulatives required for the whole chapter.

3 **Chapter Concepts** section provides a list of all the concepts that are reviewed and introduced in the chapter.

CHAPTER 2
Linear Inequalities

1 **Chapter Introduction**

2 **Chapter Materials**

graphing calculators, Teacher's Resource Master 1 (0.5-cm grid paper), Teacher's Resource Master 2 (1-cm grid paper), Teacher's Resource Master 4 (number lines), Teacher's Resource Master 5 (graphing grids), overhead projector, counters, paper cups

3 **Chapter Concepts**

Chapter 2 reviews or introduces
* solving linear inequalities in one variable
* graphing linear inequalities in one variable
* graphing linear inequalities in two variables
* solving systems of linear inequalities
* the problem solving strategies Solve a Simpler Problem, Use Logic, and Look for a Pattern

Teaching Suggestions

Direct the students to look at the graph on student text page 57. Ask:
How long can a diver stay at a depth of 30 m before requiring decompression?
What is the maximum depth that divers seem to be able to go?
If you stayed under water at a depth of 5 m, would you ever have to undergo decompression? Explain.

For question 4, ask:
What does the word "acronym" mean?
What acronym have you used in mathematics?

Integrating Technology

Internet
Use the Internet to find information about Pacific octopuses and/or scuba diving.

15 **Enrichment**

Use the graph on student text page 57 to make up a question. Exchange your problem with a classmate and solve your classmate's problem. Discuss and compare each other's solutions. Present your problem and solution to the class.

20 **Assessing the Outcomes**

Observation
You might consider some of these questions as you observe the students work.
* Do the students know how to interpret data from a graph?
* Do they work well in pairs?
* Do they persist until they find a solution?
* Do the students attempt all the questions?

2.1 Reviewing Linear Inequalities in One Variable

4 Student Text Pages
Pp. 60–64

5 Materials
graphing calculators, Teacher's Resource Master 4 (number lines), overhead projector

6 Learning Outcomes
* Solve inequalities.
* Graph inequalities.
* Solve problems involving inequalities.

7 Prerequisite Skills
1. Graph each of the following sets of numbers on a number line. x is a rational number.

a) $x > 2$

b) $x \leq -1$

c) $-5 < x \leq 3$

d) $x \geq -2$

2. Which of the given values satisfy the inequality?
a) $x + 2 > 5$; $x = 1, 2, 3, 4, 5$ [4, 5]
b) $x - 3 \leq -1$; $x = -1, 0, 1, 2, 3$ [−1, 0, 1, 2]
c) $x + 3 \geq -2$; $x = -6, -5, -4, -3$ [−5, −4, −3]
d) $x - 1 < 2$; $x = 0, 1, 2, 3, 4, 5$ [0, 1, 2]
e) $x > 0.5$; $x = 0.3, 0.4, -0.5, 0.5$ [none]

8 Mental Math
1. Copy and complete each ordered pair so that it satisfies the given equation.
a) $x + y = 7$; (2, ■)   [5]
b) $3x + y = -1$; (5, ■)   [−16]
c) $y = 3x + 7$; (5, ■)   [22]
d) $3y + 1 = -5x$; (−1, ■) $\left[\frac{4}{3}\right]$
2. Calculate.
a) 0.55^2 [0.3025]   b) 5.2^2 [27.04]
c) 0.055^2 [0.003 025]   d) 5200^2 [27 040 000]
e) 550^2 [302 500]   f) 0.52^2 [0.2704]

9 Explore/Inquire Answers
Explore: Solve the Inequalities
a) $s = 320$ and $s = 400$ b) $s \geq 320$ and $s \leq 400$

Inquire
1. 320 km/h   2. 400 km/h
3. a) 398 km/h, 399 km/h, 400 km/h
4. a) $x < 2$ b) $x > 3$ c) $x > 5$ d) $x < 16$
5. a) In order, from top to bottom: >, >, >, <, <, <
b) multiplying and dividing by a negative number

10 Teaching Suggestions
Method 1
(number lines, overhead projector, graphing calculators)
Review with the class the opening paragraphs of student text page 60. Ask:
What does the word "inequality" mean?
Where have you seen an example of an inequality in an everyday situation?

Have pairs of students look around the class and draw any imaginary straight line through the classroom area, thus, dividing the classroom area into two sections. Have them use the words "equal" and "unequal" to describe, in terms of numbers of students, the two sections of the class.

Assign to pairs of students the Explore and the Inquire sections on student text page 60. Provide them with number lines and have them draw the graphs of their solutions to the Inquire questions. For Inquire question 3, have volunteers demonstrate the answer on an overhead projector. When the students have completed the Inquire questions, have them present their results to the class. Provide an overhead projector for those who require it.

Have the students study the table following the Inquire questions on student text page 61. Ask:
What happens to the direction of the inequality sign when a number is added or subtracted from both sides of an inequality?
What type of number causes the inequality sign to be reversed when both sides of an inequality are multiplied or divided?

Review with the class the teaching examples on student text pages 61 and 62.

Method 2
(number lines, overhead projector, graphing calculators)
Provide pairs of students with number lines. Ask:
What is an inequality?
Write this inequality on the chalkboard.
$$x + 2 > 5$$
Introduce the term "satisfy." Ask:
How would you use a number line to help you solve this inequality?
Does the value 2 satisfy the inequality?
Does the value 3 satisfy the inequality?
Does the value 3.1 satisfy the inequality?

Mental math is becoming increasingly important with calculator use, which necessitates thinking about answers to determine whether they are reasonable. Discussions about strategies for doing mental math questions should be encouraged. Students who need a challenge can think of strategies for mental computation and for estimation. Such strategies often reflect an understanding of number sense and patterns.

9 Explore/Inquire Answers provides the answers to the Explore section and the Inquire questions given on the student text page.

10 Teaching Suggestions are ideas for presenting the concepts and skills in the section. Method 1 relates to the student text page, and discusses ideas about the Explore section, the Inquire questions, and the teaching example or Examples. Method 2 is an assignment in which skills are developed without the text, usually in pairs or groups, and often with materials.

Method 2 may be appropriate either for reteaching a topic or as an alternative method of approaching a topic. Some lessons, such as the Getting Started pages, the Investigating Math pages, the Technology pages, and the Connecting Math pages, may have only one teaching method.

4 Student Text Pages provides the page numbers of the section in the student text.

5 Materials provides a list of all the Teacher's Resource masters, manipulatives, and materials required for the section.

6 Learning Outcomes describes the concepts and skills the students will acquire in the section.

7 Prerequisite Skills maintains and/or reviews concepts and skills relevant to the section. The questions can be copied on the chalkboard, or an overhead projector, or on paper.

8 Mental Math presents computation questions that allow the students to practise the mental skills provided in the Getting Started section. These can be copied, and the students can read them and either record or state their answers.

Alternatively, they could be read and the students can record answers, or small groups might ask the questions orally and classmates give the answers.

11 Sample Solution provides a worked solution to one of the problems in the Applications and Problem Solving section of the student text. Tables and/or diagrams are included in these solutions.

12 **Power Problem Answer**
provides the answer to the
corresponding power problem in
the student text. Power problems
contain challenging questions
that use any math the students
have learned.

13 **Integrating Technology**
provides tips in using new
technology as it relates to the
topic in the section.

14 **Extension** assignments and
questions suggest ways to apply
the math from the section in other
related areas. They may connect
math with previously acquired skills,
with other subjects, or with topics
outside school.

15 **Enrichment** assignments and
questions present a challenge.

16 **Math Journal** requires that
students express their ideas and
feelings about math in writing.
Math Journal assignments give the
students opportunities to organize
their thinking, to clarify learning,
and to explain understanding.
Math Journal suggestions might be
followed for each lesson, for selected
lessons, once or twice in a chapter,
or according to whatever plan is
suitable.

17 **Cross-Discipline** suggests ways
to connect the math in the section
to everyday real-life situations, such
as biology, construction design, or
town planning. This can be used as
a resource for students and/or
teachers.

---

11 **Sample Solution**

Page 40, question 61

If the solution must be $(6, -5)$, then $x = 6$ and $y = -5$.
Substitute these values for x and y into the two given
equations.

$$6A - 5B = C \quad (1)$$
$$6D - 5E = F \quad (2)$$
$$6A = 5B + C$$
$$6 = \frac{5B + C}{A} \quad (3)$$
$$6D = 5E + F$$
$$6 = \frac{5E + F}{D} \quad (4)$$

Equate the right-hand sides of (3) and (4).

$$\frac{5B + C}{A} = \frac{5E + F}{D}$$
$$D(5B + C) = A(5E + F)$$
$$5BD + CD = 5AE + AF$$
$$5BD - 5AE = AF - CD$$
$$5(BD - AE) = AF - CD$$
$$5 = \frac{AF - CD}{BD - AE} \quad (5)$$

The values for $A, B, C, D, E,$ and F must satisfy the
given condition, i.e., they must be different integers.
Use a guess and check method to find values for $A, B,
C, D, E,$ and F that satisfy equation (5).
Substitute $A = 1, B = 2, C = -4, D = 3, E = 5,$ and
$F = -7$ in (5).

$$5 = \frac{AF - CD}{BD - AE} \quad (5)$$
$$5 = \frac{(1)(-7) - (-4)(3)}{(2)(3) - (1)(5)}$$
$$= \frac{-7 - (-12)}{6 - 5}$$
$$= \frac{5}{1}$$
$$= 5$$

Thus, $A = 1, B = 2, C = -4, D = 3, E = 5, F = -7$
is one set of values that satisfies all the conditions.
There are many other sets.

$$x + 2y = -4$$
$$3x + 5y = -7$$

12 **Pattern Power Answer**
The sum of the three numbers to the right of the
number in the left-hand column equals the number in
the left-hand column.
Thus, $48 = 12 + 11 + 25, 40 = 5 + 16 + 19, 74 =
29 + 27 + 18, 39 = 11 + 18 + 10,$ and $63 = x + 14 + 23.$
Thus, $x = 63 - 14 - 23 = 26.$
The missing number is 26.

---

13 **Integrating Technology**

Graphing Calculators
Check graphically the solutions to some of the systems
in questions 1 to 30 on student text pages 38 to 39
using a graphing calculator.

Computer Data Bank
Use the databases in *MATHPOWER™ 11, Western
Edition, Computer Data Bank* to find information to
create several problems that can be solved using systems
of linear equations. Display your problems for
classmates to solve.

14 **Extension**
Solve the system of equations.
Hint Think of $\frac{1}{x} = m$ and $\frac{1}{y} = n$.

$$\frac{1}{x} + \frac{1}{y} = \frac{7}{10}$$
$$\frac{3}{x} - \frac{2}{y} = \frac{11}{10}$$

16 **Math Journal**
List the steps required to solve a system of linear
equations in two variables using the elimination
process. Which method do you prefer, the method of
substitution or the method of elimination? Explain.
  Write a short paragraph explaining the usefulness
of diagrams in solving a system of linear equations.

18 **Common Errors**
- Students often forget that the division bar in a
  rational expression is a grouping symbol. This means
  that the numerator should be grouped in a set of
  brackets and any multiplication on that expression
  should apply to each term within the brackets.
  For example,

$$\frac{x + 1}{2} - \frac{y - 3}{6} = 3 \text{ and}$$
$$3x + 3 - y - 3 = 18$$

  are not equivalent equations, because the -3 of
  the term $\frac{y - 3}{6}$ in the first equation should have
  been subtracted. This would have changed -3 to $+3$.

- R_x Review the process of subtracting an expression
  by adding the opposite expression. Stress upon the
  students that, when an expression is being subtracted,
  every term of the expression is being subtracted
  and thus, the opposite of every term is added.

---

18 **Common Errors** describes
errors that students may make and
suggests approaches for remediation.
Being aware of these common errors
helps teaching and observing.

19 **Problem Levels of Difficulty**
indicates suggested text questions
as A for all students, B for most
students, and C for a challenge.

20 **Assessing the Outcomes**
provides a variety of assessment
assignments and techniques for
individuals, pairs, and groups.

Using *MATHPOWER*™ *11, Western Edition*

Each chapter contains several numbered sections.
In a typical numbered section, the following features are found.

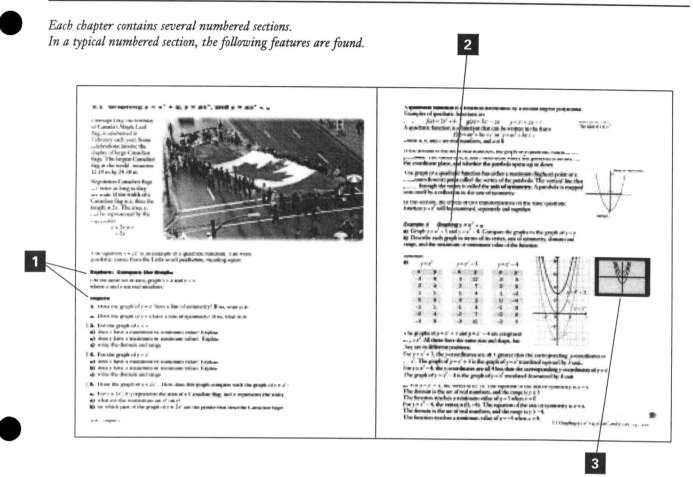

1 Explore and Inquire

You start with an exploration, followed by a set of inquire questions. The exploration and the inquire questions allow you to construct your own learning. Many explorations show how mathematics is applied in the world.

2 Examples

The examples show you how to use what you have learned.

3 Graphing Calculator Displays

These displays show you how technology can be used to solve problems.

4 Practice

By completing these questions, you practise what you have learned, so that you can stabilize your learning.

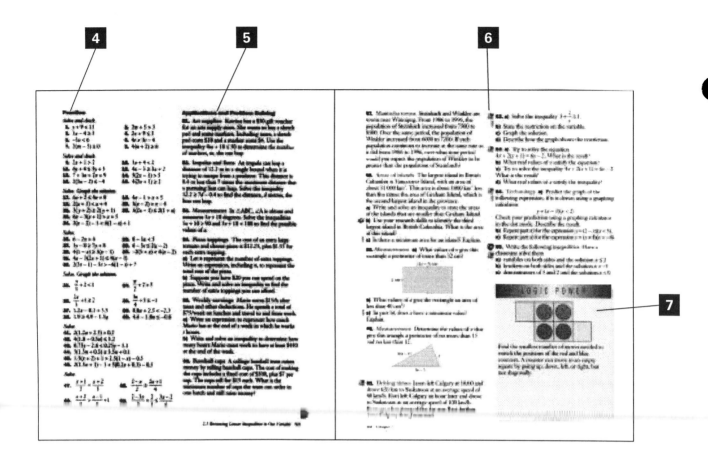

5 **Applications and Problem Solving**

These questions let you use what you have learned to solve problems, and to apply and extend what you have learned. The descriptors on many of the problems show connections to other disciplines, to other topics in mathematics, and to people's daily experiences.

6 **Logos**

The four logos indicate special kinds of problems or opportunities for research.

When you see this logo, you will be asked to demonstrate an understanding of what you have learned by writing about it in a meaningful way.

This logo signals that you will need to think critically when you answer a question.

This logo indicates an opportunity to work with a classmate or in a larger group to solve a problem.

For a problem with this logo, you will need to use your research skills to find information from the Internet, a print data bank, or some other source.

7 **Power Problems**

These problems are challenging and fun. They encourage you to reason mathematically.

Special Features of *MATHPOWER™ 11, Western Edition*

Math Standard

There are 14 Math Standard pages before Chapter 1. By working through these pages, you will explore the mathematical concepts that citizens of the twenty-first century will need to understand.

Getting Started

A Getting Started section begins each chapter. This section reviews the mathematics that you will need to use in the chapter.

Mental Math

The Mental Math column in each Getting Started section includes a strategy for completing mental math calculations.

Problem Solving

The numerous ways in which problem solving is integrated throughout the book are described on pages xiv–xv.

Technology

Each chapter includes from one to four Technology sections. These sections allow you to explore the use of graphing calculators, geometry software, spreadsheets, and the Internet to solve problems. The use of technology is also integrated into many numbered sections and feature pages. The graphing calculator displays were generated using a TI-83 or a TI-92 calculator. The geometry software displays were generated using The Geometer's Sketchpad software.

Investigating Math

The explorations in the Investigating Math sections will actively involve you in learning mathematics, either individually or with your classmates.

Connecting Math and . . .

Each chapter includes a Connecting Math section. In the explorations, you will apply mathematics to other subject areas, such as zoology, business, history, and astronomy.

Computer Data Bank

The Computer Data Bank sections are to be used in conjunction with the *MATHPOWER™ 11, Western Edition, Computer Data Bank*. In these sections, you will explore the power of a computer database program in solving problems. The explorations in these sections use ClarisWorks 4.0 and 5.0, Microsoft 4.0, and Microsoft Access 97 for Windows 95, and ClarisWorks 4.0 and 5.0 for Macintosh OS 7.0.

Career Connection

The explorations on the Career Connection pages will show you some applications of mathematics to the world of work.

Review/Chapter Check

Near the end of each chapter are sections headed Review and Chapter Check, which allow you to test your progress. The questions in each Review are keyed to section numbers in the chapter, so that you can identify any sections that require further study.

Exploring Math

At the end of the Review section in each chapter, the Exploring Math column includes an enrichment activity designed as a problem solving challenge.

Cumulative Review

Chapter 4, Chapter 8, and Chapter 9 end with cumulative reviews. The cumulative review at the end of Chapter 4 covers the work you did in Chapters 1–4. The cumulative review at the end of Chapter 8 covers Chapters 5–8, and the cumulative review at the end of Chapter 9 covers Chapters 1–9.

Data Bank

Problems that require the use of the Data Bank on pages 580–589 are included in a Data Bank box at the end of the Problem Solving: Using the Strategies page in each chapter.

Answers

On pages 591–642, there are answers to most of the questions in this book.

Glossary

The illustrated glossary on pages 643–651 explains mathematical terms.

Indexes

The book includes three indexes — an applications index, a technology index, and a general index.

Problem Solving

Students' ability to solve problems develops over time as a result of extended instruction, opportunities to solve many kinds of problems, and encounters with real-world situations. Students' progress should be assessed systematically, deliberately, and continually to effectively influence students' confidence and ability to solve problems in various contexts.

from NCTM Curriculum and Evaluation Standards for School Mathematics

Mathematics and mathematics education instruction should enable all learners to experience mathematics as a dynamic engagement in solving problems.

from NCTM Professional Standards for Teaching Mathematics

Educational research offers compelling evidence that students learn mathematics well only when they construct their own mathematical understanding.

from National Research Council, Everybody Counts: A Report to the Nation on the Future of Mathematics Education

In accordance with the NCTM *Curriculum and Evaluation Standards*, problem solving is the central focus of the *MATHPOWER™ 11, Western Edition*, program and is an integral part of most lessons and assignments in the text. Problem solving is introduced in the Math Standards at the beginning of the text, where each standard is presented with problem solving situations.

The *MATHPOWER™ 11, Western Edition*, program teaches through problem solving in the text and in the teacher's resource. In the text, students develop their understanding by exploring problem solving assignments and completing Explore sections and Inquire questions to extend and communicate their thinking. Skills and concepts are practised as students solve problems in Applications and Problem Solving.

The critical thinking logo throughout the text indicates challenging questions and problems requiring careful thought about how to apply problem solving skills.

In the teacher's resource, the students experience problem solving assignments as part of the Teaching Suggestions, Extension, Enrichment, and Assessing the Outcomes.

Confidence in problem solving is developed by a variety of experiences, by sharing ideas in groups, and by an emphasis on the process of problem solving. Students are encouraged to take risks and to try their ideas. Open-ended problems and investigations allow students to develop a sense of value for their ideas. The *MATHPOWER™ 11, Western Edition*, program offers the students frequent opportunities to be involved actively in creating problems to be solved by themselves and by classmates. Students might post problems and puzzles that they create and that they find in resource books for others to try and to discuss.

Problem solving can lead students to develop verbal and written communications skills. Connections among different topics in mathematics, and between mathematics and other subjects are part of the approach of the *MATHPOWER™, Western Edition*, program to problem solving.

In order to become successful problem solvers, students must be encouraged and supported in their efforts within the classroom environment. The process of problem solving needs to be valued as much as solutions. It is important for students to feel confidence in solving problems.

George Polya's four-stage model is presented on page xiv of *MATHPOWER™ 11, Western Edition*, as a framework for solving problems by following these stages:

- Understand the Problem
- Think of a Plan
- Carry Out the Plan
- Look Back

Problem solving strategies for stage 2 of Polya's model, Think of a Plan, are presented in Chapters 1 to 3 of the text. Each strategy is introduced with a sample problem and solution that follows Polya's model. The strategies presented in the first three chapters of *MATHPOWER™ 11, Western Edition*, are:

- Use a Diagram
- Use a Data Bank
- Solve Fermi Problems
- Solve a Simpler Problem
- Use Logic
- Look for a Pattern
- Guess and Check
- Work Backward
- Use a Table or Spreadsheet

These problem solving strategies are applied not only in Problem Solving: Using the Strategies at the end of each chapter, but also throughout the program.

The problem solving strategy Use a Data Bank is extended with a Data Bank part of each Using the Strategies page after Chapter 1. Students find resources for information to solve problems by using the Data Bank on pages 580 to 589 and other sources such as newspapers, magazines, reference books, the Internet, and discussions with classmates.

Power questions throughout the text are challenges related to different areas of mathematics.

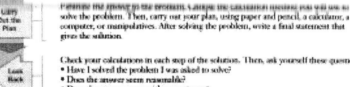

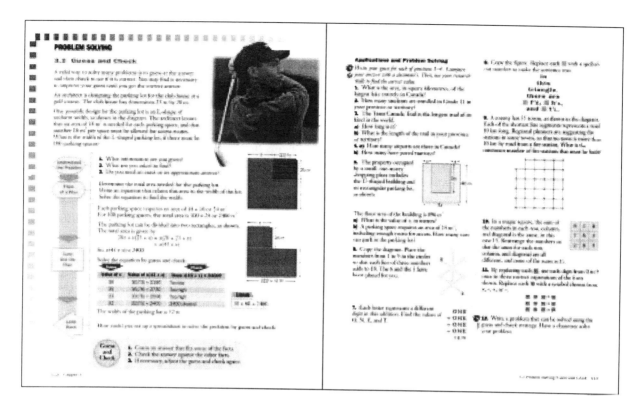

Opportunities for the students to develop problem solving skills occur throughout the student text.

In the first three chapters, there are nine numbered problem solving sections. Each section focuses on one strategy. The section provides an example of how the students can use the strategy, and includes problems that the students can solve using the strategy.

At the end of each chapter, the students will find a section headed Problem Solving: Using the Strategies. Each of these sections includes a variety of problems that can be solved using different strategies. The section ends with problems contained in a Data Bank box. To solve the Data Bank problems, the students can look up information in the Data Bank on pages 580 to 589, or they can use a data bank of their choice.

Every numbered section of the book includes the subheading Applications and Problem Solving. The problems under this sub-heading are related to that section and provide the students with many opportunities to apply problem solving strategies.

Many numbered sections include Power Problems, which have been grouped into four types—Logic Power, Pattern Power, Number Power, and Word Power. These problems are challenging and fun.

Further problem solving opportunities are to be found in the Exploring Math columns. Each of these columns allows the students to explore challenging mathematical ideas.

As described on pages T8, T19, T20, T27, T28, and MS1–MS14, many special features in the book involve explorations. These features—including Math Standard, Technology, Investigating Math, Connecting Math, Computer Data Bank, and Career Connection sections—are filled with opportunities for the students to refine their problem solving skills.

Cooperative Learning

In addition to traditional teacher demonstrations and teacher-led discussions, greater opportunities should be provided for small-group work, individual explorations, peer instruction, and whole-class discussions in which the teacher serves as a moderator.

from NCTM Curriculum and Evaluation Standards for School Mathematics

As emphasized in the NCTM *Curriculum and Evaluation Standards,* cooperative learning strategies play an important role in developing self-direction. Working in groups allows students to perform and discuss mathematics, improves their ability to communicate math ideas effectively, clarifies their thinking, and helps them become confident in their own ability as mathematicians. Cooperative learning helps students develop their sense of responsibility as they work together to plan and carry out their ideas. Each student must have the feeling of being part of the solution to reach the goal the group is working toward.

Cooperative learning provides opportunities for communication as students share and analyze ideas. Mathematics is a language, and like any language, it is best learned through speaking, listening, reading, and writing. By using all forms of communication, students forge necessary links between their own thoughts and the abstract language and symbolism of mathematics. Talking about mathematics with classmates and teachers helps students to model situations, to construct knowledge, and to develop skills necessary for making convincing arguments and defending ideas.

Cooperative learning can be used in a variety of forms, according to the needs, abilities, and attitudes of the people involved and according to the task. Such learning includes working in pairs, in small groups, in large groups, as a class, with another class, with peers outside school, with family members, with people in the community, and with other resource people. Making use of available resource people enhances a math program, showing the relevance and importance of mathematics in everyday life and in careers. It provides opportunities to apply mathematics outside school.

Home groups should be established by the teacher, with consideration given to combinations of abilities and interests in math, to leadership, to general knowledge, and to topics related to the current issue. Group sizes vary according to the task and the experience in working as a group. Groups of two or three may be appropriate as students begin cooperative learning. As group work produces successful results, the size might be increased to groups of four or six, a size that often creates an efficient working environment. Opinions about how long home groups should stay together vary. It is usually accepted, however, that students should be together long enough for them to get to know each other and to become comfortable working together, and that they need to experience different groupings throughout the year.

 The working together logo that appears throughout the *MATHPOWER™ 11, Western Edition,* text indicates work specifically designed for groups. These questions ask students to interact by comparing answers with classmates, sharing ideas with classmates, or discussing thoughts in groups.

The structure of cooperative learning may be informal or formal. For informal structures, students can turn to face nearby classmates. During mathematics lessons, informal grouping should take place whenever it assists students to learn.

For formal structures, desks can be arranged to enable the students to see and communicate with each group member easily. If a discussion area is needed, the students might move chairs into a circle, group around a table, or sit on the floor in a circle.

Active student participation in learning through individual and small-group explorations provides multiple opportunities for discussion, questioning, listening, and summarizing. Using such techniques, teachers can direct instruction away from a focus on the recall of terminology and routine manipulation of symbols and procedures toward a deeper conceptual understanding of mathematics.

from NCTM Curriculum and Evaluation Standards for School Mathematics

The *MATHPOWER*™ *11, Western Edition*, text uses both informal and formal cooperative learning. The Investigating Math pages, for the development of certain new concepts, contain assignments requiring the students to work in pairs or in small groups. The students might complete these pages with members of their home groups. Alternatively, groups can be created informally for the assignments. Assignments in the Technology sections and in the Connecting Math sections are also suitable for cooperative learning. Suggestions in the teacher's resource describe how the Mental Math, Review, Chapter Check, and Cumulative Review can be used for group work.

The Exploring Math assignment at the end of each chapter is designed to extend and enrich ideas in mathematics. These explorations could provide opportunities for the students to practise skills for formal and informal cooperative learning to develop successful group work. Keeping on task, taking turns, recording group work, involving each member, being tolerant of other students' ideas, encouraging classmates to share ideas, dividing tasks fairly, and agreeing on a consensus when necessary are skills practised and developed by such cooperative learning assignments. Suggestions to help groups work effectively could be posted, and students could add their own rules to the list as they gain experience in cooperative learning throughout the year.

- Contribute ideas by speaking quietly.
- Encourage others to participate and listen to them carefully.
- Respect the opinions of others.
- Ask for help from the teacher only when everyone in the group has the same difficulty.

Jigsaw cooperative learning assignments requires students to work with their home groups for part of an assignment and to form expert groups for other parts. The stages when students return to their home groups to combine ideas vary, but usually occur in the concluding part of the assignment. Generally, students begin as a class to brainstorm topics. Then, in home groups, they choose a topic. Each home group member is given a different task, such as a topic to research, a question to answer, or a problem to solve.

1 2 3 4 5 6		1 2 3 4 5 6

Home Groups

1 2 3 4 5 6		1 2 3 4 5 6

Then, each member leaves the home group to form an expert group with the students from the other groups who have the same task. The students in each expert group work together to complete the task.

1 1 1 1		2 2 2 2		3 3 3 3

Expert Groups

4 4 4 4		5 5 5 5		6 6 6 6

Next, the students return to their home groups, share information, and cooperate to prepare a group product. They might also evaluate the process, considering what they would change for another project.

Cooperative learning for pairs sharing their work can begin with the whole class or with individuals thinking about a topic or brainstorming ideas. Then, pairs discuss ideas or complete assigned tasks.

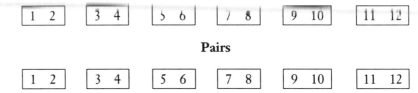

Pairs

Next, each pair pools information with the other pair who was assigned the same task.

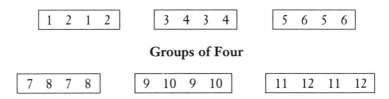

Groups of Four

The development of social skills is an important aspect of cooperative learning assignments. Through experiences in groups, students learn to cooperate as they combine work and share tasks. Cooperative learning involves the assumption that cooperative goals are established and understood so that interaction among the members of a group and among different groups is ensured.

Technology

Both the NCTM *Curriculum and Evaluation Standards* and the provincial guidelines assume that calculators and computers are available in the classroom. The emphasis is on developing an understanding of when and how to use technology and on learning how to interpret and apply results.

In *MATHPOWER™ 11, Western Edition*, calculators are considered to be a tool accessible to students at all times. Calculators are presented as one of the reasonable options when choosing a solution method. It is understood that students will have scientific or graphing calculators whenever appropriate. Using calculators allows students to solve problems with an emphasis on strategies and reasoning.

Students need to experiment with their calculators to discover and refine the key presses to perform different tasks and to interpret the results, including graphs that their calculators display. They might pose questions in pairs, post challenges on bulletin boards, or conduct group discussions.

As well as calculators being used in solutions to examples in many numbered sections, each chapter includes at least one Technology section. The Technology sections using calculators include graphing linear inequalities, exploring parabolic functions, exploring regression, and exploring rational functions. These sections, like the Solutions to Examples in the numbered sections, show calculator displays generated using a TI-83 calculator. Other Technology sections using calculators include solving inequalities, solving quadratic equations, exploring functions with two equal roots, and solving polynomial equations. These sections show displays generated using the more powerful TI-92 calculator.

In *MATHPOWER™ 11, Western Edition*, computers are considered to be a tool accessible to students at least some of the time. The Technology and the Computer Data Bank sections need not be assigned to all students in a class at the same time. The Technology sections using computers feature spreadsheets to explore the sums of the interior angles in a polygon and to calculate annuities, and geometry software to explore reflections, chord properties, properties of the angles in a circle, tangent properties, and geometric properties.

The Computer Data Bank sections in the text are used in conjunction with *MATHPOWER™ 11, Western Edition, Computer Data Bank*. When students use these sections, they direct the computer to perform tasks such as:

- find, organize, and sort data
- display data in tables and lists
- perform calculations
- summarize data
- create graphs

These tasks would be incredibly time-consuming, perhaps impossible, with large quantities of data, if they were attempted without technology. The computer does what students direct it to do. Students develop skills in using the software and the databases to accomplish what they need done. Students must understand the mathematical concepts. They create the formulas; the computer only does repetitive calculations. Students decide what types of graphs to create and what the graphs should look like; the computer only creates the graphs.

Computer software can be used
effectively for class demonstrations
and independently by students to
explore additional examples, perform
independent investigations, generate
and summarize data as part of a
project, or complete assignments.

from NCTM Curriculum and Evaluation
Standards for School Mathematics

A spirit of enquiry should pervade all
mathematics teaching and learning. In
establishing such an environment, the
teacher must be sensitive to students'
ideas and encourage mathematical
communication amount all students.
Technology can be used effectively in
creating such an environment, since
it provides a tool for making
mathematical explorations more
efficient and accessible.

from NCTM Professional Standards for
Teaching Mathematics graphs to create and
what the graphs should look like; the computer
only creates the graphs.

MATHPOWER™ 11, Western Edition, Computer Data Bank has the potential to motivate students, increase their interest in learning mathematics, and broaden their knowledge about database technology. Using *MATHPOWER™ 11, Western Edition, Computer Data Bank* allows students more time to analyze data and solve problems, to apply their understanding of mathematical concepts, to relate mathematics to other subject areas, and to solve problems involving higher-level thinking.

The importance of computers in the classroom, in careers, and in everyday life is increasing and changing rapidly. Many computer games and geometric drawing programs are available to allow students to explore math ideas and computer skills.

Internet and CD-ROM research opens many doors for students. Spreadsheets and databases can be used to organize and store information that can be accessed according to topic. Students can write about their research with word processing software and can use drawing or clip art programs to illustrate ideas. Word processing is appropriate for journal entries and for writing about mathematics. Computers provide a link among mathematics, other subjects, and everyday life. Making computer software available to students increases the interest and fun of mathematics. Since there is constant change in the computer field, students should cooperate in posting for classmates the manes of programs and web sites they have discovered.

In many sections of this teacher's resource, Integrating Technology features offer suggestions ranging from encouraging students to explain the key presses needed to accomplish specific tasks with their calculators to Internet research topics and possible web sites.

Any available technology in the classroom, at home, in a library, or in another place is an important source of information, and an opportunity to present ideas. Using technology as the development of a skill for research and for preparing one's own work should be a part of every student's classroom experience.

MATHPOWER™ 11, Western Edition, Computerized Assessment Bank

The *MATHPOWER™ 11, Western Edition, Computerized Assessment Bank* CD-ROM provides a flexible base of 50 questions per chapter. The questions, which are written to reflect the specific student outcomes of *The Common Curriculum Framework*, are either free-response or multiple choice. In both formats, some questions are dynamic and others are static. The dynamic questions are programmed so that a different question will appear each time that item is selected.

The program is fully indexed so that you, the teacher, can select questions by whatever criteria you choose. You can also edit existing questions or add your own questions to the assessment bank.

Manipulatives

Representations are crucial to the development of mathematical thinking, and through their use, mathematical ideas can be modeled, important relationships identified and clarified, and understandings fostered.

from NCTM Professional Standards for Teaching Mathematics

Students at all grade levels and at all levels within a grade must have access to appropriate manipulative materials to assist them in constructing their understanding of concepts and skills and to illustrate their understanding. Based on the view that the abstract level of mathematics follows the concrete level after conceptualization and understanding, the *MATHPOWER™ 11, Western Edition*, program assumes access to a variety of manipulatives that students can use in exploring ideas, checking answers, and solving problems, and can also use at any other stage.

The *MATHPOWER™ 11, Western Edition*, program suggests the use of the following manipulatives:

- Miras
- algebra tiles

Other commercial materials for a grade 11 mathematics classroom are:
- overhead projectors
- compasses, protractors, set squares, straightedges
- rulers, measuring tapes
- overhead algebra tiles
- interlocking cubes
- overhead graphing calculator
- geometry software
- commercial math and logic games and puzzles

Materials such as the following can be used for math assignments:
- toothpicks, straws, paper cups
- counters, coloured pencils
- scissors, string, pins
- lined paper, plain paper
- playing cards
- newspapers, magazines, maps, atlases, reference books

The Teacher's Resource Masters provide:
- grid paper
- number lines
- algebra tiles
- graphing grids
- parabola
- budget sheets

The storing of manipulatives should allow for free exploration before instructional use, efficient distribution, and easy access to material for students as they are solving problems or investigating ideas. When sufficient manipulatives are not available for the whole class, students can share materials. They can make manipulatives such as geometric figures. Providing a convenient, noticeable place for storing the items from home may encourage students to collect materials. Students might write letters home or take letters prepared by the teacher requesting supplies.

Assessment

*The assessment of students'
mathematics learning should enable
educators to draw conclusions about
their instructional needs, their progress
in achieving the goals of the
curriculum, and the effectiveness of a
mathematics program. The degree to
which meaningful inferences can be
drawn from such an assessment depends
on the degree to which the assessment
methods and tasks are aligned or are in
agreement with the curriculum.*

from NCTM Curriculum and Evaluation
Standards for School Mathematics

The NCTM *Curriculum and Evaluation Standards* discusses the importance of a variety of ways to gather information about what the students know, are able to do, and value in mathematics. Although written tests are advocated, multiple assessment techniques, including oral and demonstration formats, must be included to evaluate what mathematics the students can perform and how they feel about mathematics. Tasks with open-ended questions and investigations afford the opportunity for teachers to observe and evaluate communication skills, attitude toward mathematics, understanding of connections among math concepts, and organizational skills. Assessment is a continual process to determine the meanings students assign to ideas and the progress they are making toward achieving mathematical power.

Evaluation is a tool to inform and guide instruction. Questions that are related to stated learning outcomes demonstrate strengths and weaknesses of the students, and can be the basis for planned review and remediation.

Since problem solving is a focus of the *MATHPOWER*™, *Western Edition*, program, the assessment of problem solving skills and attitudes is important. To value learning for understanding means that both the process of solving problems and final answers need to be assessed. Any technology such as calculators or computers, or materials generally used by students, is assumed for assessment.

The NCTM *1993 Yearbook, Assessment in the Mathematics Classroom*, explains that any assessment has the following five features:

*Observing and listening to students
during class can help teachers, on the
spot, tailor their questions or tasks to
provoke and extend students' thinking
and understanding.*

from NCTM Professional Standards for
Teaching Mathematics

1. The assessment situation is presented to the students in the form of a discussion, an assignment, a question, or any action to generate student response.
2. The student's response is needed as a written numerical answer, a written paragraph about the thinking behind a solution, an oral presentation, an interview, a journal, or a portfolio.
3. The student's response is interpreted by the teacher or by a student. The interpretation requires making inferences about the understanding. This can never show the extent of the knowledge, but information from a variety of sources becomes more accurate.
4. A meaning is assigned to the interpretation of the response, perhaps by locating the response on a scale, and is presented to the student.
5. The results of the assessment are reported and recorded.

Daily observation and ongoing evaluation are essential for assessment. Whether the assessment is for mathematical understanding, for attitude, for language development, for interests, or for work habits, observations must be focussed, systematic, and recorded.

Interviews with individuals, pairs, or groups are opportunities to discover reasons for progress. They provide a chance for students to express their ideas about mathematics and their own accomplishments. Interviews with their peers can also be conducted by students.

To evaluate the students' achievement and acquire the information necessary for planning a mathematics program, the *MATHPOWER™ 11, Western Edition*, text and teacher's resource provide a variety of means of assessment. The suggestion is that choices be made about what assessments to use.

In the text, each chapter begins with a Getting Started section that can be used to assess whether students have the background appropriate to begin the chapter or whether review is needed. The Getting Started could also serve as a review of relevant topics.

Near the end of each chapter, a Review and a Chapter Check provide assessments of strengths and weaknesses in the skills and concepts presented in the chapter. At the end of Chapters 4 and 8 is a Cumulative Review with questions separated according to the chapters they review. These can be assigned at one time, or whenever an evaluation or review is needed. At the end of Chapter 9 is a cumulative review that covers Chapters 1 to 9. Although the questions are not separated by chapters, they are arranged in the same order as the material they cover is ordered in the text.

Most sections of the teacher's resource contains a Prerequisite Skills assignment designed to review or assess skills related to the learning outcome. Almost every section suggests a Math Journal topic, about which students can record their thoughts or feelings concerning the math of the section in their journals. Math Journals can be evaluated for depth of comments and questions, mathematical language, organization, and completeness.

Each teaching section in Chapters 1 to 9 of the *MATHPOWER™ 11, Western Edition, Teacher's Resource* contains an Assessing the Outcomes, and each section in the Math Standards section of the teacher's resource contains an Assessment. These evaluation tasks are based on the NCTM *Curriculum and Evaluation Standards*. They consist of individual evaluations, pair evaluations where pairs confer and present an answer that represents the pair or combine their work in some other way, and group evaluations where a group of students cooperate for a team effort that reflects their understanding. These assessments include teacher assessments, self-evaluations in which students assess their own achievements and/or confidence, and peer evaluations in which students assess the work of their classmates. It is not intended that all of these be assigned. They might be used with the section, at the end of a chapter, or weeks after the chapter has been completed.

Assessing what students know or believe about their own strengths and weaknesses in mathematics, what they think they would like to learn, and how they think this could be accomplished is an important aspect of learning math. Self-evaluation provides a chance to find out what individual students value in math. Exploring Math assignments ask students to evaluate the process and product of their group work, identifying what worked well and what they would do differently next time.

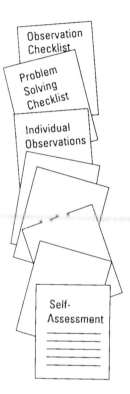

Assessment Masters on pages 405 to 414 of this teacher's resource have spaces for checks, marks, ratings, and comments made by the teacher, and comments made by the students.

- An observation checklist has blanks for marks and/or ranking.
- An attitudes assessment can be used for reporting on attitudes about mathematics, including self-confidence, curiosity, and flexibility.
- A problem solving assessment is appropriate for recording students' abilities to apply the four stages of the problem solving model and attitudes toward problem solving.
- An individual assessment can be used for recording notes about observations.
- Another individual assessment is appropriate for interviews, with space for teacher comments.
- A group assessment is appropriate for specific assignments.
- Another group assessment can be used to assess group task skills.
- A self-assessment would be completed by students evaluating strategies for working within a group.
- Another self-assessment asks students about math and what is important in math.
- A third self-assessment relates to specific math topics.

Portfolios are important parts of assessment. The collections of students' work may include problem solving tasks, investigations, research writings, reports, graphs, photographs of displays, answers for any work from the text, posters, work for Extension or Enrichment, solutions to Power problems, and any material the students themselves wish to include. The students might be responsible for choosing some or all items for their portfolios and keeping them up-to-date. Recording the date on each item is important for showing progress and trends in students' work. Portfolios can be made with large sheets of construction paper or file folders, and can be stored in a filing cabinet, a cupboard, or a cardboard box. Students should reorganize their portfolios, remove material they think is not appropriate, and add new material at reasonable intervals during the year.

The *MATHPOWER*™ *11, Western Edition*, program includes two supplementary computer products, which are designed to assist the student assessment. The *MATHPOWER*™ *11, Western Edition, Computerized Assessment Bank* is a tool for generating many more questions related to the specific student outcomes. The *MATHPOWER*™ *11, Western Edition, Outcome Tracker*™ is a sophisticated classroom assessment and management system that can help evaluate students' progress and point to concepts with which they might need further assistance. For further details on these two computer-based assessment tools, please refer to page xx of the teacher's resource.

Resources

The students should have access to a variety of reading material, such as math dictionaries, encyclopedias, almanacs, Guinness books of reference, atlases, maps, magazines, newspapers, and computer manuals, to acquire data for problems and to research information. The following resources provide teaching suggestions, theories in math education, and logical thinking puzzles.

Dishon, Dee, and Pat Wilson O'Leary. *A Guidebook for Cooperative Learning: A Technique for Creating More Effective Schools*. Holmes Beach, Fla.: Learning Publications, 1984. This guidebook presents suggestions for interacting and observing with cooperative learning and for setting cooperative learning goals.

Gardner, Martin. *Further Mathematical Diversions*. Middlesex, England: Penguin Books, 1981. This book contains challenging paradoxes and puzzles.

———. *Time Travel and Other Mathematical Bewilderments*. New York: W. H. Freeman and Company, 1988. This challenging assortment of math puzzles and questions includes polygonal numbers, anamorphic art, tiling with convex polygons, thoughts of Lewis Carroll, inductive reasoning, and probability. It also contains tangram puzzles that would extend an intermediate math program.

Hall, Godfrey. *Mind Twisters*. New York: Random House, 1992. This book contains a collection of reasoning puzzles, mazes, science experiments, and magic tricks. It includes calculator activities, Napier bones, magic squares, the Möbius strip, tangrams, tessellations, and codes.

Johnson, David W., Roger T. Johnson, and Edythe Johnson Holubec. *Circles of Learning: Cooperation in the Classroom*. Edina, Minn.: Interaction Book Company, 1986. This book describes positive interdependence, individual accountability, and collaborative skills for students working with peers. It explains the jigsaw style of cooperative learning.

Kagan, Spencer. *Cooperative Learning*. San Juan Capistrano: Calif.: Kagan Cooperative Learning, 1992. This book describes theories, methods, and lesson designs for cooperative learning. It suggests ideas for team projects and extends cooperative learning outside the classroom.

Müller, Robert. *The Great Book of Math Teasers*. New York: Sterling Publishing Co., 1989. This book presents a wide variety of puzzles with coins, dice, number patterns, magic squares, and cryptograms. Many of the puzzles are original variations of classic questions that would enhance an intermediate math program.

National Council of Teachers of Mathematics. *Mathematics Teaching in the Middle School*. Reston, Va.: The Council. This publication, printed quarterly, discusses learning needs of students in grades 5 to 9, demands placed on teachers, and mathematics issues for this level.

———. *Curriculum and Evaluation Standards for School Mathematics*. Reston, Va.: The Council, 1989. This document describes thirteen standards for the mathematics curriculum for kindergarten to grade 4, thirteen standards for grades 5 to 8, and fourteen standards for grades 9 to 12.

———. *Curriculum and Evaluation Standards for School Mathematics Addenda Series, Grades 9–12*. Edited by Christian R. Hirsch. Reston, Va.: The Council, 1991–1995. The Addenda books make suggestions about applying the *Curriculum and Evaluation Standards for School Mathematics* for grades 9 to 12. *Connecting Mathematics* focuses on connections among mathematical topics and between mathematics and real-world situations. *A Core Curriculum: Making Mathematics Count for Everyone* presents activities and lessons to cultivate students' abilities to explore, conjecture, and reason logically. *Data Analysis and Statistics Across the Curriculum* provides activities that illustrate how to integrate statistical concepts into the mathematics curriculum. *Geometry from Multiple Perspectives* provides instructional suggestions and discusses the growing use of technology. *Algebra in a Technological World* addresses teaching algebra and changes due to the graphing calculator and to computer software.

———. *Professional Standards for Teaching Mathematics*. Reston, Va.: The Council, 1991. This set of guidelines for implementing the *Curriculum and Evaluation Standards for School Mathematics* is based on the assumption that changes in education require teachers to have resources for meeting current needs.

National Research Council. *Everybody Counts: A Report to the Nation on the Future of Mathematics Education*. Washington, D.C.: National Academy Press, 1989. This report emphasizes developing the mathematical power of each student by presenting opportunities to learn by solving problems, analyzing, proving, and communicating.

Polya, G. *How To Solve It: A New Aspect of Mathematical Method*. Princeton, N.J.: Princeton University Press, 1945. Professor Polya describes the mathematical method and its application to solving problems. Polya talks about heuristic reasons and the need to challenge the curiosity of students.

Rothstein, Erica, ed. *The Dell Book of Logic Puzzles*. New York: Dell Publishing. Several Dell booklets present logic puzzles that are rated easy, medium, hard, and challenging. Grids for solutions and examples about how to use the grids are provided. *Dell Math Puzzles and Logic Problems* magazine, with similar puzzles, is published quarterly.

Smullyan, Raymond. *What is the Name of This Book? The Riddle of Dracula and Other Logical Puzzles*. Englewood Cliffs, N.J.: Prentice-Hall, 1978. This recreational puzzle book contains challenging logical puzzles, mysteries, and paradoxes.

Shortz, Will, ed. *Brain Twisters from the First World Puzzle Championships*. New York: Random House, 1993. This book contains a variety of puzzles selected from Games magazines, including grids, mazes, a rectangular tangram, geometric figures, and numbers. *Games* and *Games World of Puzzles* are published on alternate months and contain logic, number, word, and visual puzzles.

Concepts and Skills

Problem Solving

Problem solving is an integral part of the *MATHPOWER™ 11, Western Edition,* program.

Introducing Problem Solving

Problem Solving in *MATHPOWER™ 11*
Math Standard: Math as Problem Solving

Presenting the Strategies

Applying the Strategies

Other Problem Solving Features

Number

Number Concepts

Rounding and estimating are used throughout in computational parts of the MATHPOWER™ 11, Western Edition, text

Number Operations

Patterns and Relations

Patterns

Variables and Equations

Relations and Functions

Shape and Space

Measurement

3-D Objects and 2-D Shapes

Math Standards

Mathematics as Problem Solving

Students [will] use, with increasing confidence, problem-solving approaches to investigate and understand mathematical content; apply integrated mathematical problem-solving strategies to solve problems from within and outside mathematics; recognize and formulate problems from situations within and outside mathematics; apply the process of mathematical modeling to real-world situations.

from NCTM Curriculum and Evaluation Standards for School Mathematics

Student Text Page

xvi

Materials

toothpicks

Teaching Suggestions

Organize the students into pairs to solve the problems, assisting pairs as necessary. Encourage them to use whatever strategies and materials they find helpful. Assign the questions. For question 1, ask:

What information does the sentence: "The team captain is a female." provide?

Elicit from the students that since the team captain is a female, then the problem is the simpler one—finding the combinations of a team of five from three females and four males.

If they are having difficulty with question 1, suggest that they draw a tree diagram or make an organized list.

For question 2, suggest that the student pairs discuss and compare their results. Ask:

What is a magic square?

What is the first step in completing a magic square?

For question 3, suggest that the students draw a diagram for each step of the solution. When they are finished, have volunteers present their results to the class.

For question 4, ask:

Where are six identical parts on a cube?

How can this information help you find a solution to the problem?

For question 5, ask:

What formula can you use to find the number of diagonals for a polygon of n sides?

Suggest that the students find the number of diagonals for polygons of different sides and then, find which two numbers of diagonals total 14.

For question 6, provide each pair of students with 13 toothpicks and suggest they use the toothpicks to find the solution. Have the students draw a diagram of their solution. The diagram for the solution is as shown.

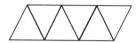

When the students have completed the questions, have volunteers present their problem solving strategies to the class. Have a class discussion about the advantages and disadvantages of each strategy.

Enrichment

Research the life and works of George Polya. Write a few sentences describing his importance to the problem solving process.

Math Journal

Choose one of the problems in the exploration, and write down an alternate strategy for solving the problem.

Assessment

Observation

Consider the following questions as the students solve the problems:

- Can they apply the four stages of the problem solving model?
- Are they able to apply different problem solving strategies to the same problem?
- Can they explain their solution and relate it to the question asked in the problem?
- Do they seem to understand other students' solutions?

Mathematics as Communication

Students [will] reflect upon and clarify their thinking about mathematical ideas and relationships; formulate mathematical definitions and express generalizations discovered through investigations; express mathematical ideas orally and in writing; read written presentations of mathematics with understanding; ask clarifying and extending questions related to mathematics they have read or heard about; appreciate the economy, power, and elegance of mathematical notation and its role in the development of mathematical ideas.

from NCTM Curriculum and Evaluation Standards for School Mathematics

Student Text Page

xvii

Teaching Suggestions

Organize the class into pairs and assign the explorations. For the question in exploration 2, ask:

Which word, uphill, downhill, or flat would you use to describe the track between points A and B? between points B and C?

Which word, increasing or decreasing, would you use to describe the speed of the train between points A and B? between points B and C?

How would you draw a line on a graph to show the speed of an object whose speed is increasing? decreasing?

The required graph for this question is the same as the graph given on student text page xvii, except it is inverted.

As well as sketching a graph for the solution to Exploration 2, have the students write a brief description of the movement of the roller coaster.

For the questions in Exploration 3, suggest that the students try simple numerical values to see if there are any patterns in the results that might help them make general conclusions about the changes in the kinetic energy and the speed of the muscle movement.

When the students have completed the exploration, have volunteers present their results to the class.

Extension

Choose a four-legged animal. Write a description of the animal, including estimates of its measurements. Do not include in your description any vocabulary that is related to the animal. For example, if you are describing a horse, do not include words such as hoofs, etc. Exchange your description with a classmate, and try to identify your classmate's animal.

Math Journal

Write a short essay describing what you like about writing instructions. Include what you found most difficult about writing instructions.

Assessment

Written Assignment

Write a set of instructions that would enable someone without the diagram to be able to recreate it.

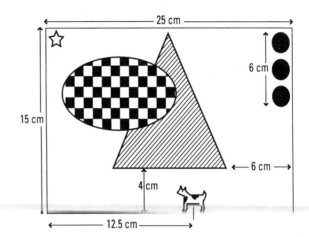

Mathematics as Reasoning

Students [will] make and test conjectures; formulate counterexamples; judge the validity of arguments; construct simple valid arguments; and ... construct proofs for mathematical assertions, including indirect proofs by mathematical induction.

from NCTM Curriculum and Evaluation Standards for School Mathematics

Student Text Page

xviii

Materials

Teacher's Resource Master 2 (1-cm grid paper)

Teaching Suggestions

(1-cm grid paper) Organize the students into pairs, and assign Exploration 1. Ask:

If there are 2 coins in each box, what are the possible amounts that are in the boxes?

What combination of coins is not in the 20¢ box? the 10¢ box? the 15¢ box?

Which box must contain coins of the same value?

If you shake the 15¢ box and a nickel falls out, what is the other coin in the box?

Which coins are left?

Then, if you shake the 20¢ box and a nickel falls out, what is the other coin in the 20¢ box?

What coins are in the 10¢ box?

Have the students find the solution when you shake the 15¢ box and a dime falls out.

For part a) of question 2, suggest that the students take each sentence and assume that it is true. If two sentences are contradictory, then the sentence that you assumed to be true must be false.

When the groups have completed the questions, have volunteers present their results to the class.

Assign Exploration 2 to pairs of students. Give them an opportunity to discuss and compare their results with other pairs. Have volunteers present their results to the class.

Math Journal

Provide an example of a choice you had to make and your reasoning for that choice.

Extension

Write a problem similar to the ones in Exploration 2. Exchange your problem with that of a classmate and solve it. Present your problem and solution to the class.

Assessment

Pair Evaluation: Critical Thinking

Have each student in the pair confer and give one answer that represents the pair.

What numbers must appear on the faces of two cubes so that there is an equal chance of rolling each number from 1 to 12.

Mathematical Connections

Students [will] recognize equivalent representations of the same concept; relate procedures in one representation to procedures in an equivalent representation; use and value the connections among mathematical topics; use and value the connections between mathematics and other disciplines.

from NCTM Curriculum and Evaluation Standards for School Mathematics

Student Text Page

xix

Materials

scientific calculator, overhead projector

Teaching Suggestions

(overhead projector)   Begin by asking:

What does the term "physiology" mean?

These assignments may be completed at different times by student pairs or by small groups of students.

For Exploration 1, ask:

What types of careers would use data similar to that given in Exploration 1?

How do you think the data could be used?

For Exploration 2, ask:

What is a scatter plot?

How can a scatter plot be used to show any relationships?

What is a linear relationship?

How do you predict data from a scatter plot?

What assumptions do you make when you make predictions from data?

Have volunteers present their results to the class. Provide an overhead projector, if necessary.

Math Journal

Describe in a few sentences a way you use mathematics in your everyday life.

Assessment

Group Evaluation: Assignment

Have each group choose a topic such as art, technology, or construction. Have the students explain and illustrate the relationship between their topic of choice and mathematics.

Algebra

Students [will] represent situations that involve variable quantities with expressions, equations, inequalities, and matrices; use tables and graphs as tools to interpret expressions, equations, and inequalities; operate on expressions and matrices, and solve equations and inequalities; appreciate the power of mathematical abstraction and symbolism; and ... use matrices to solve linear systems; demonstrate technical facility with algebraic transformations, including techniques based on the theory of equations.

from NCTM Curriculum and Evaluation Standards for School Mathematics

Student Text Page

xx

Teaching Suggestions

Ask:

How many students collect coins?

What is the study and collection of coins called?

Does anyone have the actual coin described on student text page xx?

Assign Exploration 1 to pairs of students. For question 1 c), ask:

What operation, $+$, $-$, $\times$, or $\div$, is associated with the words "How much greater?"

For question 2, ask:

What assumptions do you make to find the area of the arena?

Give students an opportunity to compare and discuss their results with other pairs of students. When they have completed the questions, have volunteers present their results to the class.

Review with the students the steps required to simplify an expression. Then, assign Exploration 2 as independent work. Ask:

What does the word "simplify" mean?

What is the first step in simplifying an expression such as the one in question 1?

Have student volunteers present their results to the class.

Math Journal

Describe in a few sentences what you think the meaning of algebra is.

Assessment

Peer Evaluation: Written Assignment

Have each student in a pair complete half of these questions. Then, have the partners trade with each other and assess each other's answers for accuracy.

1. Simplify.

a) $\dfrac{2x^2 - 5x + 3}{3x^2 - 5x + 2}$

b) $\dfrac{6x^2y}{8x^2} \times \dfrac{12x}{9y}$

c) $\dfrac{x^2 - 11x + 30}{x^2 - 6xc + 9} \div \dfrac{x^2 - 5x}{x^2 - 3x}$

d) $\dfrac{x^2 + 3x + 2}{x^2 - 5x + 6} \times \dfrac{x^2 + 3x - 10}{x^2 + 6x + 5}$

2. Simplify.

a) $\dfrac{2}{3x} + \dfrac{5}{2y}$

b) $\dfrac{2x + 3y}{9} - \dfrac{x + 4y}{2}$

c) $\dfrac{2}{x^2 - x - 12} + \dfrac{3}{x^2 - 6x + 8}$

d) $\dfrac{5}{x^2 + 7x + 12} - \dfrac{2}{x^2 + 6x + 9}$

Functions

Students [will] model real-world phenomena with a variety of functions; represent and analyze relationships using tables, verbal rules, equations and graphs; translate among tabular, symbolic, and graphical representations of functions; recognize that a variety of problem situations can be modeled by the same type of function; analyze the effects of parameter changes on the graphs of functions; and ... understand operations on, and the general properties and behaviour of, classes of functions.

from NCTM Curriculum and Evaluation Standards for School Mathematics

Student Text Page

xxi

Teaching Suggestions

Assign the explorations to pairs of students. Begin Exploration 1 by having one student provide his or her partner with a rate and asking the partner to convert the rate from one set of units to another. For example, one student could provide the rate 10 km/h and ask his or her partner to convert it to metres per second.

For question 2 of Exploration 2, ask:

What patterns do you see in the F-figures?

How many squares are added to each consecutive F-figure?

How does knowing the pattern and how many squares are added to each figure help to write the expression for the total number of squares in any figure?

When the students have completed the explorations, have volunteers present their results to the class.

Enrichment

Make up a set of diagrams of your own, similar to the ones in Exploration 2 on student text page xxi. Write a few problems related to your diagrams, and then, exchange your diagram and problems with a classmate. Solve your classmate's problems and then, discuss and compare your results.

Math Journal

Describe what you find easy about using formulas to find data. Include in your description the first step you take in using a formula to solve a problem.

Assessment

Written Assignment

1. The speed a parachutist falls depends on the mass of the parachutist and the area of the parachute. The descent speed is given by $s = \frac{50m}{a}$, where s is the descent speed in metres per second, m is the mass of the parachutist in kilograms, and a is the area of the parachute in square metres.

a) The area of a parachute is 225 m². What is the descent speed of a human with a mass of 90 kg?

b) A person with a mass of 60 kg falls with a descent speed of 30 m/s. What is the area of the parachute?

Geometry From a Synthetic Perspective

Students [will] interpret and draw three-dimensional objects; represent problem situations with geometric models and apply properties of figures; classify figures in terms of congruence and similarity and apply these relationships; deduce properties of, and relationships between, figures from given assumptions; and ... develop an understanding of an axiomatic system through investigating and comparing various geometries.

from NCTM Curriculum and Evaluation Standards for School Mathematics

Student Text Page

xxii

Materials

Teacher's Resource Master 6 (2-cm grid paper), interlocking cubes

Teaching Suggestions

(2-cm grid paper, interlocking cubes) Provide small groups of students with grid paper and assign Exploration 1. Suggest that the students copy the nets shown on student text page xxii and construct models of the cubes. One method of solving the problem is to work backward—construct a cube and label it with the letters. Then, return the cube to the net format to see the positions of the letters.

Provide the groups with interlocking cubes and grid paper, and assign Exploration 2. Suggest that the groups reconstruct the architectural model shown on student text page xxii and then, use the model to draw each view.

Have volunteers present their group's results to the class.

Extension

Create an architectural model of your own, similar to the one on student text page xxii, using objects such as interlocking cubes, marshmallows and toothpicks, or grid paper. Write a problem related to your model. Exchange your model and problem with a classmate, and solve the problem. Discuss and compare your models and solutions with your classmate.

Enrichment

Look through magazines and books and find a composite solid such as a building or a vehicle, with a variety of shapes and dimensions.

Draw the top, side and front views of your solid. Present the views of your solid to the class.

Challenge a classmate to use your views to try to recreate the shape you used.

Organize a class bulletin board of the most interesting and creative solids created by the students in the class.

Assessment

Written Assignment

Consider the following questions as the student complete these explorations:
- Can the students visualize the models from each point of view?
- Can the students draw 2-dimensional views of the 3-dimensional models?
- Can the students describe the properties of the models?
- Can the students verbally compare one model with another?

Geometry From an Algebraic Perspective

Students [will] translate between synthetic and coordinate representations; deduce properties of figures using transformations and using coordinates; identify congruent and similar figures using transformations; analyze properties of Euclidean transformations and relate translations to vectors; and...deduce properties of figures using vectors; apply transformations, coordinates, and vectors in problem solving.

from NCTM Curriculum and Evaluation Standards for School Mathematics

Student Text Page

xxiii

Materials

Teacher's Resource Master 1 (0.5-cm grid paper), Teacher's Resource Master 5 (graphing grids), overhead projector

Teaching Suggestions

(0.5-cm grid paper, graphing grids, overhead projector)
As an introduction to Exploration 1, review with the class the terms "mapping" and "transformation." Lead a class discussion about the ways in which movement can be analyzed in terms of types of motion or transformations.

Assign Exploration 1 to pairs of students. Ask:

How is a reflection line related to the original figure and its image?

In what other ways are an original figure and its image related?

Elicit from the students that for a line to be a reflection line
- the line joining an original point and its image point must be perpendicular to it
- it must bisect the line joining an original point and its image point

Furthermore,
- an original figure and its image are congruent
- the sense of the labels of an original figure and its image are reversed

Provide the students with graph paper or graphing grids, and encourage the students to write the coordinates of the image, before plotting it.

Assign Exploration 2. Ask:

How would you describe a non-linear relation?

What type of curve is shown in the diagram?

What are the properties of an original figure and its image under a rotation?

Give the students an opportunity to discuss and compare their answers with those of another pair. Encourage them to discuss any similarities and differences in their answers.

Have volunteers present their results to the class. Provide an overhead projector, if necessary.

Extension

Use geometry software such as The Geometer's Sketchpad to repeat Explorations 1 and 2 on the computer.

Math Journal

Explain the similarities and differences between geometry from an algebraic perspective and geometry from a synthetic perspective.

Assessment

Pair Evaluation: Written Assignment

Have each student confer and write a description that represents the pair.

Write a few sentences describing how algebra can be used to show that two lines are parallel.

Trigonometry

Students [will] apply trigonometry to problem situations involving triangles; explore periodic real-world phenomena using the sine and cosine functions; and...understand the connection between trigonometric and circular functions; use circular functions to model periodic real-world phenomena; apply general graphing techniques to trigonometric functions; solve trigonometric equations and verify trigonometric identities; understand the connections between trigonometric functions and polar co-ordinates, complex numbers, and series.

from NCTM Curriculum and Evaluation Standards for School Mathematics

Student Text Page

xxiv

Materials

scientific calculators, overhead projector

Teaching Suggestions

(scientific calculators, overhead projector)   Have the students read the introduction on student text page xxiv to review the primary trigonometric ratios, and the formulas for the law of sines and the law of cosines.

Assign Exploration 1 to pairs of students. Ask:

What is the first step in finding the required side lengths in questions 1 and 2?

Remind the students to check that their calculators are in Degree mode.

Assign Exploration 2. Discuss the term "angle of depression." Suggest that students work independently to obtain a sketch showing the relevant measures needed to solve each problem and then, have them compare their diagrams with a classmate's before completing the solution.

Have volunteers present their results to the class. Provide an overhead projector, if necessary.

Enrichment

Look around you in your school and chose a height that you cannot measure. Decide what measurements you could take and how you could use them to calculate the height.

Math Journal

Describe how to use a scientific calculator to find

a) an angle in a triangle when you are given three side lengths

b) an angle measure when you are given the measures of two sides of a triangle and any non-contained angle

Assessment

Written Assignment

1. Find the value of *x*.

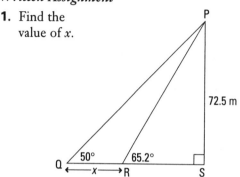

2. A roof is 10 m wide. One rafter makes an angle of 25° with the base of the roof, and the other rafter makes an angle of 60° with the base of the roof. Calculate the length of each rafter.

3. Find the width of the lake, AC.

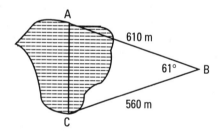

Statistics

Students [will] construct and draw inferences from charts, tables, and graphs that summarize data from real-world situations; use curve fitting to predict from data; understand and apply measures of central tendency, variability, and correlation; understand sampling and recognize its role in statistical claims; design a statistical experiment to study a problem, conduct the experiment, and interpret and communicate the outcomes; analyze the effects of data transformations on measures of central tendency and variability; and...transform data to aid in data interpretation and prediction; test hypotheses using appropriate statistics.

from NCTM Curriculum and Evaluation Standards for School Mathematics

Student Text Page

xxv

Materials

scientific calculators, overhead projector

Teaching Suggestions

(scientific calculators, overhead projector)   Ask:
Have you ever needed any advice on making a decision?
Where did you go for advice?

Students could work individually or in pairs on the questions in the explorations. Give students ample opportunity to discuss and compare their results. Have volunteers present their results to the class. Provide an overhead projector, if necessary.

Enrichment

Think of an item you would like to buy, or a place you would like to visit. Collect data that would help you make a decision about your choice. Present your data to the class and justify your choice.

Math Journal

Describe a career in which statistics is used on a daily basis. Describe why you would, or would not be, interested in pursuing this career.

Assessment

Critical Thinking

Write a short essay describing the advantages and disadvantages of buying an item directly as a result of information you gathered from an advertisement.

Probability

Students [will] use experimental or theoretical probability, as appropriate, to represent and solve problems involving uncertainty; use simulations to estimate probabilities; understand the concept of a random variable; create and interpret discrete probability distributions; describe, in general terms, the normal curve and use its properties to answer questions about sets of data that are assumed to be normally distributed; and...apply the concept of a random variable to generate and interpret probability distributions including binomial, uniform, normal, and chi square.

from NCTM Curriculum and Evaluation Standards for School Mathematics

Student Text Page

xxvi

Materials

Teacher's Resource Master 2 (1-cm grid paper)

Teaching Suggestions

(1-cm grid paper)   You might start the exploration of probability by tossing a coin. Take a vote on the result of a random toss, and then see how the actual outcome compares with the majority's choice. Ask:

What is the probability of tossing a head?

Elicit the fact that this probability means that if a coin is tossed many times, heads would occur 50% of the time. Point out that probability may be expressed as a fraction, a decimal, or a percent. Ask:

What are some examples of situations in everyday life in which probabilities are used?

Before starting the explorations, elicit and display on the chalkboard the definition of the probability of an event as follows.

$$P(\text{event}) = \frac{\text{number of favourable outcomes}}{\text{total number of outcomes}}$$

Students might find it easier to compile their data for question 1 in Exploration 2 by making a chart on grid paper.

Assign Exploration 2 to pairs of students, so that they can pool their ideas.

Math Journal

Research the meaning of the terms "experimental probability" and "theoretical probability." Write a few sentences explaining the similarities and differences between the two processes. Provide examples.

Assessment

Pair Evaluation: Conjecturing Assignment

Work together to plan an assignment in which one of the outcomes has a probability of 0.1 of occurring.

Discrete Mathematics

Students [will] represent problem situations using discrete structures such as finite graphs, matrices, sequences, and recurrence relations; represent and analyze finite graphs using matrices; develop and analyze algorithms; solve enumeration and finite probability problems; and...represent and solve problems using linear programming and difference equations; investigate problem situations that arise in connection with computer validation and the application of algorithms.

from NCTM Curriculum and Evaluation Standards for School Mathematics

Student Text Page

xxvii

Teaching Suggestions

Read with the class the opening paragraphs on student text page xxvii. Ask:

Why is there only 9 choices of digits for the first digit, but 10 choices for the second digit?

Assign Investigation 1 to pairs of students.

For Investigation 2, ask:

What is the difference between selecting a president and a treasurer, and selecting a group of two people?

Lead the students to see that in the first case if person A is selected for president, and person B is selected for treasurer, this is different than selecting person A for treasurer and person B for president. Although the same two people are chosen, their positions are different, and so each combination is different. In the second case all that is required is to select two people, that is, if you select person A and then person B, this is the same as selecting person B and then person A. Both combinations are the same, since no positions or order is indicated.

Enrichment

Research the meaning of the term "discrete" as it refers to numbers. Write a set of numbers that is discrete. Write a set of numbers that is not discrete.

Math Journal

Write two sentences describing your understanding of what is meant by the term "discrete mathematics."

Assessment

Written/Modelling Assignment

1. How many different ways can 3 men and 3 women be seated around a circular table, so that men and women alternate?

2. If you have 3 pennies, 2 nickels, and 1 dime, how many exact amounts can you pay?

Investigating Limits

Students [will] determine maximum and minimum points of a graph and interpret the results in problem situations; investigate limiting processes by examining infinite sequences and series and areas under curves; and...understand the conceptual foundations of limit, the area under a curve, the rate of change, and the slope of a tangent line, and their applications in other disciplines; analyze the graphs of polynomial, rational, radical, and transcendental functions.

from NCTM Curriculum and Evaluation Standards for School Mathematics

Student Text Page

xxviii

Teaching Suggestions

Ask the class:

What examples of limits have you seen in your everyday life?

Some examples provided by the students may be: a credit limit on a credit card, the speed limit, a maximum allowable weight on an elevator, and the height limit on a fairground ride.

Assign the investigation to small groups of students. Review with the class the meaning of $f(2)$, i.e., the value of $f(x)$ when $x = 2$. For question 2, point out that $x = 3$ is one of the inadmissible values of the function. Ask:

What other value of x is inadmissible for this function?

Ensure the students know that $x = 1$ is also an inadmissible value of the function. Explain that this is why it is important to include the value to which x approaches when writing the mathematical statement: The limit of $f(x)$ as x approaches 3 is ∎.

Give the students ample opportunity to discuss and compare their results and have volunteers present their results to the class.

Extension

For $f(x) = 2x$ and $g(x) = 1 - x$, find $\lim\limits_{x \to 0} f(x)$,

$\lim\limits_{x \to 0} g(x)$ and $\lim\limits_{x \to 0} [f(x) + g(x)]$.

How are $\lim\limits_{x \to 0} f(x)$, $\lim\limits_{x \to 0} g(x)$ and $\lim\limits_{x \to 0} [f(x) + g(x)]$ related?

b) Make up your own functions for $f(x)$ and $g(x)$ and use your own functions to find $\lim\limits_{x \to 0} f(x)$, $\lim\limits_{x \to 0} g(x)$

and $\lim\limits_{x \to 0} [f(x) + g(x)]$.

How are $\lim\limits_{x \to 0} f(x)$, $\lim\limits_{x \to 0} g(x)$ and $\lim\limits_{x \to 0} [f(x) + g(x)]$ related?

c) Repeat part b) above for another set of functions for $f(x)$, and $g(x)$. Make a conjecture that relates $\lim\limits_{x \to 0} f(x)$, $\lim\limits_{x \to 0} g(x)$ and $\lim\limits_{x \to 0} [f(x) + g(x)]$.

Enrichment

Discuss, as a group, the following paradox. A horse in a race can never finish the race because it first travels half the distance around the track, then it travels half of the remaining distance, then it travels half of the remaining distance, and so on.

a) How is this paradox related to limits?

b) What is the limit of the distance the horse travels in the race?

Math Journal

Write a paragraph about your own concept of what a limit is in mathematics.

Assessment

Written Assignment

Evaluate each limit.

1. $\lim\limits_{x \to 0} (5x + 12)$

2. $\lim\limits_{x \to 1} (x^2 + 2x - 1)$

3. $\lim\limits_{x \to 1} \dfrac{x + 2}{x + 1}$

4. $\lim\limits_{x \to 4} \dfrac{x^2 - 16}{x + 4}$

Mathematical Structure

Students [will] compare and contrast the real number system and its various sub-systems with regard to their structural characteristics; understand the logic of algebraic procedures; appreciate that seemingly different mathematical systems may be essentially the same; and...develop the complex number system and demonstrate facility with its operations; prove elementary theorems within various mathematical structures, such as groups and fields; develop an understanding of the nature and purpose of axiomatic systems.

from NCTM Curriculum and Evaluation Standards for School Mathematics

Student Text Page

xxix

Materials

Teacher's Resource Master 2 (1-cm grid paper), overhead projector

Teaching Suggestions

(1-cm grid paper, overhead projector) Provide the students with grid paper, and assign Investigation 1 to small groups. Ask:

How are the numbers in row 1, related to the numbers in row 2? row 3? row 4? row 5?

How could you write these relationships as mathematical expressions?

Give them ample opportunity to discuss and compare their results with those of other groups. Ensure that the students realize that the mathematical expressions for the numbers in row 2 are $1 + 5, 2 + 5$, etc.; for the numbers in row 3, $1 + 10, 2 + 10$, etc.; for the numbers in row 4, $1 + 15, 2 + 15$, etc.; and for the numbers in row 5, $1 + 20, 2 + 20$, etc. Have volunteers present their results to the class.

For Exploration 2, have each group do a different grid. Encourage them to write the mathematical expressions for the numbers in each row in terms of the numbers in row 1, as they did for the 5-by-5 grid above. When they have finished, have them present their results to the class. Provide an overhead projector, if necessary.

For Investigation 3, students should use the relationships expressed above in Investigation 1 to help them explain why the sums of the circled numbers are always the same. For example, for a 5-by-5 grid, suppose the number circled in row 1 is 3, the number circled in row 2 is 6 (which is $1 + 5$), the number circled in row 3 is 12 (which is $2 + 10$), the number circle in row 4 is 20 (which is $5 + 15$), and finally the

number circled in row 5 is 24, which is $(4 + 20)$. Add all the numbers

$$3 + 6 + 12 + 20 + 24$$
$$= 3 + (1 + 5) + (2 + 10) + (5 + 15) + (4 + 20)$$
$$= 3 + 1 + 2 + 5 + 4 + 5 + 10 + 15 + 20$$
$$= 1 + 2 + 3 + 4 + 5 + 50$$
$$= 15 + 50$$
$$= 65$$

As long as one number is chosen from each column, and only one number is chosen from each row, then the result will always be

$$1 + 2 + 3 + 4 + 5 + 50 = 65.$$

Extension

Create some new grids and try them out on your classmates. For example, you could create a 5-by-5 grid by beginning with the numbers 5, 6, 7, 8, and 9 in the first row. How would this affect the final total?

Create your own 6-by-6 grid and exchange your grid with a classmate. Calculate the final total for the grid. Compare your results with your partner's results.

Enrichment

1. Twin primes are prime numbers that differ by 2. For example, 5 and 7 are twin primes. Name two other sets of twin primes.

2. A number is *almost prime* if it is a product of two or less primes.

a) Which of the following numbers is almost prime? 4, 16, 15, 33, 60, 35

b) Describe a method for finding almost prime numbers.

Assessment

Pair Evaluation: Written Assignment

Have student pairs confer and give one answer that represents the pair.

Triplet primes are of the form $n, n + 2, n + 4$. Find an example of triplet primes.

MATH STANDARDS

Answers

Mathematics as Problem Solving
p. xvi

1 Solving Problems

1. 12

2. a) From left to right, top to bottom, the missing numbers are: 8; 23, 5, 16; 6, 20; 10; 25, 9
b) Yes.

3. Fill the 5-L container and empty it into the 9-L container, then fill the 5-L container again and pour water into the 9-L container to fill it. There is now 1 L of water in the 5-L container. Empty the 9-L container, pour the 1 L of water from the 5-L container into the 9-L container, refill the 5-L container and pour it into the 9-L container. There are now 6 L of water in the 9-L container.

4. a) The top vertex of each pyramid meets at the centre of the cube, with each face of the cube being a base of a pyramid.
b) 20 cm by 20 cm by 10 cm

5. pentagon, hexagon

Mathematics as Communication
p. xvii

1 Writing Solutions

1. Answers may vary.

2. Invert both timers. When the 5-min timer has expired, invert the 5-min timer again. When the 9-min timer has expired, there is still 1 min remaining on the 5-min timer. At this time, invert the 5-min timer, to time for the additional 4 min.

3 Writing and Interpreting Expressions

1. $E_k = \frac{1}{2}mv^2$

b) the bowling ball; It has the greater mass.

2. slower

Mathematics as Reasoning p. xviii

1 Using Logic

1. 1

2. a) Melissa   **b)** Paolo

2 Solving Problems

1. 15 years old and 45 years old

2. 7 dimes and 10 quarters

3. Jaleen: 17; Jamal: 14

Mathematical Connections p. xix

1 Animal Physiology

1. Mouse: 616.8 kJ/kg; Guinea pig: 320.2 kJ/kg; Rabbit: 178.4 kJ/kg; Monkey: 195.7 kJ/kg; Chimpanzee: 121.0 kJ/kg; Human: 83.7 kJ/kg; Pig: 42.2 kJ/kg; Horse: 17.7 kJ/kg; Elephant: 17.0 kJ/kg

2. The relationship is not a direct variation.

3. Answers may vary.

2 Human Physiology

b) Oxygen consumption increases as heart rate increases. The relationship is close to linear.

c) 0.95 L/min, 2.24 L/min

d) 111 beats/min

Algebra p. xx

1 Writing and Evaluating Expressions

1. a) $m = 4l - 2.825$
b) 25.175 g
c) 454.375 g

2. a) $A = 3x^2 + 16x - 12$
b) 1508 m²

3. a) $A = 4y + 10$
b) 18 m²

2 Simplifying Expressions

1. $\frac{2}{3}$

2. $\frac{x - 5}{x + 3}$

3. $\frac{2p + 1}{3p + 1}$

4. $\frac{(x + 3)(x - 2)}{(x + 1)(x - 1)}$

5. $\frac{(a - 2)^2}{(a + 1)(a - 4)}$

6. $\frac{(5x + 13)}{(x + 1)(x + 2)(x + 3)}$

Functions p. xxi

1 Using Relationships

1. a) $d = 95t$
b) 527.8 m; 1583.3 m; 3958.3 m

2. 7.2 s

2 Using Patterns

1. a) $5n + 1$
   b) 751
   c) 23
2. a) 20; 24
   b) $4n + 4$
   c) 104; 196; 452
3. a) 42; 50
   b) $8n + 10$
   c) 162; 290; 842
4. a) $P = 2s + 2$
   b) 166; 294

Geometry From an Algebraic Perspective   p. xxiii

1 Transforming a Triangle

1. a) A′(−1, 3), B′(−4, 1), C′(−5, 4)
   b) $x = 0$
2. a) A″(1, −3), B″(4, −1), C″(5, −4)
   b) $y = 0$
3. a) A‴(3, 1), B‴(1, 4), C‴(4, 5)
   b) $y = x$
4. a) A⁗(3, −1), B⁗(1, −4), C⁗(4, −5)
   b) rotation 90° clockwise about the origin

Trigonometry   p. xxiv

1 Finding Sides and Angles

1. $x = 18$ m
2. 10.7 cm
3. No.

2 Problem Solving

1. 9.8 km
2. a) H_1: 1875 m; H_2: 1089 m
   b) 822 m

Statistics   p. xxv

1 Selecting Tires

1. Baron
2. Answers may vary.

2 Purchasing Supplies

1. 156
2. Answers may vary.

3 Comparing Climates

1. Edmonton; Prince Rupert
2. Prince Rupert; Toronto
3. Toronto; There is not a lot of precipitation in the summer.
4. Prince Rupert; There is a lot of precipitation in the winter.

Probability   p. xxvi

1 Rolling Marbles

1. a) 1   **b)** 4   **c)** 6   **d)** 4   **e)** 1
2. a) 2   **b)** 8   **c)** 12   **d)** 8   **e)** 2

2 Rolling Dice

1. Regular dice: $\frac{1}{36}, \frac{1}{18}, \frac{1}{12}, \frac{1}{9}, \frac{5}{36}, \frac{1}{6}, \frac{5}{36}, \frac{1}{9}, \frac{1}{12}, \frac{1}{18}, \frac{1}{36}$;

   Irregular dice: $\frac{1}{36}, \frac{1}{18}, \frac{1}{12}, \frac{1}{9}, \frac{5}{36}, \frac{1}{9}, \frac{1}{12}, \frac{1}{18}, \frac{1}{36}$

2. Regular dice: $\frac{1}{6}$; Irregular dice: $\frac{1}{9}$

Discrete Mathematics   p. xxvii

1 Telephone Numbers

1. a) 128
   b) 640
   c) 10 000
   d) 6 400 000
   e) 819 200 000
2. Answers may vary.

2 Selecting People

1. 20
2. 10

Investigating Limits   p. xxviii

1. $f(2) = 1, f(4) = \frac{1}{3}$
2. The denominator is 0 when $x = 3$.
3. 0.666 67, 0. 588 23, 0.526 31, 0.502 51, 0.500 25; 0.400 00, 0.434 78, 0.476 19, 0.497 51, 0.499 75
4. 0.5
5. 0.5
6. 0.5
7. a) 4
   b) −2

Mathematical Structure   p. xxix

1 Investigating a Five-by-Five Grid

5. 65
6. equal

2 Investigating Other Grids

2. 111
3. 34; 15

3 Explaining Results

1. Answers may vary.

CHAPTER 1

Systems of Equations

Chapter Introduction

Chapter Materials

scientific (or graphing) calculators, Teacher's Resource Master 1 (0.5-cm grid paper), Teacher's Resource Master 2 (1-cm grid paper), Teacher's Resource Master 3 (algebra tiles), overhead algebra tiles, overhead projector, marbles, measuring tapes, toothpicks, Yellow pages, publications from Statistics Canada, Red Cross Society, Environmental Groups, miscellaneous reference books and almanacs

Chapter Concepts

Chapter 1 reviews or introduces

- methods of solving systems of equations graphically
- methods of solving systems of equations using substitution
- methods of solving systems of equations by elimination
- methods of solving systems of equations in three variables
- problem solving strategies emphasizing diagrams, data banks, and multiple estimations
- career connections, including chemistry and zoology

Teaching Suggestions

Method 1

Have the students look at the collage on the chapter opener page. Ask:

Which pictures represent sites in the east? in the west?

What clues did you use from the pictures?

How could you describe, in words, the relationship between the western sites and the eastern sites?

Look for answers such as: There are twice as many western sites as there are eastern sites; There are half as many eastern sites as western sites. Have the students write these relationships as equations. For example, if w represents the western sites and e represents the eastern sites, then, $w = 2e$ or $w = e + e$.

Challenge the students to come up with more complex relationships, such as, $w - 2e = 0$, $e = 0.5w$, or $w + e = 12$.

Instruct the students to graph the two relations. Have them create a table of ordered pairs for each equation. Point out that since neither of the variables w and e is dependent of the other, then they can choose either variable for the horizontal axis, and either variable for the vertical axis. Ask:

How would you graph each relation?

Encourage the students to change the equations to the slope y-intercept form. Remind them that if they take the two equations found in the text for the eastern and western sites and convert them to the slope y-intercept form, then they can graphically find the answer.

$w + e = 12$ becomes $w = -e + 12$, where the slope is -1 and the y-intercept is 12.

$w - 2e = 0$ becomes $w = 2e + 0$, where the slope is 2 and the y-intercept is 0.

To graph the line $w = -e + 12$, start at the vertical intercept. Find another point of the graph by moving 1 unit horizontally to the right (the run) and 1 unit vertically down (the rise). Connect the two points and you have the graph of the line $w = -e + 12$.

To graph the line $w = 2e + 0$, start at the vertical intercept. Find another point of the graph by moving 1 unit horizontally to the right (the run) and 2 units vertically up (the rise). Connect the two points and you have the graph of the line $w = 2e + 0$.

Method 2

Arrange the class into pairs. Present the following problem to the students:

> At the start of the year there were 36 students in the grade 11 math class. The teacher observed that there were three times as many girls as boys. If we wanted to present a graphical solution to the question "How many boys are there in the class?" what would we have to do?

Write two equations to represent the relationship between the numbers of boys and girls in the math class.

Have the students check their partner's equation to see if they have the same equations. Then, ask:

What does the statement "three times as many girls as boys" mean?

Elicit from the students the answers $3g = b$ and $3b = g$. Ask:

Which equation is correct? How can you tell?

Have students demonstrate by standing up with the correct ratio of boys to girls. This strategy is called mathematical modelling. If the students have difficulties, and are not sure how to proceed, help them to create a model. Ask:

What does the ratio 1:3 represent on a graph?

Which axis is the horizontal axis? the vertical axis?

Invite volunteers to come up to the chalkboard, draw and label a set of axes, and draw the line that represents the ratio of boys to girls. Then, ask:

What other information do you need to solve the problem?

Invite another volunteer to draw that line on the diagram on the chalkboard, either by connecting ordered pairs, or by writing the equation $b + g = 36$, and connecting the b-intercept and g-intercept. Ask:

What does the point where the two lines meet represent?

Integrating Technology

Internet

Use the Internet to do the research for question 4, and to find information about any of the World Heritage Sites that interest you.

Enrichment

Create your own problem about some aspect of your life (collections, food in the cupboard, number of hours of homework in two different classes, time spent doing homework to viewing TV, etc.), graph the equations, and explain the meaning of the point of intersection and the slopes of the lines.

Math Journal

Explain how you translate a situation into a mathematical equation. Describe aspects of the wording that you found difficult. Explain the meaning of slope and intercepts.

Assessing the Outcomes

Peer Evaluation: Graphing Assignment

Have one student graph the first question and the other student graph the second question on separate sheets of graph paper. Then, have the students exchange graphs to assess each other's understanding of how to create the equations.

1. Curi has five times as many CDs as Joanne. Together they have 48 CDs. How many CDs do each of them have?

2. Johal found his old hockey card collection and determined that he had seven times as many Canucks as Oilers. Altogether he had 56 hockey cards. How many cards from each team did he have?

Getting Started

Student Text Pages
Pp. 2–3

Learning Outcomes
- Study and evaluate the accuracy of Social Insurance Numbers (SINs).
- Construct SINs from check digits.

Prerequisite Skills

1. Evaluate each expression for $x = 2$ and $y = -1$.

a) $x + y$ [1]

b) $2x + y$ [3]

c) $-x - y$ [-1]

d) $5x + 3y - 2$ [5]

e) $y^2 - x^2$ [-3]

f) $2x^2 + 2 + 3y$ [7]

2. Simplify.

a) $3x + 2y - x + y$ $[2x + 3y]$

b) $5x + 2(x + y)$ $[7x + 2y]$

c) $5 - m - 2n + 1 + 3n$ $[-m + n + 6]$

d) $(3p - 5q) + (2q - p)$ $[2p - 3q]$

e) $2(p - 5q) - (p - q)$ $[p - 9q]$

f) $m^2 + 2n^2 - 3m^2 + 5n$ $[-2m^2 + 2n^2 + 5n]$

Teaching Suggestions

Social Insurance Numbers

Review with the class the first two paragraphs on student text page 2. Ask:

Who, in this class, has a social insurance number?

Encourage those students who do not have a SIN, to get one, as they will need it to apply for jobs and to pay taxes. Then, ask:

What is the first number of your SIN?

What area of the country does this first number indicate?

Have pairs of students follow the steps outlined on student text page 2 to determine if they have the correct check number. Remind them that *pqr stu vw* are variables that can be used to represent anyone's SIN.

For question 4, ask:

How many SINs are possible with a check digit of 7?

If the check digit is 7, what do you know about the digits of the SIN?

Elicit from the students that there can be an infinite number of SINs with a check digit of 7, and that a check digit of 7 means that the the last digit of the number that is subtracted from the next multiple of 10 is a 3. Thus, possible numbers to be subtracted are 13, 23, 33, 43, etc. Then, ask:

What would be the next two steps in developing a SIN with a check digit of 7?

Lead the students to see that first they need to choose a number whose last digit is 3, and then, to divide this number into two parts—one part that is the sum of the values p, r, t, and v, and the other part that is to be the total of the digits of $2q$, $2s$, $2u$, and $2w$.

Point out that the strategy of trial and error should be used in a situation like this. For example, suppose you decide to choose the number 43 to be subtracted. Each of the values chosen in the following example is just one of many possible values.

Divide 43 into 21 and 22.
Let $p + r + t + v = 21$, and let the sum of the digits of $2q$, $2s$, $2u$, and $2w$ be 22.
Remind the students that any digit can repeat any number of times.
For $p + r + t + v = 21$, let $p = 2$, $r = 4$, $t = 6$, and therefore, $v = 9$.
Four digits that total 22 are 4, 5, 6, and 7.
Then, $2q = 4$, and $q = 2$.
Since $5 = 1 + 4$, then $2s = 14$, and $s = 7$.
$2u = 6$, then $u = 3$.
Since $7 = 1 + 6$, then $2w = 16$, and $w = 8$.
Thus, one SIN could be 224 763 98 and the check digit of 7, which is 224 763 987.

Finally, ask:

Where have you seen examples of identification numbers in real life?

Warm Up

Assign some or all of the questions as individual or group work. Students could record their answers in their notebooks, or take turns asking questions orally with a partner.

When the students have finished, have them discuss the methods they used to answer the questions.

Mental Math

Students could choose, or be assigned, certain questions from each section. Alternatively, small groups could work as teams, sharing the questions and explaining the answers to the rest of the group.

Integrating Technology

Graphing Calculators

Write a graphing calculator program to calculate the 9th digit of a SIN. On a TI-83, Create New is the first item under NEW, which is the third heading when the PRGM key is pressed, and EDIT is the second heading when the PRGM key is pressed.

Extension

The ISBN is a number used to identify a book. It is 10 digits long, $d_1d_2d_3d_4d_5d_6d_7d_8d_9d_{10}$.

The formula for the ISBN is

$10d_1 + 9d_2 + 8d_3 + 7d_4 + 6d_5 + 5d_6 + 4d_7 + 3d_8 + 2d_9 + d_{10}$, where d_{10} is the check digit.

The check digit is the sum $10d_1 + 9d_2 + 8d_3 + 7d_4 + 6d_5 + 5d_6 + 4d_7 + 3d_8 + 2d_9$.

Subtract this sum from the next multiple of 11.

The number remaining is the check digit, d_{10}.

Thus, if $10d_1 + 9d_2 + 8d_3 + 7d_4 + 6d_5 + 5d_6 + 4d_7 + 3d_8 + 2d_9 = 163$, then the next multiple of 11 up from 163 is 165.

$165 - 163 = 2$.

The check digit is 2.

1. Which of the following ISBNs are incorrect?

a) 0-07-552596-8

b) 0-07-552948-6

c) 0-919028-65-9

2. Research what the letters I, S, B, and N represent.

Enrichment

With a partner, create a method of making up identification numbers for a bank card. Make up a method of calculating the check digit.

Share your method of creating bank card identification numbers with other pairs of students in your class.

Make up a class bulletin board of some of the more interesting methods.

Math Journal

Write a short paragraph suggesting why check digits are used. Describe some situations where a check digit might be necessary.

Assessing the Outcomes

Observation

You may want to consider some of the questions as the students discuss their trial and error methods.

- Do the groups share the tasks evenly?
- Are the students able to work with each other cooperatively?
- Do all of the students in each group attempt to find the answers?
- Do the students demonstrate problem solving skills?

Investigating Math

Exploring Ordered Pairs and Solutions

Student Text Pages
Pp. 4–5

Learning Outcomes
- Determine if an ordered pair satisfies an equation or system of equations.
- Check the solution of a system of linear equations graphically.

Prerequisite Skills
Evaluate each expression for $x = -1$ and $y = 3$.

a) $x + y$ [2]   **b)** $2x - y$ [−5]

c) $-5x + 3y$ [14]   **d)** $4x - 2y + 3$ [−7]

e) $x^2 + y$ [4]   **f)** $2x - y + x$ [−6]

Mental Math
1. Estimate.

a) $599 + 385$ [1000]   **b)** 2.94×0.9 [3]

c) $786 - 294$ [500]   **d)** $247 \div 8.7$ [25]

e) $76 + 192$ [300]   **f)** 801×189 [160 000]

2. Calculate.

a) 32×38 [1216]   **b)** 59×51 [3009]

c) 99×91 [9009]   **d)** 76×74 [5624]

e) 47×47 [2209]   **f)** 25×25 [625]

Teaching Suggestions
Have pairs of students complete Investigation 1 on student text page 4. Then, have volunteers present their results to the class.

Assign Investigation 2 to pairs of students. Review with the class the opening paragraph. Ask:

A system of equations involves two variables. How many equations must there be in the system in order to find the value of the two variables?

If a system of equations in two variables consists of three equations, can the system be solved? Explain.

If a system of equations in three variables consists of two equations, can the system be solved? Explain.

Have volunteers present their results to the class.

Assign Investigation 3. For question 3, ask:

If you were to remove a common factor from the second equation, what similarity would you see between the second factored equation and the first equation?

What does this tell you about the graphs of the lines represented by the equations?

How many ordered pairs satisfy both equations?

For question 4, ask:

How are the two equations similar?

How do the two equations differ?

How would you describe these two equations as they relate to each other?

How does this relationship help you to explain why no ordered pairs satisfy both equations?

Have volunteers present their results to the class.

Enrichment
Research the life and works of Gabriel D. Fahrenheit, Anders Celsius, and William Thomson Kelvin. Create a poster about the men who worked with temperatures and their formulas.

Math Journal
system of equations: Write a definition for a system of equations in your journal.

Show an example of how you would check to see if an ordered pair satisfies a system of equations.

Assessing the Outcomes

Written Assignment

These two equations show the relationship between the temperature, C, in degrees Celsius and the temperature, F, in degrees Fahrenheit.

$$F = 1.8C + 32 \quad (1)$$
$$F + C = 102 \quad (2)$$

a) The coordinates of the ordered pairs are usually given in alphabetical order, hence, the ordered pairs are (C, F). Use (1) to find the missing coordinate in each of the following ordered pairs: $(30, \blacksquare)$, $(\blacksquare, 68)$, $(15, \blacksquare)$.

b) Which ordered pairs satisfies (1) and (2)?

c) Use (1) to find the boiling point in degrees Fahrenheit, if the boiling point of water is $100°C$.

Solving Systems of Linear Equations Graphically

Student Text Pages
Pp. 6–12

Materials
graphing calculators, Teacher's Resource Master 2 (1-cm grid paper), overhead projector

Learning Outcomes
• Solve systems of equations graphically using the slope and y-intercept form.
• Solve systems of equations graphically using the intercepts.
• Find approximate solutions to systems of equations.
• Determine the number of solutions to a system of equations.
• Analyze systems of equations to determine the number of solutions.

Prerequisite Skills
1. Which point lies on the line with the given equation?
a) $x + 2y = 3$; $(2, -1)$, $(1, 1)$, $(3, 2)$ [(1, 1)]
b) $-2x + y = -1$; $(-1, -3)$, $(-1, 1)$, $(5, 4)$ [(−1, −3)]
c) $5x + 3 - 2y = 0$; $(1, 1)$, $(2, 3)$, $\left(-\frac{3}{5}, 0\right)$ $\left[\left(-\frac{3}{5}, 0\right)\right]$

2. Write three ordered pairs that satisfy each equation.
[Answers may vary.]
a) $x + 2y = 5$ $\left[(-1, 3), \left(0, 2\frac{1}{2}\right), (1, 2)\right]$
b) $3x - y = 1$ [(−1, −4), (0, −1), (1, 2)]
c) $y = -x - 4$ [(−1, −3), (0, −4), (1, −5)]

3. Write each equation in the slope and y-intercept form. Use the slope and the y-intercept of each equation to graph it.
a) $10x = 5y$ [$y = 2x$]
b) $x + 2y = 2$ $\left[y = -\frac{1}{2}x + 1\right]$
c) $3x - y = 7$ [$y = 3x - 7$]
d) $5y + 2x = 1$ $\left[y = -\frac{2}{5}x + \frac{1}{5}\right]$
e) $6x = 2y - 10$ [$y = 3x + 5$]

4. Identify the x- and y-intercepts of each equation in question 3.
$\left[\text{a) } 0, 0 \text{ b) } 2, 1 \text{ c) } \frac{7}{3}, -7 \text{ d) } \frac{9}{2}, -3 \text{ e) } \frac{1}{2}, \frac{1}{5} \text{ f) } -\frac{5}{3}, 5\right]$

5. Identify a pair of parallel lines and a pair of perpendicular lines in question 3.
[parallel: c) and f); perpendicular: a) and b)]

Mental Math
1. Evaluate each expression for $a = -1$ and $b = 2$.
a) $a + 2b$ [3]   b) $2a - b$ [−4]
c) $3a + 2b$ [1]   d) $5a - 4b$ [−13]
e) $-b - 2a$ [0]   f) $2a + 3 - 3b$ [−5]
2. Calculate.
a) 33×37 [1221]   b) 61×69 [4209]
c) 44×46 [2024]   d) 97×93 [9021]

Explore/Inquire Answers

Explore: Use a Graph
Answers may vary.
a) For example, $(1, 6)$, $(3, 4)$, $(5, 2)$
b)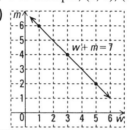

c) For example, $(1, 0)$, $(3, 2)$, $(5, 4)$
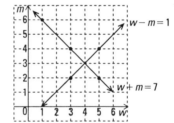

Inquire
1. a) an infinite number   b) an infinite number
2. a) $(4, 3)$
b) Substitute the values of the coordinates of the point of intersection into each equation of the system. If the coordinates satisfy both equations, then the point is on both lines.
3. a) 4   b) 3
4. a) 4   b) 6
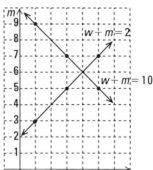
5. a) $(3, 5)$
b) $(6, -1)$
c) $(3, 3)$

Teaching Suggestions

Method 1

(1-cm grid paper, overhead projector, graphing calculators)
Read with the class the opening paragraph on student text page 6. Discuss with the class how the solution of a system of equations can be represented on a graph by the coordinates of a point that lies on all the lines represented by the equations of the system.

Arrange the class into pairs and provide each pair of students with grid paper. Assign the Explore section on student text page 6. Have the students translate each equation in the opening paragraph into words. Ask:

Is the information represented by the equations still true?

Have the students use the Internet address *www:\olympics.ca*, either at school or at home, to obtain the Barcelona summer results. Have the students compare the data on the Internet with the data in the text.

Then, ask:

Is it necessary to have the coordinates of 3 points of a line in order to draw the graph of the line?

Why is it useful to have the coordinates of 3 points of a line when drawing the graph of a line?

Have pairs of students present their results to the class. One student could display the graph on an overhead projector or construct a very large square grid, draw the graph on this large grid, and tape it to the chalkboard in front of the class. The other student could explain the steps they followed to get their results.

Then, assign the Inquire questions to pairs of students. Give the pairs of students an opportunity to compare and discuss their results with those of other pairs of students before asking them to present their results to the class.

Assign teaching example 1 on student text page 7 to the class. Review the method of finding two other points on a line, given the slope of a line and one point on the line.

If the students require more work with finding points that satisfy an equation, use the manual graphing method suggested in the text. Note that, by following the slope from the previous point (see the dotted triangles in teaching example 1), the students can easily find the pattern to get the next point without having to constantly substitute into the equation. You can reinforce this approach to manual graphing by presenting the following table of values.

$2x + y = 5$	
x	y
0	5
1	3
2	1
3	-1
4	-3

Ask:

What pattern do you see in the x values? the y values?

How are these patterns related to finding a point on the line?

Point out to the students that it is important to check the solution in both equations to determine if the answer actually satisfies both equations.

Assign teaching examples 2 to 4 to pairs of students. Have one student of each pair use paper and pencil to find the results, and the other student use a graphing calculator.

Review with the class teaching examples 4 and 5 on student text pages 9 and 10.

Method 2

(1-cm grid paper, overhead projector, graphing calculators)
Provide pairs of students with grid paper. Present this problem to the class and have pairs of students solve it.

Senga has a total of 7 dogs and fish. Three times the number of dogs she has is one more than the number of fish she has.

a) How many dogs does she have?

b) How many fish does she have?

Suggest that the variable d represent dogs and the variable f represent fish. Have the students write an equation to represent the total number of dogs and fish. Have them write an equation to represent the relationship between the number of dogs and the number of fish. Point out that there are several ways of writing each equation. For example, these are possible equations for the total number of dogs and fish: $d + f = 7$, $d = 7 - f$, or $f = 7 - d$.

Then, have the students graph both equations on the same set of axes. Give the pairs of students an opportunity to compare and discuss their results with those of other pairs of students. When the students have completed their graphs have pairs of volunteers present their results to the class. Provide an overhead projector for the students' use. Ask:

What are the coordinates of the point common to both graphs?

What do you notice when you substitute the values of d and f into one equation?

What do you notice when you substitute the values of d and f into the other equation?

The set of coordinates that satisfies each equation of a system of equations is the solution of the system of equations. Explain.

Review with the class the teaching examples on student text pages 7 to 10.

Sample Solution

Page 12, question 44

a) A system of equations that has only one solution is a pair of lines that intersects in only one point. Thus, these lines have different slopes and can have different intercepts.

The general equation of a line in the slope and y-intercept form is $y = mx + b$.
Let the point of intersection of the lines be $(3, 2)$.
Then, the general equation of a pair of lines with the intersection point $(3, 2)$ is $2 = 3x + b$.
Let the slope of one line be -1.
Then, its intercept will be
$$2 = 3(-1) + b$$
$$2 = -3 + b$$
$$2 + 3 = b$$
$$b = 5$$
Let the slope of the other line be $\frac{1}{2}$.

Then, its intercept will be
$$2 = 3\left(\frac{1}{2}\right) + b$$
$$2 = \frac{3}{2} + b$$
$$2 - \frac{3}{2} = b$$
$$b = \frac{1}{2}$$

The equations of the two lines are
$y = (-1)x + 5$ and $y = \frac{1}{2}x + \frac{1}{2}$, or
$y = -x + 5$ and $2y = x + 1$, or
$x + y = 5$ and $x - 2y = -1$.

Check by substituting the coordinates $x = 3$ and $y = 2$ into both equations.

$x + y = 5$	$x - 2y = -1$
$(3) + (2) = 5$	$(3) - 2(2) = -1$

Since the point satisfies both equations, and the slopes and intercepts are different, then this is a system of equations with only one solution.

b) A coincident system of equations has an infinite number of solutions. A pair of lines with the same slope and intercept is coincident.
Let the equation of a line be $5x + 2y = n$.
Point $(3, 2)$ is to be a point on the line.
Substitute $x = 3$ and $y = 2$ to find n.
$$5x + 2y = n$$
$$5(3) + 2(2) = 15 + 4$$
$$= 19$$
$5x + 2y = 19$ is a line containing the point $(3, 2)$.
Another line coincident with this line will also contain the point $(3, 2)$.
Multiply each term of the equation $5x + 2y = 19$ by any number, say 10.
$50x + 20y = 190$.
Then, the system $5x + 2y = 19$ and
$50x + 20y = 190$ is a coincident system with $(3, 2)$ as one of its many solutions.

Integrating Technology

Graphing Calculators: Graphing More Than One Equation

How would you use your graphing calculator to graph the pair of linear equations to find the intersection point shown in Method 2 of teaching example 1 on student text page 7? On a TI-83, a relation is graphed using an equation in the form $y =$.

Press the Y= key. Clear any equations. If Plot1 is highlighted, move the cursor to it and turn it off by pressing the ENTER key. Move the cursor back to Y1= and enter the right side of the first equation. Press the ENTER key to move the cursor to Y2= and enter the right side of the second equation. How do you enter the right side of equations such as $y = \frac{1}{2}x - 5$ from teaching example 1, and $y = -\frac{2}{5}x - 4$ and $y = \frac{5}{3}x + 5$ from teaching example 3?
You might enter $\frac{1}{2}$ and $-\frac{2}{5}$ in decimal form, 0.5 and -0.4, but $\frac{5}{3}$ is not a terminating decimal, so you can enter the right side of its equation as $5x \div 3 + 5$.
To display in the standard viewing window, press the ZOOM key and the 6 key to select ZStandard.
To use the Intersect operation, press the CALC (i.e., 2nd TRACE) key and the 5 key to select intersect. Use the arrow keys to move the cursor onto the intersection point, press the ENTER key to define the first curve, the second curve, and your guess. Then, read the coordinates of the intersection point given as $x =$ and $y =$.

Graphing Calculators: Friendly Windows

Is the standard viewing window on your graphing calculator a friendly viewing window?
On the TI-83, it is not. When you graph the system in teaching example 1 on student text page 7 in the standard viewing window and use the Trace instruction, do the values of x change by a friendly value, such as 0.1 or 0.2, or by an awkward value?
To create a friendly viewing window, set the maximum and minimum values for x and y relative to the pixel dimensions of your calculator. The size of the horizontal step, for example 0.1 or 0.2, is (Xmax − Xmin) ÷ (h − 1), where h is the horizontal pixel dimension. The size of the vertical step, for example 0.1 or 0.2, is (Ymax − Ymin) ÷ (v − 1), where v is the vertical pixel dimension.

For a TI-83, h is 95 and v is 63. Some friendly viewing windows have the following minimum and maximum values for x and y.

Xmin	Xmax	Ymin	Ymax
0	9.4	0	6.2
−1.4	8	−1.2	5
−4.7	4.7	−3.1	3.1
−9.4	9.4	−6.2	6.2
0	18.8	0	12.4
−18.8	18.8	−12.4	12.4

Why do these values create friendly viewing windows?

To set a friendly viewing window, press the WINDOW key and enter the values. Then, press the GRAPH key to view your graph.

*These values are used in the ZDecimal viewing window. ZDecimal is the fourth item under the ZOOM menu when the ZOOM key is pressed. Therefore, another way to set a friendly window is to select ZDecimal, and if the viewing window is not large enough, press the WINDOW key and multiply each value. For example, press the WINDOW key, enter ×2 beside the Xmin value of −4.7, and so on.

Graph the systems of equations in teaching examples 1, 2, and 3, using friendly viewing windows. What are some advantages and disadvantages of using friendly windows?

See *MATHPOWER™ 11, Western Edition, Blackline Masters* pp. 18 to 20 for Graphing Calculator as a Scientific Calculator. See *MATHPOWER™ 11, Western Edition, Blackline Masters* pp. 21 to 23 for Solving Linear Systems Graphically.

Calculator-Based Laboratories

Collect your own real data using a portable data collection device, a CBL (Calculator-Based Laboratory), and plot the data on a graphing calculator to find any intersection points.

Extension

Systems of equations in two variables have either no solution, one solution, or an infinite number of solutions.

A system of equations that has no solutions is called an *inconsistent* system. Otherwise the system is *consistent*.

An *independent* system of equations has exactly one solution, and a *dependent* system of equations has an infinite number of solutions.

No Solutions	1 Solution	Infinite Number of Solutions
inconsistent	consistent	consistent
neither dependent nor independent	independent	dependent

Use your graphing calculator to graph each system of equations. Identify each system as consistent or inconsistent, and as dependent, independent, or neither.

1. $3x + 5y = -2$
   $2x - y = 3$

2. $2x - y = -1$
   $4x - 2y = -2$

3. $3x + 2y = -5$
   $3x + 2y = 4$

4. $6x + y = 20$
   $-x - y = -9$

Enrichment

Draw a diagram to show the relationship between consistent, inconsistent, dependent, and independent systems of equations.

Math Journal

Write a list of the steps needed to solve a system of equations in two variables graphically.

Common Errors

- Students often forget to check the answer in the original equations.

R_x Point out to the students that, if the answer is not checked in the original equation, then some errors made at any point in their solution may not be obvious. Checking in the original equations ensures the answer arrived at is indeed the correct answer.

Problem Levels of Difficulty

A: 1–42, 48   **B:** 43–46   **C:** 47

Assessing the Outcomes

Written Assignment

1. Solve each system of equations graphically.

   a) $5x - 6y = 3$
      $-10x + 6y = -27$

   b) $4.8x + 0.04y = -1$
      $5.0x - 4.00y = 3$

2. A small business produces skateboard stickers. There is an initial machine set-up cost of $300. Then, it costs $0.50 to produce each sticker. The total cost (C) of producing any number of stickers (s) is represented by the equation $C = 0.5s + 300$. The company plans to sell the stickers for $2.00 each. This can be represented by the equation $C = 2s$.

   a) Graph the results.

   b) How many stickers need to be produced to break even?

Computer Data Bank

Using the Databases

Microsoft Works for Windows users see *Part B*, and Microsoft Access users see *Part D*, of *MATHPOWER™11, Western Edition, Computer Data Bank Teacher's Resource*.

Student Text Page
P. 13

Learning Outcomes

- Display, find, sort, calculate, summarize, graph, and analyze data in a computer database.
- Solve problems.

Prerequisite Skills

What are the steps in solving a problem? [Understand the problem. Think of a plan. Carry out the plan. Look back.]

Getting Started Blackline Masters C-1 to C-9

Teaching Suggestions

Students unfamiliar with computer databases and ClarisWorks would benefit from working through *Getting Started* Blackline Masters C-1 to C-9, noted in the *Prerequisite Skills*, prior to doing any of the explorations on this page. If they have not done so yet, you may wish to assign the *Getting Started* Blackline Masters to individuals, pairs, or small groups of students, to be completed over a period of time that allows students adequate computer time. The *Getting Started* Blackline Masters provide basic instruction in working with databases in ClarisWorks to meet the learning outcomes and provide students with an opportunity to use each of the seven databases. You may wish to delay assigning *Using the Databases* until students have had an opportunity to work through the *Getting Started* Blackline Masters. Minimally, students should have the *Getting Started* Blackline Masters available for reference.

Each exploration in *Using the Databases* is independent of the others. Some or all of the explorations can be assigned to individuals, pairs, or small groups of students, to be completed over a period of time that allows students adequate computer time. Up to two hours will be needed by some students to complete all five explorations. By working through all the explorations, students experience five of the seven databases, and gain some experience in each of the seven learning outcomes.

When assigning the explorations, inform students if you expect

- any parts of the explorations to be printed off the computer
- handwritten or word-processed answers to questions that suggest a written response
- a journal-type response about what they have learned mathematically, about using databases, and/or about the subject matter of the databases

Possible parts to assign for printing are a table to show the average inflation rate for the nations of Europe from Exploration 2; a table to show the average gross domestic product for the nations of Africa from Exploration 2; the graph from Exploration 3; the graph from Exploration 4; and a table to show the total campsite revenues from Exploration 5.

1 Seating Capacity of New Vehicles

For any vehicle available with more than one size of engine or more than one type of transmission, the road-tested vehicle, when available, is used in the database.

In question 1, use the Find feature with one comparison for *Seating* > 5 (*Getting Started* BLM C-5).

An efficient approach to question 2 is to display the records using Table 1. Count and display the number of vehicles in each type by doing the following. Create a summary field called *Vehicles by Type* for the records found in question 1, using the formula that follows. Sort by *Type*. Insert a Sub-summary section. Insert the summary field in the Sub-summary section (*Getting Started* BLM C-7). Then, note the count for each type to determine which is the greatest number.

COUNT('Vehicle')

An efficient approach to question 3 is to identify the two parts, a) and d), that are to be sorted from greatest to least and do them first. For part a), with the same records displayed using the same table as in question 1, sort *Length, m* in descending order. For part d), display the same records using Table 2 and sort *Highway Fuel Efficiency, L/100 km* in descending order (*Getting Started* BLM C-4). For part b), display the same records using Table 1 and use the Find feature with one comparison for *Mass, kg <> −1* (*Getting Started* BLM C-5). Then, sort *Mass, kg* in ascending order (*Getting Started* BLM C-4). For part c), display the same records using Table 2. Because no vehicles with seating for more than 5 were excluded by *Mass, kg <> −1*, use the Find feature with one comparison for *City Fuel Efficiency, L/100 km <> −1* (*Getting Started* BLM C-5), and then sort *City Fuel Efficiency, L/100 km* in ascending order (*Getting Started* BLM C-4).

2 Nations Around the World

All amounts of money are given in U.S. dollars, and Central American nations are considered to be on the continent of North America.

An efficient approach to question 1 is to display the records using Table 2. For each part, use the Find feature with one comparison for *Nation* nation of interest, note the government, show all the records, and use the Find feature with one comparison for *Government* government noted, showing all the records between parts (*Getting Started* BLM C-5).

An efficient approach to question 2 is to show all the records. Then, create a table to display only the *Nation*, *Continent*, and *Government* fields (*Getting Started* BLM C-2). Next, sort the continents alphabetically to see which continent occurs most frequently (*Getting Started* BLM C-4). Then, for each part except b), use the Find feature with one comparison for *Government* government of interest, noting which continent appears most frequently and showing all the records between parts. For part b), use the Find feature with one comparison for *Government* monarchy, and then, because constitutional monarchies are displayed as well, use the Find feature with one comparison for *Government* <>constitutional monarchy (*Getting Started* BLM C-5).

An efficient approach to question 3 is to show all the records, displaying them using the table created in question 2. Then, sort the governments alphabetically (*Getting Started* BLM C-4). Next, for each continent, use the Find feature with one comparison for *Continent* continent of interest, noting the number of different governments and showing all the records between continents (*Getting Started* BLM C-5).

The government types used to classify the nations are not mutually exclusive, and they reflect how each nation classifies itself. As an extension to questions 1 to 3, students could research some of the following topics.

- What is the difference between a constitutional monarchy and a monarchy?
- What is the difference between a commonwealth and a federation?
- Which government types other than democracy could be democratic? Which countries with those types are democratic?
- Which government types suggest that a nation is connected with another nation? Which nations are connected?

An efficient approach to question 4 is to show all the records and create a table displaying only the *Nation*, *Continent*, and *Inflation*, % fields (*Getting Started* BLM C-2). Then, use the Find feature with two comparisons for *Continent* Europe and *Inflation*, % <>(1 (*Getting Started* BLM C-5). Because Europe/Asia nations are displayed as well, they can be excluded, if desired, by using the Find feature with one comparison for *Continent* <>Europe/Asia. Next, determine and display the average of the inflation rates, rounded to 1 decimal place, for all the displayed records by doing the following. Create a summary field called *Average Inflation Rate*, %, using the

formula that follows. Insert a Trailing grand summary section. Insert the summary field in the Trailing grand summary section (*Getting Started* BLM C-7).

ROUND(AVERAGE('Inflation, %'),1)

An efficient approach to question 5 is to show all the records and create a table displaying only the *Nation*, *Continent*, and *GDP, $ billions* fields (*Getting Started* BLM C-2). Then, use the Find feature with two comparisons for *Continent* Africa and *GDP, $ billions* <>−1 (*Getting Started* BLM C-5). Next, determine and display the average of the gross domestic products, rounded to 3 decimal places, for all the displayed records by doing the following. Create a summary field called *Average GDP, $ billions*, using the formula that follows. Insert a Trailing grand summary section. Insert the summary field in the Trailing grand summary section (*Getting Started* BLM C-7).

ROUND(AVERAGE('GDP, $ billions'),3)

An efficient approach to question 6 is to show all the records and create a table displaying only the *Nation*, *Continent*, and *Literacy*, % fields (*Getting Started* BLM C-2). Then, use the Find feature with two comparisons for *Continent* any continent and *Literacy*, % <>−1 (*Getting Started* BLM C-5). Next, sort the literacy rates, note the highest and lowest, and determine the difference (*Getting Started* BLM C-4). Then, repeat the process for each of the other continents, showing all the records between continents.

3 Locating Craters on Earth

The craters in the database are the known terrestrial craters.

In questions 1a) to d), display the records using Full Record. For part a), use the Find feature with one comparison for *Name* Teague (*Getting Started* BLM C-5). In part b), show all the records and sort from greatest to least diameter (*Getting Started* BLM C-4). In part c), sort from greatest to least age, and in part d), sort from greatest to least rim height (*Getting Started* BLM C-4).

An efficient approach to part e) is to create a table displaying only the *Name*, *Continent*, *Apparent Depth*, *km*, and *True Depth*, *km* fields (*Getting Started* BLM C-2). Then, use the Find feature with two comparisons for *Apparent Depth, km* <>−1 and *True Depth, km* <>−1 (*Getting Started* BLM C-5). Next, create a calculation field called *Depth Difference*, *km*, using the formula that follows, to subtract the apparent depth from the true depth (*Getting Started* BLM C-6). Finally, sort from greatest to least depth difference (*Getting Started* BLM C-4).

'True Depth, km'-'Apparent Depth, km'

An efficient approach to part f) is to show all the records and create a table displaying only the *Name*, *Continent*, *Central Peak Height*, *km*, and *Central Peak*

Diameter, km fields (*Getting Started* BLM C-2). Then, use the Find feature with two comparisons for *Central Peak Height, km* −1 and *Central Peak Diameter, km* – 1 (*Getting Started* BLM C-5). Next, count and display the number of craters on each continent by doing the following. Create a summary field called *Craters by Continent*, using the formula that follows. Sort by *Continent*. Insert a Sub-summary section. Insert the summary field in the Sub-summary section (*Getting Started* BLM C-7). Then, note the count for each continent to determine which is the greatest number.

COUNT('Name')

If question 1f) has been completed with the *Craters by Continent* summary field, an efficient approach to question 2a) is to show all the records and sort again by *Continent* (*Getting Started* BLM C-4). Then, note the count for each continent.

An efficient approach to part b) is to open a new spreadsheet file and enter *Continent* and *Number* headings, and the continents and numbers found in part a). Then, use the Make Chart feature (*Getting Started* BLM C-9).

4 Summer Olympics

An efficient approach to question 1 is to use the Find feature with one comparison for *Event* event of interest (*Getting Started* BLM C-5). Then, create a table displaying only the *Year* and *Winning Distance, m* fields (*Getting Started* BLM C-2). Next, copy the *Year* and *Winning Distance, m* field values to a new spreadsheet, and use the Make Chart feature (*Getting Started* BLM C-9).

5 Camping in Western Canada

Parks with only group camping are not included.

An efficient approach to question 1 is to use the *Find* feature with two comparisons for *Province* British Columbia and *Campsites* <>−1 (*Getting Started* BLM C-5). Then, create a table displaying only the *Park*, *Type*, and *Campsites* fields (*Getting Started* BLM C-2). Next, determine and display the sum of the campsites in each type by doing the following. Create a summary field called *Total Campsites by Type*, using the formula that follows. Sort by *Type*. Insert a Sub-summary section. Insert the summary field in the Sub-summary section (*Getting Started* BLM C-7). Finally, subtract the two sums, using paper and pencil, using a calculator, or mentally.

SUM('Campsites')

An efficient approach to question 2 is to show all the records, displaying them using Full Record. Then, use the Find feature with one comparison for *Type* National (*Getting Started* BLM C-5). Next, create a table displaying only the *Park*, *Province*, and *Campsites* fields (*Getting Started* BLM C-2). Then, create a calculation field called *Campsite Revenue, $*, using the first formula that follows, where 122 is the number of days (*Getting Started* BLM C-6). Next, determine and display the sum of the campsite revenues in each province by doing the following. Create a summary field called *Total Campsite Revenue by Province, $*, using the second formula that follows. Sort by *Province*. Insert a Sub-summary section. Insert the summary field in the Sub-summary section (*Getting Started* BLM C-7). Finally, determine and display the sum of the campsite revenues for all the provinces by doing the following. Create a summary field called *Total Campsite Revenue, $*, using the second formula that follows again. Insert a Trailing grand summary section. Insert the summary field in the Trailing grand summary section (*Getting Started* BLM C-7).

'Campsites'*.8*18*122

SUM('Campsite Revenue, $')

1.2 Problem Solving: Use a Diagram

Student Text Pages
Pp. 14–15

Materials
Teacher's Resource Master 2 (1-cm grid)

Learning Outcomes
- Solve problems using diagrams.
- Apply formulas involving area, surface area, circumference, and the Pythagorean Theorem.

Prerequisite Skills
This diagram represents a garden. Describe the garden in words.

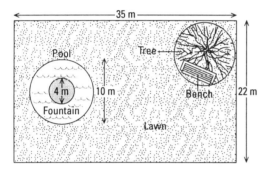

[This is a rectangular lawn measuring 35 m by 22 m. At the left-hand side of the lawn is a circular pool, 10 m in diameter, that has a circular fountain, 4 m in diameter, at its centre. At the upper right-hand side of the lawn is a tree with a bench.]

Mental Math
1. Evaluate for $x = 1$, $v = 2$, and $u = -1$.

a) $2x + v - u$ [3]

b) $x - 2u - v$ [1]

c) $-2x - 3v - 2u$ [-6]

d) $5u - x + 1$ [-5]

e) $3x - 2u - v$ [3]

f) $5 - x + u + v$ [5]

2. Calculate.

a) 0.47×43 [20.21]

b) 9.3×9.7 [90.21]

c) 410×490 [200 900]

d) 630×6.7 [4221]

e) 88×82 [7216]

f) 0.32×0.038 [0.012 16]

Teaching Suggestions

Method 1

(1-cm grid paper) The saying "A picture is worth a thousand words" could be translated into "A diagram is worth a thousand equations."

Discuss with the students how labelled diagrams (or models) are the backbone of much of the mathematics taught at this level. The importance of a well-labelled diagram, and the care taken in constructing it, cannot be over emphasized.

Review the problem solving steps on the left-hand side of student text page 14. Remind the students that drawing a diagram is a strategy for solving a problem. It is part of the plan for solving a problem.

Assign question 1 on student text page 15 to pairs of students. Challenge half of the pairs of students to solve the question with the help of a diagram, and the other half to solve the problem without a diagram. When all the students have finished, have volunteers present their results to the class. Ask:

Did those students who did not draw a diagram have difficulty in solving question 1?

How is a diagram useful in solving a problem?

Assign question 3 to the pairs of students. Ask:

What formula can you use to find the time it takes the train to pass through the tunnel?

Assign question 6 to the pairs of students. Ask:

How could a diagram be used to help you solve this question?

Discuss with the students how modelling and simulation provide a strategy that can lead to an accurate representation of a problem and correct labelling of a two-dimensional diagram. The resulting problem presented by the diagram can be solved using algebraic techniques. This strategy provides a way to make a complex three-dimensional problem into a simpler two-dimensional problem.

Provide pairs of students with 1-cm grid paper. Have them draw the net of a rectangular prism with length 10 cm, width 10 cm, and height 3 cm. Have them create a three-dimensional model of the room, including the placement of the spider and the fly. Challenge the students to use the three-dimensional model to solve the problem. Have volunteers present their results to the class.

Ensure that after they mark the location of the spider and the fly they return the rectangular prism to a two-dimensional net, draw a line joining the spider and the fly, and find the length of this line. Remind the students that the spider cannot fly, so it must travel along the surface of the rectangular prism to reach the fly.

Assign the remainder of the questions to the pairs of students. Give them a short period of time to solve their problems. Then, have volunteers present their results to the class. Provide an overhead projector for the students' use.

Method 2

Present this problem to the class.

Alice, Blake, Charlie, Dawn, and Edna are lined up, one behind the other. Blake is standing behind Alice. There are two people between Edna and Blake. Charlie is in front of Dawn. Dawn is the second-last person in the line. Who is first in line?

Have pairs of students try to solve the problem. Ask:

What do you think might help you to solve the problem?

Have volunteers present their solution to the class. Then, ask:

How many pairs of students found a diagram to be useful in solving this problem?

Then, have the class solve the problem again, only this time, have them use a diagram. Ask:

Is it easier to solve a problem using a diagram? Explain.

Integrating Technology

Internet

Work with other students on the Internet to solve problems, using web sites such as *http://forum.swarthmore.edu/mathmagic/* and Canada's SchoolNet Web Site at *http://www.schoolnet.ca*.

Extension

Draw a diagram to match this description.

A mirror with dimensions 50 cm by 35 cm has a wooden frame. The width of the vertical sides of the frame is 10 cm and the width of the horizontal sides of the frame is 7 cm. The horizontal measure of the mirror is greater than the vertical measure of the mirror. At each corner of the frame is a square decorative rosette that has a side length of 4 cm.

Math Journal

Write a short paragraph explaining why a diagram is useful in solving a problem.

Problem Levels of Difficulty

A: 1–10   **B:** 11–14

Assessing the Outcomes

Written Assignment: Diagramming

Four rods measure 2 cm, 5 cm, 7 cm, and 9 cm. How could you use these rods to measure a length of 1 cm?

Investigating Math

Translating Words Into Equations

Student Text Pages
Pp. 16–17

Learning Outcomes
- Write algebraic expressions involving two variables for word phrases.
- Use an equation to describe a relation.
- Use a system of equations to describe a pair of relations.

Prerequisite Skills

1. Write a numerical expression for each word phrase.

a) five times a number [$5x$]

b) one less than a number [$x - 1$]

c) four more than twice a number [$2x + 4$]

d) one-eighth of a number $\left[\dfrac{1}{8}x\right]$

e) the difference between a number and six [$x - 6$]

f) seven reduced by eleven times a number [$7 - 11x$]

2. Find the next two numbers of each sequence.

a) 2, 4, 6, 8, ... [10, 12]

b) 2, 4, 8, 16, ... [32, 64]

c) 5, 9, 13, 17, ... [21, 25]

d) $\dfrac{1}{128}, \dfrac{1}{64}, \dfrac{1}{32}, \dfrac{1}{16}, \ldots$ $\left[\dfrac{1}{8}, \dfrac{1}{4}\right]$

Mental Math

1. Calculate.

a) 43×47 [2021] b) 61×69 [4209]

c) 88×82 [7216] d) 55^2 [3025]

e) 16×14 [224] f) 33×37 [1221]

2. Evaluate for $m = 1$, $n = -2$, and $p = 3$.

a) $m + 2p$ [7] b) $-n + m - p$ [0]

c) $3n - 4p$ [−18] d) $2m + p - n$ [7]

e) $m - n^2 - p$ [−6] f) $m^3 - p^2$ [−8]

Teaching Suggestions

Discuss with the class how you learn to write in your mother tongue or in any language for that matter. Elicit from the students that, usually, you begin by writing words, then phrases, and then sentences. Ask:

How is this process of writing in a language similar to writing mathematical equations?

Elicit from the students that, in mathematics, first, you translate words into variables, then you translate phrases into mathematical expressions, and finally, you translate sentences into equations. Two or more sentences are translated into a system of equations. Ask:

What are the nouns in mathematics?

What are the verbs?

Point out that nouns will usually be the variables, their adjectives will often be the coefficients of the variables, verbs will usually represent the mathematical operations, and the comparatives will usually represent the equality or inequality.

Present this situation to the class.

John has five fewer CDs than Mykael. Twice the number of CDs Mykael has is three times the number of CDs John has.

If students have difficulty writing the formal "let" statements required for rigorous mathematical problem solving, you may wish to go to a less formal method and allow the students to use the first letter of the name to label the variable. For example, use j to represent the number of CDs John has and m to represent the number of CDs Mykael has.

$$j = m - 5$$
$$2m = 3j$$

If students have difficulty understanding why, in the first equation, the m and 5 have switched positions in the translation, select a student in the class who is about 5 cm shorter than you are. Then, ask:

A student is 5 cm shorter than me. Who do you start with to make the comparison?

Elicit from the students that if they start with you, then, they subtract 5 cm from your height to reach the student's height. Help the students to see that, when comparisons are made, you start with the end and then go down (or up). Hence, the comparative "than" causes a reversal in the order of the translation. The variable following "than" goes in front and the number before "than" goes at the back.

Make clear the distinction between the *number* of items and the *value* of the items. The variable represents the number of items. The value of the items is a function of price, interest rate, type of coin, etc.

For example:

If the number of dimes is d,
the value of d dimes (in pennies) is $10d$.
If the number of tickets is t, and each ticket costs $8.00, then, the value of t tickets is $8t$ (in dollars) or $800t$ (in cents).

Assign Investigations 1 to 3 on student text pages 16 and 17 to pairs of students. Point out to the students that there is no need to evaluate any of the expressions or to find values for any of the variables.

Give the students an opportunity to compare their results with those of other pairs of students in the class. Have volunteers present their results to the class. In questions 1 and 2 of Investigation 2 and question 1 of Investigation 3, point out that having the x values in an ascending or a descending order may help them to see more clearly any patterns in the numbers.

Extension

Write an algebraic expression for each statement.

a) The sum of the length and the width of a rectangle is 24 cm.

b) The school is 8 m higher than the library.

c) There are four times as many CDs as there are tapes.

d) Joya has three-quarters of the amount of money that Samuel has.

Compare your algebraic expressions with those of other students in your class.

Math Journal

Write a few sentences to describe a method you would use to find the equation that represents the relation between two sets of numbers. Compare your method with those of several other students in your class. How are your methods similar? How are they different?

Assessing the Outcomes

Written Assignment

1. Write an algebraic expression for each of the statements.

a) the difference between two numbers

b) the sum of two times a number and four times another number

c) one-quarter of a number is four more than half of another number

2. Write an algebraic expression to show the time in h hours and m minutes expressed in

a) minutes   b) seconds

3. A taxi ride costs \$2.50 for the first kilometre and \$1.25 for each additional kilometre. Write an algebraic expression to show the total cost of each journey.

a) 10 km in length

b) 17 km in length

4. Translate each statement into an equation in two variables.

a) The sum of the number of pups and twice the number of kittens is 36.

b) Seven times the number of socks is three more than four times the number of ties.

5. Write the following statements as a system of two equations in two variables.

The total length of the sides of an isosceles triangle is 15 cm. Three times the length of the shorter side is two-thirds the length of a longer side.

Investigating Math

Algebra Tiles and Substitution

Student Text Pages
Pp. 18–20

Materials
Teacher's Resource Master 2 (1-cm grid paper),
Teacher's Resource Master 3 (algebra tiles), overhead
algebra tiles, overhead projector

Learning Outcomes
- Use algebra tiles to model linear equations.
- Use algebra tiles to model systems of linear equations.
- Use algebra tiles to solve systems of linear equations
  by substitution.

Prerequisite Skills

1. Use algebra tiles to model each expression.

a) $2x + 3$

b) $-3x$

c) $x + 2y$

d) $5x - y + 1$

e) $4x - 3y - 1$
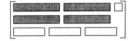

f) $-x - 3y - 3$

2. What expression could be written for the group of
   algebra tiles you would need to add to each group
   of algebra tiles to represent zero?

a)

$[-2x]$

b)

$[-x - y]$

c)

$[x - 3]$

d)

$[-2x + y]$

e)

$[2y - 3]$

f)

$[-2x + y - 2]$

Mental Math

1. Evaluate each expression for $x = 0.5$, $y = 1.5$,
   and $z = -0.1$.

   a) $x + y + z$ [1.9]   **b)** $2x + z - y$ $[-0.6]$
   c) $-x - y + 2z$ $[-2.2]$ **d)** $x^2 - 2y$ $[-2.75]$
   e) $x + 3z + 5x$ [2.7]   **f)** $2y - 5z + 3$ [6.5]

2. Calculate.

   a) 5.2×5.8 [30.16]   **b)** 6.1×6.9 [42.09]
   c) 4.4×460 [2024]   **d)** 3.3×0.37 [1.221]
   e) 88×0.82 [72.16]   **f)** 940×9.6 [9024]

Teaching Suggestions

*(algebra tiles, 1-cm grid paper, overhead algebra tiles,
overhead projector)* Provide each pair of students with
algebra tiles, and review the meaning of the values of the
tiles in the opening paragraph on student text page 18.

Provide algebra tiles and grid paper to pairs of
students, and assign Investigation 1 on student text page
18. Complete questions 1 to 3 with the class, and have
volunteers write on the chalkboard the equation
represented by each diagram. Assign questions 4 to 6.
Have one student use algebra tiles to model each
equation and have the other student draw on grid paper
a representation of each model. Provide overhead
algebra tiles and an overhead projector for volunteers
who may wish to use them to present their results.

Review with the class the opening paragraph of
Investigation 2 on student text page 18. Use overhead
algebra tiles on an overhead projector to demonstrate
each set of balanced algebra tiles, and have volunteers
explain to the class how each diagram represents the
equation to its left. Then, ask:

What is the purpose of the equals sign in an equation?

Elicit from the students that the equals sign in an
equation represents a "balancing point" and indicates
the balancing of one expression with another
expression. An understanding of this "balancing"
viewpoint of equality encourages good equation solving.

Then, have pairs of students use their algebra tiles and
grid paper to complete questions 1 to 3. Suggest that one
student set up the equation with the algebra tiles and the
other student draw the balance diagram on grid paper.
Then, have volunteers present their results to the class.

Discuss the opening paragraph of Investigation 3
with the class. Ask:

*How are the values of the first two tiles in the opening
paragraph on student text page 18 related? the next two
algebra tiles? the last two algebra tiles?*

What name can you give to these pairs of algebra tiles?

Elicit from the students that the tiles in each pair of
algebra tiles represent opposite values, and thus, each
pair represents the value zero.

Give the students some time to practise grouping tiles into equal groups. Place the following overhead algebra tiles on an overhead projector.

Ask:

If you had to group these tiles into two equal groups, what tiles would be in each group?

If you had to group these tiles into four equal groups, what tiles would be in each group?

How is the number of groups related to the number of each type of tile?

Elicit from the students that an arrangement of tiles can only be divided into a number of equal groups if each type of tile in the arrangement is a multiple of the number of groups required. Then, ask:

What mathematical operation is represented by the grouping of tiles?

Point out that, in this investigation, the second equation of each system is an equation in one variable. This second equation indicates which value must be replaced in the first equation.

Assign questions 1 to 3 to pairs of students. Have one student use the algebra tiles to model the system of equations and the other student draw the diagram and write the steps of the solution on grid paper. Have volunteers use overhead algebra tiles and the overhead projector to present their results to the class.

Review the opening paragraph in Investigation 4 on student text page 19. Ask:

How is this system of equations different from the one in the opening paragraph in Investigation 3?

When you are solving for y, why do you add two –x-tiles to each side?

Review with the class the steps required if the first step of the solution had been to solve (2) for x. Use the overhead algebra tiles and the overhead projector to demonstrate each step of the solution. Then, ask:

Which method did you prefer, solving for y first or solving for x first?

Assign questions 1 to 4. Have half of the pairs of students solve the system by solving for y in the first step and the other half of the students solve the system by solving for x in the first step. Tell the students to use their algebra tiles to model the system, draw a diagram of each step of their solution, and write the equations beside the diagrams. Have volunteers use overhead algebra tiles and the overhead projector to present their results to the class. As the volunteers present both solutions to each question, ask:

Which method was easier in this question? Explain.

Integrating Technology

Internet

Use the Internet to research the history of algebra, using web sites such as *http://www-groups.dcs.st-and.ac.uk/~history/*.

Extension

Many equations and formulas have multiple brackets and variables on both sides of the equality. Write a simplified form of each system of equations.

1. $7(x + 3) - 4(y + 1) = 3(x - 5) + 1$
$8(3 - y) + 2(x - 3) = 5 - 3(y + 1) + 6$

2. $5(x - y) - (3x - 4y) = 2x - 5$
$3x - (y - 4) = 4(x - 2)$

3. $9y - 8x + 7 - 2y = 2x + 5y - 3 + 2y$
$13 - 4(3 + 5x) + 9 = 5(3 - 4x) + 3(y - 6)$

4. $2x - (y - x) = 6(6 - y) - 1$
$3(x - y) - x = 6(-7) + 8(9)$

5. $5x - 4y - 8 = 2(x - 3y) + y - 7$
$5(x - y) - 5 = 4x - 3y - 7$

Math Journal

List the steps required to solve a system of equations by substitution. Include diagrams of algebra tiles.

Assessing the Outcomes

Written Assignment

(1-cm grid paper, algebra tiles) Students may use algebra tiles to assist them with their solutions.

Solve the system of equations by substitution. Include diagrams of algebra tiles on grid paper.

a) $x + 2y = 5$
$x + 3y = 7$

b) $2x + y = -1$
$x + 3y = 7$

1.3 Solving Systems of Linear Equations by Substitution

Student Text Pages
Pp. 21–27

Materials
graphing calculators, Teacher's Resource Master 2 (1-cm grid paper), Teacher's Resource Master 3 (algebra tiles), overhead projector

Learning Outcomes
- Solve systems of equations by substitution.
- Find the exact solutions of a system of equations.
- Solve investment problems and mixture problems involving systems of equations.

Prerequisite Skills
1. Write each equation in terms of the variable indicated.

a) $x + 3y = 4$, x $\qquad$ $[x = -3y + 4]$

b) $2y - x - 0$, y $\qquad$ $\left[y = \dfrac{x}{2}\right]$

c) $5p - 2q - 1 = 0$, q $\qquad$ $\left[q = \dfrac{5}{2}p - \dfrac{1}{2}\right]$

d) $\dfrac{1}{2}x + 3y = 6$, y $\qquad$ $\left[y = -\dfrac{1}{6}x + 2\right]$

2. Solve.

a) $x - 3 = 6$ $\qquad$ [9] $\qquad$ b) $x - 5 = -1$ $\qquad$ [4]

c) $x + 12 = 0$ $\qquad$ [−12] $\qquad$ d) $x + \dfrac{1}{2} = 1$ $\qquad$ $\left[\dfrac{1}{2}\right]$

e) $\dfrac{x}{3} = -2$ $\qquad$ [−6] $\qquad$ f) $\dfrac{3x}{4} = 9$ $\qquad$ [12]

g) $3x = 9$ $\qquad$ [3] $\qquad$ h) $5x = 0$ $\qquad$ [0]

i) $2x - 3 = 6$ $\qquad$ [4.5] $\qquad$ j) $\dfrac{2x}{3} + 1 = -2$ $\qquad$ $\left[-4\dfrac{1}{2}\right]$

Mental Math
1. Evaluate for $p = 0.5$ and $q = 0.1$.

a) $3p + q$ $\qquad$ [1.6] $\qquad$ b) $p - 2q$ $\qquad$ [0.3]

c) $2p + 7q$ $\qquad$ [1.7] $\qquad$ d) $4q + 3p$ $\qquad$ [1.9]

e) $-p^2 + q$ $\qquad$ [−0.15] $\qquad$ f) $-5p - 4q$ $\qquad$ [−2.9]

2. Calculate.

a) 310×390 $\qquad$ [120 900]

b) 940×960 $\qquad$ [902 400]

c) 770×730 $\qquad$ [562 100]

d) 690×610 $\qquad$ [420 900]

e) 190×110 $\qquad$ [20 900]

f) 520×580 $\qquad$ [301 600]

Explore/Inquire Answers

Explore: Use the Equations
The number of Siberian tigers reduced by fifteen times the number of Amur leopards is zero. The sum of the number of Siberian tigers and the number of Amur leopards is 480.

Inquire
1. $t = 15l$.

2. a) $15l + l = 480$ $\qquad$ b) $l = 30$

3. a) Substitute the value of the first variable into one of the equations.

b) $t = 450$

4. (30, 450)

5. a) either $t = 480 - l$ or $l = 480 - t$

b) either $480 - l - 15l = 0$ or $t - 15(480 - t) = 0$

c) either $l = 30$ or $t = 450$ $\qquad$ d) yes

6. a) 450 $\qquad$ b) 30

7. a) (5, 10) $\qquad$ b) (8, 1) $\qquad$ c) (3, −4)

Teaching Suggestions

Method 1
(1-cm grid paper, algebra tiles, overhead projector, graphing calculators) Read with the class the opening paragraph on student text page 21. Provide pairs of students with algebra tiles and grid paper, and assign the Explore section.

Have the pairs of students use the algebra tiles to model each equation in the Explore section. Tell the students to use the process developed in the Investigating Math: Algebra Tiles and Substitution section on student text pages 18 to 20 to solve the system of equations in the Explore section. Then, have them use grid paper to draw a diagram of each step of their solution.

Give the pairs of students an opportunity to compare and discuss their results with those of other pairs of students. Have volunteers present their results to the class. Provide an overhead projector so that one student can present the diagrams, while the partner explains the reasons for drawing the diagrams.

Then, assign the Inquire questions. Suggest the pairs of students use the diagrams they drew in the Explore section to answer questions 1 and 2. Ask:

Why do you think you are asked to write an expression for t in question 1?

When the students finish question 6, ask:

Which method did you find easier, the method in questions 1 to 3 or the method in questions 4 and 5? Explain.

Have the students use the algebra tiles and the grid paper as above to solve the systems in question 7. Ask:

What is different about the system of equations in question 7c)?

How do you decide which variable to solve for as the first step of the solution of a system of equations?

Have volunteers present their results to the class.

Review teaching examples 1 and 2 with the class. Have pairs of students work on teaching example 2. Have one student use grid paper to graph the two equations and have the other student use a graphing calculator to graph the equations. Ask:

Which method of graphing the system of equations was easier for finding the solution to the system of equations? Explain.

Which method was easier for finding the more accurate solution?

Discuss with the students how the tools of mathematics are much like the tools in a trade—some are better suited for a particular type of job than others. Point out that it is important to be able to recognize that using manual solutions to solve a difficult problem involving intersections that are not integral solutions is like using a sledge hammer when a finishing hammer is sufficient.

Review with the class teaching examples 3 and 4. For teaching example 4, help students understand how to create the second equation from the first if you first show the equation as 30% of x + 50% of y = 42% of 10. Point out that equation (2) uses the percent numbers as coefficients for the variables of equation (1). This helps students make the connection between the two equations at a conceptual level, and provides the weaker students with a visual pattern of how to create the two equations.

Method 2

(graphing calculators, 1-cm grid paper, algebra tiles, overhead projector) Present this problem to the class.

The total mass of a griffon vulture and a great bustard is 33 kg. Four times the mass of the griffon vulture is 6 kg more than twice the mass of the great bustard. What is the mass of each bird?

Provide pairs of students with algebra tiles and grid paper. Suggest that they use the letter v to represent the mass of the vulture and b to represent the mass of the bustard. Have the pairs write an equation for statement one and label it (1), and an equation for statement two and label it (2). Remind the students of the process developed in the Investigating Math: Algebra Tiles and Substitution section on student text pages 18 to 20 to solve the system of equations.

As the students work through each step of their solution, have them use algebra tiles to model each step and draw diagrams of their models. Have half the students use method 1 to solve the problem and the other half use method 2.

Method 1: Use (1) to write an expression for v in terms of b. Substitute this expression into (2). Solve this new equation for b. Use your answer for b to find a value for v.

Method 2: Use (1) to write an expression for b in terms of v. Substitute this expression into (2). Solve this new equation for v. Use your answer for v to find a value for b.

Give the students time to compare and discuss their method of solution with those of other pairs of students.

Ask volunteers to present their results to the class. Provide an overhead projector if required. Ask:

What is the mass of the griffon vulture? the great bustard?

Did you check your answer? How?

Then, ask:

Did it make any difference which method you used to find your solution? Explain.

Which method did you prefer? Explain.

Review teaching examples 1 to 4 on student text pages 22 to 25 with the class. Have some of the students use graphing calculators to find the results. Ask:

Did you find that the calculator was a better method of finding the solution to each example? Explain.

Sample Solution

Page 27, question 47

For a system of equations to have no solution, the equations must represent parallel lines, which do not coincide. This means the slope must be equal, but the y-intercepts different. The equation $2x + y - 3 = 0$, written in the slope y-intercept form, is $y = -2x + 3$. The slope of this line is -2 and the y-intercept is 3. The other equation of the system, written in the slope y-intercept form, is $y = x(m - 1) + 6$. The slope of this line is $(m - 1)$ and the y-intercept is 6.

For the slopes to be the same,

$$-2 = m - 1$$
$$-2 + 1 = m$$
$$m = -1$$

Thus, $m = -1$ gives a system with no solution.

Integrating Technology

Graphing Calculators

Investigate using the Solve feature on a graphing calculator to solve systems algebraically.

Explain why you need to know how to solve by substitution even when using a graphing calculator to solve algebraically.

See *MATHPOWER™ 11, Western Edition, Blackline Masters* pp. 24 to 26 for Solving Linear Systems Algebraically.

On a TI-83, Equation Solver is the tenth item under MATH, which is the first heading when the MATH key is pressed. Equations are entered in one variable and so that they equal 0. A guess is entered before the SOLVE (i.e., ALPHA ENTER) key is pressed. Then, that value is substituted into one of the equations which is evaluated to find the other variable.

On a TI-92, press F2 and the 1 key to get solve(. Equations are entered in one variable. Then, press , x) to indicate the equation is being solved for x or , y) to indicate the equation is being solved for y, before pressing the ENTER key. Then, that value is substituted into one of the equations, which is evaluated to find the other variable.

Extension

Use strings and flowchart shapes to create a flowchart of the steps required to solve a system of equations by substitution. Present your flowchart to the class. As a class, select the flowchart that makes the most sense to students.

Enrichment

Use the information provided in teaching example 3 on student page 24 and a spreadsheet to help you explore what the maximum and minimum amounts of money Marie could earn with her $40 000.

Math Journal

Make a list of the steps required to use the method of substitution to solve a system of equations in two variables.

Write a short paragraph describing which method you preferred to solve a system of equations, the graphical method or the method of substitution, and why.

Cross-Discipline

Have students check with either their science, computer, or business education teachers to find more information about applications of spreadsheets for solving formulas, profit and loss equations, etc. Have them present their findings in an informational bulletin board.

Problem Levels of Difficulty

A: 1–37   **B:** 38–46   **C:** 47–49

Assessing the Outcomes

Observation

You may want to consider some of these questions as you observe students working individually or in pairs:

- Do the students move quickly to either a table or equations to represent the situation?
- Do the students seem to re-read to verify the information in the table or equations before proceeding?
- Do the students follow the equation solving steps in a neat and orderly fashion?
- When they have completed solving the equations, do they check back in the reading of the problem to determine if their answer is reasonable?

Problem Solving: Use a Data Bank

Method 1

Review with the class the problem solving plan shown down the left-hand side of student text page 28. Point out that the basic problem solving strategy shown remains unchanged, but the details of the processes used to solve the particular problem change with the context of the problem.

Remind the students that this four-step plan for problem solving extends far beyond mathematics and may be applied to other disciplines, and even other areas of their lives, such as, obtaining a driver's licence, creating goals for college or university entrance, creating career goals, etc.

Ensure that the students understand how to obtain the required information from the database(s). They must learn to read the edges and labels, and to use their techniques for finding a point in the plane to obtain the required information.

Review with the class the opening paragraph on student text page 28. Ask:

Is all the information required to solve the problem given on the student text page?

Where is the information needed to solve the problem?

How do you find the number of passengers for a particular plane?

How do you find the operating costs in Canadian funds?

Direct the students to the data bank at the back of the students' text book, and have pairs of students find different information. Then, have volunteers present to the class the information they researched. Have the class check the accuracy of the information. Then, ask:

What information, other than the information found in the data bank, is required to solve the problem?

Finally, assign the problems on student text page 29 to pairs of students. Have volunteers present their results to the class.

Method 2

(miscellaneous reference books) Have pairs of students research information from reference books or the Internet, and use the information to make up a problem in which not all of the information is given. For example, What is the total surface area of the Great Lakes?

Have the students write a solution to the problem they created. Then, have them invite other pairs of students to write a solution to the problem. Give the pairs of students an opportunity to discuss and compare the solutions to the same problem. Then, have volunteers present their results to the class.

Assign, to pairs of students, student text page 28 as independent reading and the problems on student text page 29.

Student Text Pages

Pp. 28–29

Materials

miscellaneous reference books

Learning Outcome

- Solve problems using a data bank.

Prerequisite Skills

1. Evaluate each formula for the values given. Round your answer to the nearest tenth, if necessary.

a) $d = st$; $s = 50$, $t = 2.5$ [125]

b) $s = \dfrac{d}{t}$; $t = 5.5$, $d = 750$ [136.4]

c) $t = \dfrac{d}{s}$; $d = 25$, $s = 3.2$ [7.8]

d) $P = 2l + 2w$; $l = 37.5$, $w = 14.6$ [104.2]

e) $V = \dfrac{4}{3}\pi r^3$; $r = 7.6$ [1838.8]

f) $p = 2a + 3b^2$; $a = 72.9$, $b = 0.35$ [146.2]

2. Estimate each of the following.   [Answers may vary.]

a) 395×17.9 [8000]

b) 1005×2.9 [3000]

c) $78 \times 31 \times 9$ [24 000]

d) 0.81×1.93 [1.6]

e) $34.5 \times 2.2 \times 0.5$ [35]

f) $22 \times 91 \times 604$ [1 200 000]

Mental Math

1. Evaluate for $m = \dfrac{1}{2}$ and $n = \dfrac{1}{4}$.

a) $2m + 4n$ [2]   **b)** $4m - 2n$ $\left[1\dfrac{1}{2}\right]$

c) $m^2 - 2n + 3$ $\left[2\dfrac{3}{4}\right]$ **d)** $5m + 2n$ [3]

e) $-2m - 3n$ $\left[-1\dfrac{3}{4}\right]$ **f)** $7n + 5m$ $\left[4\dfrac{1}{4}\right]$

2. Estimate and then, calculate.

a) 51×59 [3000, 3009]

b) 77×73 [5600, 5621]

c) 28×22 [600, 616]

d) 66×64 [4200, 4224]

e) 82×88 [7200, 7216]

f) 49×41 [2000, 2009]

Word Power Answer

Saskatchewan or Ontario

Integrating Technology

Internet

Use the Internet to find information to create problems that require retrieving information in order to solve them. Use web sites such as Statistics Canada's Web Site *http://www.statcan.ca*. Display your problems for classmates to research and solve.

Computer Data Bank

Use the databases in *MATHPOWER™ 11, Western Edition, Computer Data Bank* to find information to create problems that require retrieving information in order to solve them. Display your problems for classmates to research and solve.

Extension

Contact some businesses such as airlines, fast-food restaurants, bus lines, automobile associations, automobile insurance companies, Statistics Canada, World Wildlife Federation, the Red Cross Society, banks, Canada Post, couriers, etc., and locate any databases they may be willing to give you. Use a database to create a problem involving systems of equations. Write a solution to your problem. Exchange your problem with that of another student in your class. Solve the other student's problem. Compare and discuss the solutions to these problems.

Enrichment

With a partner, create a poster that can be used for display for a parent-teacher interviews event at the school. Include on this poster at least one database that the students have built, two or three problems written by each pair of students, along with the solutions to their problems, and a graph.

Assessing the Outcome

Observation

Note the extent to which the students
- describe the problem in their own words
- provide a plan, and the steps they took to find the solution
- complete the solution to the problem
- check that the answer is correct
- make their presentations interesting
- include a graph or a diagram as part of their solution

Career Connection

Chemistry

Student Text Page
P. 30

Materials
graphing calculators

Learning Outcomes
- Solve systems of linear equations graphically and by substitution.
- Gain insight into careers in the field of chemistry.

Prerequisite Skills

a) What are the y-intercepts of the equations in the following system?

$$y = 30 + x$$
$$y = 40 - 2x$$ [30 and 40]

b) What would you expect to see, if you graphed the system in a standard viewing window? Explain. [only the axes]

c) Graph the system in a viewing window that allows you to solve the system.

d) What is the solution? [$(3.\overline{3}, 33.\overline{3})$]

Teaching Suggestions

Introduce the topic with a discussion about where we see chemistry happening around us. Ask what science courses students have taken or are taking that have a chemistry component. Ask if anyone knows a chemist, and, if so, what is known about the person's work.

Discuss the introduction on student text page 30 with the class, and then, assign Explorations 1 and 2 to individuals, pairs, or small groups of students.

To solve the systems in Exploration 1 using a graphing calculator, students need to use a viewing window that will show the graphs and their intersections. Encourage students to solve the systems using a graphing calculator, and to explain why they chose the viewing windows they did.

Have students compare the processes of solving graphically and solving by substitution when using equations like the solubility equations. What are the advantages and disadvantages of each?

Integrating Technology

Internet

Use the Internet to do the research for Exploration 2.

Cross-Discipline

Science What science courses have you taken that had a chemistry component? Have you taken any specific chemistry courses? How was math used in these courses?

History Trace the role of the chemical industry in Canadian history.

Assessing the Outcomes

Journal

Write about
- the most interesting thing you learned about chemistry
- what else you would like to know about chemistry, and how you could find out

Investigating Math

Exploring Equivalence

Student Text Page
P. 31

Learning Outcomes
- Create equivalent systems of equations by multiplication.
- Create other systems of equations that have the same intersection point by addition.

Prerequisite Skills

1. Evaluate for $x = 2$ and $y = -1$.

a) $x + y$ [1]   **b)** $x - y + 1$ [4]

c) $-2x + y$ [-5]   **d)** $3x - 2y$ [8]

2. Which point satisfies the equation?

a) $x + y = 3$; (0, 5), (1, 2), (3, -3)   [(1, 2)]

b) $2x - y = -1$; (5, 5), (0, 0), (0, 1)   [(0, 1)]

3. Graph each line.

a) $2x + y = 5$ **b)** $x + 6y = -1$ **c)** $y = -3x - 2$

4. Evaluate.

a) $-5 + 7$ [2]   **b)** $6 - 9$ [-3]

c) $-6 - (-2)$ [-4]   **d)** $9 + (-11)$ [-2]

e) $(-5) \times 2$ [-10]   **f)** $(-1) \times (-100)$ [100]

g) $10 \div (-5)$ [-2]   **h)** $-6 \div (-6)$ [1]

5. Simplify.

a) $2x + 3x - x$ [4x]

b) $-y - 5y + 11y$ [5y]

c) $3y + 2x + x - y$ [3x + 2y]

Mental Math

1. Evaluate for $p = 0.2$, $q = 1.1$, and $r = -0.1$.

a) $p + q + r$ [1.2]   **b)** $-p - 2r$ [0]

c) $2p - q + 3r$ [-1]   **d)** $q^2 + 5p$ [2.21]

e) $-p - 2p + 3r$ [-0.9]   **f)** $5 - 2p - q$ [3.5]

2. Calculate.

a) 54×56 [3024]   **b)** 66×64 [4224]

c) 92×98 [9016]   **d)** 81×89 [7209]

e) 29×21 [609]   **f)** 43×47 [2021]

Teaching Suggestions

Review with the class the opening paragraph of Investigation 1 on student text page 31. Ask:

How many variables occur in the equations in the opening paragraph of this investigation?

How many values satisfy the equations?

Discuss with students that, ever since they have been solving equations, they have been dealing with equivalent equations. Each step in the solution of an equation represents an equation that is equivalent to the equation in the previous step and in the following step. Thus, equivalent equations are formed by adding, subtracting, dividing, or multiplying each term of an equation by the same value or term.

Review the rules for equality. Have the students express these rules in words.

Then, assign questions 1 to 5 to pairs of students. Give the students an opportunity to compare and discuss their results with those of other pairs of students. Have volunteers present their results to the class. Then, ask:

How many variables occur in the equations in questions 1 to 5?

How many sets of points are solutions to the equations in questions 1 to 4?

Discuss with the class question 5. Ask:

How would you write an equation in two variables equivalent to another equation in two variables?

Elicit from them the use of addition, subtraction, multiplication, and division to create equivalent equations.

Point out that equations in two variables are equivalent if the solution sets of the equations are the same.

Assign Investigation 2. Ask:

In what other way can you describe an equivalent system of equations?

Remind the students of the Enrichment section in Section 1.1 in which dependent and independent systems of equations were described. An equivalent system of equations can also be described as a dependent system of equations.

Enrichment

Construct two equivalent linear systems of three equations in three variables.

Math Journal

Describe two methods you have learned to create both equivalent equations and equivalent systems.

Assessing the Outcomes

Written Assignment

1. Construct a system of equations that is equivalent to this system of equations.

$$5x - 2y = 17$$
$$2x + y = 5$$

Investigating Math

Algebra Tiles and Equivalent Equations

Student Text Pages
Pp. 32–33

Materials
Teacher's Resource Master 2 (1-cm grid paper),
Teacher's Resource Master 3 (algebra tiles), overhead
algebra tiles, overhead projector

Learning Outcomes
* Use algebra tiles to solve systems of equations using
addition and subtraction.
* Use algebra tiles to solve systems of equations using
multiplication and addition.

Mental Math
1. Evaluate each expression for $x = 5$ and $y = -2$.

a) $2x + 2y$ [6]   b) $3(x - 2y)$ [27]

c) $-x - y$ [-3]   d) $(4x + y)$ [-18]

e) $3x + 2y + x$ [16]   f) $x^2 - y^2$ [21]

2. Calculate.

a) 3.3×37 [122.1]

b) 45×450 [20 250]

c) 0.86×8.4 [7.224]

d) 710×7.9 [5609]

e) 0.92×0.98 [0.9016]

f) 6.6×6400 [42 240]

Teaching Suggestions
*(1-cm grid paper, algebra tiles, overhead algebra tiles,
overhead projector)* Review with the class the opening
assignment of Investigation 1. Provide pairs of students
with algebra tiles, and use overhead algebra tiles on an
overhead projector to demonstrate this assignment.
As you work through the assignment have the students
use their algebra tiles to model each step.

Assign questions 1 to 4. Have the students first
create each equation separately, and then, draw the
diagrams on grid paper. Instruct the students to include
on the grid paper beside the appropriate diagram the
equation for that step.

Have volunteers present their results to the class.
Encourage them to use the overhead algebra tiles on
the overhead projector.

Assign Investigation 2 to pairs of students. Draw the
students' attention to the third diagram. Ask:

*What is the equivalent operation of turning all the tiles
over in a diagram?*

Elicit from the students that this is the same as
multiplying all the terms of an equation by -1. This
may reinforce the creation of equivalent equations using
multiplication. Discuss how you start with something
you already know (equivalent fractions) and apply that
knowledge to a similar but more complex situation
(equivalent equations), and then apply this new
knowledge to solving an even more complicated process
(solution of a system of equations). By making
conscious connections between the various steps, the
complicated process of solving systems of equations
may be clarified.

Assign Investigation 3 to pairs of students. Have
volunteers present their results to the class using
overhead algebra tiles on an overhead projector.

Integrating Technology

Internet
On the Internet, discuss questions that you have
about algebra, using web sites such as
http://www.algebra-online.com.

Enrichment
Research a career that would use linear systems of
equations. Write a few sentences describing how linear
systems would be used in this career. Display your
description, along with those of other students in your
class on a class bulletin board.

Math Journal
Describe how you could use algebra tiles to solve a
system of equations. Include diagrams of your algebra
tile arrangements in your description.

Describe which system of solving a linear system of
equations you like the best. Justify your choice.

Assessing the Outcomes

Written Assignment: Diagramming
Use algebra tiles to model the solution to each system
of equations. Draw diagrams to show the steps of your
solution.

1. $x + 2y = 4$ 2. $2x + 3y = 0$

   $x + y = 1$ $4x - y = -14$

Solving Systems of Linear Equations by Elimination

Student Text Pages
Pp. 34–40

Materials
Teacher's Resource Master 2 (1-cm grid paper), Teacher's Resource Master 3 (algebra tiles), overhead algebra tiles, overhead projector

Learning Outcomes
- Solve a system of equations by elimination using addition.
- Solve a system of equations by elimination using subtraction or addition.
- Solve a system of equations by elimination using multiplication.
- Solve a system of rational equations.
- Solve problems involving systems of equations.

Prerequisite Skills
1. Find the lowest common multiple of each pair of numbers.

   a) 3, 5   [15]   b) $-2, 7$ [14]

   c) 5, 6   [30]   d) $-10, -6$ [30]

   e) 8, 12   [24]   f) $7, -21$ [21]

2. Write the opposite of each number.

   a) 7   [-7]   b) -3 [3]

   c) 16   [-16]   d) -20 [20]

   e) $-(-5)$ [-5]   f) 102   [-102]

3. Evaluate.

   a) $5 + 7$ [12]   b) $18 + (-6)$ [12]

   c) $7 + (-9)$ [-2]   d) $-11 + 11$ [0]

   e) $15 + (-15)$ [0]   f) $-2 + (-6)$ [-8]

Mental Math
1. Evaluate for $x = 1.5$ and $y = -2.4$.

   a) $x - 4y$ [11.1]   b) $-2x + y$ [-5.4]

   c) $3xy + 4$ [-6.8]   d) $-3x + 4xy + 1$ [-17.9]

   e) $5y - 3x - 2$ [-18.5]   f) $2x - y + xy$ [1.8]

2. Calculate.

   a) 75^2 [5625]   b) 65^2 [4225]

   c) 45^2 [2025]   d) 85^2 [7225]

   e) 15^2 [225]   f) 95^2 [9025]

Explore/Inquire Answers

Explore: Use the Equations
a) The total number of tracks on disc 1 and disc 2 is 60. The number of tracks on disc 1 is 8 more than the number of tracks on disc 2.

b) $x + x + y - y = 2x$ c) 68   d) $2x = 68$

Inquire
1. $x = 34$

2. a) Substitute the value of the first variable into one of the equations.

   b) Substitute $x = 34$ into equation (1).
   $$34 + y = 60$$
   $$y = 60 - 34$$
   $$= 26$$

3. $(34, 26)$

4. Substitute the coordinates $(34, 26)$ in equations (1) and (2).

$x + y = 60$	$x - y = 8$
$34 + 26 = 60$	$34 - 26 = 8$

   Thus, $(34, 26)$ satisfies both equations.

5. There are 34 tracks on disc 1 and 28 tracks on disc 2.

6. a) $(14, 3)$ b) $(9, 2)$ c) $(4, -1)$

Teaching Suggestions

Method 1
(1-cm grid paper, algebra tiles, overhead algebra tiles, overhead projector) Provide pairs of students with grid paper and algebra tiles, and assign the Explore section on student text page 34. Ask:

What does the word elimination mean?

Have one student solve the system of equations using algebra tiles, and have the other student draw the diagrams of each step of the solution on grid paper. Give the pairs of students an opportunity to discuss and compare their results with those of other pairs of students. Have volunteers present their results to the class.

Provide an overhead projector so that one student can display the diagrams of the steps of the solution and the other can explain the reasons for each step of the solution.

Then, assign the Inquire questions. Ask:

How could you have used subtraction to find an equivalent equation for the system in the Explore section?

Have the students read the paragraph following the Inquire questions on student text page 34. Remind the students that other methods of solving a system of equations, graphically or using substitution, can still be applied if desired. Ask:

How would you decide which variable to eliminate?

How would you decide whether to eliminate using addition or eliminate using subtraction?

How would you decide which method to use to satisfy a system of equations?

Look for answers such as:

If both equations are in standard form ($ax + by = c$), and the cs are multiples of their respective as and bs, then the graphical method would probably be best.

If one equation has either $y = mx + b$ or $x = ny + c$, then the method of substitution would probably be best.

If both equations are in standard form, then the method of elimination would probably be best.

Review teaching examples 1 to 3 on student text pages 34 to 36. Ask students to pay attention to the method they prefer.

In teaching example 3 on student text page 36, pay special attention to the multiplication method. Ask:

Why is equation (1) multiplied by 5 and equation (2) multiplied by –2?

Discussing such issues in class helps to focus on the decision making aspects in which the students must engage in order to choose the most suitable method of solving a system of equations.

Review with the class teaching example 4 on student text page 36. This example reinforces the fact that multiplying all the terms of an equation by the same number results in an equivalent equation.

Review with the class teaching examples 5 and 6 on student text pages 37 and 38. Discuss the use of a table as an aid in creating the system of equations needed to solve the problems. Ask:

What formula involves distance, speed, and time?

What formula did you use to find the speed in teaching example 5?

What formula did you use to find the time in teaching example 6?

Method 2

(1-cm grid paper, algebra tiles, overhead algebra tiles, overhead projector) Provide the students with this problem.

The number of lace holes in a running shoe is represented by x, and the number of lace holes in a boot is represented by y. These two equations represent the relationship between the number of holes.

$$x + y = 20 \quad (1)$$
$$2x - y = 16 \quad (2)$$

How many lace holes does the running shoe have, and how many lace holes does the boot have?

Have the students express the relationships in words. Then, have them write an equivalent equation to (1) and (2) by adding (1) and (2). Label this equation (3). Ask:

Why do you think you are asked to add (1) and (2) to find (3)?

How many variables does (3) have?

How could you solve (3)?

How could you use the solution to (3) to find the value of the other variable in (1)?

What is the solution to the given system?

How can you check your solution?

How many lace holes does the running shoe have? the boot have?

Why do you think this method of solving a system of linear equations is called the method of elimination by addition?

Then, present this system of equations to the class.

$$x - 2y = -5 \quad (4)$$
$$x + y = 1 \quad (5)$$

Have the students write an equivalent equation (6) to equations (4) and (5) by adding (4) and (5). Ask:

How many variables does (6) have?

Can you use the method of elimination by adding to solve (4) and (5)?

What could you do to equations (4) and (5) in order to eliminate one of the variables?

This method of solving a system of equations is called the method of elimination by subtraction. Explain.

What is the solution to this system of equations?

How can you check that your answer is correct?

Finally, present this system of equations to the class.

$$2x + y = 4 \quad (7)$$
$$3x - 2y = 13 \quad (8)$$

Ask:

Is it possible to eliminate one of the variables by adding or subtracting (7) and (8)?

What would you have to do to (7) so that you could use the method of elimination by addition to solve the system?

What would you have to do to (7) and (8) in order to use the method of elimination by subtraction to solve the system?

This method of solving a system of equations is called the method of elimination by multiplication. Explain.

What is the solution to this system of equations?

How can you check that your answer is correct?

Review with the class the teaching examples on student text pages 34 to 38. Encourage pairs of students to use their algebra tiles and grid paper to help them solve the systems of equations, and have volunteers present their results to the class. Provide students with overhead algebra tiles and an overhead projector, if they need them.

Sample Solution

Page 40, question 61

If the solution must be $(6, -5)$, then $x = 6$ and $y = -5$. Substitute these values for x and y into the two given equations.

$$6A - 5B = C \qquad (1)$$
$$6D - 5E = F \qquad (2)$$
$$6A = 5B + C$$
$$6 = \frac{5B + C}{A} \qquad (3)$$
$$6D = 5E + F$$
$$6 = \frac{5E + F}{D} \qquad (4)$$

Equate the right-hand sides of (3) and (4).

$$\frac{5B + C}{A} = \frac{5E + F}{D}$$
$$D(5B + C) = A(5E + F)$$
$$5BD + CD = 5AE + AF$$
$$5BD - 5AE = AF - CD$$
$$5(BD - AE) = AF - CD$$
$$5 = \frac{AF - CD}{BD - AE} \qquad (5)$$

The values for A, B, C, D, E, and F must satisfy the given condition, i.e., they must be different integers. Use a guess and check method to find values for A, B, C, D, E, and F that satisfy equation (5). Substitute $A = 1$, $B = 2$, $C = -4$, $D = 3$, $E = 5$, and $F = -7$ in (5).

$$5 = \frac{AF - CD}{BD - AE} \qquad (5)$$
$$5 = \frac{(1)(-7) - (-4)(3)}{(2)(3) - (1)(5)}$$
$$= \frac{-7 - (-12)}{6 - 5}$$
$$= \frac{5}{1}$$
$$= 5$$

Thus, $A = 1$, $B = 2$, $C = -4$, $D = 3$, $E = 5$, and $F = -7$ is one set of values that satisfies all the conditions. There are many other sets.

$$x + 2y = -4$$
$$3x + 5y = -7$$

Pattern Power Answer

The sum of the three numbers to the right of the number in the left-hand column equals the number in the left-hand column.

Thus, $48 = 12 + 11 + 25$, $40 = 5 + 16 + 19$, $74 = 29 + 27 + 18$, $39 = 11 + 18 + 10$, and $63 = x + 14 + 23$.

Thus, $x = 63 - 14 - 23 = 26$.

The missing number is 26.

Integrating Technology

Graphing Calculators

Check graphically the solutions to some of the systems in questions 1 to 30 on student text pages 38 to 39 using a graphing calculator.

Computer Data Bank

Use the databases in *MATHPOWER*™ 11, *Western Edition, Computer Data Bank* to find information to create several problems that can be solved using systems of linear equations. Display your problems for classmates to solve.

Extension

Solve the system of equations.

Hint: Think of $\frac{1}{x} = m$ and $\frac{1}{y} = n$.

$$\frac{1}{x} + \frac{1}{y} = \frac{7}{10}$$
$$\frac{3}{x} - \frac{2}{y} = \frac{11}{10}$$

Math Journal

List the steps required to solve a system of linear equations in two variables using the elimination process. Which method do you prefer, the method of substitution or the method of elimination? Explain.

Write a short paragraph explaining the usefulness of diagrams in solving a system of linear equations.

Common Errors

- Students often forget that the division bar in a rational expression is a grouping symbol. This means that the numerator should be grouped in a set of brackets and any multiplication on that expression should apply to each term within the brackets. For example,

$$\frac{x + 1}{2} - \frac{y - 3}{6} = 3 \text{ and}$$
$$3x + 3 - y - 3 = 18$$

are not equivalent equations, because the -3 of the term $\frac{y - 3}{6}$ in the first equation should have been subtracted. This would have changed -3 to $+3$.

R_x Review the process of subtracting an expression by adding the opposite expression. Stress upon the students that, when an expression is being subtracted, every term of the expression is being subtracted and thus, the opposite of every term is added.

- Students often forget to multiply the constant term on the right side of the equation by the common denominator. For example,

$$\frac{x+7}{3} - \frac{y-2}{6} = 3$$
$$2x + 14 - y + 2 = 3$$

are not equivalent because the right side of the equation was not multiplied by 6.

R_x Provide the students with practice in multiplying rational equations with brackets in the numerators by integers.

Cross-Discipline

Navigation When navigating on large rivers like the St. Lawrence, Nile, Mississippi, or Amazon, which have fairly strong currents, it is important to keep a schedule, while conserving fuel. So often times, it is the time to complete a journey and the speed of the river current that are the variables, while the captain can read the speed of his boat from the odometer. The problem is a simplified version of real problems that must be solved to create a reasonable schedule for ferries and other boats that travel in currents, whose speed may be variable.

Problem Levels of Difficulty

A: 1–53, 63   **B:** 54–60   **C:** 61, 62

Assessing the Outcomes

Written Assignment

1. Solve each system of equations.

a) $x - y = -1$
    $3x + y = 13$

b) $2x + 2y = -6$
    $-x + 2y = 0$

c) $2x - 3y = 16$
    $x + 5y = -5$

2. At a dog show in Vancouver, between the number of humans and the number of dogs, there were a total of 36 heads and 102 legs in the ring. How many dogs were in the ring?

1.6 Solving Systems of Linear Equations in Three Variables

Student Text Pages
Pp. 41–46

Materials
graphing calculators, Teacher's Resource Master 2 (1-cm grid paper), Teacher's Resource Master 3 (algebra tiles), overhead algebra tiles, overhead projector

Learning Outcomes
- Solve systems of linear equations in three variables by elimination.
- Solve problems involving systems of linear equations in three variables.

Prerequisite Skills
1. Solve.

a) $x + 3 = 5$ [2]

b) $x - 4 = -2$ [2]

c) $\frac{x}{9} = -5$ [−45]

d) $5x = 75$ [15]

e) $3x + 2 = -1$ [−1]

f) $\frac{2x}{5} - 3 = 1$ [10]

2. Find the lowest common multiple of each group of numbers.

a) 2, 3, 4   [12]

b) −2, 4, 9   [36]

c) 3, 3, 5   [15]

d) 10, 3, 2   [30]

3. Evaluate each expression for the given values of the variables.

a) $v = u + at$; $u = 3$, $a = -0.5$, $t = 5$ [0.5]

b) $I = Prt$; $P = 500$, $r = 0.04$, $t = 3.5$ [70]

c) $D = \frac{M}{V}$; $M = 1500$, $V = 800$ [1.875]

Mental Math
1. Evaluate for $k = \frac{1}{3}$ and $m = -\frac{2}{3}$.

a) $-k - m$ $\left[\frac{1}{3}\right]$

b) $-3k + 6m$ [−5]

c) $k^2 + m^2$ $\left[\frac{5}{9}\right]$

d) $2k^2 + 3k - 2$ $\left[-\frac{7}{9}\right]$

e) $k + 4m + m$ [−3]

f) $2m^2 - 2k$ $\left[\frac{2}{9}\right]$

2. Estimate.

a) 3.6×34 [120]

b) 0.41×490 [200]

c) 0.77×73 [56]

d) 940×9.6 [9000]

e) 5.2×5.8 [30]

f) 280×220 [60 000]

Explore/Inquire Answers

Explore: Use the Equations
The total number of public art galleries in Canada is 28. The number of public art galleries in Central Canada and Eastern Canada is four more than the number of public art galleries in Western Canada.
The number of public art galleries in Central Canada and Western Canada is ten more than twice the number of public art galleries in Eastern Canada.

Inquire
1. a) w b) $2c + 2e = 32$

2. a) w b) $2c - e = 14$

3. $3e = 18$, $e = 6$; $c = 10$

4. a) Substitute the value of the variables found in question 3 into the equation in question 1b).

   b) $w = 12$

5. There are 10 public art galleries in Central Canada, 6 public art galleries in Eastern Canada, and 12 public art galleries in Western Canada.

6. Substitute the values of the three variables into each of the equations. If the three variables satisfy all the equations, then the values are correct.

7. a) $x = 4, y = 2, z = 1$ b) $a = 1, b = 4, c = 3$

Teaching Suggestions

Method 1
(1-cm grid paper, algebra tiles, overhead algebra tiles, overhead projector) Read with the class the opening paragraph on student text page 41. Ask:

How many equations are needed to solve a system that involves two variables?

How many equations are needed to solve a system that involves three variables?

Discuss with the students the relationship between the number of variables in an equation and the graph formed. Ask:

What geometric shape is formed when an equation in two variables is graphed?

What geometric shape is formed when an equation in three variables is graphed?

Elicit from the students that a straight line that crosses the axes is formed when an equation in two variables is graphed, and a plane is formed when an equation in three variables is graphed. Point out that the solution to a system of three equations in three variables is an ordered triple.

Assign the Explore section to pairs of students. Remember that some of the equations can be expressed in more than one way. For example, there are two ways that equation (2) can be expressed: the sum of the numbers in Central Canada and in Eastern Canada is four more than the number in Western Canada, and the number in Central Canada plus the number in Eastern Canada minus the number in Western Canada is four. Encourage the students to express each equation in as many ways as possible. Have volunteers present their results to the class.

Provide pairs of students with algebra tiles and grid paper, and assign the Inquire questions on student text page 41. Ask:

How would you describe the equation formed in question 1b)? in question 2b)?

Have half the pairs of students solve the system of equations in two variables by the method of elimination and the other half by the method of substitution. Suggest that the students use their algebra tiles and draw a diagram on grid paper for each step of their solution.

When the students have completed question 6, have volunteers present their results to the class. Provide overhead algebra tiles and an overhead projector for the students, if necessary. Ask:

What is the first step required in solving a system of three equations in three variables?

What is the second step? the third step?

Are there any other steps you would insert or add to this list?

What should be the final step of any solution?

Assign Inquire question 7 to pairs of students. Have the students use their algebra tiles to help them with their solutions. Suggest they draw a diagram on grid paper of each step of their results. Have volunteers present their results to the class. Let them use overhead algebra tiles and an overhead projector, if they wish. Remind the students that the first step in the solution is to reduce the system of three equations in three variables to a system of two equations in two variables. Then, the students are able to use the algebra tiles to solve the system of two equations in two variables.

Finally, review teaching examples 1 and 2 on student text pages 42 and 43.

Method 2

(1-cm grid paper, algebra tiles, overhead algebra tiles, overhead projector) Provide the students with grid paper and algebra tiles, and present the following system of equations in three variables.

$x + y - z = 4$ (1)
$x - y - z = 3$ (2)
$2x + y + 2z = 3$ (3)

Ask:

What does the solution of a system of three equations in three variables look like?

Elicit from the students that the solution of a system of three equations in three variables is an ordered triple of the form (x, y, z).

What does the graph of such an ordered triple represent?

Point out that, when this ordered triple is graphed, it represents a point in space. Then, ask:

How could you eliminate a variable from equations (1) and (2)?

What other variable could you eliminate from equations (1) and (2)? How?

How could you eliminate a variable from equations (2) and (3)?

How would you describe the system of equations that is the result of eliminating a variable from (1) and (2) and of eliminating the same variable from (2) and (3)?

What would be the next step in finding the solution to the three equations in three variables?

What would be the final step of the solution?

Have the students use their algebra tiles and grid paper to help them solve the system of two equations in two variables. Ask:

Now that you have solved the system of two equations in two variables, how can you find the solution for the system of three equations in three variables?

Have volunteers present their results to the class. Provide overhead algebra tiles and an overhead projector, if necessary.

Review with the class teaching examples 1 and 2 on student text pages 42 and 43.

Sample Solution

Page 46, question 60

There are many solutions to this problem. Let the three variables be a, b, and c, where $a = 2$, $b = 3$, and $c = -1$. Use these three values to make up true statements. For example,

$5(2) + 3 - (-1) = 10 + 3 + 1$
$\qquad\qquad\qquad = 14$
Then, $5a + b - c = 14$.
$-2(2) + 3(3) + 7(-1) = -4 + 9 - 7$
$\qquad\qquad\qquad\qquad = -2$
Then, $-2a + 3b + 7c = -2$.
$2 + 3 + (-1) = 4$
Then, $a + b + c = 4$.
One system is $5a + b - c = 14$
$\qquad\qquad\qquad -2a + 3b + 7c = -2$
$\qquad\qquad\qquad\qquad a + b + c = 4$

Logic Power Answer

K_C	Q_S	A_S
Q_H	A_H	K_D

Integrating Technology

Graphing Calculators

Solve the system in teaching example 1 on student text page 42 using Method 2, and compare your graph with the one shown. Try this method with some of the questions on student text page 44. Try the standard viewing window and friendly viewing windows.

Internet

Use the Internet to find data to create problems that can be solved using a system of three linear equations in three variables. Display your problems for classmates to solve.

Extension

Another method for solving systems of equations in two or three variables is called the method of comparison. For systems in two variables, both equations are solved for one variable in terms of the other. The resulting right sides are equated, and the resulting equation is solved.

$x + y = 7$ (1)

$x - y = 5$ (2)

Solve (1) for x in terms of y.

$x = 7 - y$ (3)

Solve (2) for x in terms of y.

$x = 5 + y$ (4)

Equate the right sides of (3) and (4).

$$7 - y = 5 + y$$
$$7 - 5 = y + y$$
$$2 = 2y$$
$$1 = y$$

Substitute $y = 1$ in (1).

$$x + 1 = 7$$
$$x = 6$$

Thus, $x = 6, y = 1$ is the solution to the system. Check the solution by substituting $x = 6$ and $y = 1$ in (2).

$x - y = 5$ (2)

L.S. $= x - y$ R.S. $= 5$

     $= 6 - 1$

     $= 5$ L.S. = R.S. Checks.

Use the method of elimination to rewrite a system of three equations in three variables as a system of two equations in two variables. Then, use the comparison method to solve the resulting system of two equations in two variables.

Use the method of comparison to solve each system of three equations in three variables.

1. $\begin{aligned} 3x + y - z &= 10 \\ x + y + z &= 4 \\ 2x + y + 2z &= 3 \end{aligned}$ **2.** $\begin{aligned} x + y + z &= 2 \\ 2x + y - z &= -4 \\ -x + 3y + z &= 0 \end{aligned}$

Enrichment

Research the life and works of Colin Maclaurin. Write a few sentences describing his contribution to the solution of systems of equations.

Math Journal

Make a list of the steps required to solve a system of three equations in three variables.

In point form, list at least two advantages and two disadvantages for each of the three methods presented for solving systems of three equations in three variables: the method of elimination, the graphical method in teaching example 1, and the method of substitution in teaching example 2 on student pages 42 and 43.

For students who complete the Extension section, include two advantages and disadvantages of the comparison method.

Problem Levels of Difficulty

A: 1–18, 23–30, 41–57, 61
B: 19–22, 31–35, 58
C: 36–40, 59, 60

Assessing the Outcomes

Written Assignment

Solve each of the following systems of equations in two different ways.

1. $\begin{aligned} 2x - y + z &= -3 \\ -x + y + 2z &= -2 \\ x + 3y - z &= 14 \end{aligned}$ **2.** $\begin{aligned} x + y - z &= -4 \\ 2x + 3y + z &= -7 \\ -2x + 2y + 3z &= 1 \end{aligned}$

Technology

Exploring Non-linear Systems With a Graphing Calculator

Student Text Page
P. 47

Materials
graphing calculators

Learning Outcomes
- Graph non-linear equations using a graphing tool.
- Graph systems containing non-linear equations using a graphing tool.

Prerequisite Skills
Graph each system of equations using a graphing calculator.

a) $y = 5 - r$
$y = x + 2$
[(1.5, 3.5)]

b) $y = 2x + 1$
$y = 0.5x - 1$
$[(-1.\overline{3}), -1.\overline{6})]$

Teaching Suggestions
Discuss the graphs that the students create in Exploration 1. Ask them to compare not only the graphs with those of linear equations, but the given equations with linear equations.

In Exploration 2, all the systems prior to question 6 have been chosen to show the intersections in the standard viewing window, because of the introductory nature of the section with respect to non-linear equations. Question 4 draws attention to the fact that only a portion of the graphs can be seen in the viewing window.

Encourage students to compare the viewing windows they used in questions 6 and 7 with those of their classmates.

See *MATHPOWER™ 11, Western Edition, Blackline Masters* pp. 27 to 29 for Setting Viewing Windows.

Extension
1. Find the solutions by graphing, using viewing windows that allow intersection points to be seen.

a) $y = x^3 + 1$
$y = 16 - x$

b) $y = 3^x$
$y = 3x + 20$

2. Graph each non-linear equation in a viewing window so that the portion seen gives the impression that the equation is linear.

a) $y = 2^x$

b) $y = x^2 - 5$

Assessing the Outcomes

Written Assignment

Write about the similarities and differences when graphing linear equations and non-linear equations using a graphing calculator.

1.7 Problem Solving: Solve Fermi Problems

Student Text Pages
Pp. 48–49

Materials
Yellow Pages, publications from Statistics Canada, the Red Cross Society and Environmental Groups, reference books, almanacs, marbles, measuring tapes

Learning Outcome
• Solve Fermi problems.

Prerequisite Skills

1. Estimate.   [Answers may vary.]

a) 909×54 [50 000]

b) 3.9×2.1 [8]

c) $471 + 69 + 31$ [575]

d) $369 + 503 - 194$ [700]

e) $289 \div 58$ [5]

f) $8771 \div 999$ [9]

2. Round each calculation as indicated.

a) 1.49×2.7, 1 decimal place   [4.0]

b) 37×652, nearest hundred   [24 100]

c) $15.65 \div 0.78$, 2 decimal places   [20.06]

d) $934.5 \div 16.2$, nearest whole number   [58]

e) $16.5 \times 3.2 \div 22$, nearest tenth   [2.4]

f) $105.29 \div 0.0027 + 25.4$,
nearest thousandth   [39 021.696]

3. Calculate. Round your answer to 2 decimal places, if necessary.

a) $3.6 \times 10^4 \times 1.9 \times 10^3$ [6.84×10^7]

b) $2.15 \times 10^{-4} \times 8.03 \times 10^2$ [1.73×10^{-1}]

c) $1.579 \times 10^8 \div 6.4 \times 10^{-2}$ [2.47×10^9]

d) $9.2 \times 10^5 \div 4.3 \times 10^7$ [2.14×10^{-2}]

Mental Math

1. Evaluate for $a = 2$ and $b = -3$.

a) $-a - b$ [1]   **b)** $-3a + 5b$ [−21]

c) $b^2 + 2a^2$ [17]   **d)** $3b^2 + 3b - 2$ [16]

e) $b + 4a - a$ [3]   **f)** $6a^2 - 2b$ [30]

2. Estimate.

a) 36×2.4 [90]   **b)** 6.1×490 [300]

c) 0.87×7.3 [7]   **d)** 9.60×9.4 [9000]

e) 4.2×68 [280]   **f)** 280×220 [60 000]

Teaching Suggestions

Method 1

(Yellow Pages, publications from Statistics Canada, the Red Cross Society, and Environmental Groups, reference books, almanacs)   Fermi problems are fun and enjoyable, and provide a fantastic opportunity for the not-so-committed mathematicians to shine!

The key to getting students involved is to get them hooked on creating the problems they would like to solve—the more outrageous, the better.

Discuss with the class the nature of Fermi problems. Explain that Fermi problems often involve comparing an object of known dimensions with an object of very large or very small dimensions. Although it might not seem like there is enough information, by making assumptions and using estimates, the answer can usually be found.

Make reference books available for students' use. Review with the class the opening paragraph and the problem on student text page 48. Ask:

How many students have ever visited the Royal Centre?

What is the actual shape of a soccer ball?

How would the answer to the problem on student text page 48 change if you were to assume the soccer ball is a sphere?

Which answer do you prefer? Explain.

Lead students to realize that they can use mathematical formulas, make close estimates, and use facts from around the globe. They can use compensation techniques and calculators, if they so choose, although the game "I can get a better estimate than you can, and faster! And I didn't use anything but my fine mind!" is much more fun with just scrap paper, sharpened minds, and a playful attitude.

Help students realize that, while the answers are estimates, they are based on facts found in the library, on the Internet, in a reference book, a glossary, or a dictionary.

Have pairs of students choose different questions on student text page 49 to solve. Give the pairs of students who choose the same problem an opportunity to compare and discuss their results. Have volunteers present their results to the class.

Set up a bulletin board and display any solutions to the problems that are particularly inventive or creative.

Method 2

(marbles, measuring tapes)   Provide pairs of students with marbles and measuring tapes, and have them choose one of the following problems.

How many marbles would it take to fill this classroom?

How many times could the people of the world, with their arms outstretched at their sides and holding hands, go around the equator?

Have pairs of students write down a list of steps they are going to take to solve their problem. Then, ask:

What would be your first step in solving these problems?

What information do you need to solve the problem?

Discuss the process of solving a Fermi problem. Remind the students that the solutions to Fermi problems are just estimates. Thus, there are many different answers possible, depending on the facts they use to estimate the solution. Point out that it is useful to include the facts used to solve the problem as part of the answer to the problem.

Have pairs of students volunteer to present their solution to their problem of choice to the class.

Number Power Answer

Number the bags from 0 to 9. Put 2^n coins in bag number n, i.e., put 2^0 coins, or 1 coin, in bag number 0, 2^1 coins, or 2 coins, in bag number 1, 2^6 coins, or 64 coins, in bag number 6. For any number between 1 and 1023, choose the combination of bags whose total is the requested number. For example, if the requested number is 89, choose bags 1, 3, 4, and 6, since these bags contain $2^0 + 2^3 + 2^4 + 2^6 = 1 + 8 + 16 + 64$, or 89 coins.

Integrating Technology

Internet

Use the Internet to find information to create problems that require retrieving information in order to solve them. Use web sites such as Statistics Canada's Web Site *http://www.statcan.ca*. Display your problems for classmates to research and solve.

Computer Data Bank

Use the databases in *MATHPOWER™ 11, Western Edition, Computer Data Bank* to find information to create problems that require retrieving information in order to solve them. Display your problems for classmates to research and solve.

Enrichment

A googol is 10^{100}.

A googolplex is a googol to the power of a googol. Thus,

1 googolplex $= (1 \text{ googol})^{1 \text{ googol}}$

$= (10^{100})^{10^{100}}$

If you were able to write the digits of a googolplex, how long would it take you, and how long would the number be?

Math Journal

How do you feel when you answer a Fermi problem? How does this compare with finding the answer to a system of three equations in three variables? Explain.

Cross-Discipline

Environmental Studies   Research some environmental issues, such as, how much pollution is being released from local pulp mills or how much acid rain is being formed over the Great Lakes. Use the data you have collected to create a Fermi problem and write a solution to your problem. Exchange your problem with that of another student in the class. Write a solution to this problem, and compare your solution with that of the other student. Display your Fermi problem and solution on a class bulletin board.

Problem Levels of Difficulty

A: 1–13, 19   **B:** 14–18

Assessing the Outcomes

Group Evaluation: Presentation

With a partner, write your own Fermi problem and its solution. Then, in an oral report, present the problem, the reasoning behind the solution to the problem, the plan to solve the problem, and the solution.

Written Assignment

Find a solution to each problem.

1. How many cans of paint are required to paint a line 1 m wide around the equator?

2. How many $2 coins would you need, if you wanted to cover completely, without any overlap, the surface of all the Great Lakes?

Connecting Math and Zoology

Ape/Monkey Populations

Student Text Pages
Pp. 50–51

Learning Outcomes
- Interpret graphs to make predictions about a population.
- Make inferences and generalizations based on population data.

Prerequisite Skills

1. Two points on a line are given. Write the equation of each line in standard form.
   a) $(3, 11)$, $(7, 5)$ $[3x + 2y = 31]$
   b) $(-2, -4)$, $(3, 3)$ $[7x - 5y = 6]$
   c) $(0, 4)$, $(-2, -1)$ $[5x - 2y = -8]$

2. Calculate what percent the first number is of the second number. Round your answer to the nearest whole percent, if necessary.
   a) 5, 20   [25%]
   b) 78, 92   [85%]
   c) 125, 90   [139%]
   d) 6.5, 8.3   [78%]

3. Evaluate.
   a) $|-5|$ [5]
   b) $|2 - 3|$ [1]
   c) $|5 + 6 - 3|$ [8]
   d) $-|9 - 11|$ [2]

Mental Math

1. Evaluate each expression for $x = 2$ and $y = -3$.
   a) $2x + 3y$ $[-5]$
   b) $-x - 6y$ $[16]$
   c) $2x^2 + y^2$ $[17]$
   d) $-5y + 2 + x$ $[19]$

2. Calculate.
   a) 7.5^2 [56.25]
   b) 650^2 [422 500]
   c) 0.35^2 [0.1225]
   d) 9.5^2 [90.25]

Teaching Suggestions

This section provides a rare opportunity for students to read information together, investigate the data presented by some graphs, and then argue, defend, and interpret information provided and questions posed.

Have three different students each read aloud a paragraph on student text page 50. Ask:

Which students in the class are taking biology?

What is the difference between a monkey and an ape?

Why do you think the ape population decreased so much and the monkey population increased so much over the course of millions of years?

Assign Investigations 1 and 2 to pairs of students. Give them an opportunity to compare and discuss their results with those of other pairs of students. Have volunteers present their results to the class.

Assign Investigation 3 to pairs of students. Of particular interest are questions 3 and 4. They help to clarify some issues around positive and negative slope, and their dependence on the usual starting point of (0, 0). If the "years ago" horizontal points were labelled with negative numbers, this would work. Give the pairs of students plenty of opportunity to compare and discuss their results. Also, allow them the time on the Internet to research the ape/monkey populations. Have volunteers present their results to the class.

Integrating Technology

Internet

To learn more about zoology, research the topic using the Internet.

Enrichment

Research the life and work of Jane Goodall and Diane Fossey, as they relate to monkeys and apes. Make up a poster about these two women, and include on your poster artwork, data, graphs, etc. Present your poster to your class.

Math Journal

Describe how you feel about the declining population of apes. Use numerical estimates and predictions to explain your opinions and any suggestions you have for changing the situation.

Assessing the Outcome

Group Evaluation: Presentation

Have small groups of students choose a type of animal, say birds. The groups should research a bird that has become extinct and a bird whose numbers have increased significantly. Suggest that they find at least two sets of data for each bird of the form (year, number), and construct a graph of the change over time in the population of each bird. Have the groups make a class display of the graphs.

Observation

You might consider some of these questions as you observe the students work:
- Are the students able to read the values from the graph accurately?
- Are the students able to interpret the information shown in a graph?
- Are the students able to verbalize their answers?

Review

Student Text Pages
Pp. 52–53

Materials
Teacher's Resource Master 1 (0.5-cm grid paper),
Teacher's Resource Master 2 (1-cm grid paper)

Learning Outcome
- Review the skills and concepts in Chapter 1.

Using the Review
Have the students work independently to complete the
Review. Meeting in small groups, the students can mark
and discuss the work. Groups can then share their
solutions and report any questions that caused them
difficulty. Discuss these questions with the class.

Reteaching Suggestions
For those students having difficulty with the chapter
material, form small groups and use the following exercises.
   If you feel that the class has had particular difficulty
mastering any concept, you may wish to work through a
problem from each section as a model of excellence of
solution, which some students require just prior to
assessment.

Solving Systems of Linear Equations Graphically
1. Solve each system by graphing. Check your
   solutions.

a) $y = -x + 1$
   $y = x - 3$

b) $x + 2y = -7$
   $x - 3y = -8$

c) $2x - y = 2$
   $3x + 2y = -8$

d) $1.45x + y = 2.3$
   $2x + 3y = -0.15$

2. Without graphing, determine whether each system has
   one solution, no solution, or infinitely many solutions.

a) $-2x + y = 5$
   $4x - 2y = -10$

b) $4x - y = -5$
   $x + 2y = -8$

c) $x - 2y = -10$
   $x - 2y = -14$

d) $y = 2x + 11$
   $y = \frac{1}{5}x - 45$

3. The sum of two integers is -2. The difference
   between the integers is 20. Find the integers.

Solving Systems of Linear Equations by Substitution
1. Solve each system of equations by substitution.
   Check each solution.

a) $3x + 2y = 14$
   $5x - y = 6$

b) $x + 6y = 17$
   $3x - 7y = 1$

2. An apartment building contains sixty units.
   One-bedroom apartments rent for $725 per month.
   Two-bedroom apartments rent for $925 per month.
   When the building is entirely rented, the total
   monthly rental income is $48 700. How many
   apartments of each type are there?

Solving Systems of Linear Equations by Elimination
1. Solve each system of equations by elimination.
   Check each solution.

a) $x - y = 2$
   $x + y = 6$

b) $x - 2y = 0$
   $3x + 2y = 16$

c) $3x - 2y = 6$
   $6x = 11 + 4y$

d) $5x + 2y = -19$
   $-3x + 2y = 5$

e) $2x + y = 5$
   $3x - 4y = 2$

f) $3y - x + 10 = 0$
   $3x + 4y = -22$

2. Nine times the larger of two numbers plus 4 times
   the smaller is 135. Six times the larger less 5 times
   the smaller is 21. Find the numbers.

Solving Systems of Linear Equations in Three Variables
Solve each system of equations.

a) $x + y + 3z = 12$
   $x - y + 4z = 11$
   $2x + y + 3z = 13$

b) $3x - 2y + 5z = 1$
   $4x + 5y - 3z = 17$
   $7x - 3y + 2z = 36$

Answers to Reteaching Suggestions

Solving Systems of Linear Equations Graphically
1. a) $(2, -1)$
   b) $\left(\frac{-37}{5}, \frac{1}{5}\right)$
2. c) $\left(-\frac{4}{7}, -\frac{22}{7}\right)$
   d) $(3, -2.05)$
2. a) infinite   b) one   c) no   d) one
3. $9, -11$

Solving Systems of Linear Equations by Substitution
1. a) $(2, 4)$ b) $(5, 2)$
2. 34 one-bedrooms, 26 two-bedrooms

Solving Systems of Linear Equations by Elimination
1. a) $(4, 2)$ b) $(4, 2)$ c) no solution
   d) $(-3, -2)$ e) $(2, 1)$ f) $(-2, -4)$
2. $11, 9$

Solving Systems of Linear Equations in Three Variables
a) $(1, 2, 3)$ b) $(5, -3, 4)$

Exploring Math

Tiling Squares With L-Shaped Triominoes

(grid paper) This is a nice exploration that reinforces the idea of mathematics as a language of patterns.

You may direct the students to read this on their own, whenever they are finished their work in class, or perhaps at the end of a test.

Have the students provide a record of their attempts and present their conclusions on grid paper, in such a way that locations where the square can be removed, or cannot be removed, show up on the same graph.

1	1	2	2
1	■	3	2
4	3	3	5
4	4	5	5

■	1	2	2
1	1	3	2
4	3	3	5
4	4	5	5

1	■	2	2
1	1	3	2
4	3	3	5
4	4	5	5

They should provide a different grid for each of the 3 by 3, 4 by 4, and 5 by 5 situations. Some students may wish to extend this to thinking about 6 by 6, ..., *n* by *n* situations.

The following diagrams are the answers to question 3.

3. a)

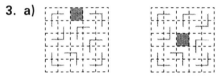

or any rotation of these.

3. b)

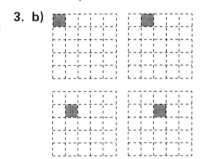

or any rotation of these.

Chapter Check

Student Text Page
P. 54

Learning Outcome
- Evaluate the skills and concepts in Chapter 1.

Assessing the Outcomes

Observation

If you assign the Chapter Check as a student assessment, look for the following:
- When graphing, do they use either the x- and y-intercepts or the slope and y-intercept to graph, or do they plot points?
- Can they describe systems of equations that are intersecting, coincident, or parallel?
- Do they immediately know which equation should be used to create an equivalent equation for use with substitution?
- Do they quickly decide which variable to eliminate when they are using elimination?
- Do they have problems with decimals or fractions in the equations or do they immediately realize that they need to clear the denominators?
- Do they consistently remember that the division bar is a grouping symbol?
- Do they make sign errors when transforming equations from one form to another?
- Can they analyze a word problem and create appropriate tables, graphs, or equations?
- Do they check their work in all equations to ensure accuracy?

Problem Solving

Student Text Page
P. 55

Materials

Teacher's Resource Master 2 (1-cm grid paper), toothpicks

Learning Outcome

- Use problem solving strategies to solve problems.

Using the Strategies

The problems on this page allow the students to use the problem solving strategies discussed in Chapter 1. These strategies are
- Use a Diagram
- Use a Data Bank
- Solve Fermi Problems

Teaching Suggestions

(grid paper, toothpicks)   Encourage the students to work in pairs or small groups. When students have completed the problems, have them share and discuss their strategies and solutions with other students.

For question 1, ask:

What do you notice about the two numbers that are squared?

Lead the students to see that the two numbers are consecutive numbers, and when the difference of squares is applied to these numbers, the factors become 1 and the sum of the numbers. Thus, if you want to find the number 15 written as a difference of two squares, think of two consecutive numbers that total 15. Two consecutive numbers that total fifteen are 7 and 8. Thus,

$$8^2 - 7^2 = (8 - 7)(8 + 7) = 1 \times 15 = 15.$$

If students are having difficulty with problem 4, point out that the square is made up of 16 unit squares.

If the large square is to be divided into 4 congruent shapes, then each shape must have 4 unit squares. This is the required answer.

For problem 5, the next number is generated by squaring the units digit or the previous number and adding it to the tens digit of the previous number.

For problem 7, suggest that the students divide the shape into squares and right triangles. Remind the students that the distance between two parallel lines is the perpendicular line between the lines. Thus, the height of the right triangles is 8 cm. The formula for the area of a triangle may also be used. If this is used, then the length of the sides need to be determined.

For question 10, provide pairs of students with toothpicks, and have them present their results to the class. These are two possible diagrams.

For question 11, if necessary, point out that the diagonal of the cube is the diameter of the sphere.

For question 12, remind the students that no one said you couldn't fold the paper!

Assessing the Outcome

Observation

As you make your problem solving assessment of each student, consider the following:
- Do they understand the problem?
- Do they consider a variety of strategies?
- Do they use an organized approach?
- Do they create and use diagrams effectively?
- Do they show persistence?

CHAPTER 1

Student Text Answers

Chapter Opener   p. 1
1. a) (8, 4)   b) 8; 4
2. b) (8, 4)
3. They are the same.

Getting Started   pp. 2–3
Social Insurance Numbers
1. 10; The next highest multiple of 10 is 10 greater than a multiple of 10. In this case, the check digit is 0.
2. a) 9   b) 9   c) 2   d) 8
3. a) No; the check digit is incorrect.
   b) Yes; the check digit is correct.
   c) Yes; the check digit is correct.
4. Answers may vary. 444 142 517; 535 253 520
5. a) $10 - m$ b) 10
   c) m is the ones digit from step 4. Subtract m from 10 to find the check digit.

Warm Up
1. $x + 2$ 2. $2x + 8$ 3. $3y - 5$ 4. $-5a + 3$
5. $6x$ 6. $-2c$ 7. x 8. $3n$
9. $x + 2y$ 10. $3p - r$ 11. 8   12. 2
13. -6 14. -5 15. 2   16. 12
17. $-\dfrac{1}{2}$ 18. $\dfrac{3}{2}$ 19. 4   20. -5
21. $-\dfrac{5}{3}$ 22. -4 23. -1 24. -4
25. $x = 11 - 3y$ 26. $x = 5y - 8$
27. $x = 2y - 4$ 28. $x = 2y + 4$
29. $y = 3 - 2x$ 30. $y = x - 2$
31. $y = \dfrac{-1 - 2x}{4}$ 32. $y = \dfrac{3x - 4}{2}$

Mental Math
Evaluating Expressions
1. 4   2. 1   3. -5 4. 12
5. 3   6. 8   7. 0   8. 3
9. -2 10. -1 11. 20   12. -9

Multiplying Special Pairs of Numbers
1. 2016   2. 7221   3. 3024   4. 5609
5. 216   6. 4225   7. 12.24   8. 56.25
9. 6.16   10. 200 900   11. 902 100   12. 421 600
13. a) $100n^2 + 100n + 10x - x^2$
   b) $100n^2 + 100n + 10x - x^2 = 100n(n + 1) + x(10 - x)$; The first term multiplies the tens digit by the next whole number. The second term multiplies the ones digits.

Investigating Math   pp. 4–5
1 Ordered Pairs and One Equation
1. a) (1, 13), (24, −10)   b) (5, −3)
   c) (−2, −4), (−12, 0)   d) (2, 3)   e) (−2, −10)
2. a) 3, 9, 10, −2   b) 2, −9, 11, −2
   c) −1, 5, 13, 10   d) 5, 3, −4, −7

2 Ordered Pairs and Two Equations
1. a) (1, 2)   b) (−3, 1)   c) (2, 3)
   d) (6, −8)   e) (−2, −5)   f) (−4, 7)
2. a) (4, −3)   b) (6, 3)   c) (−1, 0)
   d) Answers may vary. (0, 0)

3 Problem Solving
1. a) 38   b) Victoria: 17 m; Prince Rupert: 38 m
2. a) 40   b) lynx: 16 kg; wolf: 40 kg
3. a) The equations represent the same line on a coordinate grid.
   b) Answers may vary. (−2, 3), (−3, 4)
4. The equations represent parallel lines on a coordinate grid. They do not intersect.

Section 1.1   pp. 11–12
Practice (Section 1.1)
1. (3, −1)   2. (−1, 6)   3. (4, −1)
4. infinitely many solutions
5. (6, 0)   6. (−3, 4)   7. no solution
8. (−2, −1)   9. (2, −1)   10. (−3, −2)   11. (4, 1)
12. no solution   13. (5, −1)
14. infinitely many solutions
15. $\left(\dfrac{1}{2}, 2\right)$ 16. $\left(2, \dfrac{3}{2}\right)$ 17. $\left(-1, \dfrac{1}{2}\right)$ 18. $\left(\dfrac{3}{2}, \dfrac{5}{2}\right)$
19. (1.5, −0.8)   20. (6.7, 1.7)   21. (3.9, −0.3)
22. (−2.7, 0.3)   23. (2.3, 3)   24. (−2.6, 5.1)
25. one solution   26. no solution
27. infinitely many solutions   28. one solution
29. no solution   30. no solution

Applications and Problem Solving (Section 1.1)
31. Austria: 9; Germany: 16
32. a) (20, 500)   b) 20   c) Champion
33. a) 3 mg   b) 7 mg
34. Montreal: 15 km/h; Victoria: 10 km/h
35. a) (50, 1000)   b) 50
   c) less than 50   d) greater than 50
36. north: 125 000; south: 5000
37. (−6, 3)   38. (3, −1), (5, $\tfrac{1}{3}$), (4, 0)
39. parallelogram

40. Answers may vary.
   a) (0, 0), (1, 1), (1, 2)   **b)** (−2, 0), (0, 4), (1, 6)
41. Answers may vary.
   a) $x + y = 6$ **b)** $2x + 2y = 8$ **c)** $x + 2y = 4$
42. a) (3, 5)   **b)** (2, 3) and (−1, 0)
43. a) For less than 8 h/month, Plan A is least expensive.
   For between 8 h/month and 22 h/month, Plan B is
   least expensive. For greater than 22 h/month,
   Plan C is least expensive.
   b) For less than 11 h/month, Plan C is most
   expensive. For greater than 11 h/month,
   Plan A is most expensive.
44. Answers may vary.
   a) $x + y = 5$, $2x + y = 8$
   b) $x + y = 5$, $2x + 2y - 10 = 0$
45. A linear system can have one solution, no solution,
   or infinitely many solutions. It cannot have only
   two solutions. This system must have infinitely
   many solutions.
47. a) $\left(-\dfrac{25}{2}, 9\right)$; (48, 24); (−16, −18)

Computer Data Bank   p. 13

1 Seating Capacity of New Vehicles

1. 55
2. minivan
3. a) Dodge Ram 1500
   b) Mercury Grand Marquis
   c) Honda Odyssey, Isuzu Oasis, and Toyota Avalon
   d) GMC Yukon and Land Rover Discovery

2 Nations Around the World

1. a) 31, including Canada
   b) 18, including Greenland
   c) 5, including China
2. a) Europe
   b) Asia
   c) Africa and Europe
   d) Africa
3. Asia, 10; South America, 5
4. 18.4%
5. $23.388 billion
6. Africa, 83%

3 Locating Craters on Earth

1. a) Oceania
   b) Africa
   c) Europe
   d) North America
   e) North America
   f) Europe
2. a) Africa, 16; Asia, 19; Europe, 44;
   North America, 51; Oceania, 19; South America, 7

4 Summer Olympics

1. Answers will vary.
2. Answers will vary.

5 Camping in Western Canada

1. Provincial, 9524
2. Alberta, $8 703 187.20; British Columbia,
   $2 419 113.60; Manitoba, $1 073 404.80;
   Saskatchewan, $894 211.20; all four,
   $13 089 916.80

Section 1.2   p. 15

Applications and Problem Solving (Section 1.2)

1. 67 m   **2.** 65 cm   **3.** 20 s
4. Timid swimmer and Bold swimmer cross in boat;
   Timid swimmer returns in boat; Timid swimmer
   and Bold cross in boat; Bold swimmer returns in
   boat; Bold swimmer and Timid cross in boat,
   Bold swimmer returns in boat; Bold swimmer and
   Timid cross in boat; Bold swimmer returns in boat;
   Bold and Bold swimmer cross in boat.
5. Train A is heading to the right, Train B, to the left.
   Train A pulls into the siding with 20 cars, leaving
   20 cars on the track. Train B pushes these cars back
   until it clears the way for Train A to back out of the
   siding. Train B unhitches 20 of its cars. Train A
   picks them up and pulls them down the track. Train
   B backs its remaining 20 cars into the siding and
   Train A backs down the track to pick up its 20 cars.
   Train A now pulls 60 cars — its 40 plus 20 from
   Train B in the middle — to the right. Train B exits
   the siding, then backs up the track to get 20 cars
   from train A, pulling them forward and backing
   them into the siding. Train B backs up to collect its
   remaining 20 cars, pulls forward and hitches up the
   20 cars from Train A in the siding, pulling them
   onto the track. Train A backs up to hitch up its 20
   cars. Both trains proceed to their destinations.
6. 17.1 m   **7.** $3\sqrt{2}$ cm   **8.** (3, 10) and (9, 6)
9. 24   **10.** 5.8 cm or 10 cm   **13.** 1300 m

Investigating Math   pp. 16–17

1 Expressions in Two Variables

1. a) $x + y$ **b)** $6x + 2y$ **c)** $5y - x$
2. a) $x - y$ **b)** $x + y$
3. a) $x + 7y$ **b)** $x + 15y$
4. a) $x + y$ **b)** $10x$
   c) $5y$ **d)** $10x + 5y$
5. a) $10x + 25y$ **b)** $0.1x + 0.25y$
6. a) $x + y$ **b)** $0.07x$
   c) $0.06y$ **d)** $0.07x + 0.06y$

2 Equations in Two Variables

1. $x + y = 8$ **2.** $y = x - 5$
3. $y = x^2 - 1$ **4.** $x - 2y + 1 = 0$
5. $l + w = 40$ **6.** $c - q = 6$
7. $g = 2t - 7$ **8.** $2b + 3t = 61$

3 Systems of Equations

1. $x + y = 7, x - y = 3$
2. $y = 2x, y = x - 4$
3. a) $x + y = 256$ **b)** $5x + 2y = 767$
4. $p + r = 295, p = r + 11$
5. $r = \frac{2}{3}c, c - r = 1700$
6. $b + f = 331, 10b + 15f = 3915$
7. $q + l = 73, 0.25q + l = 37$
8. $x + y = 180, y = 3x - 4$

Investigating Math   pp. 18–20

1 Representing Equations

1. $x + y = 3$ **2.** $2x - y = -1$ **3.** $x + 3 = -2y$

3 Solving Systems by Substitution, I

1. $(4, -1)$ **2.** $(1, 3)$ **3.** $(-3, 1)$ **4.** $(2, 2)$

4 Solving Systems by Substitution, II

1. $(2, 1)$ **2.** $(2, -1)$ **3.** $(0, -1)$ **4.** $(1, 0)$

Section 1.3   pp. 25–27

Practice (Section 1.3)

1. $x = 8 - 3y$ **2.** $x = -4y - 13$
3. $x = 7y + 7$ **4.** $x = 2y - 1$
5. $y = 11 - 6x$ **6.** $y = -5x - 9$
7. $y = x + 2$ **8.** $y = 3x + 4$
9. $(3, 2)$ **10.** $(4, -5)$
11. $(5, 0)$ **12.** $(-2, 3)$
13. $(-2, -2)$ **14.** $\left(\frac{1}{2}, -1\right)$
15. $(-1, 1)$ **16.** $\left(\frac{7}{11}, -\frac{1}{11}\right)$
17. $\left(3, -\frac{6}{5}\right)$ **18.** $(-3, -4)$
19. $(1, 0)$ **20.** $\left(1, -\frac{1}{3}\right)$
21. $(1, 3)$ **22.** $\left(-1, \frac{2}{7}\right)$
23. $\left(\frac{4}{3}, \frac{11}{3}\right)$ **24.** $\left(-\frac{32}{5}, -\frac{18}{5}\right)$

Applications and Problem Solving (Section 1.3)

25. a) $(24, -18)$ **b)** $(-3, 2)$
c) $\left(\frac{3}{2}, 2\right)$ **d)** $\left(-\frac{5}{3}, \frac{1}{6}\right)$

26. If the system reduces to an impossible equation, there is no solution. If the system reduces to $0 = 0$, there are infinitely many solutions. Otherwise, there is one solution.
a) no solution   **b)** $(3, -1)$; one solution
c) infinitely many solutions
d) $(-1, -5)$; one solution   **e)** no solution
f) infinitely many solutions
27. a) Fairweather Mountain is 3831 m higher than Baldy Mountain. The height of Fairweather Mountain is 329 m less than 6 times the height of Baldy Mountain.
b) Baldy Mountain: 832 m;
Fairweather Mountain: 4663 m
28. $x = 34, y = 10$
29. a) $(5, 4)$ **b)** $(4, 5)$ **c)** $(-1, -5)$
30. 463, 289
31. 2.5
32. short span: 890 m; long span: 1780 m
33. For less than 4.5 h, Quality is cheaper. For greater than 4.5 h, ABC is cheaper.
34. owls: 14; pigeons: 3
35. 21°, 69°
36. 323 adult tickets; 227 student tickets
37. $6000 at 4%; $9000 at 5%
38. a) 84 km   **b)** 132 km
39. "Macbet": 12 years; "Macbeth": 336 years
40. 5% solution: 10 mL; 10% solution: 40 mL
41. 18-carat gold: 100 g; 9-carat gold: 50 g
42. 25 mL
43. a) 1.8 h   **b)** 135 km
44. a) No; we get two equivalent equations, and cannot solve the system.
b) yes; We get two different equations, and can solve the system.
45. 68   **46. a)** $(1, 4, -2)$ **b)** $(2, -1, 3)$
47. -1 **48.** $\frac{1}{2}$ **49.** $x + y = q, x - y = r$

Section 1.4   p. 29

Applications and Problem Solving (Section 1.4)

1. a) $14\,835   **b)** $9.06/km
c) $0.031 per passenger-kilometre   **d)** 11:00
2. a) DC-9: 1.15 h; B737: 1.11 h
b) DC-9: $4.58/km; B737: $4.35/km
c) DC-9: $0.038 per passenger-kilometre;
B737: $0.039 per passenger-kilometre
3. Answers may vary.
4. a) 191 000   **b)** Answers may vary.
c) Answers may vary.
5. 5915 km
6. a) Jupiter   **b)** 45 591 km/h
c) approximately 27 times faster than Earth; approximately 6 times faster than the sun
7. Prince Edward Island; Northwest Territories

Career Connection p. 30

1 Comparing Solubilities

1. a) 16 °C   b) 26 g/100 g
2. a) 13 °C   b) 26 g/100 g
3. a) no   b) Yes; if it is not parallel, it must intersect.
4. sodium chloride, ammonium chloride, and potassium iodide. The slopes of their graphs are positive.

Investigating Math p. 31

1 Equivalent Forms

1. Answers may vary. (1, 5), (2, 4), (3, 3)
2. a) $2x + 2y = 12$ b) yes
3. a) $-3x - 3y = -18$ b) yes
4. Yes; they represent the same line on a coordinate grid.
5. Answers may vary.
   a) $-x + y = -2, 2x - 2y = 4, 3x - 3y = 6$
   b) $-2x - y = -7, x + \frac{1}{2}y = \frac{7}{2}, 4x + 2y = 14$
   c) $2y = 8x - 6, 3y = 12x - 9, 4y = 16x - 12$
   d) $2y = x + 5, 4y = 2x + 10, 6y = 3x + 15$

2 Equivalent Systems

1. (3, 4)
2. (3, 4)
3. a) $4x - 2y = 4, -x - y = -7$ b) (3, 4)
4. They all have the same point of intersection.
5. Answers may vary. $2x + y = 10, x + 2y = 11$

3 Adding Equations

1. (2, 1)   2. $2x + y = 5$
3. They all pass through (2, 1).
4. They are equivalent systems. They all have the same solution.
5. They are equivalent systems. They all have solution $(3, -2)$.

Investigating Math pp. 32–33

1 Solving Systems by Addition

1. (2, 1)   2. $(-1, 2)$
3. (0, 1)   4. (1, 1)

2 Solving Systems by Subtraction

1. (2, 1)   2. $(-1, 1)$ 3. (0, 2)   4. $(-1, -1)$

3 Solving Systems by Multiplication

2. $(2, -1)$ 3. (1, 0)   4. $(-2, -2)$

Section 1.5 pp. 38–40

Practice (Section 1.5)

1. (2, 6)   2. $(-1, -3)$ 3. $(-4, 1)$
4. $(3, -2)$ 5. $(-2, 1)$ 6. (5, 3)

7. $(1, -2)$ 8. $(-2, -2)$ 9. (3, 1)
10. no solution   11. (1, 0)
12. infinitely many solutions
13. (4, 2)   14. $(-3, 2)$ 15. $(-2, -3)$ 16. $(0, -5)$
17. $(9, -4)$ 18. $(-3, 8)$ 19. (4, 11)   20. $(2, -1)$
21. $\left(\frac{1}{3}, 1\right)$ 22. $\left(-2, \frac{1}{2}\right)$ 23. $\left(\frac{5}{9}, \frac{1}{9}\right)$
24. infinitely many solutions
25. $\left(\frac{4}{5}, \frac{3}{5}\right)$ 26. no solution   27. $(-1, -3)$
28. (1, 6)   29. $(-2, 3)$ 30. (2, 1)
31. (3, 4)   32. (5, 4)   33. $(4, -2)$
34. (4, 1)   35. $(-1, -3)$ 36. $(-0.2, 0.1)$

Applications and Problem Solving (Section 1.5)

37–42. Answers may vary.
43. a) The total number of provinces is 10. Three times the number of provincial names with First Nations origins is equal to twice the number of provincial names with other origins.   b) 4
44. adult: 206 bones; baby: 350 bones
45. $x = 32, y = 20$
46. $-28, 38$
47. boat: 16 km/h; current: 4 km/h
48. plane speed: 495 km/h; wind speed: 55 km/h
49. 200 km at 100 km/h and 270 km at 90 km/h
50. chicken sandwich by $0.75
51. 2.7 m by 1.2 m
52. 30 min
53. a) 3 V and 6 V   b) 5
54. (4, 6)
55. (3, 2), (0, -2), (-2, 4)
56. A = 3, B = 2
57. $a = -2, b = 3$
58. a) 10   b) 6
59. a) -2 b) 3
60. (2, 5); The solution is not affected by multiplication by a constant.
61. Answers may vary. $3x + 2y = 8, 5x - 7y = 65$
62. Answers may vary.
    a) $3x - 4y = -14, 4x - 3y = -7$
    b) $2x + 3y = 13, 4x + 3y = 5$
    c) $2x - 3y = 4, 4x + 9y = -2$

Section 1.6 pp. 44–46

Practice (Section 1.6)

1. yes   2. no   3. no   4. no   5. yes
6. no   7. no   8. yes   9. yes   10. no
11. (2, 1, 3)   12. $(0, 1, -2)$ 13. $(2, -1, -3)$
14. $(-1, -2, -3)$ 15. (2, 3, 2)   16. $(4, -3, 2)$
17. $(-2, 0, -7)$ 18. $(5, 6, -2)$ 19. $(-2, 4, 1)$
20. $(-3, -4, -2)$ 21. (4, 2, 5)   22. $(3, -3, -2)$
23. $\left(-1, \frac{1}{3}, \frac{1}{2}\right)$ 24. $\left(0, \frac{1}{4}, \frac{3}{4}\right)$

25. $\left(\frac{33}{4}, -\frac{17}{4}, \frac{9}{2}\right)$ **26.** $\left(\frac{27}{5}, \frac{7}{5}, -\frac{27}{5}\right)$

27. $(2, 3, 9)$ **28.** $(1, 2, -1)$ **29.** $(6, -5, 3)$
30. $(3, -1, 5)$ **31.** $(-2, -3, 4)$ **32.** $(-3, 0, -2)$
33. $(-3, 8, 1)$ **34.** $(4, -3, 1)$ **35.** $(3, 2, 4)$
36. $(-3, -2, -4)$ **37.** $(6, 8, 6)$ **38.** $(-4, -6, 12)$
39. $\left(\frac{1}{5}, 0, \frac{2}{3}\right)$ **40.** $\left(\frac{1}{2}, -\frac{1}{3}, \frac{1}{4}\right)$

Applications and Problem Solving (Section 1.6)

41. a) The sum of the points won by the first, second, and third place finishers is 159. The second place finisher had 6 more points than the third place finisher. The first place finisher had 3 less than twice the number of points of the second place finisher. **b)** first: 81; second: 42; third: 36
42. $x = 50, y = 55, z = 25$
43. 8, 14, 31 **44.** 20, 10, -5
45. 82°, 43°, 55° **46.** 120°, 40°, 20°
47. a) 3 gold, 6 silver, 4 bronze
b) biathlon: 7.5-km sprint and 15 km
48. Saturn: 18; Uranus: 17; Neptune: 8
49. 42 years
50. Batman: $134 000; Captain Marvel: $60 000; Superman: $144 000
51. 21 $5 bills, 18 $10 bills, 32 $20 bills
52. Canada: 240 000 km; United States: 20 000 km; Mexico: 10 000 km
53. British Columbia: 630 000 km²; Alberta: 350 000 km²; Manitoba: 350 000 km²
54. $3000 at 4%; $9000 at 5%; $8000 at 7%
55. $a = -5, b = 200, c = 0$
56. $a = -1, b = 100, c = 500$
57. 50 g of X, 30 g of Y, 20 g of Z
58. $a = 2, b = 4$, and $c = 7$ cannot be the side lengths of a triangle, because $c > a + b$.
59. a) Use elimination. **b)** $(2, 3, 1, 4)$
60. Answers may vary.
$x + y + z = 4, 2x + y + z = 6, 3x + y + z = 8$

Technology p. 47

1 Graphing Non-linear Equations

2. a) The graphs are congruent parabolas with different vertices and different directions of opening.
b) Graphs with a positive coefficient of x^2 open up. Graphs with a negative coefficient of x^2 open down.
4. The graphs start close to horizontal and then either increase to positive infinity or decrease to negative infinity.
6. The graphs are cubics. The ones with a positive coefficient of x^3 start in the 3rd quadrant and end in the 1st quadrant. The ones with a negative coefficient of x^3 start in the 2nd quadrant and end in the 4th quadrant.

2 Solving Systems Containing Non-linear Equations

1. a) $(-3, 7), (3, 7)$ **b)** $(2, -2), (-2, -6)$
c) $(1, -1), (4, 5)$ **d)** $(-0.62, 2.62), (1.62, 0.38)$
2. a) $(3, 8)$ **b)** $(1, -2)$ **c)** $(-1, 0.5)$
d) $(-0.79, 0.42), (1.44, 4.89)$
3. a) $(2, 9)$ **b)** $(2, -7)$ **c)** $(0, 0), (-2, -8), (2, 8)$
d) $(0.84, 2.29)$
4. Answers may vary.
5. a) 0 **b)** infinitely many
c) 0 **d)** 1 **e)** 2 **f)** 2
6. a) $t_n = 36 + 4n$ **b)** $t_n = n^2 - n$
c) First quadrant; all the ordered pairs have positive coordinates. **d)** $(9, 72)$
e) The value of term 9 is 72 for both sequences.
7. b) 2063 **c)** Answers may vary.

Connecting Math and Zoology p. 51

1 Interpreting the Graph

1. 14 million years ago
2. a) 6% **b)** 94%
3. a) 94% **b)** 6%
4. 4 million years ago

2 Solving Algebraically

1. apes: $y = 5x - 20$; monkeys: $y = -5x + 120$
2. a) $(14, 50)$
b) the point where the populations were equal

3 Critical Thinking

1. Answers may vary.
2. Answers may vary.
3. On the graph, the time for "years ago" is positive instead of negative. This reverses the signs of the slopes.
4. They are equal. The monkey population increased at the same rate as the ape population decreased.
5. No, it shows only percents, not numbers.

Review pp. 52–53

1. $(4, -1)$ **2.** $(-4, 3)$ **3.** $(2, 2)$ **4.** $\left(\frac{1}{2}, 5\right)$
5. $(1.9, -2.2)$ **6.** $(0.1, 0.7)$
7. infinitely many solutions
8. no solution
9. one solution
10. no solution
11. Sahara: 9 million km²; Australian: 4 million km²
12. a) d represents the number of dollars; p represents the number of paddles
b) $(62.5, 1125)$ **c)** at least 63
13. $(2, 2)$ **14.** $(1, -1)$ **15.** $(-1, 5)$ **16.** $\left(1, \frac{1}{3}\right)$
17. 75 kg of 24% nitrogen and 25 kg of 12% nitrogen
18. $(3, -2)$ **19.** $(1, 1)$

20. $5000 Canada Savings Bond;
    $10 000 provincial government bond
21. Mount Pleasant: 16; Centreville: 15
22. $(-1, 2)$ 23. $(-2, 1)$ 24. $(3, 2)$ 25. $(4, 1)$
26. $(-4, -5)$ 27. $(1, 1)$ 28. $\left(2, \frac{1}{2}\right)$ 29. $(-1, 2)$
30. 36 cars, 9 vans
31. $(-2, -3)$ 32. $(3, 4)$ 33. $(0.6, -0.5)$
34. wind speed: 40 km/h; plane speed: 280 km/h
35. $(2, 1, -3)$ 36. $(2, 1, 4)$ 37. $(7, -1, 2)$
38. $(1, 2, -2)$
39. a) 13 b) 4 c) 33
40. Cross-Cedar Lake: 10 billion m³; Kinbasket Lake:
    25 billion m³; Williston Lake: 70 billion m³

Exploring Math p. 53

2. a) no b) 3, due to symmetry
3. a) corner, middle side, middle
   b) between corner and middle side, between middle
   and corner, between middle and middle side
   c) 6
4. yes

Chapter Check p. 54

1. $(4, 3)$ 2. $(-2, -3)$ 3. $(-1, 0)$
4. $(1, -2)$ 5. $(-0.7, 3.7)$ 6. $(2.4, 1.1)$
7. a) The lines intersect at one point.
   b) The lines are parallel. c) The lines coincide.

8. $(2, 2)$ 9. $\left(-3, \frac{1}{2}\right)$ 10. $(-1, -1)$

11. $(2, 1)$ 12. $(3, 2)$ 13. $(2, -2)$
14. infinitely many solutions
15. no solution
16. $(-6, 4)$ 17. $\left(\frac{2}{3}, \frac{1}{3}\right)$ 18. $\left(-\frac{4}{7}, -\frac{2}{7}\right)$

19. $(4, 1)$ 20. $(2, 0, 3)$ 21. $(1, 2, -1)$
22. Lindros: 16; Modano: -8
23. Yukon: 3185 km; Mackenzie: 4241 km
24. 240 g of 30% fruit granola;
    360 g of 15% fruit granola
25. Yellowknife: 111 days; Peace River: 93 days
26. $4000 at 4%; $9000 at 6%
27. wind speed: 50 km/h; plane speed: 550 km/h
28. Western Canada: 21; Central Canada: 42;
    Eastern Canada: 16

Using the Strategies p. 55

1. $11 = 6^2 - 5^2$; $12 = 4^2 - 2^2$; $15 = 8^2 - 7^2$;
   $16 = 5^2 - 3^2$; $17 = 9^2 - 8^2$; $19 = 10^2 - 9^2$
2. Monday, Tuesday, Wednesday
3. 400
5. 9 and 81
6. Answers may vary.
7. 512
8. 1049
9. 9
11. 192.5 cm³

Data Bank

1. Answers may vary.
2. b) 2011
3. Answers may vary.

CHAPTER 2

Linear Inequalities

Chapter Introduction

Chapter Materials

graphing calculators, Teacher's Resource Master 1 (0.5-cm grid paper), Teacher's Resource Master 2 (1-cm grid paper), Teacher's Resource Master 4 (number lines), Teacher's Resource Master 5 (graphing grids), overhead projector, counters, paper cups

Chapter Concepts

Chapter 2 reviews or introduces
* solving linear inequalities in one variable
* graphing linear inequalities in one variable
* graphing linear inequalities in two variables
* solving systems of linear inequalities
* the problem solving strategies Solve a Simpler Problem, Use Logic, and Look for a Pattern

Teaching Suggestions

Direct the students to look at the graph on student text page 57. Ask:

How long can a diver stay at a depth of 30 m before requiring decompression?

What is the maximum depth that divers seem to be able to go?

If you stayed under water at a depth of 5 m, would you ever have to undergo decompression? Explain.

For question 4, ask:

What does the word "acronym" mean?

What acronym have you used in mathematics?

Integrating Technology

Internet

Use the Internet to find information about Pacific octopuses and/or scuba diving.

Enrichment

Use the graph on student text page 57 to make up a question. Exchange your problem with a classmate and solve your classmate's problem. Discuss and compare each other's solutions. Present your problem and solution to the class.

Assessing the Outcomes

Observation

You might consider some of these questions as you observe the students work.
* Do the students know how to interpret data from a graph?
* Do they work well in pairs?
* Do they persist until they find a solution?
* Do the students attempt all the questions?

Getting Started

Student Text Pages
Pp. 58–59

Learning Outcomes
- Interpret information presented in tables.
- Create compound inequalities.

Prerequisite Skills

1. In each of the following, round your answer to 1 decimal place, if necessary.

   a) What percent is 50 of 100?   [50%]

   b) What percent is 180 of 300?   [60%]

   c) What percent is 2500 of 7000?   [35.7%]

   d) What percent is 3.75 of 250?   [0.15%]

2. In each of the following, reduce the fraction to lowest terms, if necessary.

   a) What fraction is 250 of 1000? $\left[\dfrac{1}{4}\right]$

   b) What fraction is 700 of 2000? $\left[\dfrac{7}{20}\right]$

   c) What fraction is 25 of 35? $\left[\dfrac{5}{7}\right]$

   d) What fraction is 1600 of 2200? $\left[\dfrac{8}{11}\right]$

Teaching Suggestions

Frequency Ranges

Display the following statement on the chalkboard.

     Robins eat grasshoppers and cats eat robins.

     Ask:

What does the word "predator" mean?

What does the word "prey" mean?

Have the students use the statement on the chalkboard and the data in the table on student text page 58 to explain how it is possible for a robin to be both a predator and prey.

Remind students that a range depicts the minimum and maximum values of an occurrence. Ask:

What is the possible range of percentage marks in an examination?

For questions 3 and 7 on student text page 58, have the students write compound inequalities for the ranges given.

Warm Up

Assign some or all of the questions as individual or group work. Students could record their answers in their notebooks, or take turns asking questions orally with a partner.

     When the students have finished, have them discuss the methods they used to answer the questions.

Mental Math

Students could choose, or be assigned, certain questions from each section. Alternatively, small groups could work as teams, sharing the questions and explaining the answers to the rest of the group.

Integrating Technology

Internet

Use the Internet to find more information about sound frequency ranges or other data that are presented in ranges. Use the data to create problems involving compound inequalities. Display your problems for classmates to solve.

Enrichment

Think of other properties of animals that could have a frequency range, such as speed, wingspan, etc. Choose one of these properties and research the frequency ranges for at least 5 animals. Construct a table of your data and use the data in your table to write a problem. Present your table, your problem, and its solution to the class.

Assessing the Outcomes

Observation

You may want to consider some of the following skills as the students complete this lesson.
- Do the students understand the process of reading from a table a value from a range of values?
- Are the students able to interpret the data in the table on student text page 58?
- Do the students understand the concept of a compound inequality?

2.1 Reviewing Linear Inequalities in One Variable

Student Text Pages

Pp. 60–64

Materials

graphing calculators, Teacher's Resource Master 4 (number lines), overhead projector

Learning Outcomes

- Solve inequalities.
- Graph inequalities.
- Solve problems involving inequalities.

Prerequisite Skills

1. Graph each of the following sets of numbers on a number line. x is a rational number.

a) $x > 2$
b) $x \leq -1$
c) $-5 < x \leq 3$
d) $x \geq -2$

2. Which of the given values satisfy the inequality?

a) $x + 2 > 5$; $x = 1, 2, 3, 4, 5$ [4, 5]
b) $x - 3 \leq -1$; $x = -1, 0, 1, 2, 3$ [−1, 0, 1, 2]
c) $x + 3 \geq -2$; $x = -6, -5, -4, -3$ [−5, −4, −3]
d) $x - 1 < 2$; $x = 0, 1, 2, 3, 4, 5$ [0, 1, 2]
e) $x > 0.5$; $x = 0.3, 0.4, -0.5, 0.5$ [none]

Mental Math

1. Copy and complete each ordered pair so that it satisfies the given equation.

a) $x + y = 7$; (2, ■)   [5]
b) $3x + y = -1$; (5, ■)   [−16]
c) $y = 3x + 7$; (5, ■)   [22]
d) $3y + 1 = -5x$; (−1, ■) $\left[\dfrac{4}{3}\right]$

2. Calculate.
a) 0.55^2 [0.3025]   **b)** 5.2^2 [27.04]
c) 0.055^2 [0.003 025]   **d)** 5200^2 [27 040 000]
e) 550^2 [302 500]   **f)** 0.52^2 [0.2704]

Explore/Inquire Answers

Explore: Solve the Inequalities

a) $s = 320$ and $s = 400$ **b)** $s \geq 320$ and $s \leq 400$

Inquire

1. 320 km/h   **2.** 400 km/h
3. a) 398 km/h, 399 km/h, 400 km/h
4. a) $x < 2$ **b)** $x > 3$ **c)** $x > 5$ **d)** $x < 16$
5. a) In order, from top to bottom: $>$, $>$, $>$, $<$, $>$, $<$
b) multiplying and dividing by a negative number

Teaching Suggestions

Method 1

(number lines, overhead projector, graphing calculators)
Review with the class the opening paragraphs of student text page 60. Ask:

What does the word "inequality" mean?

Where have you seen an example of an inequality in an everyday situation?

Have pairs of students look around the class and draw any imaginary straight line through the classroom area, thus, dividing the classroom area into two sections. Have them use the words "equal" and "unequal" to describe, in terms of numbers of students, the two sections of the class.

Assign to pairs of students the Explore and the Inquire sections on student text page 60. Provide them with number lines and have them draw the graphs of their solutions to the Inquire questions. For Inquire question 3, have volunteers demonstrate the answer on an overhead projector. When the students have completed the Inquire questions, have them present their results to the class. Provide an overhead projector for those who require it.

Have the students study the table following the Inquire questions on student text page 61. Ask:

What happens to the direction of the inequality sign when a number is added or subtracted from both sides of an inequality?

What type of number causes the inequality sign to be reversed when both sides of an inequality are multiplied or divided?

Review with the class the teaching examples on student text pages 61 and 62.

Method 2

(number lines, overhead projector, graphing calculators)
Provide pairs of students with number lines. Ask:

What is an inequality?

Write this inequality on the chalkboard.

$$x + 2 > 5$$

Introduce the term "satisfy." Ask:

How would you use a number line to help you solve this inequality?

Does the value 2 satisfy the inequality?

Does the value 3 satisfy the inequality?

Does the value 3.1 satisfy the inequality?

Chapter 2, Linear Inequalities   **51**

Have the students write the set of all the numbers that satisfies this inequality. Point out that the domain of the solution set is the set of real numbers.

Review with the students the steps for solving an inequality algebraically. Discuss with the class the teaching examples on student text pages 61 and 62.

Sample Solution

Page 64, question 62

a)
$$3 + \frac{2}{x} \geq 1$$
$$3x + 2 \geq x$$
$$3x - x + 2 \geq x - x$$
$$2x + 2 \geq 0$$
$$2x + 2 - 2 \geq 0 - 2$$
$$2x \geq -2$$
$$\frac{2x}{2} \geq \frac{-2}{2}$$
$$x \geq -1$$

b) $x \neq 0$

c)
$$\begin{array}{ccccccc} & | & | & \bullet & \circ & | & | \\ -2 & -1 & 0 & 1 & 2 \end{array}$$

d) The open dot means that x cannot equal zero, but x can equal any value less than zero, or greater than zero.

Logic Power Answer

16 moves

Integrating Technology

Graphing Calculators

How would you use your graphing calculator to create the graphs in question 64 on student text page 64? On a TI-83, the Y=, TEST, and MODE keys are used. For the first graph, press the Y= key, and enter $(x - 3)(x$. Press the TEST (i.e., 2nd MATH) key and the 5 key to select <.
Then, enter 2).
Press the MODE key, and use the arrow keys to reach Dot (to the right of Connected), and then, press the ENTER key.
Press the ZOOM key and the 6 key to select ZStandard.

Internet

Use the Internet to find data to create problems that can be solved using an inequality in one variable. Display your problems for classmates to solve.

Computer Data Bank

Use the databases in *MATHPOWER™ 11, Western Edition, Computer Data Bank* to find information to create problems that can be solved using an inequality in one variable. Display your problems for classmates to solve.

Math Journal

Write a short report describing the similarities and the differences between the steps used to solve an equation and the steps used to solve an inequality.

Common Errors

- Students often substitute only one value from the solution of an inequality to check to see if the solution is correct. For example, suppose a student made the following mistake:

$$y + 2 < 5$$
$$y < 7$$

If the student substituted the value $y = 1$ into $y + 2 < 5$, the result would be

L.S. $= y + 2$	R.S. < 5
$= 1 + 2$	
$= 3$	L.S. $<$ R.S. Checks.

But, substituting $y = 5$ results in

L.S. $= y + 2$	R.S. < 5
$= 5 + 2$	
$= 7$	L.S. $>$ R.S. Does not check.

This means that $y = 5$ cannot be a solution, and thus, $y < 7$ must be incorrect.

R_x Stress upon the students that they should check more than one value in the original inequality.

Problem Levels of Difficulty

A: 1–48, 51–54, 64 **B:** 49–50, 55–59 a), b) **C:** 59 c)–63

Assessing the Outcomes

Written Assignment

Solve. Graph the solution.

a) $3x - 1 \geq 2$

b) $3(4x + 1) < -1$

c) $2y + 7 > y - 5$

d) $4y - 2(y + 3) \leq 11y$

e) $1.5(2y + 0.5) < 3.5$

f) $3(2.5y + 1) \leq 5(1.2y + 3) - 7$

g) $\frac{2x}{5} > \frac{x}{4}$

h) $\frac{x - 2}{3} \geq \frac{3x + 1}{6}$

Technology

Solving Inequalities With a Graphing Calculator

Student Text Page
P. 65

Materials
graphing calculators

Learning Outcome
- Display the solution to a linear inequality in one variable using a graphing calculator.

Prerequisite Skills

1. Show the keystrokes for each.

   a) $Y_1 = \frac{3}{4}x$ [(3 ÷ 4)x or .75x]

   b) $Y_1 = \frac{x-5}{6}$ [(x − 5) ÷ 6]

Mental Math

1. For each inequality, write three different ordered pairs that include the given coordinate and that satisfy the inequality.   [Answers may vary.]

   a) $x - 2y > 1$; (3, ■)   [(3, −2), (3, −3), (3, −4)]

   b) $y \geq x - 3$; (■, 2)   [(5, 2), (3, 2), (0, 2)]

   c) $y \leq 1 + 2x$; (■, −2)   [(−1, −2), (1, −2), (5, −2)]

   d) $x - 2y > 3$, (−1, ■)   [(−1, −4), (−1, −5), (−1, −6)]

2. Calculate.

   a) 53^2 [2809]   b) 54^2 [2916]

   c) 59^2 [3481]   d) 58^2 [3364]

   e) 55^2 [3025]   f) 51^2 [2601]

Teaching Suggestions

Discuss the graph displayed in Exploration 1. Ask students how they would create the graph on their graphing calculators. On a TI-83, the Y=, TEST, and MODE keys are used.
Press the Y= key, and enter $2x + 1$.
Press the TEST (i.e., 2nd MATH) key and the 5 key to select < .
Enter the $3x - 2$.
Press the MODE key, and use the arrow keys to reach Dot (to the right of Connected), and then, press the ENTER key.
Press the ZOOM key and the 6 key to select ZStandard.

In question 3, on a TI-83, press the TRACE key, and use the arrow keys to move along the x-axis to find the last value of x before the graph.
In question 4, on a TI-83, one way to use the Zoom function is to press the ZOOM key and the 1 key to select Zbox.
Use the arrow keys to create a small box around the start of the graph and x-axis just before it.
Press the TRACE key, and use the arrow keys to find the last value of x before the graph.
On a TI-83, to use tables, with the graph displayed, press the TBLSET (i.e., 2nd WINDOW) key.
Enter a start value such as 2.9 and then, an increment value such as .01.
Press the TABLE (i.e., 2nd GRAPH) key to see the table.
Use the down arrow key to move through the values to find the last value of x before $y = 1$.
On a TI-83, to use a friendly window for this graph, press the WINDOW key, and enter 0 as Xmin, 9.4 as Xmax, 0 as Ymin, and 6.2 as Ymax.
Press the GRAPH key, and then, the TRACE key.
Use the arrow keys to move along the x-axis to find the last value of x before the graph. For more information about friendly windows, see *Graphing Calculators: Friendly Windows* in *Integrating Technology* in Section 1.1 on page 8 of this teacher's resource.
In question 7, on a TI-83, ≤ is the sixth item in the TEST menu.
For questions 9 to 12 in Exploration 2, students need to use brackets and division to show fractions.
For algebraic solutions in question 15, on a TI-92, use Solve, which is the first item in the Algebra menu. The symbols < and > are the second functions of the 0 and . keys respectively. The symbols ≤ and ≥ are found by pressing the CHAR (i.e., 2nd +) key, pressing the 2 key for Math, and pressing the C key for ≤ and the E key for ≥.

Assessing the Outcome

Written Assignment

Explain the difference between graphing a solution to an inequality and solving an inequality by graphing.

2.2 Solve a Simpler Problem

Student Text Pages
Pp. 66–67

Learning Outcome
- Use the Solve a Simpler Problem strategy to solve problems.

Prerequisite Skills
1. Find the area of each figure.

a) rectangle; 3 cm wide and 9 cm long   [27 cm²]

b) triangle; base 5 m, height 6 m   [15 m²]

2. Write the next two numbers in each sequence.

a) 5, 6, 8, 11, ?, ?   [15, 20]

b) 5, 25, 125, ?, ?   [625, 3125]

c) –5, –3, –1, 1, ?, ?   [3, 5]

Mental Math
1. For each inequality, write three different ordered pairs that include the given coordinate and that satisfy the inequality.   [Answers may vary.]

a) $x - y < 1$; ($\blacksquare$, −1)   [(−1, −1), (−2, −1), (−3, −1)]

b) $y < -x + 3$; (3, $\blacksquare$)   [(3, −1), (3, −2), (3, −3)]

c) $x + 3y > -2$; ($\blacksquare$, 1)   [(−3, 1), (0, 1), (2, 1)]

d) $3x + y < 1$; ($\blacksquare$, 1)   [(−1, 1), (−2, 1), (−3, 1)]

2. Calculate.

a) 5.2^2 [27.04]   b) 5.3^2 [28.09]

c) 5.7^2 [32.49]   d) 5.5^2 [30.25]

e) 5.1^2 [26.01]   f) 5.9^2 [34.81]

Teaching Suggestions
Display the table shown on student text page 66 on the chalkboard. Describe the problem and what the table represents. Have a few students demonstrate the situation given in the text. Point out that this is called making a model or a simulation, and is an important strategy. Students may not think of starting with 1 actor, but may begin with 3 or 4 actors.

Suggest that they complete the table for 3 or 4 actors, and leave room in the table for the simpler cases of less than 3 actors.

Have pairs of students try to solve the problem before reading the solution in the text. Give the pairs of students an opportunity to discuss and compare their results.

When the students have completed their solutions, have volunteers present their results to the class. Then, have the class review the solution shown on student text page 66. Ask:

Did you use the Solve a Simpler Problem strategy to solve the problem? Explain.

Point out to the students that, when using this strategy to solve a problem, you are often looking for patterns. Ask:

What patterns did you see in the exponent numbers?

Review the steps of the Solve a Simpler Problem strategy given at the bottom of student text page 66.

Number Power Answer
a) 0, 2   b) 10, 25

Integrating Technology
Internet

Work with other students on the Internet to solve problems, using web sites such as *http://forum.swarthmore.edu/mathmagic/* and Canada's SchoolNet Web Site at *http://www.schoolnet.ca.*

Enrichment
Review the works of Martin Gardner in the library or on the Internet to find problems similar to those in this section. Present to the class any interesting problems for them to solve.

Math Journal
Write the steps of the Solve a Simpler Problem strategy in your math journal.

Write a few sentences describing where you think this method of solving a problem could be used.

Problem Levels of Difficulty
A: 1–8, 13   **B:** 9–12

Assessing the Outcome
Observation

Assign the problems on student text page 67 and note the extent to which the students
- understand the problems
- use the Solve a Simpler Problem strategy
- demonstrate a willingness to solve new problems
- show persistence
- work cooperatively

Investigating Math

Graphing Inequalities in the Coordinate Plane

Student Text Pages
Pp. 68–70

Materials

graphing calculators, Teacher's Resource Master 1 (0.5-cm grid paper), Teacher's Resource Master 5 (graphing grids), overhead projector

Learning Outcomes

- Represent linear inequalities in one variable as a boundary.
- Represent linear inequalities in two variables as a boundary.
- Identify regions represented by inequalities in one variable.
- Identify regions represented by inequalities in two variables.

Prerequisite Skills

Graph each line.

a) $x = 2$

b) $y = -5$

c) $y = 2x - 3$

d) $y = -5x + 1$

e) $3x + 5y = 15$

f) $-2y + x = 0$

Mental Math

1. Calculate.

a) 0.53^2 [0.2809]

b) 0.051^2 [0.002 601]

c) 5.8^2 [33.64]

d) 590^2 [348 100]

e) 560^2 [313 600]

f) 5.2^2 [27.04]

2. Copy and complete each ordered pair, so that it satisfies the given equation.

a) $-x + y = 2$; ($\blacksquare$, 2)   [(0, 2)]

b) $y = 2x - 3$; (3, $\blacksquare$)   [(3, 3)]

c) $3x - y = 5$; ($\blacksquare$, −1) $\left[\left(\frac{4}{3}\right), -1\right]$

d) $3x + 2y = -3$; (−1, $\blacksquare$)   [(−1, 0)]

e) $y = -x + 5$; ($\blacksquare$, −2)   [(7, −2)]

f) $2x - y + 5 = 0$; (−2, $\blacksquare$)   [(−2, 1)]

Teaching Suggestions

(0.5-cm grid paper, graphing grids, overhead projector, graphing calculators) Ask the students:

How would you describe a boundary? a region?

How are boundaries and regions related?

Provide pairs of students with grid paper or graphing grids. Have them plot the following points on a grid.

$$(3, 2), (3, -4), (3, 0), (3, -1)$$

Ask:

What do you notice about the coordinates of the points?

How would you describe the points you plotted on your graph?

Elicit from the students that the x-coordinate of each set of points is 3, and the plotted points are located immediately above each other in the graph. Then, ask:

If the dots were connected with a straight line, what would the equation of the line be?

If you were to shade the region to the right of the line, and include the boundary line, what inequality would you use to represent this region?

If you were to shade the region to the right of the line, and exclude the boundary line, what inequality would you use to represent this region?

Elicit from the students that an equation such as $x > 4$ excludes the points on the line $x = 4$, but an equation such as $x \geq 4$ includes the points on the line $x = 4$. Ask:

Is the region represented by $x > 4$ above or below the line $x = 4$?

Similarly, an equation such as $y < 7$ excludes the points on the line $y = 7$, but an equation such as $y \leq 7$ includes the points on the line $y = 7$. Ask:

Is the region represented by $y \leq 7$ to the right or to the left of the line $y = 7$?

Discuss with the class the opening paragraph on student text page 68.

Assign Investigation 1 to pairs of students. Ask:

How would you describe the line represented by an inequality in one variable?

Point out the use of the open and closed dots. Ask:

How can you use the coordinates of any point in a plane to decide whether it belongs in a region represented by a system of inequalities?

How can you use the coordinates of a point on the line of a graph to decide whether the boundary line should be drawn solid or broken?

Discuss question 7 with the class. Ask:

How would you translate into words the equation $y \neq 6$?

Which points are not included in the region?

Elicit from the students that $y \neq 6$ means all of the points except those on the line $y = 6$ are included in the region. This means that all the points in the plane are included except those on the line $y = 6$. Ask:

How would you draw such a plane?

Ensure that the students shade in the whole coordinate plane, but represent the line $y = 6$ with a broken line, to indicate that points on the line $y = 6$ are not included in the region.

Have volunteers present their results to the class. Provide an overhead projector, if necessary.

Assign Investigation 2 to pairs of students. Ask:

How would you compare the regions represented by inequalities in two variables with the regions represented by inequalities in one variable?

Elicit from the students answers such as:
- Regions represented by inequalities in one variable are parallel to one of the axes.
- Regions represented by inequalities in two variables lean to the left or to the right.

Have volunteers present their results to the class. Assign Investigation 3. Ask:

What does the term "restriction" mean?

How can you tell whether there are restrictions on the variables?

Elicit from the students that if the restrictions are not given, then care must be taken to interpret the given information. For example, if the variables represent measurements, then the variables cannot be less than or equal to zero. If the variables represent whole numbers, then the variables cannot be fractional or decimal values.

Have volunteers present their results to the class.

Extension

Describe in words the region defined by the following system of linear inequalities. Identify the shape of each region.

1. $y > 0, x + 2y \leq 7, y \geq -x + 3$

2. $x - 3y \geq -11, x > -2, x \leq 4, y > -x - 3$

Enrichment

On grid paper, draw a diagram of your backyard, your school yard, or a parking lot close to your home. Superimpose a set of axes and scales, and use these axes and scales to write a set of inequalities for the region that represents your space.

Exchange your system of inequalities with that of a classmate and use your classmate's system of equations to draw a diagram of his or her space. Discuss and compare your results with the classmate.

Math Journal

boundary point, region Write a definition for each of these terms in your journal. Include a diagram for clarity.

Common Errors

- Students often want to use pens when graphing, and then make errors in shading.

R_x Suggest that students use pencils and cross hatching in different directions. In this way, the students will see clearly where the overlapped shading occurs. Students could also use colouring pencils for more complex drawings.

Assessing the Outcomes

Written Assignment

1. a) Graph this system of linear inequalities.
$$x < 6, x \geq -6, y \geq -6, y < 6$$

b) Shade this region formed by the system of inequalities and describe the shape of the region.

2. a) Graph this system of linear inequalities.
$$x \geq 2, x \leq 5, y = -x + 7, x + y = 12$$

b) Shade the region formed by the system of inequalities and describe the shape of the region.

c) Find the area of the shaded region.

Technology

Graphing Linear Inequalities With a Graphing Calculator

Student Text Page
P. 71

Materials
graphing calculators

Learning Outcome
• Graph linear inequalities in two variables using a graphing calculator.

Prerequisite Skills
Graph each equation using a graphing calculator. Then, state which side of the graph would be shaded if it was an inequality with the given sign.

1. $y = x - 4, \geq$ [above]
2. $y = 2x + 1, \leq$ [below]
3. $2x + y = 3, \geq$ [above]

Mental Math
1. Evaluate for $p = 1$, $q = -1$, and $r = 2$.

a) $p + q + r$ [2]   b) $2p + r - q$ [5]
c) $p^2 - 2r$ [−3]   d) $-p - q + 3r$ [6]
e) $4r + 2 - q$ [11]   f) $-(q - r + 3p)$ [0]

2. Calculate.

a) 53^2 [2809]   b) 57^2 [3249]
c) 5.6×5.6 [31.36]   d) 5900×0.059 [348.1]
e) 0.51×51 [26.01]   f) 5.4×540 [2916]

Teaching Suggestions
Discuss the graph displayed before Exploration 1. Ask students how they would create the graph on their graphing calculators.

On a TI-83, changing the graphing style from a line to shading can be used.

To graph the inequality in question 1 in Exploration 1 by changing the graphing style from a line to shading, press the Y= key, clear any previous entries, and enter the right side of the inequality $x + 1$ at the Y1= prompt. Use the left arrow key to move the cursor to the diagonal line at the left of Y1, and press ENTER twice until the shade above option appears. Press the ZOOM key and the 6 key to select ZStandard.

To graph the inequality in question 2 in Exploration 1 by changing the graphing style from a line to shading, press the Y= key, clear any previous entries, and enter

the right side of the inequality $x - 2$ at the Y1= prompt. Use the left arrow key to move the cursor to the diagonal line at the left of Y1, and press ENTER three times until the shade below option appears. Press the ZOOM key and the 6 key to select ZStandard.

On a TI-83, the Shade instruction can also be used. Lower and upper boundaries are specified, with the lower boundary specified first. If $y \geq$, then the rest of the inequality is the lower boundary and Ymax is the upper boundary. Similarly if $y \leq$, then Ymin is the lower boundary and the rest of the inequality is the upper boundary.

To graph the inequality in question 1 in Exploration 1 using the Shade instruction, press the DRAW (i.e., 2nd PRGM) key and the 7 key to select Shade. At the Shade(prompt, enter the right side $x + 1$ as the lower boundary, and then, a comma. Then, to enter the upper boundary, press the VARS key, press the 1 key to select Window, and the 5 key to select Ymax. Enter a closing bracket, and press the ENTER key.

To graph the inequality in question 2 in Exploration 1 using the Shade instruction, press the CLEAR key, the DRAW (i.e., 2nd PRGM) key, the 1 key to select ClrDraw, and the ENTER key to clear the previous shading. Just pressing the CLEAR key does not clear shaded graphs. Press the DRAW (i.e., 2nd PRGM) key and the 7 key to select Shade.

At the Shade(prompt, press the VARS key, the 1 key to select Window, and the 4 key to select Ymin as the lower boundary, and then, enter a comma. Then, enter the right side $x - 2$ as the upper boundary. Enter a closing bracket, and press the ENTER key.

In Exploration 2, the inequalities must be solved for y first.

See *MATHPOWER™ 11, Western Edition, Blackline Masters* pages 43 to 45 for Graphing Linear Inequalities.

Math Journal
Write about the similarities and the differences when graphing linear equations and linear inequalities using a graphing calculator.

Common Errors
• Students often become confused by the details of the keystrokes required using the Shade instruction.

$\mathbf{R}_x$ Write generic keystrokes for each of $y \geq$ and $y \leq$, including the clearing step.

Assessing the Outcome
Journal

Is it necessary to know how to graph an inequality in the coordinate plane to be able to graph it using a graphing calculator? Explain.

2.3 Graphing Linear Inequalities in Two Variables

Student Text Pages
Pp. 72–76

Materials

graphing calculators, Teacher's Resource Master 1 (0.5-cm grid paper), Teacher's Resource Master 5 (graphing grids), overhead projector

Learning Outcomes

- Graph inequalities with boundary lines in the form $y = mx + b$.
- Graph inequalities with boundary lines in the form $ax + by = c$.
- Graph inequalities by rewriting the inequalities in the form $y = mx + b$.
- Solve word problems involving inequalities.

Prerequisite Skills

1. Find the intercepts of each equation of a line.
a) $x + 2y = 4$ [x-intercept 4, y-intercept 2]
b) $2y - 3x = 6$ [x-intercept −2, y-intercept 3]
c) $5x - 2y = -10$ [x-intercept −2, y-intercept 5]
d) $\frac{1}{2}x + \frac{1}{3}y = 2$ [x-intercept 4, y-intercept 6]

2. Rewrite each equation in the form $y = mx + b$.
a) $2x + y = 4$ $[y = -2x + 4]$

b) $3y - x = -2$ $\left[y = \frac{1}{3}x - \frac{2}{3} \right]$

c) $\frac{1}{4}x + 3y = -1$ $\left[y = -\frac{1}{12}x - \frac{1}{3} \right]$

d) $12x - 6y = -15$ $\left[y = 2x + \frac{5}{2} \right]$

3. Graph each line.
a) $2x + y = -3$ b) $-x + 3y + 9 = 0$
c) $y = -\frac{1}{2}x - 3$ d) $y = 1 + 5x$

Mental Math

1. Calculate.
a) 0.53^2 [0.2809]   b) 550^2 [302 500]
c) 5.6^2 [31.36]   d) 0.57^2 [0.3249]
e) 580^2 [336 400]   f) 5100^2 [26 010 000]

2. Copy and complete each ordered pair, so that it satisfies the given equation.
a) $x - y = 6$, $(\blacksquare, -1)$ [5]
b) $2x + 3 = y$; $(-2, \blacksquare)$ [−1]
c) $2x - y = -2$; $(-2, \blacksquare)$ [−2]
d) $y = -5x + 2$; $(\blacksquare, 4)$ $\left[-\frac{2}{5} \right]$
e) $3x + 5y = 2$; $(-1, \blacksquare)$ [1]
f) $2y = -x + 2$; $(\blacksquare, 3)$ [−4]

Explore/Inquire Answers

Explore: Interpret the Data

a) The number of wins and losses is 18. Thus, the team played in every league game.

b) The number of wins and losses is less than 18. Thus, the team did not play in every league game.

Inquire

1.

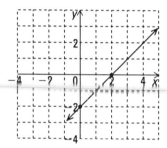

2. $x - y \leq 2$
$(0) - (0) \leq 2$
The point (0, 0) satisfies $x - y \leq 2$.

3. Since (0, 0) satisfies $x - y \leq 2$, then the region containing (0, 0) should be shaded. (0, 0) is above the line $x - y = 2$. Then, the shading should be above the line $x - y = 2$.

4. $y \geq x - 2$ 5. Shade above the boundary line.   6. yes

7. a)

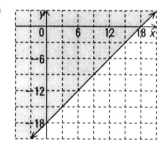

b) Points on the line $x + y = 18$ are part of the region. This is indicated by the solid line used as the boundary line.

c) Choose two points, one from the region on one side of the boundary line, and the other from the region on the other side of the boundary line. Substitute the values of x and y of each point. The region containing the point that satisfies the inequality is the one to shade.

Teaching Suggestions

(0.5-cm grid paper, graphing grids, overhead projector, graphing calculators)   Read with the class the opening paragraph on student text page 72. Assign the Explore section and discuss with the students the possible outcomes of a football game, i.e., win, loss, or tie. Elicit from the students that $x + y = 18$ means that there were no ties in the season, and $x + y < 18$ means that there were some ties in the season. Ask:

How can you find the number of ties in the season?

Elicit from the students that if the numbers of wins and losses are known, then the number of ties is 18 minus the total number of wins and losses.

Provide pairs of students with graphing grids or grid paper and assign the Inquire questions. Ask:

Why do you think the point (0, 0) is chosen to substitute in the inequality?

For question 3, elicit from the students that once you have decided whether the point you have chosen satisfies the inequality, then you can say that all the other points on the same side of the boundary line as the chosen point also do not satisfy the inequality.

For question 7, ask:

How would you indicate the restrictions on x and y in a graph?

Elicit from the students that since x and y represent wins and losses, they cannot be negative numbers. Thus, the graph of the line can only occur in the first quadrant, since x and y can only have values greater than or equal to zero.

Have pairs of students present their results to the class. Provide an overhead projector for students who wish to display their graphs to the class.

Review with the class the paragraph at the bottom of student text page 72 and teaching examples 1 to 3 on student text pages 73 to 75.

Sample Solution

Page 76, question 43

a) Since $y \neq x + 4$, then, $y < x + 4$ and $y > x + 4$.

These inequalities represent the whole plane except the points lying on the line $y = x + 4$.

b) Since $y \not> x - 3$, then, $y \leq x - 3$.

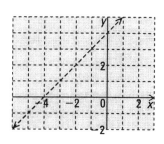

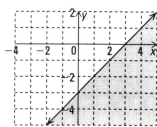

Integrating Technology

Graphing Calculators

Use the skills learned in *Technology: Graphing Linear Inequalities With a Graphing Calculator* on pages 57 and 58 of this teacher's resource to graph the inequalities in the examples and the questions on student text pages 75 and 76. Remember to clear shading between questions, and to identify whether or not the boundary line is included in the solution.

Math Journal

Write a list of the steps required to identify the regions into which a plane is divided by a system of inequalities.

Common Errors

* Students often forget to reverse the inequality sign when multiplying or dividing each side of an inequality by the same negative value. For example,

  if $-3 > -4$, then $\frac{-3}{-2} < \frac{-4}{-2}$ and $\frac{3}{2} < 2$

  if $-5y > 6$, then $-5y(-2) > 6(-2)$ and $10y > -12$.

R$_x$ Demonstrate the principal with numerical inequalities and give the students practice with numerical inequalities. Point out that the effect of multiplying or dividing each side of an inequality by the same negative value holds true for inequalities containing variables, as well as numerical inequalities.

Problem Levels of Difficulty

A: 1–52, 60   **B:** 53–55, 57   **C:** 56, 58, 59

Assessing the Outcomes

Written Assignment

1. Graph each inequality.

a) $x - y \leq 1$ b) $2x + 3y > -2$

c) $5x \geq 2y - 1$ d) $y \leq \frac{3x}{2} - \frac{1}{3}$

2. Given the restrictions on the variables, graph the inequality.

   $x > 2y + 5, x > 0, y \leq 0$

3. Two positive real numbers, p and q, are related by the inequality $4p - q \geq 3$.

a) What are the restrictions on p and q?

b) Graph the inequality.

c) Write three ordered pairs in the form (p, q) that satisfy the inequality.

Computer Data Bank

Nations of the World

Microsoft Works for Windows users see *Part B*, and
Microsoft Access users see *Part D*, of *MATHPOWER™ 11*,
Western Edition, Computer Data Bank Teacher's Resource.

Student Text Pages

P. 77

Learning Outcomes

- Display, find, sort, calculate, and analyze data
  in a computer database.
- Interpret inequalities.
- Write and solve inequalities.

Prerequisite Skills

Express symbolically.

a)	at most five	[≤ 5]
b)	no more than seven	[≤ 7]
c)	between three and eleven	[3 ≤ x ≤ 11]
d)	at least nine	[≥ 9]
e)	within three degrees of freezing	[−3°C ≤ x ≤ 3°C]

Getting Started Blackline Masters C-1, C-2,
C-4 to C-6, and C-8

Teaching Suggestions

Students unfamiliar with computer databases and
ClarisWorks would benefit from working through
Getting Started Blackline Masters C-1, C-2, C-4 to
C-6, and C-8, noted in the *Prerequisite Skills*, prior to
doing any of these explorations. If they have not done
so yet, you may wish to assign the *Getting Started*
Blackline Masters to individuals, pairs, or small groups
of students, to be completed over a period of time that
allows students adequate computer time. The *Getting
Started* Blackline Masters provide basic instruction in
working with databases in ClarisWorks to meet the
learning outcomes and provide students with an
opportunity to use each of the seven databases. You may
wish to delay assigning *Nations of the World* until
students have had an opportunity to work through
Getting Started Blackline Masters C-1, C-2, C-4 to
C-6, and C-8. Minimally, students should have *Getting
Started* Blackline Masters C-1, C-2, C-4 to C-6, and
C-8 available for reference.

Each exploration in *Nations of the World* is
independent of the others. However, answering
question 14 in Exploration 1 may provide students with
an idea for answering Exploration 3. Some or all of the

explorations can be assigned to individuals, pairs, or
small groups of students, to be completed over a period
of time that allows students adequate computer time.
Up to 1.5 h will be needed by some students to
complete all three explorations.

Nations of the World is an opportunity for
cross-curricular learning.

When assigning the explorations, inform students if
you expect

- any parts of the explorations to be printed off the
  computer
- handwritten or word-processed answers to questions
  that suggest a written response
- a journal-type response about what they have learned
  mathematically, about using databases, and/or about
  the subject matter of the database

Possible parts to assign for printing are a table to show
the nations with the calculation field giving their labour
forces as percents of the populations that satisfy the given
inequality from Exploration 1; a table to show the
nations with the calculation field giving their educational
expenditures in billions of dollars that satisfy the given
inequality from Exploration 1; a table to show the
nations with the calculation field giving their GDP per
capita that satisfy the given inequality from Exploration
1; and a table to justify answers to Exploration 3.

All amounts of money are given in U.S. dollars.
Central American nations are considered to be on the
continent of North America.

1 Comparing Nations

For questions 1 to 11, display the records using Full
Record. For question 1, use the Find feature with
one comparison for *Population* >=30000000
(*Getting Started* BLM C-5).

For question 2, show all the records and use the Find
feature with one comparison for *Nation* France, noting
the area. Then, show all the records and use the Match
feature with the following formula (*Getting Started*
BLM C-5).

AND('Area, km^2' <>−1,'Area, km^2'<547030)

An efficient approach to question 3 is to deselect
the records from the previous question, show all the
records, and use the Find feature with one comparison
for *Nation* New Zealand, noting the coastline (*Getting
Started* BLM C-5). Then, show all the records and use
the Match feature with the following formula (*Getting
Started* BLM C-5).

AND('Coastline, km'>=10134,'Coastline, km'<=20134)

For question 4, deselect the records from the
previous question, show all the records, and use the
Match feature with the following formula (*Getting
Started* BLM C-5).

AND('GDP, \$ billions'<>−1,'GDP, \$ billions'<=10)

For question 5, deselect the records from the previous question, show all the records, and use the Find feature with one comparison for *Nation* Canada, noting the expenditures. Then, show all the records and use the Match feature with the following formula (*Getting Started* BLM C-5).

AND('Expenditures, \$ billions'<>−1,'Expenditures, \$ billions'<=115.2)

An efficient approach to question 6 is to deselect the records from the previous question, show all the records, and use the Find feature with one comparison for *Nation* Australia, noting the inflation rate (*Getting Started* BLM C-5). Then, show all the records and use the Match feature with the following formula (*Getting Started* BLM C-5).

AND('Inflation, %'>=2.1,'Inflation, %'<=4.1)

For question 7, deselect the records from the previous question, show all the records, and use the Find feature with one comparison for *Nation* Japan, noting the labour force. Then, show all the records and use the Find feature with one comparison for *Labour Force* >67230000 (*Getting Started* BLM C-5).

For question 8, show all the records and use the Match feature with the following formula (*Getting Started* BLM C-5).

AND('Area, km^2'<>−1,'Coastline, km'<>−1,'Coastline, km'>'Area, km^2')

For question 9, deselect the records from the previous question, show all the records, and use the Match feature with the following formula (*Getting Started* BLM C-5).

AND('Exports, \$ billions'<>−1,'Imports, \$ billions'<>−1,'Exports, \$ billions'>'Imports, \$ billions')

For question 10, deselect the records from the previous question, show all the records, and use the Find feature with one comparison for *Nation* nation of interest, noting the educational expenditure rate. Then, show all the records and use the Find feature with one comparison for *Education Expenditure, %* >educational expenditure rate of interest (*Getting Started* BLM C-5).

An efficient approach to question 11 is to show all the records and use the Find feature with one comparison for *Nation* nation of interest, noting the literacy rate. Then, show all the records and use the Match feature with the following formula (*Getting Started* BLM C-5).

AND('Literacy, %'>=*x*,'Literacy, %'<=*y*)
 where *x* and *y* are 10 less than and 10 greater than the literacy rate of interest, respectively

An efficient approach to question 12 is to deselect the records from the previous question, show all the records, and create a table displaying only the *Nation*, *Population*, and *Labour Force* fields (*Getting Started* BLM C-2). Then, create a calculation field called *Labour Force as Percent of Population*, using the first formula that follows, to express labour force as a percent of population, rounded to 2 decimal places (*Getting Started* BLM C-6). Next, use the Match feature with the second formula that follows (*Getting Started* BLM C-5).

ROUND('Labour Force'/'Population'*100,2)

AND('Population'<>−1,'Labour Force'<>−1, 'Labour Force as Percent of Population'>=40, 'Labour Force as Percent of Population'<=50)

An efficient approach to question 13 is to deselect the records from the previous question, show all the records, and create a table displaying only the *Nation*, *Expenditures, \$ billions*, and *Education Expenditure, %* fields (*Getting Started* BLM C-2). Then, add a calculation field called *Education Expenditure, \$ billions*, using the formula that follows, to express educational expenditure in billions of dollars, rounded to 1 decimal place (*Getting Started* BLM C-6). Next, use the Find feature with three comparisons for *Expenditures, \$ billions* <>−1, *Education Expenditure, %* <>−1, and *Education Expenditure, \$ billions* >6 (*Getting Started* BLM C-5).

ROUND('Education Expenditure, %'/100*'Expenditures, \$ billions',1)

An efficient approach to question 14 is to show all the records and create a table displaying only the *Nation, Population*, and *GDP, \$ billions* fields (*Getting Started* BLM C-2). Then, create a calculation field called *GDP, \$/person*, using the formula that follows, to determine the GDP per capita, rounded to 0 decimal places (*Getting Started* BLM C-6). Next, use the Find feature with one comparison for *Nation* Sweden, noting the GDP per capita (*Getting Started* BLM C-5). Finally, show all the records and use the Find feature with three comparisons for *Population* <>−1, *GDP, \$ billions* <>−1, and *GDP, \$/person* <20790 (*Getting Started* BLM C-5).

ROUND('GDP, \$ billions'*1000000000/'Population',0)

2 Forested Areas in South America

In question 1, show all the records, displaying them using Table 1. Then, use the Find feature with two comparisons for *Continent* South America and *Area, km^2* >250000 (*Getting Started* BLM C-5). Next, sort the areas and use the least and the greatest to write the restrictions on *x* (*Getting Started* BLM C-4).

In question 2, construct the graph showing a region in the first quadrant shaded below a solid boundary line ($y = 0.67x$, where $283\ 560 \leq x \leq 8\ 511\ 965$), using a graphing calculator, using a spreadsheet, or by hand.

In question 3, read the area of Venezuela from the records displayed.

In question 4, multiply the area of Venezuela by 0.67, using a calculator, or interpolate the value of y, when x is the area of Venezuela.

In question 5, find the percent of forested area in Venezuela, using print or electronic sources.

3 Standard of Living

In question 1, some students might consider the *Continent* field to be a strong indicator, because Canadians and Americans, in North America, enjoy a high standard of living. Some might consider any or all of the monetary fields, thinking that money either coming in or being spent would reflect standard of living. Some might consider the *Unemployment, %* field and/or the *Literacy, %* field to give clues to standard of living. Others might consider some or all of the monetary fields in conjunction with the *Population* field to look at the picture per capita. Some might consider the *GDP, $/person* field calculated in Exploration 1 to be a strong indicator.

An efficient approach to question 2 is to decide on a strong indicator, such as GDP per capita. Then, show all the records and use the table created in Exploration 1 question 14, where the *GDP, $/person* field was created. Next, use the Find feature with two comparisons for *GDP, $ billions* $<>-1$ and *Population* $<>-1$ to eliminate the records without meaningful *GDP, $/person* field values (*Getting Started* BLM C-5). Then, sort the GDP per capita to determine the greatest, the least, and Canada (*Getting Started* BLM C-4).

2.4 Problem Solving: Use Logic

Student Text Pages
Pp. 78–79

Materials
Teacher's Resource Master 2 (1-cm grid paper), counters, paper cups

Learning Outcome
- Use the problem solving strategy Use Logic to solve problems.

Prerequisite Skills

1. State whether each statement is always true (T), sometimes true (S), or never true (F).

a) This sentence contains two misteaks. [T]

b) The sum of five and two is eight. [F]

c) When an obtuse angle is bisected, the two angles formed are acute. [S]

d) If the total cost of a pineapple and a banana is $5, and the pineapple costs $4 more than the banana, then, the banana costs $1. [F]

2. Which of the cubes labelled A, B, C, D, and E can be made using the net shown? [E]

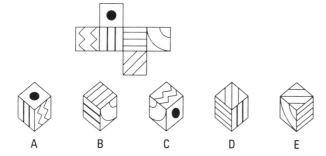

A   B   C   D   E

Mental Math

1. For each inequality, write three different ordered pairs that include the given coordinate and that satisfy the inequality. [Answers may vary.]

a) $x + y > 2$; $(5, \blacksquare)$ $[(5, -1), (5, -2), (5, 3)]$

b) $y < 2x + 1$; $(\blacksquare, 2)$ $[(6, 2), (8, 2), (10, 2)]$

c) $y \geq 5 + 2x$; $(\blacksquare, -1)$ $[(-3, -1), (-4, -1), (-5, -1)]$

d) $2x - y > 5$, $(-1, \blacksquare)$ $[(-1, -8), (-1, -9), (-1, -10)]$

2. Calculate.

a) 51^2 [2601]   **b)** 54^2 [2916]

c) 57^2 [3249]   **d)** 58^2 [3364]

e) 52^2 [2704]   **f)** 56^2 [3136]

Teaching Suggestions

Method 1

(counters, paper cups) Begin by asking the students: *What does the word "logical" mean?*

Discuss with the class the problem on student text page 78. Elicit from the students that as long as both journeys take place between the same two time periods, at some point the two paths must cross. Ask:

Look at the graph on student text page 78. How would you describe the point at which Justine is the same distance from the cottage at exactly the same time on both days?

Is this the only possible answer? Explain.

Have pairs of students draw a sketch of a possible graph for each of the questions given at the bottom of student text page 78. Give the students an opportunity to compare and discuss their sketches. Have volunteers present their graphs to the class. Ask:

Are all the graphs the same? Explain.

Is there enough information to find the answer? Explain.

Elicit from the students graphs such as

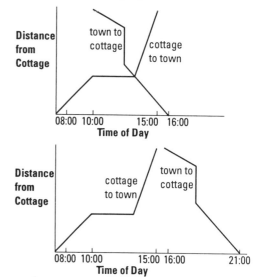

Then, ask:

What type of skill do you think is required to solve logical problems?

Discuss with the students how this type of problem develops skills with deductive reasoning.

Review with the class the steps of the Use Logic strategy given at the bottom of student text page 78.

Provide pairs of students with 11 counters and two paper cups. Assign the problem at the top of student text page 79, and suggest that one student manipulate the counters and the paper cups, while the other draws diagrams of the steps of the solution. Then, have volunteers present their results to the class. Encourage pairs of students who have different solutions to present them to the class.

Method 2

(1-cm grid paper, overhead projector) On the chalkboard, present this problem to the class.

Adams, Beam, Cliffe, and Dalton are an artist, a dentist, an editor, and a plumber. Adams and her husband went to dinner with the dentist and his wife. The editor said he bowled with Cliffe last week. The plumber congratulated Dalton on her golf score. Identify each person as male or female, and determine each person's occupation.

Have pairs of students copy and complete a table such as this one.

	Adams	Beam	Cliffe	Dalton	Male	Female
Artist					X	✓
Dentist	X				✓	X
Editor					✓	X
Plumber					X	✓

Ask:

What information is suggested by the sentence, "Adams and her husband went to dinner with the dentist and his wife"?

Suggest that the students decide which fact can be concluded from each statement, and indicate that fact with a √. Once you know one fact you can automatically indicate more information. For example, if you know that Adams is a female, then, you can indicate with an X that she is not a male.

Ask:

What information is given in each sentence?

What clues are given in each sentence that help you to come up with some information?

How can logical reasoning be used to solve problems in real life?

Point out to the students that the table is an organizational tool. The √ indicates facts and the Xs indicate fictional information. Once you have indicated all the possibilities, you will see the solution.

Once the pairs of students have completed the table, suggest that they compare and discuss their results with those of other students. Have volunteers present their results to the class.

Sample Solution

Page 79, question 3

Substitute $a + b = c$ into $c + d = e$.
Thus, $a + b + d = e$ ....(1)

Substitute (1) into $a + e = f$.
Thus, $a + a + b + d = f$ ....(2)

Substitute (2) into $f + g = h$.
$$a + a + b + d + g = h$$
$$2a + b + d + g = h$$ ....(3)

Substitute $a = 4$ into (3).
$$2(4) + b + d + g = h$$
$$8 + b + d + g = h$$
$$b + d = h - g - 8$$ ....(4)

But, $b + d + f = 30$.
$$b + d = 30 - f$$ ....(5)

Equate the right-hand sides of (4) and (5).
$$h - g - 8 = 30 - f$$
$$h - g + f = 30 + 8$$
$$h - g + f = 38$$ ....(6)

But, $f + g = h$
$$f = h - g$$ ....(7)

Substitute (7) into (6).
$$h - g + h - g = 38$$
$$2h - 2g = 38$$
$$h - g = 19$$
$$h = g + 19$$ ....(8)

Any pair of values of h and g that makes equation (8) true is a correct pair of values. For example, if $g = 1$, then $h = 20$, if $g = 2$, then $h = 21$, if $g = 3$, then $h = 22$, and so on.

Integrating Technology

Internet

Work with other students on the Internet to solve problems, using web sites such as *http://forum.swarthmore.edu/mathmagic/* and Canada's SchoolNet Web Site at *http://www.schoolnet.ca.*

Enrichment

Research careers in which logical reasoning skills would be useful. Discuss and compare your research with that of your classmates.

Math Journal

Write the three steps of the Use Logic strategy in your journal.

Problem Levels of Difficulty

A: 1–6, 10   **B:** 7–9

Assessing the Outcome

Observation

Some of the questions you might want to consider while the students complete this section include:
• Do the students understand the problems?
• Do the students show persistence?
• Do the students draw conclusions from the information?

2.5 Solving Systems of Linear Inequalities

Student Text Pages
Pp. 80–87

Materials
graphing calculators, Teacher's Resource Master 1 (0.5-cm grid paper), Teacher's Resource Master 5 (graphing grids), overhead projector

Learning Outcomes
- Solve systems of linear inequalities whose boundary line equations are in the form $y = mx + b$.
- Solve systems of linear inequalities whose boundary line equations are in the form $ax + by = c$.
- Solve problems involving systems of linear inequalities.

Prerequisite Skills
1. Graph each of the following lines.

a) $y = 2x - 1$ b) $y = -3x + 2$

c) $y = \frac{1}{2}x + 5$ d) $y = -\frac{3}{4}x$

2. Write the intercepts and the slope of each line.

a) $3x + y = 6$ [x-intercept 2, y-intercept 6, slope -3]

b) $-2x + 5y + 10 = 0$

$$\left[\text{x-intercept } 5,\ \text{y-intercept } -2,\ \text{slope } \frac{2}{5} \right]$$

c) $y = 3x - 2$ $\left[\text{x-intercept } \frac{2}{3},\ \text{y-intercept } -2,\ \text{slope } 3 \right]$

d) $x + 5y = 15$ $\left[\text{x-intercept } 15,\ \text{y-intercept } 3,\ \text{slope } -\frac{1}{5} \right]$

Mental Math
1. Evaluate each expression for $a = -1$ and $b = -2$.

a) $2a - b$ [0]   b) $-a + 5b$ [-9]

c) $a^2 + b^2$ [5]   d) $3a - 2b + a$ [0]

e) $5b - a^2$ [-11]   f) $-b - 2a$ [4]

2. Calculate.

a) 57×530 [30 210]   b) 5.4×56 [302.4]

c) 72×7.8 [561.6]   d) 39×31 [1209]

e) 0.81×89 [72.09]   f) 45^2 [2025]

Explore/Inquire Answers

Explore: Draw a Graph
a), b)

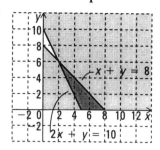

Inquire
1. The region represents number of games won and lost. There are no negative values for wins or losses. Thus, points with negative coordinates are invalid for the given situation.

2. a) Segments of each line for which $x \geq 0$ and $y \geq 0$ are included in the solution.   b) yes

3. a) The values in the ordered pairs of $x + y \leq 8$ represent games won or lost. Since there can only be whole numbers of games, then the ordered pairs are made up of whole numbers. The values in the ordered pairs of $2x + y \geq 10$ represent numbers of points. Since there can only be whole numbers of points, then the ordered pairs are made up of whole numbers.

b) (2, 6), (3, 5), (4, 2), (4, 4), (5, 0), (5, 1), (5, 2), (5, 3), (6, 0), (6, 1), (6, 2), (7, 0), (7, 1), (8, 0)

4. 14

Teaching Suggestions

Method 1
(graphing grids, grid paper, overhead projector, graphing calculators)   Read with the class the opening paragraph on student text page 80. Review with the class the rules for isolating one variable of an inequality in two variables. Ask:

A system of two equations in two variables can be used to write a corresponding system of two inequalities in two variables by substituting the inequality signs for the equals signs. How is the solution of the system of equations related to the points of intersection of the system of inequalities?

Provide pairs of students with graphing grids or grid paper and assign the Explore section and the Inquire questions. Suggest that, after the pairs have graphed their results, they should compare their graphs with those of other students in the class. Have volunteers present their results to the class. Provide an overhead projector for those students who wish to present their graphs to the class. Ask:

What region of the graph represents all the possible solutions to question 4?

Review with the class the paragraph at the bottom of student text page 80. Ask:

What examples can you provide for the use of the word "intersection"?

Look for an example such as the intersection of two roads.

Review with the class teaching examples 1 and 2 on student text pages 81 to 83. Ask:

How does the format of the inequalities given in teaching example 1 differ from that in teaching example 2?

Which format do you find easier to use when you are using a calculator to graph a system? Explain.

Which format do you find easier to use when you are graphing manually? Explain.

Review with the class teaching example 3 on student text page 83.

Method 2

(graphing grids, grid paper, overhead projector, graphing calculators) Provide pairs of students with grid paper or graphing grids. Present these two inequalities to the class.

$$x + 2y > 6 \qquad 3x - 9y \leq 5$$

Ask:

The set of points in the x-y plane that is the solution of an inequality represents a plane. Explain.

The set of points in the x-y plane that is the solution of an equation represents a straight line. Explain.

Have each pair of students draw on the same set of axes the graphs of the lines represented by the equations. Ask:

How could you indicate whether the solution of the inequality includes the points on the boundary line?

Instruct the students to label with letters or Roman numerals the regions of the graph into which the intersecting lines divide the grid.

Challenge the students to think of a method of deciding whether a point on the grid is inside, outside, or on the boundary of a region of the grid. Give the students an opportunity to compare and discuss any methods they may have thought of. Then, have volunteers present their ideas to the class. One student of each pair could present any graphs drawn to illustrate their ideas, while the other student describes the idea to the class.

Lead the students to see that they can choose a point in each region, and substitute the coordinates of the point into each inequality. If the point satisfies both inequalities, then it lies in the region. This region can be shaded. If the point satisfies the equation of the boundary line, then the boundary line is included in the solution and should be drawn as a solid line. Introduce the term "intersection" and ask:

How would you use the word "intersection" to describe the solution of a system of inequalities?

Review with the class the teaching examples on student text pages 81 to 84.

Sample Solution

Page 87, question 59

All answers may vary.

a) A system of lines must meet the following conditions to represent the perimeter of a rectangle.

- A pair of parallel lines that do not coincide.
- A second pair of parallel lines that do not coincide and that is perpendicular to the first pair of parallel lines.

The general equation of a line is $y = mx + b$.
Parallel lines that do not coincide have the same slope but different y-intercepts.
Let the slope of a line be 2, and the y-intercept be 3.
The equation of this line is $y = 2x + 3$.
The equation of a non-coincidental line parallel to this line has slope 2 and y-intercept, say 8. The equation of this line is $y = 2x + 8$.
Perpendicular lines have slopes that are reciprocals of each other. Since the second pair of parallel lines must be perpendicular to the first pair of parallel lines, their slopes must be the negative reciprocal of 2, i.e., $-\frac{1}{2}$.

Let the y-intercepts of the lines be 3 and -2.
Then, the equations of the lines are $y = -\frac{1}{2}x + 3$ and $y = -\frac{1}{2}x - 2$.

Thus, the equations of the sides of the rectangle are $y = 2x + 3$, $y = 2x + 8$, $y = -\frac{1}{2}x + 3$, and $y = -\frac{1}{2}x - 2$.

Since the line $y = 2x + 8$ is above the line $y = 2x + 3$ on the grid, then the inequalities for the points between these lines are $y < 2x + 8$ and $y > 2x + 3$. Since the line $y = -\frac{1}{2}x + 3$ is above the line $y = -\frac{1}{2}x - 2$ on the grid, then the inequalities of the points between these lines are $y < -\frac{1}{2}x + 3$ and $y > -\frac{1}{2}x - 2$.

Thus, the inequalities of the lines representing the sides of the rectangle and the points inside the rectangle are

$y \geq 2x + 3$, $y \leq 2x + 8$,
$y \leq -\frac{1}{2}x + 3$, and
$y \geq -\frac{1}{2}x - 2$.

b) The graph of the rectangle is given at the right. The area of a rectangle is the product of its length and width.

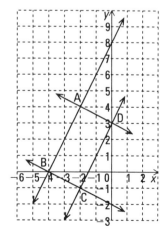

The coordinates of the rectangle are A(−2, 4), B(−4, 0), C(−2, −1), and D(0, 3).
The length AB is

$$\sqrt{[-2-(-4)]^2 + [4-(-1)]^2} = \sqrt{2^2 + 4^2}$$
$$= \sqrt{20}$$
$$= 2\sqrt{5}$$

The width BC is

$$\sqrt{[(-4)-(-2)]^2 + [0-(-1)]^2} = \sqrt{(-2)^2 + 1^2}$$
$$= \sqrt{5}$$

Area of rectangle = length AB × width BC
$$= 2\sqrt{5} \times \sqrt{5}$$
$$= 2 \times 5$$
$$= 10$$

The area of the rectangle is 10 square units.

Integrating Technology

Graphing Calculators

How would you graph the solution to teaching example 1 on student text page 81 using your graphing calculator?

On a TI-83, the Shade instruction can be used. Press the CLEAR key, the DRAW (i.e., 2nd PRGM) key, the 1 key, and the ENTER key to clear any previous shading.
Press the DRAW (i.e., 2nd PRGM) key and the 7 key to select Shade.
At the Shade(prompt, enter $2x - 1$, $-x + 5$) and then, press the ENTER key. $2x - 1$ is the lower boundary, and $-x + 5$ is the upper boundary. This results in the graph shown.
Changing the graphing style from a line to shading can also be used on a TI-83.
Press the Y= key, clear any previous entries, and enter the right side of the first inequality $-x + 5$ at the Y1= prompt.
Use the left arrow key to move the cursor to the diagonal line at the left of Y1, and press ENTER twice until the shade above option appears.
Enter the right side of the second inequality $2x - 1$ at the Y2= prompt.
Use the left arrow key to move the cursor to the diagonal line at the left of Y2, and press ENTER three times until the shade below option appears.
Press the ZOOM key and the 6 key to select ZStandard. This results in a graph with three areas of shading like the graph drawn manually.

How would you graph the solution to teaching example 3 on student text pages 83 and 84 using your graphing calculator?

On a TI-83, the Shade instruction can be used. Press the DRAW (i.e., 2nd PRGM) key, the 1 key, and the ENTER key to clear the previous shading. Press the WINDOW key, and then enter 20 as Xmin, 70 as Xmax, 100 as Ymin, and 170 as Ymax, and suitable scales.
Press the DRAW (i.e., 2nd PRGM) key and the 7 key to select Shade.
At the Shade(prompt, enter .7(220 − x), .8(220 − x)) and then, press the ENTER key. .7(220 − x) is the lower boundary, and .8(220 − x) is the upper boundary. This results in the graph shown.
Changing the graphing style from a line to shading can also be used on a TI-83.
Press the Y= key, clear any previous entries, and enter the right side of the first inequality .8(220 − x) at the Y1= prompt.
Use the left arrow key to move the cursor to the diagonal line at the left of Y1, and press ENTER three times until the shade below option appears.
Enter the right side of the second inequality .7(220 − x) at the Y2= prompt.
Use the left arrow key to move the cursor to the diagonal line at the left of Y2, and press ENTER twice until the shade above option appears.
Press the WINDOW key, and then enter 20 as Xmin, 70 as Xmax, 100 as Ymin, and 170 as Ymax, and suitable scales.
Press the GRAPH key to view the graph in that viewing window. This results in a graph with three areas of shading like the graph drawn manually.

Use your graphing calculator to graph the questions on student text pages 85 to 87.

See *MATHPOWER™ 11, Western Edition, Blackline Masters* pages 46 to 48 for Solving Systems of Linear Inequalities Graphically.

Extension

Construct a system of linear inequalities whose solution

a) is a square with an area of 16 square units.

b) is a triangle with an area of 5 square units.

Enrichment

Create a design on a grid, using straight lines. Write a system of linear inequalities to represent your design. Exchange your system of linear inequalities with that of a classmate. Use your classmate's system of linear inequalities to recreate his or her design. Compare and discuss your results with your classmate. Present your results to the class.

Math Journal

List the steps required to find the vertices of the graph of a system of linear inequalities.

Problem Levels of Difficulty

A: 1–54, 56   **B:** 55, 57–65   **C:** 66, 67

Assessing the Outcomes

Written Assignment

1. Solve each system of inequalities by graphing.

a) $y < 3x - 1, y \geq 5x$

b) $2x - 3y > 6, 3x + 4y \leq 12$

2. Tony has $200. He would like to buy at least 7 magazines and books for gifts. The magazines cost $5 and the books cost $15.

a) Graph the system of inequations where m represents the number of magazines and b represents the number of books.

   $b + m \geq 7$

   $15b + 5m \leq 200$

b) How many presents can Tony buy?

2.6 Problem Solving: Look for a Pattern

Student Text Pages

Pp. 88–89

Learning Outcome

• Use the problem solving strategy Look for a Pattern to solve problems.

Prerequisite Skills

1. Write the next two terms in each sequence.

a) 2, 5, 8, 11, ...   [14, 17]

b) 507, 506, 504, 501, ...   [497, 492]

c) 6, 9, 13.5, 20.25, ...   [30.375, 45.5625]

d) 2, 5, 10, 17, ...   [26, 37]

2. Write the second, third, and fourth terms of each sequence.

a) The first term is 5. Each subsequent term is decreased by 3.   [2, −1, −4]

b) The first term is −64. Each subsequent term is divided by −2.   [32, −16, 8]

c) The first term is $\frac{1}{2}$. Each subsequent term is increased by $\frac{1}{3}$. $\left[\frac{5}{6}, \frac{7}{6}, \frac{3}{2}\right]$

d) The first term is 0.2. Each subsequent term is the square of the previous term.

[0.04, 0.0016, 0.000 002 56]

Mental Math

1. For each inequality, write three different ordered pairs that include the given coordinate and that satisfy the inequality.

a) $x + y < 2$; (■, 1)   [(0, 1), (−1, 1), (−2, 1)]

b) $-x - y > 5$; (1, ■)   [(1, −7), (1, −8), (1, −9)]

c) $y \geq 2x + 3$; (3, ■)   [(3, 9), (3, 10), (3, 11)]

d) $2x - 3y + 1 \leq 0$; (■, −1)   [(−2, −1), (−3, −1), (−4, −1)]

2. Calculate.

a) 6.2×6.8 [42.16]

b) 23×27 [621]

c) 370×0.33 [122.1]

d) 190×1100 [209 000]

e) 4.4×46 [202.4]

f) 96×9.4 [902.4]

Teaching Suggestions

Method 1

Discuss with the class the term "pattern." Ask:

What pattern do you see in the first three terms of the sequence 1, 2, 4, ...?

What do you think the next term of the sequence is?

Look for more than one answer to this question. For example, some students may say, "A term of the sequence is formed by multiplying the previous term by 2. The next term is 8." or "The first term is 1. Each consecutive term is increased by each of the consecutive whole numbers, starting with 1. Thus, 1 + 1 = 2, 2 + 2 = 4, and 4 + 3 = 7. The next term is 7."

Then, ask:

How many terms of a sequence are necessary in order to be able to identify a pattern?

Assign the problem on student text page 88 to pairs of students. Give the pairs of students an opportunity to discuss the steps of the problem. Ask:

What other method could you use to find a formula for the number of side pieces and the number of inner pieces?

A jigsaw is m pieces long and n pieces wide. How many corners does it have?

What expression represents the total number of pieces it has?

What expression represents the total number of pieces it has with at least one straight edge?

What expression represents the number of edge pieces along its length? along its width?

What expression represents the total number of pieces with 1 straight edge?

What expression represents the total number of inner pieces?

Have volunteers present their results to the class.

Finally, have the students discuss the steps of the Look for a Pattern strategy at the top of student text page 89.

Method 2

Present to the class the following numbers on the chalkboard.

$$
\begin{aligned}
4 \times 6 &= 24 \\
14 \times 16 &= 224 \\
24 \times 26 &= 624 \\
34 \times 36 &= 1224 \\
44 \times 46 &= \boxed{} \\
54 \times 56 &= \boxed{} \\
64 \times 66 &= \boxed{}
\end{aligned}
$$

Have pairs of students study the numbers in each equation. Tell the students not to find the values of the last three multiplication statements at this time. Ask:

What patterns do you see in the first numbers in each equation?

What patterns do you see in the second numbers in each equation?

How are the last two digits of the numbers on the right side of the equations related to the numbers on the left side of the equations?

How are the digits in front of the last two digits of the numbers on the right side of the equations related to the numbers on the left side of the equations?

After discussing the students' results, have the students find the values of the last three multiplication statements from the patterns they found in the numbers. Have volunteers present their results to the class.

Sample Solution

Page 89, question 8

Look for a pattern in the values of the powers of 2.

$2^1 = 2$	$2^2 = 4$	$2^3 = 8$	$2^4 = 16$
$2^5 = 32$	$2^6 = 64$	$2^7 = 128$	$2^8 = 256$
$2^9 = 512$	$2^{10} = 1024$	$2^{11} = 2048$	$2^{12} = 4096$

The powers in column 1 have exponents beginning at 1 and increase by multiples of 4. The final digit of each value of the power is 2.

The powers in column 2 have exponents beginning at 2 and increase by multiples of 4. The final digit of each value of the power is 4.

The powers in column 3 have exponents beginning at 3 and increase by multiples of 4. The final digit of each value of the power is 8.

The powers in column 4 have exponents beginning at 4 and increase by multiples of 4. The final digit of each value of the power is 6.

$75 = 3 + 4 \times 18$

Thus, the final digit of 2^{75} is 8.

Any number whose final digit is 8, when divided by 10, has a remainder of 8.

Integrating Technology

Internet

Work with other students on the Internet to solve problems, using web sites such as *http://forum.swarthmore.edu/mathmagic/* and Canada's SchoolNet Web Site at *http://www.schoolnet.ca.*

Enrichment

In these diagrams, the three outside numbers are related to the centre number by the same rule.

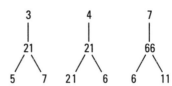

Study the diagrams and find the rule.

Use the rule to find the unknown values in each diagram below.

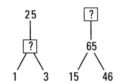

Create a similar problem. Exchange problems with a classmate, and try to find the rule for your classmate's problem. Discuss and compare your results. Present any interesting problems to the class.

Math Journal

List the steps of the Look for a Pattern strategy in your journal.

Problem Levels of Difficulty

A: 1–9   **B:** 10–12

Assessing the Outcome

Written Assignment

1. What is the last digit of 2^{355}?

2. Find a rule that relates *a* and *b*.

a	7	4	−1	5
b	13	7	−3	9

Investigating Math

Polygonal Regions

Student Text Pages
Pp. 90–91

Materials

graphing calculators, Teacher's Resource Master 1 (0.5-cm grid paper), Teacher's Resource Master 5 (graphing grids)

Learning Outcomes

- Identify convex and concave polygons.
- Find the maximum and minimum values of a region.
- Graph polygonal regions, given a system of linear inequalities.
- Use graphing calculators to graph polygonal regions and find the vertices of the regions graphed.

Prerequisite Skills

1. Evaluate each expression for the given values of the variables.

   a) $3x + 5y$; $x = -1, y = 2$ [7]

   b) $-2x + y = 1$; $x = 3, y = 1$ [−5]

   c) $3y - x = 0$; $x = 10, y = 15$ [35]

   d) $x - 2y - 3$; $x = -0.5, y = 1.5$ [−6.5]

2. Graph each line.

   a) $2x + y = 10$ **b)** $3x - 2y = 5$

   c) $y = -2$ **d)** $x = 9$

   e) $y = -2x - 3$ **f)** $y = 5x + 1$

Mental Math

1. Copy and complete each ordered pair, so that it satisfies the given equation.

   a) $x - y = 3$; (4, ■)   [(4, 1)]

   b) $-3x - 2y = -2$; (2, ■)   [(2, −2)]

   c) $2x + y - 3 = 0$; (■, 1)   [(1, 1)]

   d) $y = 3x + 7$; (■, −2)   [(−3, −2)]

   e) $3x - 2y = 2$; (−1, ■) $\left[\left(-1, -\frac{5}{2}\right)\right]$

   f) $-2x + y - 1 = 0$; (3, ■)   [(3, 7)]

2. Evaluate each expression for $m = 2$ and $n = -3$.

   a) $3m + 2n$ [0]   **b)** $2(m + n)$ [−2]

   c) $(m + n)^2$ [1]   **d)** $-3(m - n)$ [−15]

   e) $m - 3n - 2m$ [7]   **f)** $3(-m + 4n) + 5$ [−37]

Teaching Suggestions

(0.5-cm grid paper, graphing grids, graphing calculators)
Provide pairs of students with grid paper or graphing grids. Assign Investigation 1. Ask:

What does the term "maximum" mean?

What does the term "minimum" mean?

How would you describe the lines used to make the polygonal region?

What are the general equations of lines such as these?

Have the students complete the investigation and present their results to the class.

Assign Investigations 2 and 3 and have volunteers present their results to the class.

Work through Investigation 4 with the class.

Integrating Technology

Graphing Calculators

How would you find the vertices of the polygonal region in Exploration 4 using your graphing calculator?

On a TI-83, changing the graphing style from a line to shading results in three shadings which is difficult to read, but can be used.

Press the Y= key and enter the right side of each of the first three inequalities.

Use the left arrow key to move the cursor to the diagonal line at the left of each of Y1, Y2, and Y3 to change to shade below, shade below, and shade above respectively.

Press the WINDOW key to enter 0 as Xmin, 0 as Ymin, and 10, for example, as Xmax and Ymax.

Press the GRAPH key to view the graph in that viewing window.

Press the CALC (i.e., 2nd TRACE) key and the 5 key to select intersect to find each intersection points of these boundary lines.

Alternatively, press the Y= key and enter the right side of each of the first three inequalities as three equations.

Press the WINDOW key to enter 0 as Xmin, 0 as Ymin, and 10, for example, as Xmax and Ymax.

Press the GRAPH key to view the graph in that viewing window.

Press the CALC (i.e., 2nd TRACE) key and the 5 key to select intersect to find each intersection point of these boundary lines.

Enrichment

Make up a system of linear inequalities in two variables whose solution is a region with the following shape.

1. triangle
2. rectangle
3. parallelogram
4. square

Math Journal

convex polygon, concave polygon   Write a definition for these two terms in your journal. Include a diagram to help you clarify each definition.

Assessing the Outcomes

Journal

List the steps you would follow to graph a polygonal region. Describe how you would use the vertices of the polygonal region to find the maximum and minimum values of an expression over a polygonal region.

Connecting Math and Business

Linear Programming

Student Text Pages
Pp. 92–93

Materials
graphing calculators, Teacher's Resource Master 1 (0.5-cm grid paper), Teacher's Resource Master 5 (graphing grids)

Learning Outcomes
* Analyze problems to find the objective quantity, the constraints, and the feasible region.
* Solve problems involving linear programming.

Prerequisite Skills
1. Evaluate each expression for the given values of the variables.

a) $x - y$; $x = 2, y = 5$ [−3]
b) $2x + y$; $x = −1, y = 2.5$ [0.5]
c) $3y + 2x$; $x = −2, y = −1$ [−7]
d) $−x − 2y$; $x = 0.5, y = −1.5$ [−2.5]

2. Graph each of the following lines.

a) $x + y = 5$ b) $2x − 3y = −1$
c) $2.5x + 5y = 7.5$ d) $500x + 200y = 3000$

Mental Math
1. Calculate.

a) 3.7×33 [122.1]   b) 6.2×6.8 [42.16]
c) 960×94 [90 240]   d) 81×89 [7209]
e) 0.58×52 [30.16]   f) 45^2 [2025]

2. Copy and complete each ordered pair so that it satisfies the given equation.

a) $2x + y = 3$; (5, ■)   [(5, −7)]

b) $y = −3x − 1$; (■, −2) $\left[\left(\frac{1}{3}, −2\right)\right]$

c) $−4x + y = 0$; (−3, ■)   [(−3, −12)]

d) $x − 2y + 1 = 0$; (2, ■) $\left[\left(2, \frac{3}{2}\right)\right]$

e) $x − y − 2 = 1$; (■, 3)   [(6, 3)]

f) $y = −2 + 5x$; (■, −1) $\left[\left(\frac{1}{5}, −1\right)\right]$

Teaching Suggestions

(grid paper, graphing grids) Provide small groups of students with grid paper or graphing grids, and assign Exploration 1 on student text page 92. Ask:

What does the word "feasible" mean?

How would you find the vertices of the system of linear equations given in the opening paragraph of this exploration?

Once you find the coordinates of the vertices, what can you do with them?

Give the groups an opportunity to complete this exploration, and discuss and compare their results with other groups. Have volunteers present their results to the class. Provide an overhead projector so that students can present their graphs to the class. This graph represents the system of inequalities.

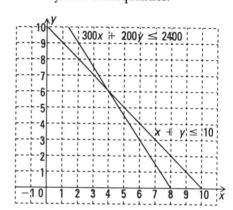

Ensure that the students realize that for question 4, the coordinates of the vertex representing the maximum values should be substituted into the expression to find the maximum number of times the advertisement should be heard.

Assign Exploration 2. Divide the class into four groups and assign question 1 to all the groups. Have each group chose one of the remaining four questions, ensuring that all of the questions are chosen. For each question, instruct the groups to identify the objective quantity, the feasible region, the constraints, and the required answers.

When the groups have completed question 1, ensure that the groups are on the right track by having volunteers present their results to the class. Then, assign the other question that the groups have to do. Give the groups an opportunity to compare and discuss their results. Have volunteers present their results to the class.

Because the groups will not be completing all of the questions, give the groups ample opportunity to question and discuss the method of solution used by each group.

Integrating Technology

Graphing Calculator

How would you find the coordinates of the vertices of the feasibility region in Exploration 1?

On a TI-83, the Shade instruction can not be used because $x + y \leq 10$ and $300x + 200y \leq 2400$ are both $y \leq$, but changing the graphing style from a line to shading can be used.

Rewrite the last two inequalities in terms of y, i.e., $y \leq 10 - x$ and $y \leq (2400 - 300x)/200$.

Press the Y= key and enter the right side of each of these two inequalities.

Use the left arrow key to move the cursor to the diagonal line at the left of each of Y1 and Y2 to change to shade below.

Press the WINDOW key to enter 0 as Xmin, 0 as Ymin, and 15, for example, as Xmax and Ymax.

Press the GRAPH key to view the graph in that viewing window.

Press the CALC (i.e., 2nd TRACE) key and the 5 key to select intersect to find the intersection point of these boundary lines.

Alternatively, press the Y= key and enter the right side of each of the last two inequalities as two equations.

Press the WINDOW key to enter 0 as Xmin, 0 as Ymin, and 15, for example, as Xmax and Ymax.

Press the GRAPH key to view the graph in that viewing window.

Press the CALC (i.e., 2nd TRACE) key and the 5 key to select intersect to find each intersection point of these boundary lines.

Internet

To learn more about linear programming, research the topic using the Internet.

Enrichment

Research the topic of linear programming. Write a few sentences describing how is was developed and why. Share your findings with your classmates.

Math Journal

constraints, feasible region, objective quantity

Write a definition for each of these terms in your journal. Copy a question involving linear programming in your journal, and use the question to help give an example of each of the terms.

Assessing the Outcomes

Observation

You might consider some of these questions as you observe the students work:

- Are the students able to analyze the questions and write the objective quantity?
- Can the students graph the inequalities and find the feasible region?
- Do the students use their graphing calculators to identify the maximum point of the region?
- Do all the students of the groups participate in the exploration?
- Do the students listen to the points of view of the other participants in the group?

Review

Student Text Pages
Pp. 94–95

Materials
Teacher's Resource Master 1 (0.5-cm grid paper),
Teacher's Resource Master 2 (1-cm grid paper)

Learning Outcome
• Review the skills and concepts in Chapter 2.

Using the Review
Have the students work independently to complete
the Review.

Meeting in small groups, the students can mark and
discuss the work.

Groups can then share their solutions and report any
questions that caused them difficulty. Discuss these
questions with the class.

Reteaching Suggestions
For those students having difficulty with the chapter
material, form small groups and use the following exercises.

If you feel that the class has had particular difficulty
mastering any concept, you may wish to work through
a problem from each section as a model of excellence
of solution, which some students require just prior to
assessment.

Reviewing Linear Inequalities in One Variable
1. Solve. Graph the solution.

a) $5x - 2 \geq 5 - x$

b) $2(x + 1) < x + 1$

c) $\frac{3x}{2} > 2x - 5$

d) $5(1.5x + 2) \leq 3.5x - 1$

2. Solve.

a) $\frac{x - 2}{3} > \frac{2x}{5}$

b) $\frac{1 + x}{3} + \frac{x}{2} \leq \frac{2x - 5}{3}$

Graphing Linear Inequalities in Two Variables
1. Graph each inequality.

a) $x - 3y \leq 5$

b) $-x + 2y - 1 > 0$

c) $5x + y < -2$

2. Given the restrictions on the variables, graph each
inequality.

a) $y \leq 5x + 2; x \geq 0, y < 0$

b) $2x - y > -1; x > 0, y \geq 0$

c) $3x + 2y > 15; x < 0, y > 0$

3. The length of a rectangle is l metres. The length of
the rectangle is greater than or equal to 5 m less
than twice the width of the rectangle.

a) Write an inequality that relates the length and the
width of the rectangle.

b) What are the restrictions on the length and the width?

c) Graph l versus w for the inequality.

d) Write three possible sets of dimensions for the
rectangle.

Solving Systems of Linear Inequalities
Solve each system of inequalities by graphing.

a) $y \geq -x + 1; x < 0, y \geq 0$

b) $x + 2y < 5; x > -2, x \leq 4, y > 0, y \leq 3$

Answers to Reteaching Suggestions

Reviewing Linear Inequalities in One Variable

1. a) $x \geq \frac{7}{6}$ **b)** $x < -1$

    c) $x < 10$ **d)** $x \leq \frac{-11}{4}$

2. a) $x < -10$ **b)** $x \leq -12$

Graphing Linear Inequalities in Two Variables

3. a) $l \geq 2w - 5$ **b)** $w > 0, l > 0$

c) Answers may vary. For example, (3, 1), (3, 2), (4, 3),
(4, 4), etc.

Exploring Mathematics

Midpoint Polygons
(grid paper) Provide pairs of students with grid paper.
Have students work in pairs or small groups. Give the
groups an opportunity to discuss their results with other
groups and to compare the similarities and differences
in their results.

Chapter Check

Learning Outcome
- Evaluate the skills and concepts in Chapter 2.

Assessing the Outcome

Observation

If you assign the Chapter Check as a student assessment, look for the following.
- Can they solve inequalities in one variable?
- Can they graph inequalities in one variable on a number line?
- Can they graph inequalities in two variables on a grid?
- Can they determine the region created by a system of linear inequalities in two variables?

Problem Solving

Materials
counters of two different colours

Learning Outcome
- Use problem solving strategies to solve problems.

Using the Strategies

The problems on this page allow the students to use the problem solving strategies discussed in Chapters 1 and 2. These strategies are
- Use a Diagram
- Use a Data Bank
- Solve Fermi Problems
- Solve a Simpler Problem
- Use Logic
- Look for a Pattern

Teaching Suggestions

(counters of two different colours) Encourage the students to work in pairs or small groups. When students have completed the problems, have them share and discuss their strategies and solutions with other students.

For question 1, ask:
What number can D not be?

Lead the students to see that because D is the first digit of the number in the sum of the numbers, it cannot be zero.

For question 2, provide pairs of students with 8 counters, 4 of one colour and 4 of another colour. Encourage students to use the counters to sort out the solution. Suggest that they record each step as they move the counters.

For question 4, start the students off by asking:

What two variables are you asked to find?

Which of the given equations contain both the required variables?

What do you notice about the value of the third variable of this equation?

For question 7, ask:

How are distance, speed, and time related when travelling in a straight line?

For question 9, ask:

If two sides of a triangle are equal, what other fact do you know about the triangle?

Lead the students to see that an algebraic solution is required for this problem.

In $\triangle CED$, $y = 180° - 2x$
In $\triangle ABC$, $y = 180° - 2b - 50°$
Thus,
$$180° - 2x = 180° - 2b - 50°$$
$$-2x = -2b - 50°$$
$$x = b + 25°$$
$$b = x - 25°$$
In $\triangle DEC$, $x = a + b$
$$= a + x - 25°$$
Then, $a = 25°$.

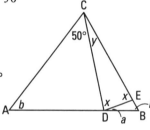

If students are having difficulty with question 10, demonstrate the method of finding the solution by asking:

What is the units digit in the answer to the first subtraction?

How can you use this information in the second subtraction to find a value for Y?

Have volunteers present their results to the class.

Assessing the Outcome

Observation

As you make your problem solving assessment of each student, consider the following:
- Do they understand the problem?
- Do they consider a variety of strategies?
- Do they use an organized approach?
- Do they create and use diagrams effectively?
- Do they show persistence?

CHAPTER 2

• Student Text Answers

Chapter Opener   p. 57

1. a) 50 min   **b)** 120 min   **c)** 10 min
2. 50 min
3. a) no   **b)** yes   **c)** no   **d)** yes
   e) yes   **f)** no
4. self-contained underwater breathing apparatus

Getting Started   pp. 58–59

Frequency Ranges

1. a) $250 \leq f \leq 21\,000$ **b)** $760 \leq f \leq 1520$
2. a) dolphin   **b)** dolphin   **c)** frog
   d) grasshopper   **e)** dog   **f)** cat
3. a) yes   **b)** no
4. a) yes   **b)** yes
5. a) grasshopper   **b)** 91.4%
6. a) $10\,000 \leq f \leq 20\,000$ **b)** 9.1%
7. a) the soprano hitting high notes   **b)** No;
   the frequency of a normal speaking voice is too low.

Warm Up

1. <   **2.** >   **3.** ≤   **4.** ≥   **5.** ≥   **6.** ≥
7. >   **8.** ≤   **9.** ≤   **10.** <   **11.** ≤   **12.** ≥
13. $x \geq -3$ **14.** $x < 2$
15. $x > -4$ **16.** $x \leq -2$
17. $-1 \leq x \leq 7$ **18.** $-3 < x < 1$
19. $-2 \leq x < 4$ **20.** $-6 < x \leq -2$
21. same; order does not matter
22. same; order does not matter
23. same; order does not matter
24. same; order does not matter

Mental Math

Equations and Inequalities

1. $(3, 1)$ **2.** $(-2, -7)$ **3.** $(2, 2)$
4. $(-1, 1)$ **5.** $(0, -2)$ **6.** $(2, 3)$
7–12. Answers may vary.
7. $(1, 2), (1, 3), (1, 4)$
8. $(2, -2), (2, -3), (2, -4)$
9. $(-1, 1), (0, 1), (1, 1)$
10. $(-1, 3), (0, 3), (1, 3)$
11. $(1, 3), (1, 4), (1, 5)$
12. $(-2, 7), (-2, 6), (-2, 5)$

Squaring Two-Digit Numbers Beginning in 5

1. 3364   **2.** 2601   **3.** 3136
4. 2809   **5.** 3025   **6.** 3481
7. 29.16   **8.** 291 600   **9.** 26.01
10. 270 400   **11.** 31.36   **12.** 348 100

13. 2601   **14.** 2809   **15.** 30 250
16. 33 640 000   **17.** 31.36   **18.** 3249
19. a) $100(25 + x) + x^2$; The first term represents adding 25 to the ones digit. The second term represents affixing the square of the ones digit.

Section 2.1   pp. 63–64

Practice (Section 2.1)

1. $y < 2$ **2.** $w > -1$ **3.** $x \geq 3$
4. $z \leq -3$ **5.** $x > -2$ **6.** $t > -4$
7. $m \leq 3$ **8.** $n \geq 0$ **9.** $x > \frac{1}{2}$
10. $x < -\frac{2}{3}$ **11.** $y \leq -1$ **12.** $z \geq 5$
13. $x < 2$ **14.** $x > 1$ **15.** $x \leq 0$
16. $x \geq -\frac{1}{4}$ **17.** $x \leq 3$ **18.** $x > 2$
19. $x < -2$ **20.** $x > 1$ **21.** $y \geq -4$
22. $z \leq \frac{5}{4}$ **23.** $x > 4$ **24.** $x < \frac{5}{3}$
25. $x < 1$ **26.** $x > 1$ **27.** $y \leq -4$
28. $c \geq 2$ **29.** $x \leq 1$ **30.** $x > \frac{1}{3}$
31. $x \geq \frac{3}{2}$ **32.** $t < -\frac{3}{5}$ **33.** $y < -3$
34. $w > 2$ **35.** $x \geq \frac{3}{2}$ **36.** $z \leq -8$
37. $x > 3$ **38.** $x < -6$ **39.** $q \geq 2$
40. $n \geq 3$ **41.** $a > -2$ **42.** $x \geq 1$
43. $y < -1$ **44.** $n \geq -2$ **45.** $x > -\frac{1}{2}$
46. $x < 0$ **47.** $x < 1$ **48.** $x \leq \frac{3}{4}$
49. $z > 6$ **50.** $x \geq 1$

Applications and Problem Solving (Section 2.1)

51. 8   **52.** 1.8 m   **53.** $16 < x < 34$
54. a) $12.25 + 1.55n$ **b)** $12.25 + 1.55n \leq 20$; 5
55. a) $15t - 75$ **b)** $15t - 75 \geq 450$; 35 h
56. 63   **57.** 2056 to 2066
58. a) $a < \frac{31\,000 + 1000}{5}$; $a < 6400$
   c) An island must have an area greater than 0 km².
59. a) $x > 7$ **b)** $x < 9$
   c) $x > \frac{7}{3}$, because the area has to be greater than 0
60. $\frac{5}{2} \leq x \leq 3$
61. between 10:00 and 14:00

62. a) $x \geq -1$ **b)** $x \neq 0$

63. a) $0 = 4$ **b)** no real values   **c)** $4 > 0$
   d) all real values

64. a) graph of $y = x - 3$ to the left of $x = 2$
   b) graph of $y = 2 - x$ to the left of $x = 5$
   c) graph of $y = x + 4$ to the right of $x = -4$

65. Answers may vary.
   a) $1 + 2x \leq 3 + x$
   b) $2(2x + 1) > -2(2 - x)$
   c) $\dfrac{x - 2}{2} < \dfrac{x - 3}{3}$

Technology   p. 65

1 Displaying a Solution

1. $x > 3$

2. The calculator displays the solution on a coordinate grid instead of on a number line.

3. $x > 3$

5. a) 1
   b) The graph would not show if it was on the x-axis.

6. The connected mode shows a small vertical piece of the graph that is not accurate.

7. b) no

2 Solving Inequalities

1. $x \geq 2$ **2.** $x < 3$ **3.** $x > 1$
4. $x \leq -3$ **5.** $x \geq 1$ **6.** $x \leq 4$
7. $x \geq -2$ **8.** $x < -3$ **9.** $x \leq 3$
10. $x > 2$ **11.** $x < -1$ **12.** $x \geq 3$
13. $x \leq -\dfrac{1}{2}$ **14.** $x > \dfrac{1}{3}$

Section 2.2   p. 67

Applications and Problem Solving (Section 2.2)

1. 29 square units   **2.** -100 **3.** 55

4. 11 111 111 100 000 000 000

5. 728 units   **6.** 46   **7.** 37   **9.** 21

10. a) $\dfrac{n(n + 1)}{2}$ **b)** 741   **c)** 1562

11. 1 000 000

12. a) 1, 8, 27   **b)** 4913; 970 299

Investigating Math   pp. 68–70

1 Inequalities in One Variable

1. a) Answers may vary. (3, 2)
   b) Answers may vary. (2, 2)
   c) equal   **d)** less than

2. a) yes   **b)** Points that satisfy the inequality; they all have x-coordinates less than or equal to 3.

3. a) no   **b)** broken line

5. b) $y < 2$, $y \leq 2$, $y > 2$, $y \geq 2$

2 Linear Inequalities in Two Variables

1. b) Answers may vary. (1, 3)
   c) Answers may vary. (1, 4)
   d) equal   **e)** greater than   **f)** yes; no
   g) above; These points satisfy the inequality.
   h) The line would be broken for $y > x + 2$.

2. b) Answers may vary. (2, 1)
   c) Answers may vary. (2, 0)
   d) equal   **e)** less   **f)** yes; no
   g) Below; these points satisfy the inequality.
   h) The line would be broken for $y < x - 1$.

4. a) below   **b)** below   **c)** above   **d)** above

3 Restricting the Variables

1. a) The graph of $b < 2a - 3$ does not include the points on the axes, and the graph does not extend above the x-axis or to the right of the y-axis.
   b) Only negative numbers are included in $b < 2a - 3$.

3. a) no   **b)** no   **c)** yes   **d)** no

7. a) 4   **b)** 12   **c)** 1   **d)** 28

Technology   p. 71

1 Solving for y and Graphing

1. $y > x - 2$ **2.** $y < x + 1$ **3.** $y \leq -2x - 3$

4. $y \geq \dfrac{x - 4}{2}$ **5.** $y > x - 3$ **6.** $y \leq \dfrac{2x + 6}{3}$

7. $y \geq \dfrac{3x + 2}{2}$ **8.** $y > x - 1$ **9.** $y > 2(x + 1)$

Section 2.3   pp. 75–76

Practice (Section 2.3)

1. (2, 2), (1, −2), (0, 0)   **2.** (0, 0), (−3, 8)
3. (5, −1)   **4.** (2, 5), (−4, 0)

Applications and Problem Solving (Section 2.3)

35. a) $m > 0$, $n > 0$
   c) Answers may vary. (16, 1), (15, 1), (14, 1)

36. a) $l \geq 2w - 1$ **b)** $l > 0$, $w > 0$
   d) Answers may vary. (1, 1), (2, 3), (3, 5)

37. a) $125d + 50b \geq 500$ **b)** $d \geq 0$, $b \geq 0$

38. a) $w + t \leq 10$ **b)** yes, with 7 wins and 1 tie, for example; no, there are not enough games

39. a) $l + w > 2$

40. a) $\dfrac{1}{2}x + y \leq 30$

41. a) the half plane that lies below the boundary line $y = mx + b$
   b) the half plane that lies above the boundary line $y = mx + b$
   c) the half plane that lies below and includes the boundary line $y = mx + b$
   d) the half plane that lies above and includes the boundary line $y = mx + b$

e) the half plane that lies above the boundary line $y = b$

f) the half plane that lies below and includes the boundary line $y = b$

g) the half plane that lies to the left of the boundary line $x = c$

h) the half plane that lies to the right and includes the boundary line $x = c$

i) the half planes that lie on either side of the boundary line $x = c$

42. a) $y \leq 2x - 2$ **b)** $y > -2x - 3$

44. a) No, there is only one intercept.

45. No, the point is on the line.

47. Answers may vary. $x + y \geq -11$

Computer Data Bank p. 77

1 Comparing Nations

1. 34   **2.** 182

3. 5, including New Zealand

4. 108

5. 188, including Canada

6. 38, including Australia

7. 4   **8.** 15   **9.** 61

10. Answers will vary.

11. Answers will vary.

12. 56   **13.** 20   **14.** 203

2 Forested Areas in South America

1. $y \leq 0.67x$; $283\ 560 \leq x \leq 8\ 511\ 965$

3. vertical line segment from $912\ 050$ km^2 to the boundary line

4. $0 \leq y \leq 611\ 073.5$

5. Answers will vary.

3 Standard of Living

1. Answers will vary.

2. Answers will vary. Using GDP per capita, United Arab Emirates is the highest, Democratic Republic of Congo is the lowest, and Canada is the 9th.

Section 2.4 p. 79

Applications and Problem Solving (Section 2.4)

1. Empty the 7-L container into the 19-L container. Fill the 19-L container from the 13-L container, leaving 1 L in the 13-L container. Fill the 7-L container from the 19-L container. Empty the 7-L container into the 13-L container. There is now 8 L of water in the 13-L container.

2. Vancouver vs. Boston; Toronto vs. Calgary; Edmonton vs. Detroit; Chicago vs. Montreal

3. $g = 3$, $h = 22$

4. 6, 1, 10, 8; 5, 9, 2; 4, 7; 3

5. a) one thousand   **b)** one billion

6. Double the pile of 7 from the pile of 11; double the pile of 6 from the resulting pile of 14; double the pile of 4 from the resulting pile of 12.

7. Tonya   **8.** Sharif   **9.** Donna

Section 2.5 pp. 85-87

Practice (Section 2.5)

1. $(-1, 0)$, $(-2, -2)$, $(1, 3)$

2. $(4, 2)$, $(5, -1)$

3. $(0, 0)$, $(2, 3)$, $(-3, -3)$

4. $(0, 3)$, $(4, -2)$, $(0, 4)$

5. $(3, 2)$, $(10, 9)$

6. $(0, 0)$, $(-4, -2)$

7. $y \geq 3 - x$, $y \geq x - 1$

8. $x + y \geq 3$, $x - y \geq 3$

9. $x + y < 4$, $y \geq 3x + 1$

10. $y < \frac{1}{2}x + 1$, $y < x + 1$

11. a) $y \geq 1 - x$, $y \geq x + 2$ **b)** $y \leq 1 - x$, $y \geq x + 2$

12. a) $y < 1 - x$, $y < x + 2$ **b)** $y > 1 - x$, $y < x + 2$

13. a) $y > 1 - x$, $y \geq x + 2$ **b)** $y > 1 - x$, $y \leq x + 2$

Applications and Problem Solving (Section 2.5)

46. b) $(5, 0)$, $(6, 0)$, $(4, 1)$, $(5, 1)$, $(3, 2)$, $(4, 2)$, $(2, 3)$, $(3, 3)$, $(1, 4)$, $(2, 4)$, $(3, 4)$, $(0, 5)$, $(1, 5)$, $(2, 5)$, $(0, 6)$, $(1, 6)$, $(0, 7)$, $(0, 8)$

47. a) $2w + t \geq 80$, $w + t \leq 82$ **b)** $w \geq 0$, $t \geq 0$

48. Graph the system $x + y < 8$, $x + y > 4$, $x \geq 0$, $y \geq 0$.

49. $12x + 15y \leq 90$, $x + y \geq 6$, $x \geq 0$, $y \geq 0$, where x represents the \$12 pizzas, and y represents the \$15 pizzas; $(6, 0)$, $(7, 0)$, $(5, 1)$, $(6, 1)$, $(4, 2)$, $(5, 2)$, $(3, 3)$, $(2, 4)$, $(1, 5)$, $(0, 6)$

50. $10x + 15y \geq 180$, $x + y \leq 14$, $x \geq 0$, $y \geq 0$

51. part c); If you isolate y in the other systems, they are the same.

54. a) infinitely many solutions; One of the four regions determined by the boundary lines will be the solution set.

b) infinitely many solutions; The solution set consists of the boundary line together with a half plane, or just the boundary line itself.

c) infinitely many solutions or no solutions; The solution set consists of a half plane in the event that the inequality signs do not conflict.

d) infinitely many solutions; The solution set consists of the half plane above the upper boundary line, the half plane below the lower boundary line, or the strip between the boundary lines, if there are solutions.

55. all real numbers

56. a) $y \leq \frac{2}{3}x - 2$, $y \geq -2x - 4$

b) $y > 3x - 3$, $y \geq \frac{1}{2}x + 2$

59. a) Answers may vary. $0 \leq x \leq 2$, $0 \leq y \leq 2$ **b)** 4

60. a) 9 **b)** 18

61. a) $x + y \le 12\,000$, $0.04x + 0.05y > 500$, $x \ge 0$, $y \ge 0$
b) $9999; If she invests more than $9999 at 4%, she will not earn more than $500 in interest.

62. a) irregular pentagon **b)** 29.5 m^2

63. a) $j + w \le 8$, $\frac{j}{10} + \frac{w}{6} \ge \frac{1}{2}$, $\frac{j}{10} + \frac{w}{6} \le 1$, $j \ge 0$, $w \ge 0$
b) Answers may vary. (5, 1), (1, 5), (6, 2)

64. Answers may vary.
a) $0 \le x \le 50$, $-20 \le y \le 50$
b) $-20 \le x \le 10$, $-30 \le y \le 5$
c) $0 \le x \le 10$, $0 \le y \le 40$
d) $-50 \le x \le 0$, $0 \le y \le 30$

65. a) $x + y \ge 50$, $0.35x + 0.12y \le 10$, $x \ge 0$, $y \ge 0$
b) 83.3 g

66. a) Shade between the solid lines $y = 4$ and $y = -4$.
b) Shade to the right of the broken line $x = 1$ and to the left of the broken line $x = -1$.

67. b) The points on the line $y = 2x + 2$ that are on and above the line $x + y = 8$.

Section 2.6 p. 89

Applications and Problem Solving (Section 2.6)

1. a) corner pieces: 4, side pieces: $4m - 8$, inner pieces: $(m - 2)^2$
b) corner pieces: 4, side pieces: 152, inner pieces: 1444

2. corner pieces: 4, side pieces: 128, inner pieces: 1015

3. 3 333 333 266 666 667

4. a) 2002, 3003, 4004, 5005, 6006
b) If the second factor in the product is $n \times 7$, the product is $1000n + n$. **c)** 14 014

5. a) $y = 4x + 6$; 42, 23, 214
b) $y = x^2 + 2$; 66, 11, 227
c) $y = 2x - 1$; 9, 64, 19
d) $y = \dfrac{x + 3}{2}$; 7, 37, 51

6. 49; In each row, the sum of the middle two numbers equals the sum of the outer two numbers.

7. a) 35 **b)** $n^2 + 2n$ **c)** 960; 2600
8. 8 **9.** 17, 10 **10.** 5
11. a) equal **b)** The sum is divisible by 9.
c) Answers may vary. 111 211 111; 12 222 122 221; 211 211 121 121 112

Investigating Math pp. 90–91

1 Maximum and Minimum Values

1. $x \ge 3$, $x \le 7$, $y \ge 2$, $y \le 6$
2. a) A: 21; B: 13; C: 25; D: 33 **b)** D; 33 **c)** B; 13
3. a) Answers may vary.
E(7, 4); F(3, 4); G(5, 3); H(5, 4)
b) E: 29; F: 17; G: 21; H: 23; None of these values is less than the minimum or greater than the maximum.

4. the vertices
5. a) maximum = 22 at B(5, 4); minimum = 0 at O(0, 0)
b) maximum = 28 at C(7, 0); minimum = −6 at A(0, 6)
c) maximum = 12 at A(0, 6); minimum = −21 at C(7, 0)

6. a) maximum = 26 at C(5, 3); minimum = 0 at O(0, 0)
b) maximum = 12 at D(6, 0); minimum = −35 at A(0, 5)
c) maximum = 25 at A(0, 5); minimum = −6 at D(6, 0)

7. a) maximum = 43 at B(5, 7); minimum = 0 at O(0, 0)
b) maximum = 32 at C(8, 4); minimum = −8 at A(0, 4)
c) maximum = 12 at A(0, 4); minimum = −10 at D(5, 0)

2 Graphing Polygonal Regions, I

1. (1, 2), (1, 7), (8, 2), (8, 7)
a) maximum = 51; minimum = 12
b) maximum = 4; minimum = −22
2. (0, 0), (8, 0), (2, 6), (0, 6)
a) maximum = 20; minimum = 0
b) maximum = 8; minimum = −24
3. (2, 0), (10, 0), (10, 8), (8, 8), (2, 2)
a) maximum = 80; minimum = 8
b) maximum = 20; minimum = −8
4. (0, 2), (5, 2), (8, 5), (8, 9), (3, 9), (0, 6)
a) maximum = 15; minimum = −1
b) maximum = −1; minimum = −24

3 Graphing Polygonal Regions, II

1. (0, 0), (4, 0), (2, 4), (0, 5)
a) maximum = 20; minimum = 0
b) maximum = 8; minimum = −15
2. (0, 0), (3, 0), (8, 10), (0, 2)
a) maximum = 28; minimum = 0
b) maximum = 3; minimum = −42
3. (0, 0), (5, 0), (5, 3), (2, 6), (0, 5)
a) maximum = 13; minimum = 0
b) maximum = 16; minimum = −5
4. (10, 0), (6, 8), (2, 4)
a) maximum = 20; minimum = 0
b) maximum = 12; minimum = −20

4 Technology

1. Yes. Graph the inequalities.
2. Graph the first three inequalities, and set the viewing window to show only the first quadrant.

Connecting Math and Business
pp. 92–93

1 Radio Advertising

2. (0, 0), (8, 0), (4, 6), (0, 10)
3. 0, 64 000, 68 000, 60 000
4. 68 000
5. 4 between 06:00 and 09:00 and 6 between 16:00 and 18:00

2 More Business Applications

1. a) $x + y \geq 10\,000$, $x + y \leq 15\,000$
   b) $x \geq 3000$, $x \leq 4000$
   d) (3000, 7000), (3000, 12 000), (4000, 6000), (4000, 11 000)
   e) $3x + 1.2y$
   f) maximum = $25 200; minimum = $17 400
2. 10 h at the hardware store, 5 h at the fitness centre
3. 12 Mogul and 8 Speed
4. 5 regular and 6 deluxe
5. a) 80 classic and 20 deluxe
   b) No. The feasible region has no outside boundary. The store can buy as many dishwashers as it can sell.

Review   pp. 94–95

1. $y < 6$
2. $w > 2$
3. $x \geq -1$
4. $z \leq 2$
5. $k > -2$
6. $t > -8$
7. $m \leq 4$
8. $n \geq -4$
9. $x > -4$
10. $y < 0$
11. $m \leq -1$
12. $z > 11$
13. $b > 8$
14. $q > 1$
15. $b \leq 2$
16. $n \leq 4$
17. $m \leq 3$
18. $w < 2$
19. $x < 17$
20. $z \leq 1$
21. $y \leq -2$
22. $n < 3$
23. $x > 8$
24. $w \leq -9$
25. $m < 2$
26. $p \leq -2$
27. $x > 0$
28. $w \leq 5$
29. $y > -2$
30. $k \leq 4$
31. more than 255 tickets
32. a) $x \geq 7$ **b)** $x < 9$
33. (−1, 6), (3, 13)
34. (−1, −5), (2, −9)
55. a) $2x + 3y \leq 18$ **b)** $x \geq 0, y \geq 0$
56. a) $\frac{2}{3}x + y \leq 10$ **b)** $x \geq 0, y \geq 0$
57. (15, 21)
58. (0, −3), (−2, 1)
59. $y \geq x + 1, y \geq 2 - x$
60. $x + y \leq 2, x - y \leq 5$
61. $y > 1 - x, y \leq 2 + 0.5x$
62. $2x + y < 2, y < x + 5$
73. $x + y < 12, x - y \geq 6$; (12, 0), (11, 1), (10, 2), (9, 3)

Exploring Math   p. 95

1. scalene triangle
2. isosceles triangle
3. equilateral triangle
4. rhombus
5. square
6. rectangle
7. parallelogram
8. rectangle
9. parallelogram
10. rhombus
11. rectangle
12. rectangle
13. regular hexagon
14. irregular hexagon
15. square
16. scalene, isosceles, and equilateral triangles; square; regular hexagon
17. yes
18. no

Chapter Check   p. 96

1. $m < 17$
2. $w > 4$
3. $x \geq -3$
4. $n \leq 3$
5. $k > -5$
6. $t > -11$
7. $m < -5$
8. $z \geq -8$
9. $b \leq -11$
10. $y < 13$
11. $x > -1$
12. $z < 11$
13. $m \leq 4$
14. $w < 2$
15. $g > -6$
16. $z \leq -3$
17. $y \leq 12$
18. $n < \frac{1}{3}$
19. $x \geq 25$
20. $m > 7$
21. $q < 1$
22. $w \leq \frac{1}{2}$
23. $b < 8$
24. $k \geq -15$
25. $p < 0$
26. $y < 5$
27. (1, 1), (−1, 6), (0, 0)   **28.** (0, 0)
29. (−2, 3)
60. $200 + 25x \leq 4000$; at most 252 people
61. a) $0.4x + y \leq 20$

Using the Strategies   p. 97

1. D = 1; F = 9
2. Move the 2nd and 3rd counters to the right end. In the new configuration, move the 3rd and 4th counters to fill the gap made on the previous move. In the new configuration, move the 6th and 7th counters to fill the gap made on the previous move. Move the first and second counters to fill the gap made on the previous move.
3. Answers may vary.
4. E = 10; F = 14
5. 7
6. a) $y = \dfrac{b(x - 2b)}{x + b}$
   b) $y = 1, x = 15$
7. 9 km
8. A: 60 kg; E: 61 kg; B: 62 kg; D: 63 kg; C: 64 kg
9. 25°
10. X = 2; Y = 7
11. 1¢, 2¢, 4¢, 7¢

Data Bank

1. Answers may vary.
2. Answers may vary.
3. Answers may vary.

CHAPTER 3

Quadratic Functions

Chapter Introduction

Chapter Materials

graphing calculators, Teacher's Resource Master 1 (0.5-cm grid paper), Teacher's Resource Master 2 (1-cm grid paper), Teacher's Resource Master 3 (algebra tiles), Teacher's Resource Master 4 (number lines), Teacher's Resource Master 5 (graphing grids), Teacher's Resource Master 6 (2-cm grid paper), algebra tiles, overhead algebra tiles, overhead projector, counters, paper cups

Chapter Concepts

Chapter 3 reviews or introduces
• graphing equations of the form $y = x^2 + q$, $y = ax^2$, $y = ax^2 + q$, and $y = a(x - p)^2 + q$
• graphing equations of the form $y = ax^2 + bx + c$ by completing the square
• the problem solving strategies Guess and Check, Work Backward, and Use a Table or Spreadsheet

Teaching Suggestions

Review with the class the opening paragraphs of student text page 99. Ask:

How would you describe, in words, the shape of gravity's rainbow curve?

Where do you think the maximum point is?

How would you describe the speed of the object at the maximum point?

What is the speed of the object at the maximum point of the curve?

How would you describe the speed of the object at different points of gravity's rainbow curve?

Elicit from the students that there are two times an object moving in gravity's rainbow curve has the same speed, once going up and once going down.

Have small groups of students complete questions 1 to 4 on student text page 99. When they have completed the questions, invite volunteers to present their results to the class.

Complete question 5 as a class discussion. Look for examples such as water from a water fountain and the flight path of a golf ball after being hit by a golf club.

Integrating Technology

Internet

Use the Internet to find information about situations described by gravity's rainbow curve.

Enrichment

Make up a question involving a quadratic equation. Exchange problems with a classmate and solve your classmate's problem. Discuss and compare your solutions. Present your problem and solution to the class.

Math Journal

gravity's rainbow curve Write a description of the behaviour of an object moving in gravity's rainbow curve in terms of speed and position. Include a diagram of a curve and include the maximum point in the diagram.

Assessing the Outcomes

Observation

You might consider some of these questions as you observe the students work.
• Can the students substitute values for x into quadratic equations?
• Do the students work together to find the maximum height?
• Do the students know how to substitute into a radical equation?
• Do all the students try to come up with a suggestion for an example of gravity's rainbow curve?

Getting Started

Student Text Pages
Pp. 100–101

Materials
scientific (or graphing) calculators, Teacher's Resource Master 1 (0.5-cm grid paper), overhead projector

Learning Outcomes
- Generate algebraic formulas that represent number patterns.
- Generate the minimum or maximum values for a given rule.

Teaching Suggestions

Number Games
(0.5-cm grid paper, calculators, overhead projector)
Provide pairs of students with grid paper and assign question 1 on student text page 100. Ask:

What do the terms "maximum" and "minimum" mean?

After a while, have the students discuss and compare their guesses. Have the class decide on the value of the integer that gives the maximum result.
Ask:

How would you describe the graph you have drawn, linear or non-linear?

Provide an overhead projector and have the students present their graphs to the class.

Then, assign questions 2 and 3, and have the pairs of students present their results to the class.

Warm Up
Assign some or all of the questions as individual or group work. Students could record their answers in their notebooks, or take turns asking questions orally with a partner.

When the students have finished, have them discuss the methods they used to answer the questions.

Mental Math
Students could choose, or be assigned, certain questions from each section. Alternatively, small groups could work as teams, sharing the questions and explaining the answers to the rest of the group.

Integrating Technology

Scientific Calculators
Use a calculator to perform repeated calculations in Number Games.

Math Journal
Write a short paragraph explaining to someone how to determine whether a quadratic equation has a maximum or a minimum value.

Assessing the Outcomes

Observation
You may want to consider some of these questions as the students discuss their guessing methods.
- Do the groups share the tasks evenly?
- Are the students able to work with each other co-operatively?
- Do all of the students in each group attempt to find the answers?
- Do the students demonstrate problem solving skills?

Investigating Math

Exploring Transformations

Student Text Pages
Pp. 102–103

Materials
Teacher's Resource Master 1 (0.5-cm grid paper), graphing calculators, overhead graphing calculator, overhead projector

Learning Outcomes
- Graphically perform and algebraically identify horizontal and vertical translations on absolute value functions.
- Graphically perform and algebraically identify horizontal and vertical reflections on absolute value functions.
- Graphically perform and algebraically identify dilatations and compressions on absolute value functions.
- Describe the patterns of these transformations in terms of the changes that occur in the coordinates of the graph and the coefficients of the equations.
- Identify axes of symmetry, vertices, and directions of opening of absolute value functions.

Prerequisite Skills
1. Evaluate.

a) $|-5|$ [5]   b) $1 + |-3 - 5|$ [9]

c) $2|-2|$ [4]   d) $3|5 - 2| - 20$ [-11]

2. Evaluate each expression for $x = -10$.

a) $|x|$ [10]   b) $3|2x + 5|$ [45]

c) $|5 - x|$ [15]   d) $-|-3x|$ [-30]

Mental Math
1. Evaluate each expression for the given values of x.

a) $x^2 + 5$, $x = -1, 0, 1, 2$ [6, 5, 6, 9]

b) $2x^2 - 1$, $x = 2, 4, 6, 8$ [7, 31, 71, 127]

c) $-x^2 - 4$, $x = -5, -4, -3, -2$ [$-29, -20, -13, -8$]

d) $x^2 - x$, $x = 0, 1, 2, 3$ [0, 0, 2, 6]

e) $(x - 2)^2 + 2$, $x = -3, -1, 1, 2$ [27, 11, 3, 2]

f) $(x + 3)^2 - 1$, $x = 5, 6, 7, 8$ [63, 80, 99, 120]

2. Calculate.

a) 37×33 [1221]   b) 61×69 [4209]

c) 16×14 [224]   d) 54×56 [3024]

e) 92×98 [9016]   f) 41×49 [2009]

Teaching Suggestions
(0.5-cm grid paper, overhead projector, overhead graphing calculator, graphing calculators) Provide small groups of students with grid paper and graphing calculators, if possible. Ask:

What is the absolute value of -2? of 500? of $-2x$?

What type of graph is the function $y = |x|$?

What do the terms "domain" and "range" mean?

What is the vertex of a curve?

Have the students copy and complete this table of values for every required graph.

x	y
-3	
-2	
-1	
0	
1	
2	
3	

Students could also graph the functions on a graphing calculator.

Have volunteers present their results to the class. Provide an overhead projector and an overhead graphing calculator so that students who used a graphing calculator to find the graphs can show their results to the class.

For Investigation 1, ask:

Can you think of another function that would have the same graph as the graph of the function $y = |x|$?

How is the graph of this function different from the graph of the function $y = |x|$?

For Investigation 2, ask:

How would you describe the range of absolute value functions?

For Investigation 3, ask:

How can you tell the horizontal shift of the graph by looking at the equation of the graph?

For Investigation 4, ask:

How can you identify the vertex of the graph from the equation of the graph?

What information can you deduce from the coordinates of the vertex of a graph?

For Investigation 5, ask:

What is the effect of a on the absolute value function $y = a|x|$?

For Investigation 6, have the students summarize in writing the effect of a on the absolute value function $y = a|x - p| + q$. This would be a good time to come to an agreement with the students as to how to describe the graph of an absolute value function.

For Investigation 7, discuss with the class the effect of the x- and y-intercepts on the absolute value function $y = a|x - p| + q$.

Integrating Technology

Graphing Calculators

How would you graph the absolute value functions on student text pages 102 and 103 on your graphing calculator? On a TI-83, the absolute value function abs(is used. It is the first item under the second menu NUM when the MATH key is pressed.
To graph $y = x|x - 2| + 3$, press the Y= key.
Press the MATH key, the right arrow key once to get to the NUM menu, and the 1 key to select abs(.
At the abs(prompt, enter $x - 2$, a closing bracket, and + 3.
Press the ZOOM key and the 6 key to select ZStandard.

See *MATHPOWER™ 11, Western Edition, Blackline Masters* pages 63 to 65 for Graphing Absolute Value Functions.

Math Journal

Write a summary of the effect of the value of a on the absolute value function $y = a|x - p| + q$.

Assessing the Outcomes

Written Assignment

Graph each of the following functions. State the vertex of each function.

1. $y = |x - 2| - 4$
2. $y = -3|x - 2| - 4$
3. $y = 3|x + 2| - 4$

Extension

For each graph, write

a) *the equation*
b) *the coordinates of the vertex*
c) *the direction of opening*
d) *the x- and y-intercepts, if any exist*

1.

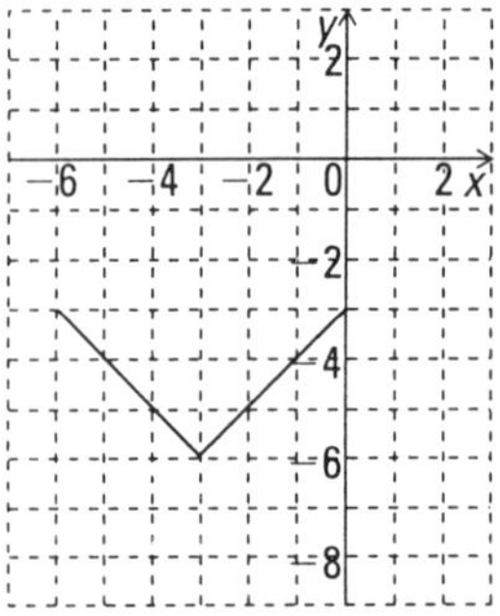

2.

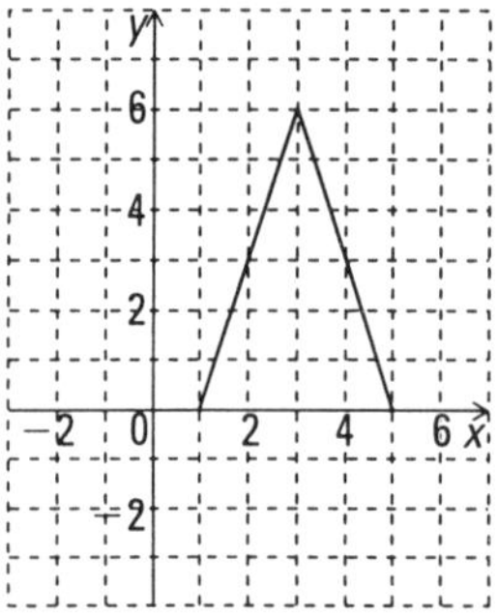

3.

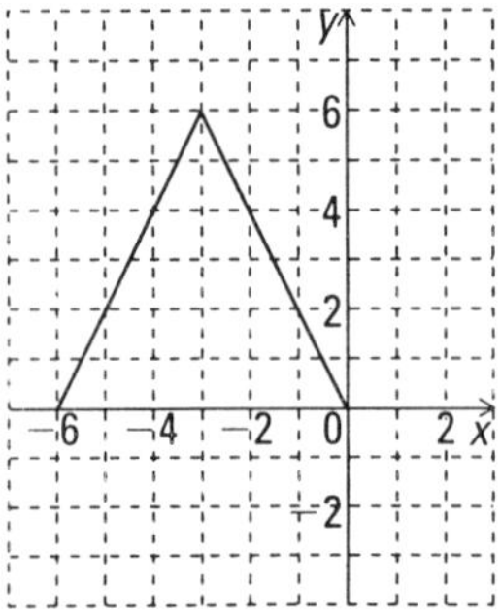

3.1 Graphing $y = x^2 + q$, $y = ax^2$, and $y = ax^2 + q$

Student Text Pages
Pp. 104–111

Materials
graphing calculators, Teacher's Resource Master 2 (1-cm grid paper), Teacher's Resource Master 6 (2-cm grid paper), overhead projector

Learning Outcomes
- Graph equations of the form $y = x^2 + q$, $y = ax^2$, and $y = ax^2 + q$.
- Describe the vertex, axis of symmetry, domain, range, maximum value, minimum value, and intercepts of equations of the form $y = x^2 + q$, $y = ax^2$, and $y = ax^2 + q$.
- Write the equation of a parabola given its vertex and a point on its graph.
- Solve problems involving equations of the form $y = x^2 + q$, $y = ax^2$, and $y = ax^2 + q$.

Prerequisite Skills
For each relation
a) construct a table of values
b) write the table of values as a set of coordinate points
c) graph the points in b)
d) name the intercepts of each relation
e) find the value of y for $x = 1.5$
f) find the value of x for $y = -2$

1. $y = 2x + 1$
2. $x + 2y - 3 = 0$

1. a)

x	y
-2	-3
-1	-1
0	1
1	3
2	5

b) $(-2, -3)$, $(-1, -1)$, $(0, 1)$, $(1, 3)$, $(2, 5)$

2. a)

x	y
-2	$\frac{5}{2}$
-1	2
0	$\frac{3}{2}$
1	1
2	$\frac{1}{2}$

b) $\left(-2, \frac{5}{2}\right)$, $(-1, 2)$, $\left(0, \frac{3}{2}\right)$, $(1, 1)$, $\left(2, \frac{1}{2}\right)$

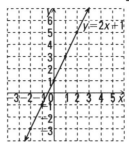

c)

d) x-intercept $-\frac{1}{2}$; y-intercept 1

e) 4

f) $\frac{3}{4}$

c)

d) x-intercept; 3 y-intercept $\frac{3}{2}$

e) $\frac{3}{4}$

f) 7

Mental Math
1. Multiply in two steps.
   a) 3.6×22 [79.2]
   b) 9.1×12 [109.2]
   c) 2.9×1.3 [3.77]
   d) 37×0.51 [18.87]
   e) 52×140 [7280]
   f) 91×0.9 [81.9]

2. Evaluate for $x = -1$ and $y = 2$.
   a) $3x - y$ [−5]
   b) $-2x - 2y$ [−2]
   c) $-x + 5y$ [11]
   d) $4x + y$ [−2]
   e) $x^2 + y$ [3]
   f) $3y + 4x$ [2]

Explore/Inquire Answers

Explore: Compare the Graphs

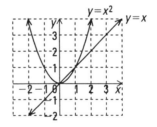

Inquire
1. yes; $x = 0$
2. yes; $y = -x$
3. a) no   b) no   c) R, R
4. a) no   b) Yes; a minimum of 0
   c) $R, \{x \in R: x \geq 0\}$
5. $y = 2x^2$ is a vertical stretch of $y = x^2$
6. a) $x \geq 0, y \geq 0$ b) the points in the first quadrant

Teaching Suggestions

Method 1

(grid paper, overhead projector) Review with the class the opening paragraph on student text page 104. Discuss the meaning of the word "quadratic." Ask:

Why do you think the word "quadratic" was used to name a quadratic equation?

What other words have the same root as the word "quadratic"?

Provide pairs of students with grid paper and assign the Explore section. Have the students describe their methods of drawing the graph of an equation. Ask:

How would you describe the graph of $y = x$?

How would you describe the graph of $y = x^2$?

Assign the Inquire questions to the pairs of students. Ask:

How would you define a line of symmetry?

Have the students identify an item in class that has a line of symmetry. Ask:

Where is the line of symmetry?

Is there more than one line of symmetry?

Introduce the terms *maximum*, *minimum*, *domain*, *range*, and *restrictions*. Have the students provide an example of each term.

For question 5, ask:

How could you use the table of values you used to draw the graph of $y = x^2$ to help you draw the graph of $y = 2x^2$?

Elicit from the students that if they constructed a table of values for the equation $y = x^2$, they could use the same x-values to construct a table of values for $y = 2x^2$.

Have volunteer pairs present their results to the class. Suggest that one student present the graphs on an overhead projector, while the other student describes the steps of the solution.

Review with the class the material at the top of student text page 105. Ask:

What examples can you think of that demonstrate the shape of a parabola?

Elicit from the students examples such as the path of water from a drinking fountain, the curve a person makes when diving into a pool of water, and the surface of a satellite dish.

Review with the class the teaching examples on student text pages 105 to 107. Discuss the differences between the instructions "Graph ...," "Draw the graph of ...," and "Sketch ..." Ask:

What are the differences in the instructions "Graph..." and "Sketch..." as they are used in this section?

Lead the students to see that a sketch is a rough drawing of an object, with only the main features indicated, while a graph is more exact, since points are plotted on a grid. Thus, in this text, the instructions "Graph ..." and "Draw the graph of ..." indicate that a table of values or a graphing calculator is required. When the instruction "Sketch ..." is given, then the required diagram is less detailed and includes only the main features of the transformation.

Point out to the class that teaching examples 1 and 2 each demonstrate one transformation, while teaching example 3 demonstrates a combination of two transformations. Ask:

What are the two transformations completed in teaching example 3?

Give me an example of the equation of a parabola that opens upward; that opens downward.

Finally, review with the class teaching examples 4 and 5 on student text pages 107 and 108.

Method 2

(2-cm grid paper, overlays of the graphs of $y = x^2$, $y = 2x^2$, and $y = \frac{1}{2}x^2$, overhead projector, 1-cm grid paper) Turn off the lights in the classroom and toss a ball between a screen and an overhead projector shining on the screen. Begin at one side of the screen and have a student catch the ball at the other side of the screen. Instruct students to observe the path of the ball, and then, ask:

How would you describe the path of the ball?

Introduce the term "parabola," and indicate that in general, paths of objects thrown in the air are parabolic curves.

Draw a sketch of a parabola and use the sketch to introduce and demonstrate the terms "vertex" and "axis of symmetry." Ask:

How would you describe the path of a swimmer after diving into a pool?

Elicit from the students that such paths are similar to those of balls tossed in the air, except that they open in the opposite direction. Ask:

How is the path of a ball and the path of a diver similar? How do they differ?

Lead the students to see that the difference between the two types of paths is that a ball reaches a maximum point, whereas a diver reaches a minimum point. Thus, the path of a ball opens downward, while the path of a diver opens upward.

Prepare on 2-cm grid paper a set of axes showing the four quadrants. As well, prepare an overlay for the graph of each of the following functions: $y = x^2$, $y = 2x^2$, and $y = \frac{1}{2}x^2$. Place the graph of the function $y = x^2$ on top of the overlay on the overhead projector with the vertex at the origin. Ask:

Which path does this graph model, the path of the ball, or the path of the diver?

Elicit from the students that the path models the path of the diver. Explain that the path of the diver is a model of the function $y = ax^2$. Ask:

What would I have to do to this graph to model the path of a ball?

Lead the students to see that the result of reflecting the graph through the x-axis is the model of the path of a ball, and is described by the function $y = -ax^2$.

Provide pairs of students with grid paper. Have them study the effects of changes in the value of a in the functions $y = ax^2$ and $y = -ax^2$. Suggest they construct tables of values for $y = 2x^2$, $y = -2x^2$, $y = \frac{1}{2}x^2$, $y = -\frac{1}{2}x^2$, and draw the graphs on grid paper. Then, suggest that different pairs choose their own values of a, construct a table of values, and draw the graph.

Ensure that the pairs choose a variety of whole numbers and fractional numbers for values of a in $y = ax^2$ and $y = -ax^2$.

When the pairs have completed this investigation, have volunteer pairs present their results to the class. Challenge the students to make a general statement about the shape of the graphs of the functions $y = ax^2$ and $y = -ax^2$, depending on the value of a. Encourage the students to identify the vertex of each parabola.

Sample Solution

Page 111, question 77

a) $A = 25 \times 16 - s^2$
$\quad = 400 - s^2$

b) Since none of the square can extend beyond the rectangle, the maximum length of the side must be the lesser of the dimensions of the rectangle. The maximum length of the square is 16.

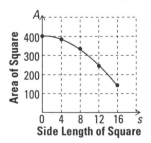

d) domain $0 \le s \le 16$, $s \in R$;
range $144 \le A \le 400$, $A \in R$.

Number Power Answer

The sum of the numbers in the corners is 100.
Thus, the missing number is
$100 - 33 - 15 - 24 = 28$.

Integrating Technology

Graphing Calculators

How would you use your graphing calculator to create the graphs in the examples on student text pages 105 to 107?

On a TI-83, the Y= key is used.
Press the Y= key, and enter the right side of the first equation at the Y1= prompt.
Press the ENTER key to move to Y2=, and enter the right side of the second equation.
Press the ENTER key to move to Y3=, and enter the right side of the third equation.
After all the equations to be graphed have been entered, press the ZOOM key and the 6 key to select ZStandard.

For teaching example 5 on student text page 108, the standard viewing window is not useful. On a TI-83, Zoom Fit can be selected to create a graph where the Ymax and the Ymin are recalculated to include the maximums and minimums between the Xmax and Xmin that were selected in the last graph. Zoom Fit is the tenth item under the ZOOM menu when the ZOOM key is pressed. Use the down arrow key to see the last items.

Alternatively, the viewing window can be created based on given information. Here the graph opens down with a maximum value of 192 when d is 0, and height is never negative. The window uses an Xmin of -100, an Xmax of 100, a Ymin of 0, a Ymax of 200, and scales of 10.

Teaching examples 3 and 5 show ways to find the x-intercepts when they are not easily read from the graph.

On a TI-83, the Zero operation is the second item when the CALC (i.e., 2nd TRACE) key is pressed. With the graph displayed, press the CALC (i.e., 2nd TRACE) key and the 2 key to select zero.
Use the arrow keys to move the cursor slightly to the left of one of the x-intercepts, and press the ENTER key to define the Left Bound.
Use the arrow keys to move the cursor slightly to the right of the same x-intercept, and press the ENTER key to define the Right Bound.
Use the arrow keys to move the cursor onto the same x-intercept, and press the ENTER key to define your Guess.
Read the x-intercept given as $x=$.
Repeat the steps for the other x-intercept.
On a TI-83, to use tables, with the graph displayed, press the TBLSET (i.e., 2nd WINDOW) key.
Enter a start value and then, an increment value.
Press the TABLE (i.e., 2nd GRAPH) key to see the table.
Use the arrow keys to move through the values.
On a TI-83, one way to use the Zoom and Trace instructions is to press the ZOOM key and the 1 key to select ZBox.
Use the arrow keys to create a small box around the x-intercept.

Press the TRACE key, and use the arrow keys to find the value of x when y is zero.

You can also use a graphing calculator to find the y-intercepts when they are not easily read from the graph. This is shown in teaching example 3 on student text page 117 of Section 3.3. On a TI-83, use the Value operation, which is the first item when the CALC (i.e., 2nd TRACE) key is pressed.
With the graph displayed, press the CALC (i.e., 2nd TRACE) key and the 1 key to select value.
At the $x=$ prompt, enter 0 and press the ENTER key. Read the y-intercept given as $y=$.

Use your graphing calculator to create the graphs and find the x-intercepts in questions 42 to 47 on student text page 109.

Use your graphing calculator to create the graphs in questions 67, 69 to 71, and 76 to 77 on student text pages 110 and 111.

To determine a suitable viewing window in question 67, consider that the graph opens up with a minimum of 0 when b is 0, and neither area nor height can be negative. Try 0 and 20 as the Xmin and Xmax, and 0 and 100 as the Ymin and Ymax, with suitable scales.

To determine a suitable viewing window in question 69, consider that the graph opens up with a minimum of 2 when d is 0, height cannot be negative, and the distance between the towers is 1280. Try -700 and 700 as the Xmin and Xmax, and 0 and 100 as the Ymin and Ymax, with suitable scales.

To determine a suitable viewing window in question 70, consider that the graph opens down with a maximum of 134 when t is 0, and neither time nor height can be negative. Try 0 and 10 as the Xmin and Xmax, and 0 and 150 as the Ymin and Ymax, with suitable scales.

To determine a suitable viewing window in question 76, consider that the graph opens up with a minimum of 0 when r is 0, and neither area nor radius can be negative. Try 0 and 10 as the Xmin and Xmax, and 0 and 100 as the Ymin and Ymax, with suitable scales.

To determine a suitable viewing window in question 77, consider that the graph opens down with a maximum of 400 when s is 0, and neither area nor side length can be negative. Try 0 and 50 as the Xmin and Xmax, and 0 and 450 as the Ymin and Ymax, with suitable scales.

In question 71, the intersection points can be found after graphing the equations. On a TI-83, use the Intersect instruction, which is the fifth item when the CALC (i.e., 2nd TRACE) key is pressed, and a friendly viewing Window such as -4.7 and 4.7 as the Xmin and Xmax, and 0 and 12.4 as the Ymin and Ymax. For more information about the Intersect operation and friendly windows, see *Integrating Technology* in Section 1.1 on page 8 of this teacher's resource.

The inequalities in questions 72 and 78 on student text page 111 can be graphed using a graphing calculator. For more information about graphing inequalities, see *Technology: Graphing Linear Inequalities With a Graphing Calculator* on page 57 in Chapter 2 of this teacher's resource.

In question 80 on student text page 111, show the graph in the standard viewing window, and then, select a portion of the graph by changing the Xmin, Xmax, and Xscl values to meet each required condition.

See *MATHPOWER*™ 11, *Western Edition, Blackline Masters* pages 24 to 26 for Setting Viewing Windows. See *MATHPOWER*™ 11, *Western Edition, Blackline Masters* pages 66 to 68 for Graphing Quadratic Functions and Finding Intercepts.

Calculator-Based Laboratories
Collect your own real data, using a portable data collection device, a CBL (Calculator-Based Laboratory), and plot the data on a graphing calculator.

Enrichment
Describe each transformation of $y = x^2$ represented by the equations $y = ax^2$, $y = x^2 + q$, and $y = ax^2 + q$. Use sketches to help you describe each transformation. Indicate the meaning of negative values for a and q, and fractional values for a.

Math Journal
quadratic function, parabola, maximum point, minimum point, axis of symmetry Write a definition for each of these terms in your journal. Include a diagram to illustrate your definitions.

Common Errors
- When substituting for x in a function such as $y = ax^2 + k$, students often multiply the value of a by the value of x, and then square this result.

- R_x Review the order of operations, emphasizing that the exponent is calculated first, before any multiplication is done.

Problem Levels of Difficulty
A: 1–64, 70, 80   **B:** 65–69, 71–77   **C:** 78, 79

Assessing the Outcomes
Written Assignment
Sketch the graph of each parabola and state
a) the direction of opening
b) the coordinates of the vertex
c) the equation of the axis of symmetry
d) the domain and range
e) the maximum or minimum value
  1. $y = -4x^2 + 12$ **2.** $5x^2 - y = 8$

3.2 Problem Solving: Guess and Check

Student Text Pages
Pp. 112–113

Materials
overhead projector

Learning Outcome
• Use the Guess and Check strategy to solve problems.

Prerequisite Skills
The length of a rectangle is twice the width. If the perimeter of the rectangle is 24 units, what are the dimensions of the rectangle?   [8 units by 4 units]

Mental Math
1. Multiply in two steps.

a) 3.6×22 [79.2]   **b)** 9.1×12 [109.2]

c) 2.9×1.3 [3.77]   **d)** 37×0.51 [18.87]

e) 52×140 [7280]   **f)** 91×0.9 [81.9]

2. Evaluate for $x = -1$ and $y = 2$.

a) $3x - y$ [−5]   **b)** $-2x - 2y$ [−2]

c) $-x + 5y$ [11]   **d)** $4x + y$ [−2]

e) $x^2 + y$ [3]   **f)** $3y + 4x$ [2]

Teaching Suggestions

Method 1
(overhead projector)   Read with the class the problem given in the opening paragraphs on student text page 112. Ask:

What do you need to know to solve the problem?

What information in the problem will help you find the answer?

Display a copy of the chart on an overhead projector, and have volunteers make guesses and fill in the chart.

When the students have found the required answer, review the solution given on the student text page. Ask:

How does your answer compare with the answer on the text page?

Review with the class the steps of problem solving given down the left side of the student text page.

Discuss the guess and check procedure outlined at the bottom of the student text page.

Method 2
Display this problem on the chalkboard.

Each letter represents a different digit. Find the value of each letter.

$$\begin{array}{r} C\,2\,D \\ 8\overline{)X\,9\,Y} \end{array}$$

Have pairs of students copy the problem and give them several moments to consider it. Direct students to plan a solution to the problem. Ask:

What information are you given?

What information are you required to find?

What plan would you use to solve the problem?

Have volunteers present their solutions to the class. Discuss the students' answers, encouraging responses that suggest guessing. Then, ask:

What do you think the expression "educated guess" means?

What information can you use that will help you come up with an educated guess?

Lead students to see that some digits can be eliminated from the guess work. For example, because C and X are the first digits of two of the numbers in the problem, they cannot be zero; because the divisor 8 is an even number and because there is no remainder, then the letter Y must be an even number. Ask:

How can you use your guess to help you find the answer?

Review with the class the problem solving steps given down the left side and the Guess and Check procedure given at the bottom of student text page 112.

Integrating Technology

Computer Spreadsheets
To use a computer spreadsheet to make the table on student text page 112, enter the headings and your guesses. Then, enter the formula $=(A2*(43+A2))$ in cell B2, copy it, and paste it in cells B3, B4, and so on, until the correct value of x is found.

Use a computer spreadsheet to create tables of guess and check values to solve some of the problems on student text page 113.

Internet
Use the Internet to find the answers to questions 1 to 4 on student text page 113.

Work with other students on the Internet to solve problems, using web sites such as *http://forum.swarthmore.edu/mathmagic/* and Canada's SchoolNet Web Site at *http://www.schoolnet.ca.*

Math Journal

Write a short paragraph explaining how the Guess and Check strategy works.

Describe a situation where you would use, or have used, the guess and check strategy to solve a problem.

Problem Levels of Difficulty

A: 1–7, 12   **B:** 8, 9   **C:** 10, 11

Assessing the Outcome

Pair Evaluation: Written Assignment

Ask each student pair to confer and give one answer that represents the pair.

The total mass of 4 boxes is 240 kg. The mass of the lightest box is 12 times less than the total mass of the 2 middle boxes. Each box has a mass 3 times greater than the one before it. What is the mass of each box?

3.3 Graphing $y = a(x - p)^2 + q$

Student Text Pages
Pp. 114–121

Materials

graphing calculators, Teacher's Resource Master 1 (0.5-cm grid paper), overhead projector

Learning Outcomes

- Sketch the graphs of quadratic functions of the form $y = a(x - p)^2 + q$.
- Describe the directions of opening, the vertices, the axes of symmetry, the domains, the ranges, and the maximum or the minimum values of the graphs of quadratic functions of the form $y = a(x - p)^2 + q$.
- Find the intercepts of the graphs of quadratic functions of the form $y = a(x - p)^2 + q$.
- Write the equations of parabolas given characteristics such as vertices and points on the graph.
- Solve problems involving quadratic functions of the form $y = a(x - p)^2 + q$.

Prerequisite Skills

1. Find the intercepts of each line.

a) $2x - y = 4$ [x-intercept 2; y-intercept −4]

b) $y = -\frac{1}{2}x + 5$ [x-intercept 10: y-intercept 5]

c) $3x + y - 6 = 0$ [x-intercept 2; y-intercept 6]

d) $y = 5x - 2$ [x-intercept $\frac{2}{5}$; y-intercept −2]

2. Write the coordinates of two points on each line.
[Answers may vary. For example,

a) $x + 2y = -8$ $\left[(0, -4), \left(1, -4\frac{1}{2}\right)\right]$

b) $x - 5y = 1$ $\left[\left(-1, -\frac{2}{5}\right), (1, 0)\right]$

c) $y = 4x + 3$ [(2, 11), (0, 3)]

d) $y = -2x - 1$ [(0, −1), (2, −5)]

3. Find the values of y for the given values of x.

a) $y = 3x + 1$; $x = -3, 1, 5$ [−8, 4, 16]

b) $2x + 5y = -1$; $x = 0, 1, 2$ $\left[-\frac{1}{5}, -\frac{3}{5}, -1\right]$

c) $x - 3y = 7$; $x = -1, 0, 1$ $\left[-\frac{8}{3}, -\frac{7}{3}, -2\right]$

4. Write in standard form the equation of the line with the given intercepts.

a) x-intercept $\frac{1}{3}$; y-intercept −1   [$3x - y = 1$]

b) x-intercept −2; y-intercept 3   [$3x - 2y = -6$]

Mental Math

1. Evaluate each expression for the given values of x.

a) $-x^2 + 1$, $x = 0, 1, 2, 3$ [1, 0, −3, −8]

b) $5x^2 - 1$, $x = 3, 2, 0, -1$ [44, 19, −1, 4]

c) $-2x^2 + 1$, $x = -5, -3, 1, 2$ [−49, −17, −1, −7]

d) $x^2 + 2x$, $x = -2, -1, 0, 1$ [0, −1, 0, 3]

e) $(x + 1)^2 + 1$, $x = -4, -3, -2, -1$ [10, 5, 2, 1]

f) $-(x + 2)^2$, $x = 1, 3, 4, 6$ [−9, −25, −36, −64]

2. Calculate.

a) 7.6×7.4 [56.24]   b) 3.7×3.3 [12.21]

c) 4.4×4.6 [20.24]   d) 2.9×2.1 [6.09]

e) 8.1×8.9 [72.09]   f) 9.4×9.6 [90.24]

Explore/Inquire Answers

Explore: Compare the Graphs

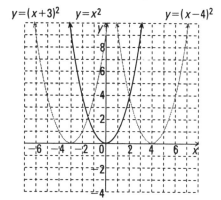

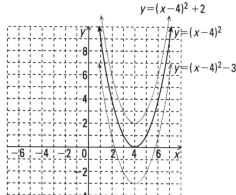

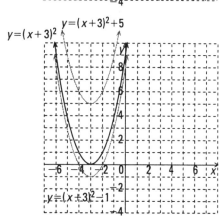

		Function	Vertex	Axis of Symmetry
Group 1	a)	$y - x^2$	(0, 0)	$x = 0$
	b)	$y = (x - 4)^2$	(4, 0)	$x = 4$
	c)	$y = (x + 3)^2$	(−3, 0)	$x = -3$
Group 2	a)	$y = (x - 4)^2$	(4, 0)	$x = 4$
	b)	$y = (x - 4)^2 + 2$	(4, 2)	$x = 4$
	c)	$y = (x - 4)^2 - 3$	(4, −3)	$x = 4$
Group 3	a)	$y = (x + 3)^2$	(−3, 0)	$x = -3$
	b)	$y = (x + 3)^2 + 5$	(−3, 5)	$x = -3$
	c)	$y = (x + 3)^2 - 1$	(−3, −1)	$x = -3$

Inquire

1. a) 4 units right b) 3 units left
2. a) $(7, 0); x = 7$ b) $(-9, 0); x = -9$
3. a) 2 units upward b) 3 units downward
4. a) $(7, 6); x = 7$ b) $(6, -5); x = 6$
5. a) 5 units upward b) 1 unit downward
6. a) (9, 1); x = −9 b) (−5, −7); x = −5

Teaching Suggestions

Method 1

(0.5-cm grid paper, overhead projector) Review with the class the opening paragraph on student text page 114. Ask:

What type of function is $h(t) = -4.9(t - 5)^2 + 124$?

How would you describe the shape of the graph of this function?

How can you tell just by looking at the function whether the vertex is a maximum or a minimum?

How is the equation $h(t) = -4.9(t - 5)^2 + 124$ similar to the equation $y = 2x^2$ given on student page 104?

How do these equations differ?

For the last two questions, elicit from the students responses such as these.
similarities: both equations are quadratic equations, the second degree variables have coefficients greater than 1
differences: one equation has a constant term, the signs of the coefficients of the squared variable are different

Divide the class into 6 groups, provide the groups with grid paper, and assign the Explore section. Have two student groups complete Group 1 functions, another two student groups Group 2 functions and the last two student groups Group 3 functions. Give the student groups who are working on the same group of functions an opportunity to discuss and compare their graphs and then, combine their results in the table.

Have volunteers from different student groups present their results to the class. Provide an overhead projector for any students who wish to display their graphs. Ask:

How are the coordinates of the vertex and the equation of the graph related?

How is the axis of symmetry and the equation of the graph related?

Assign the Inquire questions and have volunteers present their results to the class.

Review with the class student text page 115. Ask:

How can you tell by looking at two or more quadratic functions when their graphs represent congruent parabolas?

Is it possible for the graphs of two quadratic functions that open up in different directions to be congruent? Explain.

A parabolic curve is symmetric. What information could this fact be used to determine?

Review with the class teaching examples 1 and 2 on student text page 116. Then, analyze the table given at the top of student text page 117. Have volunteers express, in their own words, the information given in the chart.

Review with the class teaching examples 3 to 5 on student text pages 117 and 118. For teaching example 5 ask:

How would you describe the position of the rocket at t = 0?

What does the value −4.9 represent?

Assign the Practice and Applications and Problem Solving section to the students. Ensure that the students understand the difference between the instructions "Sketch ..." and "Graph ..." Remind them that a sketch only involves the general characteristics of a graph, but a graph involves setting up a table of values, drawing the curve on a grid, and indicating the exact values of any characteristics such as the intercepts, the vertex, and the line of symmetry.

Method 2

(0.5-cm grid paper, overhead projector) Provide students with grid paper and divide the class into groups of 4. Write the following equations on the chalkboard.

Column 1	Column 2
$y = (x + 5)^2$	$y = (x + 5)^2 + 1$
$y = (x - 3)^2$	$y = (x - 3)^2 + 2$
$y = 2(x + 4)^2$	$y = -2(x + 4)^2 + 1$
$y = -\frac{1}{2}(x - 1)^2$	$y = \frac{1}{2}(x - 1)^2 - 5$

Have two groups graph the equations in column 1 and the other two groups graph the equations in column 2. Give the groups that are working on the same column of equations opportunity to discuss and compare their progress and results. Tell the groups to indicate the vertices and the axes of symmetry for their equations on their graphs.

Give volunteer group representatives an opportunity to present their results to the class. Ensure that each group is given an opportunity to present its results. Discuss with the class any patterns that can be seen from the graphs. Some suggested patterns may be the following: the x-value of the vertex is the opposite of the sign and numerical part of the squared bracket, the y-value of the vertex is the same as the sign and the constant numerical part of the equation outside of the squared bracket, and so on.

Present the following general standard form of a quadratic function on the chalkboard.

$$y = a(x - p)^2 + q$$

Have the students compare the equations in columns 1 and 2 with this general form and identify the values of a, p, and q for each quadratic equation. Challenge the students to identify the type of transformation that each value generates. For example, the sign and the numerical value inside the squared bracket generates a horizontal translation, the constant numerical value outside the squared bracket generates a vertical translation, different values of the coefficient of the squared bracket generate stretches and compressions, and different signs in front of the coefficient of the squared bracket generate reflections.

Review with the class teaching examples 1 and 2 on student text page 116. Have them copy and complete the following table in their math journal and sketch an example of each type of graph.

Equation of Graph	Description of the Graph
$y = x^2$	
$y = ax^2$	
$y = ax^2 + q$	
$y = ax^2 - q$	
$y = a(x - p)^2$	
$y = a(x - p)^2 + q$	
$y = a(x - p)^2 - q$	

Give volunteers an opportunity to present their descriptions to the class. Provide an overhead projector in case some students wish to present their sketches as an aid in their descriptions.

Review teaching examples 3 to 5 on student text pages 117 and 118, and assign the Practice and Applications and Problem Solving sections.

Word Power Answer

ring, rink, bilk, bill, bell

Integrating Technology

Graphing Calculators

As an introduction to this section, you might use the SHIFT function on a Sharp EL-9600 to investigate p and q in the standard form of a quadratic function. Press the SHIFT/CHANGE (i.e., 2nd F EZ) key and the 1 key to select $y = x^2$.
Use the arrow keys to translate the graph of the function.
Press the ENTER key to see the translated graph and the new equations.

Use the skill discussed in *Integrating Technology* in Section 3.1 on page 91 of this teacher's resource to create the graphs and find the x- and y-intercepts in the teaching examples on student text pages 115 to 117.

Use your graphing calculator to create the graphs and find the x- and y-intercepts in questions 38 to 45 on student text page 119.

Use your graphing calculator to create the graphs in questions 83 to 85 on student text pages 120 and 121.

To determine a suitable viewing window in question 83, consider that the graph opens up with a minimum of -0.25 when t is 0.5, but neither number of teams nor number of games can be negative. Try 0 and 10 as the Xmin and Xmax, and 0 and 60 as the Ymin and Ymax, with suitable scales.

In question 85, the intersection points can be found after graphing the equations. On a TI-83, use the Intersect operation, which is the fifth item when the CALC (i.e., 2nd TRACE) key is pressed, and a friendly viewing window such as -4.7 and 4.7 as the Xmin and Xmax, and -6.2 and 6.2 as the Ymin and Ymax. For more information about the Intersect operation and friendly windows, see *Integrating Technology* in Section 1.1 on page 8 of this teacher's resource.

In question 92 on student text page 121, show the graph in a suitable viewing window, such as 10 and 40 as the Xmin and Xmax, and 50 and 150 as the Ymin and Ymax, with suitable scales, to see the parabolic shape, and then, select a portion of the graph by changing the Xmin, Xmax, and Xscl values to meet each required condition.

Calculator-Based Laboratories

Collect your own real data, using a portable data collection device, a CBL (Calculator-Based Laboratory), and plot the data on a graphing calculator.

Enrichment

The "Ring of Fire" is a group of volcanoes that extends from Northern California through British Columbia. Earthquakes are predicted, and it is thought that these may cause tsunamis.

a) Research and write a few sentences about tsunamis.

b) The equation of a tsunami is given by $d = 0.1s^2$, where d is the depth of the tsunami, in metres, and s is the speed of the wave, in metres per second. Draw a sketch of the tsunami wave.

Math Journal

Write a general function for a quadratic equation with vertex (p, q), and indicate how you would identify a translation, a reflection, and a stretch transformation.

Common Errors

- Students often write the vertex of $y = a(x - p)^2 + q$ as $(-p, q)$.

R_x Emphasize that the sign of p is opposite the sign inside the squared bracket.

- Students often mistake the value of q in the quadratic function $y = a(x - p)^2 + q$ as the y-intercept.

R_x Point out that q is the y-intercept only when $x = p$. Remind students, to find the y-intercept, substitute $x = 0$ and simplify to find the value of y.

- Students often mistake the value of p in the quadratic function $y = a(x - p)^2 + q$ as the x-intercept.

R_x Point out that students must substitute $y = 0$ and solve the resulting equation for x.

- When given the vertex and a point on the parabola, students often try to substitute the point into the equation first and get an equation in 3 variables. At this point they become confused.

R_x Stress the importance of first substituting the values of the vertex (p, q), and then, substituting the given point (x, y) to obtain a value for a.

Problem Levels of Difficulty

A: 1–78, 92   **B:** 79–87   **C:** 88–91

Assessing the Outcomes

Written Assignment

1. Without graphing, state the vertex, the axis of symmetry, and the direction of opening.

   a) $y = -(x - 3)^2 + 4$ b) $f(x) = 3(x + 4)^2 - 5$

2. *(grid paper)* Graph each parabola and state its equation.

   a) vertex at $(3, -4)$, through point $(4, -6)$

   b) axis of symmetry $x = -5$, congruent to $y = -4x^2$, x-intercepts -6 and -4

   c) vertex $(-1, 2)$, y-intercept -1

3. The height of a basketball thrown from the free-throw line is defined by $h(d) = -0.16(d - 3.35)^2 + 3.66$.

   a) If the centre of the hoop is 5.18 m away from the player, how tall is the basketball hoop, to the nearest tenth of a metre, if the player makes the shot?

   b) Sketch a graph of the path of the ball after the player makes the shot.

**Problem Solving:
Work Backward**

Student Text Pages
Pp. 122–123

Learning Outcome
• Use the Work Backward strategy to solve problems.

Prerequisite Skills
1. What are the first two terms of this sequence?
   ___, ___, 11, 14, 17, 21, ...   [5, 8]
2. Write an equation that has a solution $x = 2$.
   [Answers may vary. For example, $x + 3 = 5$, $x + 11 = 13$]

Mental Math
1. Multiply in two steps.

   a) 13×6.8 [88.4]   b) 0.8×51 [40.8]

   c) 3.7×18 [66.6]   d) 8.8×12 [105.6]

   e) 41×1.2 [49.2]   f) 9.2×16 [147.2]

2. Evaluate for $x = 0.5$ and $y = 0.1$.

   a) $x - 4y$ [0.1]   b) $2x + 3y$ [1.3]

   c) $2y - 5x$ [−2.3]   d) $x^2 + 3y$ [0.55]

   e) $-y^2 - 2x$ [−1.01]   f) $4x + 10y - 1$ [2]

Teaching Suggestions

Method 1
Read with the class the opening paragraph and the problem at the top of student text page 122. Have pairs of students try to solve the problem. Then, invite volunteers to present their results to the class. Encourage students to include any paper work they generated in solving the problem.

Read with the class the solution given on student text page 122. Have the students compare their solutions with the one on the student text page. As a class, discuss any similarities and differences.

Review with the class the steps of the problem solving process given down the left side of student text page 122.

Discuss the work backward procedure outlined at the top of student text page 123.

Method 2
Have pairs of students solve this problem.

Tony wants to buy running shoes that cost $172.50, including 7% PST and 8% GST. He has $60 saved already, and decides to save the rest in 4 equal weekly installments. How much does Tony have to save each week?

Ask:

What information are you asked to find?

What information are you given?

What must you calculate first, before you can work backward to find the answer?

When the students have completed the problem, have them discuss and compare their solutions with other pairs of students. Then, have volunteer pairs share their solution with the class. Ask:

How can you check your answer to the problem?

Review with the class the steps of the problem solving process given down the left side of student text page 122.

Discuss the work backward procedure outlined at the top of student text page 123.

Integrating Technology

Internet
Use the Internet to answer question 6 on student text page 123.

Work with other students on the Internet to solve problems, using web sites such as *http://forum.swarthmore.edu/mathmagic/* and Canada's SchoolNet Web Site at *http://www.schoolnet.ca*.

Use the Internet to find data to create problems that can be solved by working backward. Display your problems for classmates to solve.

Computer Data Bank
Use the databases in *MATHPOWER™11, Western Edition, Computer Data Bank* to find information to create problems that can be solved by working backward. Display your problems for classmates to solve.

Extension
Draw a diagram to help you and a partner explain the solution to this problem. When you have written a solution to this problem, compare and discuss your solution with another pair of students in the class. Discuss any similarities and differences in your solutions. Present your solution to the class.

On a long train journey between Edmonton and Toronto, Siu-Hyun slept sporadically. She first fell asleep after she had completed half the trip. She slept for a while and then woke up and found she still had to travel half the distance that she travelled while she was asleep. She tried to stay awake, but fell asleep again after she had gone one-half of the distance left to travel. When she awoke for the second time, she discovered she still had half the distance to go from when she had fallen asleep for the second time. For what fraction of the trip did she sleep?

Enrichment

Work with a partner and write a problem that can only be solved by working backward. Write the solution to your problem. Exchange your problem with that of another pair of students in the class. Solve the problem and discuss and compare your solutions with the other pair of students. Present your problem to the class.

Math Journal

Write a few sentences describing the problem solving strategy of working backward.

Common Errors

- Students often forget to reverse the operation when working backward to solve a problem.

- R_x Suggest that students write the operation(s) required to work forward in these types of problems, before they begin to calculate each answer.

Problem Levels of Difficulty

A: 1–5, 7, 8   **B:** 6

Assessing the Outcome

Group Evaluation: Presentation

Display the following problem and have the students work in small groups to solve it. Then, have them present their findings, encouraging them to be creative.

Janice is a school bus driver. One day, she picked up the bus at Brendan along with the initial number of students. First, she stopped at Quince, dropped off 5 students and picked up 2 students. Then, she stopped at Drimen, dropped off 3 students and picked up 11 students. Next, she stopped at Niven and dropped off 6 students. Finally, she dropped off 9 students at Ranger. How many students were on the bus to begin with?   [10]

Computer Data Bank

Jumping and Throwing Events

Microsoft Works for Windows users see *Part B*, and Microsoft Access users see *Part D*, of *MATHPOWER™ 11, Western Edition, Computer Data Bank Teacher's Resource*.

Student Text Page
P. 124

Learning Outcomes
- Display, find, sort, calculate, and analyze data in a computer database.
- Interpret quadratic functions.
- Model using quadratic functions.

Prerequisite Skills
1. Write a quadratic equation for the parabola with vertex (2, 3), passing through (4, 11).

$$[y = 2(x - 2)^2 + 3]$$

Getting Started Blackline Masters C-1, C-2, C-4 to C-6, and C-8

Teaching Suggestions
Students unfamiliar with computer databases and ClarisWorks would benefit from working through *Getting Started* Blackline Masters C-1, C-2, C-4 to C-6, and C-8, noted in the *Prerequisite Skills*, prior to doing any of these explorations. If they have not done so yet, you may wish to assign the *Getting Started* Blackline Masters to individuals, pairs, or small groups of students, to be completed over a period of time that allows students adequate computer time. The *Getting Started* Blackline Masters provide basic instruction in working with databases in ClarisWorks to meet the learning outcomes and provide students with an opportunity to use each of the seven databases. You may wish to delay assigning *Jumping and Throwing Events* until students have had an opportunity to work through *Getting Started* Blackline Masters C-1, C-2, C-4 to C-6, and C-8. Minimally, students should have *Getting Started* Blackline Masters C-1, C-2, C-4 to C-6, and C-8 available for reference.

Each exploration in *Jumping and Throwing Events* is independent of the other. One or both of the explorations can be assigned to individuals, pairs, or small groups of students, to be completed over a period of time that allows students adequate computer time. Up to 1.5 h will be needed by some students to complete both explorations.

When assigning the explorations, inform students if you expect
- any parts of the explorations to be printed off the computer
- handwritten or word-processed answers to questions that suggest a written response
- a journal-type response about what they have learned mathematically, about using databases, and/or about the subject matter of the database

Possible parts to assign for printing are a table to show the long jumps with the calculation fields and the values of *a* sorted from Exploration 1, and a table to show the percent increases sorted from greatest to least from Exploration 2.

1 Long Jump

In question 1, some students will sketch the start of the path at the origin; others will sketch the path symmetrically about the vertical axis. The responses that follow are for the sketches of the start of the path at the origin.

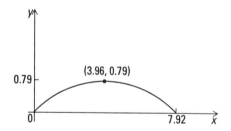

In question 2, *p* is half of the horizontal distance, and *q* is the maximum height.

In question 3, the value of *a* is found by substituting the values of *p* and *q* found in question 2 and values for *x* and *y* using a point on the parabola, such as (0, 0) or (7.92, 0), into $y = a(x - p)^2 + q$, and solving.

An efficient approach to question 4 is to analyze the equation solved for *a* in question 3.

$$y = a(x - p)^2 + q, \text{ where } y = 0, x = 0,$$
$$p = 3.96, \text{ and } q = 0.79$$
$$0 = a(0 - 3.96)^2 + 0.79$$
$$\frac{-0.79}{(-3.96)^2} = a$$
$$\frac{-0.79}{3.96^2} = a$$
$$\text{i.e., } \frac{-q}{p^2} = a$$

Then, use the Find feature with one comparison for *Event* Long Jump (*Getting Started* BLM C-5). Next, create a table displaying only the *Event* and *Winning Distance*, *m* fields (*Getting Started* BLM C-2). Then, create three calculation fields called *p*, *q*, and *a*, using the formulas that follow, to determine *p*, which is the winning distance less the distance that feet land ahead of the centre of gravity all divided by 2, and q, which is the height of a typical long jump, with a rounded to 3 decimal places (*Getting Started* BLM C-6). Finally, for each long jump, the values for p, q, and a can be substituted into $y = a(x - p)^2 + q$ to model the path of the jumper's centre of gravity.

('Winning Distance, m'–0.65)/2

0.79

ROUND($-$'q'/'p'^2,3)

In question 6, sort from least to greatest value of a (*Getting Started* BLM C-4).

2 Winning Distances

An efficient approach to question 1 is to show all the records and display them using Table 1. Then, use the Find feature with one comparison for *Event* event of interest (*Getting Started* BLM C-5). Next, sort the records chronologically, noting the winning distance or height of the first record (*Getting Started* BLM C-4). Then, create a table displaying only the *Event, Year,* and *Winning Distance, m* fields (*Getting Started* BLM C-2). Next, create a calculation field called *Percent Increase*, using the formula that follows, to express the difference between each winning distance or height and the first winning distance or height as a percent of the first winning distance or height, rounded to 2 decimal places (*Getting Started* BLM C-6). Finally, sort from greatest to least percent increase (*Getting Started* BLM C-4).

ROUND(('Winning Distance, m'$(x)/x$*100,2)
        where x is the winning distance or
        height the first year the event was held.
        For *Pole Vault, Men*, for example, x is 3.30.

An efficient approach to question 3 is to show all the records and use the Find feature with one comparison for *Event* next event of interest (*Getting Started* BLM C-5). Then, sort the records chronologically, noting the winning distance or height of the first record (*Getting Started* BLM C-4). Next, modify the formula for the *Percent Increase* field, replacing the winning distance or height the first year the event was held, x in the above formula, from the previous event with the winning distance or height the first year the event was held for the next event (*Getting Started* BLM C-6). Finally, sort from greatest to least percent increase (*Getting Started* BLM C-4).

Investigating Math

Algebra Tiles and Perfect Squares

Student Text Page
P. 125

Materials

Teacher's Resource Master 2 (1-cm grid paper), Teacher's Resource Master 3 (algebra tiles), algebra tiles, overhead algebra tiles, overhead projector

Learning Outcome

- Use algebra tiles to model perfect squares.

Prerequisite Skills

Write each expression in expanded form.

a) $(x - 1)^2$ $[x^2 - 2x + 1]$
b) $(x + 3)^2$ $[x^2 + 6x + 9]$
c) $(2x + 1)^2$ $[4x^2 + 4x + 1]$

Mental Math

1. Evaluate each expression for the given values of x.

a) $x^2 + 6$, $x = 1, 2, 3, 4$ [7, 10, 15, 22]
b) $4x^2 - 1$, $x = 0, -2, -4, -6$ [−1, 15, 63, 143]
c) $-x^2 + 3$, $x = 2, 5, 6, 10$ [−1, −22, −33, −97]
d) $x^2 + 3x$, $x = -3, 0, 3, 6$,   [0, 0, 18, 54]
e) $(x + 2)^2 + 7$, $x = -1, 0, 1, 2$ [8, 11, 16, 23]
f) $(x + 1)^2 - 4$, $x = -3, -2, -1, 0$ [0, −3, −4, −3]

2. Calculate.

a) 28×22 [616]   **b)** 75^2 [5625]
c) 76×74 [5624]   **d)** 19×11 [209]
e) 82×88 [7216]   **f)** 51×59 [3009]

Teaching Suggestions

(algebra tiles, 1-cm grid paper, overhead projector, overhead algebra tiles) Provide pairs of students with algebra tiles and grid paper. Review with the class the use and meaning of algebra tiles. Assign the investigations and suggest that the students draw diagrams of their algebra tile arrangements. Give the pairs of students opportunity to discuss and compare their results with other students in the class.

For Investigation 1, question 2, ask:

What does "expanded form" mean?

For Investigation 2, question 5, ask:

How does the number of x-tiles along the horizontal side compare to the number of x-tiles down the vertical side of the square?

If there are 10 x-tiles altogether, how many x-tiles are along each side of the square?

Elicit from the students that since the number of x-tiles is the same along the horizontal side as down the vertical side, then, if there are 10 x-tiles, 5 of them must be along the horizontal side and 5 must be down the vertical side.

Have volunteers present their results to the class. One student could use an overhead projector and overhead algebra tiles to demonstrate the results, while the other student explains each step of their results.

Extension

(1-cm grid paper) Draw diagrams to represent how you would use algebra tiles to complete the square of each of the following.

1. $3x^2 + 6x$
2. $5x^2 + 20x$
3. $2x^2 + 20x$

Math Journal

Write a few sentences explaining how to complete the square without using algebra tiles.

Assessing the Outcome

Written Assignment: Diagramming

(1-cm grid paper) Draw diagrams to represent the arrangements of algebra tiles you would use to complete the square.

1. $x^2 + 4x$
2. $x^2 + 10x$
3. $4x^2 + 4x$

3.5 Graphing $y = ax^2 + bx + c$ by Completing the Square

Student Text Pages
Pp. 126–134

Materials
graphing calculators, Teacher's Resource Master 1 (0.5-cm grid paper), overhead projector

Learning Outcomes
- Rewrite quadratic equations in general form as quadratic equations in standard form.
- Find the maximum or minimum values of quadratic functions by rewriting quadratic equations in general form as quadratic equations in standard form.
- Find the vertices of quadratic functions by rewriting quadratic equations in general form as quadratic equations in standard form.
- Solve problems involving quadratic functions given in general form by rewriting them as quadratic equations in standard form.

Prerequisite Skills

1. Write each expression as a perfect square.

a) $x^2 + 6x + 9$ $[(x + 3)^2]$

b) $x^2 + x + \frac{1}{4}$ $\left[\left(x + \frac{1}{2}\right)^2\right]$

c) $4x^2 - 4x + 1$ $[(2x - 1)^2]$

d) $9x^2 - 12x + 4$ $[(3x - 2)^2]$

2. Rewrite each equation in standard form.

a) $y = x^2 + 3x + 2$ $\left[y = \left(x + \frac{3}{2}\right)^2 - \frac{1}{4}\right]$

b) $y = x^2 - x - \frac{1}{4}$ $\left[y = \left(x - \frac{1}{2}\right)^2 - \frac{1}{2}\right]$

c) $y = -x^2 - 6x - 13$ $[y = -(x + 3)^2 - 4]$

d) $y = 4x^2 - 4x + 4$ $[y = (2x - 1)^2 + 3]$

3. Rewrite each equation in general form.

a) $y = (x - 1)^2 + 2$ $[y = x^2 - 2x + 3]$

b) $y = -(x + 1)^2 - 5$ $[y = -x^2 - 2x - 6]$

c) $y = (2x - 3)^2 + 1$ $[y = 4x^2 - 12x + 10]$

d) $y = -(3x - 2)^2 - 1$ $[y = -9x^2 + 12x - 5]$

Mental Math

1. Evaluate each expression for the given values of x.

a) $-x^2 - 2$, $x = -1, 0, 3, 4$ $[-3, -2, -11, -18]$

b) $x^2 + 3$, $x = -3, -2, -1, 0$ $[12, 7, 4, 3]$

c) $4x^2 - 1$, $x = -1, 0, 1, 2$ $[3, -1, 3, 15]$

d) $3x^2 + x$, $x = 0, 1, 2, 3$ $[0, 4, 14, 30]$

e) $(x + 5)^2 + 2$, $x = -3, -2, -1, 1$ $[6, 11, 18, 38]$

f) $(x - 10)^2 - 1$, $x = 1, 2, 3, 4$ $[80, 63, 48, 35]$

2. Calculate.

a) 33×370 $[12\ 210]$ b) 520×580 $[301\ 600]$

c) 17×130 $[2210]$ d) 79×710 $[56\ 090]$

e) 420×480 $[201\ 600]$ f) 610×69 $[42\ 090]$

Explore/Inquire Answers

Explore: Look for a Pattern

Trinomial, $x^2 + bx + c$	Value of b	Value of c	Factored Form, $(x - p)^2$	Value of p
$x^2 + 6x + 9$	6	9	$(x + 3)^2$	-3
$x^2 + 2x + 1$	2	1	$(x + 1)^2$	-1
$x^2 + 10x + 25$	10	25	$(x + 5)^2$	-5
$x^2 - 2x + 1$	-2	1	$(x - 1)^2$	1
$x^2 - 8x + 16$	-8	16	$(x - 4)^2$	4
$x^2 - 14x + 49$	-14	49	$(x - 7)^2$	7

Inquire

1. a) Half the value of b and square it.

b) The negative of half the value of b.

2. a) $x^2 + 12x + 36 = (x + 6)^2$, -6

b) $x^2 + 16x + 64 = (x + 8)^2$, -8

c) $x^2 - 20x + 100$, $(x - 10)^2$, 10

d) $x^2 - 4x + 4$, $(x - 2)^2$, 2

e) $x^2 + 1.6x + 0.64$, $(x + 0.8)^2$, -0.8

f) $x^2 - 3x + 2.25 = (x - 1.5)^2$, 1.5

Teaching Suggestions

(0.5-cm grid paper, overhead projector) Discuss with the students the opening paragraph on student text page 126. Ask:

How can you tell that the graph given by the quadratic function $h(t) = -10t^2 + 300t + 9750$ is parabolic in shape?

In what direction will the parabola given by the quadratic function $h(t) = -10t^2 + 300t + 9750$ open?

What does it mean to "analyze a quadratic function"?

The standard form of a quadratic function is more convenient for analysis than the general form of a quadratic function. Explain.

Look for answers such as the following: The function $h(t) = -10t^2 + 300t + 9750$ is quadratic in nature with $a = -10$, $b = 300$, and $c = 9750$; The parabola given by the function $h(t) = -10t^2 + 300t + 9750$ opens upward because the coefficient of the term in x^2 is negative; To analyze a function means to describe the shape of the function by indicating whether the parabola is congruent to the graph of $y = x^2$, any transformations that have occurred, the intercepts, the turning point and whether it is a maximum or a minimum, and whether the graph opens upward or downward; The standard form is more convenient because all of the basic characteristics of the curve can be determined by inspecting the function.

Assign the Explore section and the Inquire questions to pairs of students. Have the students copy and complete the table in the Explore section on student text page 126. Ask:
What is the value of a in each of the trinomials given in the table?

Before the class begins question 1, ask:
What are the steps for writing an expression such as ax² + bx + c as a perfect square binomial?

For part b) of question 1, ensure that the students realize that to find the value of p for an expression such as $(x + a)^2$, they must rewrite the expression inside the bracket so that the sign is negative. Thus, $(x + 5)^2$ must be rewritten as $[x - (-5)]^2$, so that $p = -5$.

Have pairs of volunteers present their results to the class.

Discuss with the students the method given on student text page 127 for graphing a quadratic function using a table of values. Point out that when choosing values of x to substitute into the function to find y, it is often best to start with the value $x = 0$, and then choose values on either side of 0, such as 1, -1, 2, -2, etc.

Review with the class teaching examples 1 and 2 on student text pages 127 and 128. Provide pairs of students with graph paper and give them time to sketch the graphs for themselves. Discuss the difference between a graph and a sketch, i.e., a sketch is a more generalized picture of a curve, and only has to give the general characteristics of the curve, whereas a graph requires a table of values so that exact points can be plotted.

Point out to the students the importance of checking the rewritten functions. Discuss the two methods of checking given after teaching example 2 and in teaching example 3 on student text pages 128 and 129.

Have pairs of students work through teaching examples 4 to 6 on student text pages 129 and 130. Discuss the importance of symmetry in the parabolic curve. Give the students an opportunity to sketch the graphs of the parabolic functions in teaching examples 4 and 5 and have volunteers present their results to the class. Provide an overhead projector in case students wish to present their parabolic sketches to the class.

Sample Solution

Page 134, question 88

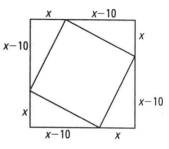

Side length of outer square is 10 cm. If one section of a side has length x cm, then the other section has length $(x - 10)$ cm. Using the Pythagorean Theorem, the side length of the inner square is $\sqrt{x^2 + (x - 10)^2}$.

Thus, the area of the inner square, A, is
$$A = \left(\sqrt{x^2 + (x - 10)^2}\right)^2$$
$$= x^2 + (x - 10)^2$$
$$= x^2 + x^2 - 20x + 100$$
$$= 2x^2 - 20x + 100$$

The equation for the area is quadratic, and the coefficient of x^2 is positive. Thus, the vertex represents the point at which the minimum area occurs.
$$A = 2x^2 - 20x + 100$$
$$= 2(x^2 - 10x) + 100$$
$$= 2(x^2 - 10x + 25 - 25) + 100$$
$$= 2(x^2 - 10x + 25) - 50 + 100$$
$$= 2(x - 5)^2 + 50$$

The minimum area is 50 cm² and occurs when $x = 5$ cm.

Pattern Power Answer

When you read aloud the numbers in one line, the words describe the digits and their frequency in the previous line. For example,
For line 2 read one one. There is one 1 in line 1.
For line 3 read two one. There are two 1's in line 2.
For line 4 read one two one one. There is one 2 and two 1's in line 3.
For line 5 read one one one two two one.
There is one 1, one 2, and two 1's in line 4.
The next row of the table is 1113213211.

Integrating Technology

Graphing Calculators

How would you use your graphing calculator to find the coordinates of the vertex of a quadratic function as shown in Solution 2 of teaching example 3 on student text page 129?

On a TI-83, use the Maximum operation, which is the fourth item when the CALC (i.e., 2nd TRACE) key is pressed. (The Minimum operation is the third item.) Press the Y= key and enter the right side of the equation.

Press the ZOOM key and the 6 key to select Zstandard. Press the CALC (i.e., 2nd TRACE) key and the 4 key to select maximum.

Use the arrow keys to move the cursor slightly to the left of the maximum, and press the ENTER key to define the Left Bound.

Use the arrow keys to move the cursor onto the maximum, and press the ENTER key to define your guess. Read the coordinates of the vertex given as $x=$ and $y=$.

How would you use a graphing calculator to create the graph for teaching example 4 on student text page 129 without rewriting the equation in standard form? To determine a suitable viewing window, consider that the graph opens down, $h(0) = 9750$, and neither height nor time can be negative. Try 0 and 50 as the Xmin and Xmax, and 0 and 14 000 as the Ymin and Ymax, with suitable scales.

Use your graphing calculator to graph the functions and find their x-intercepts in questions 64 to 69 on student text page 131.

Use your graphing calculator and the method of Solution 2 in teaching example 3 to find some of the maximum values in the questions on student text pages 132 and 133.

In question 97 on student text page 134, you can either complete the square or use what is known from the general form (the graph opens down and $y = -52$ when $x = 0$) and guess and check to determine a suitable viewing window to see the parabolic shape. After viewing the parabolic shape in a viewing window, such as -1 and 5 as the Xmin and Xmax, and -200 and -50 as the Ymin and Ymax, with suitable scales, select a portion of the graph by changing the Xmin, Xmax, and Xscl values to meet each required condition.

See *MATHPOWER™ 11, Western Edition, Blackline Masters* pages 69 to 71 for Finding Maximums or Minimums.

Calculator-Based Laboratories

Collect your own real data, using a portable data collection device, a CBL (Calculator-Based Laboratory), and plot the data on a graphing calculator.

Internet

Use the Internet to answer questions 89 and 98 on student text page 134.

Extension

Write an example of completing the square for a quadratic function that involves fractional or decimal values of a. Compare your example with those of your classmates, and discuss any similarities or differences.

Math Journal

Describe how to rewrite a quadratic function in general form as a quadratic function in standard form, and use it to sketch the graph of the quadratic function.

Common Errors

• Students often forget to subtract the square that is added to the expression as a consequence of completing the square.

R_x Remind the students that when they are rewriting a quadratic expression by completing the square, each subsequent expression must be equivalent to the original expression. Encourage them to check their work by expanding and collecting terms to see if the expression in each step is still the same as the one they started with.

Problem Levels of Difficulty

A: 1–76, 98, 99   **B:** 77–89, 91   **C:** 90, 92–97

Assessing the Outcomes

Written Assignment

1. Write each function in the form $y = a(x - p)^2 + q$. Sketch the graph, showing the coordinates of the vertex, the equation of the axis of symmetry, and the coordinates of two other points on the graph.

   a) $y = x^2 + 4x + 3$ **b)** $y = -x^2 + 25x + 1$

2. Find the coordinates of the vertex.

   a) $y = -x^2 + 6x - 1$ **b)** $y = 2x^2 - 4x + 1$

3. Graph each function. Find any x-intercepts. Round to the nearest tenth, if necessary.

   a) $y = 4x^2 + 3x - 2$ **b)** $y = -2x^2 - x + 10$

Investigating Math

Exploring Patterns in $y = ax^2 + bx + c$

Student Text Page
P. 135

Materials
graphing calculators

Learning Outcomes
- Determine the axes of symmetry of quadratic functions of the form $y = a^2x + bx + c$ from the values of a and b.
- Determine the values of p of quadratic equations of the form $y = a(x - p)^2 + q$ from the values of a and b of quadratic functions of the form $y = a^2x + bx + c$.

Prerequisite Skills
Draw the axis or axes of symmetry, if any, of each letter of the alphabet.

a) M [M]   b) C [C]

c) H [H]   d) Z   [none]

Mental Math
1. Multiply in two steps.

a) 62×24	[1488]	b) 73×16	[1168]
c) 49×8	[392]	d) 65×13	[845]
e) 96×12	[1152]	f) 58×22	[1276]

2. Evaluate for $x = -2$, $y = -1$, and $z = 5$.

a) $x + y + z$	[2]	b) $-x - y + 2z$	[13]
c) $2y + x - 3z$	[−19]	d) $x^2 + 2y + 5z$	[27]
e) $z^2 + 4x - y^2$	[16]	f) $2x - 3y^2 + z$	[−2]

Teaching Suggestions
Have pairs of students work on the explorations. Give them opportunity to discuss and compare their results with other students in the class. Remind students to be vigilant in checking their work as they go along. Each expression should be equivalent to the previous expression. Thus, expanding can be used to check each expression. Invite volunteers to present their results to the class.

Integrating Technology

Graphing Calculators
Use your graphing calculator to graph the equations in question 1 of Investigation 1 in order to find the axes of symmetry.

Extension
Two forms of the quadratic function are $y = ax^2 + bx + c$ and $y = a(x - p)^2 + q$. Show algebraically that the axis of symmetry is given by $x = -\dfrac{b}{2a}$.

Assessing the Outcomes

Written Assignment

1. Without graphing, write an equation for the axis of symmetry for each of the following.

a) $y = x^2 + 6x$ b) $y = -x^2 - 10x + 3$
c) $y = 4x^2 + 24x + 5$ d) $y = -3x^2 - 15x$

2. Without completing the square, rewrite each of the following equations in standard form.

a) $y = x^2 - 9x$ b) $y = -x^2 + 18x + 2$
c) $F(x) = 5x^2 + 30x - 1$ d) $f(x) = -7x^2 - 21x - 11$

Technology

Graphing Calculators and Parabolic Functions

Student Text Pages
Pp. 136–137

Materials
scientific (or graphing) calculators

Learning Outcome
- Compare graphing quadratic functions using a graphing calculator and manually.

Prerequisite Skills

1. Show the key strokes for each.

a) $y = -(x - 3)^2 + 4$ [Y = (−) (x − 3)^2 + 4]

b) $y = 0.5(x + 2.5)^2 - 0.75$ [Y = .5(x + 2.5)^2 − .75]

2. Describe the graph of each function in question 1.

[a) opens down, axis of symmetry $x = 3$, vertex (3, 4), maximum is 4 at $x = 3$, translated 3 units to the right and 4 units up relative to $y = -x^2$

b) opens up, axis of symmetry $x = -2.5$, vertex $(-2.5, -0.75)$, minimum is -0.75 at $x = -2.5$, translated 2.5 units left and 0.75 units down, and shrunk vertically by a scale factor of 0.5 relative to $y = x^2$]

Teaching Suggestions

Students use the skills discussed earlier in this chapter for graphing quadratic functions and using the Maximum, Minimum, Zero, and Value operations. On a TI-83, these operations are found when the CALC (i.e., 2nd TRACE) key is pressed. They are used when the values cannot be read directly from the graph.

In the questions on student text page 137, the coefficients and constants are increasingly awkward. In some cases, constructing a table of values would be very time consuming, and rearranging the equation into standard form, next to impossible.

While graphing calculators ease many burdens, they sometimes give only approximate coordinates, as was the case in teaching example 3 on student text page 128 of Section 3.5.

While the equations in question 6 on student text page 136 and the problems on student text page 137 are extremely awkward to graph manually, the standard viewing window on a graphing calculator does not provide a useful graph for several of the equations, and the Zoom Fit window is only useful where the maximum or minimum occurs between the last used Xmin and Xmax values.

In question 6 e) on student text page 136, for example, you know the graph opens up and $f(0) = 0$. In the standard viewing window, the graph appears to be a line going up to the right through the origin. This suggests that the Zoom Fit window will not help, and a much larger viewing window is needed. Since the graph opens up, the viewing window should focus on the third quadrant. Try -700 and 100 as the Xmin and Xmax, and -700 and 100 as the Ymin and Ymax, with suitable scales.

In question 6 g) on student text page 136, for example, you know the graph opens down and y is -25 when x is 0. Nothing appears in the standard viewing window. The Zoom Fit window may or may not be useful. Try it. It works. Alternatively, try a larger viewing window such as -100 and 100 as the Xmin and Xmax, and -100 and 100 as the Ymin and Ymax, with suitable scales. This shows a parabola below the x-axis, symmetric about the y-axis. Now the viewing window could be reduced to focus on the area of interest. Try -20 and 20 as the Xmin and Xmax, and -100 and 0 as the Ymin and Ymax, with suitable scales.

In question 2 on student text page 137, for example, you know the graph opens down, $s(0) = 0$, and time cannot be negative. In the standard viewing window, the graph appears to be a slight curve, with a maximum close to, but to the right of, the origin. This could be used, and it suggests that the Zoom Fit window could be used, but a more suitable viewing window would take into account that the graph opens down, with a maximum very near the x-axis, and time cannot be negative. Try 0 and 10 as the Xmin and Xmax, and 0.05 and 0.1 as the Ymin and Ymax, with suitable scales.

Common Errors

- Some students might prefer not to clear previous equations, type over when possible, and use the INS (i.e., 2nd DEL) key to insert when needed to enter the next equations when they are graphing many equations. This can lead to errors.

R_x Suggest that the students always check what they have entered before pressing the keys to create the graph. If the students are getting errors frequently, they should clear between entering equations.

Assessing the Outcome

Written Assignment

Create an example of a quadratic equation that you would definitely prefer to graph using a graphing calculator and an example of one you would just as soon sketch manually, and explain why.

3.6 Problem Solving: Use a Table or Spreadsheet

Student Text Pages
Pp. 138–139

Learning Outcome
- Use a Table or Spreadsheet strategy to solve problems.

Prerequisite Skills
1. Construct a table of values for each relation. Use the domain {−3, −2, −1, 0, 1, 2, 3}.

a) $y = −3x + 2$
b) $2x + y = −5$

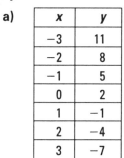

a)

x	y
−3	11
−2	8
−1	5
0	2
1	−1
2	−4
3	−7

b)

x	y
−3	1
−2	−1
−1	−3
0	−5
1	−7
2	−9
3	−11

2. Evaluate each expression for the given values of the variables.

a) $x − 3y + 5$; $x = 2, y = −1$ [10]
b) $2x + 7y − 11$; $x = −1, y = 5$ [22]
c) $−5x + y^2$; $x = 1.5, y = 0.5$ [−7.25]
d) $x^2 + 2x − 3y$; $x = −1, y = −3$ [8]

Mental Math
1. Multiply in two steps.

a) $97 × 1.9$ [184.3]   b) $15 × 2.9$ [43.5]
c) $0.23 × 61$ [14.03]   d) $4.9 × 17$ [83.3]
e) $7.3 × 11$ [80.3]   f) $32 × 6.1$ [195.2]

2. Evaluate for $x = 1, y = 3$, and $z = −1$.

a) $x + 2y − z$ [8]   b) $2x − y − z$ [0]
c) $5y + x + z$ [15]   d) $3y − 5z$ [14]
e) $2x − 3y + 4z$ [−11]   f) $x^2 + 2z$ [−1]

Teaching Suggestions
Read with the class the problem given on student text page 138. Ask:

What is a spreadsheet?

What is the purpose of a table or spreadsheet?

Then, read with the class the solution to the problem.
Challenge pairs of students to set up a spreadsheet to solve the problem. Ask:

What expression would you insert into the cell to calculate the profit each month?

What expression would you insert into the cell to calculate the net financial position each month?

Once they have set up the spreadsheet and filled it in, have them print the spreadsheet and compare it with the solution on student text page 138. Give the students an opportunity to compare and discuss their printed results.

Review with the class the problem solving steps down the left side of the student text pages.

Integrating Technology

Computer Spreadsheets

How would you create the table on student text page 138 using a computer spreadsheet? You could enter the headings and the first row of data, and then, create formulas to complete the columns for the other 19 rows. To complete the *Month* column, enter the formula =(A2+1) in cell A3, copy it, and paste it in each cell to A21. To complete the *Profit ($)* column, enter the formula =(B2+100) in cell B3, copy it, and paste it in each cell to B21. To complete the *Net Financial Position ($)* column, enter the formula =(C2+B3) in cell C3, copy it, and paste it in each cell to C21.

Use a computer spreadsheet to create the tables in the questions on student text page 139.

Graphing Calculators

How would you create the quadratic function on student text page 138 with your graphing calculator? The values from the table facilitate selecting values for the viewing window. On a TI-83, press the Y= key and enter the right side of the equation. Press the WINDOW key, and enter 0 and 20 as Xmin and Xmax, −4000 and 4000 as Ymin and Ymax, with suitable scales. Then, press the GRAPH key.

Internet

Work with other students on the Internet to solve problems, using web sites such as *http://forum.swarthmore.edu/mathmagic/* and Canada's SchoolNet Web Site at *http://www.schoolnet.ca*.

Enrichment

Research careers that you think require the use of spreadsheets. Write a short description of such a career, including how the spreadsheet would be used, and present it to your class.

Math Journal

Write a few sentences describing the usefulness of using a table or a spreadsheet to solve a problem.

Problem Levels of Difficulty

A: 1–4, 9   **B:** 5–7   **C:** 8

Assessing the Outcomes

Observation

You may want to consider some of these questions as the students discuss their skills with tables or spreadsheets.
- Do the students understand the problem?
- Are the students able to organize the data?
- Do the students know how to use a spreadsheet?
- Do the students work well together?

Connecting Math and History

Galileo's Experiments on Gravity

Student Text Pages
Pp. 140–142

Learning Outcome
- Use patterned thinking to find the value of the force of gravity, g.

Prerequisite Skills
1. Rewrite each formula in terms of the indicated variable.

a) $P = 2l + 2w$; w $\qquad$ $\left[w = \dfrac{P - 2l}{2} \right]$

b) $S = 4\pi r^2$; r $\qquad$ $\left[r = \sqrt{\dfrac{S}{4\pi}} \right]$

c) $V = \dfrac{4}{3}\pi r^3$; r $\qquad$ $\left[r = \sqrt[3]{\dfrac{3S}{4\pi}} \right]$

2. a) Draw the next two diagrams.

Diagram 1 $\quad$ Diagram 2 $\quad$ Diagram 3

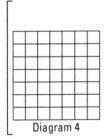 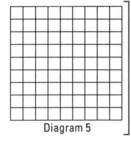

Diagram 4 $\qquad$ Diagram 5

b) How many unit squares are in Diagram 10? $\qquad$ [361]

3. Use the diagram to write a ratio for each of the following.

a) sin A $\qquad$ $\left[\dfrac{CB}{AC} \right]$

b) cos C $\qquad$ $\left[\dfrac{CB}{AC} \right]$

c) tan A $\qquad$ $\left[\dfrac{CB}{AB} \right]$

4. Solve each equation.

a) $3x + 7 = 5x - 11$ $\quad$ [9] $\qquad$ **b)** $15x = 7.5$ $\quad$ [0.5]

c) $\dfrac{3x - 1}{2} = \dfrac{2x}{3}$ $\quad$ [0.6] $\qquad$ **d)** $-2x - 5 = 9$ $\quad$ [−7]

Mental Math

1. Multiply in two steps.

a) 83×9 $\quad$ [747] $\qquad$ **b)** 48×25 $\quad$ [1200]

c) 64×14 $\quad$ [896] $\qquad$ **d)** 62×31 $\quad$ [1922]

e) 11×36 $\quad$ [396] $\qquad$ **f)** 91×18 $\quad$ [1638]

2. Evaluate for $x = -3$ and $y = 5$.

a) $-x + y$ $\quad$ [8] $\qquad$ **b)** $7x + 8y$ $\quad$ [19]

c) $5y - 4x$ $\quad$ [37] $\qquad$ **d)** $2x - 3y + 1$ $\quad$ [−20]

e) $x^2 - 2y - 3$ $\quad$ [−4] $\qquad$ **f)** $-x^2 - y^2$ $\quad$ [−34]

Teaching Suggestions

Assign these explorations to small groups of students. Give them an opportunity to discuss and compare their results. Ask:

What is the difference between velocity and acceleration?

Have volunteers present their results to the class.

Integrating Technology

Internet

Use the Internet to answer question 6 of Exploration 1 and to research Galileo's experiments on gravity, using web sites such as *http://www-groups.dcs.st-and.ac.uk/~history/*.

Enrichment

Research the terminal velocity of other planets of our solar system. Which planet has the greatest terminal velocity? the least terminal velocity?

Display any interesting information you find on a class bulletin board.

Assessing the Outcome

Observation

Some skills to watch for in this lesson are:
- Do the students show patience for a lengthy assignment?
- Do the pairs co-operate to help make the work easier?
- Are the students willing to help other students who do not understand parts of the explorations?

Career Connection

Volcanology

Student Text Page
P. 143

Materials
graphing calculators

Learning Outcomes
- Model height over time using a quadratic function.
- Gain insight into careers in the field of volcanology.

Prerequisite Skills
a) Graph $h(t) = -3t^2 + 40t$, where h is the height in metres and t is the time in seconds.

b) Describe the viewing window you used.

[Answers may vary. For example, Xmin = 0, Xmax = 15, Ymin = 0, and Ymax = 150]

c) Find the maximum height reached, to the nearest tenth of a metre. [133.3 m]

d) At what time, to the nearest tenth of a second, was the maximum height reached? [6.7 s]

Mental Math

1. Evaluate each expression for the given values of x.

a) $x^2 - 2$, $x = 1, 3, 5, 7$ [−1, 7, 23, 47]

b) $3x^2 + 1$, $x = 2, 3, 4, 5$ [13, 28, 49, 76]

c) $-x^2 + 4$, $x = -1, 0, 1, 2$ [3, 4, 3, 0]

d) $x^2 - 2x$, $x = 0, 1, 2, 3$ [0, −1, 0, 3]

e) $(x + 3)^2 + 2$, $x = -3, -2, -1, 0$ [2, 3, 6, 11]

f) $(x - 1)^2 - 1$, $x = -5, -6, -7, -8$ [35, 48, 63, 80]

2. Calculate.

a) 4.9×41 [200.9]   b) 36×3.4 [122.4]

c) 24×2.6 [62.4]   d) 9.3×97 [902.1]

e) 88×8.2 [721.6]   f) 16×1.4 [22.4]

Teaching Suggestions

Introduce the topic with a discussion about volcanoes. Ask:

Does anyone remember the last time a volcanic eruption was reported in the news?

Where did the eruption take place?

Does anyone know about any volcanic eruptions in Canada?

Where are the likeliest places in North America for a volcanologist to live?

Discuss with the class the introduction on student text page 143 and then, assign the explorations to pairs or small groups.

Suggest students consider from where the lava is ejected and where it lands in order to answer parts d) and e) of Question 2 in Exploration 1.

Integrating Technology

Internet

Use the Internet to research the information for Explorations 1 and 2.

Graphing Calculator

Use a graphing calculator to graph the quadratic function in Exploration 1.

Cross-Discipline

Geography Research the answers to the following questions.

Have you taken any geography courses in which you studied volcanoes?

How are volcanoes formed?

What causes volcanoes to erupt?

Environmental Studies Research the answers to the following questions.

Have you taken any environmental studies courses in which you studied volcanoes?

What are the effects of volcanic eruptions on the immediate environment? the greater environment?

Assessing the Outcomes

Journal

- Write about the most interesting thing you learned about volcanology.
- Write about what else you would like to know about volcanology, and how you could find the information.

Review

Learning Outcome

• Review the skills and concepts in Chapter 3.

Using the Review

Have the students work independently to complete the Review.

Meeting in small groups, the students can mark and discuss the work.

Groups can then share their solutions and report any questions that caused them difficulty. Discuss these questions with the class.

Reteaching Suggestions

Assign the questions to the students. Direct the students to compare their answers with those of other students and report any questions that caused them difficulty. Discuss these questions with the class. For those students who are having difficulty with the chapter material, form small groups and use the following exercises.

Graphing $y = x^2 + q$, $y = ax^2$, and $y = ax^2 + q$

Sketch the graph of each parabola and state
a) *the direction of opening*
b) *the coordinates of the vertex*
c) *the equation of the axis of symmetry*
d) *the domain and the range*
e) *the maximum or minimum*
f) *any intercepts*

1. $y = x^2 - 3$ **2.** $y = -x^2 + 1.5$
3. $y = 2x^2 + 5$ **4.** $y = -5x^2 - 1$

Write an equation for a parabola with
5. vertex $(0, 0)$ and $a = 5$
6. vertex $(0, -1)$ and $a = -2$
7. vertex $(0, 2)$ and passing through $(1, 4)$

Graphing $y = a(x - p)^2 + q$

Without sketching each parabola, state
a) *the direction of opening*
b) *how the parabola is stretched or shrunk, if at all*
c) *the coordinates of the vertex*
d) *the equation of the axis of symmetry*
e) *the domain and the range*
f) *the maximum or minimum*

1. $y = (x - 5)^2 + 1$
2. $y = -(x + 1)^2 - 5$
3. $y = 2(x + 3)^2 + 1.5$

Write an equation that defines each parabola.
4. vertex $(4, 3)$, $a = -3$
5. congruent to $y = x^2$, opens down, vertex $(-1, 1)$
6. $a = \frac{1}{2}$, axis of symmetry $x = 2$, maximum value 3

Graphing $y = ax^2 + bx + c$ by Completing the Square

Find the value of c that will make each expression a perfect square trinomial.
1. $x^2 + 9x + c$ **2.** $x^2 - 7x + c$

Write each function in the form $y = a(x - p)^2 + q$. Sketch the graph, showing the coordinates of the vertex, the equation of the axis of symmetry, and the coordinates of two other points on the graph.
3. $y = x^2 + 9x + 2$ **4.** $y = -x^2 + 4x + 3$

Find the coordinates of the vertex.
5. $y = -x^2 + 5x - 1$ **6.** $y = 3x^2 - 2x + 5$

Graph each function. Find any x-intercepts. Round to the nearest tenth, if necessary.
7. $y = 3x^2 + 5x - 2$ **8.** $y = -2x^2 + x + 11$

Answers to Reteaching Suggestions

Graphing $y = x^2 + q$, $y = ax^2$, and $y = ax^2 + q$

1. a) up   **b)** $(0, -3)$ **c)** $x = 0$
     d) $D = \{x \in R\}$, $R = \{y \mid y \geq -3, y \in R\}$
     e) min -3 **f)** $(\sqrt{3}, 0), (-\sqrt{3}, 0), (0, -3)$

2. a) down   **b)** $(0, 1.5)$ **c)** $x = 0$
     d) $D = \{x \in R\}$, $R = \{y \mid y \leq 1.5, y \in R\}$
     e) max 1.5 **f)** $\left(\frac{\sqrt{6}}{2}, 0\right), \left(-\frac{\sqrt{6}}{2}, 0\right), (0, 1.5)$

3. a) up   **b)** $(0, 5)$ **c)** $x = 0$
     d) $D = \{x \in R\}$, $R = \{y \mid y \geq 5, y \in R\}$
     e) min 5   **f)** $(0, 5)$

4. a) down   **b)** $(0, -1)$ **c)** $x = 0$
     d) $D = \{x \in R\}$, $R = \{y \mid y \leq -1, y \in R\}$
     e) max -1 **f)** $(0, -1)$

5. $y = 5x^2$ **6.** $y = -2x^2 - 1$ **7.** $y = 2x^2 + 2$

Graphing $y = a(x - p)^2 + q$

1. a) up   **b)** none   **c)** $(5, 1)$
     d) $x = 5$ **e)** $D = \{x \in R\}$, $R = \{y \mid y \geq 1, y \in R\}$
     f) min 1

2. a) down   **b)** none   **c)** $(-1, -5)$
     d) $x = -1$ **e)** $D = \{x \in R\}$, $R = \{y \mid y \leq -5, y \in R\}$
     f) max -5

3. a) up   **b)** shrink   **c)** $(-3, 1.5)$
     d) $x = -3$ **e)** $D = \{x \in R\}$, $R = \{y \mid y \geq 1.5, y \in R\}$
     f) min 1.5

4. $y = -3(x - 4)^2 + 3$

5. $y = -(x + 1)^2 + 1$

6. $y = -\frac{1}{2}(x - 2)^2 + 3$

Graphing $y = ax^2 + bx + c$ by Completing the Square

1. $\frac{81}{4}$ **2.** $\frac{49}{4}$

3. $y = \left(x + \frac{9}{2}\right)^2 - \frac{73}{4}$; $V\left(\frac{-9}{2}, \frac{-73}{4}\right)$; $x = -\frac{9}{2}$;

   $(0, 2), (1, 12)$

4. $y = -(x - 2)^2 + 7$; $V(2, 7)$; $x = 2$; $(0, 3), (4, 3)$

5. $\left(\frac{5}{2}, \frac{21}{4}\right)$ **6.** $\left(\frac{1}{3}, \frac{14}{3}\right)$

7. $-2, \frac{1}{3}$ **8.** $2.6, -2.1$

Exploring Math

Analyzing a Game

(coloured counters) Provide pairs of students with 9 counters and have them play the game. Ensure that the student pairs fully understand the rules of the game.

Ask:

What does the word "strategy" mean?

Where do you use strategies?

Encourage the students to write their scores down, so that they can use their results to explain their reasoning.

After a time, suggest that pairs of students compare and discuss their results. Then, have volunteers present their results to the class.

Chapter Check

Student Text Page
P. 146

Learning Outcome
- Evaluate the skills and concepts in Chapter 3.

Assessing the Outcome

If you assign the Chapter Check as a student assessment, look for the following:
- Do they understand the concept of a quadratic function?
- Do they understand the relation between a quadratic function and a parabolic curve?
- Can they analyze a quadratic function to give the characteristics of the parabola represented by the quadratic function?
- Can they draw the graph of a quadratic function without constructing a table of values?

Problem Solving

Student Text Page
P. 147

Materials
Teacher's Resource Master 1 (0.5-cm grid paper)

Learning Outcome
- Use problem solving strategies to solve problems.

Using the Strategies

The problems on this page allow the students to use the problem solving strategies discussed in Chapters 1 to 3. These strategies are
- Use a Diagram
- Use a Data Bank
- Solve Fermi Problems
- Solve a Simpler Problem
- Use Logic
- Look for a Pattern
- Guess and Check
- Work Backward
- Use a Table or Spreadsheet

Teaching Suggestions

(0.5-cm grid paper) Provide pairs of students with grid paper and assign the questions.

For question 6, ask:

What formula can you use to find the distance?

For question 8, ask:

What does it mean when a number is written in standard form?

For question 10, ask:

What is the mean of a set of numbers?

If you know the mean of a set of numbers, what do you know about the sum of the numbers in the set?

Give the students an opportunity to discuss and compare their results. Have volunteers present their results to the class.

Assessing the Outcome

Observation

As you make your problem solving assessment of each student, consider the following:
- Do they follow the four-step method?
- Do they choose the appropriate strategy to solve each problem?
- Do they consider a variety of strategies?
- Can they implement the strategy correctly?
- Do they attempt all the questions?

CHAPTER 3

Student Text Answers

Chapter Opener p. 99
Height: 0, 45, 80, 105, 120, 125, 120, 105, 80, 45, 0
1. 125 m **2.** 5 s **3.** 10 s **4.** 40 km

Getting Started pp. 100–101
Number Games
1. c) 40 **d)** 40, 2000; 41, 1999; 42, 1996;
43, 1991; 44, 1984, 39, 1999; 38, 1996; 37, 1991;
36, 1984 **f)** no **g)** $y = -x^2 + 80x + 400$
2. c) 35 **d)** 35, 75; 36, 76; 37, 79; 38, 84;
39, 91; 34, 76; 33, 79; 32, 84; 31, 91
f) no **g)** $y = x^2 - 70x + 1300$
3. a) $m = 100 - n^2 + 50n$; The equation gives a
greater amount of money, \$725, for $n = 25$.
b) $m = 400 + n^2 - 20n$; The equation has no
maximum. Since there is no limit on the value of n,
there is no limit on the value of m.

Warm Up
1. Domain: {1, 2, 3, 4, 5}; Range: {2, 4, 6, 8, 10}
2. Domain: {5, 8, 12, 15, 28}; Range: {4, 7, 11, 14, 27}
3. Domain: {1, 4, 8, 22, 53}; Range: {1}
4. function; Domain: R; Range: $y \geq 0$
5. not a function; Domain: $x \geq 0$; Range: R
6. a) -4 **b)** -1 **c)** -7 **d)** 2
e) -19 **f)** -2 **g)** 0.5 **h)** 71
7. a) 0 **b)** 1 **c)** 1 **d)** 9
e) 9 **f)** $\frac{1}{4}$ **g)** $\frac{1}{4}$ **h)** 2.25
8. a) -1 **b)** 4 **c)** -4 **d)** 11
e) 44 **f)** $\frac{5}{4}$ **g)** -4 **h)** 15.25
9. $x^2 - 3x$ **10.** $x^2 + 2x$ **11.** $x^2 - 3x$
12. $x^2 + 4x$ **13.** $x^2 - \frac{1}{2}x$ **14.** $x^2 - \frac{5}{2}x$
15. $x^2 - 14x$ **16.** $x^2 - 3x$ **17.** $x^2 - 6x$
18. $x^2 + 10x$ **19.** $x^2 + 0.3x$ **20.** $x^2 + 60x$
21. $x^2 - \frac{5}{2}x$ **22.** $x^2 - 30x$
23. 1 **24.** 2 **25.** 2
26. 3 **27.** 2 **28.** 4

Mental Math
Evaluating Expressions
1. 7, 19, 7, 19 **2.** 1, 1, 17, 17
3. 2, 0, 6, 42 **4.** 1, -3, -3, -24
5. 4, 7, 15, -1.25 **6.** -3, 3, 3, 9
7. 10, 2, 26, 5 **8.** -3, -4, 0, 5

Multiplying in Two Steps
1. 220 **2.** 609 **3.** 324
4. 143 **5.** 900 **6.** 1005
7. 377 **8.** 650 **9.** 2952
10. 2550 **11.** 1750 **12.** 3857
13. 31.5 **14.** 102.6 **15.** 34.83
16. 0.0288 **17.** 70.2 **18.** 0.1825
19. a) $100xm + 10xn + 10ym + yn$
b) $100xm + 10xn + 10ym + yn$
c) $100xm + 10xn + 10ym + yn$
d) All three expressions are equivalent.

Investigating Math pp. 102–103
1 Exploring $y = |x|$
2. up
3. All values of y are greater than or equal to 0.
4. a) y-axis **b)** $x = 0$
5. (0, 0)
6. a) R **b)** $y \geq 0$

2 Comparing $y = |x|$ and $y = |x| + q$
2. The three graphs are congruent, with the same
domain and axis of symmetry, but a different
range and vertex.
3. a) (0, 0), (0, 3), (0, -7) **b)** $x = 0$
c) Domain: R; Range: $y \geq 0$, $y \geq 3$, $y \geq -7$
4. a) [0, 3] **b)** [0, -7]
5. a) (0, 11); Domain: R; Range: $y \geq 11$
b) (0, -10); Domain: R; Range: $y \geq -10$
c) (0, -22); Domain: R; Range: $y \geq -22$
d) (0, 44); Domain: R; Range: $y \geq 44$

3 Comparing $y = |x|$ and $y = |x - p|$
2. a) (0, 0), (4, 0), (-6, 0)
b) $x = 0$, $x = 4$, $x = -6$
c) Domain: R; Range: $y \geq 0$
3. a) 4 units to the right
b) 6 units to the left
4. a) (9, 0), $x = 9$
b) (-7, 0), $x = -7$
c) (11, 0), $x = 11$
d) (-13, 0), $x = -13$

4 Comparing $y = |x|$ and $y = |x - p| + q$
2. a) (0, 0), (1, 5), (6, -3)
b) $x = 0$, $x = 1$, $x = 6$
c) Domain: R; Range: $y \geq 0$, $y \geq 5$, $y \geq -3$
3. a) [1, 5] **b)** [6, -3]

5. a) $(0, 0)$, $(-5, 6)$, $(-8, -7)$
   b) $x = 0$, $x = -5$, $x = -8$
   c) Domain: R; Range: $y \geq 0$, $y \geq 6$, $y \geq -7$
6. a) $[-5, 6]$ **b)** $[-8, -7]$
7. a) $(3, 4)$, $x = 3$ **b)** $(-2, -5)$, $x = -2$
   c) $(11, -3)$, $x = 11$ **d)** $(-13, 6)$, $x = -13$

5 Comparing $y = |x|$ and $y = a|x|$

2. a) up: $y = |x|$, $y = 2|x|$, $y = 0.5|x|$;
     down: $y = -|x|$, $y = -2|x|$, $y = -0.5|x|$
   b) the sign of the coefficient
3. a) $(0, 0)$ **b)** $x = 0$
   c) Domain: R;
     Range: $y \geq 0$, $y \leq 0$, $y \geq 0$, $y \leq 0$, $y \geq 0$, $y \leq 0$
4. reflection in the x-axis
5. vertical stretch   **6.** vertical shrink

6 Combining Transformations

1. a) $(0, -9)$ **b)** $x = 0$
   c) Domain: R; Range: $y \geq -9$
   d) up   **e)** stretch
2. a) $(0, 7)$ **b)** $x = 0$
   c) Domain: R; Range: $y \leq 7$
   d) down   **e)** stretch
3. a) $(0, -2)$ **b)** $x = 0$
   c) Domain: R; Range: $y \leq -2$
   d) down   **e)** congruent
4. a) $(3, 6)$ **b)** $x = 3$
   c) Domain: R; Range: $y \geq 6$
   d) up   **e)** stretch
5. a) $(-4, 0)$ **b)** $x = -4$
   c) Domain: R; Range: $y \leq 0$
   d) down   **e)** congruent
6. a) $(-6, -3)$ **b)** $x = -6$
   c) Domain: R; Range: $y \leq -3$
   d) down   **e)** congruent
7. a) $(7, 0)$ **b)** $x = 7$
   c) Domain: R; Range: $y \geq 0$
   d) up   **e)** shrink
8. a) $(5, -8)$ **b)** $x = 5$
   c) Domain: R; Range: $y \leq -8$
   d) down   **e)** shrink

7 Exploring Intercepts

1. a) y-intercept: 2, x-intercepts: none
   b) y-intercept: -3, x-intercepts: 3, -3
   c) y-intercept: 1, x-intercept: 1
   d) y-intercept: 5, x-intercept: -5
   e) y-intercept: 5, x-intercepts: none
   f) y-intercept: 2, x-intercepts: 2, 4
   g) y-intercept: 5, x-intercepts: none
   h) y-intercept: 1, x-intercepts: -1, -5
   i) y-intercept: 0, x-intercept: 0
   j) y-intercept: 2, x-intercept: 1
   k) y-intercept: 6, x-intercept: -2

   l) y-intercept: 0, x-intercept: 0
   m) y-intercept: -3, x-intercept: -1
   n) y-intercept: -6, x-intercept: 3
   o) y-intercept: 1, x-intercepts: 0.5, -0.5
   p) y-intercept: -2, x-intercepts: none
   q) y-intercept: 7, x-intercepts: none
   r) y-intercept: 2, x-intercepts: -1, -5
   s) y-intercept: 1, x-intercepts: -0.5, 2.5
   t) y-intercept: -5, x-intercepts: none
2. a) one   **b)** 0, 1, or 2
   c) There is no relationship between the number of
   x-intercepts and the value of p. If $aq > 0$, then
   there are no x-intercepts. If $q = 0$, then there is
   one x-intercept. If $aq < 0$, then there are two
   x-intercepts.

Section 3.1   pp. 109–111

Practice (Section 3.1)

1. a) up   **b)** $(0, 5)$ **c)** $x = 0$
   d) Domain: R; Range: $y \geq 5$
   e) min: 5 at $x = 0$
2. a) up   **b)** $(0, -2)$ **c)** $x = 0$
   d) Domain: R; Range: $y \geq -2$
   e) min: -2 at $x = 0$
3. a) down   **b)** $(0, -1)$ **c)** $x = 0$
   d) Domain: R; Range: $y \leq -1$
   e) max: -1 at $x = 0$
4. a) down   **b)** $(0, 3)$ **c)** $x = 0$
   d) Domain: R; Range: $y \leq 3$
   e) max: 3 at $x = 0$
5. a) up   **b)** $(0, 0)$ **c)** $x = 0$
   d) Domain: R; Range: $y \geq 0$
   e) min: 0 at $x = 0$
6. a) down   **b)** $(0, 0)$ **c)** $x = 0$
   d) Domain: R; Range: $y \leq 0$
   e) max: 0 at $x = 0$
7. a) up   **b)** $(0, 2)$ **c)** $x = 0$
   d) Domain: R; Range: $y \geq 2$
   e) min: 2 at $x = 0$
8. a) down   **b)** $(0, 0)$ **c)** $x = 0$
   d) Domain: R; Range: $y \leq 0$
   e) max: 0 at $x = 0$
9. a) down   **b)** $(0, -3)$ **c)** $x = 0$
   d) Domain: R; Range: $y \leq -3$
   e) max: -3 at $x = 0$
10. a) up   **b)** $(0, 1)$ **c)** $x = 0$
   d) Domain: R; Range: $y \geq 1$
   e) min: 1 at $x = 0$
11. a) down   **b)** $(0, 7)$ **c)** $x = 0$
   d) Domain: R; Range: $y \leq 7$
   e) max: 7 at $x = 0$
12. a) down   **b)** $(0, -6)$ **c)** $x = 0$
   d) Domain: R; Range: $y \leq -6$
   e) max: -6 at $x = 0$

13. The graph of $y = x^2 - 4$ is the graph of $y = x^2$ translated 4 units downward.

14. The graph of $y = -x^2 + 5$ is the graph of $y = -x^2$ translated 5 units upward.

15. The graph of $y = 3x^2$ is a vertical stretch of the graph of $y = x^2$ by a factor of 3.

16. The graph of $y = -\frac{1}{3}x^2$ is a vertical shrink of the graph of $y = -x^2$ by a factor of $\frac{1}{3}$.

17. The graph of $y = 2x^2 - 2$ is the graph of $y = 2x^2 + 7$ translated 9 units downward.

18. The graph of $y = -0.25x^2$ is the reflection of the graph of $y = 0.25x^2$ in the x-axis.

19. a) $y = -2x^2 + 3$ **b)** $y = 2x^2 - 3$
 c) $y = 2x^2 + 3$ **d)** $y = -2x^2 - 3$

20. a) down **b)** $(0, 0)$
 c) Domain: R; Range: $y \leq 0$
 d) max: 0 at $x = 0$

21. a) up **b)** $(0, -11.4)$
 c) Domain: R; Range: $y \geq -11.4$
 d) min: -11.4 at $x = 0$

22. a) down **b)** $(0, 4.7)$
 c) Domain: R; Range: $y \leq 4.7$
 d) max: 4.7 at $x = 0$

23. a) up **b)** $(0, -3)$
 c) Domain: R; Range: $y \geq -3$
 d) min: -3 at $x = 0$

24. a) down **b)** $(0, -8.3)$
 c) Domain: R; Range: $y \leq -8.3$
 d) max: -8.3 at $x = 0$

25. a) up **b)** $(0, 9.9)$
 c) Domain: R; Range: $y \geq 9.9$
 d) min: 9.9 at $x = 0$

26. a) up **b)** $(0, 3.5)$
 c) Domain: R; Range: $y \geq 3.5$
 d) min: 3.5 at $x = 0$

27. a) down **b)** $(0, -0.5)$
 c) Domain: R; Range: $y \leq -0.5$
 d) max: -0.5 at $x = 0$

28. $(2, 13)$ **29.** $(2, -1)$ **30.** $(2, -2)$ **31.** $(2, -2)$
32. a) $(0, -9)$ **b)** y-intercept: -9, x-intercepts: $-3, 3$
33. a) $(0, 1)$ **b)** y-intercept: 1
34. a) $(0, 4)$ **b)** y-intercept: 4, x-intercepts: $-2, 2$
35. a) $(0, -8)$ **b)** y-intercept: -8, x-intercepts: $-2, 2$
36. a) $(0, 16)$ **b)** y-intercept: 16, x-intercepts: none
37. a) $(0, 18)$ **b)** y-intercept: 18, x-intercepts: $-3, 3$
38. a) $(0, -3)$ **b)** y-intercept: -3, x-intercepts: none
39. a) $(0, 5)$ **b)** y-intercept: 5, x-intercepts: $-1, 1$
40. a) $(0, 8)$ **b)** y-intercept: 8, x-intercepts: $-4, 4$
41. a) $(0, -1)$ **b)** y-intercept: -1, x-intercepts: $-2, 2$
42. $-1.4, 1.4$ **43.** $-1.7, 1.7$ **44.** no x-intercepts
45. $-2.2, 2.2$ **46.** $-1.4, 1.4$ **47.** $-2.4, 2.4$
48. $y = 5x^2$ **49.** $y = -6x^2$ **50.** $y = -8x^2 - 7$
51. $y = 0.2x^2 + 3$ **52.** $y = 0.1x^2 - 2.5$
53. $y = -0.6x^2 + 6.5$ **54.** $y = 4x^2$

55. $y = -2x^2$ **56.** $y = 3x^2 - 7$
57. $y = -x^2 + 3$ **58.** $y = -0.5x^2 - 5$
59. $y = \frac{1}{6}x^2 + \frac{3}{2}$ **60.** $y = 2x^2$
61. $y = -0.5x^2 - 2$ **62.** $y = -x^2 + 5$
63. $y = 2x^2 - 8$

Applications and Problem Solving (Section 3.1)
64. -15
65. -7.5; The parabola is symmetric about the y-axis.
66. $y = -\frac{2}{3}x^2 + 6$
67. a) $A = \frac{1}{2}b^2$ **c)** $(0, 0)$
 d) Domain: $b > 0$; Range: $A > 0$
68. b) Domain: $x \geq 0$; Range: R
 c) No; the vertical line test fails.
69. b) 2 m **c)** 150 m **d)** 17 m
70. b) first quadrant; t and h must be greater than or equal to 0
 c) 5.2 s **d)** 12.9 s
71. a) $(2, 2)$, $(-3, 7)$
72. a) $A \leq s^2$
73. a) $y = x^2 + 2$ **b)** $y = -x^2 - 1$
 c) $y = 2x^2 - 3$ **d)** $y = -0.5x^2 + 4$
74. a) $y = -\frac{9}{12\,100}x^2$ **b)** $y = -\frac{9}{12\,100}x^2 + 49$
75. a) $n = 2p^2 - 4$ **b)** $n = -2p^2 + 4$
 c) They are reflections in the x-axis.
76. a) $A = \pi r^2$
 c) No; the radius must be non-negative.
 d) $r \geq 0, A \leq 0$
77. a) $A = 400 - s^2$ **b)** 16
 d) $0 \leq s \leq 16, 144 \leq A \leq 400$
79. a) no relationship; always one y-intercept
 b) If $aq > 0$, then there are no x-intercepts.
 If $q = 0$, then there is one x-intercept.
 If $aq < 0$, then there are two x-intercepts.

Section 3.2 p. 113
Applications and Problem Solving (Section 3.2)
1. Great Bear Lake: 31 792 km^2
3. a) 15 000 km **b)** Answers may vary.
4. a) 1255
5. a) 8 m **b)** 16
6. Beginning at the top and moving left to right, place the numbers in the order 2, 6, 3, 7, 8, 5, 9, 4, 1.
7. O = 1, N = 8, E = 2, T = 7
8. three, four, five
9. 13
10. 7, 5, 8; 6, 1, 4; 3, 2, 9
11. $8 - 7 = 1$; $20 \div 5 = 4$; $9 - 6 = 3$

Practice (Section 3.3)

1. a) up   **b)** $(-5, 0)$ **c)** $x = -5$
   d) Domain: R; Range: $y \geq 0$
   e) min: 0 at $x = -5$

2. a) down   **b)** $(-1, 0)$ **c)** $x = -1$
   d) Domain: R; Range: $y \leq 0$
   e) max: 0 at $x = -1$

3. a) up   **b)** $(3, 0)$ **c)** $x = 3$
   d) Domain: R; Range: $y \geq 0$
   e) min: 0 at $x = 3$

4. a) up   **b)** $(-2, 4)$ **c)** $x = -2$
   d) Domain: R; Range: $y \geq 4$
   e) min: 4 at $x = -2$

5. a) down   **b)** $(2, -5)$ **c)** $x = 2$
   d) Domain: R; Range: $y \leq -5$
   e) max: -5 at $x = 2$

6. a) up   **b)** $(-3, -5)$ **c)** $x = -3$
   d) Domain: R; Range: $y \geq -5$
   e) min: -5 at $x = -3$

7. a) up   **b)** $(-6, 2)$ **c)** $x = -6$
   d) Domain: R; Range: $y \geq 2$
   e) min: 2 at $x = -6$

8. a) up   **b)** $(5, -4)$ **c)** $x = 5$
   d) Domain: R; Range: $y \geq -4$
   e) min: -4 at $x = 5$

9. a) down   **b)** $(-4, 3)$ **c)** $x = -4$
   d) Domain: R; Range: $y \leq 3$
   e) max: 3 at $x = -4$

10. a) down   **b)** $(6, -1)$ **c)** $x = 6$
   d) Domain: R; Range: $y \leq -1$
   e) max: -1 at $x = 6$

11. a) up   **b)** $(5, 0)$ **c)** $x = 5$
   d) Domain: R; Range: $y \geq 0$
   e) min: 0 at $x = 5$

12. a) down   **b)** $(-4, 0)$ **c)** $x = -4$
   d) Domain: R; Range: $y \leq 0$
   e) max: 0 at $x = -4$

13. a) up   **b)** $(2, 1)$ **c)** $x = 2$
   d) Domain: R; Range: $y \geq 1$
   e) min: 1 at $x = 2$

14. a) down   **b)** $(-1, -2)$ **c)** $x = -1$
   d) Domain: R; Range: $y \leq -2$
   e) max: -2 at $x = -1$

15. a) up   **b)** stretched by a factor of 2
   c) $(1, 0)$ **d)** $x = 1$ **e)** min: 0 at $x = 1$

16. a) down   **b)** shrunk by a factor of 0.5
   c) $(-7, 0)$ **d)** $x = -7$ **e)** max: 0 at $x = -7$

17. a) down   **b)** stretched by a factor of 2
   c) $(4, 7)$ **d)** $x = 4$ **e)** max: 7 at $x = 4$

18. a) up   **b)** stretched by a factor of 4
   c) $(-3, -4)$ **d)** $x = -3$ **e)** min: -4 at $x = -3$

19. a) down   **b)** stretched by a factor of 3
   c) $(5, 6)$ **d)** $x = 5$ **e)** max: 6 at $x = 5$

20. a) down   **b)** shrunk by a factor of 0.4
   c) $(8, -1)$ **d)** $x = 8$ **e)** max: -1 at $x = 8$

21. a) up   **b)** shrunk by a factor of $\frac{1}{3}$
   c) $(-6, -7)$ **d)** $x = -6$ **e)** min: -7 at $x = -6$

22. a) up   **b)** shrunk by a factor of 0.5
   c) $(-1, -5)$ **d)** $x = -1$ **e)** min: -5 at $x = -1$

23. a) up   **b)** stretched by a factor of 2.5
   c) $(-1.5, -9)$ **d)** $x = -1.5$
   e) min: -9 at $x = -1.5$

24. a) down   **b)** stretched by a factor of 1.2
   c) $(2.6, 3.3)$ **d)** $x = 2.6$
   e) max: 3.3 at $x = 2.6$

25. a) $y = -3(x + 1)^2 + 2$ **b)** $y = 3(x - 1)^2 + 2$
   c) $y = 3(x + 1)^2 - 2$ **d)** $y = -3(x - 1)^2 - 2$

32. a) y-intercept: 4, x-intercept: 2
   b) Answers may vary. $(4, 4)$, $(3, 1)$

33. a) y-intercept: -5, x-intercepts: -5, 1
   b) Answers may vary. $(2, 7)$, $(3, 16)$

34. a) y-intercept: 8, x-intercepts: 2, 4
   b) Answers may vary. $(1, 3)$, $(3, -1)$

35. a) y-intercept: -3, x-intercepts: -3, -1
   b) Answers may vary. $(-2, 1)$, $(1, -8)$

36. a) y-intercept: -18, x-intercepts: none
   b) Answers may vary. $(-1, -9)$, $(-2, -6)$

37. a) y-intercept: -6, x-intercepts: -3, 1
   b) Answers may vary. $(-1, -8)$, $(2, 10)$

38. y-intercept: -2, x-intercepts: 0.7, -2.7
39. y-intercept: -2, x-intercepts: -0.4, 2.4
40. y-intercept: -3, x-intercepts: 0.5, 1.5
41. y-intercept: -47, x-intercepts: none
42. y-intercept: 1, x-intercepts: -0.5
43. y-intercept: $-\frac{2}{9}$, x-intercept: $\frac{1}{3}$
44. y-intercept: 4, x-intercept: -4
45. y-intercept: -2.5, x-intercepts: -1, -5
46. $y = (x - 7)^2$ **47.** $y = -(x + 5)^2$
48. $y = 2(x - 3)^2 - 5$ **49.** $y = -3(x - 6)^2 + 7$
50. $y = -0.5(x + 1)^2 - 1$ **51.** $y = 1.5(x + 8)^2 + 9$
52. $y = (x - 1)^2 + 5$ **53.** $y = -(x + 3)^2$
54. $y = 3(x - 4)^2 - 2$ **55.** $y = -2(x - 2)^2 - 3$
56. $y = 0.4(x + 3)^2 - 3$ **57.** $y = 5(x - 4.5)^2$
58. $y = -4(x - 3)^2$ **59.** $y = 2(x + 5)^2 - 6$
60. $y = (x + 4)^2 - 5$ **61.** $y = -(x - 3)^2 + 2$
62. $y = -(x - 1)^2 + 6$ **63.** $y = 3(x + 2)^2 + 3$
64. $y = -2(x + 5)^2 - 3$ **65.** $y = \frac{1}{2}(x - 6)^2 + 4$
66. $y = 2(x - 1)^2 + 2$ **67.** $y = -(x + 2)^2 + 3$
68. $y = \frac{1}{2}(x - 2)^2 - 4$ **69.** $y = -\frac{1}{4}(x + 4)^2 - 1$

Applications and Problem Solving (Section 3.3)

70. 4   **71.** -11
72. $x = -1$; This is halfway between the x-intercepts.
73. $x = -3$
74. a) 83 m   **b)** 6 s
75. $a = 2$, $q = 4$

76. $a = -1$, $q = -4$ **77.** $a = -2$, $q = 5$

78. a) 10 m **b)** 20 m **c)** 40 m **d)** 7.5 m
e) No; the player would need to be able to reach 5.1 m, which is impossible.
f) $h(d) = -0.025d^2$

79. a) 38.5 m **b)** 1 m **c)** 5 s **d)** 25 m

80. a) 6 m **b)** 20 m **c)** 2 m; 2 m
d) 38 m **e)** 2.76 m

81. a) Domain: $s \geq 0$; Range: $d \geq 0$
b) (0, 0), (−30, 0) **c)** 24 m; 78 m
d) Answers may vary. 30 km/h or 40 km/h
e) Answers may vary. 10.8 m at 30 km/h or 19.5 m at 40 km/h

82. b) The part in the first quadrant since t and h must be greater than or equal to 0. **c)** 253 m

83. b) (0, 0), (1, 0); No games will be played if there are no teams or one team.
c) $g = t(t - 1)$ **d)** $g = t(t - 1)$

84. a) The graphs are the same.
b) $(x - p)^2 = (p - x)^2 = x^2 - 2px + p^2$

85. (1, 6), (−2, −3)

86. a) $m = n$ **b)** $m > n$ **c)** $m < n$

87. a) $A = (x - 2)^2 + 3$ **c)** 2 m **d)** 0
e) Shade above the parabola $A = (x - 2)^2 + 3$.

88. a) $y = -3(x - 2)^2 - 1$ **b)** $y = 3(x + 2)^2 + 1$
c) $y = -3(x + 2)^2 - 1$

89. a) 17, 19, 23 **b)** 289

90. a) (−30, 0.36), (30, 0.36)
b) $y = 0.0004x^2$
c) $y = 0.0004(x + 30)^2 - 0.36$
d) $y = 0.0004(x - 30)^2 - 0.36$
e) 0.16 cm

91. $y = 2(x - 1)^2 + 3$

Section 3.4 p. 123

Applications and Problem Solving (Section 3.4)

1. Scott: 6; Ivan: 11; Enzo: 4
2. $3500
3. (−2, 4)
4. WNWWWNN; 43 km
5. 6 cm by 4 cm

Computer Data Bank p. 124

1 Long Jump

1. Answers will vary.
2. For the start of the path at the origin, $p = 3.96$ and $q = 0.79$.
3. a) Substitute values for all the variables except a into $y = a(x - p)^2 + q$, and solve for a.
b) −0.050
4. Answers will vary.
6. For the parabola opening down, from least flat to most flat

2 Winning Distances

1. Answers will vary.
3. Answers will vary.

Investigating Math p. 125

1 Making Squares

2. a) $x^2 + 4x + 4 = (x + 2)^2$
b) $x^2 + 6x + 9 = (x + 3)^2$

2 Completing the Square

1. 16
2. $x^2 + 8x + 16 = (x + 4)^2$
3. a) 25; $x^2 + 10x + 25 = (x + 5)^2$
b) 36; $x^2 + 12x + 36 = (x + 6)^2$
4. the square of half the coefficient of x
5. a) 49 **b)** 64 **c)** 100 **d)** 225
6. a) $x^2 + 14x + 49 = (x + 7)^2$
b) $x^2 + 16x + 64 = (x + 8)^2$
c) $x^2 + 20x + 100 = (x + 10)^2$
d) $x^2 + 30x + 225 = (x + 15)^2$

Section 3.5 pp. 130–134

Practice (Section 3.5)

1. 49 **2.** 36 **3.** 1 **4.** 81
5. 25 **6.** 100 **7.** 2.25 **8.** 6.25
9. 0.25 **10.** 0.25 **11.** 0.16 **12.** 0.000 625
13. 1.44 **14.** 46.9225 **15.** $\frac{1}{9}$ **16.** $\frac{1}{144}$

17. $y = (x + 3)^2 - 6$; (−3, −6); $x = -3$; Points may vary. (0, 3), (1, 10)
18. $y = (x - 2)^2 - 5$; (2, −5); $x = 2$; Points may vary. (0, −1), (1, −4)
19. $y = (x + 5)^2 + 5$; (−5, 5); $x = -5$; Points may vary. (0, 30), (1, 41)
20. $y = (x - 1)^2 + 2$; (1, 2); $x = 1$; Points may vary. (0, 3), (2, 3)
21. $y = (x + 6)^2 - 8$; (−6, −8); $x = -6$; Points may vary. (0, 28), (1, 41)
22. $y = (x - 4)^2 - 4$; (4, −4); $x = 4$; Points may vary. (0, 12), (1, 5)
23. a) $y = x^2 - 4$ **b)** $y = -x^2 + 4x$
c) $y = x^2 - 4x$ **d)** $y = x^2 + 4x$
e) $y = -x^2 + 4$ **f)** $y = -x^2 - 4x$
24. (1, −9); $x = -1$; y-intercept: −8, x-intercepts: −2, 4; $y \geq -9$
25. (3, 1); $x = 3$; y-intercept: 10, x-intercepts: none; $y \geq 1$
26. (−2, −4); $x = -2$; y-intercept: 0, x-intercepts: −4, 0; $y \geq 4$
27. (6, 4); $x = 6$; y-intercept: 40, x-intercepts: none; $y \geq 4$
28. $y = -(x - 4)^2 + 5$; (4, 5); $x = 4$; Points may vary. (0, −11), (1, −4)
29. $y = -(x + 4)^2 + 9$; (−4, 0); $x = -4$; Points may vary. (−7, 0), (−1, 0)

30. $y = -(x + 2)^2 - 3$; $(-2, -3)$; $x = -2$;
Points may vary. $(0, -7)$, $(1, -12)$
31. $y = -(x + 1)^2 + 1$; $(-1, 1)$; $x = -1$;
Points may vary. $(-2, 0)$, $(0, 0)$
32. $(-1, 4)$; $x = -1$; y-intercept: 3, x-intercepts: -3, 1;
$y \leq 4$
33. $(-2, -8)$; $x = -2$; y-intercept: -12, x-intercepts:
none; $y \leq -8$
34. $(4, 4)$; $x = 4$; y-intercept: -12, x-intercepts: 2, 6;
$y \leq 4$
35. $(5, 0)$; $x = 5$; y-intercept: -25, x-intercept: 5;
$y \leq 0$
36. min: -7 at $x = -3$
37. max: 5 at $x = -2$
38. max: 16 at $x = 4$
39. min: 0 at $x = 6$
40. min: -30 at $m = -5$
41. max: 13 at $t = -3$
42. min: -28 at $x = 7$
43. max: -3 at $k = -5$
44. min: 1 at $x = -1$
45. max: 6 at $x = 5$
46. max: 7 at $x = -3$
47. max: -1 at $x = 3$
48. min: -2 at $x = 2$
49. min: 2 at $x = 1$
50. max: 8 at $x = 2$
51. max: 0 at $x = 1$
52. min: -1.25 at $x = -1.5$
53. min: -2.25 at $x = 0.5$
54. max: 7 at $x = 3$
55. max: -0.875 at $x = 0.75$
56. max: 6.25 at $x = -2.5$
57. max: 0.97 at $x = 0.1$
58. max: -1.92 at $x = -0.2$
59. min: 1.5 at $x = -1$
60. max: $\frac{4}{3}$ at $x = \frac{2}{3}$
61. min: -0.18 at $x = 0.6$
62. max: -3.19 at $x = 0.9$
63. max: 20 at $x = 100$
64. -3.5, 0
65. -1.7, 1
66. -0.3
67. -1.3, 1.3
68. no x-intercepts
69. 0, 2.9

Applications and Problem Solving (Section 3.5)
70. a) y-intercept: 3, x-intercepts: -1, -3; $(-2, -1)$
b) y-intercept: 2, x-intercepts: -2, 1; $(-0.5, 2.25)$
c) y-intercept: 9, x-intercept: 1.5; $(1.5, 0)$
d) y-intercept: -2, x-intercepts: -0.5, 2; $(0.75, -3.125)$
e) y-intercept: 3, x-intercepts: 0.5, 1.5; $(1, -1)$
f) y-intercept: 6, x-intercepts: -2, 1; $(-0.5, 6.75)$

71. a) $y = x^2 - 8x + 35$ **b)** 4
72. a) $y = 375 - 10x - x^2$ **b)** -5
73. 5, -5
74. 17, 17
75. 17, 17
76. a) 20 m   **b)** 100 m   **c)** 200 m
77. a) 4.25 m   **b)** 5 m   **c)** 2 m
78. a) Earth: 7 m, Jupiter: 4 m, Mars: 14.5 m,
Neptune: 6.2 m
b) Earth: 1 s, Jupiter: 0.4 s, Mars: 2.5 s,
Neptune: 0.83 s
79. a) 46 m   **b)** 480 m   **c)** 17 m
80. a) 84 m   **b)** 75 m   **c)** 31 m
81. a) 100 m by 100 m   **b)** 10 000 m²
82. 10 m by 30 m
83. 15 m by 30 m
84. a) $R(x) = (2000 - 100x)(8 + x)$
b) $(6, 19\,600)$ **c)** \$14   **d)** 1400
85. \$30
86. a) 12.5 cm²   **b)** 21.125 cm²
87. a) 176.6 m   **b)** 8.5 s
88. 50 cm²
89. a) They are reflections in the x-axis.
b) They are opposites.
90. a) The graph is a straight line.
b) The parabola has an axis of symmetry of the
y-axis.
91. $y = x^2 - 2x - 3$
92. $y = -2x^2 + 4x + 6$
93. No; the graphs never intersect.
94. $b = 0$; If $f(x) = f(-x)$ for all x, then the axis of
symmetry is $x = 0$ and this means that $b = 0$.
95. a) $k = 9$ **b)** $k < 9$ **c)** $k > 9$
96. a) $k = -8$ **b)** $k > -8$ **c)** $k < -8$
99. Answers may vary.
a) $y = x^2 - 6x + 8$ **b)** $y = -x^2 - 6x + 7$
c) $y = 2x^2 - 4x + 22$ **d)** $y = -0.5x^2 + 6x - 18$

Investigating Math   p. 135

1 Relating $y = ax^2 + bx + c$ to the Axis of Symmetry
1. a) $a = 1$, $b = -4$, $c = 0$; $x = 2$
b) $a = 1$, $b = -4$, $c = 3$; $x = 2$
c) $a = 1$, $b = 6$, $c = 0$; $x = -3$
d) $a = 1$, $b = 6$, $c = -5$; $x = -3$
e) $a = -1$, $b = 8$, $c = 0$; $x = 4$
f) $a = -1$, $b = 8$, $c = -4$; $x = 4$
g) $a = 0.5$, $b = -3$, $c = 0$; $x = 3$
h) $a = 0.5$, $b = -3$, $c = 2$; $x = 3$
i) $a = -2$, $b = -4$, $c = 0$; $x = -1$
j) $a = -2$, $b = -4$, $c = -7$; $x = -1$
2. No; if the value of c changes, the axis of symmetry
does not change.
3. Divide the negative of b by twice a.

4. $x = -\dfrac{b}{2a}$

5. a) $x = -2$ **b)** $x = 8$ **c)** $x = -6$ **d)** $x = 4.5$
   e) $x = -2$ **f)** $x = -2$ **g)** $x = -2$ **h)** $x = 2.5$
   i) $x = -3$ **j)** $x = -1.5$ **k)** $x = 0.75$ **l)** $x = \dfrac{4}{3}$

2 Relating $y = ax^2 + bx + c$ to $y = a(x - p) + q$

1. the x-coordinate

2. Substitute the coordinate into the equation to find the other coordinate.

3. a) $(-3, -5)$ **b)** $(-6, 35)$ **c)** $(1, -7)$
   d) $(-10, -50)$ **e)** $(-0.75, -2.75)$ **f)** $(3, -1)$

4. The coordinates of the vertex are (p, q).

5. Divide the negative of b by twice a.

6. $p = -\dfrac{b}{2a}$

7. Find $p = -\dfrac{b}{2a}$ and then substitute $x = -\dfrac{b}{2a}$ in the equation $ax^2 + bx + c = a(x - p)^2 + q$ to find q.

8. a) $y = (x - 3)^2 - 9$
   b) $f(x) = 2(x + 1)^2 - 7$
   c) $y = -5(x - 2)^2 + 22$
   d) $f(x) = -(x + 1.5)^2 + 0.25$
   e) $y = (x + 2.5)^2 - 4.25$
   f) $f(x) = 3(x - 0.5)^2 - 0.75$
   g) $y = -1.5(x - 1)^2 + 2.5$
   h) $y = 0.4(x + 1.25)^2 - 0.625$

Technology   pp. 136–137

1 Comparing Graphing Calculator and Manual Methods

1. a) $(0, 5)$; y-intercept: 5, x-intercepts: none
   b) $(0, -3)$; y-intercept: -3, x-intercepts: -1.7, 1.7
   c) $(0, 4)$; y-intercept: 4, x-intercepts: -2, 2
   d) $(0, 8)$; y-intercept: 8, x-intercepts: -2.8, 2.8

2. a) $(0, -9)$; y-intercept: -9, x-intercepts: -2.1, 2.1
   b) $(0, 2)$; y-intercept: 2, x-intercepts: none
   c) $(0, 12)$; y-intercept: 12, x-intercepts: -2, 2
   d) $(0, 4)$; y-intercept: 4, x-intercepts: -2.6, 2.6

3. a) $(2, -3)$; y-intercept: 1, x-intercepts: 0.3, 3.7
   b) $(-2, 1)$; y-intercept: 9, x-intercepts: none
   c) $(-3, 1)$; y-intercept: -8, x-intercepts: -4, -2
   d) $(1, 6)$; y-intercept: 5.5, x-intercepts: -2.5, 4.5
   e) $(4.5, 0)$; y-intercept: 5.1, x-intercept: 4.5
   f) $(-5, 0)$; y-intercept: -5, x-intercept: -5

4. a) $(2.5, -9.25)$; y-intercept: -3, x-intercepts: -0.5, 5.5
   b) $(3, 5)$; y-intercept: -4, x-intercepts: 0.8, 5.2
   c) $(-1, 6)$; y-intercept: 5, x-intercepts: -3.4, 1.4
   d) $(-3.5, 24.5)$; y-intercept: 12.25, x-intercepts: -8.4, 1.4
   e) $(0.75, -3.125)$; y-intercept: -2, x-intercepts: -0.5, 2
   f) $(-7, 21.5)$; y-intercept: -3, x-intercepts: -13.6, -0.4

5. a) $(1.5, 2.3)$; y-intercept: 0, x-intercepts: 0, 3
   b) $(-1, 1)$; y-intercept: 0, x-intercepts: -2, 0
   c) $(-2.5, -0.6)$; y-intercept: 0, x-intercepts: -5, 0
   d) $(0.4, 0.04)$; y-intercept: 0, x-intercepts: 0.75, 0
   e) $(1.3, -0.9)$; y-intercept: 0, x-intercepts: 0, 2.5
   f) $(-0.9, 2.8)$; y-intercept: 0, x-intercepts: -1.8, 0

6. a) $(4.58, -6.30)$; y-intercept: 0, x-intercepts: 0, 9.17
   b) $(0.18, 0.16)$; y-intercept: 0, x-intercepts: 0.36, 0
   c) $(-1.14, -0.42)$; y-intercept: 1, x-intercepts: -1.75, -0.52
   d) $(0.56, 1.03)$; y-intercept: 0.8, x-intercepts: -0.64, 1.77
   e) $(-291.67, -510.42)$; y-intercept: 0, x-intercepts: -583.33, 0
   f) $(-242.13, -243.25)$; y-intercept: -1.12, x-intercepts: -484.82, 0.56
   g) $(0.21, -24.90)$; y-intercept: -25, x-intercepts: none
   h) $(-31.73, 54.66)$; y-intercept: 2.3, x-intercepts: -64.15, 0.69

2 Problem Solving

1. a) 2.1 m   **b)** 4.43 m   **c)** 3.05 m

2. a) 0.09 mm²/h; 3.57 h
   b) The number of cells was decreasing.
   c) 7.14 h

3. a) 1.46   **b)** $x = 0.83$

4. a) 32.33 m   **b)** 54.9 m   **c)** 32.08 m

5. a) $y = x^2 - 4$ and $y = |x^2 - 4|$ are the same for $x \le -2$, $x \ge 2$; $y = x^2 - 4$ and $y = |x^2 - 4|$ are reflections in the x-axis for $-2 < x < 2$
   b) $y = x^2 - 4$ and $y = 4 - x^2$ are reflections in the x-axis
   c) $y = |x^2 - 4|$ and $y = |4 - x^2|$ are identical

Section 3.6   p. 139

Applications and Problem Solving (Section 3.6)

1. b) 23rd month
   c) $y = 100(x - 11)^2 - 12\,100$

2. 5 months sooner

3. 14

4. a) 276   **b)** 312

5. b) 5 s   **c)** 122.5 m
   d) $h(t) = 49t - 4.9t^2$
   e) $0 \le t \le 10$, $0 \le h \le 122.5$

6. 49

7. 10

8. To follow this plan, eventually Ray must save more in a month than what he earns.

Connecting Math and History
pp. 140–142

1 Falling Objects

1. 5, 125, 50; 6, 180, 60
2. $f = 5t^2$
3. 245 m; 320 m
4. 10 m/s^2
5. $\frac{1}{2}$ of g
6. Answers may vary.

2 The Path of a Cannonball

1. a) 60, 90, 120, 150, 180
2. c) 45 m   d) 3 s   e) $h(t) = 30t - 5t^2$
   f) 44.2 m; 28.8 m   g) 6 s
3. a) $h(t) = 50t - 5t^2$ b) 125 m   c) 5 s
   d) 100.8 m   e) 10 s

3 Distances Travelled by a Cannonball

1. a) $H = D\sin A$ b) $h(t) = D\sin A - 5t^2$
   c) $h(t) = vt\sin A - 5t^2$
2. a) 75 m   b) yes   c) 80 m; 8 s
3. a) $d = D\cos A$ b) $d = vt\cos A$
   c) 554 m
4. 355 m; 106 m
5. no
6. a) $v = \dfrac{d}{t\cos A}$
   b) 64 m/s

Career Connection p. 143

1. The tallest building in Canada, the CN Tower, is 553 m, which is 53 m taller than the fountain of lava.
2. b) 151 m   c) 5.5 s
   d) The lava may fall on land that is below the crater, and therefore take longer to get to the ground.
   e) The equation is only a model of the situation. It does not account for any external factors that might affect the way the lava falls.
3. British Columbia: 1.9 cm; Alberta: 2.8 cm; Saskatchewan: 2.9 cm; Manitoba: 2.8 cm

Review pp. 144–145

1. The graph of $y = x^2 - 3$ is a translation of the graph of $y = x^2$, 3 units downward.
2. The graph of $y = -4x^2$ is a vertical stretch of the graph of $y = -x^2$ by a factor of 4.
3. a) up   b) (0, 4)   c) $x = 0$
   d) Domain: R; Range: $y \geq 4$
   e) min: 4 at $x = 0$
   f) y-intercept: 4, x-intercepts: none
4. a) down   b) (0, −2)   c) $x = 0$
   d) Domain: R; Range: $y \leq -2$

e) max: −2 at $x = 0$
f) y-intercept: −2, x-intercepts: none
5. a) up   b) (0, 0)   c) $x = 0$
   d) Domain: R; Range: $y \geq 0$
   e) min: 0 at $x = 0$
   f) y-intercept: 0, x-intercept: 0
6. a) down   b) (0, 3)   c) $x = 0$
   d) Domain: R; Range: $y \leq 3$
   e) max: 3 at $x = 0$
   f) y-intercept: 3, x-intercepts: 1, −1
7. a) down   b) (0, 0)
   c) Domain: R; Range: $y \leq 0$
   d) max: 0 at $x = 0$
8. a) down   b) (0, 3.5)
   c) Domain: R; Range: $y \leq 3.5$
   d) max: 3.5 at $x = 0$
9. a) down   b) (0, −7)
   c) Domain: R; Range: $y \leq -7$
   d) max: −7 at $x = 0$
10. a) up   b) (0, 3)
    c) Domain: R; Range: $y \geq 3$
    d) min: 3 at $x = 0$
11. −2.6, 2.6   12. −1.4, 1.4
13. no x-intercepts   14. −2.1, 2.1
15. $y = 2x^2$ 16. $y = -3x^2 - 2$
17. $y = -5x^2$ 18. $y = x^2 - 5$
19. a) 2.13 m   b) 12 m   c) 1.2 m
20. a) down   b) stretched by a factor of 3
    c) (3, 1)   d) $x = 3$
    e) Domain: R; Range: $y \leq 1$
    f) max: 1 at $x = 3$
21. a) up   b) not stretched or shrunk
    c) (−7, −2)   d) $x = -7$
    e) Domain: R; Range: $y \geq -2$
    f) min: −2 at $x = -7$
22. a) up   b) shrunk by a factor of 0.5
    c) (−1, 5)   d) $x = -1$
    e) Domain: R; Range: $y \geq 5$
    f) min: 5 at $x = -1$
23. a) down   b) not stretched or shrunk
    c) (−3, −1)   d) $x = -3$
    e) Domain: R; Range: $y \leq -1$
    f) max: −1 at $x = -3$
24. a) up   b) not stretched or shrunk
    c) (−1, −1)   d) $x = -1$
    e) Domain: R; Range: $y \geq -1$
    f) min: −1 at $x = -1$
25. a) down   b) stretched by a factor of 4
    c) (1, 0)   d) $x = 1$
    e) Domain: R; Range: $y \leq 0$
    f) max: 0 at $x = 1$
26. a) down   b) stretched by a factor of 2
    c) (4, −3)   d) $x = 4$
    e) Domain: R; Range: $y \leq -3$
    f) max: −3 at $x = 4$

27. a) up   **b)** shrunk by a factor of 0.25
    c) $(-2, 1)$ **d)** $x = -2$
    e) Domain: R; Range: $y \geq 1$
    f) min: 1 at $x = -2$
28. a) $(3, 0)$ **b)** min: 0 at $x = 3$
    c) y-intercept: 9, x-intercept: 3
    d) Answers may vary. $(1, 4), (2, 1)$
29. a) $(-2, -4)$ **b)** min: -4 at $x = -2$
    c) y-intercept: 0, x-intercepts: $-4, 0$
    d) Answers may vary. $(1, 5), (2, 12)$
30. a) $(3, -8)$ **b)** min: -8 at $x = 3$
    c) y-intercept: 10, x-intercepts: 1, 5
    d) Answers may vary. $(2, -6), (3, -8)$
31. a) $(-2, 9)$ **b)** max: 9 at $x = -2$
    c) y-intercept: 5, x-intercepts: $-5, 1$
    d) Answers may vary. $(-4, 5), (-3, 8)$
32. $-4.2, 0.2$
33. $-0.2, 2.2$
34. $y = 2(x - 3)^2 + 4$
35. $y = (x - 2)^2 - 3$
36. $y = 2(x + 3)^2 - 4$
37. $y = -4(x - 1)^2 + 3$
38. $y = \frac{1}{2}(x + 2)^2 + 1$
39. a) 13 m   **b)** 0.9 m   **c)** 4.9 s   **d)** 8.9 m
40. 16   **41.** 49   **42.** 6.25   **43.** 0.09
44. $y = (x + 2)^2 - 3$; $(-2, -3)$; $x = -2$;
    Points may vary. $(0, 1), (1, 6)$
45. $y = (x - 5)^2 - 10$; $(5, -10)$; $x = 5$;
    Points may vary. $(0, 15), (1, 6)$
46. $y = -(x + 3)^2 + 4$; $(-3, 4)$; $x = -3$;
    Points may vary. $(0, -5), (1, -12)$
47. $y = -(x + 2)^2 + 7$; $(-2, 7)$; $x = -2$;
    Points may vary. $(0, 3), (1, -2)$
48. $(-3, -9)$; $x = -3$; y-intercept: 0,
    x-intercepts: $-6, 0$; $y \geq -9$
49. $(4, -4)$; $x = 4$; y-intercept: 12,
    x-intercepts: 2, 6; $y \geq -4$
50. $(-2, -5)$; $x = -2$; y-intercept: -9,
    x-intercepts: none; $y \leq -5$
51. $(-4, -1)$; $x = -4$; y-intercept: 15,
    x-intercepts: $-5, -3$; $y \geq -1$
52. $(2.5, -3.25)$
53. $(0.5, -3.75)$
54. $(-2, 3)$
55. $(-1.5, 10.5)$
56. $(-0.25, -1.25)$
57. $(-1.5, 1.125)$
58. no x-intercepts
59. $-0.3, 1$
60. $-0.5, 0$
61. $-1.6, 1.6$
62. a) 4.5 m   **b)** 4 m   **c)** 2.5 m
63. $6, -6$
64. a) 150 m by 150 m   **b)** 22 500 m²

Exploring Math   p. 145

1. Player 1 takes 1 counter, leaving 8. Player 2 takes 1, 2, or 3 counters, leaving 7, 6, or 5. Player 1 takes 3 counters if Player 2 left 7, 2 counters if Player 2 left 6, and 1 counter if Player 2 left 5. There are now 4 counters left for Player 2. Player 2 takes 1, 2, or 3 counters, leaving 3, 2, or 1. Player 1 can take all the remaining counters, and win.
2. Player 1 takes 1, 2, or 3 counters, leaving 7, 6, or 5. Player 2 takes 3 counters if Player 1 left 7, 2 counters if Player 1 left 6, and 1 counter if Player 1 left 5. Therefore, there are now 4 counters left for Player 1. Player 1 takes 1, 2, or 3 counters, leaving 3, 2, or 1. Player 2 can take all the remaining counters, and win.
3. F, F, F, S, F, F, F, S, F, F, F, S, F
4. a) first player
    b) Take 2 counters.
    c) Any first move that results in a number of counters divisible by 4 results in a win for the first player.
5. a) second player
    b) Take away the number of counters that will result in a number divisible by 4.
    c) Any second move that results in a number of counters divisible by 4 results in a win for the second player.
6. a) first player   **b)** second player
    c) first player   **d)** second player

Chapter Check   p. 146

1. a) up   **b)** $(0, -1)$ **c)** $x = 0$
    d) Domain: R; Range: $y \geq -1$
    e) min: -1 at $x = 0$
2. a) down   **b)** $(0, 5)$ **c)** $x = 0$
    d) Domain: R; Range: $y \leq 5$
    e) max: 5 at $x = 0$
3. a) down   **b)** $(0, 0)$ **c)** $x = 0$
    d) Domain: R; Range: $y \leq 0$
    e) max: 0 at $x = 0$
4. a) down   **b)** $(0, -3)$ **c)** $x = 0$
    d) Domain: R; Range: $y \leq -3$
    e) max: -3 at $x = 0$
5. no x-intercepts
6. $-3.2, 3.2$
7. $-1.6, 1.6$
8. $-2.4, 2.4$
9. $y = -4x^2$
10. $y = -0.5x^2 - 3$
11. $y = 3x^2$
12. $y = 2x^2 - 5$
13. a) up   **b)** neither stretched nor shrunk
    c) $(-3, -1)$ **d)** $x = -3$
    e) Domain: R; Range: $y \geq -1$
    f) min: -1 at $x = -3$

14. a) up   **b)** stretched by a factor of 3
   c) $(1, 0)$ **d)** $x = 1$
   e) Domain: R; Range: $y \geq 0$
   f) min: 0 at $x = 1$

15. a) down   **b)** stretched by a factor of 2
   c) $(5, -2)$ **d)** $x = 5$
   e) Domain: R; Range: $y \leq -2$
   f) max: -2 at $x = 5$

16. a) down   **b)** shrunk by a factor of 0.5
   c) $(-2, 3)$ **d)** $x = -2$
   e) Domain: R; Range: $y \leq 3$
   f) max: 3 at $x = -2$

17. a) $(1, 0)$ **b)** min: 0 at $x = 1$
   c) y-intercept: 1, x-intercept: 1
   d) Answers may vary. $(2, 1)$, $(3, 4)$

18. a) $(-1, -4)$ **b)** min: -4 at $x = -1$
   c) y-intercept: -3, x-intercepts: -3, 1
   d) Answers may vary. $(2, 5)$, $(3, 12)$

19. a) $(5, -9)$ **b)** min: -9 at $x = 5$
   c) y-intercept: 16, x-intercepts: 2, 8
   d) Answers may vary. $(1, 7)$, $(3, -5)$

20. a) $(-6, 18)$ **b)** max: 18 at $x = -6$
   c) y-intercept: -54, x-intercepts: -9, -3
   d) Answers may vary. $(-2, -14)$, $(-1, -32)$

21. -4.1, 0.1

22. 0.3, 3.7

23. $y = (x + 3)^2 + 1$

24. $y = -2(x + 5)^2 + 4$

25. $y = -2(x - 1)^2 + 4$

26. $y = \dfrac{4}{9}(x + 3)^2 + 1$

27. $y = (x + 4)^2 - 8$; $(-4, -8)$; $x = -4$;
Points may vary. $(0, 8)$, $(1, 17)$

28. $y = (x - 4)^2 - 7$; $(4, -7)$; $x = 4$; Points may vary.
$(0, 9)$, $(1, 2)$

29. $y = (x - 2)^2 + 1$; $(2, 1)$; $x = 2$; Points may vary.
$(0, 5)$, $(1, 2)$

30. $y = -(x + 5)^2 + 21$; $(-5, 21)$; $x = -5$;
Points may vary. $(0, -4)$, $(1, -15)$

31. $(-4, -14)$; $x = -4$; y-intercept: 2;
x-intercepts: -0.3, -7.7; $y \geq -14$

32. $(5, -25)$; $x = 5$; y-intercept: 0;
x-intercepts: 0, 10; $y \geq -25$

33. $(-3, -1)$; $x = -3$; y-intercept: $(0, -10)$,
x-intercepts: none; $y \leq -1$

34. $(-3, 2)$; $x = -3$; y-intercept: $(0, 11)$,
x-intercepts: none; $y \geq 2$

35. $(3.5, -11.25)$

36. $(0.5, 12.25)$

37. $(-1, 9)$

38. $(-1.25, 1.875)$

39. a) 3 m   **b)** 3.2 m   **c)** 2.7 m

40. a) 86 m   **b)** 2 m   **c)** 8 s

41. $12

Using the Strategies   p. 147

1. A: 11 kg, B: 13 kg, C: 14 kg, D: 9 kg, E: 7 kg

2. a) Astros: 2, 0, 1, 1, 2, 4; Bears: 2, 0, 1, 1, 3, 7;
   Colts: 2, 2, 0, 0, 7, 1
   b) Astros: 2, Bears: 2; Colts: 2, Astros: 0;
   Colts: 5, Bears: 1

3. 34

5. 11

6. 12 km

7. by rows: 19, 22, 7; 4, 16, 28; 25, 10, 13

8. 9

9. a) 60 or 48

10. a) 68   **b)** no

Data Bank

1. a) $y = 0.0144x^2 - 0.09$ **b)** 5.76 cm

2. Answers may vary. 2036

3. Answers may vary. Northwest Territories

CHAPTER 4

Quadratic and Polynomial Equations

Chapter Introduction

Chapter Materials

graphing calculators, Teacher's Resource Master 1
(0.5-cm grid paper), Teacher's Resource Master 2
(1-cm grid paper), Teacher's Resource Master 3 (algebra
tiles), Teacher's Resource Master 7 (parabola), overhead
algebra tiles, overhead projector, overhead graphing
calculator, rulers, compasses

Chapter Concepts

Chapter 4 reviews or introduces
* solving quadratic equations graphically
* using factoring to solve quadratic equations
* solving quadratic equations by completing the square
* developing the quadratic formula
* defining, adding, subtracting, multiplying, and
  dividing complex numbers
* understanding and applying the use of the
  discriminant to analyze the nature of the roots of a
  quadratic equation
* developing and applying the remainder theorem to
  polynomial equations
* developing and applying the factor theorem to
  polynomial equations
* reviewing and applying the methods of solving
  polynomial equations

Teaching Suggestions

Direct the students to look at the graph on student text
page 149. Ask:

*Why can the word "cyclic" be used to describe the graph on
this page?*

*How could you use the diagram of the graph to describe a
wavelength?*

Elicit from the students that a wavelength is the
distance between two corresponding points on the
graph. Thus, it could be the distance between one of
the highest points on the graph and the next highest
point, or it could be the distance from the lowest point
on the graph to the next lowest point on the graph.

Have volunteers present their results to the class.

Enrichment

Research and identify situations in nature or a career that
would require the study of the speed of waves. Write a
brief description of such a situation or career and present
your results to the class. Contribute to a class bulletin
board of some of the more interesting situations and
careers presented by you and your classmates.

Assessing the Outcomes

Observation

You might consider some of these questions as you
observe the students work.
* Do the students know how to interpret data from
  a graph?
* Do they work well in pairs?
* Do they persist until they find a solution?
* Do the students attempt all the questions?

Getting Started

Student Text Pages
Pp. 150–151

Learning Outcomes
- Find a pattern in the sum of two consecutive squares.
- Find a pattern in the difference between alternate squares.
- Study patterns in four consecutive Fibonacci numbers.

Prerequisite Skills
1. Evaluate the expression $5m^3$ for each value of m.

a) 4   [320]   b) -3 $[-135]$ c) $\frac{2}{3}$ $\left[\frac{40}{27}\right]$

2. Write the next three consecutive numbers greater than each number.

a) 55   [56, 57, 58]   b) -4 $[-3, -2, -1]$

Teaching Suggestions

Investigating Patterns in Fibonacci Numbers
Review with the class the opening paragraphs on student text page 150. Ask:

What is the meaning of the term "consecutive"?

Discuss the use of subscripts in the terms and their meanings. Ask:

If you are given the third and fourth Fibonacci numbers, how can you find the fifth Fibonacci number?

Assign Investigation 1 to pairs of students. Give the students an opportunity to discuss and compare their results with those of another pair of students in the class.

Have volunteers present their results to the class. Elicit from the students that the sum of the squares of the term numbers of the Fibonacci numbers equals the square of the term number of the result.

Assign Investigation 2 to pairs of students. Ask:

What does the word "alternate" mean in reference to Fibonacci numbers?

What two alternate Fibonacci numbers are possible for the Fibonacci number 34?

Elicit from the students that alternate means not the next one, but the one after that, or not the previous one, but the one before that. Thus, for the Fibonacci number 34, the next one is 55 and the one after that is 89. So the next alternate Fibonacci number to 34 is 89. Also, the Fibonacci number before 34 is 21, and the one before that is 13, so the previous alternate Fibonacci number to 34 is 13.

Assign Investigation 3 to pairs of students. Have the students discuss and compare their results with those of other students.

Ensure that all the students in the class come to the same conclusion. Ask volunteers to present the results in words, and then, have them develop a generalization similar to those in Investigation 1, question 4 and in Investigation 2, question 3. The generalization should take this form:

$$t_n \times t_{n+3} = t_{n+2}^2 - t_{n+1}^2$$

Warm Up
Assign some or all of the questions as individual or group work. Students could record their answers in their notebooks, or take turns asking questions orally with a partner.

When the students have finished, have them discuss the methods they used to answer the questions.

Mental Math
Students could choose, or be assigned, certain questions from each section. Alternatively, small groups could work as teams, sharing the questions and explaining the answers to the rest of the group.

Integrating Technology

Internet
Use the Internet to find information about Leonardo Fibonacci and the Fibonacci sequence.

Assessing the Outcomes

Observation
You may want to consider some of the following skills as the students complete this lesson.
- Do the students understand the use of subscripted variables?
- Are the students able to perform mathematical operations on subscripted variables?
- Do the students understand the concept of Fibonacci numbers?

4.1 Solving Quadratic Equations by Graphing

Student Text Pages
Pp. 152–156

Materials

graphing calculators, Teacher's Resource Master 1 (0.5-cm grid paper), Teacher's Resource Master 2 (1-cm grid paper), Teacher's Resource Master 7 (parabola), overhead graphing calculator, overhead projector

Learning Outcomes

- Solve quadratic equations with unequal roots by graphing.
- Solve quadratic equations with equal roots by graphing.
- Solve quadratic equations with no real roots by graphing.
- Solve problems involving quadratic equations by graphing.

Prerequisite Skills

1. Evaluate each expression for the given value of the variable.

   a) $2x + 5; x = -2$ [1]

   b) $5x^2 + x; x = 2$ [22]

   c) $-3x^2 - 2x + 1; x = \frac{1}{2}$ $\left[-\frac{3}{4}\right]$

   d) $0.5x^2 + 1.5x - 11; x = 0.1$ [-10.845]

2. Write a mathematical expression for each literal expression. Use the variable y.

   a) twice a number increased by 5   [$2y + 5$]

   b) three more than half a number $\left[\frac{y}{2} + 3\right]$

   c) ten decreased by five times a number   [$10 - 5y$]

   d) six times a number increased by the square of the number   [$6y + y^2$]

Mental Math

1. Simplify.

   a) $\sqrt{20}$ [$5\sqrt{2}$]   b) $\sqrt{63}$ [$3\sqrt{7}$]

   c) $\sqrt{75}$ [$3\sqrt{5}$]   d) $\sqrt{48}$ [$4\sqrt{3}$]

   e) $\sqrt{108}$ [$6\sqrt{3}$]   f) $\sqrt{150}$ [$5\sqrt{6}$]

2. Evaluate, if possible.

   a) $\sqrt{81}$ [9]

   b) $\sqrt{-25}$ [not possible]

   c) $\sqrt{14 + 11}$ [5]

   d) $\sqrt{26 - 8}$ [$3\sqrt{2}$]

   e) $\sqrt{5^2 + 75}$ [10]

   f) $\sqrt{3(-7) + 12}$ [not possible]

Explore/Inquire Answers

Explore: Interpret the Graphs

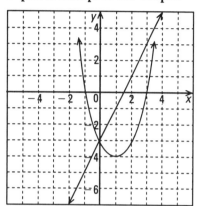

Straight Line: x-intercept $\frac{3}{2}$; y-intercept -3

Parabola: x-intercepts $3, -1$; y-intercept -3

Inquire

1. $\left(\frac{3}{2}, 0\right)$; $x = \frac{3}{2}$ produces $y = 0$

2. $(-1, 0)$, $(3, 0)$; either $x = -1$ or $x = 3$ produces $y = 0$

3. b) $2, -3$ c) yes

4. a) $4, -2$ b) $1, -4$ c) -1

Teaching Suggestions

Method 1

(0.5-cm grid paper, overhead graphing calculator) Review with the class the opening paragraphs of student text page 152. Suggest that students use their graphing calculators to graph the function given in the opening paragraphs. Point out that since the variables in the function are h and d, the horizontal axis should be called the d-axis and the vertical axis should be called the h-axis. Ask:

What values of d and h are inadmissible?

What does the d-intercept of 0 represent?

What does the other d-intercept represent?

What does the vertex of the graph of the height of the kicked ball represent?

What does the axis of symmetry of the graph represent?

Provide pairs of students with grid paper and have them draw the graph of $h(d) = -0.025d^2 + d$, indicating the vertex and the d-intercepts.

Elicit from the students that because distances and heights cannot be negative, negative values of d and h

are inadmissible, the d-intercept of 0 represents the horizontal distance of 0 m before the ball is kicked, the other d-intercept represents the horizontal distance the y-value of the ball has travelled when it lands on the ground, the vertex represents the maximum height of the ball, and the axis of symmetry is the line such that for every h-value before the d-value of the line of symmetry there is a corresponding h-value after the d-value of the line of symmetry. Ask:

How many h-values are there for each d-value? Explain.

How many d-values are there for each h-value? Explain.

Provide pairs of students with graphing calculators and grid paper, and have them complete the Explore section and the Inquire questions. Review how to use the Zoom and the Trace keys of the graphing calculator to locate the intercepts. Ask volunteers to present their results to the class. Provide an overhead projector and an overhead graphing calculator for students to show the graphs they drew or their calculator outputs.

Discuss with the students how a quadratic equation sometimes does not show up on the graphing screen. This means that the graphing calculator window will have to be adjusted in order to see the vertex and intercepts.

Review the meaning of "zeros" and "roots," as shown at the bottom of student text page 152.

Work through with the class teaching examples 1 to 4 on student text pages 153 and 154, ensuring that the students follow along with their own graphing calculators. Have a volunteer demonstrate on the overhead graphing calculator, while you assist the students and facilitate their understanding of the Window, Zoom, Trace, Variable, and Graph keys on their calculators.

Review with the class teaching examples 5 and 6 on student text pages 154 and 155. Remind the students that using a graphing calculator to solve a quadratic equation results in approximate values for the solutions. Many times approximate values are more than sufficient, but if an exact value is required, then the solution would have to be found algebraically. Have volunteers present their results to the class.

Method 2

(0.5-cm grid paper, 1-cm grid paper, overhead graphing calculator, overhead projector, plastic sheet with the graph of $y = -x^2$ drawn on a 1-cm grid) Put a 1-cm grid on the overhead projector and superimpose the graph of $y = -x^2$ so that the vertex is at (0, 4). Ask:

What are the coordinates of the vertex of the graph on the overhead projector?

What are the x-intercepts of this graph?

How many roots does the equation of the graph have?

How would I move the graph so that there is only one x-intercept?

How many roots does the equation of the graph have?

Is it possible to move the graph so that there are no x-intercepts?

What are the coordinates of the vertex of the shifted graph?

How many roots does the equation of this graph have?

Write the following problem on the chalkboard.

The path of a thrown beach ball is given by the function $h = -0.625d^2 + 2.5d$, where h is the height of the ball in metres and d is the distance travelled in metres. How far does the ball travel before landing on the ground?

Organize the class into small groups and have the groups use graphing calculators to graph the equation in the problem. Also, have one student work on an overhead graphing calculator. Give oral directions for inputting the equation. Have the students pay particular attention to the x-intercepts, the vertex, and the number of distinct roots. Be sure to show them the use of the Zoom and Trace keys. Ask:

How would you find the horizontal distance travelled by the ball?

Encourage the students to draw diagrams of their results on grid paper.

Review with the class teaching examples 1 to 6 on student text pages 153 to 155. Remind the students that using a graphing calculator to solve a quadratic equation results in approximate values for the solutions. If exact values are required, then the equation must be solved algebraically. Have volunteers present their results to the class.

Integrating Technology

Graphing Calculators

How would you use your graphing calculator to create the graphs in the teaching examples on student text pages 153 to 155? On a TI-83, the Y= key is used. Press the Y= key, and enter the right side of the first equation at the Y1= prompt.

Then, press the ZOOM key and the 6 key to select ZStandard.

Teaching example 1 shows how to find the x-intercepts when they are not easily read from the graph.

On a TI-83, the Zero operation is the second item when the CALC (i.e., 2nd TRACE) key is pressed. With the graph displayed, press the CALC (i.e., 2nd TRACE) key and the 2 key to select zero.

Use the arrow keys to move the cursor slightly to the left of one of the x-intercepts, and press the ENTER key to define the Left Bound.

Use the arrow keys to move the cursor slightly to the right of the same x-intercept, and press the ENTER key to define the Right Bound.

Use the arrow keys to move the cursor onto the same x-intercept, and press the ENTER key to define your Guess.

Read the x-intercept given as $x =$.

Repeat the steps for the other x-intercept.

On a TI-83, one way to use the Zoom and Trace instructions is to press the ZOOM key and the 1 key to select Zbox.

Use the arrow keys to create a small box around the x-intercept.

Press the TRACE key, and use the arrow keys to find the value of x when y is zero.

For teaching example 4 on student text page 154, the standard viewing window is not useful. The viewing window can be created based on given information. Here the graph opens down, and neither height nor distance can be negative. To set the maximums, use reasonable values for the distance and height a soccer ball is kicked. The window shown uses an Xmin of 0, an Xmax of 50, a Ymin of 0, a Ymax of 12, and suitable scales.

For teaching example 5 on student text page 154, the standard viewing window can be used because it gives the x-intercepts, but not the minimum. If you want to see the minimum, Zoom Fit can be selected to create a graph where the Ymax and Ymin are recalculated to include the maximums and minimums between the Xmax and Xmin that were selected in the last graph. Zoom Fit is the tenth item under the ZOOM menu when the ZOOM key is pressed. Use the down arrow key to see the last items. The window shown uses an Xmin of -10, an Xmax of 10, a Ymin of -50, a Ymax of 20, and suitable scales.

For teaching example 6 on student text page 155, solution 1 follows the method of the previous examples, using the Zero operation. Solution 2 involves graphing a system of equations. The solution is found by finding the intersection using the Intersect operation, which is the fifth item when the CALC (i.e., 2nd TRACE) key is pressed.

See *MATHPOWER™ 11, Western Edition, Blackline Masters* pages 27 to 29 for Setting Viewing Windows. See *MATHPOWER™ 11, Western Edition, Blackline Masters* pages 93 to 98 for Solving Quadratic Equations Graphically.

Computer Data Bank

Use the databases in *MATHPOWER™ 11, Western Edition, Computer Data Bank* to find information to create problems that can be solved by solving a quadratic equation. Display your problems for classmates to research and solve.

Calculator-Based Laboratories

Collect your own real data using a portable data collection device, a CBL (Calculator-Based Laboratory), plot the data on a graphing calculator, and solve the resulting quadratic equation.

Extension

Find the approximate solutions of each equation. Round your answers to 1 decimal place.

1. $0.6x^2 - 1.8x + 4.8 = 0$
2. $-0.2x^2 - 2.8x + 5.4 = 0$

Math Journal

Write a short description of the difference between a quadratic function and a quadratic equation.

Write a short paragraph explaining how the graph of a quadratic function can be used to solve the quadratic equation. Include a diagram.

Common Errors

• Students often leave all the windows of their graphing calculators in standard form. Sometimes this precludes seeing the vertex and the x-intercepts.

R_x Give them time to practise shifting the window to include x-values of the axis from -100 to 100. Then, have them use the Zoom and Trace keys to find approximate values of the x-intercepts.

• Because of work with slope and its definition, "rise over run," students often confuse which coordinate is read first, the horizontal or the vertical.

R_x When finding slope, get the students in the habit of reading across first and then, up or down. This will help them remember to read the horizontal coordinate first and then, the vertical coordinate.

Problem Levels of Difficulty

A: 1–44   **B:** 45–57   **C:** 58–61

Assessing the Outcomes

Written Assignment

1. Solve each equation graphically.
a) $5x^2 + 7x + 9 = 3x^2 + 3x + 5$
b) $2(x - 1)^2 + 3 = 0$
c) $\dfrac{3x + 5}{x + 1} + \dfrac{2}{x} = \dfrac{2}{x + 1}$
2. Identify the vertex, the axis of symmetry, the x-intercepts, and the y-intercept of each equation in question 1.

4.2 Solving Quadratic Equations by Factoring

Student Text Pages
Pp. 157–162

Materials
graphing calculators, Teacher's Resource Master 1 (0.5-cm grid paper)

Learning Outcomes
- Solve quadratic equations by factoring.
- Solve rational equations by factoring.
- Write quadratic equations given the roots of the equations.
- Solve problems involving quadratic equations.

Prerequisite Skills
1. Add.

a) $\dfrac{2}{x+1} + \dfrac{3}{x-1}$ $\left[\dfrac{5x+1}{x^2-1}\right]$

b) $\dfrac{x}{2x-1} + \dfrac{1}{x}$ $\left[\dfrac{x^2+2x-1}{2x^2-x}\right]$

2. Subtract.

a) $\dfrac{5}{x} - \dfrac{3x}{x+1}$ $\left[\dfrac{-3x^2+5x+5}{x^2+x}\right]$

b) $\dfrac{2x}{x+1} - \dfrac{3}{2x+3}$ $\left[\dfrac{4x^2+3x-3}{2x^2+5x+3}\right]$

3. Solve.

a) $x + 5 = 9$ [4]   b) $2x - 1 = 11$ [6]

c) $3x + 1 = 16$ [5]   d) $\dfrac{2x}{3} - 1 = 0$ $\left[\dfrac{3}{2}\right]$

Mental Math
1. Subtract.

a) $74 - 52$ [22]   b) $156 - 49$ [107]

c) $94 - 68$ [26]   d) $32 - 17$ [15]

e) $203 - 57$ [146]   f) $186 - 79$ [107]

2. Simplify, if possible.

a) $\sqrt{300}$ $[10\sqrt{3}]$ b) $\sqrt{50}$ $[5\sqrt{2}]$

c) $\sqrt{45}$ $[3\sqrt{5}]$ d) $\sqrt{28}$ $[2\sqrt{7}]$

e) $\sqrt{242}$ $[11\sqrt{2}]$ f) $\sqrt{432}$ $[12\sqrt{3}]$

Explore/Inquire Answers

Explore: Solve an Equation

a) $x + 12$ b) $x(x+12)$ c) $x(x+12) = 28$

Inquire
1. $x^2 + 12x - 28 = 0$
2. $(x-2)(x+14) = 0$
3. a) $x = 2$ or -14 b) 2 m, 14 m
4. a) $-2, -3$ b) $4, -1$ c) $1, 2$

Teaching Suggestions

Method 1
(0.5-cm grid paper) Review with the class the opening paragraphs on student text page 157. Write some quadratic equations on the chalkboard, and have the students practise identifying the values of a, b, and c from each equation.

Write on the chalkboard the general quadratic equation in standard form: $ax^2 + bx + c = 0$. Discuss with the class the properties of a quadratic equation. Ask:

What values of a are inadmissible?

What values of b are inadmissible?

What values of c are inadmissible?

Elicit from the students that a cannot be equal to zero, but b and c can be any value.

Review with the class the zero property of factors, i.e., if $ab = 0$, then $a = 0$ or $b = 0$.

Have some students use graphing calculators to find the x-intercepts of the quadratic equations you wrote on the chalkboard, and have some students find the solutions to the quadratic equations by factoring and by using the zero property of factors. In this way, the students are able to see that the x-intercepts and the roots of the quadratic equations are the same.

Provide the students with grid paper, and assign the Explore section and the Inquire questions to pairs of students. Have them sketch the graphs of the quadratic functions as a way of checking their results. Give them an opportunity to discuss and compare their results with those of other pairs of students.

Review with the class teaching examples 1 to 5 on student text pages 158 to 160. Remind the students to always ensure that the quadratic equation is in standard form before finding the roots. If the students are having difficulty in rewriting quadratic equations involving rational expressions in standard form, work through this process. Point out that if there are any denominators in the equation, they should be eliminated by multiplying each term of the equation by the common denominator. Remind the students that the inadmissible values of the variable must be stated.

Work through teaching example 6 on student text page 160 with the class. Ask:

How can you find the equation if you know the roots of an equation?

Point out that the problem solving strategy of working backward can be used to find the equation. In other words, if the roots are a and b, then,

$$x = a \quad \text{and } x = b.$$

Thus, $x - a = 0$ and $x - b = 0$.

Thus, $(x - a)(x - b) = 0$.

Have volunteers present their results to the class.

Method 2

Review with the class the general quadratic equation $ax^2 + bx + c = 0$. Point out that this quadratic equation is written in standard form.

Write these quadratic equations on the chalkboard.

$$3x^2 + 2x - 5 = 0 \qquad -4x = -3x^2 + 5$$

$$x^2 - 1.5x = 3.75 \qquad -x^2 - 7x + 4 = 0$$

Have the students rewrite them in standard form and then, identify the values of a, b, and c. Ask:

Which variable, a, b, or c, cannot be zero for a quadratic equation?

Write this quadratic equation on the chalkboard.

$$x^2 - 8x + 15 = 0$$

Use this equation to review with the class the method of solving a quadratic equation. First, have them factor the expression on the left side of the equation and then, set each factor equal to zero. Remind the students about the zero property of factors, i.e., if $ab = 0$, then, $a = 0$ or $b = 0$.

Arrange the class into 4 groups. Write the following quadratic equations on the chalkboard.

$$x^2 - 11x + 24 = 0 \qquad x^2 - 5x - 24 = 0$$

$$x^2 - 10x + 24 = 0 \qquad x^2 - 2x - 24 = 0$$

$$x^2 - 14x + 24 = 0 \qquad x^2 - 10x - 24 = 0$$

$$x^2 - 25x + 24 = 0 \qquad x^2 - 23x - 24 = 0$$

Have two of the groups solve the equations in column 1 and the other two groups solve the equations in column 2. Have them factor the left side of each equation and equate each factor to zero. Then, suggest that one student in each group use a graphing calculator to graph each quadratic equation and find the x-intercepts of the equation.

Give the groups who are solving the same set of equations an opportunity to discuss and compare their results. Then, have all the groups discuss and compare their results. Ask:

How are the solutions to the quadratic equation related to the x-intercepts of the graph of the equation?

Have volunteers present their results to the class.

Review with the class teaching examples 1 to 6 on student text pages 158 to 160.

Sample Solution

Page 162, question 90

a) If -3 is a root of $3x^2 + mx + 3 = 0$, then $(x + 3)$ is a factor of the equation, and the remainder is zero. Divide $3x^2 + mx + 3$ by $(x + 3)$.

$$
\begin{array}{r}
3x + (m - 9) \\
x + 3 \overline{)\, 3x^2 + mx + 3} \\
\underline{3x^2 + 9x} \\
(m - 9)x + 3 \\
\underline{(m - 9)x + 3(m - 9)} \\
3 - 3(m - 9)
\end{array}
$$

The remainder is $3 - 3(m - 9)$ and equals zero.

$$3 - 3(m - 9) = 0$$
$$3 = 3(m - 9)$$
$$1 = m - 9$$
$$10 = m$$

Thus, $m = 10$.

b) The quadratic equation can now be written as

$$3x^2 + 10x + 3 = 0.$$
$$(3x + 1)(x + 3) = 0$$
$$(3x + 1) = 0 \text{ or } (x + 3) = 0$$
$$x = -\frac{1}{3} \text{ or } \qquad x = -3$$

The other root is $-\frac{1}{3}$.

Pattern Power Answer

1. The sums of the rows are consecutive numbers.

2. 25

Integrating Technology

Graphing Calculators

Use the skills discussed in *Integrating Technology* in Section 4.1 on pages 126 and 127 to visualize solutions to some of the questions on student text pages 160 to 162.

Investigate using a graphing calculator with the capacity to factor. On a TI-92, factor is the second item under F2 Algebra. When it is pressed, factor(appears on the screen. It is useful to have the Pretty Print mode on. ON is the default setting. Pretty Print is the 8th item when the MODE key is pressed. To factor, press the F2 key and the 2 key, enter the polynomial and a final), and then, press the ENTER key.

Computer Data Bank

Use the databases in *MATHPOWER™ 11, Western Edition, Computer Data Bank* to find information to create problems that can be solved by solving a quadratic equation. Display your problems for classmates to research and solve.

Calculator-Based Laboratories

Collect your own real data using a portable data collection device, a CBL (Calculator-Based Laboratory), plot the data on a graphing calculator, and solve the resulting quadratic equation.

Extension

The roots of a quadratic equation are $-\frac{1}{2}$ and $\frac{2}{3}$. Write the quadratic equation.

Math Journal

Explain in a few sentences which method of solving a quadratic equation you prefer, using a graphing calculator or using an algebraic method. Explain the differences in the accuracy of the results between the two methods.

Problem Levels of Difficulty

A: 1–38, 47–64, 69–80, 91
B: 39–46, 65–68, 81–88 a), b)
C: 88 c)–90

Assessing the Outcomes

Written Assignment

1. Write each equation in standard form, identify the values of *a*, *b*, and *c*, and solve each equation.

a) $5x^2 + 7x + 9 = 3x^2 + 3x + 5$

b) $2(x - 1)^2 + 3 = 0$

c) $\frac{3x + 5}{x + 1} + \frac{2}{x} = \frac{2}{x + 1}$

2. Explain what a double root means in terms of factors.

Quadratic Equations—
The Square Root Principle

Student Text Pages
Pp. 163–167

Materials
scientific or graphing calculators, Teacher's Resource Master 2 (1-cm grid paper), overhead projector

Learning Outcomes
- Solve quadratic equations using the square root principle.
- Solve problems involving quadratic equations and the square root principle.

Prerequisite Skills

1. Solve.

a) $2x^2 = 18$ $\qquad$ [± 3]

b) $-4x^2 + 9 = 0$ $\qquad$ $\left[\pm\dfrac{3}{2} \right]$

c) $3x^2 - 1 = 26$ $\qquad$ [± 3]

d) $5(x^2 - 1) - 20 = 0$ $\qquad$ [$\pm\sqrt{5}$]

2. Factor.

a) $x^2 + 3x + 2$ $\qquad$ [$(x + 1)(x + 2)$]

b) $x^2 + 5x$ $\qquad$ [$x(x + 5)$]

c) $4x^2 - 6x + 2$ $\qquad$ [$2(2x - 1)(x - 1)$]

d) $-3x^2 + 15x$ $\qquad$ [$-3x(x - 5)$]

Mental Math

1. Subtract.

a) $2.7 - 1.9$ [0.8] $\qquad$ b) $8.5 - 4.9$ [3.6]

c) $15.7 - 8.8$ [6.9] $\qquad$ d) $36.4 - 13.7$ [22.7]

e) $7.4 - 3.6$ [3.8] $\qquad$ f) $5.8 - 2.9$ [2.9]

2. Multiply in two steps.

a) 92×11 [1012] $\qquad$ b) 37×12 [444]

c) 15×27 [405] $\qquad$ d) 15×69 [1035]

e) 7×63 [441] $\qquad$ f) 82×19 [1558]

Explore/Inquire Answers

Explore: Use the Diagram

a) $4x$ $\qquad$ b) $16x^2$

Inquire

1. $16x^2 = 144$ $\qquad$ 2. $x^2 = 9$ $\qquad$ 3. $x = \pm 3$

4. Yes; -3 must be rejected since a length is always positive.

5. $100x^2 = 400$; 2 m

6. a) $64s^2$ $\qquad$ b) 3 cm $\qquad$ c) 3.5 cm

7. a) $x = \pm 6$ $\qquad$ b) $y = \pm 7$ $\qquad$ c) $w = \pm 11$

d) $n = \pm 2$ $\qquad$ e) $t = \pm 5$ $\qquad$ f) $r = \pm\dfrac{6}{5}$

Teaching Suggestions

Method 1

(1-cm grid paper, overhead projector) Review with the class the opening paragraphs on student text page 163. Ask:

What everyday situation or activity have you seen that involves the use of a grid?

Elicit from the students activities such as tiling a floor, police search and rescue work, creating layout pages in the printed media, laying out farm lands on the Prairies, and designing wallpapers.

Provide pairs of students with grid paper and assign the Explore section and the Inquire questions. Encourage the students to use the grid paper to model each question. Give them an opportunity to compare and discuss their results. Have volunteers present their results to the class. Provide an overhead projector for those students who wish to use their diagrams as part of their explanation.

Work through teaching examples 1 to 4 on student text pages 164 and 165. Ask:

What is an exact value?

Which type of method of solving quadratic equations, graphical or algebraic, tends to result in an approximate value? Explain.

For teaching example 1, have one student in each pair use the square root principle and the other use factoring. Ask one or two pairs to explain to the class which method they prefer.

For teaching example 2, challenge some students to solve the equation by factoring. Ask:

How would you write the terms of $9y^2 - 21 = 0$ as a difference of squares?

Lead the students to see that $9y^2 - 21 = 0$ can be written $(3y)^2 - (\sqrt{21})^2 = 0$.

Thus, $(3y)^2 - (\sqrt{21})^2 = 0$

$$(3y - \sqrt{21})(3y - \sqrt{21}) = 0$$

$(3y - \sqrt{21}) = 0$ $\quad$ or $(3y + \sqrt{21}) = 0$

$3y = \sqrt{21}$ or $\qquad$ $3y = -\sqrt{21}$

$y = \dfrac{\sqrt{21}}{3}$ or $\qquad$ $y = -\dfrac{\sqrt{21}}{3}$

Have volunteers present their results to the class.

Method 2

Review with the class the standard form of a quadratic equation, i.e., $ax^2 + bx + c = 0$. Ask:

What would the equation become if $b = 0$?

How would you solve such an equation?

Elicit from the students that to solve an equation of the form $ax^2 + c = 0$, c would be subtracted from each side, each side would then be divided by a, and the square root of each side would be found. Ask:

How many answers are possible?

Ensure that the students realize that when the square root is found, there are two values; if the value is a measurement, then only the value that gives a positive measurement is allowed.

Work through teaching examples 1 to 4 on student text pages 164 and 165 with the class.

Sample Solution

Page 167, question 92

a) $x^2 < 9$

Then, $|x| < 3$

b) $x^2 \geq 25$

Then, $|x| \geq 5$.

Word Power Answer

silk, bilk, balk, bark, barn, born, worn, worm

Integrating Technology

Graphing Calculators

How would you calculate the square root shown in part b) of the solution to teaching example 2 on student text page 164? On a TI-83, the $\sqrt{}$ (i.e., 2nd x^2) key is used. Discuss why the closing bracket is entered after 21.

Use the $\sqrt{}$ key to find the solutions to questions 21 to 32 on student text page 165, and when appropriate, to the questions on student text pages 166 and 167.

Use the skills discussed in *Integrating Technology* in Section 4.1 on pages 126 and 127 of this teacher's resource to visualize solutions to some of the questions on student text pages 165 to 167.

See *MATHPOWER™ 11, Western Edition, Blackline Masters* pages 18 to 20 for Graphing Calculator as a Scientific Calculator.

Computer Data Bank

Use the databases in *MATHPOWER™ 11, Western Edition, Computer Data Bank* to find information to create problems that can be solved by solving a quadratic equation. Display your problems for classmates to research and solve.

Calculator-Based Laboratories

Collect your own real data using a portable data collection device, a CBL (Calculator-Based Laboratory), plot the data on a graphing calculator, and solve the resulting quadratic equation.

Math Journal

Explain the difference between the procedures for solving $(2x + 1)^2 = 16$ and $2x^2 + 1 = 16$.

Problem Levels of Difficulty

A: 1–76, 94   B: 77–88   C: 89–93

Assessing the Outcomes

Written Assignment

1. Solve each equation and state all the roots using the square root principle.

a) $(3x + 1)^2 = 25$ b) $3x^2 + 1 = 25$

2. A picture has the same area as the mat of uniform width that surrounds it. The dimensions of the picture are 32 cm by 50 cm.

a) What is the width of the mat?

b) What are the outside dimensions of the mat?

4.4 Solving Quadratic Equations by Completing the Square

Student Text Pages
Pp. 168–173

Materials
scientific or graphing calculators, Teacher's Resource Master 2 (1-cm grid paper), Teacher's Resource Master 3 (algebra tiles), overhead graphing calculator, overhead algebra tiles, overhead projector

Learning Outcomes
- Solve quadratic equations by completing the square.
- Solve quadratic equations with irrational roots.
- Solve problems involving quadratic equations.

Prerequisite Skills

1. Factor each expression.

a) $4x^2 + 4x + 1$ $[(2x + 1)^2]$

b) $9x^2 - 12x + 4$ $[(3x - 2)^2]$

c) $-2x^2 + 20x - 50$ $[2(x - 5)^2]$

d) $16x^2 + 40x + 25$ $[(4x + 5)^2]$

2. Expand and simplify.

a) $(1 + \sqrt{2})^2$ $[3 + 2\sqrt{2}]$

b) $(3 - \sqrt{5})^2$ $[4 - 6\sqrt{5}]$

c) $(-2 + \sqrt{3})^2$ $[7 - 4\sqrt{3}]$

d) $2(\sqrt{7} - 2)^2$ $[6 - 8\sqrt{7}]$

Mental Math

1. Evaluate for $m = 2$ and $n = -3$.

a) $m + n$ $[-1]$ **b)** $2n - m$ $[-8]$

c) $3m + 2n$ $[0]$ **d)** $m^2 + n^2$ $[13]$

e) $2m^2 - n^2$ $[-1]$ **f)** $5 + n^2 + m$ $[16]$

2. Evaluate, if possible.

a) $\sqrt{3 + 2(3)}$ $[3]$

b) $\sqrt{2(5^2) + 5(10)}$ $[10]$

c) $\sqrt{37 - 53}$ [not possible]

d) $\sqrt{-8^2 - (-3)(-5)}$ [not possible]

e) $\sqrt{19 + 17}$ $[6]$

f) $\sqrt{10^2 - 7(-3)}$ $[11]$

Explore/Inquire Answers

Explore: Use a Diagram

a) $x^2 + 120x$ **b)** $x^2 + 120x = 6400$

Inquire

1. a) $x^2 + 120x + 3600$

b) to preserve the equality of both sides

2. $(x + 60)^2 = 10\ 000$

3. $x + 60 = \pm100$

4. $x = 40$ or $x = -160$

5. -160 must be rejected since a width cannot be negative

6. a) 40 m   **b)** 160 m

7. a) $2, -6$ **b)** $3, -1$ **c)** $-2, -4$

Teaching Suggestions

Method 1

(1-cm grid paper, overhead graphing calculators) Read with the class the opening paragraphs on student text page 168 and then, assign the Explore section and the Inquire questions to pairs of students. Have volunteers present their results to the class.

Point out to the students that since measurements must be positive, any values of the variable that give negative measurements are to be rejected.

Work through teaching examples 1 to 4 on student text pages 169 to 171. Provide an overhead graphing calculator so that volunteers can graph the equations in the teaching examples as you go along.

Remind the students that a radical root value is more exact when left in the form of a radical expression than by finding the approximate value of the radical, and that most solutions of quadratic equations found on the graphing calculator are approximate values.

Method 2

(1-cm grid paper, algebra tiles, overhead algebra tiles, overhead projector) Organize the students into small groups and provide each group with algebra tiles. Write this quadratic equation on the chalkboard.

$$x^2 + 2x = 0$$

Have the students try to arrange one x^2-tile and two x-tiles into a square. Ask:

How many unit squares do you need to complete the square?

What is the side length of your square?

How could you rewrite the equation $x^2 + 2x = 0$ to include the unit tiles you had to add to your group of tiles to make a perfect square?

How could you use the rewritten equation to solve the original equation $x^2 + 2x = 0$?

What is the solution to the equation $x^2 + 2x = 0$?

Elicit from the students that one unit square needs to be added to make a square arrangement. The equation $x^2 + 2x = 0$ can now be written as $x^2 + 2x + 1 = 1$, which can be rewritten as $(x + 1)^2 = 1$. Thus,

$$(x + 1)^2 - 1 = 0$$
$$[(x + 1) - 1][(x + 1) + 1] = 0$$
$$(x + 1 - 1)(x + 1 + 1) = 0$$
$$x(x + 2) = 0$$
$$x = 0 \text{ or } x + 2 = 0$$
$$x = -2$$

The solutions to the equation are 0 and -2.

Provide the students with grid paper and have them repeat the process above with the quadratic equation $x^2 + 4x + 1 = 0$.

Instruct the students to draw the diagram for each step of their solutions on grid paper and have volunteers present their results to the class. Provide overhead algebra tiles and an overhead projector so that students can demonstrate their results with the tiles or with their diagrams. Have them present the solution to the equation. Ask:

How did you write 3 as a square term?

Discuss the difference between exact and approximate values with solutions involving radical numbers. Point out that unless asked, solutions should always be left in radical form, as they are more exact. Have them repeat the same process with these equations:

$$x^2 + 2x - 3 = 0$$
$$x^2 + 6x + 4 = 0$$

Give the students an opportunity to discuss and compare their results with those of other students, and have volunteers present their results to the class.

Review with the class the teaching examples on student text pages 169 to 171. Have a student use an overhead graphing calculator to graph the results as you work through the examples.

Pattern Power Answer

$9322 - 109 = 9213$
$4710 - 898 = 3812$
$6033 - 415 = 5618$
Missing number is 8.

Integrating Technology

Graphing Calculators

How would you calculate the square roots shown in the solution to teaching example 3 on student text page 171? On a TI-83, the $\sqrt{}$ (i. e., 2nd x^2) key is used. Discuss the placement of the brackets around the numerator and around 33. Remind the students that they do not need to re-enter the expression for the subtraction of the square root. Recall the previous expression and edit it, by pressing the ENTRY (i. e., 2nd ENTER) key, using the left arrow key to move the cursor to the + sign, entering a − sign, and pressing the ENTER key.

Use the $\sqrt{}$ key to find the solutions to questions 45 to 54 on student text page 172, and when appropriate, to the questions on student text pages 172 and 173.

Use the skills discussed in *Integrating Technology* in Section 4.1 on pages 126 and 127 in this teacher's resource to visualize solutions to some of the questions on student text pages 172 and 173.

See *MATHPOWER™ 11, Western Edition, Blackline Masters* pages 18 to 20 for Graphing Calculator as a Scientific Calculator.

Computer Data Bank

Use the databases in *MATHPOWER™ 11, Western Edition, Computer Data Bank* to find information to create problems that can be solved by solving a quadratic equation. Display your problems for classmates to research and solve.

Calculator-Based Laboratories

Collect your own real data using a portable data collection device, a CBL (Calculator-Based Laboratory), plot the data on a graphing calculator, and solve the resulting quadratic equation.

Enrichment

The equation for a parabola whose vertex is at (p, q) is of the form $a(x - p)^2 + q = 0$. Use this form of the equation and the equation of a parabola in standard form, $ax^2 + bx + c = 0$, to develop an expression for p and for q in terms of a, b, and c.

Use the expressions to write the vertex of the quadratic equation $5x^2 + 2x - 10 = 0$ without graphing the equation.

Math Journal

Write a list of the methods you can use to solve a quadratic equation. Write a few sentences explaining which method you prefer and why.

Problem Levels of Difficulty

A: 1–48, 51–54, 74
B: 49–50, 55–71
C: 72, 73

Assessing the Outcomes

Diagramming Assignment

a) Use algebra tiles to show the steps of the solution to $5x^2 + 50x = 141$.

b) Draw diagrams of each step of your solution on grid paper.

Materials

scientific or graphing calculators, overhead projector, overhead graphing calculator

Learning Outcomes

- Use the quadratic formula to solve quadratic equations with rational roots.
- Use the quadratic formula to solve quadratic equations with irrational roots.
- Use the quadratic formula to solve rational equations with variables in the denominator.
- Use the quadratic formula to solve problems involving quadratic equations.

Prerequisite Skills

1. Add or subtract.

a) $\dfrac{3}{x} + \dfrac{2}{x + 1}$ $\left[\dfrac{5x + 3}{x^2 + x}\right]$

b) $\dfrac{5x}{2} - \dfrac{7}{3x}$ $\left[\dfrac{15x^2 - 14}{6x}\right]$

c) $\dfrac{100}{2x + 1} + \dfrac{50}{3x}$ $\left[\dfrac{400x + 50}{6x^2 + 3x}\right]$

d) $\dfrac{17}{3x - 1} - \dfrac{2}{4x}$ $\left[\dfrac{31x + 1}{6x^2 - 2x}\right]$

2. Evaluate. Round your answers to 1 decimal place.

a) $\dfrac{1 + \sqrt{8}}{2}$ [1.9]   b) $3\sqrt{5} - 1$ [5.7]

c) $2\sqrt{7} + \sqrt{2}$ [6.7]   d) $5 - 9\sqrt{3}$ [−10.6]

Mental Math

1. Evaluate for $x = -2$ and $y = 1$.

a) $3x - y$ [−7]   b) $x - 5y$ [−7]
c) $4x + 7y$ [−1]   d) $x^2 + 2y$ [6]
e) $-y^2 - 3x$ [5]   f) $2x^2 + y^3$ [9]

2. Subtract.

a) $4.9 - 2.7$ [2.2]   b) $39.2 - 17.5$ [21.7]
c) $11.7 - 6.8$ [4.9]   d) $6.8 - 3.9$ [2.9]
e) $5.7 - 2.9$ [2.8]   f) $9.1 - 6.4$ [2.7]

Explore/Inquire Answers

Explore: Describe the Steps

1. Divide both sides by a.
2. Subtract $\dfrac{c}{a}$ from both sides.
3. Add $\dfrac{b^2}{4a^2}$ to both sides to complete the square on the left side.
4. Factor to a perfect square on the left side.
5. Write the fractions on the right side with a common denominator, and subtract.
6. Take the square root of both sides.
7. Use the exponent law $\sqrt{\dfrac{a}{b}} = \dfrac{\sqrt{a}}{\sqrt{b}}$ to simplify the right side.
8. Subtract $\dfrac{b}{2a}$ from both sides.
9. Simplify the left side.
10. Simplify the right side.

Inquire

1. 1, 3, 2   2. a) 1   b) 1   c) −1   d) −2
4. a) −3, −1   b) 3, −4   c) 1, −5

Teaching Suggestions

Method 1

(overhead projector, overhead graphing calculator)
Read with the class the opening paragraphs on student text page 174. Ask:

How would you describe the path of the skier?

What features of the quadratic function for the path of the skier help you to describe the path of the skier?

Organize the class into small groups, and assign the Explore section and the Inquire questions. Give the groups an opportunity to discuss and compare each other's results. Have volunteers present their results to the class. Provide an overhead projector, if necessary.

Review with the class the teaching examples on student text pages 175 to 178. Have some students work alongside the rest of the class with a graphing calculator and find the graphs of the equations. Give these students an opportunity to show their results on an overhead graphing calculator.

For teaching example 4 on student text page 177, ask:

What formula relates distance, speed, and time?

If you know the distance and the speed, how do you find the time?

Emphasize that the chart is there to help them visualize the relationships among the variables. It is a problem-solving tool.

Method 2

Review with the class the meaning of standard form of a quadratic equation. Ask:

Why is it important to write the quadratic equation in standard form?

Elicit from the students that the values of *a*, *b*, and *c* can only be identified when the quadratic equation is in standard form.

Present the general form of the quadratic equation and have pairs of students use algebraic skills to find the roots of the equation. This process is given in the Explore section on student text page 174. Give the students an opportunity to discuss and compare their results with those of other students. Have volunteers present their results to the class.

Then, assign the students these quadratic equations, $x^2 + 3x = 4$ and $3x^2 - 21x + 15 = 0$, and have them use their formula to find the roots of the equations.

Ensure that they begin by writing the quadratic equation in standard form, and that if the values of the roots involve a radical sign, then a more exact solution includes the radical number rather than an approximate value for the radical number. Point out that in the second equation, a common factor of 3 exists. It is useful to remove any common factors, so that the calculations do not have to be any more complicated than necessary.

Work through teaching examples 1 to 5 on student text pages 175 to 178. Have some students use their graphing calculator to find the solutions as a check.

Sample Solution

Page 180, question 84 a)

$2x^2 + 17xy + 8y^2 = 0$

Substitute $a = 2$, $b = 17y$, and $c = 8y^2$ into

$$x = \frac{-b \pm \sqrt{b^2 - 4ac}}{2a}$$

$$= \frac{-17y \pm \sqrt{(17y)^2 - 4(2)(8y^2)}}{2(2)}$$

$$= \frac{-17y \pm \sqrt{289y^2 - 64y^2}}{4}$$

$$= \frac{-17y \pm \sqrt{225y^2}}{4}$$

$$= \frac{-17y \pm 15y}{4}$$

$$= \frac{-2y}{4} \text{ or } \frac{-32y}{4}$$

$$= \frac{-y}{2} \text{ or } -8y$$

Thus, $x = \frac{-y}{2}$ or $-8y$.

Integrating Technology

Graphing Calculators

How would you calculate the square roots shown in the solutions to teaching example 3 on student text page 176 and teaching example 5 on student text page 178? On a TI-83, the $\sqrt{\ }$ (i. e., 2nd x^2) key is used. Discuss the placement of the brackets around the numerator and around 17 and 12.65. Remind the students that they do not need to re-enter the expression for the subtraction of the square root. See *Integrating Technology* in Section 4.4 on page 134 of this teacher's resource for more information about not re-entering expressions.

Teaching example 4 on student text page 177 illustrates using the ANS (i. e., 2nd (−)) key to recall the previous answer. Discuss the placement of the brackets around −1270.

Use the $\sqrt{\ }$ key to find the solutions to questions 31 to 40, 41 to 46, and 47 to 50 on student text page 178, and when appropriate, to the questions on student text pages 179 and 180.

Use the skills discussed in *Integrating Technology* in Section 4.1 on pages 126 and 127 of this teacher's resource to visualize solutions to some of the questions on student text pages 178 to 180.

See *MATHPOWER™ 11, Western Edition, Blackline Masters* pages 18 to 20 for Graphing Calculator as a Scientific Calculator.

Computer Data Bank

Use the databases in *MATHPOWER™ 11, Western Edition, Computer Data Bank* to find information to create problems that can be solved by solving a quadratic equation. Display your problems for classmates to research and solve.

Calculator-Based Laboratories

Collect your own real data using a portable data collection device, a CBL (Calculator-Based Laboratory), plot the data on a graphing calculator, and solve the resulting quadratic equation.

Extension

Consider the solutions of each of the following equations. You may use factoring, completing the square, or the quadratic formula. Explain why the first has two distinct roots, the second has two equal roots, and the third has no real roots. Use diagrams to help your explanations.

1. $x^2 - 2x - 15 = 0$

2. $4x^2 + 4x + 1 = 0$

3. $x^2 - 6x + 11 = 0$

Enrichment

Research who first discovered the quadratic formula and any present day applications. Write a short paragraph of your findings and share them with the class.

Math Journal

Write the general form of the quadratic equation in standard form and the quadratic formula associated with the general form of the quadratic equation. Describe how you would use the formula to find the roots of a quadratic equation.

Common Errors

*   Students often forget to include any negative signs when identifying the values of a, b, and c for substitution into the quadratic formula. They also often forget the minus sign in front of the b and in front of the $4ac$ in the quadratic formula.

* R_x Remind the students that it is important to encapsulate the value, including any negative signs, in brackets. They will avoid extraneous or imaginary roots by multiplying the resulting value by the negative sign in front of b or in front of $4ac$.

Problem Levels of Difficulty

A: 1–65, 86, 87   **B:** 66–77   **C:** 78–85

Assessing the Outcomes

Written Assignment

Solve each of the following equations, if possible. You may use factoring, completing the square, or the quadratic formula.

1. $9x^2 - 1 = 0$

2. $x^2 - 6x - 9 = 0$

3. $2x^2 + 6x + 9 = 0$

4. $15x^2 = 16x - 15$

5. $6x^2 - 11x - 10 = 0$

4.6 Complex Numbers

Student Text Pages
Pp. 181–186

Materials
graphing calculators

Learning Outcomes
- Study the concept of complex numbers.
- Simplify expressions involving complex numbers.
- Add and subtract complex numbers.
- Multiply and divide complex numbers.
- Solve quadratic equations whose roots are complex numbers using the square root principle.
- Solve quadratic equations whose roots are complex numbers using the quadratic formula.
- Solve quartic equations whose roots are complex numbers.
- Find the output values of fractal equations.

Prerequisite Skills
1. Simplify.

a) $\sqrt{9} \times \sqrt{16}$ [12]   b) $2\sqrt{4} \times 3\sqrt{25}$ [60]

c) $\sqrt{8} \times \sqrt{27}$ $[6\sqrt{6}]$ d) $3\sqrt{5} \times \sqrt{45}$ [45]

2. Simplify.

a) i^2 $[-1]$ b) i^7 $[-i]$ c) i^6 $[-1]$

d) i^8 $[1]$ e) i^{17} $[i]$ f) i^{202} $[-1]$

Mental Math
1. Calculate.

a) 2.1×2.9 [6.09]   b) 5.6×5.4 [30.24]

c) 7.5^2 [56.25]   d) 4.2×4.8 [20.16]

e) 9.3×9.7 [90.21]   f) 6.6×6.4 [42.24]

2. Evaluate for $k = -1$, $m = 3$, and $n = \frac{1}{2}$.

a) $k + 2m - n$ $\left[4\frac{1}{2}\right]$ b) $-m^2 + 2n$ $[-8]$

c) $n - m - 3k$ $\left[\frac{1}{2}\right]$ d) $2k + 3m + 5n$ $\left[9\frac{1}{2}\right]$

e) $2k + n^3$ $\left[-1\frac{7}{8}\right]$ f) $3 + m - n$ $\left[5\frac{1}{2}\right]$

Explore/Inquire Answers

Explore: Use the Definitions
a) $i\sqrt{3}$ b) $3i$ c) $4i$ d) $2i\sqrt{2}$ e) $2i\sqrt{5}$

Inquire
1. Factor out the $\sqrt{-1}$ and simplify the remaining radicals.
2. a) $i\sqrt{10}$ b) $3i\sqrt{2}$ c) $2i\sqrt{7}$ d) $5i\sqrt{2}$
3. a) -25 b) -6 c) -4 d) -12 e) 10 f) 18

Teaching Suggestions
Review with the class the opening paragraphs of student text page 181. Discuss the definition of the imaginary unit i. Practise finding the values of different powers of i. Ask:

What are all the possible values of powers of i?

Elicit from the students that the powers of i have one of four values, i, $-i$, 1, or -1.

Assign the Explore section and the Inquire questions to pairs of students. Give the students an opportunity to discuss and compare their results and then, have volunteers present their results to the class.

Review with the class the paragraphs at the top of student text page 182 and work through teaching examples 1 to 3 on student text pages 182 and 183. Ask:

Are all real numbers also complex numbers? Explain.

Review with the class the final paragraphs on student text page 183 and assign teaching examples 4 to 7 on student text pages 184 and 185. Have volunteers present their results to the class.

Sample Solution
Page 186, question 97
The general term for an even number is $2n$.
The general terms for two consecutive even numbers are $2n$ and $2n + 2$.
The square of the product of two consecutive even numbers is $[2n(2n + 2)]^2$.

$$\text{Thus, } [2n(2n + 2)]^2 = 28\,224$$
$$[4n(n + 1)]^2 = 168^2$$
$$[n(n + 1)]^2 = \frac{168^2}{4^2}$$
$$= 42^2$$
$$(n^2 + n)^2 = 42^2$$
$$(n^2 + n)^2 - 42^2 = 0$$
$$[(n^2 + n) - 42][(n^2 + n) + 42] = 0$$
$$(n^2 + n - 42)(n^2 + n + 42) = 0$$
$$(n^2 + n - 42) = 0 \text{ or } (n^2 + n + 42) = 0$$
$$(n + 7)(n - 6) = 0 \qquad \text{or} \qquad n = \frac{-1 \pm \sqrt{1^2 - 4(1)(42)}}{2}$$
$$n = -7 \text{ or } 6 \quad \text{or} \quad n = \frac{-1 \pm \sqrt{-167}}{2}$$

Since $n = \dfrac{-1 \pm \sqrt{-167}}{2}$ are complex numbers and not integers, they are inadmissible.

Thus, $n = -7$ or 6.

The even numbers for $n = -7$ are $2(-7)$ and $2(-7) + 2$, or -14 and -12.

The even numbers for $n = 6$ are $2(6)$ and $2(6) + 2$, or 12 and 14.

Integrating Technology

Graphing Calculators

Investigate using complex numbers on a graphing calculator. On a TI-83, complex number mode is set by pressing the MODE key, using the arrow key to move to a + bi to the immediate right of Real, and pressing the ENTER key.

In complex number mode, simplify questions 1 to 18 on student text page 185.

Internet

Use the Internet to find information about fractals.

Extension

Describe the pattern in the values of i^n for real values of n. How would you use this pattern to find the value of the following powers of i?

1. i^{372} **2.** i^{355} **3.** i^{97} **4.** i^{150}

5. i^{7601} **6.** i^{768} **7.** i^{1051} **8.** i^{5622}

Enrichment

Research the history of fractals and how they are related to the Mandelbrot set. Write a short report on your research and present your results to the class.

Math Journal

Describe the three possible types of solutions there are for quadratic functions. Include a diagram to demonstrate each type of solution.

Cross-Discipline

Electrical Engineering Complex numbers are used to calculate the impedance of AC electrical circuits. Impedance (Z) is how a device resists the flow of electricity in an AC signal. The impedance of a basic component is given as a complex number, $a + ib$. When two basic components are combined in series, the overall impedance is given by

$$Z = Z_1 + Z_2.$$

When two basic components are combined in parallel, the overall impedance is given by

$$Z = \frac{Z_1 Z_2}{Z_1 + Z_2}.$$

1. The impedance of one of the basic components is $1.000\,000 + 1.000\,000i$ and of the other component is $0.500\,000 - 0.499\,999i$. Calculate the overall impedance in the complex circuit, if the basic components are connected

  a) in series   **b)** in parallel

2. The impedance of one of the basic components is $10.000\,000 + 100.000\,000i$ and of the other component is $1.000\,023 - 99.990\,005i$. Calculate the overall impedance in the complex circuit, if the basic components are connected

  a) in series   **b)** in parallel

Problem Levels of Difficulty

A: 1–73, 78–81, 88, 89

B: 74–77, 82–87, 90–94   **C:** 95–97

Assessing the Outcomes

Written Assignment

1. The roots of a quadratic equation are $3i$ and $2i$. Find the original quadratic equation.

2. The roots of a quadratic equation are ai and bi. Find the original quadratic equation.

4.7 The Discriminant

Student Text Pages
Pp. 187–190

Materials
graphing calculators, Teacher's Resource Master 1 (0.5-cm grid paper), overhead projector

Learning Outcomes
- Learn the concept of discriminant.
- Use the discriminant to find the nature of the roots of quadratic equations.
- Use the nature of the roots of a quadratic equation to find the coefficients of the quadratic equation.
- Solve problems involving quadratic equations using the formula for the discriminant.

Prerequisite Skills
1. Write each equation in standard form.
   a) $2x - 5 = 3x^2$ $[3x^2 - 2x + 5 = 0]$
   b) $3 + x^2 = -5x + 1$ $[x^2 + 5x + 2 = 0]$
   c) $-2x^2 - 3 = 7x$ $[2x^2 + 7x + 3 = 0]$
   d) $-7 + 3x = -11x^2$ $[11x^2 + 3x - 7 = 0]$

2. Expand and simplify.
   a) $x(3x - 5)$ $[3x^2 - 5x]$
   b) $-2x(7 + 4x)$ $[-8x^2 - 14x]$
   c) $3(5x + 2x^2)$ $[6x^2 + 15x]$

Mental Math
1. Subtract.
   a) $62 - 29$ [33]   b) $810 - 350$ [460]
   c) $9.1 - 4.7$ [4.4]   d) $72 - 25$ [47]

2. Calculate.
   a) 58^2 [3364]   b) 5200^2 [27 040 000]
   c) 5.4^2 [29.16]   d) 530^2 [280 900]

Explore/Inquire Answers

Explore: Complete the Table

Equation	Type of Solutions	Value of $b^2 - 4ac$
$x^2 + 2x + 1 = 0$	real and equal	0
$x^2 + 6x + 9 = 0$	real and equal	0
$x^2 + 4x + 3 = 0$	real and distinct	4
$x^2 + 6x + 7 = 0$	real and distinct	8
$x^2 + 5x + 7 = 0$	imaginary	−3
$x^2 + 6x + 10 = 0$	imaginary	−4

Inquire
1. a) real and equal   b) real and distinct
   c) imaginary
2. a) $2d^2 - 4d + 2.1 = 0$; -0.8
   b) No; the equation has no real solutions.
3. If $b^2 - 4ac$ is a perfect square, then the roots are rational; otherwise, they are irrational.

Teaching Suggestions

Method 1
Review with the class the opening paragraphs on student text page 187.

Assign the Explore section and the Inquire questions to pairs of students. Give the students ample opportunity to discuss and compare their results with other students. Have volunteers present their results to the class. Ask:

How are the solutions of a quadratic equation and the x-intercepts of the quadratic equation related?

In what form must the quadratic equation be, in order for you to use the discriminant to find the nature of the roots of the equation?

Why do you think it is useful to know the nature of the roots of a quadratic function?

Review with the class the material at the top of student text page 188 and suggest they copy this chart into their journals. Work through teaching examples 1 to 3 on student text pages 188 and 189. Point out that teaching example 3 demonstrates why knowing the discriminant, and thus, the nature of the roots is useful. It can save a lot of time and effort.

Method 2
(0.5-cm grid paper, overhead projector)   Review with the class the quadratic formula for finding the roots of a quadratic equation.

$$x = \frac{-b \pm \sqrt{b^2 - 4ac}}{2a}$$

Tell the class that the part under the square root sign, $b^2 - 4ac$, is called the discriminant.

Write these quadratic equations on the chalkboard.

Column 1	Column 2	Column 3
$x^2 - 3x + 2 = 0$	$x^2 + 2x + 1 = 0$	$x^2 - 2x = 0$
$x^2 - 2x - 3 = 0$	$x^2 - 4x + 4 = 0$	$x^2 - x + 4 = 0$
$x^2 + x + 10 = 0$	$x^2 + 6x + 9 = 0$	$x^2 - 4x + 6 = 0$
$x^2 - 5x + 4 = 0$	$x^2 + 4x + 4 = 0$	$x^2 + 3x + 5 = 0$
$x^2 + 3x - 10 = 0$	$x^2 - 10x + 25 = 0$	$x^2 + 2x + 7 = 0$

Organize the class into 6 groups with about the same number of students in each group and provide each group with grid paper. Have two groups work on the quadratic equations in column 1, two groups on the quadratic equations in column 2, and two groups on the quadratic equations in column 3.

Instruct the students to write down the values of a, b, and c, use the quadratic formula to find the roots of each equation, and sketch a graph of the equation, showing the x-intercepts of the graph. Tell them to keep a record of the value of the discriminant for each equation.

Give the groups who are working on the same columns of equations an opportunity to discuss and compare their results.

Then, ask:

What pattern do you see in the value of the discriminant for the quadratic equations in your column?

How would you describe the roots of the equations in your column?

What do the sketches of the graphs of the equations have in common?

Have a member from each group present his or her results to the class. Provide an overhead projector so that the sketches of the graphs of the quadratic equations can be shown.

Challenge the students to make up some rules for the nature of the roots of a quadratic equation from the discriminant.

Lead the students to see that when the discriminant is greater than zero, there are two real roots; when the discriminant is zero, there are two equal roots; and when the discriminant is less than zero, the equation has no real roots.

Discuss the usefulness of such a result, i.e., by evaluating the discriminant alone, you can tell whether a quadratic equation has two solutions, 1 solution, or no real number solution. Ask:

How does the sketch of the graph of a quadratic equation indicate the nature of the roots of a quadratic equation?

Review with the class the teaching examples on student text pages 188 and 189.

Pattern Power Answer

1. 10, 21, 32, 43, 54, 65, 76, 87, 98

2. a) 20, 31, 42, 53, 64, 75, 86, 97

b) 30, 41, 52, 63, 74, 85, 96

c) 40, 51, 62, 73, 84, 95

3. The tens digit must exceed the units digit by the subtracted number divided by 9.

4. a) 60, 71, 82, 93   **b)** 80, 91

Extension

Show that if a and c have different signs, then the quadratic equation $ax^2 + bx + c = 0$, $a \neq 0$ has two real roots.

Enrichment

Research the person who first discovered the significance of the discriminant. Write a few sentences about this person and any present day applications of the discriminant. Present your research to the class.

Math Journal

discriminant Write a few sentences describing the discriminant, and what the value of the discriminant indicates.

Write a few sentences explaining how knowledge of the value of the discriminant tells you the nature of the roots of the equation $2x^2 + 9 = 6x$.

Common Errors

- Students often use $\sqrt{b^2 - 4ac}$ to evaluate the discriminant instead of $b^2 - 4ac$.

R$_x$ Remind the students that only $b^2 - 4ac$ needs to be evaluated and analyzed.

Problem Levels of Difficulty

A: 1–47   **B:** 48–53   **C:** 54–55

Assessing the Outcomes

Pair Evaluation: Student Assignment

Have pairs of students work together on this project and submit a report that represents the work done by the pair.

a) Determine if a rectangular garden with a perimeter of 60 m can have an area of 189 m^2.

b) Find the dimensions of the garden if the garden does exist.

Written Assignment

For each of the following, list the values of a, b, and c, and without solving the equation, decide if the roots of the equation are real and distinct, real and equal, or imaginary.

1. $9x^2 - 1 = 0$

2. $-6x + x^2 = -9$

3. $2x^2 + 9 = 6x$

4. $16x = 15x^2 + 15$

5. $6x^2 - 11x - 10 = 0$

6. $x^2 + x = -\dfrac{1}{4}$

Career Connection

Package Design

Student Text Page
P. 191

Learning Outcomes
- Define the dimensions of a package.
- Gain insight into careers in the field of package design.
- Solve problems involving the design of packages.

Mental Math
1. Evaluate for $m = -2$ and $n = -1$.

a) $2m + n$ $[-5]$ b) $2n - m$ $[0]$

c) $m + 2n$ $[-4]$ d) $m^2 + 2n^2$ $[6]$

e) $m^2 - n^2$ $[3]$ f) $2 + n^2 - m$ $[5]$

2. Evaluate, if possible.

a) $\sqrt{4 + 2(3) - 1}$ $[3]$

b) $\sqrt{25 + 20}$ $[10]$

c) $\sqrt{27 - 43}$ [not possible]

d) $\sqrt{19 + 17}$ $[6]$

Teaching Suggestions
Introduce the topic with a discussion about designing packages. Ask:

Does any student in the class know of anyone who designs packages?

Supply packages, or have the students bring to class packages that they find attractive, and discuss what features the packages have that make them attractive or unattractive.

Assign Investigation 1 to pairs of students. Ask:

What formulas would you use for the surface area and the volume of a rectangular solid?

Have volunteers present their results to the class.

Then, organize the class into 5 groups of approximately the same size. Assign one question in Investigation 2 to each group, ensuring that all the questions are assigned. Have each group complete the research for that question and present their results to the class.

Assessing the Outcomes

Journal

Write about
- the most interesting thing you learned about designing packages
- what else you would like to know about designing packages and how you could find out

Investigating Math

Sum and Product of the Roots

Student Text Pages
Pp. 192–193

Materials
graphing calculators

Learning Outcomes

- Develop the relationships between the coefficients of a quadratic equation in standard form and the sum and product of the roots of a quadratic equation.
- Develop the form of the quadratic equation involving the sum of the roots and the product of the roots.
- Solve problems involving the roots of a quadratic equation.

Mental Math

1. Evaluate for $x = 0.5$ and $y = -1.2$.

a) $3x - y$	[2.7]	**b)** $-x - y$	[0.7]
c) $x^2 + y^2$	[1.69]	**d)** $x + y + 5$	[4.3]
e) $-2x + 3y$	[-4.6]	**f)** $y^2 + 2y$	[-0.96]

2. Subtract.

a) $39 - 21$	[18]	**b)** $94 - 77$	[17]
c) $46 - 38$	[8]	**d)** $114 - 36$	[78]
e) $255 - 129$	[126]	**f)** $582 - 377$	[205]

Teaching Suggestions

Assign Investigation 1 to pairs of students. Give the students an opportunity to compare and discuss their results with those of other students in the class. Have volunteers present their results to the class. Ask:

Do you think knowing the sum and the product of the roots of a quadratic equation is useful?

How could you use this knowledge?

Assign Investigation 2 to pairs of students. Ask:

What would be your first step in adding the equations for the roots?

Remind the students that these expressions obey the same rules as the addition of fractions and that all fractions should be reduced to lowest terms.

For question 2, ask:

What would be your first step in multiplying the equations for the roots?

What is special about the product of the numerators of the expressions for the roots?

Ensure that the students realize that the product of the numerator is the product of the sum and the difference of terms, and can be simplified like this

$$(a - b)(a + b) = a^2 - b^2$$

Assign Investigations 3 and 4 to pairs of students, and give them ample opportunity to discuss and compare their results with those of other students in the class. Have volunteers present their results to the class.

Math Journal

Include in your journal the formulas for the sum and the products of the roots of a quadratic equation.

Also include in your journal the form of the quadratic equation found at the end of student text page 192, which involves the sum and the product of the roots.

Assessing the Outcomes

Written Assignment

1. Without solving, find the sum and the product of the roots of each equation.

a) $x^2 + 8x + 15 = 0$

b) $2x^2 - 5x - 3 = 0$

2. Write a quadratic equation with

a) a sum of roots of -7 and a product of 12

b) a sum of roots of 2 and a product of $-\frac{5}{4}$

3. One of the roots of $6x^2 + mx - 14 = 0$ is $\frac{2}{3}$.

a) Find the other root.

b) Find the value of m.

Connecting Math and Esthetics

The Golden Ratio

Student Text Pages
Pp. 194–196

Materials
scientific or graphing calculators, Teacher's Resource Master 2 (1-cm grid paper), rulers, compasses, overhead projector

Learning Outcomes
- Develop the value for the ratio ϕ.
- Construct geometric shapes whose measures conform to the ratio ϕ.
- Discover the relationships between the Fibonacci numbers and the golden ratio.
- Discover the relationship between the golden ratio, ϕ, and examples in architecture, nature, and art.

Mental Math
1. Simplify.
a) $\sqrt{8} \times \sqrt{27}$ $[6\sqrt{6}]$ b) $\sqrt{5} \times \sqrt{45}$ $[15]$
c) $2\sqrt{9} \times \sqrt{16}$ $[24]$ d) $2\sqrt{4} \times 3\sqrt{25}$ $[60]$

2. Evaluate each expression for the given values of the variables.
a) $3x + y - 5$; $x = -2, y = 1$ $[-5]$
b) $2x + y - 11$; $x = -5, y = 1$ $[-20]$
c) $5x - 2y^2$; $x = 0.5, y = -0.5$ $[2]$
d) $x^2 + 5x + y$; $x = 1, y = 3$ $[9]$

Teaching Suggestions
(1-cm grid paper, rulers, compasses, overhead projector)
Review with the class the opening paragraphs on student text page 194. Ask:

If the golden ratio is ϕ, what are the terms of the ratio?

Ensure that the students realize that the terms of the ratio are 1 and ϕ.

Draw the students' attention to the diagram of a rectangle and the proportion involving w beside the diagram of the rectangle. Ask:

Does any student have a bank card?

Is this card an example of a golden rectangle?

Why do you think designers of bank cards use the golden ratio to decide on the dimensions of a card?

If one dimension of a rectangle is 20 cm, what would the other dimension of the rectangle have to be in order for the rectangle to be a golden rectangle? Is there more than one answer?

Assign Investigation 1 to pairs of students. Project a copy of the Mondrian painting on the chalkboard and have volunteers present their results to the class, by identifying the golden rectangles from the painting and justifying their choices.

For question 4, ask:

What is the first step in showing the validity of each equation?

What other method could you use to show the validity of each equation?

Elicit from the students that substituting the exact value into the right side of each equation and simplifying should result in the exact value of ϕ. The other way of showing the validity of each equation is to simplify each equation by multiplying each side by the denominator, and then, solving the resultant quadratic equation.

For question 5, ask:

What pattern do you see in the index number of each term and the power of ϕ?

Have volunteers present their results to the class.

Organize the class into groups of four. Provide half of the groups with rulers, compasses, and grid paper and assign them Investigation 2. Assign Investigation 3 to the other half of the groups. Encourage groups who have been assigned the same investigation to discuss and compare their results. Have volunteers present their results to the class. Provide an overhead projector and encourage the students to present any diagrams they created as part of their results of the investigation.

For Investigation 2, question 4, the construction in question 1 could be constructed by placing the compasses on centre A and radius AF, draw an arc of a circle, and with centre F and radius AB draw an arc to cut the arc with centre A and radius AF at G. Then, since $\triangle$AFG is isosceles and the ratio of one of its equal sides, AF to the base FG (which is equal to AB) is equal to ϕ, it is a golden triangle.

Assign one question in Investigation 4 to pairs of students. Give the students time to research any information they need, and ensure every question in Investigation 4 is assigned. Give the pairs of students who have been assigned the same question an opportunity to discuss and compare their results. Have volunteers present their results to the class. Create a class bulletin board of all the interesting information presented by the students.

Integrating Technology

Graphing Calculators

See *MATHPOWER*™ *11, Western Edition, Blackline Masters* pages 18 to 20 for Graphing Calculator as a Scientific Calculator.

Internet

Use the Internet to find information about Aristotle, Kepler, Pythagoras, Phidias, Piet Mondrian, the golden ratio, and the golden rectangle.

Extension

The Lucas numbers are formed in the same way as the Fibonacci numbers, except the first two terms are 2 and 1.
Lucas numbers: 2, 1, ...

a) Write the first 10 terms of the Lucas numbers.

b) Calculate the ratio of succeeding terms.

c) To what number does the succeeding ratios tend?

Enrichment

Research the life and works of Albrecht Dürer. Write a short essay on his work involving the golden ratio and the human body, and present your essay to the class.

Math Journal

golden ratio, golden rectangle   Write a short description of the meaning of each of these terms, and how they apply to art. Compare your essay with those of others in your class.

Assessing the Outcomes

Journal

Write a short essay about the most interesting thing you learned about the golden ratio.

Observation

You might consider some of these questions as you observe the students work.

- Do the students understand the concept of the golden ratio?
- Do the students demonstrate a willingness to work cooperatively with classmates?
- Do the students use enough resources to obtain new information?
- Do the students show persistence?

Technology

Solving Quadratic Equations With a Graphing Calculator

Student Text Page

P. 197

Materials

graphing calculators

Learning Outcomes

- Find the real roots of quadratic equations algebraically using a graphing calculator.
- Interpret solutions found algebraically using a graphing calculator.

Prerequisite Skills

Graph each equation using a graphing calculator. Then, find the x-intercepts.

a) $2x^2 - 5 = 9x$ [0.5, 5]

b) $6x^2 + 6 = 15x$ [0.666…, 1.5]

Teaching Suggestions

Discuss how to use a graphing calculator to solve algebraically quadratic equations like those on student text page 197. On a TI-83, guesses must be entered. So, it is helpful to graph the equation first. The equation must be written with 0 on one side. There is not a lot of advantage to change from the default bounds.

For example, to solve the equation in question 24, rewrite the equation as $5(2x^2 - 5) + 2(4 - x) = 0$.
Then, enter the left side at the Y1= prompt.
Press the ZOOM key and the 6 key to select ZStandard. Observe that there are two real roots — one between -1 and -2 and the other between 1 and 2.
To solve algebraically, press the MATH key and the 0 key to select Solver. (Use the down arrow key to see the last items.)

Press the up arrow key once and the CLEAR key to clear any previous equation.
At the eqn:0 = prompt, either enter the equation or press the VARS key, the right arrow key to select Y-VARS, the 1 key to select Function, the 1 key to select Y1, and the ENTER key.
At the X= prompt, enter a guess such as -1, based on what you observed when the equation was graphed, and then, press the SOLVE (i. e., ALPHA ENTER) key. (If the ENTER key is pressed after the guess, the up arrow key must be pressed to return to the variable line before the SOLVE (i. e., ALPHA ENTER) key is pressed.) Observe that one root is (1.207 669 683…
At the X= prompt, enter a second guess such as 1, based on what you observed when the equation was graphed.
Then, press the SOLVE (i. e., ALPHA ENTER) key. Observe that the other root is 1.407 669 683 0…

On a TI-92, solve is the first item under F2 Algebra. At the solve(prompt, enter the equation. Then, press , x) to indicate the equation is being solved for x, or whatever letter is used as the variable, before pressing the ENTER key. Observe that the two roots for the equation in question 24 are $(3\sqrt{19} + 1)/10$ and $-(3\sqrt{19} + 1)/10$. To get the decimal approximations, press the ≈ (i.e., ◆ ENTER) key.

In Exploration 1, all solutions are real roots, while there are some imaginary roots in Exploration 2.
A TI-83 does not find non-real roots. However, by graphing the quadratic equation first, you can tell if the roots are real and distinct, real and equal, or not real. Imaginary roots must be found another way. With a TI-92, if a solution gives only one root, you know there is a second equal root, and if a solution gives no roots (i.e., false), the roots are imaginary and can be found using cSolve, which is the first item in A: Complex under F2 Algebra. At the cSolve(prompt, enter the equation. Then, press , x) to indicate the equation is being solved for x, or whatever letter is used as the variable, before pressing the ENTER key.

See *MATHPOWER™ 11, Western Edition, Blackline Masters* pages 99 to 101 for Solving Quadratic Equations Algebraically.

Common Errors

- Students frequently proceed without having the cursor in the correct place.

R_x When solving for a variable, remember the cursor must be on the variable line before pressing the SOLVE (i.e., ALPHA ENTER) key.

Assessing the Outcomes

Journal

Write about the advantages and disadvantages of solving quadratic equations algebraically using a graphing calculator, and whether you prefer solving graphically or algebraically when using a graphing calculator, and why.

4.8 The Remainder Theorem

Student Text Pages
Pp. 198–203

Materials
graphing calculators

Learning Outcomes
- Develop the concept of the remainder theorem.
- Use the remainder theorem to find the remainder when one polynomial is divided by another polynomial.
- Use the remainder theorem to find the coefficient of a polynomial.
- Use the remainder theorem to find a system of equations that can be used to find the coefficients of a polynomial.
- Use the remainder theorem to find a remainder of a polynomial whose leading coefficient is not 1.
- Solve problems using the remainder theorem.

Prerequisite Skills
1. For $P(x) = 7x^2 - 3x - 1$, find the following.

a) $P(0)$ [−1]   b) $P(-3)$ [71]

c) $P(5)$ [159]   d) $P\left(-\frac{1}{2}\right)$ $\left[\frac{9}{4}\right]$

2. Solve each equation.

a) $3x - 2 = 7$ [3]   b) $5x + 4 = -11$ [−3]

c) $-2x - 4 = 0$ [−2]   d) $\frac{5x}{4} + 2 = 7$ [4]

Mental Math
1. Evaluate.

a) $\sqrt{3^2 + 4^2}$ [5]   b) $2\sqrt{5^2 + (3)(-8)}$ [2]

c) $\sqrt{8^2 + 5(4^2)}$ [12]   d) $3\sqrt{10^2 - 91}$ [9]

e) $\sqrt{7(9) + 106}$ [13]   f) $-\sqrt{20^2 - 3(13)}$ [−19]

2. For each inequality, write three different ordered pairs that include the given coordinate and that satisfy the inequality.

a) $x + y > -1$; ($\blacksquare$, 2)   [(0, 2), (−1, 2), (−2, 2)]

b) $-x - y < 2$; (3, $\blacksquare$)   [(3, 7), (3, 8), (3, 9)]

c) $y \leq -x + 1$; (2, $\blacksquare$)   [(2, −2), (2, −3), (2, −4)]

d) $3x - 4y + 1 \geq 0$; ($\blacksquare$, 1)   [(2, 1), (3, 1), (4, 1)]

Explore/Inquire Answers

Explore: Discover the Relationship

Quotient	Remainder	P(b)
$x - 4$	4	4
$2x + 7$	6	6
$3x + 2$	0	0
$x^2 + 4x + 1$	−1	−1
$x^2 - 2x - 2$	−2	−2
$2x^2 - 3x + 1$	2	2

Inquire
1. $P(b)$ equals the remainder.

2. a) Evaluate $P(4)$.   b) Evaluate $P(-3)$.

3. a) −6   b) 6   c) 0   d) 10

4. 0

5. a) 5

b) the height of the shot at $t = 1$, or after 1 s

Teaching Suggestions

Method 1
Review with the class the opening paragraph on student text page 198. Write this problem on the chalkboard.

Divide $4x^4 - 3x^3 + 7x - 10$ by $x + 5$.

Review with the class the process of dividing one polynomial by another. Remind the students that if a power of x is missing, then space must be left for that power in the answer.

Arrange the class into groups of three and assign the Explore section and the Inquire questions. Have each student work on two of the polynomials in the table in the Explore section. Ensure that all of the equations in the table are completed by each group.

Have the students of each group combine their results and discuss any similarities and differences in their results.

For Inquire question 2, suggest that the students look at any patterns they see in their results that might help them answer this question.

Have volunteers present their results to the class.

Review with the class the development of the relationship with the factor theorem given at the top of student text page 199. Be sure that the students understand that if the remainder is a constant, then it actually represents the value of the function at $x = b$. Ask:

Why is the remainder theorem useful?

Ensure that the students realize that the remainder theorem is a real time-saving tool.

Review with the class teaching example 1 on student text page 199. Point out that the remainder theorem avoids doing division, and uses substitution to determine the remainder.

Before reviewing teaching examples 2 and 3 on student text pages 199 and 200, you may want to review the process of synthetic division. Ask:

If there is one coefficient missing, how many divisors must you know?

If there are two coefficients missing, how many divisors must you know? Explain.

Ensure that the students realize that just as in the solution of any system of equations, if there are two variables, then you need a system of two equations in the two variables; if there are three variables, then you need a system of three equations in the three variables.

Review the paragraphs given at the top of student text page 201. Ensure that the students know how to find the value to be substituted for the variable if the coefficient of the variable of the given divisor is more than 1. For example, if the divisor given is $3x + 4$, then by equating $3x + 4$ to zero, you can find the value to be substituted.

$$3x + 4 = 0$$
$$3x = -4$$
$$x = -\frac{4}{3}$$

The value to be substituted is $-\frac{4}{3}$.

Remind the students that although this method is the same one used to find a solution for the equation, given the factor of an equation, the divisors in teaching examples 1 to 4 are not factors of the equation. Ask:

What condition would have to exist for the divisors of an equation to be factors of the equation?

Ensure that the students understand that a factor divides a number or an expression evenly with no remainder. So a divisor is a factor only when the remainder is zero. This information will be very important in the following section.

Review with the class teaching examples 4 and 5 on student text pages 201 and 202. Ask:

How is $-\frac{5}{2}$ determined to be the value to be substituted in the polynomial in teaching example 4?

Method 2

Ask the students:

When you divide 32 by 10, what is the remainder?

What equation involving the dividend, the divisor, the quotient, and the remainder can you write for this problem?

Elicit from the students that
$$32 \div 10 = 3 \times 10 \text{ R } 2.$$

Give the students a few more examples like this. These examples will help with the development of the remainder theorem, since these examples are numerical cases of the general case of the remainder theorem.

Write the following polynomials and divisors on the chalkboard.

Polynomial	Divisor	$P(x)$
$x^2 + x - 12 = 0$	$(x + 3)$	$P(-3)$
$x^2 - 6x - 1 = 0$	$(x - 7)$	$P(7)$
$2x^2 + 11x + 7 = 0$	$(2x + 1)$	$P\left(-\frac{1}{2}\right)$

Have pairs of students divide each polynomial by the given divisor and find the value of the polynomial for the given value of x. Remind the students that they can use the process of synthetic division to speed up the assignment. Give students an opportunity to discuss and compare their results with other students. Ask:

What pattern do you see in the remainder when the polynomial is divided by the given divisor and the value of the polynomial for the given value of x?

Then, write these polynomials and divisors on the chalkboard and have the students complete the same process as with the above polynomials.

Polynomial	Divisor	$P(x)$
$x^3 - x^2 + 10 = 0$	$(x - 3)$	$P(3)$
$2x^3 + x^2 + 4x + 3 = 0$	$(x + 1)$	$P(-1)$
$2x^4 + 7x^3 - 19x^2 - 8x - 5 = 0$	$(2x - 3)$	$P\left(\frac{3}{2}\right)$

Ask:

Does the pattern that you saw above also apply to polynomials of degree greater than 2?

Have volunteers present their results. Ask:

How would you describe in words the relation between a polynomial, its divisor, its quotient, and its remainder?

Have pairs of students create some of their own polynomial expressions and divisors, and share them with each other to test the theorem for themselves. Give the students an opportunity to discuss and compare similarities and differences before asking volunteers to present their results to the class.

Review with the class the material at the top of student text pages 199 and 201, and the teaching examples on student text pages 199 to 202.

Integrating Technology

Graphing Calculators

The screen with the solution to teaching example 1 on student text page 199 shows finding a remainder by dividing. A TI-92 is used to divide a polynomial by a polynomial using propFraction, which is the seventh item under F2 Algebra. The division is entered at the propFraction(prompt. Discuss the placement of brackets around the numerator and the denominator, and a closing bracket at the end.

Enrichment

Cardan's solution of a cubic equation such as $x^3 + mx + n = 0$ is

$$x = \left[-\frac{1}{2}n + \sqrt{R}\right]^{\frac{1}{3}} + \left[-\frac{1}{2}n - \sqrt{R}\right]^{\frac{1}{3}},$$

where $R = \left(\frac{1}{2}b\right)^2 + \frac{a^3}{27}$.

Use the method above to solve each cubic equation. Round your answers to 3 decimal places, if necessary.

1. $x^3 - 15x - 4 = 0$

2. $x^3 + 5x + 1 = 0$

3. $x^3 - 3x - 6$

Research Girolama Cardan, and write a few sentences about his life and works.

Math Journal

The Remainder Theorem   Describe the remainder theorem for a polynomial of any degree. Write a description of the steps you would follow to find the missing coefficient of a polynomial, given a divisor and a remainder.

Problem Levels of Difficulty

A: 1–56, 63   **B:** 57–60   **C:** 61–62

Assessing the Outcomes

Written Assignment

1. Use two different methods to find the remainder when $6a^3 + 11a^2 - 5$ is divided by $a - 5$.

2. When $12s^3 + ms^2 + 13s + 20$ is divided by $s + 4$, the remainder is -310. What is the value of m?

3. When $8y^3 + ay^2 + by - 45$ is divided by $2x + 7$, the remainder is -10. When the same polynomial is divided by $x + 5$, the remainder is -455. What are the values of a and b?

The Factor Theorem

Explore/Inquire Answers

Explore: Discover the Relationship

	Remainder, $P(b)$	Factor? (Yes or No)		Remainder, $P(b)$	Factor? (Yes or No)
1.	0	Yes	7.	0	Yes
2.	−6	No	8.	24	No
3.	0	Yes	9.	0	Yes
4.	0	Yes	10.	−18	No
5.	−10	No	11.	144	No
6.	0	Yes	12.	−120	No

Student Text Pages
Pp. 204–211

Materials

graphing calculators, overhead graphing calculator, overhead projector

Learning Outcomes

- Verify that a divisor is a factor of a polynomial.
- Define the integral zero theorem.
- Use the integral zero theorem to factor a polynomial.
- Use the factor theorem to find the factors of a polynomial.
- Define the rational zero theorem.
- Use the rational zero theorem to factor a polynomial.
- Solve problems involving the factor theorem.

Inquire

1. Yes **2.** No

3. a) ±1, ±2, ±5, ±10 **b)** $x - 2, x - 1, x + 5$

4. a) $x(x - 4)(x - 5)$ **c)** 6 m by 2 m by 1 m

Teaching Suggestions

Method 1

(overhead graphing calculator) Review with the class the opening paragraphs of student text page 204. Ask:

What is the difference between a factor of a polynomial and a divisor of a polynomial?

Elicit from the students that a factor of a polynomial divides a polynomial evenly and there is no remainder. A divisor of a polynomial may or may not result in a remainder.

Assign the Explore section and the Inquire questions to pairs of students. Suggest that they use synthetic division to complete the table in the Explore section. Ask:

How will you recognize when a divisor is a factor of the polynomial?

Ensure that the students realize that the divisor is a factor of a polynomial when the remainder is zero. Have volunteers present their results to the class.

Review with the class the lesson and the teaching examples on student text pages 206 to 209. As you work through the teaching examples, have several students simultaneously use a graphing calculator to find the solutions of the equations given in the teaching examples. Students could use an overhead graphing calculator to present their results to the class. Ask:

If the divisor of a polynomial is $3x + 5$, what value of x would you substitute in the polynomial? Explain.

Prerequisite Skills

1. For $f(x) = 3x^2 + 2x - 1$, find

a) $f(-3)$ [20] **b)** $f(2)$ [15]

c) $f\left(\frac{1}{4}\right)$ $\left[-\frac{5}{16}\right]$ **d)** $f(0)$ [−1]

2. Divide.

a) $(x^2 + 3x + 2) \div (x + 1)$ [x + 2]

b) $(2x^2 - 5x - 3) \div (x - 3)$ [2x + 1]

c) $(2x^2 - 11x + 5) \div (2x - 1)$ [x − 5]

d) $(-x^2 + 2x + 15) \div (5 - x)$ [x + 3]

3. Write the prime factors of each number.

a) 24 [1, 2, 3, 4, 6, 8, 12, 24]

b) 60 [1, 2, 3, 4, 5, 6, 10, 12, 15, 20, 30, 60]

c) 49 [1, 7, 49]

Mental Math

1. Simplify.

a) $\sqrt{20}$ [$2\sqrt{5}$] **b)** $\sqrt{32}$ [$4\sqrt{2}$]

c) $\sqrt{147}$ [$7\sqrt{3}$] **d)** $\sqrt{200}$ [$10\sqrt{2}$]

e) $\sqrt{45}$ [$3\sqrt{5}$] **f)** $\sqrt{243}$ [$9\sqrt{3}$]

2. Calculate.

a) 0.52^2 [0.2704] **b)** 5.5^2 [30.25]

c) 0.052^2 [0.002 704] **d)** 5500^2 [30 250 000]

e) 520^2 [270 400] **f)** 0.55^2 [0.3025]

Method 2

(overhead graphing calculator, overhead projector)   Review with the class the remainder theorem. Ask:

How would you describe a divisor that divided evenly into the polynomial so that the remainder was zero?

Discuss the case of the divisor, $(x - a)$, that divides a polynomial so that the remainder is zero. Point out that in this case, the divisor is a factor, and one solution of the polynomial equation is $x = a$. Tell the students that this is a special case of the remainder theorem, and is called the factor theorem.

Review with the class the division statement for a polynomial.

Dividend = Quotient × Divisor + Remainder

Use this division statement as a basis for writing the factor theorem statement on the chalkboard.

For a polynomial $P(x)$ with a divisor $(x - a)$ that results in a quotient $Q(x)$ and a zero remainder,

$P(x) = (x - a) \times Q(x)$, if, and only if, $P(a) = 0$.

Write the polynomial function

$$y = x^3 + 2x^2 - 11x - 12$$

on the chalkboard and have pairs of students use their graphing calculators to find the x-intercepts of the function. Ask:

How are the x-intercepts related to the roots of the function $y = x^3 + 2x^2 - 11x - 12$?

Remind the students that the x-intercepts are also called the roots or the zeros of the function.

How could you use the x-intercepts to write the factors of the function $y = x^3 + 2x^2 - 11x - 12$?

How could you use the x-intercepts to write the function $y = x^3 + 2x^2 - 11x - 12$ as a product of its factors?

How could you check that the product of the factors represents the function $y = x^3 + 2x^2 - 11x - 12$?

Have the same pairs of students repeat the process above with the following equations:

$$y = 2x^3 - x^2 - 16x + 15$$
$$y = x^3 - 0.75x^2 - 55.75x + 14$$

Give the students an opportunity to discuss and compare their results and then, have volunteers present their results to the class. Provide an overhead graphing calculator, if possible.

Review with the class the lesson and the teaching examples on student pages 205 to 209.

Sample Solution

Page 211, question 91

a) If $x + y$ is to be a factor of $x^4 + y^4$, then, $x = -y$ must satisfy $x^4 + y^4 = 0$.
Substitute $x = -y$ in $x^4 + y^4 = 0$.
$$(-y)^4 + y^4 = y^4 + y^4$$
$$= 2y^4$$
Then, $x = -y$ does not satisfy $x^4 + y^4 = 0$.
Thus, $x + y$ is not a factor of $x^4 + y^4$.
If $x - y$ is to be a factor of $x^4 + y^4$, then, $x = y$ must satisfy $x^4 + y^4 = 0$.
Substitute $x = y$ in $x^4 + y^4 = 0$.
$$(y)^4 + y^4 = y^4 + y^4$$
$$= 2y^4$$
Then, $x = y$ does not satisfy $x^4 + y^4 = 0$.
Thus, $x - y$ is not a factor of $x^4 + y^4$.
b) Substitute $x = -y$ in $x^4 - y^4 = 0$.
$$(-y)^4 - y^4 = y^4 - y^4$$
$$= 0$$
Then, $x + y$ is a factor of $x^4 - y^4$.
Substitute $x = y$ in $x^4 - y^4 = 0$.
$$(y)^4 - y^4 = y^4 - y^4$$
$$= 0$$
Then, $x - y$ is a factor of $x^4 - y^4$.
c), d), e), f), g), h) As in parts a) and b), $x + y$ is a factor of $x^5 + y^5$, $x - y$ is not a factor of $x^5 + y^5$, $x + y$ is not a factor of $x^5 - y^5$, $x - y$ is a factor of $x^5 + y^5$; $x + y$ is not a factor of $x^6 + y^6$, $x - y$ is not a factor of $x^6 + y^6$, $x + y$ is a factor of $x^6 - y^6$, $x - y$ is a factor of $x^6 - y^6$; $x + y$ is a factor of $x^7 + y^7$, $x - y$ is not a factor of $x^7 + y^7$, $x + y$ is not a factor of $x^7 - y^7$, $x - y$ is a factor of $x^7 - y^7$.
i) In general,
$x + y$ is not a factor of $x^n + y^n$ when n is even, $x + y$ is a factor of $x^n + y^n$ when n is odd,
$x - y$ is never a factor of $x^n + y^n$,
$x + y$ is a factor of $x^n - y^n$ when n is even,
$x + y$ is not a factor of $x^n - y^n$ when n is odd,
$x - y$ is always a factor of $x^n - y^n$
j) Since n is even, $x + y$ and $x - y$ are factors of $x^8 - y^8$.
k) Since n is odd, $x + y$ is a factor of $x^{11} + y^{11}$.

Logic Power Answer

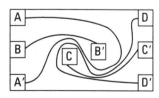

Integrating Technology

Graphing Calculators

The screen with the solution to teaching example 2 on student text page 206 shows the division of a polynomial by a polynomial. A TI-92 is used to divide a polynomial by a polynomial. The division is entered with brackets around the numerator and the denominator.

How would you use your graphing calculator to create the graphs in the solutions to teaching example 2 on student text page 206 and teaching example 6 on student text page 209? On a TI-83, a polynomial function is graphed like other functions, using the Y= key. The x-intercepts for the first function can be read from the graph. For the second function, two of the three x-intercepts can be read from the graph, and the other is found using the Zero operation. As pointed out, the Zero operation gives a decimal approximation to $\frac{1}{3}$.

Use your graphing calculator to graph some of the functions in questions 1 to 54 on student text pages 209 and 210 to determine if the stated polynomial is a factor.

Extension

You are told that the polynomial $2x^4 + 3x^3 + 8x^2 - 15x + 6$ has four real roots, and that two of them are -1 and -3. What are the other two roots?

Math Journal

Write a short essay describing the difference between the remainder theorem and the factor theorem.

Problem Levels of Difficulty

A: 1–50, 55–58, 65–68, 75–77
B: 51–54, 59–64, 69–74, 78–88
C: 89–93

Assessing the Outcomes

Written Assignment

1. In each of the following, a polynomial and one of its factors is given. Find the other factors of the polynomial.

a) $x^3 - 6x^2 - x + 30, (x + 2)$

b) $2x^3 - x^2 - 5x - 2, (2x + 1)$

2. Factor.

a) $x^3 + x^2 - 14x - 24$

b) $x^4 - x^3 - 3x^2 + x + 12$

Technology

Exploring Polynomial Functions With a Graphing Calculator

Student Text Pages
Pp. 212–213

Materials
graphing calculators

Learning Outcomes

- Graph cubic, quartic, and quintic functions, and functions of the form $y = x^n$ using a graphing calculator.
- Relate the x-intercepts of cubic, quartic, and quintic functions, and functions of the form $y = x^n$ to the solutions of their related equations.
- Solve cubic, quartic, and quintic equations graphically using a graphing calculator.

Prerequisite Skills

Sketch the graph of a quadratic function for which the related equation has each type of roots.

a) distinct real roots

b) equal real roots

c) imaginary roots

d) a real root and an imaginary root   [not possible]

Teaching Suggestions

Discuss how to use a graphing calculator to create the graphs on student text page 212. On a TI-83, a polynomial function is graphed like other functions, using the Y= key. Sometimes the x-intercepts of a function can be read from the graph. Other times the Zero operation is needed.

Have the students graph the cubic and quartic functions given before Exploration 1, and compare their graphs with those shown. Then, use the skills discussed in *Integrating Technology* in Section 4.1 on pages 126 and 127 of this teacher's resource to find the roots.

Discuss terms such as local maximums, local minimums, and turning points, and their use in describing graphs.

Assign each exploration, discussing the findings of each before proceeding with the next. Remind the students of the importance of sketching graphs to have a record for later comparisons and interpretation.

See *MATHPOWER™ 11, Western Edition, Blackline Masters* pages 102 to 104 for Polynomial Functions and Polynomial Equations.

Assessing the Outcomes

Written Assignment

Summarize features of quadratic, cubic, quartic, and quintic functions in a table using headings such as the following.

Name
Degree
General form
y-intercept
Greatest number of x-intercepts
Greatest number of turning points

4.10 Solving Polynomial Equations

Student Text Pages
Pp. 214–221

Materials
graphing calculators, Teacher's Resource Master 1 (0.5-cm grid paper), overhead graphing calculator, overhead projector

Learning Outcomes
- Solve polynomial equations that contain a common factor.
- Solve polynomial equations that have integral, rational, irrational, and imaginary roots.
- Solve problems involving polynomial equations.

Prerequisite Skills
1. Find the intercepts of each function.

a) $y = 2x + 5$ $\left[x\text{-intercept } -\frac{5}{2}; y\text{-intercept } 5\right]$

b) $y = -3x - 7$ $\left[x\text{-intercept } \frac{7}{3}; y\text{-intercept } -7\right]$

c) $y = x^2 - 3x + 2$ [x-intercepts 1, 2; y-intercept 2]

d) $y = x^2 + 4x + 3$ [x-intercepts −1, −3; y-intercept 3]

2. Evaluate $x^2 + x - 5$ for each value of x. Round your answers to 1 decimal place, if necessary.

a) -2 [−3]   b) $\sqrt{2} - 1$ [−4.4]

c) $\dfrac{2 + \sqrt{3}}{3}$ [−2.2]   d) $\dfrac{\sqrt{5} - 2}{2}$ [−4.9]

3. Factor.

a) $x^2 + 4x + 4$ [$(x + 2)^2$]

b) $x^2 - 5x + 6$ [$(x - 2)(x - 3)$]

c) $2x^2 - 4x - 6$ [$2(x + 1)(x - 3)$]

Mental Math
1. Simplify.

a) $\sqrt{32}$ [$4\sqrt{2}$]   b) $\sqrt{18}$ [$3\sqrt{2}$]

c) $\sqrt{96}$ [$4\sqrt{6}$]   d) $\sqrt{99}$ [$3\sqrt{11}$]

e) $\sqrt{147}$ [$7\sqrt{3}$]   f) $\sqrt{162}$ [$9\sqrt{2}$]

2. For each inequality, write three different ordered pairs that include the given coordinate and that satisfy the inequality.

a) $x + y \geq 5$; ($\blacksquare$, 1)   [(5, 1), (6, 1), (7, 1)]

b) $-x - y < -1$; (1, $\blacksquare$)   [(1, 1), (1, 2), (1, 3)]

c) $y \leq 3x - 1$; (3, $\blacksquare$)   [(3, 8), (3, 7), (3, 6)]

d) $x + 3y + 1 > 0$; ($\blacksquare$, −1)   [(3, −1), (4, −1), (5, −1)]

Explore/Inquire Answers

Explore: Interpret the Graph

a), d)

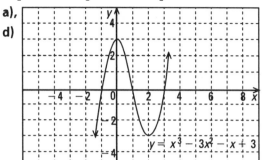

b) $-1, 1, 3$ c) 3

Inquire
1. $(-1, 0), (1, 0), (3, 0)$ The x-values of these three points give zero y-values. Thus, the x-values satisfy the equation $x^3 - 3x^2 - x + 3$. Values that satisfy an equation are solutions of the equation.

2. a) $(x + 1)(x - 1)(x - 3)$

   b) Equate each factor to zero and solve for the variable.

3. a) $-2, 1, 2$ b) $-2, 1, 3$ c) $-2, -1, 3$ d) $1, 1, 1$

Teaching Suggestions
(graphing calculators, overhead graphing calculator, 0.5-cm grid paper) Review with the class the opening paragraphs on student text page 214. Provide pairs of students with grid paper and assign the Explore section and the Inquire questions.

Have one student draw a graph on the grid paper while the partner uses a graphing calculator to find the x- and y-intercepts and to solve the equations. Ask:

If a polynomial is of degree n, how many roots does it have?

How can you use this fact to help you decide whether all of the required x-intercepts of a polynomial function graphed on a graphing calculator are present on the screen?

Give the students ample opportunity to discuss and compare similarities and differences in their results and diagrams with those of other pairs of students. Have volunteers present their results to the class. Provide an overhead projector for those students who drew diagrams on grid paper, and an overhead graphing calculator for those students who used the graphing calculator. Ask:

How are the x-intercepts and the factors of the equation related?

How are the factors of an equation related to the roots of the equation?

Review with the class the paragraphs at the top of student text page 215. Point out that this material is a review of much of the work covered in the rest of the chapter.

Work through teaching examples 1 to 6 on student text pages 215 to 219. Have some students work along with the class and graph the required equations with a graphing calculator.

For teaching example 1, ask:

Why is the origin a root of the equation?

How does the fact that the origin is a root relate to the common factor that was removed?

For teaching example 2, ask:

How many roots does the equation have? Explain.

Elicit from the students that there are three roots, because the equation is cubic. If they see the solution 1, -2 for a cubic equation, they should know that one of the roots has to be a double root. They won't know which root is the double root without further checking. Point out that the roots of the equation are written as 1, -2, -2 to avoid any ambiguity as to the number of roots. This is why teaching example 2 has 3 roots, although two of them are equal.

In teaching example 3, point out that once you are faced with quadratic equations, it is acceptable to apply regular factoring skills, if you wish. The quadratic formula could also be used.

Sample Solution

Page 221, question 104 a)

The general cubic function is given by
$y = ax^3 + bx^2 + cx + d$.
The y-intercept is the value of the cubic equation when $x = 0$.
The y-intercept is -5.
Substitute $x = 0$ and $y = -5$ in
$\quad y = ax^3 + bx^2 + cx + d$
$-5 = a(0) + b(0) + c(0) + d$
$-5 = d$

Then, the general cubic function becomes
$y = ax^3 + bx^2 + cx - 5$.
If the x-intercepts are $\sqrt{5}$, $-\sqrt{5}$, and -1, then the values of the cubic function are zero when $x = \sqrt{5}$, $-\sqrt{5}$, and -1.

For $x = \sqrt{5}$, $\quad 0 = ax^3 + bx^2 + cx - 5$
$\qquad\qquad 0 = 5\sqrt{5}a + 5b + \sqrt{5}c - 5 \dots\dots(1)$
For $x = -\sqrt{5}$, $0 = ax^3 + bx^2 + cx - 5$
$\qquad\qquad 0 = -5\sqrt{5}a + 5b - \sqrt{5}c - 5 \dots\dots(2)$
For $x = -1$, $\quad 0 = ax^3 + bx^2 + cx - 5$
$\qquad\qquad 0 = -a + b - c - 5 \dots\dots\dots\dots(3)$

Add (1) and (2).
$0 = 5\sqrt{5}a + 5b + \sqrt{5}c - 5 \dots\dots\dots\dots\dots(1)$
$0 = -5\sqrt{5}a + 5b - \sqrt{5}c - 5 \dots\dots\dots\dots(2)$
$0 = 10b - 10$
$10 = 10b$
$b = 1$

Subtract (2) from (1).
$\qquad 0 = 5\sqrt{5}a + 5b + \sqrt{5}c - 5 \dots\dots\dots\dots(1)$
$\qquad 0 = -5\sqrt{5}a + 5b - \sqrt{5}c - 5 \dots\dots\dots\dots(2)$
$\qquad 0 = 10\sqrt{5}a + 2\sqrt{5}c$
$-10\sqrt{5}a = 2\sqrt{5}c$
$\qquad -5a = c \dots\dots\dots\dots\dots\dots\dots\dots(4)$

Substitute $b = 1$ and $c = -5a$ in (3).
$0 = -a + b - c - 5 \dots\dots\dots\dots\dots\dots(3)$
$0 = -a + 1 - (-5a) - 5$
$0 = -a + 1 + 5a - 5$
$0 = 4a - 4$
$4a = 4$
$a = 1$

Thus, from (4), $-5a = c$
$\qquad\qquad -5(1) = c$
$\qquad\qquad\quad c = -5$
The cubic function is $y = x^3 + x^2 - 5x - 5$.

Logic Power Answer

1st row: 1, 4
2nd row: 3, 10, 7, 11
3rd row: 8, 12, 2, 5
4th row: 6, 9

Integrating Technology

Graphing Calculators

How would you use your graphing calculator to create the graphs in the solutions to the teaching examples on student text pages 215 to 219? On a TI-83, a polynomial function is graphed like other functions, using the Y= key. Sometimes the x-intercepts of a function can be read from the graph. Other times the Zero operation is needed.

Use the skills discussed in *Integrating Technology* in Section 4.1 on page 109 of this teacher's resource to solve some of the polynomial equations on student text pages 219 to 221.

How would you calculate the square root shown in part b) of the solution to teaching example 4 on student text page 217? On a TI-83, the $\sqrt{}$ (i.e., 2nd x^2) key is used. Discuss the placement of the brackets around the numerator and around 5. Remind students that they do not need to re-enter the expression for the subtraction of the square root. See *Integrating Technology* in Section 4.4 on page 134 of this teacher's resource for more information about not re-entering expressions.

Use the $\sqrt{}$ key to evaluate the roots in questions 47 to 52 on student text page 220, and when appropriate, in the questions on student text page 221.

See *MATHPOWER™ 11, Western Edition, Blackline Masters* pages 102 to 104 for Polynomial Functions and Polynomial Equations.

Extension

Create a polynomial function from each of the following.

1. The roots of the function are 1, −2, 3, and 4.

2. The roots of the function are $\frac{1}{2}$, $-\frac{1}{3}$, and 0.

3. The function has any 3 roots of your choice, provided two of them are opposite in value.

Math Journal

Make a list of the processes you could use to solve a polynomial equation. Compare your list with that of your classmate's, and add any processes you missed.

Common Errors

- Students often confuse the sign of the root of an equation when they know a factor of the equation. For example, if a factor of an equation is $(x + 2)$, they often identify the root of the equation as 2 instead of −2.

R_x Remind the students that in order to find the roots of the equation by factoring, the original equation must be factored and the equation rewritten as a product of factors. Then, each factor is equated to zero. Thus, for a factor such as $(x + a)$, when it is equated to zero, and the equation solved by adding the opposite of a, i.e., $-a$ to each side, it can be seen that the root is $-a$.

If the factor is of the form $(ax + b)$, then in order to isolate x, $-b$ must be added and then both sides divided by a. Thus, the root becomes $x = -\frac{b}{a}$.

Problem Levels of Difficulty

A: 1–77   **B:** 78–101   **C:** 102–106

Assessing the Outcomes

Written Assignment

1. Solve and check.
   a) $x^2 - 9x = 0$
   b) $x^3 - 6x - 6 = 0$
   c) $2x^3 + 9x^2 - 6x - 5 = 0$

2. a) Find the exact solutions of $x^3 - 2x^2 - 7x + 2 = 0$.
   b) Evaluate the solutions. Round to the nearest hundredth, if necessary.

3. Find the exact roots of $x^3 = -8$.

4. Write an equation with the given roots.
   a) $2, \frac{2}{3}, -5$ b) $1 - 2i, 5, 1 + 2i$

5. Find three consecutive integers with a product of −990.

Technology

Solving Polynomial Equations With a Graphing Calculator

Student Text Page
P. 222

Materials
graphing calculators

Learning Outcomes
- Solve polynomial equations algebraically using a graphing calculator.
- Interpret solutions found algebraically using a graphing calculator, particularly when fewer roots are shown than expected.

Prerequisite Skills
1. State the possible numbers of each type of roots for a cubic equation.

a) distinct real roots	[1, 2, 3]
b) equal real roots	[2, 3]
c) imaginary roots	[0, 2]

2. Repeat question 1 for a quartic equation.

[a) 0, 1, 2, 3, 4; b) 0, 2, 3, 4; c) 0, 2, 4]

Teaching Suggestions
Discuss how to use a graphing calculator to solve algebraically quadratic equations like those on student text page 222.

In Exploration 1, all the equations have real roots. On a TI-92, solve, which is the first item under F2 Algebra, finds all real roots. At the solve(prompt, enter the equation. Then, press , x) to indicate the equation is being solved for x, or whatever letter is used as the variable, before pressing the ENTER key. For non-integer roots, press the $\approx$ (i.e., ◆ ENTER) key to get the decimal approximations.

In Exploration 2, some of the roots are imaginary. On a TI-92, cSolve, which is the first item in A: Complex under F2 Algebra, finds all roots. At the cSolve(prompt, enter the equation. Then, press , x) to indicate the equation is being solved for x, or whatever letter is used as the variable, before pressing the ENTER key.

To avoid missing imaginary roots that might exist, use cSolve.

Discuss how, for example, when the calculator gives two real roots for a cubic equation, it is impossible to tell which of the two is the double root. This can be determined by graphing the corresponding function.

To use a TI-83 to find real roots, see *Technology: Solving Quadratic Equations With a Graphing Calculator* on page 146 of this teacher's resource.

See *MATHPOWER™ 11, Western Edition, Blackline Masters* pages 105 to 107 for Solving Polynomial Equations Algebraically.

Common Errors
- Students often forget that when the Solve instruction is being used, the variable for which they are solving must be entered, after a comma following the equation, before the closing bracket.

R_x Record general instructions, such as solve(equation, x) and cSolve(equation, x).

Assessing the Outcomes

Written Assignment

Write about the advantages and disadvantages of solving polynomial equations using
- a calculator with the ability to solve equations algebraically like a TI-92
- a calculator with the ability to solve equations algebraically like a TI-83
- a calculator to solve graphically
- paper and pencil

Investigating Math

Exploring Finite Differences

Student Text Pages
Pp. 223–228

Materials
graphing calculators, overhead projector

Learning Outcomes
- Construct a difference table for a given set of coordinates.
- Calculate the coefficients of the terms of a linear, quadratic, or cubic function from the difference table.
- Write an equation that represents a given set of coordinates.
- Solve problems using a difference table.

Mental Math

1. Subtract.

a) $64 - 45$ [19]   b) $126 - 79$ [47]

c) $93 - 67$ [26]   d) $72 - 57$ [15]

e) $503 - 57$ [446]   f) $182 - 89$ [93]

2. Multiply in two steps.

a) 2.6×32 [83.2]   b) 2.1×19 [39.9]

c) 1.9×2.3 [4.37]   d) 57×0.31 [17.67]

e) 42×150 [6300]   f) 9.1×0.9 [8.19]

Teaching Suggestions

(overhead projector) Discuss with the class the terms "dependent variable" and "independent variable." Ask:

Along which axis, the horizontal axis or the vertical axis, would you plot the dependent variable? the independent variable?

Assign Investigation 1 to pairs of students. Have volunteers present their results to the class. Provide an overhead projector, so that students may display their tables for the class to see. For question 2, ask:

What do you notice about the value of the differences?

How would you describe the relation between the degree of the function whose differences you found and the number of differences you found before you reached a constant difference?

For question 3, ask:

How many differences did you find before you reached the constant difference?

Elicit from the students that only one set of differences had to be found before the differences were constant. Also, the degree of the equation whose differences they found was 1.

Then, ask:

For each equation in question 1, how is the difference related to the equation?

What other pattern can you see that relates the differences and the equation?

Help the students see that the constant difference is the same as the coefficient of the x-variable in the equation, and the y-value at $x = 0$ is the constant term of the equation. Ask:

If you are given a set of coordinates for a linear relation, how can you use differences to write an equation for the relation?

Assign Investigations 2 and 3 to pairs of students. Give them an opportunity to discuss and compare their results with those of other pairs of students. Ask:

How is the set of constant differences related to the degree of the equation for the function?

If you are given a set of coordinates for a quadratic relation, how can you use differences to write an equation for the relation?

If you are given a set of coordinates for a cubic relation, how can you use differences to write an equation for the relation?

Have the students express the relation between the values in the chart and the coefficients of the terms of the function in words. Then, have them write relations for the values of the coefficients of the given function.

Ensure the students recognize that for a quadratic equation, a is half the value of the second difference, b is the first difference minus a, and c is the value of y when $x = 0$.

Ask:

How would you use a set of coordinates for a quadratic or cubic relation to write an equation for the relation?

Assign Investigation 4 to pairs of students. Give the students ample opportunity to discuss and compare their results with those of other students. Ask:

If you are given a table of values that represents a function, what is the first step you need to take to help you write an equation for that function?

Elicit from the students that the first step is to construct a difference table, and identify which differences are constant. From this you can write a general form of the required relation. Once this is ascertained, then the values of the coefficients for the relation can be calculated and substituted into the generalized form of the relation.

For the problems on student text page 228, point out that the data could be written as a table of values, and from this table of values, a difference table could be constructed. This would help the students find a relation that could be used to make predictions and find other information. For example, the table of values that could be set up for problem 15 is

Diagram Number, d	Number of Asterisks, n	First Differences
1	11	5
2	16	5
3	21	5
4	26	

From this table, you know that the equation required is linear and of the form $y = mx + b$.
You know that m is 5.
Thus, the relation is $n = 5d + b$.
When d is 1, n is 11.
Thus, $11 = 5 + b$
and $b = 6$.
Now the required equation is $n = 5d + 6$.
This equation can be used to make predictions about the values for n and d.

For problems 17 and 18, point out that the term number is the independent variable, and the term is the dependent variable.

Have students present their results to the class. Provide an overhead projector, if necessary.

Math Journal

method of finite differences List the steps you would follow when using the method of finite differences to help you find a linear relation, or a quadratic relation, or a cubic relation between the values in a set of coordinate points.

Assessing the Outcomes

Journal

Describe the use to which you could put the method of finite differences to make predictions about the terms in a sequence.

Written Assignment

1. Write an equation for each function.

a)

x	y
0	2
1	5
2	8
3	11
4	14

b)

x	y
0	1
1	0
2	1
3	4
4	9

2. Write an equation for each function.

a)

x	y
0	2
1	−5
2	−16
3	−31
4	−50

b)

x	y
0	−1
1	5
2	33
3	101
4	227

3. The first five numbers in a sequence are 7, 4, −5, −20, and −41.

a) Write an equation in the form $m = \blacksquare d$ that relates each number, m, to its position in the sequence, d.

b) In which position in the sequence is the number −7507?

c) What is the 25th number in the sequence?

Technology

Exploring Regression With a Graphing Calculator

Student Text Pages
Pp. 229–231

Materials
graphing calculators

Learning Outcomes
- Determine the equation of a function, given points on its graph, using a Regression instruction on a graphing calculator.
- Construct a scatter plot of points, draw the line of best fit, and determine the equation of the line of best fit, using a graphing calculator.

Prerequisite Skills
Use the method of finite differences to determine for which type of function these values are solutions.

0, 11, 46, 117, 236   [cubic]

Teaching Suggestions
Discuss how to use a graphing calculator to perform regressions like those on student text pages 229 and 230. On a TI-83, the SetUp Editor and Edit instructions, the fifth and first items under the EDIT menu when the STAT key is pressed, are used to generate the lists. A statistical plot, found by pressing the STAT PLOT (i.e., 2nd Y=) key, is used to plot the points. Then, a Regression instruction (the fourth, fifth, or sixth item under the CALC menu when the STAT key is pressed) is used to determine the equation.
Press the STAT key and the 5 key to select SetUp Editor, and then, press the ENTER key.
Press the STAT key and the 1 key to select Edit. Clear previous lists by moving the cursor to the L1 and L2 headings, and pressing the CLEAR key.
Return to the first row of the L1 column, and enter the x-coordinates, pressing the ENTER key after each.
Use the right arrow key to move to the first row of the L2 column, and enter the y-coordinates, pressing the ENTER key after each.
Then, press the Y= key, clear any equations that exist, and turn off any plots that are highlighted.
Press the STAT PLOT (i.e., 2nd Y=) key and the 1 key to select Plot1.
Press the ENTER key to select On.

If scatter plot (the first option) is highlighted as the Type, L1 is given for Xlist and L2 is given for Ylist, press the ZOOM key and the 9 key to select ZoomStat and graph the points. (Use the down arrow key to see the last items.)
If not, use the arrow keys to move to scatter plot and press the ENTER key to select it, the down arrow key, the L1 (i.e., 2nd 1) key, the ENTER key, the L2 (i.e., 2nd 2) key, and the ENTER key before pressing the ZOOM key and the 9 key to select ZoomStat and graph the points.
Next, press the STAT key, the right arrow key, and the 4 key to select LinReg. QuadReg is 5 and CubicReg is 6.
Press the L1 (i.e., 2nd 1) key, the comma key, the L2 (i.e., 2nd 2) key, the comma key, the VARS key, the right arrow key, the 1 key, the 1 key again, and the ENTER key to define the regression as x-values from L1, y-values from L2, and plotting Y1.
Read the coefficient values and write the equation.
Press the GRAPH key to display the regression line or curve.

Assign the explorations, ensuring the students know how to perform linear regressions in Exploration 1 before moving on to the next exploration. Discuss why more points are needed for quadratic functions than for linear functions, and for cubic functions than for quadratic functions.

In Exploration 5, the lists are generated, the points are plotted, and the regression lines are determined and graphed, using the same method as in Explorations 1 to 3.

See *MATHPOWER™ 11, Western Edition, Blackline Masters* pages 108 to 110 for Scatter Plots and Regression Lines.

Common Errors
- Often students have difficulty remembering what to enter at the regression prompt, for example, at LinReg(ax + b).

R$_x$ Record the entry that is used.
L1, L2, Y1

Assessing the Outcomes

Written Assignment

Write a flow-chart type set of instructions for performing regressions using a graphing calculator.

Review

Student Text Pages
Pp. 232–233

Materials
Teacher's Resource Master 1 (0.5-cm grid paper),
Teacher's Resource Master 2 (1-cm grid paper)

Learning Outcome
• Review the skills and concepts in Chapter 4.

Using the Review
Have the students work independently to complete the
Review. Meeting in small groups, the students can mark
and discuss the work. Groups can then share their
solutions and report any questions that caused them
difficulty. Discuss these questions with the class.

Reteaching Suggestions
For those students having difficulty with the chapter
material, form small groups and use the following exercises.

   If you feel that the class has had particular difficulty
mastering any concept, you may wish to work through a
problem from each section as a model of excellence of
solution, which some students require just prior to
assessment.

Solving Quadratic Equations by Graphing
1. Solve by graphing a related function.
   a) $x^2 - 2x - 15 = 0$ b) $(x - 3)^2 - 4 = 0$
2. Solve by graphing a related system of equations.
   a) $x^2 - 10x = -25$ b) $-x^2 + x = -6$

Solving Quadratic Equations by Factoring
1. Write each equation in standard form. Then, solve
   and check each equation.
   a) $x^2 + 6x = -8$ b) $64 = (x + 3)^2$
2. Write a quadratic equation with the given roots.
   a) $3, -5$ b) $-\frac{2}{5}, 2$

Quadratic Equations—The Square Root Principle
1. Solve.
   a) $2x^2 = 128$ b) $y^2 - 11 = 70$
2. Solve. Round your answers to the nearest hundredth.
   a) $m^2 - 50 = 5$ b) $2p^2 + 5 = -p^2 - 9$
3. Find the exact solutions, and then, calculate the
   solutions, to the nearest hundredth.
   a) $(n - 2)^2 = 13$ b) $2(a + 5)^2 - 2 = 48$

Solving Quadratic Equations by Completing the Square
1. Solve by completing the square. Express solutions in
   simplest radical form.
   a) $y^2 + 3x + 11 = 0$ b) $4y^2 + 2y + 1 = 0$
2. Solve. Round solutions to the nearest hundredth.
   a) $\frac{a^2}{4} + \frac{1}{8} = -a$ b) $10w - 4 = -5w^2$
3. A square of side length $(v + 2)$ has an area of 11 square
   units. Find the value of v, to the nearest hundredth.

The Quadratic Formula
1. Solve, using the quadratic formula. Express answers
   in simplest radical form.
   a) $-d^2 + 4 = -2d$ b) $5m^2 = 18$
2. Solve. Round answers to the nearest hundredth.
   a) $\frac{15}{g - 2} - 2 = \frac{15}{g}$ b) $0.34k^2 - 0.06 = 0.4k$
3. The sum of the squares of two even consecutive
   integers is 452. Find the integers.

Complex Numbers
1. Simplify.
   a) $(3 + 5i) + (4 - 3i)$ b) $(9 - 2i) - (3 + 5i)$
   c) $7i(4 + i)$ d) $(6 + 5i)(6 - 5i)$
2. Solve.
   a) $-b = \frac{-3}{b - 1}$ b) $\frac{4}{m^2 - 4} = \frac{3}{m^2 - 1}$
3. Evaluate $(7 + 2i)(7 - 2i)$.
4. Write a quadratic equation that has $2 - i$ and $2 + i$
   as roots.

The Remainder Theorem
1. Find the remainder when the polynomial
   $3x^3 - 7x^2 + x + 1$ is divided by $x - 3$.
2. When the polynomial $m^3 + km^2 - 5m + 7$ is
   divided by $m + 3$, the remainder is 4. What is the
   value of k?
3. Find the remainder when $3x^3 - 2x^2 + 4$ is divided
   by $3x - 4$.

The Factor Theorem
1. Show that $x + 4$ is a factor of $x^3 + 6x^2 + 5x - 12$.
2. Factor.
   a) $x^3 + 8x^2 + x - 42$
   b) $2n^3 - 3n^2 + 3n - 10$

Solving Polynomial Equations
1. Solve and check.
   a) $w^3 - 9w^2 + 15w - 7 = 0$
   b) $(5x + 1)(x - 1)(x - 2) = 0$
   c) $64b^3 - 49b = 0$

2. Find the exact roots.

a) $10d - 25 = -d^3 - 8d^2$

b) $7v^3 + 4v = 0$

Answers to Reteaching Suggestions

Solving Quadratic Equations by Graphing

1. a) $-3, 5$ **b)** $5, 1$

2. a) 5 **b)** $3, -2$

Solving Quadratic Equations by Factoring

1. a) $x^2 + 6x + 8 = 0; -2, -4$

b) $x^2 + 6x - 55 = 0, 5; -11$

2. a) $x^2 + 2x - 15 = 0$

b) $5x^2 - 8x - 4 = 0$

Quadratic Equations — The Square Root Principle

1. a) $8, -8$ **b)** $9, -9$

2. a) $-\sqrt{55}, \sqrt{55}$ **b)** no solution

3. a) $2 - \sqrt{13}, 2 + \sqrt{13}, -1.61, 5.61$

b) $0, -10$

Solving Quadratic Equations by Completing the Square

1. a) $\dfrac{-3 + i\sqrt{35}}{2}, \dfrac{-3 - i\sqrt{35}}{2}$

b) $\dfrac{-1 + i\sqrt{3}}{4}, \dfrac{-1 - i\sqrt{3}}{4}$

2. a) $-0.13, -3.87$ **b)** $0.34, -2.34$

3. 1.32

The Quadratic Formula

1. a) $-\sqrt{5} + 1, \sqrt{5} + 1$ **b)** $\dfrac{3\sqrt{10}}{5}, \dfrac{-3\sqrt{10}}{5}$

2. a) $5, -3$ **b)** $\dfrac{\sqrt{151} + 10}{17}, \dfrac{-\sqrt{151} + 10}{17}$

3. a) $14, 16$ and $-14, -16$

Complex Numbers

1. a) $7 + 2i$ **b)** $6 + 3i$ **c)** $-7 + 28i$ **d)** 61

2. a) $\dfrac{\sqrt{13} + 1}{2}, \dfrac{-\sqrt{13} + 1}{2}$ **b)** $2\sqrt{2}i, -2\sqrt{2}i$

3. 53

4. $x^2 - 4x + 5 = 0$

The Remainder Theorem

1. 22 **2.** 1 **3.** $\dfrac{68}{9}$

The Factor Theorem

1. $f(-4) = 0$ or $(x - 1)(x + 3)(x + 4)$

2. a) $(x - 2)(x + 3)(x + 7)$

b) $(n - 2)(2n^2 + n + 5)$

Solving Polynomial Equations

1. a) $7, 1$ **b)** $\dfrac{-1}{5}, 1, 2$ **c)** $\dfrac{7}{8}, \dfrac{-7}{8}, 0$

2. a) $\dfrac{-\sqrt{29} - 3}{2}, \dfrac{\sqrt{29} - 3}{2}, -5$ **b)** $\dfrac{2\sqrt{7}i}{7}, \dfrac{-2\sqrt{7}i}{7}, 0$

Exploring Mathematics

Investigating the Argand Plane

(grid paper) Provide pairs of students with grid paper. Have students work in pairs or small groups. Ask:

Where on the Argand plane does the point $0 + 5i$ occur?

Where on the Argand plane does the point $3 + 0i$ occur?

Have students take turns practising plotting complex numbers. One student could plot a complex point and the other student could identify the coordinates of the point.

Give the groups an opportunity to discuss their results with other groups and to compare the similarities and differences in their results.

Ensure that the students realize that the diagonal of the parallelogram represents the sum of the two complex numbers. Thus, the coordinates of the end point of the diagonal represents the sum of the complex numbers. Ask:

Is it possible for a diagonal to represent more than one sum of complex numbers? Explain.

Lead the students to see that although the two following sums are the same, the two numbers being added in each case are different.

$(5 + 7i) + (2 - 2i) = (7 + 5i)$

$(3 - i) + (4 + 6i) = (7 + 5i)$

Thus, since each sum is the same, the diagonal representing each sum is the same, but the individual numbers being added are different.

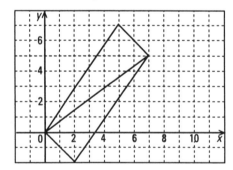

$(5 + 7i) + (2 - 2i)$
$= 7 + 5i$

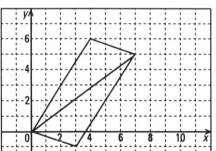

$(3 - i) + (4 + 6i)$
$= 7 + 5i$

Chapter Check

Student Text Page
P. 234

Learning Outcome

- Evaluate the skills and concepts in Chapter 4.

Assessing the Outcomes

Observation

If you assign the Chapter Check as a student assessment, look for the following:

- Can they solve quadratic equations graphically?
- Can they solve quadratic equations by the principle of the square root?
- Can they solve quadratic equations by completing the square?
- Can they solve quadratic equations by using the quadratic formula?
- Can they add, subtract, and multiply complex numbers?
- Can they use the discriminant to analyze the nature of the roots of quadratic equations?
- Can they solve polynomial equations?

Problem Solving

Student Text Page
P. 235

Learning Outcome

- Use problem solving strategies to solve problems.

Using the Strategies

The problems on this page allow the students to use the problem solving strategies discussed in Chapters 1 to 3. These strategies are

- Use a Diagram
- Use a Data Bank
- Solve Fermi Problems
- Solve a Simpler Problem
- Use Logic
- Look for a Pattern
- Guess and Check
- Work Backward
- Use a Table or Spreadsheet

Teaching Suggestions

Encourage the students to work in pairs or small groups. When students have completed the problems, have them share and discuss their strategies and solutions with other students.

For question 3, ask:

How are distance, speed, and time related when travelling in a straight line?

Lead the students to see that the distance Rashad drove was the same as the distance Tyson drove.

For question 6, remind the students that there are 4 variables, and so a system of 4 equations is required to find all 4 values.

Have students present their results to the class.

Assessing the Outcome

Observation

As you make your problem solving assessment of each student, consider the following:

- Do they understand the problem?
- Do they consider a variety of strategies?
- Do they use an organized approach?
- Do they create and use diagrams effectively?
- Do they show persistence?

Cumulative Review, Chapters 1–4

Learning Outcome

- Review skills and concepts in Chapters 1 to 4.

Teaching Suggestions

Method 1

The review of these four chapters can take several days.

Divide the class into groups of four. Each group is to decide which chapter each student will review. The students who are assigned the same chapter are to then form expert groups. They are to decide on strategies for reviewing the questions and solutions with their home groups. They are also to be the discussion leaders for the questions in these groups, ensuring that all of the group members can complete each question and explain each solution.

Each student from the expert group is to then return to his or her home group and lead a review of the chapter he or she was assigned.

Method 2

Have pairs of students choose one question from every section in each of the chapter reviews. The partner may correct the answers. If a student is having difficulty with any particular type of question, reteach the concepts to the student, and assign other similar questions for reinforcement.

Reteaching Suggestions

Chapter 1 Systems of Equations

1. Solve by graphing.

a) $y = 2x - 7$
$y = -x + 2$

b) $3x - y = -7$
$-2x - 5y = -1$

2. Solve each system by substituting. Check each solution.

a) $x - 2y = 1$
$-2x + y = -8$

b) $4m - n = -1$
$3m + 2n = -9$

3. Solve each system by elimination. Check each solution. If there is not exactly one solution, does the system have no solution or infinitely many solutions?

a) $4a - b = 20$
$-a + 2b = -5$

b) $2p + 7q = 1$
$4p + 14q = 2$

c) $2w - z = 3$
$4w - 2z = -9$

d) $5c - d = -7$
$11c - 2d = -16$

4. Solve and check.

a) $x - y - z = 0$
$2x + y + z = 3$
$-y - z = -1$

b) $2g + h - k = 7$
$-g - h + 3k = -13$
$2g - 5h + 2k = -26$

5. Liam took 4 h to drive 360 km from his home to his brother's home. For part of the trip he drove at 96 km/h. For the rest of the trip he drove at 80 km/h. How far did he drive at each speed?

6. A box contains dice, counters, and paper clips. The total number of objects in the box is 16. The number of counters is one less than three times the number of dice. Twice the number of counters minus five times the number of dice is one less than three times the number of paper clips. How many counters are in the box?

Chapter 2 Linear Inequalities

1. Solve and check.

a) $x - 2 < 5$
b) $3y + 4 \geq -2$
c) $2(p + 5) > 10$
d) $3m + 7 < -m - 5$
e) $-(n + 2) - 2 > 3n + 2(n + 1)$
f) $\frac{w}{5} + 2 \leq -1$
g) $\frac{3z}{5} - 4 > 2$
h) $\frac{p - 1}{3} < \frac{2p + 3}{2}$
i) $9.2 + 1.5x \geq 1.7$
j) $\frac{2z}{5} + \frac{1}{2} \leq \frac{z}{10}$

2. Graph each inequality.

a) $y > 2x + 3$
b) $x - y \leq -2$
c) $3 + x - 2y \geq 5$
d) $\frac{x}{3} + \frac{y}{2} < -1$

3. Which of the given ordered pairs are solutions to the system of inequalities?

$x + 2y > 4$
$3x - y \leq 5$
$(2, 4), (0, 0), (-2, -5), (0, 3), (3, 7)$

4. Solve each system of inequalities by graphing.

a) $y > x - 2$
$y < 2x$

b) $y > 3x + 1$
$y \geq -x + 2$

c) $x + y < 5$
$2x - 3y \geq -1$

d) $3 + 2x - y \geq 0$
$3x + y - 6 \leq 0$

5. The perimeter of a rectangle is more than 16 cm and less than 30 cm. Show graphically all the possible values for the length and width of the rectangle.

Chapter 3 Quadratic Functions

Sketch the graph of each parabola and state
a) *the direction of opening*
b) *the coordinates of the vertex*
c) *the equation of the axis of symmetry*
d) *the domain and the range*
e) *the maximum or minimum*
f) *any intercepts*

1. $y = x^2 + 5$
2. $y = -x^2 - 1$
3. $y = 2x^2 + 5$
4. $y = -3x^2 + 1$

5. Write an equation for a parabola with

a) vertex $(0, 0)$ and $a = 2$

b) vertex $(1, 2)$ and $a = -3$

c) vertex $(0, -1)$ and passing through $(1, -4)$

Without sketching each parabola, state
a) the direction of opening
b) how the parabola is stretched or shrunk, if at all
c) the coordinates of the vertex
d) the equation of the axis of symmetry
e) the domain and the range
f) the maximum or minimum

6. $y = (x - 2)^2 - 1$

7. $y = -\frac{1}{2}(x + 3)^2 - 4$

8. $y = 2(x - 1)^2 + 2.5$

9. Write an equation that defines each parabola.

a) vertex $(4, 3)$, $a = -2$

b) congruent to $y = -x^2$, vertex $(2, 2)$

c) $a = \frac{1}{2}$, axis of symmetry $x = -3$, minimum value 2

10. Find the value of c that will make each expression a perfect square trinomial.

a) $x^2 + 4x + c$ **b)** $x^2 - 11x + c$

11. Write each function in the form $y = a(x - p)^2 + q$. Sketch the graph, showing the coordinates of the vertex, the equation of the axis of symmetry, and the coordinates of two other points on the graph.

a) $y = x^2 + 9x + 2$ **b)** $y = -x^2 + 4x + 3$

12. Find the coordinates of the vertex.

a) $y = -x^2 + 4x - 2$ **b)** $y = 2x^2 - 3x + 4$

13. Graph each function. Find any x-intercepts. Round to the nearest tenth, if necessary.

a) $y = 2x^2 - 5x - 2$ **b)** $y = -4x^2 + x + 7$

Chapter 4 Quadratic and Polynomial Equations

1. Solve by graphing.

a) $x^2 + 3x - 10 = 0$ **b)** $-7x + 3 = -2x^2$

c) $3x^2 = 2x$ **c)** $5 = -3x^2 - x$

2. Solve by factoring and check.

a) $x^2 + 7x - 18 = 0$ **b)** $4x^2 - 11x - 3 = 0$

c) $3x^2 - 7x = 0$ **d)** $\frac{4}{x - 1} - \frac{3}{x + 2} = 2$

3. Write a quadratic equation with the given roots.

a) $3, -1$ **b)** $-\frac{2}{3}, -2$

4. Find and check exact solutions.

a) $x^2 - 125 = 275$ **b)** $b^2 + 10 = 59$

c) $(x + 3)^2 = 100$ **d)** $3(x - 5)^2 = 75$

5. Solve by completing the square. Express each irrational solution in simplest radical form and to the nearest hundredth.

a) $x^2 - 6x + 2 = 0$ **b)** $x^2 - 10x + 1 = 0$

c) $7m + 2 = -m^2$ **d)** $p^2 - 1 = -11p$

e) $0.4x^2 - 0.1x = 0.5$

6. Solve using the quadratic formula. Express radical solutions in simplest radical form.

a) $x^2 + 6x + 8 = 0$ **b)** $2m^2 - 3m + 1 = 0$

c) $x^2 - 2x - 4 = 0$ **d)** $2 = 3z^2 + 8z$

e) $1 = 5d^2$ **f)** $4x^2 = 14 - 4x$

7. Solve to the nearest hundredth.

a) $y^2 - 0.1y - 0.06 = 0$

b) $0.1t^2 + 0.2 = 0.45t$

8. Solve. Express radical roots in simplest form.

a) $\frac{n^2}{2} - \frac{n}{4} - 1 = 0$ **b)** $\frac{3}{v + 2} - 2 = -\frac{2}{v - 3}$

9. Simplify.

a) $\sqrt{-25}$ **b)** $\sqrt{-200}$

c) $\sqrt{-8p^5}$ **d)** $3i^2$

e) $i(-i)^3$ **f)** $(-i\sqrt{7})^2$

g) $(2 + 5i) + (6 - 7i)$ **h)** $(1 - 6i) - (3 + 4i)$

i) $(8 + i)(11 - 3i)$ **j)** $(4 + 5i)^2$

10. Solve and check.

a) $x^2 + 121 = 0$ **b)** $2y^2 + 10 = 0$

c) $n^2 + 3n + 11 = 0$ **d)** $q^2 - 7q + 15 = 0$

e) $25x^4 = 16$

11. Determine the nature of the roots.

a) $x^2 - 8x + 16 = 0$ **b)** $x^2 - x - 5 = 0$

c) $x^3 + 3x + 10 = 0$ **d)** $\frac{x - 1}{2} - x^2 - 3 = 0$

12. Determine the value of m that gives the type of solution indicated.

a) $x^2 - 4x + m = 0$; equal

b) $x^2 + 3x - 2m = 0$; imaginary

c) $mx^2 - 2x + 1 = 0$; real, unequal

13. Use the remainder theorem to determine the remainder for each division.

a) $(x^3 + 2x^2 + 3x + 7) \div (x - 1)$

b) $(m^3 - m^2 + 7m - 4) \div (m + 1)$

14. For each polynomial, find the value of k if the remainder is 3.

a) $(x^2 - x + k) \div (x - 1)$

b) $(x^2 + kx - 17) \div (x - 2)$

15. Show that the binomial is a factor of the first polynomial.
   a) $x^3 - x^2 - 5x - 3$; $x + 1$
   b) $8x^4 + 32x^3 + x + 4$; $2x + 1$

16. Factor.
   a) $x^3 - 6x^2 + 11x - 6$
   b) $4m^3 - 7m - 3$

17. Solve and check.
   a) $n^3 - 3n^2 - 4n + 12 = 0$
   b) $3a^3 + a^2 - 3a - 1 = 0$
   c) $x^3 - 4x^2 - x + 12 = 0$
   d) $w^4 + w^3 + 2w - 4 = 0$

18. Find two consecutive even numbers whose product is 80.

19. A lidless box is constructed from a square piece of tin by cutting a 10-cm square from each corner and bending up the sides for the box. If the volume of the box is 1210 cm³, find the dimensions of the box.

Answers to Cumulative Review, Chapters 1–4

Chapter 1
1. a) $(3, -1)$ b) $(-2, 1)$
2. a) $(5, 2)$ b) $(-1, -3)$
3. a) $(5, 0)$ b) infinitely many
   c) no solution   d) $(-2, -3)$
4. a) $(1, -1, 2)$ b) $(0, 4, -3)$
5. 2.5 h at 96 km/h, 1.5 h at 80 km/h
6. 11 counters

Chapter 2
1. a) $x < 7$ b) $y \geq -2$ c) $p > 0$
   d) $m < -3$ e) $n < -1$ f) $w \leq -15$
   g) $z > 10$ h) $p > -\frac{11}{4}$ i) $x \geq -5$
   j) $z \leq -\frac{5}{3}$
3. $(2, 4), (0, 3), (3, 7)$

Chapter 3
5. a) $y = 2x^2$ b) $y = -3(x - 1)^2 + 2$ c) $y = -3x^2 - 1$
6. a) upward   b) no stretch or shrinkage
   c) $(2, -1)$ d) $x = 2$
   e) x is any real number, $y \geq -1$ f) minimum -1
7. a) downward   b) stretch
   c) $(-3, -4)$ d) $x = -3$
   e) x is any real number, $y \leq -4$ f) maximum -4
8. a) upward   b) shrinkage
   c) $(1, 2.5)$ d) $x = 1$
   e) x is any real number, $y \geq 2.5$ f) minimum 2.5

9. a) $y = -2(x - 4)^2 + 3$ b) $y = -(x - 2)^2 + 2$
   c) $y = \frac{1}{2}(x + 3)^2 + 2$
10. a) 4   b) $\frac{121}{4}$
11. a) $y = \left(x + \frac{9}{2}\right)^2 - \frac{73}{4}$ b) $y = -(x - 2)^2 + 7$
12. a) $(2, 2)$ b) $\left(\frac{3}{4}, \frac{23}{8}\right)$
13. a) $2.9, -0.4$ b) $-1.2, -1.5$

Chapter 4
1. a) $2, -5$ b) $\frac{1}{2}, 3$ c) $0, \frac{2}{3}$ d) $\frac{-1 \pm i\sqrt{59}}{6}$
2. a) $2, -9$ b) $-\frac{1}{4}, 3$ c) $0, \frac{7}{3}$ d) $-3, \frac{5}{2}$
3. a) $x^2 - 2x - 3 = 0$ b) $3x^2 + 8x + 4 = 0$
4. a) ± 20 b) ± 7 c) $7, -13$ d) $0, 10$
5. a) $3 + \sqrt{7}, 3 - \sqrt{7}, 5.65, 0.35$
   b) $5 \pm 2\sqrt{6}$; 0.10, 9.90
   c) $\frac{-7 \pm \sqrt{41}}{2}$; $-0.30, -6.70$
   d) $\frac{-11 \pm \sqrt{1}}{2}$; 0.09, -11.09
   e) $\frac{1}{8} \pm \frac{9}{8}$; 1.25, -1.00
6. a) $-2, -4$ b) $\frac{1}{2}, 1$ c) $1 \pm \sqrt{5}$
   d) $\frac{-4 \pm \sqrt{22}}{3}$ e) $\pm\frac{\sqrt{5}}{5}$ f) $\frac{-1 \pm \sqrt{15}}{2}$
7. a) $0.3, -0.2$ b) $0.50, 4.00$
8. a) $\frac{1 \pm \sqrt{33}}{4}$ b) $\frac{7 \pm \sqrt{105}}{4}$
9. a) $5i$ b) $10i\sqrt{2}$ c) $2p^2 i\sqrt{2p}$
   d) -3 e) -1 f) -7
   g) $8 - 2i$ h) $-2 - 10i$
   i) $91 - 13i$ j) $-9 + 40i$
10. a) $11i, -11i$ b) $\pm i\sqrt{5}$ c) $\frac{-3 \pm i\sqrt{35}}{2}$
    d) $\frac{7 \pm i\sqrt{11}}{2}$ e) $\pm\frac{2}{\sqrt{5}}$
11. a) real, equal   b) real, distinct
    c) imaginary   d) imaginary
12. a) 4   b) $m < -\frac{9}{8}$ c) $m < 1$
13. a) 13   b) -13
14. a) 3   b) 8
16. a) $(x - 1)(x - 2)(x - 3)$ b) $(m + 1)(2m + 1)(2m - 3)$
17. a) $2, 3, -2$ b) $1, -1, -\frac{1}{3}$
    c) $3, \frac{1 \pm \sqrt{17}}{2}$ d) $-2, 1 \pm i\sqrt{2}$
18. 8, 10 or $-8, -10$ 19. 11 cm × 11 cm × 10 cm

CHAPTER 4

• Student Text Answers

Chapter Opener p. 149

1. $s^2 = 16$
2. $s = \pm 4$
3. -4; speed is non-negative
4. 4 m/s
5. a) 2 m/s **b)** 6 m/s **c)** 1.2 m/s

Getting Started pp. 150–151

1 The Sum of Consecutive Squares

2. The sum of the term numbers is equal to the term number of the result.
3. a) t_{19} **b)** t_{43} **4.** $t_n^2 + t_{n+1}^2 = t_{2n+1}$

2 The Difference Between Alternate Squares

2. The sum of the term numbers is equal to the term number of the result.
3. $t_{n+2}^2 - t_n^2 = t_{2n+2}$

3 Four Consecutive Fibonacci Numbers

1. The product of the first and last numbers is equal to the difference between the squares of the middle two numbers.
2. $t_n \times t_{n+3} = t_{n+2}^2 - t_{n+1}^2$

Warm Up

1. $3x(x - 1)$
2. $2xy(2x + 5y)$
3. $(y + 1)(y + 7)$
4. $(s + 2)(s - 3)$
5. does not factor
6. $(c + 5)^2$
7. does not factor
8. $(2a + 1)(2a - 1)$
9. $(3v - 1)(v + 4)$
10. $(2x - 5)^2$
11. $2(t - 1)(t - 12)$
12. does not factor
13. ± 1 **14.** ± 3 **15.** ± 2 **16.** ± 5
17. $0, 1$ **18.** $0, -2$ **19.** $0, -4$ **20.** $0, 3$
21. $2\sqrt{5}$ **22.** $3\sqrt{6}$ **23.** $2\sqrt{15}$ **24.** $4\sqrt{6}$
25. $6\sqrt{2}$ **26.** $20\sqrt{3}$ **27.** $42\sqrt{2}$ **28.** $8\sqrt{13}$
29. $21\sqrt{11}$ **30.** $\sqrt{2}$ **31.** $\sqrt{3}$ **32.** $2\sqrt{2}$
33. 5
34. $2\sqrt{10}$
35. $2\sqrt{5}$
36. $\dfrac{3 - 2\sqrt{3}}{2}$
37. $-\dfrac{1}{2}$
38. $2 + \sqrt{5}$
39. 5
40. $\dfrac{-1 - \sqrt{7}}{3}$
41. $x + 2$
42. $x - 3$ R-1
43. $x + 1$
44. $3x + 5$ R1
45. $x^2 + 3x + 1$
46. $4x + 1$ R2
47. $3x + 4$
48. $5x - 1$
49. $x^2 + 2x + 1$ R-2
50. $x^2 - 4x + 4$ R3

Mental Math

Simplifying and Evaluating Square Roots

1. $2\sqrt{2}$ **2.** $3\sqrt{2}$ **3.** not possible
4. $2\sqrt{3}$ **5.** not possible **6.** $2\sqrt{6}$
7. $3\sqrt{3}$ **8.** $2\sqrt{11}$ **9.** $3\sqrt{5}$
10. $5\sqrt{2}$ **11.** $3\sqrt{7}$ **12.** $4\sqrt{5}$
13. 7 **14.** not possible **15.** 11
16. 9 **17.** 4 **18.** 6
19. 8 **20.** 8 **21.** 9
22. 5 **23.** 10 **24.** 5

Subtracting in Two Steps

1. 25 **2.** 25 **3.** 54 **4.** 28
5. 39 **6.** 36 **7.** 64 **8.** 61
9. 87 **10.** 86 **11.** 81 **12.** 83
13. 1.9 **14.** 1.9 **15.** 2.6 **16.** 10.8
17. 17.6 **18.** 16.7 **19.** 350 **20.** 380
21. 290 **22.** 470 **23.** 530 **24.** 880

Section 4.1 pp. 155–156

Practice (Section 4.1)

1. $-3, 2$ **2.** $4, 1$ **3.** $-5, -1$
4. -2 **5.** no real roots **6.** $-5, 1$
7. ± 2 **8.** $0, -3$ **9.** ± 3
10. no real roots **11.** 1 **12.** no real roots
13. $0, 5$ **14.** $2, -1$ **15.** 3
16. $-4, 1$ **17.** no real roots **18.** $1, 2$
19. $-1, 1.5$ **20.** $-0.5, 3$ **21.** no real roots
22. -0.5 **23.** $0, 2.5$ **24.** $-2.9, 0.6$
25. $1.3, -0.5$ **26.** 2.7 **27.** $-0.6, 0.4$
28. $-0.8, 0.5$ **29.** $-1.6, 3.6$ **30.** no real roots
31. $0, -3.3$ **32.** -1.7 **33.** $1, 3$
34. $-3, 1$ **35.** no real roots **36.** 3
37. 1 **38.** $-0.5, -1.5$ **39.** 1
40. $-7, 1$

Applications and Problem Solving (Section 4.1)

41. $w = 8$ m, $l = 9$ m **42.** 20 m
43. 45 m **44.** 11 cm by 3 cm
45. 6 m, 8 m **46.** 12 cm, 5 cm
47. 5 m **48.** 35 m by 65 m
49. $l = 26$ m, $w = 14$ m **50.** 4.8 cm by 6.4 cm
51. 14, 16 or $-16, -14$ **52.** 18.3 m by 9.1 m
53. 7, 8, 9
54. a) $x^2 - x - 12 = 0$ **b)** $4, -3$ **c)** opposites
55. a) $-0.3, 2$ **56. a)** $-0.5, 2$

57. a) $c < 0$ **b)** $c = 0$ **c)** $c > 0$
58. a) $c = 49$ **b)** $c < 49$ **c)** $c > 49$
59. a) $b = \pm 10$ **b)** $b < -10, b > 10$
    c) $-10 < b < 10$
60. a) $b = 0$ **b)** $0, -b$
61. a) $x \le -4, x \ge 4$ **b)** $-5 \le x \le 5$

Section 4.2 pp. 160–162

Practice (Section 4.2)

1. $-1, -2$ **2.** $-3, 1$ **3.** 5 **4.** $2, -3$
5. $-\dfrac{1}{2}, 3$ **6.** $-\dfrac{4}{3}, \dfrac{1}{2}$ **7.** $0, -9$ **8.** $0, 4$
9. $x^2 - 2x - 6 = 0$ **10.** $2y^2 - 3y + 2 = 0$
11. $3z^2 + 4z + 3 = 0$ **12.** $x^2 + 2x - 3 = 0$
13. $4m^2 - 3m = 0$ **14.** $2x^2 - x - 2 = 0$
15. $3x^2 + 2x - 6 = 0$ **16.** $8x^2 - x - 13 = 0$
17. $x^2 - 5 = 0$ **18.** $y^2 + 2y - 1 = 0$
19. $2t^2 + 3t - 4 = 0$ **20.** $10x^2 - 6x + 15 = 0$
21. $-3, -4$ **22.** $1, 2$ **23.** $-2, 3$ **24.** 4
25. $-7, 5$ **26.** $9, -2$ **27.** $-2, \dfrac{1}{2}$ **28.** $\dfrac{1}{3}, 1$
29. $-5, -\dfrac{1}{2}$ **30.** $\dfrac{2}{3}, -3$ **31.** $-\dfrac{1}{2}, \dfrac{3}{2}$ **32.** $\dfrac{3}{5}, 1$
33. $0, -2$ **34.** $0, 3$ **35.** $0, -\dfrac{2}{3}$ **36.** $0, \dfrac{8}{5}$
37. $0, 4$ **38.** $0, -\dfrac{4}{3}$ **39.** $-3, 5$ **40.** $7, 3$
41. $-3, 1$ **42.** $\dfrac{3}{2}$ **43.** $0, \dfrac{2}{5}$ **44.** $2, 18$
45. $-6, -2$ **46.** $0, 6$ **47.** $-1, 2$ **48.** $5, 1$
49. $-\dfrac{2}{3}, 2$ **50.** $-3, -2$ **51.** $-3, 2$ **52.** $-\dfrac{4}{3}, 3$
53. $-1, -\dfrac{1}{2}$ **54.** $-2, \dfrac{8}{3}$ **55.** $x^2 + 8x + 15 = 0$
56. $x^2 - 4x + 4 = 0$ **57.** $x^2 - 9 = 0$
58. $2x^2 - 7x - 4 = 0$ **59.** $9x^2 - 9x + 2 = 0$
60. $8x^2 + 10x - 3 = 0$ **61.** $x^2 + 5x = 0$
62. $3x^2 - 4x = 0$ **63.** $0, 1$
64. $-\dfrac{1}{2}, 2$ **65.** $-4, 2$ **66.** $\dfrac{1}{2}$
67. $-4, 3$ **68.** $\dfrac{8}{3}, 6$

Applications and Problem Solving (Section 4.2)

69. a) $0 = -5t^2 + 9t + 2$ **b)** 2 s
70. 5, 11 or $-11, -5$ **71.** 9, 10 or $-10, -9$
72. -2 or 3   **73.** 16, 18 or $-18, -16$
74. 0 or -10 **75.** 9 cm by 4 cm
76. $\dfrac{3}{2}$ or $\dfrac{2}{3}$ **77.** -1 or 2
78. 18 m by 1 m   **79.** 20 cm by 122 cm
80. $\dfrac{8}{3}$ m by 6 m   **81.** 8 cm, 15 cm
82. 11   **83.** 4
84. 0.5 m
85. a) 70 mm by 135 mm   **b)** The dimensions of a Canadian \$20 bill are 70 mm by 153 mm.
86. a) -3; one   **b)** $-3, -3$; two equal roots

87. $x^2 - (p + q)x + pq = 0$
88. a) $-4y, -y$ **b)** $3y, -\dfrac{y}{2}$ **c)** $\dfrac{y}{2}$ **d)** $-2y, \dfrac{y}{4}$
    e) $0, -\dfrac{y}{5}$ **f)** $0, \dfrac{7y}{3}$
89. a) $6x^2 - x - 2 = 0$ **b)** Yes. Multiply the equation by any non-zero constant.
90. a) 10   **b)** $-\dfrac{1}{3}$
91. a) $x^2 + 4x + 4 = 0$ **b)** $x^2 - 5x + 6 = 0$
    c) $2x^2 - x - 3 = 0$

Section 4.3 pp. 165–167

Practice (Section 4.3)

1. ± 9 **2.** ± 8 **3.** $\pm \dfrac{5}{2}$ **4.** ± 4
5. ± 5 **6.** ± 6 **7.** ± 4 **8.** ± 10
9. ± 1 **10.** ± 0.5 **11.** ± 6 **12.** ± 4
13. ± 4 **14.** ± 3 **15.** ± 2 **16.** ± 7
17. ± 1.1 **18.** ± 0.7 **19.** ± 1 **20.** ± 5
21. ± 3.87 **22.** ± 4.47 **23.** ± 6.32 **24.** ± 2.45
25. ± 4.12 **26.** ± 3.46 **27.** ± 3.16 **28.** ± 3.61
29. ± 0.76 **30.** ± 1.67 **31.** ± 0.82 **32.** ± 4.12
33. $\pm 2\sqrt{3}$ **34.** $\pm 5\sqrt{3}$ **35.** $\pm 3\sqrt{5}$ **36.** $\pm 3\sqrt{2}$
37. $\pm 2\sqrt{2}$ **38.** $\pm 6\sqrt{3}$ **39.** $\pm \dfrac{\sqrt{15}}{3}$ **40.** $\pm \dfrac{2\sqrt{10}}{5}$
41. $\pm \dfrac{\sqrt{2}}{2}$ **42.** $\pm \dfrac{\sqrt{13}}{2}$ **43.** $\pm \dfrac{3\sqrt{2}}{2}$ **44.** $\pm \dfrac{3\sqrt{5}}{2}$
45. 1 **46.** $-5, 1$ **47.** $-2, 0$ **48.** $-1, 7$
49. $-1, 0$ **50.** $1, -\dfrac{1}{3}$ **51.** $-1, 4$ **52.** $-3, 4$
53. $-3, -7$ **54.** $-\dfrac{5}{4}, \dfrac{7}{4}$ **55.** $-10, 6$ **56.** $5, -4$
57. $-\dfrac{2}{3}$ **58.** $2, -\dfrac{3}{2}$ **59.** $-\dfrac{5}{2}, -\dfrac{9}{2}$ **60.** $0, \dfrac{6}{5}$
61. 0.75, 0.25   **62.** 0.01, -0.21
63. $-0.15, -0.85$ **64.** $\dfrac{2}{3}, -\dfrac{1}{3}$
65. $\pm\sqrt{3} + 5$; 6.73, 3.27
66. $\pm 2\sqrt{2} - 3$; $-0.17, -5.83$
67. $\dfrac{\pm\sqrt{5} + 1}{3}$; 1.08, -0.41
68. $\dfrac{\pm 2\sqrt{5} - 3}{4}$; 0.37, -1.87
69. $\pm \dfrac{\sqrt{7}}{2} - 3$; $-1.68, -4.32$
70. $\dfrac{\pm 3\sqrt{2} + 5}{2}$; 4.62, 0.38

Applications and Problem Solving (Section 4.3)

71. a) $28 - x^2 = 19$; $x = 3$; 3 m by 3 m
    b) $28 - x^2 = 19$; $x = \pm 3$ **c)** A flower bed can only have positive dimensions.
72. ± 12 **73.** ± 5

74. a) $2w$ **b)** $2w^2$
     c) $2w^2 = 800$; $w = 20$; 20 cm by 40 cm
75. a) $2\sqrt{10}$ s   **b)** 6.3 s
76. a) 2 s   **b)** 10.5 s
77. ± 4 **78.** ± 2.5 **79.** ± 2.65
80. -14 or 20 **81.** $\pm \frac{1}{2}$
82. a) $\pm \frac{10\sqrt{7}}{7}$ **b)** ± 3.78
83. 9   **84.** 4
85. 11 cm by 11 cm   **86.** 3.5 cm
87. a) 4 cm by 4 cm, 8 cm by 8 cm
     b) 3 cm by 3 cm, 9 cm by 9 cm
88. a) $\pm \frac{5}{3}$ **b)** ± 3 **c)** $\pm \frac{\sqrt{10}}{2}$
     d) $\pm \frac{\sqrt{17}}{2}$ **e)** $\pm \sqrt{10}$ **f)** $\pm \sqrt{2}$
     g) ± 1 **h)** $\pm 2\sqrt{2}$ **i)** $\pm \frac{3\sqrt{11}}{11}$
89. a) ± 2 **b)** ± 1.4 **c)** ± 2.8
     d) ± 0.7 **e)** 1.5, 2.5   **f)** $-0.3, -1.7$
90. No. The equation reduces to $3 = 1$ if the left side is expanded and simplified. This is impossible.
91. a) 8.5 cm   **b)** 72 cm^2
92. a) $-3 < x < 3$ **b)** $x \leq -5$, $x \geq 5$
93. No. A square must always be non-negative.

Section 4.4   pp. 172–173

Practice (Section 4.4)

1. 1; $(x + 1)^2$ **2.** 25; $(x + 5)^2$
3. 16; $(t - 4)^2$ **4.** 49; $(w - 7)^2$
5. $\frac{9}{4}$; $\left(m + \frac{3}{2}\right)^2$ **6.** $\frac{49}{4}$; $\left(x + \frac{7}{2}\right)^2$
7. $\frac{25}{4}$; $\left(p - \frac{5}{2}\right)^2$ **8.** $\frac{121}{4}$; $\left(q - \frac{11}{2}\right)^2$
9. $\frac{4}{9}$; $\left(x + \frac{2}{3}\right)^2$ **10.** $\frac{1}{9}$; $\left(d - \frac{1}{3}\right)^2$
11. $\frac{1}{16}$; $\left(x - \frac{1}{4}\right)^2$ **12.** $\frac{1}{100}$; $\left(r + \frac{1}{10}\right)^2$
13. 0.49; $(x + 0.7)^2$ **14.** 0.0009; $(x - 0.03)^2$
15. $0, -6$ **16.** $9, 11$
17. $-\frac{2}{3}, -\frac{4}{3}$ **18.** $-\frac{1}{2}, -\frac{7}{2}$
19. $1 \pm 2\sqrt{2}$ **20.** $4 \pm 2\sqrt{3}$
21. $-\frac{5}{2}, \frac{3}{2}$ **22.** $\frac{1 \pm \sqrt{7}}{3}$
23. $\frac{-3 \pm \sqrt{3}}{4}$ **24.** $\frac{-6 \pm \sqrt{6}}{4}$
25. $1.6, -0.6$ **26.** $-0.3, -0.5$
27. $-3 \pm \sqrt{5}$ **28.** $2 \pm \sqrt{15}$
29. $-4 \pm \sqrt{23}$ **30.** $5 \pm 2\sqrt{7}$
31. $\frac{7 \pm \sqrt{13}}{2}$ **32.** $\frac{5 \pm \sqrt{17}}{2}$

33. $\frac{-1 \pm \sqrt{13}}{2}$ **34.** $10 \pm 4\sqrt{6}$
35. $\frac{-4 \pm \sqrt{6}}{2}$ **36.** $\frac{3 \pm \sqrt{3}}{3}$
37. $\frac{-5 \pm \sqrt{5}}{4}$ **38.** $\frac{-2 \pm \sqrt{10}}{3}$
39. $\frac{-3 \pm \sqrt{57}}{12}$ **40.** $2, -\frac{1}{3}$
41. $\frac{-1 \pm \sqrt{31}}{5}$ **42.** $\frac{-1 \pm \sqrt{6}}{5}$
43. $-1 \pm 3\sqrt{3}$ **44.** $\frac{1 \pm \sqrt{10}}{3}$
45. $0.41, -2.41$ **46.** $3.73, 0.27$
47. $1.45, -3.45$ **48.** $2.19, -3.19$
49. $3.58, 0.42$ **50.** $0.34, -2.34$
51. $-0.72, -2.78$ **52.** $4.10, -1.10$
53. $-0.13, -3.87$ **54.** $3.81, -1.31$

Applications and Problem Solving (Section 4.4)

55. 40 m by 110 m   **56.** 4.3 cm
57. 3.6 m by 5.6 m   **58.** 8.1 m by 6.1 m
59. 11.2 m   **60.** 7.4 cm by 5.4 cm
61. -15 or 14 **62.** 1.45
63. a) $7 \pm 2\sqrt{3}$ **b)** 10.464, 3.536
64. $1 \pm 3\sqrt{3}$ **65.** 23.7 cm by 29.7 cm
66. a) $\frac{-7 \pm 3\sqrt{5}}{2}$ **b)** $\frac{9 \pm \sqrt{73}}{2}$
     c) $2 \pm \sqrt{6}$ **d)** $-3 \pm 2\sqrt{2}$
67. a) $\frac{1 \pm \sqrt{5}}{2}$, $x \neq 0$ **b)** $\frac{5 \pm \sqrt{73}}{4}$, $z \neq -\frac{1}{2}$
     c) $\frac{1 \pm 2\sqrt{34}}{3}$, $y \neq \pm\sqrt{15}$
     d) $\frac{3 \pm \sqrt{89}}{8}$, $x \neq \pm 1$
68. a) 4.1 s   **b)** 2 s
69. a) Let x represent the number of 10¢ increases. The number of loaves sold is $50 - 2x$. The price of each loaf is $1.50 + 0.1x$. The total revenue is $(50 - 2x)(1.50 + 0.1x)$. For revenue of $80, solve $(50 - 2x)(1.50 + 0.1x) = 80$, which reduces to $0.2x^2 - 2x + 5 = 0$.   **b)** 5   **c)** $2
     d) between $1.80 and $2.20
70. ± 7
71. a) $-1 \pm \sqrt{k + 1}$ **b)** $\frac{1 \pm \sqrt{k^2 + 1}}{k}$
     c) $\frac{k \pm \sqrt{4 + k^2}}{2}$
72. a) $x^2 - 5 = 0$ **b)** $x^2 - 6x + 7 = 0$
     c) $x^2 + 2x - 11 = 0$ **d)** $4x^2 - 24x + 23 = 0$
73. 5, 9   **74.** $x = \frac{-b \pm \sqrt{b^2 - 4c}}{2}$

Section 4.5 pp. 178–180

Practice (Section 4.5)

1. $-5, -1$ **2.** $-4, 2$ **3.** $3, -1$
4. $5, 7$ **5.** -2 **6.** 1
7. $1, \frac{1}{2}$ **8.** $3, -\frac{1}{5}$ **9.** $4, -\frac{3}{2}$
10. $\frac{1}{3}$ **11.** $\frac{3}{4}, -\frac{3}{2}$ **12.** $-\frac{1}{2}, \frac{2}{3}$
13. $\pm\frac{3}{2}$ **14.** $-\frac{5}{2}, -\frac{3}{2}$ **15.** $0, \frac{5}{2}$
16. $-\frac{5}{3}, -2$ **17.** $-2 \pm \sqrt{2}$ **18.** $3 \pm \sqrt{10}$
19. $2 \pm \sqrt{3}$ **20.** $1 \pm \sqrt{2}$ **21.** $-2 \pm \sqrt{3}$
22. $\frac{1 \pm \sqrt{17}}{2}$ **23.** $\frac{1 \pm \sqrt{15}}{7}$ **24.** $\frac{-1 \pm \sqrt{5}}{2}$
25. $\frac{-4 \pm \sqrt{22}}{2}$ **26.** $\frac{1 \pm \sqrt{21}}{2}$ **27.** $\frac{-1 \pm \sqrt{6}}{2}$
28. $1 \pm \sqrt{5}$ **29.** $\pm\frac{2\sqrt{3}}{3}$ **30.** $\frac{2 \pm \sqrt{7}}{3}$
31. $0, 1.6$ **32.** $1.3, -0.3$ **33.** $3.4, -1.4$
34. $3.9, -0.9$ **35.** $6.6, -0.6$ **36.** $2.8, -1.3$
37. $-0.3, -2$ **38.** $10.7, 1.3$ **39.** $6.2, 0.8$
40. $1.9, 0$ **41.** $0.65, 1.65$ **42.** $-1.16, 5.16$
43. $1.31, -0.13$ **44.** $1.67, -0.5$ **45.** $-0.04, -1.05$
46. $-12.44, 9.94$ **47.** $-3, 5$ **48.** $20, -2.78$
49. $-1.61, 5.61$ **50.** $6.16, -0.16$ **51.** $2, -1.5$
52. $-1, -2$ **53.** $0, -10$ **54.** $7 \pm \sqrt{58}$
55. $-1 \pm \sqrt{7}$ **56.** $\frac{1 \pm \sqrt{13}}{2}$ **57.** $\frac{1 \pm \sqrt{33}}{2}$
58. $4 \pm 2\sqrt{7}$

Applications and Problem Solving (Section 4.5)

59. a) 2.25 m   **b)** 3.8 s
60. 82 m   **61.** 1160 m
62. $\pm\frac{9}{2}$ **63.** 56 m by 116 m
64. 600 km/h   **65.** -24 or 25
66. 75 km/h   **67.** $-29, -27$ or $27, 29$
68. 2.5 km/h   **69.** 2.8 cm
70. 10 km/h   **71.** 12 cm, 16 cm
72. a) 7.5 cm   **b)** 6562.5 cm^3
73. a) $0, -\frac{3}{4}$ **b)** $-\frac{11}{4}, 2$ **c)** $-\frac{1}{4}, -\frac{1}{2}$
74. 10 km/h   **75.** 13 cm by 8 cm
76. b) 17.72 cm
77. a) $110; \$160$ **b)** $\$120; 130$
78. a) 1. Multiply both sides by $4a$. 2. Add b^2 to both sides. 3. Subtract $4ac$ from both sides. 4. Factor the perfect square trinomial on the left-hand side. 5. Take the square root of both sides. 6. Subtract b from both sides. 7. Divide both sides by $2a$. **b)** Yes. Terms are added and subtracted from both sides to make the left side a perfect square. **c)** 1. $36x^2 + 24x - 48 = 0$

2. $36x^2 + 24x - 48 + 4 = 4$
3. $36x^2 + 24x + 4 = 52$ 4. $(6x + 2)^2 = 52$
5. $6x + 2 = \pm\sqrt{52}$
6. $6x = -2 \pm \sqrt{52}$
7. $x = \frac{-2 \pm \sqrt{52}}{6}$, which reduces to $x = \frac{-1 \pm \sqrt{13}}{3}$

79. 3.58 units
80. a) $6, 10$ **b)** $s = \frac{p^2 - p}{2}$ **c)** 11
d) No. The solution to the quadratic must be an integer.
81. $b^2 - 4ac$ is a perfect square.   **82.** $b^2 - 4ac = 0$
83. 2.1 cm
84. a) $-8y, -\frac{y}{2}$ **b)** $(-1 \pm \sqrt{2})y$
85. a) $40x^2 + 2x - 3 = 0$ **b)** $x^2 - 6x + 4 = 0$
c) $4x^2 - 4x - 11 = 0$

Section 4.6 pp. 185–186

Practice (Section 4.6)

1. $3i$ **2.** $5i$ **3.** $9i$
4. $i\sqrt{5}$ **5.** $i\sqrt{13}$ **6.** $i\sqrt{23}$
7. $2i\sqrt{3}$ **8.** $2i\sqrt{10}$ **9.** $3i\sqrt{6}$
10. $-2i$ **11.** $-2i\sqrt{5}$ **12.** $5i\sqrt{y}$
13. $6ix$ **14.** $3ix^2\sqrt{2}$ **15.** $2iz^2\sqrt{5z}$
16. 6 **17.** 6 **18.** $2ix^2y\sqrt{10xy}$
19. $-i$ **20.** 1 **21.** i
22. -20 **23.** -5 **24.** i
25. -12 **26.** 64 **27.** 18
28. -2 **29.** 5 **30.** 6
31. -12 **32.** -50 **33.** 40
34. $7 - 2i$ **35.** $3 - 11i$ **36.** $2 - 5i$
37. $1 + 6i$ **38.** $-2 + 13i$ **39.** $5i - 11$
40. $-3 - i$ **41.** $+24 - 3i$ **42.** $14 - 17i$
43. $-12i + 7$ **44.** $8 - 6i$ **45.** $3i - 6$
46. $-12i - 20$ **47.** $8 - 2i$ **48.** $14 + 2i$
49. $29 - 3i$ **50.** $-7 - 19i$ **51.** 26
52. $-3 + 4i$ **53.** $-7 - 24i$ **54.** $-2i$
55. 4 **56.** $\pm3i$ **57.** $\pm2i$
58. $\pm2i\sqrt{5}$ **59.** $\pm2i\sqrt{3}$ **60.** $\pm2i\sqrt{2}$
61. $\pm3i\sqrt{2}$ **62.** $-1 \pm i$ **63.** $2 \pm 2i$
64. $\frac{-5 \pm i\sqrt{7}}{2}$ **65.** $\frac{3 \pm i\sqrt{3}}{2}$ **66.** $\frac{1 \pm 3i\sqrt{3}}{2}$
67. $\frac{3 \pm 3i\sqrt{3}}{2}$ **68.** $\frac{-3 \pm i\sqrt{15}}{4}$ **69.** $\frac{2 \pm i\sqrt{2}}{3}$
70. $\frac{-5 \pm i\sqrt{15}}{10}$ **71.** $\frac{2 \pm i}{5}$ **72.** $\pm i\sqrt{6}$
73. $\pm i$ **74.** $\frac{1 \pm i\sqrt{11}}{2}$ **75.** $1 \pm i$
76. $\frac{-1 \pm i\sqrt{23}}{6}$ **77.** $\pm2i\sqrt{2}$ **78.** ±2
79. $\pm i$ **80.** $\pm1, \pm2i$ **81.** $\pm\sqrt{3}, \pm\sqrt{2}$

82. $\pm\sqrt{3}, \pm i\sqrt{2}$ **83.** $\pm 1, \pm\dfrac{\sqrt{6}}{3}$ **84.** $\pm i, \pm\dfrac{i\sqrt{6}}{2}$

85. $\pm\dfrac{\sqrt{6}}{2}, \pm i\sqrt{2}$ **86.** $\pm\dfrac{\sqrt{2}}{2}, \pm\dfrac{i\sqrt{2}}{2}$ **87.** $0, \pm\dfrac{2}{3}$

Applications and Problem Solving (Section 4.6)

88. a) $a^2 + b^2$; real **b)** 74
  c) $(3 + 4i)(3 - 4i) = 25$, $(4 + 3i)(4 - 3i) = 25$
89. a) $i, -1 + i, -i$ **b)** $-i, -1 - i, i$
  c) $3i, -9 + 3i, 72 - 51i$ **d)** $2 + i, 5 + 5i, 2 + 51i$
90. a) $-1, -i, 1, i, -1, -i, 1, i, -1, -i, 1$
  b) The pattern $-1, -i, 1, i$ repeats.
  c) Divide n by 4. If the remainder is 1, $i^n = i$. If the remainder is 2, $i^n = -1$. If the remainder is 3, $i^n = -i$. If the remainder is 0, $i^n = 1$. **d)** $1; -1; i; -i$
91. a) $s = 3, t = 4$ **b)** $s = 3, t = -1$
  c) $s = 2, t = 1$
92. b) An error message appears.
93. a) $x^2 + 4 = 0$ **b)** $x^2 - 2x + 2 = 0$
  c) $4x^2 - 12x + 13 = 0$
94. a) 1 s and 9 s **b)** 5 s **c)** no
95. No. Imaginary roots occur in complex conjugate pairs.
96. a) 2; equal **b)** $2, -1$; equal
  c) $0, 2, -1$; equal **d)** $\pm i, \pm\sqrt{2}$; equal
  e) $0, \pm i, \pm\sqrt{2}$; equal
97. 12, 14 or $-14, -12$

Section 4.7 pp. 189–190

Practice (Section 4.7)

 1. two equal real roots **2.** two distinct real roots
 3. two imaginary roots **4.** two imaginary roots
 5. two distinct real roots **6.** two equal real roots
 7. two imaginary roots **8.** two distinct real roots
 9. two distinct real roots **10.** two imaginary roots
11. two imaginary roots **12.** two distinct real roots
13. two equal real roots **14.** two distinct real roots
15. two imaginary roots **16.** two equal real roots
17. two distinct real roots **18.** two distinct real roots
19. two equal real roots **20.** two imaginary roots
21. two distinct real roots **22.** two distinct real roots
23. two imaginary roots **24.** two imaginary roots
25. two imaginary roots **26.** two distinct real roots
27. 2 **28.** 0
29. 2 **30.** 1
31. 0 **32.** 1
33. $k = 9$ **34.** $k < 1, k \neq 0$
35. $k < -2$ **36.** $k < \dfrac{2}{3}, k \neq 0$
37. $k > \dfrac{3}{4}$ **38.** $k = \pm\dfrac{1}{2}$
39. $k < -\dfrac{4}{3}$ **40.** $k > -\dfrac{9}{16}$

41. $k > -\dfrac{4}{3}$ **42.** $k = 2$

43. a) $m > -\dfrac{4}{3}, m \neq 0$ **b)** $m = -\dfrac{4}{3}$ **c)** $m < -\dfrac{4}{3}$

Applications and Problem Solving (Section 4.7)

44. a) 16, 15 **b)** no **c)** $\dfrac{55}{2}, \dfrac{7}{2}$
45. a) 5 m by 20 m or 10 m by 10 m **b)** no
46. a) no **b)** 11 cm by 11 cm **c)** 9 cm by 13 cm
47. Yes, after 2 s.
48. a) 6000 at \$26 or 6500 at \$24
  b) No. The discriminant is negative and the function has no zeros.
  c) prices from \$20 to \$30
49. two distinct real roots; If $ac < 0$, then $b^2 - ac > 0$, since $b^2 > 0$ and $-ac > 0$.
50. $\dfrac{1}{2}$ **51.** $25i$ and $-6i$
52. a) If $a = k$, then $b = -k^2 - 1$ and $c = k$, where $k \neq 0$, then the equation $ax^2 + bx + c = 0$ has roots k and $\dfrac{1}{k}$.
  b) Answers may vary. $x^2 - 2x + 1 = 0$ has roots 1 and 1; $3x^2 - 10x + 3 = 0$ has roots 3 and $\dfrac{1}{3}$
53. a) $k < -8, k > 8$ **b)** $k = 2$ **c)** $-4 < k < 4$
54. a) $\left(-\dfrac{1}{2}, 5\right), \left(-\dfrac{3}{2}, 7\right)$ **b)** no
55. a) $-2\sqrt{6} < m < 2\sqrt{6}$ **b)** $m = \pm 3\sqrt{3}$

Career Connection p. 191

1 Defining the Dimensions of a Package
 1. a) 6.25 cm by 10 cm by 16 cm; 7.2 cm by 11.4 cm by 18.3 cm **b)** 843 cm^2; 1072 cm^2
 2. 5.8 cm by 9.4 cm by 15.0 cm

2 Locating Information
1–5. Answers may vary.
 1. math, design, economics
 2. artistic, advertising, consumer awareness
 3. A package with a colour and shape that stands out and is attractive may influence a buyer.
 5. all companies that package goods for display in stores

Investigating Math pp. 192–193

1 Exploring the Relationships
 1. b) 5, 4; 9; 20; 1, -9, 20
  c) 2, -6; -4; -12; 1, 4, -12
  d) 3, $\dfrac{1}{2}$; $\dfrac{7}{2}$; $\dfrac{3}{2}$; 2, -7, 3
  e) $-\dfrac{1}{2}, -1$; $-\dfrac{3}{2}$; $\dfrac{1}{2}$; 2, 3, 1
  f) $\dfrac{2}{3}, -3$; $-\dfrac{7}{3}$; -2; 3, 7, -6
  g) 0, -8; -8; 0; 1, 8, 0
  h) 4, -4; 0; -16; 1, 0, -16

2. a and b **3.** $-\dfrac{b}{a}$

4. c and a **5.** $\dfrac{c}{a}$

6. a) sum = -6, product = 8
b) sum = 3, product = -4
c) sum = $\dfrac{3}{2}$, product = $-\dfrac{5}{2}$
d) sum = $-\dfrac{9}{5}$, product = 0
e) sum = $-\dfrac{1}{2}$, product = $\dfrac{9}{4}$
f) sum = $-\dfrac{2}{3}$, product = $-\dfrac{8}{3}$
g) sum = 0, product = $\dfrac{9}{2}$
h) sum = $-\dfrac{3}{2}$, product = 2
i) sum = $\dfrac{3}{4}$, product = $\dfrac{1}{4}$

2 Using Algebra

1. a) $r_1 + r_2 = -\dfrac{b}{a}$ **b)** equal

2. a) $r_1 \times r_2 = \dfrac{c}{a}$ **b)** equal

3. sum of roots = $-\dfrac{b}{a}$; product of roots = $\dfrac{c}{a}$

3 Working Backward

1. a) $x^2 - 2x + 3 = 0$ **b)** $x^2 + x + 5 = 0$
c) $x^2 + 2x - 2 = 0$ **d)** $x^2 - 3 = 0$
e) $x^2 + 4x = 0$ **f)** $4x^2 - 12x + 1 = 0$
g) $2x^2 - x + 2 = 0$ **h)** $6x^2 + 4x - 3 = 0$
i) $10x^2 + 4x + 3 = 0$
2. a) $x^2 - 8x + 15 = 0$ **b)** $x^2 - 3x - 4 = 0$
c) $3x^2 + 7x - 6 = 0$ **d)** $2x^2 + x = 0$
e) $16x^2 - 24x + 9 = 0$ **f)** $9x^2 - 1 = 0$
g) $x^2 - 5 = 0$ **h)** $x^2 - 2x - 1 = 0$
i) $x^2 - 4x - 14 = 0$ **j)** $x^2 + 4 = 0$
k) $x^2 - 2x + 10 = 0$ **l)** $4x^2 - 8x + 1 = 0$

4 Problem Solving

1. a) $-\dfrac{2}{3}$ **b)** -2
2. $\pm 33, \pm 12, \pm 3$ **3.** ± 9 **4.** -14
5. $x^2 - 2x - 9 = 0$ **6.** 1
7. a) $k = 1$ **b)** $k = -\dfrac{1}{5}$ **c)** $k = -\dfrac{4}{9}$ **d)** $k = 5$

8. a) $\dfrac{1}{r_1} + \dfrac{1}{r_2} = \dfrac{r_1 + r_2}{r_1 r_2} = \dfrac{-\frac{b}{a}}{\frac{c}{a}} = -\dfrac{b}{a} \times \dfrac{a}{c} = -\dfrac{b}{c}$

b) $r_1, r_2, c \neq 0$

Connecting Math and Esthetics pp. 195–196

1 Investigating φ

1. a) $\phi = \dfrac{1 + \sqrt{5}}{2}$ **b)** 1.618

2. a) $\dfrac{3 + \sqrt{5}}{2}$ **b)** 2.618   **c)** 2.618 − 1.618 = 1

d) $\dfrac{3 + \sqrt{5}}{2} - \dfrac{1 + \sqrt{5}}{2} = 1$; equal

3. a) $\dfrac{-1 + \sqrt{5}}{2}$ **b)** 0.618   **c)** 1.618 − 0.618 = 1

d) $\dfrac{1 + \sqrt{5}}{2} - \left(\dfrac{-1 + \sqrt{5}}{2}\right) = 1$; equal

4. a) $\dfrac{1}{\phi - 1} = \dfrac{1}{\frac{1 + \sqrt{5}}{2} - 1} = \dfrac{1}{\frac{-1 + \sqrt{5}}{2}} = \dfrac{2}{-1 + \sqrt{5}}$

$= \dfrac{2(1 + \sqrt{5})}{4} = \dfrac{1 + \sqrt{5}}{2} = \phi$

b) $2 - \dfrac{1}{\phi^2} = 2 - \dfrac{1}{\frac{3 + \sqrt{5}}{2}} = 2 - \dfrac{2}{3 + \sqrt{5}} =$

$2 - \dfrac{2(3 - \sqrt{5})}{4} = 2 - \dfrac{3\sqrt{5}}{2} = \dfrac{1 + \sqrt{5}}{2} = \phi$

5. a) $t^6 = \phi^5$, $t_{22} = \phi^{21}$, $t_n = \phi^{n-1}$ **b)** $\dfrac{3 + \sqrt{5}}{2}$
c) t^3 **d)** $2 + \sqrt{5}$ **e)** t_4
f) t_5, t_{10}, t_{n+2} **g)** Fibonacci sequence

2 Geometry and φ

1. $EF = \sqrt{5}$, $AE = 1$, $AF = 1 + \sqrt{5}$, $AB - 2$,
$\dfrac{AF}{AB} = \dfrac{1 + \sqrt{5}}{2} = \phi$
2. $AC^2 = AB^2 + BC^2 = AB^2 + \left(\dfrac{1}{2}AB\right)^2 = \dfrac{5AB^2}{4}$,

$AC = \dfrac{\sqrt{5}AB}{2}$, $CD = CB = \dfrac{1}{2}AB$, $AE = AD =$

$AC - CD = \dfrac{\sqrt{5}AB}{2} - \dfrac{1}{2}AB = \dfrac{\sqrt{5} - 1}{2}AB$,

$\dfrac{AB}{AE} = \dfrac{AB}{\frac{\sqrt{5} - 1}{2}AB} = \dfrac{2}{\sqrt{5} - 1} = \dfrac{2(\sqrt{5} + 1)}{4} =$

$\dfrac{1 + \sqrt{5}}{2} = \phi$

3. $a^2 = 1^2 + 1^2 - 2(1)(1)\cos 108°$, $a \approx 1.618 \approx \phi$

3 Fibonacci Numbers and φ

1. 377, 610
2. a) $\dfrac{5}{3}$ **b)** $\dfrac{13}{8}$ **c)** The denominator and numerator are consecutive terms of the Fibonacci sequence.

d) $1 + \cfrac{1}{1 + \cfrac{1}{1 + \cfrac{1}{1 + \cfrac{1}{1 + \cfrac{1}{1 + \cfrac{1}{1 + 1}}}}}}$

3. a) 2, 5, 7, 12, 19, 31, 50, 81, 131, 212

b) 2.5, 1.4, 1.7143, 1.5833, 1.6316, 1.6129, 1.62, 1.6173, 1.618; ϕ

c) Answers may vary. **i)** 1, 10, 11, 21, 32, 53, 85, 138, 223, 361 **ii)** 10, 1.1, 1.9091, 1.5238, 1.6563, 1.6038, 1.6235, 1.6159, 1.6188; ϕ

4 ϕ in Architecture, Design, and Nature

1. 18 m
2. approximately ϕ
3. approximately ϕ

Technology p. 197

1 Solving Algebraically

1. 4, -1
2. 2, -5
3. -1, -5
4. 6, 1
5. 8
6. ± 0.7
7. $\frac{1}{2}$, -1
8. $\frac{3}{2}$, $-\frac{2}{3}$
9. 0, $-\frac{3}{7}$
10. $-\frac{1}{3}$, -2
11. 3, -5
12. 1, -4
13. 2, $-\frac{4}{3}$
14. -8, $\frac{1}{2}$
15. $-\frac{33}{10}$, 3
16. $-2 \pm \sqrt{11}$
17. $3 \pm \sqrt{5}$
18. $\frac{5 \pm \sqrt{17}}{2}$
19. $\frac{-7 \pm \sqrt{145}}{4}$
20. $\frac{-5 \pm \sqrt{13}}{6}$
21. $\frac{6 \pm \sqrt{105}}{3}$
22. $\frac{-31 \pm \sqrt{2611}}{15}$
23. $\frac{1 \pm 3\sqrt{5}}{2}$
24. $\frac{1 \pm 3\sqrt{19}}{10}$
25. $-1 \pm \sqrt{5}$
26. $\frac{7 \pm \sqrt{39}}{5}$
27. $\frac{-7 \pm \sqrt{113}}{3}$
28. 2, 1
29. ± 3
30. $\frac{1 \pm \sqrt{13}}{3}$

2 Nature of the Roots

1. **a)** $-1 \pm 2i\sqrt{3}$ **b)** Answers may vary.
2. $\frac{3}{2}$, 1
3. $\frac{-3 \pm i\sqrt{11}}{4}$
4. $\pm \frac{i\sqrt{3}}{5}$
5. **a)** 0, $\pm i$ **b)** ± 1, $\pm i$ **c)** $\pm \sqrt{5}$, $\pm i\sqrt{3}$

Section 4.8 pp. 202–203

Practice (Section 4.8)

1. -3
2. -2
3. 0
4. 12
5. 0
6. -4
7. -3
8. -24
9. 6
10. -2
11. -18
12. 22
13. -23
14. 85
15. 5
16. $\frac{9}{2}$
17. -9
18. 0
19. 1
20. 4
21. -2
22. 0
23. -7
24. -3
25. 0
26. -55
27. 12
28. 10
29. -1
30. 11
31. -10
32. -16
33. -45
34. 0
35. 22
36. 70
37. 136
38. 0
39. 11
40. -3
41. 19
42. 0
43. $-\frac{3}{8}$
44. 6

45. $\frac{8}{3}$
46. -37
47. 2
48. 4
49. -1
50. 3
51. $m = 2$, $n = -3$
52. $p = 1$, $q = 2$
53. $v = 6$, $w = -11$

Applications and Problem Solving (Section 4.8)

54. 7
55. -20
56. **a)** 14 **b)** When the height is $\frac{7}{2}$ units, the area is 14 square units.
57. **a)** 12 **b)** When $n = -\frac{1}{2}$, the product of the two numbers is 12.
58. **a)** 77 **b)** 77 **c)** equal; $h(500) = h(-500)$
59. **a)** $-0.017d + 0.45$ R25
b) When the horizontal distance is 50 m, the height is 25 m.
c) $-0.017d - 0.06$ R-2.3
d) No. The hammer cannot have a negative height.
60. 1, 4
61. **a)** $ba^2 + ca + d = 0$ **b)** $a = \frac{-c \pm \sqrt{c^2 - 4bd}}{2b}$
62. **a)** $-Q(x)$, R **b)** $\frac{P(x)}{x - b} = Q(x) + \frac{R}{x - b}$.
Multiply both sides by -1. $\frac{P(x)}{b - x} = -Q(x) + \frac{R}{b - x}$
63. **a)** $x^2 - 3x - 4 = 0$
b) $x^3 - 2x^2 - 8x + 3 = 0$
c) $8x^4 - 4x^3 + 2x^2 - x + 1 = 0$

Section 4.9 pp. 209–211

Practice (Section 4.9)

1. yes
2. no
3. no
4. yes
5. yes
6. no
7. no
8. yes
9. yes
10. no
11. yes
12. yes
13. yes
14. yes
15. no
16. yes
17. no
18. yes
19. $P(-1) = 0$
20. $P(2) = 0$
21. $P(3) = 0$
22. $P(-3) = 0$
23. $P(-2) = 0$
24. $P(-5) = 0$
25. no
26. no
27. yes
28. yes
29. yes
30. yes
31. yes
32. no
33. yes
34. yes
35. no
36. yes
37. no
38. yes
39. yes
40. no
41. no
42. yes
43. $P\left(-\frac{1}{2}\right) = 0$
44. $P\left(\frac{3}{2}\right) = 0$
45. $P\left(\frac{1}{3}\right) = 0$
46. $P\left(-\frac{1}{3}\right) = 0$
47. $P\left(-\frac{2}{3}\right) = 0$
48. $P\left(\frac{2}{3}\right) = 0$ 49. no
50. yes
51. yes
52. yes
53. no
54. no
55. $(x - 1)(x - 2)(x - 3)$
56. $(x + 1)(x + 3)(x + 4)$
57. $(x - 2)(x + 3)(x - 3)$
58. $(x + 3)(x^2 + x - 1)$
59. $(z + 2)(z + 4)(z - 5)$
60. $(x + 1)(x - 4)(x + 4)$

61. $(x - 4)(x^2 + 2x + 2)$　　**62.** $(k - 3)(k + 4)(k + 5)$
63. $(x - 5)(x^2 + 5x - 2)$　　**64.** $(x - 3)(x + 1)(x + 6)$
65. $(2x - 1)(x - 1)(x - 3)$　　**66.** $(y + 1)(2y + 1)(2y - 3)$
67. $(x + 2)(3x - 1)(x - 3)$　　**68.** $(x + 2)(3x - 2)(x - 2)$
69. $(x + 4)(2x + 3)(x + 1)$　　**70.** $(x - 2)(2x^2 + x + 5)$
71. $(3x + 5)(2x - 1)(x - 3)$
72. $(p + 2)(2p + 1)(2p - 1)$
73. $(3w - 1)(2w^2 + 6w - 5)$
74. $(x + 1)(x - 1)(4x + 3)$

Applications and Problem Solving (Section 4.9)

75. a) $h(h - 1)^2$　　　　　　**b)** 0.5 m by 0.5 m
76. a) $l(3l - 4)(l + 1)$　　　**b)** 9.8 m by 5.6 m
77. a) $(h + 2)(h + 1)(3h - 1)$　**b)** 4 m by 3 m by 5 m
78. a) $(x + 4)(x + 2)(x + 1)(x - 3)$
　b) $(x + 3)(x + 2)(x + 1)(x - 1)(x - 2)$
79. a) $(2x + 1)^2(2x - 1)$　**b)** $(2x + 1)(2x - 1)(2x - 3)$
80. They are consecutive integers starting at -3.
81. $P(-y) = y^2(y^2 - 1) - y^2(1 + y^2) + y^2 + y^2 = y^4 - y^2$
　$- y^2 - y^4 + y^2 + y^2 = 0$
82. a) 3　　　　**b)** -72
83. 2 m by 2 m by 3 m
84. a) $(x - 2)$, $(x + 4)$, $(3x + 1)$　**b)** No. A cubic
　polynomial has only three factors.
85. $m = 3$, $n = -8$
86. $P(a) = a^3 - a^3 + ba^2 - a^2b + ca - ac = 0$
87. The edge length of the larger cube is 2 more than
　the edge length of the smaller cube.
88. a) $(x - 1)(x^2 + x + 1)$　**b)** $(x + 1)(x^2 - x + 1)$
　c) $(x - 3)(x^2 + 3x + 9)$　**d)** $(x + 4)(x^2 - 4x + 16)$
　e) $(2x - 1)(4x^2 + 2x + 1)$
　f) $(4x + 1)(16x^2 - 4x + 1)$
　g) $(x + y)(x^2 - xy + y^2)$
　h) $(x - y)(x^2 + xy + y^2)$
　i) $(2x + 5)(4x^2 - 10x + 25)$; $(3x - 4)(9x^2 + 12x + 16)$
　j) $(x^2 + y^3)(x^4 - x^2y^3 + y^6)$
89. a) yes; yes; $P(-1) = P(1) = 0$　**b)** yes; no;
　$P(-1) = 0$, $P(1) = 0$
90. $r + 3$
91. a) neither　**b)** both　**c)** $x + y$　**d)** $x - y$
　e) neither　**f)** both　**g)** $x + y$　**h)** $x - y$
　i) $x + y$ is a factor of $x^n + y^n$ if n is odd; $x - y$ is a
　factor of $x^n - y^n$ if n is odd; $x + y$ and $x - y$ are
　factors of $x^n - y^n$ if n is even; neither $x + y$ nor
　$x - y$ is a factor of $x^n + y^n$ if n is even
　j) $x - y$, $x + y$　　　**k)** $x + y$
92. If there is more than one zero, there must be 3
　zeros. Since they are all integers, the factors must
　be of the form $x - m$ or $m - x$, where m is an
　integer. When these three factors are multiplied,
　the coefficient of x^3 will be ± 1.
93. a) $P(1) = 0$; thus $a + b + c + d = 0$　**b)** yes
　c) no　　**d)** yes

Technology pp. 212–213

1 Cubic or Third-Degree Functions and Equations

4. With the exception of the region between any local
　maximum or minimum values, when $a > 0$ the
　cubic function increases from left to right and when
　$a < 0$ the cubic function decreases from left to
　right.
5. the y-intercept
6. a) $-2, 1, 3$
　b) Yes. The x-intercepts occur when $y = 0$.
7. a) 3　　**b)** 2　　**c)** 1　　**d)** 1
　e) 3　　**f)** 1　　**g)** 2　　**h)** 1
8. a) 1, 2, 3　**b)** 2, 3　　**c)** 0, 2
9. No. The term involving x^3 will dominate all others
　in the cubic function for sufficiently large (positive)
　x and for sufficiently small (negative) x. Thus, the
　function will assume both negative and positive
　values and, since it is continuous, it must cross the
　x-axis at least once.

2 Quartic or Fourth-Degree Functions and Equations

4. If $a > 0$, the function decreases from the left and
　then increases again to the right. If $a < 0$, the
　function increases from the left and then decreases
　again to the right.
5. the y-intercept
6. a) $-3, -1, 1, 2$
　b) Yes. The x-intercepts occur when $y = 0$.
7. a) 4　　**b)** 2　　**c)** 0　　**d)** 1
　e) 2　　**f)** 2　　**g)** 0　　**h)** 4
　i) 3　　**j)** 1
8. a) 0, 1, 2, 3, 4　　**b)** 0, 2, 3, 4　　**c)** 0, 2, 4
9. No. There could be two pairs of equal roots.

3 Quintic or Fifth-Degree Functions

1. If the function is expanded, the highest power of x
　is 5.
2. $0, \pm 1, \pm 2$; These values of x produce $y = 0$.
5. a) 2 distinct real roots, 3 equal real roots
　b) 1 distinct real root, 2 pairs of equal real roots
　c) 2 equal real roots, 1 distinct real root,
　2 imaginary roots
　d) 2 pairs of equal real roots, 1 distinct real root

4 Functions in the Form $y = x^n$

1. b) All have a similar shape to the parabola.
　c) $(0, 0)$, $(-1, 1)$, $(1, 1)$
　d) The solutions are $x = 0$, and all graphs pass
　through the origin.
2. b) All increase from left to right, without any
　maximum or minimum values.
　c) $(0, 0)$, $(-1, -1)$, $(1, 1)$
　d) The solutions are $x = 0$, and all graphs pass
　through the origin.

174 *Chapter 4 Answers*

Practice (Section 4.10)

1. $-1, 4, -5$ 2. $2, 7, -6$ 3. $0, -3, 8$
4. $-6, 3$ 5. $0, -3, 2$ 6. $0, -4, -3$
7. $0, 2, 2$ 8. $0, \pm 3$ 9. $-3, \pm 1$
10. $3, \pm 2$ 11. $-4, 1, 1$ 12. $\pm 4, 3$
13. $-1, 2, 3$ 14. $-2, 3, 3$ 15. $1, 2, 3$
16. $-5, \pm 1$ 17. $-5, -1, 4$ 18. $-2, -2, 5$
19. $1, 1, 7$ 20. $-3, 2, 6$ 21. $-3, -2, 5$
22. $-4, 3, 5$ 23. $-1, 2, 4$ 24. $1, 1, 3$

25. $-6, -1, -1$ 26. $-2, -1, 4$ 27. $-\frac{1}{2}, 1, 3$
28. $-\frac{1}{4}, \frac{1}{3}, -1$ 29. $\frac{2}{3}, \frac{1}{2}, \frac{1}{2}$ 30. $0, 4, -\frac{2}{5}$
31. $0, -\frac{1}{2}, 2$ 32. $0, 3, \frac{1}{3}$ 33. $0, \pm \frac{2}{3}$
34. $0, -\frac{1}{4}, -\frac{1}{4}$ 35. $-3, -1, -\frac{1}{2}$ 36. $\frac{2}{3}, 1, 1$
37. $-1, \frac{2}{5}, 2$ 38. $-1, -1, \frac{7}{2}$ 39. $-\frac{5}{2}, -\frac{1}{2}, 1$
40. $\frac{1}{2}, 1, 5$ 41. $-2, \frac{1}{3}, 1$ 42. $-\frac{1}{4}, \frac{1}{2}, 3$
43. $-\frac{1}{2}, 3, 3$ 44. $-2, \pm \frac{2}{3}$ 45. $1, \frac{4}{3}, \frac{3}{2}$
46. $\frac{1}{2}, \pm 1$

47. **a)** $0, \pm 2\sqrt{2}$ **b)** $0, \pm 2.83$
48. **a)** $3, \dfrac{-3 \pm \sqrt{13}}{2}$ **b)** $3, 0.30, -3.30$
49. **a)** $4, 1 \pm \sqrt{3}$ **b)** $4, 2.73, -0.73$
50. **a)** $-5, 1 \pm \sqrt{6}$ **b)** $-5, 3.45, -1.45$
51. **a)** $-3, -1 \pm \sqrt{7}$ **b)** $-3, 1.65, -3.65$
52. **a)** $-2, \dfrac{-3 \pm \sqrt{17}}{2}$ **b)** $-2, 0.56, -3.56$
53. $0, \pm \dfrac{5\sqrt{2}}{2}$ 54. $2, \pm \dfrac{\sqrt{5}}{2}$
55. $1, \dfrac{1 \pm \sqrt{61}}{6}$ 56. $-3, \dfrac{-1 \pm \sqrt{10}}{3}$
57. $-4, \dfrac{-1 \pm \sqrt{33}}{4}$ 58. $3, \dfrac{-2 \pm \sqrt{29}}{5}$
59. $0, \pm i$ 60. $-1, \dfrac{1 \pm i\sqrt{7}}{2}$
61. $2, \dfrac{1 \pm i\sqrt{7}}{2}$ 62. $-2, 1 \pm i\sqrt{3}$
63. $1, -1 \pm \sqrt{5}$ 64. $-5, \dfrac{-3 \pm \sqrt{29}}{2}$
65. $-1, \dfrac{-3 \pm i\sqrt{3}}{3}$ 66. $0, \pm \dfrac{i\sqrt{15}}{5}$
67. $4, \pm \dfrac{i\sqrt{10}}{2}$ 68. $1, \dfrac{2 \pm i\sqrt{2}}{3}$
69. $-2, \dfrac{-3 \pm i\sqrt{31}}{4}$ 70. $3, \dfrac{-3 \pm i\sqrt{23}}{8}$

Applications and Problem Solving (Section 4.10)

71. $\frac{1}{2}, \frac{1}{2}, \frac{1}{2}$ 72. $\frac{1}{2}, -\frac{2}{3}, -\frac{2}{3}$
73. $\frac{1}{5}, -\frac{1}{3}, -\frac{1}{2}$ 74. $\frac{1}{3}, \pm \frac{3}{2}$
75. $\frac{1}{3}, \dfrac{-3 \pm \sqrt{5}}{2}$ 76. $-\frac{3}{2}, \dfrac{3 \pm 3i\sqrt{3}}{4}$
77. $0, \pm \dfrac{\sqrt{6}}{3}$ 78. $2, 2, -\frac{3}{4}$
79. $1, \pm i$ 80. $0, \dfrac{3 \pm \sqrt{5}}{2}$
81. **a)** $k = 3; -4, 3$ **b)** $k = -5; \dfrac{-1}{3}, 1$
82. **a)** 4 **b)** $0, 2, 2$
83. **a)** $x^3 - 6x^2 + 3x + 10 = 0$
    b) $x^3 + 3x^2 - 10x - 24 = 0$
    c) $x^3 - 3x^2 + x + 1 = 0$
    d) $x^3 - 2x - 4 = 0$ Yes. Multiply each equation by any non-zero constant and the roots remain the same.
84. $-9, -8, -7$ 85. $0, -1, 2, 3$
86. $-3, -2, 1, 2$ 87. $-2, -2, 3, 3$
88. $\pm 1, \pm \sqrt{3}$ 89. $-3, 2, 1 \pm \sqrt{3}$
90. $\pm 1, \pm i$ 91. $-1, -1, -1, \frac{1}{2}$
92. $1, 2, -\frac{1}{2}, -\frac{1}{2}$ 93. 2 cm by 3 cm by 7 cm
94. 3 cm by 3 cm by 15 cm
95. 5 cm by 20 cm by 25 cm
96. 12 cm by 12 cm by 7 cm
97. $-3, \pm 1, \pm 2$
98. 5 m by 20 m by 1 m
99. Answers may vary. $x^3 - 7x^2 + x - 7 = 0$
100. Yes. Multiply the equation by any non-zero constant to get a different graph.
101. 100 m by 300 m by 300 m
102. 6 cm by 9 cm by 20 cm
103. 4 m by 3 m by 0.25 m
104. **a)** $y = x^3 + x^2 - 5x - 5$
    b) $y = 2x^3 + 2x^2 - 10x - 10$; Multiplying the right-hand side by 2 does not affect the roots, but changes the y-intercept to -10.
105. n must be odd, since imaginary roots always occur in pairs.
106. **a)** never true; Imaginary roots occur in conjugate pairs.
    b) always true; Take into account repeated and imaginary roots.
    c) sometimes true; for example, $x^4 + 1 = 0$
    d) sometimes true; for example, $(x - 1)(x - \sqrt{5})(x + \sqrt{5})$
    e) sometimes true; for example, $(x - \sqrt{2})^4 = 0$
    f) never true; Imaginary roots occur in conjugate pairs and an imaginary number never equals its conjugate.

Technology p. 222

1 Solving Algebraically

1. $-5, -3, 2$
2. $-8, 6, 9$
3. $-5, -4, 1, 3$
4. $-6, -5, -3, 1$
5. $-5, -\frac{5}{2}, -1$
6. $-\frac{7}{3}, -\frac{1}{2}, \frac{2}{3}$
7. $\pm\frac{1}{2}, 2, 4$
8. $\frac{1}{4}, \frac{1}{3}, \frac{2}{3}, \frac{3}{2}$
9. $-2, -1.41, 1.41$
10. $-0.54, 2.07, 4.97$
11. $\pm1.73, \pm2.24$
12. $-1.65, \pm0.45, 3.65$
13. $-3.65, 1.65, 4.5$
14. $0, -1, \pm0.63$
15. The number of roots found was equal to the degree of the equation in each case.

2 Nature of the Roots

1. a) $-1, -1, -1$ **b)** $3, -1 \pm i\sqrt{2}$ **c)** $3, 4, 3$
  The graphing calculator does not show repeated roots or imaginary roots.
2. Answers may vary. Use the pencil-and-paper method.
3. $-1, -1, -1, -1$
4. $-2, -2, \frac{3}{2}$
5. $\frac{1}{2}, \frac{1 \pm 2i\sqrt{2}}{3}$
6. $\pm\sqrt{2}, \frac{1}{3}, \frac{1}{3}$
7. $1, 1, -1, \pm i$
8. $\pm i, \pm i\sqrt{2}$

3 Problem Solving

1. $12, 14, 16, 18$ or $-18, -16, -14, -12$
2. 35 m, 21 m

Investigating Math pp. 223–228

1 Exploring Linear Functions, $y = mx + b$

1. a) $9, 11, 13; 2, 2, 2$ **b)** $6, 10, 14; 4, 4, 4$
  c) $-5, -8, -11; -3, -3, -3$
2. The differences are equal to m.
3. The constant term is the value of y when $x = 0$.
4. a) $y = 2x + 3$ **b)** $y = 5x - 4$ **c)** $y = -6x + 2$
  d) $y = -0.5x + 5$
5. a) $3m + b, 4m + b; m, m, m, m$ **b)** A unit increase in the x-coordinate produces an increase or decrease in the y-coordinate of an amount equal to the slope.

2 Exploring Quadratic Functions, $y = ax^2 + bx + c$

1. a) $13, 21; 6, 8; 2, 2$ **b)** $11, 20, 33; 1, 5, 9, 13; 4, 4, 4$
  c) $-1, 4, 15, 32, 55; 5, 11, 17, 23; 6, 6, 6$
2. They are equal.
3. The second difference is equal to $2a$.
4. a) $5a + b, 7a + b; 2a, 2a, 2a$
  b) The second difference is equal to $2a$, which gives the value for a. The first entry in the first difference column is equal to $a + b$, which gives the value for b. The y-value when $x = 0$ is equal to c.
5. a) $5, 9, 13, 17; 4, 4, 4$ **b)** 1 **c)** 2 **d)** 3
  e) $y = 2x^2 + 3x + 1$

6. a) $y = x^2 + 2x + 3$ **b)** $y = 4x^2 - x - 2$
  c) $y = -2x^2 + 3x + 4$ **d)** $y = -x^2 + 4x$

3 Exploring Cubic Functions, $y = ax^3 + bx^2 + cx + d$

1. a) $9, 25, 57, 111; 6, 16, 32, 54, 4, 10, 16, 22; 6, 6, 6$
  b) $-4, -5, 6, 41, 112, 231; -1, 11, 35, 71, 119; 12, 24, 36, 48; 12, 12, 12$
2. a) 3rd column **b)** The third difference is equal to $6a$.
3. a) $27a + 9b + 3c + d, 64a + 16b + 4c + d; 7a + 3b + c, 19a + 5b + c, 37a + 7b + c; 6a + 2b, 12a + 2b, 18a + 2b; 6a, 6a$ **b)** When $x = 0$, the value of y is equal to d. The third difference is equal to $6a$. The first entry in the second difference column is $6a + 2b$, from which b can be found. When $x = 1$, the value of y is $a + b + c + d$. Use this to find c.
4. a) $-3, 1, 11, 27; 4, 10, 16; 6, 6$ **b)** 1 **c)** -1
  d) -3 **e)** -2 **f)** $y = x^3 - x^2 - 3x - 2$
5. a) $y = x^3 + 2x^2 - 4x + 3$
  b) $y = 2x^3 + x^2 + 3x + 2$
  c) $y = -x^3 + 4x^2 + x - 4$ **d)** $y = -3x^3 + 5x - 8$

4 Problem Solving

1. $y = x^3 - 3x + 7$
2. $y = -2x + 6$
3. $y = x^3 + x^2 - x - 1$
4. $y = -3x + 5$
5. $y = 5x^2 + 2$
6. $y = -2x^3 + 9x^2$
7. $y = 3x^3 - 4x^2 - 6x$
8. $y = -3x^2 + 4x - 5$
9. $1, 16; 3, 3, 3, 3; 0, 0, 0, 0; 0, 0, 0; y = 3x + 1$
10. $-1; 1, 3, 5, 7, 9; 2, 2, 2, 2; 0, 0, 0; y = x^2 - 1$
11. $3, 1, -5; -2, -6, -10, -14, -18, -22; -4, -4, -4, -4, -4; y = -2x^2 + 3$
12. $1; 1, 7, 19, 37, 61; 6, 12, 18, 24; 6, 6, 6; y = x^3 + 1$
13. $0; 0, 10, 32, 66, 112; 10, 22, 34, 46; 12, 12, 12; y = 2x^3 - x^2 - x$
14. $5, 8; 3, 5, 1, -9, -25, -47; 2, -4, -10, -16, -22; -6, -6, -6, -6; y = -x^3 + 4x^2 + 5$
15. a) $n = 5d + 6$ **b)** 81 **c)** 25
16. a) $n = \frac{l^2 + l}{2}$ **b)** 55 **c)** 14
17. $-54, -79, -108$
18. a) $n = 2p^3 - 3p - 1$ **b)** 8 **c)** 1969
19. a) $V = p^3 + 3p^2 + 2p, p \geq 1$ **b)** 10
  c) 9240 cm^3 **d)** $p(p + 1)(p + 2)$
  e) 1 cm by 2 cm by 3 cm; 2 cm by 3 cm by 4 cm; 3 cm by 4 cm by 5 cm; 4 cm by 5 cm by 6 cm; 5 cm by 6 cm by 7 cm; 6 cm by 7 cm by 8 cm
  f) No. For example, the following dimensions fit the pattern of the first 6 given volumes: 1 cm by 1 cm by 6 cm; 2 cm by 2 cm by 6 cm; 2 cm by 5 cm by 6 cm; 2 cm by 6 cm by 10 cm; 3 cm by 7 cm by 10 cm; 4 cm by 7 cm by 12 cm

Technology pp. 229–231

1 Linear Functions

1. a) $y = 2x + 4$ b) $y = -x + 2$
   c) $y = -12x + 11$ d) $y = \frac{1}{2}x - 2$

2. a) $n = -8p + 13$ b) -123 c) 35

2 Quadratic Functions

1. a) $y = x^2 - 3x + 2$ b) $y = 2x^2 + x - 6$
   c) $y = -3x^2 - x + 9$ d) $y = -4x^2 + 6x$

2. a) $n = 4p^2 + 2p - 3$ b) 269 c) 12

3. $n = p^2 + \frac{2}{3}p + \frac{1}{9}$

4. a) Substitute the points into the equation $y = ax^2 + bx + c$, then solve the system of three equations for a, b, and c. b) $y = x^2 - 2x - 1$

3 Cubic Functions

1. a) $y = x^3 - 3x^2 - x + 2$
   b) $y = x^3 + 2x^2 + 3x - 1$
   c) $y = -x^3 - x^2 + 4x + 5$
   d) $y = -2x^3 + 4x + 6$

2. a) $n = 2p^3 - 8$ b) 424 c) 20

4 Using Finite Differences

1. a) linear; $n = 3p - 7, p \geq 1$
   b) cubic; $n = 2p^3 - 3p + 1, p \geq 1$
   c) quadratic; $n = -4p^2 - 5, p \geq 1$

2. a) 1, 7, 19, 37 b) quadratic c) $h = 3r^2 - 3r + 1$
   d) 271 e) 15

3. a) 14, 30, 55 b) cubic
   c) $n = \frac{1}{3}l^3 + \frac{1}{2}l^2 + \frac{1}{6}l$ d) 385

4. a) 5 points b) Answers may vary.

5 Scatter Plots and Lines of Best Fit

1. b) 57 000 c) 2011 d) Answers may vary.
   e) about -4.3 f) the decrease in Armed Forces in thousands per year

2. b) $37 billion; $49 billion c) $84 billion
   d) Answers may vary. e) about 1.7 f) the increase in education spending in billions of dollars per year

Review pp. 232–233

1. $-3, 1$ 2. no real roots
3. $-4, 1$ 4. $2, 2$
5. no real roots 6. $-5, -1$
7. $3, 6$ 8. $\frac{3}{2}, \frac{3}{2}$
9. $\pm\frac{3}{2}$ 10. $-3, \frac{5}{2}$
11. 4 cm by 9 cm 12. $4, -7$
13. $2, 3$ 14. $-5, -2$

15. $-3, \frac{1}{2}$ 16. $-9, \frac{3}{2}$
17. $0, \frac{3}{8}$ 18. $1, \frac{4}{3}$
19. $1, -4$ 20. $3, -2$
21. $x^2 - 4x - 5 = 0$ 22. $2x^2 - 9x + 4 = 0$
23. 5 m by 45 m 24. ± 5
25. ± 8 26. $-7, 11$
27. $-10, 4$ 28. $\pm 5\sqrt{2}$
29. $\pm 2\sqrt{3}$ 30. $\pm 2\sqrt{2}$
31. $\pm\frac{3\sqrt{2}}{2}$ 32. 2
33. $4, -2$ 34. $-4 \pm \sqrt{11}$
35. $\frac{-5 \pm \sqrt{21}}{2}$ 36. $\frac{3 \pm \sqrt{17}}{2}$
37. $\frac{5 \pm \sqrt{61}}{2}$ 38. $\frac{-3 \pm \sqrt{21}}{2}$
39. $\frac{-5 \pm \sqrt{13}}{6}$ 40. $\frac{-1 \pm \sqrt{31}}{6}$
41. $2 \pm \sqrt{2}$ 42. $-\frac{1}{6}, 1$
43. 2.5 m 44. $6, -7$
45. $\frac{1}{2}, 3$ 46. $\frac{2}{7}, 1$
47. $-\frac{1}{2}, \frac{3}{2}$ 48. $5 \pm \sqrt{34}$
49. $-3 \pm \sqrt{3}$ 50. $\frac{3 \pm 3\sqrt{33}}{16}$
51. $\frac{-5 \pm \sqrt{73}}{6}$ 52. $0.74, -0.90$
53. $0.33, -0.75$ 54. $\frac{1}{2}, 4$
55. $\frac{-1 \pm \sqrt{41}}{2}$ 56. 650 km/h
57. $7i$ 58. $3i\sqrt{2}$
59. $2yi\sqrt{14y}$ 60. -50
61. 8 62. -3
63. $12 - 3i$ 64. $-2 - 6i$
65. $-25 + 19i$ 66. $-5 - 12i$
67. $\pm 4i$ 68. $\pm 3i$
69. $-1 \pm i\sqrt{6}$ 70. $\frac{5 \pm i\sqrt{11}}{2}$
71. $\frac{-1 \pm i\sqrt{2}}{2}$ 72. $\frac{1 \pm i\sqrt{11}}{3}$
73. $\pm\sqrt{5}, \pm i\sqrt{2}$ 74. $\pm\frac{\sqrt{6}}{3}, \pm\frac{i\sqrt{6}}{3}$
75. $-2i, -4 - 2i, 12 + 14i$ 76. two distinct real roots
77. two imaginary roots 78. two equal real roots
79. two distinct real roots 80. two equal real roots
81. two imaginary roots 82. $k < \frac{9}{4}$
83. $k = \frac{25}{8}$ 84. $k > \frac{9}{8}$
85. Yes; 15 cm by 8 cm 86. 6
87. 7 88. -2
89. 14 90. 11

91. 4
92. 7
93. $P(1) = 0$
94. $P(-2) = 0$
95. $P\left(-\frac{3}{2}\right) = 0$
96. $P\left(\frac{1}{3}\right) = 0$
97. $(x + 1)^2(x - 3)$
98. $(x + 4)(x^2 + x - 1)$
99. $(x + 1)(2x - 1)(x - 1)$
100. $(y - 1)(y + 4)(3y + 4)$
101. $0, \pm 3$
102. $-1, -1, 2$
103. $-2, \frac{1}{2}, 3$
104. $\frac{2}{3}, 1$
105. $1 \pm \sqrt{2}, 1$
106. $-2, \frac{2 \pm \sqrt{7}}{2}$
107. $\pm 4i, -1$
108. $3, -1 \pm i\sqrt{3}$
109. 5 cm by 20 cm by 25 cm

Exploring Math   p. 233

1. a) $-4 - 3i$; rotation of 180°
   b) $3 - 4i$; rotation of 270° counterclockwise
   c) $4 + 3i$; rotation of 360°
   d) $8 + 6i$; vertical stretch by a factor of 2
   e) $12 + 9i$; vertical stretch by a factor of 3
   f) $16 + 12i$; vertical stretch by a factor of 4
2. b) $2 + 5i$
   e) The sum is the diagonal of the parallelogram.
3. a) $5 - 2i$ **b)** $-7 + 7i$ **c)** $-2 - 2i$ **d)** $-3 + 0i$

Chapter Check   p. 234

1. $-4, 2$
2. $1, -3$
3. $\frac{1}{2}, 5$
4. $\frac{-3 \pm i\sqrt{23}}{4}$
5. $-5, 3$
6. $3, 8$
7. $-4, \frac{1}{2}$
8. $-\frac{1}{3}, \frac{2}{3}$
9. $-3, 2$
10. $1, 2$
11. $x^2 + 4x = 0$
12. $8x^2 - 2x - 3 = 0$
13. ± 12
14. $\pm \frac{\sqrt{7}}{2}$
15. $-11, 1$
16. $2, 6$
17. 4
18. $-3, 6$
19. $\frac{1 \pm \sqrt{22}}{3}$; 1.90, -1.23
20. $\frac{1 \pm \sqrt{6}}{?}$; $-0.29, 0.69$
21. $-2, -2$
22. $-1, -\frac{2}{5}$
23. $-\frac{2}{3}, \frac{1}{6}$
24. $-\frac{1}{3}, \frac{3}{4}$
25. $\frac{3 \pm \sqrt{37}}{2}$
26. $\frac{4 \pm \sqrt{11}}{5}$
27. $\frac{-7 \pm \sqrt{13}}{6}$
28. $-1, \frac{7}{4}$
29. $0.19, 3.47$
30. $2.67, -1$
31. $6i$
32. $4i\sqrt{3}$
33. -45
34. $13 - 8i$
35. $-2 + 8i$
36. $27 + 24i$
37. 50
38. $\pm 3i\sqrt{2}$
39. $\pm i$
40. $\pm 2i$
41. $\frac{5 \pm i\sqrt{3}}{2}$
42. $\frac{-3 \pm \sqrt{31}}{4}$
43. $\pm \frac{\sqrt{2}}{2}, \pm i\sqrt{3}$
44. two imaginary roots
45. two distinct real roots
46. two equal real roots
47. two distinct real roots
48. $k < \frac{25}{4}$
49. $k > 4$
50. 14
51. -10
52. 0
53. -2
54. $m = -4, n = -9$
55. $P(5) = 0$
56. $P(-3) = 0$
57. $P\left(\frac{2}{3}\right) = 0$
58. $P\left(\frac{1}{4}\right) = 0$
59. $(x + 6)(x - 1)(x - 3)$
60. $(x + 1)(3x - 1)(x - 4)$
61. $0, -2, -2$
62. $3, \pm 2$
63. $-2, -2, 2$
64. $-1, 3 \pm 2\sqrt{2}$
65. $-2, -1 \pm 2i$
66. $8, 1, \frac{1}{3}$
67. 27 cm by 10 cm
68. 3.5 m
69. 12 km/h

Using the Strategies   p. 235

1. 8
2. a) 35 cm^2; 440 cm^2; $n^2 + 2n \text{ cm}^2$
   b) 43 cm; 58 cm; 99 cm
3. 528 km from Vancouver at 15:36
4. 1.8   **5.** 0, 0, 0, 6, 6, 6
6. last row sum: 21; last column sum: 22
8. $\frac{qst}{prx}$ **9.** 13 cm, 14 cm, 15 cm
10. Q   **11.** 10 240
12. Danielle: 3 or 4, Jessica: 5; For the products 15, 20, 24, and 28, the possible pairs of numbers are (1, 15), (3, 5), (1, 20), (2, 10), (4, 5), (1, 24), (2, 12), (3, 8), (4, 6), (1, 28), (2, 14), and (4, 7). If either one had 15, 20, 10, 24, 12, 8, 6, 28, 14, or 7, she would know what the other's number was, so the pairs including those numbers can be eliminated. This leaves two pairs: (3, 5) and (4, 5). Since Jessica doesn't know what Danielle's number is, Jessica must have the 5.

Data Bank

1. a) Dash 8–100   **b)** yes
3. a) Quebec   **b)** Manitoba

Cumulative Review, Chapters 1–4
pp. 236–237

Chapter 1
1. $(-14, -41)$ **2.** $\left(\frac{1}{2}, -3\right)$
3. $(-1, 1)$ **4.** $(1, 0)$

5. $(2, 2)$ **6.** infinitely many solutions

7. $(-3, -4)$ **8.** $\left(0, \frac{1}{2}\right)$

9. $(5, 4, 1)$ **10.** $(1, 3, 2)$

11. a) 7 mg   **b)** 3 mg

12. 600 g portobello, 400 g shiitake

13. 20 km/h, 4 km/h

14. 4 par 3 holes, 11 par 4 holes, 3 par 5 holes

Chapter 2

1. $n < -3$ **2.** $w > 6$ **3.** $d \geq 5$

4. $k \leq 5$ **5.** $m > 5$ **6.** $y \geq -8$

7. $x \leq -6$ **8.** $h > 3$ **9.** $p > 2$

10. $q \leq 7$ **11.** $c < 0$ **18.** $(3, -1)$

25. $2y - 900 \leq 10\ 300; y \leq 5600$

26. a) $x + 2y \leq 3.5, x \geq 0, y \geq 0$

27. $9 < l + w < 11$

Chapter 3

1. a) down   **b)** $(0, 0)$ **c)** $x = 0$
   d) domain: all real numbers, range: $y \leq 0$
   e) x-intercept: 0, y-intercept: 0

2. a) up   **b)** $(0, -3)$ **c)** $x = 0$
   d) domain: all real numbers, range: $y \geq -3$
   e) x-intercepts: $\pm\sqrt{3}$, y-intercept: -3

3. a) up   **b)** $(-3, 0)$ **c)** $x = -3$
   d) domain: all real numbers, range: $y \geq 0$
   e) x-intercept: -3, y-intercept: 9

4. a) down   **b)** $(2, 1)$ **c)** $x = 2$
   d) domain: all real numbers, range: $y \leq 1$
   e) x-intercepts: 1, 3, y-intercept: -3

5. a) up   **b)** $(4, 3)$ **c)** $x = 4$
   d) domain: all real numbers, range: $y \geq 3$
   e) x-intercepts: none, y-intercept: 11

6. a) down   **b)** $(-5, -2)$ **c)** $x = -5$
   d) domain: all real numbers, range: $y \leq -2$
   e) x-intercepts none, y-intercept: -77

7. x-intercepts: -4.4, -1.6, y-intercept: 7

8. x-intercepts: 2.6, 5.4, y-intercept: -7

9. $y = x^2 - 4$ **10.** $y = -2(x - 1)^2 + 5$

11. $y = -(x - 5)^2 + 4$ **12.** $y = 2(x + 1)^2 + 2$

13. $y = -(x + 1)^2 - 2$; $(-1, -2)$, $x = -1$, $(0, -3)$, $(1, -6)$

14. $y = 0.5(x - 4)^2 - 7$; $(4, -7)$, $x = 4$, $(0, 1)$, $(2, -5)$

15. a) 18.2 m   **b)** 38 m   **c)** 5.3 m

16. $22

Chapter 4

1. $-1, \frac{3}{2}$ **2.** 3, 4   **3.** ± 6

4. $-2, 8$ **5.** $-\frac{1}{2}, 4$ **6.** $-4, 3$

7. $\frac{1}{3}$ **8.** $\frac{-1 \pm i\sqrt{7}}{4}$ **9.** $\frac{-1 \pm i\sqrt{35}}{2}$

10. $-8, 6$ **11.** $-5, -\frac{2}{3}$ **12.** $\frac{1 \pm \sqrt{13}}{2}$

13. $-2, 6$ **14.** $-2 \pm 2\sqrt{2}$

15. two distinct real roots   **16.** two equal real roots

17. two imaginary roots   **18.** two distinct real roots

19. $-0.67, 0.14$ **20.** $1.67, -1.07$

21. $2x^2 - 5x - 3 = 0$ **22.** $k > \frac{9}{4}$

23. 0   **24.** 0

25. $(x + 1)(x - 4)(x - 5)$ **26.** $(x + 1)(4x - 3)(x - 3)$

27. $2, \frac{3 \pm \sqrt{5}}{2}$ **28.** $-1, 6, 6$

29. $1, 1 \pm i$ **30.** $\pm 3, \frac{1}{2}$

31. base: 6 cm, height: 8 cm **32.** 80 km/h

CHAPTER 5

Functions

Chapter Introduction

Chapter Materials

graphing calculators, Teacher's Resource Master 1
(0.5-cm grid paper), Teacher's Resource Master 2
(1-cm grid paper), Teacher's Resource Master 6
(2-cm grid paper), MIRAs or reflection mirrors,
straightedges, overhead projector, overhead graphing
calculator, geometry software

Chapter Concepts

Chapter 5 reviews or introduces
- determining the domain, range, and values for
  rational, radical, and absolute value functions
- performing operations with functions
- finding the composition of functions
- finding the inverse of functions
- solving polynomial equations
- solving polynomial inequalities
- understanding absolute value functions
- solving absolute value equations and inequalities
- understanding rational functions
- solving rational equations and inequalities
- understanding radical functions
- solving radical equations and inequalities

Prerequisite Skills

1. The diameter of Earth is about 13 000 km.
   Write this number in scientific notation.

2. The diameter of the sun is about 1 400 000 km.
   Write this number in scientific notation.

3. Insert a word in each blank to make a true
   statement.

While the radius of the sun is about _____ times
as large as the radius of Earth, its volume is about
_____ times that of Earth.

Teaching Suggestions

Review with the class the table on the opening page of
Chapter 5. Have the students rewrite the mean radius
of the orbit for each planet as a decimal numeral and
then, read the numbers aloud. For example, ensure the
students read the mean radius of Mercury as 57 billion
900 million. Remind the students that 10^9 means
billions, while 10^{12} means trillions.

Discuss with the students the method of multiplying
and dividing numbers written in scientific notation.
Point out that the laws of exponents can be applied to
calculate the required values. Remind them that the
final answer must be given in scientific notation, i.e.,
the product of the numerical part that is greater than or
equal to 1 and less than or equal to 10 and a power of
10. For example, to find R^3 for Mercury, you calculate

$$(5.79 \times 10^{10})^3 = 5.79^3 \times 10^{30}$$
$$= 194.10 \times 10^{30}$$
$$= 1.94 \times 10^{32}$$

Ask:

Were you surprised by the answer you found in question 2a)?

To what use do you think the Kepler constant can be put?

Point out to the students that the Kepler constant
can be used to find information that might otherwise be
impossible to find. This is illustrated in questions 3 and 4.

Integrating Technology

Internet

Use the Internet to check the mean radius of the orbit
of Pluto, and to find more information about Johannes
Kepler, Sir Isaac Newton, and the orbit of the planets.

Enrichment

Research the life and works of Johannes Kepler and discover another of Kepler's Laws. Write a short essay describing this law and its application, and include a diagram for clarity. Present your essay to the class.

Assessing the Outcomes

Observation

You might consider some of these questions as you observe the students work.

- Do the students know how to apply the laws of exponents?
- Do the students know how to write numbers in scientific notation?
- Do the students know how to multiply, divide, and find powers of numbers written in scientific notation?
- Do the students work well in pairs?
- Do the students persist until they find a solution?
- Do the students attempt all the questions?

Getting Started

Student Text Pages
Pp. 240–241

Materials
graphing calculators

Learning Outcome
• Determine the equations of lines and parabolas from their graphs.

Prerequisite Skills
Describe the graph of each function.

a) $y = 3x - 1$ [a line going up to the right, with a slope of 3 and a y-intercept of -1]

b) $y = (x + 1)^2 - 4$ [a parabola opening upwards, symmetrical about $x = -1$, with vertex at $(-1, -4)$]

Teaching Suggestions

Designing With Functions

Before assigning question 1, elicit from the students that if you can identify the y-intercept and the slope from the graph of a line, you have m and b in the equation $y = mx + b$. There are two lines in the design for which the y-intercepts are not shown, but students could mentally extrapolate to find them. Alternatively, they could use the slope and the coordinates of any point to determine b for those lines.

Similarly, before assigning question 2, elicit from the students that if you can identify the vertex from the graph of a parabola, you have p and q in the equation $y = a(x - p)^2 + q$, and using those values with the coordinates of any point, you can determine a.

For questions 1 to 3, students might find it useful to set the given viewing window and graph each equation as they determine it. In so doing, they complete part b) at the same time as part a).

When assigning question 4, suggest that students select a viewing window symmetrical about one or both axes, or one that uses only one quadrant. Encourage students to be creative and to experiment with different equations.

Warm Up

Assign some or all of the questions as individual or group work. Students could record their answers in their notebooks, or take turns asking questions orally with a partner.

When the students have finished, have them discuss the methods they used to answer the questions.

Mental Math
Students could choose, or be assigned, certain questions from each section. Alternatively, small groups could work as teams, sharing the questions and explaining the answers to the rest of the group.

Extension
Use absolute value functions as well as quadratic functions to create a design.

Math Journal
Write a few sentences about what you like or dislike about creating designs on a graphing calculator. Discuss and compare your ideas with other students in the class.

Assessing the Outcome

Observation

While students are working, do they
• use the screens displayed in the student text, or sketch the screens in their notebooks and add scales to the axes?
• use paper and pencil or mental calculations to find the coefficients?
• use trial and error to create their designs?
• create designs similar to those given?
• create designs with symmetry?

5.1 Operations With Functions

Student Text Pages
Pp. 242–250

Materials
graphing calculators, Teacher's Resource Master 1 (0.5-cm grid paper), overhead projector

Learning Outcomes
- Develop the definitions of the combination of functions.
- Write expressions for the combination of functions.
- Evaluate combined functions
- Graph the sums of functions.
- Identify and state the restrictions on the variables of combined functions.
- Solve problems involving combined functions.

Prerequisite Skills

1. Evaluate each expression for the given values of the variables.

a) $x + 3y; y = 2, x = -1$ [5]

b) $-2p^2 - 5; p = \frac{1}{2}$ $\left[-5\frac{1}{2}\right]$

c) $5w + 2z - 15; w = 0.1, z = 1.5$ [−11.5]

d) $a^2 - 2b^2; a = 20, b = 15$ [−50]

e) $3m - 2n + r; m = -2, n = 5, r = 0$ [−16]

f) $x^3 + y^2; x = -2, y = \frac{1}{4}$ $\left[-7\frac{15}{16}\right]$

2. Simplify each expression.

a) $2x + 5y - x + 11y$ $[x + 16y]$

b) $(5z + 2w) - (z - w)$ $[4z + 3w]$

c) $-2xy \times (-3x^2y^3)$ $[6x^3y^4]$

d) $\left(\frac{1}{3}m^4\right)^2 \times \frac{18}{m^3}$ $[2m^5]$

e) $6w^5 \div -3w^2$ $[-2w^3]$

f) $\frac{2x^2}{y} \div \frac{3xy}{-6xy^2}$ $[-4x^2]$

Mental Math

1. If $t(x) = \frac{5}{2x + 1}$, find

a) $t(4)$ $\left[\frac{5}{9}\right]$ b) $t(-8)$ $\left[\frac{-1}{3}\right]$

c) $t(500)$ $\left[\frac{5}{1001}\right]$ d) $t(5.75)$ $[0.4]$

e) $t(-50)$ $\left[-\frac{5}{99}\right]$ f) $t\left(\frac{1}{4}\right)$ $\left[\frac{10}{3}\right]$

2. Multiply in two steps.

a) 35×41 [1435]   b) 28×19 [532]

c) 77×18 [1386]   d) 81×22 [1782]

e) 23×41 [943]   f) 53×31 [1643]

Explore/Inquire Answers

Explore: Complete the Table

A: $x^2 + 2x + 1$, 25; B: $x^2 - 1$, 15;
C: $x^3 + 2x^2 + x$, 100; D: x, 4

Inquire

1. 20, 5   2. a) 25   b) 15   c) 100   d) 4

3. equal

4. $g(x) \neq 0, x \neq -1$; cannot divide by zero

6. a) $2x^2 + 6x$ b) $2x^2 + 2x$ c) $-2x^2 - 2x$

d) $4x^3 + 8x^2$ e) $x + 2$

7. a) $l(x) = 11x + 3$ b) 80 m by 6 m

Teaching Suggestions

Method 1

(overhead projection) Read with the class the opening paragraphs on student text page 242. Then, review and discuss the concepts of domain and range. Remind the students that the relations or functions discussed in this section assume the domain and range are the set of real numbers, unless otherwise stated. Ask:

How is a relation different from a function?

How can you tell from looking at the graph of a relation whether it is a function?

Elicit from the students that the vertical line test can be used to test whether a relation is a function. Ask:

In how many ways can you represent a relation or a function?

Help the students to identify all of the methods of representing a relation or function: a table of values, a set of coordinates, an arrow diagram, a graph, an equation, or a verbal sentence.

Assign the Explore section and the Inquire questions to pairs of students. Have volunteers present their results to the class.

Instruct each student to make up a function. Have pairs of students combine their functions using addition, subtraction, multiplication, and division, to see if their results are similar to those found in the Explore section. Have pairs of students present their functions and their results to the class. Remind the students that any restrictions on the variables must be identified.

Review with the class teaching example 1 on student text page 243. Ask:

How could you check your answers in this example?

Elicit from the students that they could use substitution in the original functions and in the combined function to see if the values agree. Draw attention to the fact that restrictions on the variables must be noted.

Assign teaching examples 2 and 3 on student text pages 243 and 244. Point out that in teaching example 2, the functions are combined and then values of the variable are substituted. In teaching example 3, the values of the variable are substituted and then, the results are combined. Ask:

What patterns do you see in the degrees of the original functions and in the degrees of the combined functions?

Assign teaching example 4 to pairs of students, and have one of them work alongside his or her partner with a graphing calculator demonstrating how the functions are graphed.

Review with the class teaching example 5. Point out that in part b), the restrictions on the variable must be noted, not just for the last step of the solution, but for all the steps of the solution. Thus, the restrictions $x \neq 2$, -5 come from line 2 of the solution, while the restriction $x \neq 0$ comes from line 3 of the solution.

Review with the class teaching example 6. If the students have difficulty with the process of rationalizing denominators, have a volunteer demonstrate the process to the class. Point out that with radical functions, the restrictions on the variable are not just limited to the values that make the denominator equal to zero. With square roots, values of the variable that make the expression under the radical less than zero are also possible restricted values.

Assign to pairs of students teaching examples 6 and 7 on student text page 246 as independent study.

Method 2

(0.5-cm grid paper, overhead projector) Discuss with the class the difference between a function and a relation, and the meaning of the concepts of domain and relation. Ask:

Which is the more general term: relation or function? Explain.

Challenge the students to identify as many ways as possible of representing a function. Then, ask:

How can you tell whether or not a relation is a function?

Have volunteers present their results to the class. Ensure that the students identify a table of values, an ordered pair, an equation, a mapping, a graph, and a verbal sentence as methods of representing a function. Remind them to use the vertical line test to identify whether or not a graph represents a function.

Write the following functions on the chalkboard.

$$f(x) = 2x^2 + 5x - 1 \qquad h(x) = 3x - 2$$

Have pairs of students find the following:

$$f(x) + h(x)$$
$$f(x) - h(x)$$
$$f(x) \times h(x)$$
$$f(x) \div h(x)$$

Challenge students to find the domain and the restrictions on the variable of the resulting function.

Provide pairs of students with grid paper and have each student make up his or her own function. Have pairs of students use their made-up functions to find each of the combined functions above. Encourage the students to graph their functions on grid paper or a graphing calculator. Give the students ample time to discuss and compare their results with those of other pairs of students in the class. Have volunteers present their results to the class.

Review with the class teaching examples 1 to 8 on student text pages 243 to 247.

Sample Solution

Page 250, question 74

The vertex of the parabola is (0, 0), the graph opens upward, and the points $(-2, 4)$, $(0, 0)$, and $(2, 4)$ lie on the graph.
The equation of the parabola is $y = x^2$.
Thus, $f(x) = x^2$.
The points $(1, -1)$ and $(-3, -5)$ lie on the straight line.
The equation of the line is given by
$$\frac{y - y_1}{x - x_1} = \frac{y_2 - y_1}{x_2 - x_1}.$$
$(x_1, y_1) = (1, -1)$ and $(x_2, y_2) = (-3, -5)$
$$\frac{y - (-1)}{x - 1} = \frac{(-5) - (-1)}{(-3) - 1}$$
$$\frac{y + 1}{x - 1} = \frac{-5 + 1}{-3 - 1}$$
$$= \frac{-4}{-4}$$
$$= 1$$
$$y + 1 = x - 1$$
$$y = x - 2$$

Thus, $g(x) = x - 2$.
$h(x) = (f + g)(x)$
$\quad = x^2 + x - 2$
Thus, $h(x) = x^2 + x - 2$.

Number Power Answer

A = 1, B = 2, C = 2, D = 6, E = 7

Integrating Technology

Graphing Calculators

How would you use your graphing calculator to create the graphs in teaching example 4 on student text pages 244 and 245? On a TI-83, the Y= key and the VARS key are used.

Press the Y= key, clear any equations that exist, and turn off any plots that are highlighted.

Enter the equations at Y1= and Y2=.

Press the VARS key, the right arrow key, the 1 key, and the 1 key again to select Y1.

Press the + key, and then the VARS key, the right arrow key, the 1 key, and the 2 key to select Y2.

Press the ZOOM key and the 6 key to select ZStandard.

To change the operation sign, press the Y= key, and use the arrow keys to move the cursor to the + sign, and press the − key, and so on.

To see the error in the Y3 column of the table, press the TABLE (i.e., 2nd GRAPH) key, and move the cursor down to 1, and then press the right arrow key three times.

To see the break in the graph of $(f/g)(x)$, use the decimal viewing window. Press the ZOOM key and the 4 key to select Zdecimal.

Use your graphing calculator to graph the operations with functions in questions 14 to 19 on student text page 247, and in question 68 on student text page 249.

See *MATHPOWER*™ 11, *Western Edition, Blackline Masters* pages 128 to 130 for Operations With Functions and Composition of Functions.

Computer Spreadsheets

In question 69 on student text page 250, the formulas =2*A1+3 and =A1^2−4 describe functions f and g. Use a spreadsheet for other operations on f and g, as well as addition.

Enrichment

Leonard Euler was the first to use the notation $f(x)$. Research the works of this mathematician and write a short essay on his accomplishments.

Math Journal

Make a list of the operations that can be applied to two or more functions to define new functions. Make up functions of your own, and use these functions to demonstrate each point in your list.

Common Errors

• Students often forget to put brackets around a value being substituted into an expression, especially when the value is negative or when the variable is raised to an exponent.

R_x Review with the students the different results when brackets are included and excluded for negative values of the variable, especially when the variable is raised to an exponent.

• Sometimes students forget that rational expressions, like rational numbers, must be written with common denominators before being added or subtracted.

R_x A reminder of the general formula
$$\frac{a}{b} \pm \frac{c}{d} = \frac{ad \pm bc}{bd}$$
can help refocus the students.

Problem Levels of Difficulty

A: 1–50, 54, 55, 77
B: 51–53, 56–69
C: 70–76

Assessing the Outcomes

Written Assignment

For each pair of functions f and g, find each of the following. State any restrictions on the variables.

a) $f + g$
b) $f - g$
c) fg
d) $\dfrac{f}{g}$
e) $2f$
f) gg
g) $3f - 2g$

1. $f(x) = x^2 - 3$; $g(x) = 2x + 1$
2. $f(x) = \dfrac{x^2}{x + 1}$; $g(x) = 5x$
3. $f(x) = \sqrt{2x - 1}$; $g(x) = 2\sqrt{x}$

5.2 Composition of Functions

Student Text Pages
Pp. 251–259

Materials

graphing calculators

Learning Outcomes

- Develop the concept of the composition of functions.
- Find the composition of functions.
- Evaluate the composition of functions.
- Find the composition of radical, absolute value, and rational functions.
- Solve problems involving the composition of functions.

Prerequisite Skills

A function is given as a table of values.

x	y
−5	−5
−3	−1
−1	3
0	5
2	9
4	13

a) Write an equation that relates x and y.   [$y = 2x + 5$]

b) Write the function as a set of coordinate points.
    [$(−5, −5), (−3, −1), (−1, 3), (0, 5), (2, 9), (4, 13)$]

c) Write the domain and the range of the relation.
    [domain: {−5, −3, −1, 0, 2, 4}; range: {−5, −1, 3, 5, 9, 13}]

Mental Math

1. Divide.

a) $95 ÷ 5$ [19]   b) $165 ÷ 15$ [11]

c) $152 ÷ 8$ [19]   d) $204 ÷ 17$ [12]

e) $372 ÷ 6$ [62]   f) $234 ÷ 13$ [18]

2. Subtract.

a) $3.5 − 2.9$ [0.6]   b) $8.9 − 5.6$ [3.3]

c) $92 − 65$ [27]   d) $237 − 149$ [88]

e) $72 − 43$ [29]   f) $496 − 288$ [208]

Explore/Inquire Answers

Explore: Use the Formulas

a) 220 000   b) 720 000   c) 264 000

Inquire

1. $l(d) = 1320d$

2. $g(l) = \dfrac{l}{6}$

3. $d(g) = \dfrac{g}{220}$

4. $d(l) = \dfrac{l}{1320}$

5. a) $j(d) = 92d$ b) $d(j) = \dfrac{j}{92}$

Teaching Suggestions

Method 1

Read with the class the opening paragraphs of student text page 251. Ask:

Has anyone travelled abroad?

Do you recall any of the exchange rates that you used?

How are exchange rates used?

Review with the class the concept of function, domain, and range. Ask:

What is the difference between a relation and a function?

Assign the Explore section and the Inquire questions to pairs of students. Give students an opportunity to discuss and compare their results with those of other students, and have volunteers present their results to the class.

Work through teaching examples 1 to 8 on student text pages 252 to 255. Ensure that the students understand the necessity for defining the domain and the range of the original functions as well as the composition of the functions. Emphasize the restrictions on the variables of absolute value, rational, and radical functions.

Method 2

Write these two functions on the chalkboard.

$$f(x) = x^2 + 2x − 3 \qquad g(x) = −5x + 1$$

Explain that the compositions of two functions, $f(x)$ and $g(x)$, are found by substituting $g(x)$ for x in $f(x)$ and by substituting $f(x)$ for x in $g(x)$. Use the two functions above to demonstrate this point. When $g(x)$ is substituted for x in $f(x)$, this is the composition $(f \circ g)(x)$, and when $f(x)$ is substituted for x in $g(x)$, this is the composition $(g \circ f)(x)$.

$$f(x) = x^2 + 2x − 3 \qquad g(x) = −5x + 1$$
$$
\begin{aligned}
(f \circ g)(x) &= (−5x + 1)^2 + 2(−5x + 1) − 3 \\
&= 25x^2 − 10x + 1 − 10x + 2 − 3 \\
&= 25x^2 − 20x \\
(g \circ f)(x) &= −5(x^2 + 2x − 3) + 1 \\
&= −5x^2 − 10x + 15 + 1 \\
&= −5x^2 − 10x + 16
\end{aligned}
$$

Discuss the concept of domain as it relates to the composition of functions. Stress that for $(f \circ g)(x)$, the domain of f must include the range of g, and for $(g \circ f)(x)$, the domain of g must include the range of f.

Arrange the students into pairs and have the students make up one function of their own.

Then, have pairs of students use their functions to find $(f \circ g)(x)$ and $(g \circ f)(x)$. Remind the students to define the domain for each composition. Give the students an opportunity to compare and discuss their results with other pairs of students, and present their results to the class.

Work through teaching examples 1 to 8 on student text pages 252 to 255. Ensure that the students understand the necessity for defining the domain and the range of the original functions, as well as the composition of the functions. Emphasize the restrictions on the variables of absolute value, rational, and radical functions.

Sample Solution

Page 259, question 95 a), b)

a) $(h \circ g \circ f)(x)$ is the same as $h(g(f(x)))$

$f(x) = 5x$ and $g(x) = x + 9$

Then, $g(f(x)) = 5x + 9$

$h(x) = 3$

$h(g(f(x))) = 3$

b) $(g \circ f \circ h)(x)$ is the same as $g(f(h(x)))$

$h(x) = 3$ and $f(x) = 5x$

Then, $f(h(x)) = 5(3) = 15$

$g(x) = x + 9$

Then, $g(f(h(x))) = (15) + 9 = 24$

$(g \circ f \circ h)(x) = 24$

Integrating Technology

Graphing Calculators

How would you use your graphing calculator to create the graphs in teaching example 3 on student text page 253? On a TI-83, the Y= key and the VARS key are used, and $f(g(x))$ is entered as Y1(Y2).

Press the Y= key, clear any equations that exist, and turn off any plots that are highlighted.

Enter the equations at Y1= and Y2=.

Press the VARS key, the right arrow key, the 1 key, and the 1 key again to select Y1.

Press the (key, and then the VARS key, the right arrow key, the 1 key, and the 2 key to select Y2.

Press the) key, and then the ZOOM key and the 6 key to select ZStandard.

Use your graphing calculator to visualize some of the compositions of functions on student text pages 256 and 257, and to graph the composition in question 97 on student text page 259.

See *MATHPOWER™ 11, Western Edition, Blackline Masters* pages 128 and 129 for Operations With Functions and Composition of Functions.

Use the Internet to find foreign currency exchange rates. Then, use the information to create problems similar to question 69 on student text page 257 and question 75 on student text page 258. Display your problems for classmates to solve.

Extension

Create two functions, $f(x)$ and $g(x)$, so that $f(g(x)) = g(f(x))$. Compare your functions with those of your classmates, and present your functions to the class.

Math Journal

In your own words describe the difference between
a) $f(g(x))$ and $g(f(x))$ **b)** $fg(x)$ and $f(g(x))$

Cross-Discipline

Science To change from degrees Fahrenheit (F) to degrees Celsius (C) you can use the formula

$$C = \frac{5}{9}(F - 32).$$

To change from degrees Celsius (C) to kelvins (K) you can use the formula

$$K = C + 273.15.$$

a) Write a formula to change from kelvins (K) to degrees Fahrenheit (F).
b) Write a formula to change from degrees Fahrenheit (F) to kelvins (K).
c) Change 77°F to kelvins.
d) Change 320 K to degrees Fahrenheit.

Common Errors

- Students often confuse $f(g(x))$, $g(f(x))$, and $f(g(x)) \times g(f(x))$.

R_x Provide two functions, one linear and one second degree, to demonstrate that the product of a linear and a second degree function is a third degree function, whereas the composition of a linear function and a second degree function is a second degree function.

Problem Levels of Difficulty

A: 1–70   **B:** 71–92   **C:** 93–97

Assessing the Outcomes

Written Assignment
a) Given $F(x) = -(x^2 + 5)$ and $g(x) = \frac{1}{x}$, find $(f \circ g)(x)$ and $(g \circ f)(x)$.
b) Find $(f \circ g)(x)$ and $(g \circ f)(x)$ for $x = -2, -1, 0, 1, 2$.

Math Journal
Explain any similarities or differences in your results in part b) above.

Technology

Exploring Reflections With Geometry Software

Student Text Page
P. 260

Materials
geometry software

Learning Outcomes
- Reflect objects in the x-axis, in the y-axis, and in the line $y = x$ using geometry software.
- Identify and interpret reflections in the x-axis, in the y-axis, and in the line $y = x$.

Prerequisite Skills

1. Give the coordinates of each point.

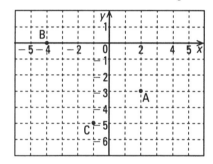

[A(2, −3), B(−4, 0), C(−1, −5)]

2. Give the coordinates of each image.

a) (6, −3) reflected in the x-axis   [(6, 3)]

b) (−5, −7) reflected in the y-axis   [(5, −7)]

3. Name three points on the line $y = x$.

[Answers may vary. For example, (5, 5), (−3, −3), (0, 0)]

Teaching Suggestions

Vertices and other points are not named to avoid the extra, time-consuming work that would be required by students to label their constructions to match.

When using Geometer's Sketchpad,
- always select the object or objects needed before selecting the menu item that you want to apply
- change from segment to line and vice versa as needed by clicking the tool at the left of the screen to display the options
- return the cursor to a pointer by clicking the pointer tool at the left of the screen
- select more than one object at a time by pressing the Shift key while clicking all the objects after the first one

Before assigning Activity 1, discuss constructing triangles, reflecting them in the x- and y-axes, and finding the coordinates of the images using geometry software. With Geometer's Sketchpad, the process is as follows:
Click Show Grid from the Graph menu.
Click Plot Points from the Graph menu.
Enter the coordinates of the points, pressing Tab between them, and then, press OK.
Click Segment from the Construct menu, resulting in a triangle because all three points were selected (highlighted) immediately after they were plotted.
Click the x-axis.
Click Mark Mirror "x" from the Transform menu.
Click one side of the triangle, and while pressing the Shift key, click each of the other two sides to select the triangle.
Click Reflect from the Transform menu.
Click one vertex of the triangle, and while pressing the Shift key, click each of the other two vertices to select all three vertices.
Click Coordinates from the Measure menu.
Click the y-axis.
Click Mark Mirror "y" from the Transform menu.
Click one side of the triangle, and while pressing the Shift key, click each of the other two sides to select the triangle.
Click Reflect from the Transform menu.
Click one vertex of the triangle, and while pressing the Shift key, click each of the other two vertices to select all three vertices.
Click Coordinates from the Measure menu.

Discuss the students' findings and summarize reflecting in the axes before assigning the next activity.

Before assigning Activity 2, discuss graphing lines, plotting points, constructing line segments, finding coordinates of points of intersection, and measuring distances, angles, and slope using geometry software. With Geometer's Sketchpad, the process is as follows:
Click New Sketch from the File menu.
Click Show Grid from the Graph menu.
Click Plot Points from the Graph menu.
Enter the coordinates of points such as (0, 0) and (5, 5), which lie on the line $y = x$, pressing Tab between each, and then, press OK.
Click the segment tool at the left of the screen to display the options, and drag to the line tool.
Click Line from the Construct menu, resulting in the line $y = x$ because two points were selected (highlighted) immediately after they were plotted.
Click Plot Points from the Graph menu.
Enter the coordinates of the points, pressing Tab between the coordinates, and then, press OK.
Click the line tool at the left of the screen to display the options, and drag to the segment tool.

Click Segment from the Construct menu.
Click the pointer tool at the left side of the screen to return the cursor to a pointer.
While pressing the Shift key, click the line $y = x$ to select it while the line segment just constructed is still selected.
Click Point At Intersection from the Construct menu.
Click Coordinates from the Measure menu.
While pressing the Shift key, click one of the end points of the segment to select it while the point of intersection is still selected.
Click Distance from the Measure menu.
Click the other end point of the segment, and while pressing the Shift key, click the point of intersection to select the two points.
Click Distance from the Measure menu.
While pressing the Shift key, click one of the points on the line $y = x$ to select it while one of the end points of the segment and the point of intersection are still selected, ensuring that the three points are selected with the point of intersection (vertex) in the middle.
Click Angle from the Measure menu.
Click the other end point of the segment, and while pressing the Shift key, click the point of intersection and one of the points on the line $y = x$ to select the three points, ensuring that the three points are selected with the point of intersection (vertex) in the middle.
Click Angle from the Measure menu.
Since both angles measure 90°, there is no need to measure any others.
Click the segment.
Click Slope from the Measure menu.
Click the line $y = x$.
Click Slope from the Measure menu.

Discuss the students' findings and summarize reflecting in the line $y = x$ before assigning the next activity.

In Activity 3, students experiment, constructing squares and rectangles to help answer the questions.

Common Errors

• Students often forget to select the object or objects necessary for a construction, resulting in the construction they want not being available.

R_x Suggest that students print the Construction Help, noting the constructions being used. Then, before each construction, they check what is needed.

• Some students have difficulty selecting more than one object at a time when needed.

R_x Remind students to press the Shift key while clicking all the objects after the first one. Frequently, the last object constructed is one of the objects needed for the next.

Assessing the Outcomes

Written Assignment

Describe in words the relationship between the coordinates of a point and its reflection image in each of the x-axis, the y-axis, and the line $y = x$.

5.3 Inverse Functions

Materials

graphing calculators, Teacher's Resource Master 2 (1-cm grid paper), Teacher's Resource Master 6 (2-cm grid paper), MIRAs or reflective mirrors, straightedges, overhead projector

Learning Outcomes

- Develop the concept of inverse functions.
- Write the inverse of a function by interchanging the coordinates, by interchanging the variables, and by interchanging the domain and the range of a mapping diagram.
- Verify an inverse function.
- Solve problems involving inverse functions.

Prerequisite Skills

Rewrite each relation so that the variable x is isolated on one side.

a) $2x + 6y = 14$ $\qquad$ $[x = -3y + 7]$

b) $-5y - 2x + 15 = 0$ $\qquad$ $\left[x = \dfrac{-5}{2}y + \dfrac{15}{2}\right]$

c) $y - 3x + 5 = -2y$ $\qquad$ $\left[x = y + \dfrac{5}{3}\right]$

Mental Math

1. If $f(x) = \dfrac{-2}{3x - 1}$, find

a) $f(3)$ $\qquad \left[-\dfrac{1}{4}\right]$ $\qquad$ b) $f(-5)$ $\qquad \left[\dfrac{1}{8}\right]$

c) $f(100)$ $\qquad \left[-\dfrac{2}{299}\right]$ $\qquad$ d) $f(0.5)$ $\qquad [-4]$

e) $f(-20)$ $\qquad \left[\dfrac{2}{61}\right]$ $\qquad$ f) $f\left(\dfrac{1}{4}\right)$ $\qquad [8]$

2. Subtract.

a) $47 - 19$ $\quad$ [28] $\qquad$ b) $126 - 77$ $\quad$ [49]

c) $92 - 65$ $\quad$ [27] $\qquad$ d) $237 - 149$ $\quad$ [88]

e) $72 - 43$ $\quad$ [29] $\qquad$ f) $496 - 288$ $\quad$ [208]

Explore/Inquire Answers

Explore: Complete the Table

5, 12.5; 3, 7.5; 1.5, 3.75; 0.8, 2; 0.4, 1; 0.2, 0.5

Inquire

1. a) $d(n) = 0.4n$ $\qquad$ b) multiplication by 0.4

c) (12.5, 5), (7.5, 3), (3.75, 1.5), (2, 0.8), (1, 0.4), (0.5, 0.2)

2. a) $n(d) = 2.5d$ $\qquad$ b) multiplication by 2.5

c) (5, 12.5), (3, 7.5), (1.5, 3.75), (0.8, 2), (0.4, 1), (0.2, 0.5)

3. x- and y-coordinates are interchanged

4. yes $\qquad\qquad$ 5. equal

6. $(d \circ n)(x) = x$, $(n \circ d)(x) = x$

7. a) $g(x) = \dfrac{x}{2}$ $\qquad$ b) $g(x) = \dfrac{4}{3}x$

c) $g(x) = x - 2$ $\qquad$ d) $g(x) = x + 4$

Teaching Suggestions

Method 1

(2-cm grid paper, overhead projector) Read with the class the opening paragraphs on student text page 261. Ask:

What does the word "inverse" mean to you?

Have you ever heard the word "inverse" used outside of this class? Explain.

Before beginning the Explore section, write the following coordinates on the chalkboard and ask the class to write the inverse of this function.

$$(2, 6), (3, 9), (4, 12), \text{ and } (5, 15)$$

Ensure that the students realize that the inverse is found by switching the coordinates.

$$(6, 2), (9, 3), (12, 4), \text{ and } (15, 5)$$

Now, assign the Explore section and the Inquire questions to pairs of students. Have volunteers present their results to the class. Ask:

Is the inverse of a function always a function?

Draw the students' attention to the method of finding the inverse of a function given at the top of student text page 262.

Review with the class teaching examples 1 to 8 on student text pages 262 to 267.

For teaching example 1, place a large 2-cm grid on the chalkboard. Provide the coordinates of about ten points and have volunteers set up a coordinate plane, plot the line $y = x$ on the plane, and plot the points whose coordinates you provided. Have the students reverse the coordinates of each point you provided, and plot these points on the grid. Ask:

What do you notice about the points provided and the points of the reversed coordinates?

Ensure that the students realize that reversing the coordinates of a point is the same as reflecting the point in the line $y = x$.

For teaching example 5, review with the students the vertical line test. Point out that the vertical line test is a quick visual check to determine whether a graph represents a function.

For teaching example 6, ask:

Why must the domain of the original function be limited?

How are the domain of a function and the range of the inverse of the function related?

Elicit from the students that if the inverse function involves a radical expression, then the domain of the original function must be limited so that values of the expression beneath the square root are always positive. Also, the domain of a function and the range of the inverse of the function are the same.

Assign teaching examples 7 and 8 to pairs of students as independent study. Have volunteers present their results.

Method 2

(1-cm grid paper, 2-cm grid paper, MIRAs or reflective mirrors, straightedges) Provide pairs of students with grid paper, a straightedge, and a MIRA (reflective mirror). Have each pair of students create a table of values for the function $y = 2x + 3$, and write the table of values as a set of coordinates. Then, use the coordinates to graph the function $y = 2x + 3$.

Next, have the students rewrite the set of coordinates with the y-values as the first coordinate and the x-values as the second coordinate. Have them graph this set of coordinates on the same set of axes as they used to graph the function $y = 2x + 3$. Point out to the students that this graph of the reversed coordinates is the graph of the inverse relation of $y = 2x + 3$. Ask:

What is the equation of the line of the inverse relation?

Is this inverse relation a function? Explain.

Next, on a new set of axes, have the pairs of students construct the graphs of the functions $y = 2x + 3$ and $y = x$. Then, have them lay a MIRA along the graph of the line $y = x$ and plot the points that are the reflections of the points on the graph of the line $y = 2x + 3$. Tell the students to connect the plotted points with a straight line. Ask:

How is the line that you constructed for the reversed coordinates in your first diagram related to the reflected line in the second diagram?

What relation relates the second coordinates of the set of reversed coordinates with the first coordinates?

What other method, apart from reversing the coordinates, can you use to construct the inverse of the graph of a line?

Guide the students to see that the graph of the original function reflected in the line $y = x$ is the graph of the inverse of the function. Ask:

What is the equation of the reflected line?

What pattern do you see between the relation for the original line and the relation for the reversed coordinates and the relation for the reflected line?

Ensure that the students realize that by reversing the variables in the original function and then simplifying the results gives the relation of the inverse of the function. Thus, if the original function is $y = -\frac{1}{3}x + 4$, then the relation of the inverse is

$$x = -\frac{1}{3}y + 4$$
$$3x = -y + 12$$
$$3x - 12 = -y$$
$$y = -3x + 12$$

Have the students repeat these steps for the function $y = x^2 + 1$. Ask:

Is the relation $y = x^2 + 1$ a function? Explain.

Is the relation of the inverse of the function $y = x^2 + 1$ a function? Explain.

Have volunteers present their results to the class. One student could display the diagrams on an overhead projector or draw the diagram on a large 2-cm grid that has been superimposed on the chalkboard. The other student could explain the results of each step.

Have students present a list of the ways of writing the relation for the reverse of a function. Ensure that they include reversing the coordinates, reflecting the original line in the line $y = x$, and reversing the variables of the original relation.

Finally, have the pairs of students take each function $f(x)$ and its inverse $g(x)$ and find each composition $f(g(x))$ and $g(f(x))$. Ask:

What do you notice about the compositions $f(g(x))$ and $g(f(x))$?

How could you use compositions to show that two relations are inverses of each other?

Ensure that the students realize that if they have two relations, $f(x)$ and $g(x)$, and if $f(g(x)) = g(f(x))$, the functions are inverses of each other.

Review with the class teaching examples 1 to 8 on student text pages 262 to 267.

Logic Power Answer

Total number of green tiles was 36.
Total number of white tiles was 28.
The number of tiles required to surround a rectangle equals the number of tiles in the perimeter of the rectangle plus 4 corner tiles.
The area of the white centre rectangle has to be 28 square units.

Possible Rectangles	Perimeter of Rectangle	Tiles Required to Surround the Rectangle
1 × 28	58	58 + 4 = 62
2 × 14	32	32 + 4 = 36
4 × 7	22	22 + 4 = 26

Since the number of green tiles available was 36, then the white rectangle with dimensions 2 × 14 was the required rectangle.
The dimensions of the patio were 2 tiles by 14 tiles.

Integrating Technology

Graphing Calculators

How would you use your graphing calculator to create the graphs in teaching examples 4 and 5 on student text page 265? On a TI-83, the Y= key, the Draw instruction, and the VARS key are used.

Press the Y= key, clear any equations that exist, and turn off any plots that are highlighted.

Enter the function at Y1=.

Press the ZOOM key and the 6 key to select ZStandard.

The viewing window can be squared so that the symmetry between the function and its inverse will be visible when the inverse is graphed.

Press ZOOM 5 to select ZSquare.

Press the DRAW (i.e., 2nd PRGM) key and the 1 key to select ClrDraw.

Press the DRAW (i.e., 2nd PRGM) key and the 8 key to select DrawInv. (Use the down arrow key to see the last items.)

Press the VARS key, the right arrow key, the 1 key, and the 1 key again to select Y1.

Then, press the ENTER key to display the inverse of the function graphed with the function.

How would you use your graphing calculator to graph a function with a restricted domain, so that its inverse will also be a function? On a TI-83, enter the function in brackets at the Y= prompt and enter the restriction in brackets after the function. Inequality signs are under the Test menu when the TEST (i.e., 2nd MATH) key is pressed. Press the 4 key for greater than or equal to. The steps to display the graph and then the inverse with it are as above.

Use your graphing calculator to graph the functions and their inverses, restricting the domain of the function when necessary, in questions 19 to 24 and 36 to 41 on student text page 268, questions 60 to 65 and 76 to 83 on student text page 269, and question 93 on student text page 270.

See *MATHPOWER™ 11, Western Edition, Blackline Masters* pages 131 to 133 for Inverses of Functions.

Enrichment

Explain in a short essay how the following represents the definition of the inverse of a function.

$$[f \circ f^{-1}](x) = x \text{ and } [f^{-1} \circ f](x) = x$$

Math Journal

Make a list of the different ways of finding the inverse of a relation.

Compare your list with that of a classmate's. Discuss any omissions, and ensure that you have all of the possible methods listed in your journal.

Common Errors

- Students often mistake the -1 of the inverse function notation $f^{-1}(x)$ as the exponent -1.

$\mathbf{R}_x$ Demonstrate the differences by making up a function such as $f(x) = 2x + 1$ and finding $f^{-1}(2)$, $f(2^{-1})$, and $(f(3))^{-1}$.

Problem Levels of Difficulty

A: 1–83, 102   **B:** 84–95   **C:** 96–101

Assessing the Outcomes

Journal

Describe three ways to find the inverse of a function.

Written Assignment

Find the inverse of each of the following in two different ways. Then, graph the function and its inverse.

a) $f(x) = -3x - 1$ **b)** $f(x) = \dfrac{x}{2x - 5}$

Computer Data Bank

New Vehicles

Microsoft Works for Windows users see *Part B*, and Microsoft Access users see *Part D*, of *MATHPOWER™ 11, Western Edition, Computer Data Bank Teacher's Resource*.

Student Text Page
P. 271

Learning Outcomes

- Display, find, sort, calculate, summarize, and analyze data in a computer database.
- Investigate and evaluate functions.

Prerequisite Skills

Velocity, v, is a function of both distance, d, and time, t; specifically, $v = \frac{d}{t}$. Is each statement true or false?

a) If the time is fixed, then the greater the distance, the less the velocity.   [false]

b) If the distance is fixed, then the greater the time, the less the velocity.   [true]

Getting Started Blackline Masters C-1, C-2, and C-4 to C-8.

Teaching Suggestions

Students unfamiliar with computer databases and ClarisWorks would benefit from working through *Getting Started* Blackline Masters C-1, C-2, and C-4 to C-8, noted in the *Prerequisite Skills*, prior to doing any of the explorations on this page. Minimally, students should have *Getting Started* Blackline Masters C-1, C-2, and C-4 to C-8 available for reference.

Each exploration in *New Vehicles* is independent of the others. Some or all of the explorations can be assigned to individuals, pairs, or small groups of students, to be completed over a period of time that allows students adequate computer time. Up to two hours will be needed by some students to complete all three explorations.

When assigning the explorations, inform students if you expect
- any parts of the explorations to be printed off the computer
- handwritten or word-processed answers to questions that suggest a written response
- a journal-type response about what they have learned mathematically, about using databases, and/or about the subject matter of the database

Possible parts to assign for printing are tables to show the averages from Exploration 1; tables to show the vehicles with the specified differences from Exploration 2; and tables to show the vehicles meeting the specified criteria from Exploration 3.

For any vehicle available with more than one size of engine or more than one type of transmission, the road-tested vehicle, when available, is used in the database.

1 The "Average" Vehicle

For questions 2a) to c), display the records using Table 1.

An efficient approach to question 2a) is to use the Find feature with one comparison for *Mass, kg* $<> -1$ (*Getting Started* BLM C-5). Then, determine and display the average of the masses, rounded to 0 decimal places, in each type by doing the following. Create a summary field called *Average Mass by Type, kg*, using the formula that follows. Sort by *Type*. Insert a Sub-summary section. Insert the summary field in the Sub-summary section (*Getting Started* BLM C-7). Finally, manually sort the nine averages from greatest to least.

ROUND(AVERAGE('Mass, kg'),0)

For part b), show all the records and use the Find feature with one comparison for *Length, m* $<> -1$ (*Getting Started* BLM C-5). Then, create a summary field called *Average Length by Type, m*, using the formula that follows, and insert the summary field in the Sub-summary section created in the previous part to determine and display the average of the lengths, rounded to 1 decimal place, in each type (*Getting Started* BLM C-7). Finally, manually sort the nine averages from greatest to least.

ROUND(AVERAGE('Length, m'),1)

For part c), repeat the process in part b), using the *Width, m* field in place of the *Length, m* field.

For parts d) to f), create a table displaying only the *Vehicle, Type, Power, hp, Highway Fuel Efficiency, L/100 km*, and *City Fuel Efficiency, L/100 km* fields (*Getting Started* BLM C-2).

For part d), show all the records and use the Find feature with one comparison for *Power, hp* $<> -1$ (*Getting Started* BLM C-5). Then, determine and display the average of the powers, rounded to 0 decimal places, in each type by doing the following. Create a summary field called *Average Power by Type, hp*, using the formula that follows. Sort by *Type*. Insert a Sub-summary section. Insert the summary field in the Sub-summary section (*Getting Started* BLM C-7). Finally, manually sort the nine averages from greatest to least.

ROUND(AVERAGE('Power, hp'),0)

For parts e) and f), repeat the process in part b), using the *Highway Fuel Efficiency, L/100 km* and *City Fuel Efficiency, L/100 km* fields in place of the *Length, m* field.

2 Acceleration Times

In question 2, show all the records, displaying them using Table 2. Then, use the Find feature with two comparisons for *Time to Accelerate from 0-48 km/h, s* <>−1 and *Time to Accelerate from 0-96 km/h, s* <>−1 (*Getting Started* BLM C-5).

In question 3, sort the *Time to Accelerate 0-48 km/h, s* field from least to greatest, and repeat for the *Time to Accelerate 0-96 km/h, s* field (*Getting Started* BLM C-4).

An efficient approach to question 5 is to show all the records and create a table to display only the *Vehicle* and *Time to Accelerate 0-48 km/h, s* fields (*Getting Started* BLM C-2). Then, use the Find feature with one comparison for *Time to Accelerate 0-48 km/h, s* <>−1 (*Getting Started* BLM C-5). Next, create two calculation fields called *Theoretical Time for 0-48 km/h, s* and *Difference in Times for 0-48 km/h, s*, using the first two formulas that follow, to determine the theoretical time and the difference in the times, rounded to 1 decimal place (*Getting Started* BLM C-6). Then, use the Match feature with the third formula that follows (*Getting Started* BLM C-5). Finally, express the number of records displayed as a percent of the number of records found in question 2, using a calculator.

ROUND((48^2*'Mass, kg')/(6024.67*'Power, hp'),1)

ROUND('Time to Accelerate 0-48 km/h, s'−'Theoretical Time for 0-48 km/h, s',1)

AND('Difference in Times for 0-48 km/h, s'<=0.5, 'Difference in Times for 0-48 km/h, s'>=−0.5)

An efficient approach to question 7 is to use the same approach as for question 5, ensuring that different field names are used for the calculation fields. Deselect the records from the previous question and show all the records. Then, create a table to display only the *Vehicle* and *Time to Accelerate 0-96 km/h, s* fields (*Getting Started* BLM C-2). Next, use the Find feature with one comparison for *Time to Accelerate 0-96 km/h, s* <>−1 (*Getting Started* BLM C-5). Then, create two calculation fields called *Theoretical Time for 0-96 km/h, s* and *Difference in Times for 0-96 km/h, s*, using the first two formulas that follow, to determine the theoretical time and the difference in the times, rounded to 1 decimal place (*Getting Started* BLM C-6). Next, use the Match feature with the third formula that follows (*Getting Started* BLM C-5). Finally, express the number of records displayed as a percent of the number of records found in question 2, using a calculator.

ROUND((96^2*'Mass, kg')/(10378.64*'Power, hp'),1)

ROUND('Time to Accelerate 0-96 km/h, s'−'Theoretical Time for 0-96 km/h, s',1)

AND('Difference in Times for 0-96 km/h, s'<=1,'Difference in Times for 0-96 km/h, s'>=−1)

3 Buying a Vehicle

An efficient approach to question 1 is to deselect the records from the previous exploration and show all the records, displaying them using Full Record. Then, use the Match feature with the following formula (*Getting Started* BLM C-5).

AND('Highway Fuel Efficiency, L/100 km'<>−1, 'Highway Fuel Efficiency, L/100 km'<=7.5, 'Seating'>=5,'Type'<>"minivan", 'Type'<>"small car")

An efficient approach to question 2 is to deselect the records from the previous question, show all the records, and use the Match feature in a manner similar to the one used for question 1 (*Getting Started* BLM C-5).

Technology

Exploring Polynomial Functions With a Graphing Calculator

Student Text Pages
Pp. 272–273

Materials
graphing calculators

Learning Outcomes
- Graph linear, quadratic, cubic, quartic, and quintic functions using a graphing calculator.
- Relate the end behaviours of functions to the degree of the polynomial and the sign of its leading coefficient.

Prerequisite Skills
State the degree and classify each function.

a) $y = 2x^4 - 3x^2 + 1$ [4th, quartic]

b) $y = -5x - 1$ [1st, linear]

c) $y = -2x^5 - x^4 + 2x^2 - x + 1$ [5th, quintic]

d) $y = x^3$ [3rd, cubic]

e) $y = -4x^2 - 3x + 5$ [2nd, quadratic]

Teaching Suggestions

Review how to use a graphing calculator to create the graphs on student text page 272. On a TI-83, a function is graphed using the Y= key. The Maximum and Minimum operations are used to find the coordinates of the relative maximums and relative minimums.

Discuss the following terms — relative maximums, relative minimums (sometimes called local maximums, local minimums), turning points, leading coefficient, even-degree, and odd-degree.

Assign the explorations, discussing the findings of Exploration 1 before proceeding with the next.

See *MATHPOWER™ 11, Western Edition, Blackline Masters* pages 102 to 104 for Polynomial Functions and Polynomial Equations.

Assessing the Outcomes

Journal

Summarize the features of linear, quadratic, cubic, quartic, and quintic functions in a table using headings such as the following.

Name
Degree
General form
End behaviour direction
End behaviour when a is positive
End behaviour when a is negative
Greatest number of turning points possible

Polynomial Functions and Inequalities

Student Text Pages

Pp. 274–285

Materials

graphing calculators, Teacher's Resource Master 1 (0.5-cm grid paper), overhead projector

Learning Outcomes

- Identify polynomial functions.
- Interpret graphs of polynomial functions.
- Graph polynomial functions.
- Solve polynomial inequalities.
- Solve problems involving polynomial equations and inequalities.

Prerequisite Skills

1. Find the x- and y-intercepts of each expression.

a) $2x + 3y = 0$ [x-intercept 0; y-intercept 0]

b) $5x - y = -1$ $\left[x\text{-intercept } -\frac{1}{5}; y\text{-intercept } 1\right]$

c) $-3x + 2y = 5$ $\left[x\text{-intercept } -\frac{5}{3}; y\text{-intercept } \frac{5}{2}\right]$

d) $y = x^2 - 9$ [x-intercept ± 3; y-intercept -9]

e) $3x + y^2 = 1$ $\left[x\text{-intercept } \frac{1}{3}; y\text{-intercept } \pm 1\right]$

f) $-x - 7y - 14 = 0$ [x-intercept -14; y-intercept -2]

2. Factor each expression.

a) $x^2 + 4x - 5$ [$(x - 1)(x + 5)$]

b) $x^2 + 5x + 6$ [$(x + 3)(x + 2)$]

c) $2x^2 - 14x + 20$ [$2(x - 2)(x - 5)$]

d) $-2x^2 + 5x + 3$ [$-(2x + 1)(x - 3)$]

Mental Math

1. If $d(x) = 2|-x - 2|$, find

a) $d(-4)$ [4]   **b)** $d(5)$ [14]

c) $d\left(\frac{1}{2}\right)$ [5]   **d)** $d(-0.5)$ [3]

e) $d(40)$ [84]   **f)** $d(-10)$ [16]

2. Evaluate, if possible.

a) $\sqrt{14 + 11}$ [5]   **b)** $\sqrt{-49}$ [Impossible]

c) $\sqrt{24 - 8}$ [4]   **d)** $\sqrt{5^2 - 4^2}$ [3]

e) $\sqrt{7^2 - 13}$ [6]   **f)** $2\sqrt{36 + 28}$ [16]

Explore/Inquire Answers

Explore: Draw a Graph

(0, 60), (20, 40), (40, 28), (50, 25), (60, 24), (70, 25), (80, 28), (100, 40)

Inquire

1. 24 m   **2. a)** $0 \le d \le 100$, $24 \le h \le 60$ **3.** 2

4. No. The height is never 0 for $0 \le d \le 100$.

5. Yes. The height of the roller-coaster varies continuously.

Teaching Suggestions

(0.5-cm grid paper, overhead projector) Review with the class the methods of solving polynomial equations. Help them identify these methods.

- removing a common factor
- using factoring
- using the square root principle
- completing the square
- using the factor theorem

Read with the class the opening paragraph on student text page 274. Provide pairs of students with grid paper and assign the Explore section and the Inquire questions. Ask:

How would you describe the graph of the function given in the Explore section?

Have volunteers present their results to the class. Provide an overhead projector for those who wish to display their graphs. Remind the students that the number of times the graph of a function intersects the x-axis is the number of real roots of the function. Ask:

The points at which the graph of a function crosses the x-axis are called zeros of the function. Explain.

Review with the class teaching examples 1 to 8 on student text pages 275 to 281.

Integrating Technology

Graphing Calculators

How would you use your graphing calculator to graph the polynomial functions in teaching example 3 on student text page 276 and teaching example 4 on student text page 277? On a TI-83, the Y= key is used. To find maximums and minimums, the Maximum and Minimum operations are used.

Press the Y= key, clear any equations that exist, and turn off any plots that are highlighted. Enter the function at Y1=.

Press the ZOOM key and the 6 key to select ZStandard. Press the CALC (i.e., 2nd TRACE) key and the 3 key to find a minimum, or the 4 key to find a maximum.

How would you use your graphing calculator to determine the double root of 0 for the polynomial equation in teaching example 5 on student text page 278? On a TI-83, the Y= key is used, and interpretation of the shape of the graph at the origin identifies the double root as 0.

How would you use your graphing calculator to solve the polynomial inequalities in teaching example 6 on student text page 279 and teaching example 7 on student text page 280? On a TI-83, the Y= key and the Zero operation are used.

Write the inequality < 0, > 0, ≤ 0, or ≥ 0.

Press the Y= key, clear any equations that exist, and turn off any plots that are highlighted.

Enter the left side of the inequality at Y1=.

Press the ZOOM key and the 6 key to select ZStandard.

Press the CALC (i.e., 2nd TRACE) key and the 2 key to select the Zero operation and confirm the x-intercepts.

Interpret the graph, that is, identify the values of x for which the function is below (< 0), above (> 0), on or below (≤ 0), or on or above (≥ 0) the x-axis.

The Y= key and the Intersect operation can also be used to solve the inequalities in the teaching examples. When the inequality is written with a non-zero expression on each side of the inequality sign, graph the function corresponding to each side of the inequality, and find the intersection points.

Press the Y= key, clear any equations that exist, and turn off any plots that are highlighted.

Enter the left side of the inequality at Y1=.

Enter the right side of the inequality at Y2=.

Press the ZOOM key and the 6 key to select ZStandard.

Press the CALC (ie., 2nd TRACE) key and the 5 key to select the Intersect operation and confirm the intersection points.

Interpret the graphs, that is, identify the values of x for which one function is above (> 0), below (< 0), above or the same as (≥ 0), or below or the same as (≤ 0) the other. For each inequality solved in the teaching examples, solve using this method, and check that the solutions are the same. For example, in teaching example 6 on student text page 279 where $x^2 + x < 6$, graph $y = x^2 + x$ and $y = 6$.

How would you use your graphing calculator to solve the problem in teaching example 8 on student text page 281? On a TI-83, the Y= key and the Intersect operation are used.

Press the Y= key, clear any equations that exist, and turn off any plots that are highlighted.

Enter the first function at Y1=.

Enter the second function at Y2=.

The standard viewing window is not useful. Create a viewing window based on the given information. Both graphs open down. The maximum value is 80 when t is 0 in the first function. Neither time nor height can be

negative. The window shown uses an Xmin of 0, an Xmax of 5, an Xscl of 1, a Ymin of 0, a Ymax of 80, and a Yscl of 10.

Press the CALC (i.e., 2nd TRACE) key and the 5 key to select the Intersect operation.

Use your graphing calculator to graph the polynomial functions in questions 17 to 40 on student text pages 282 and 283, to solve the polynomial inequalities in questions 41 to 56 on student text page 283, and when appropriate, to answer the questions on student text pages 283 to 285.

A method for graphing the solution to an inequality is presented in question 57 on student text page 283. Inequality signs are under the Test menu when the TEST (i.e., 2nd MATH) key is pressed.

See *MATHPOWER™ 11, Western Edition, Blackline Masters* pages 102 to 104 for Polynomial Functions and Polynomial Equations. See *MATHPOWER™ 11, Western Edition, Blackline Masters* pages 27 to 29 for Setting Viewing Windows.

Enrichment

Graph the following functions.

1. $y = x^2$ 2. $y = 2x^3$
3. $y = -x^3$ 4. $y = 4x^3$
5. $y = 5x^4$ 6. $y = -2x^4$
7. $y = -x^5$ 8. $y = 4x^5$
9. $y = 5x^6$ 10. $y = -2x^6$
11. $y = -x^7$ 12. $y = 4x^7$

Study any patterns you see in the shapes of the graphs. Use your graphs to describe the general characteristics of

a) polynomial functions of even degree

b) polynomial functions of odd degree

Refer to
• the continuity of the graphs,
• the number of turns in the graphs, and
• the effect of the sign of the leading coefficient.

Math Journal

critical numbers, test intervals   Define these terms for polynomial functions. Include diagrams for clarity.

Problem Levels of Difficulty

A: 1–56, 77   **B:** 57–71   **C:** 72–76

Assessing the Outcomes

Journal

Write three examples of a polynomial function and three examples of functions that are not polynomial functions.

Written Assignment

1. Graph each of the following functions. Determine
- the domain and the range
- the real zeros
- the y-intercept
- the intervals where $f(x) > 0$ and $f(x) \leq 0$
- any symmetry
- the end behaviour

a) $f(x) = x^3 - 2x$

b) $f(x) = (x + 1)(x - 2)(x - 1)(x - 3)$

2. Solve each inequality.

a) $x^3 + 2x^2 - 5x < 6$ **b)** $x^2 + 11x + 28 \geq 0$

c) $x^4 - 2x^3 + x^2 \leq 0$ **d)** $x^3 > -3x^2 + 4x$

Technology

Exploring Functions With Two Equal Roots

Student Text Pages

Pp. 286–287

Materials

graphing calculators

Learning Outcomes

- Verify equal roots of polynomial functions.
- Find a pattern and predict values of the constant term of a polynomial function for which the function has equal roots.

Prerequisite Skills

Find the factors.

a) $x^3 + 2x^2 + x$ $[(x)(x + 1)(x + 1)]$

b) [illegible] [illegible]

c) $2x^3 + 3x^2 - 3x - 2$ $[(x - 1)(x + 2)(2x + 1)]$

Teaching Suggestions

Have the students graph $f(x) = x^3 - 4x^2 + k$ for different values of k to estimate the values for k for which $f(x) = 0$. After they conclude that 0 and approximately 9.5 appear to be values for k for which $f(x) = 0$, have them graph $f(x) = x^3 - 4x^2$ and use the Zero operation to verify that the equal roots are 0. Then, have them graph $f(x) = x^3 - 4x^2 + \frac{256}{27}$ and use the Zero operation to verify that the equal roots are $2.\overline{6}$ or $\frac{8}{3}$.

For the first graph in Exploration 1, discuss how interpretation of the shape of the graph identifies the double root as 0 and the single root as 2. Similarly, for the second graph, the double root is $1.\overline{3}$ and the single root is $-0.\overline{6}$. The related polynomial can be factored to verify the equal roots of the function. The factor theorem can be used to find the factors, when needed.

Discuss how to use a graphing calculator to solve algebraically polynomial equations like the equation on student text page 286. On a TI-92, solve, which is the first item under F2 Algebra, finds all real roots. At the solve(prompt, enter the equation. Then, press , x) to indicate the equation is being solved for x, or whatever letter is used as the variable, before pressing the ENTER key.

Alternatively, on a TI-92, factor, which is the second item under F2 Algebra, can be used to find the factors of the related polynomial. At the factor(prompt, enter the polynomial and a closing bracket, and then press the ENTER key. Factoring shows if any factor is repeated, identifying the equal roots of the function.

To use the Equation Solver on a TI-83 to find real roots, see *Technology: Solving Quadratic Equations With a Graphing Calculator* on page 146 of this teacher's resource.

In question 1, it is difficult in the standard viewing window to determine if there are equal roots. Change the viewing window to see the details near the origin using an Xmin of −3, an Xmax of 3, an Xscl of 1, a Ymin of −1, a Ymax of 1, and a Yscl of 1, for example. Use the Zero operation to determine the single root is $-0.\overline{3}$ and the double roots is $0.\overline{6}$. Alternatively, factor the polynomial to determine the roots. In questions 2 and 3, interpret the shape of the graph to determine that there are equal roots. Use the Zero operation to determine what they, and the single root, are. Record the roots to use in Exploration 2.

In question 2 in Exploration 2, the pattern is found between successive sets of roots.

See *MATHPOWER™ 11, Western Edition, Blackline Masters* pages 102 to 104 for Polynomial Functions and Polynomial Equations.

Assessing the Outcomes

Journal

Write about the different approaches that can be used to determine that equal roots exist for a polynomial function — by graphing it in an appropriate viewing window, by solving the related equation, and by factoring the related polynomial.

5.5 Absolute Value Functions, Equations, and Inequalities

Student Text Pages
Pp. 288–298

Materials
graphing calculators

Learning Outcomes
- Develop the concept of absolute value equations.
- Solve absolute value equations.
- Identify extraneous solutions of absolute value equations.
- Solve absolute value inequalities.
- Graph absolute value functions.
- Solve problems involving absolute value functions.

Prerequisite Skills
1. Evaluate each expression for the given values of the variables.

a) $2x^2 + 1; x = -2$ [9]

b) $-3x + 2y; x = 1, y = -1$ [−5]

c) $x^2 + y^2; x = -1, y = 2$ [5]

d) $5y^2 - x; x = 2, y = -3$ [43]

2. Solve each inequality. x is an integer.

a) $2x > 12$ [$x > 6, x \in I$]

b) $-3x + 2 \leq 14$ [$x > -4, x \in I$]

c) $-4 + x \geq 2x - 5$ [$x \leq 1, x \in I$]

d) $\frac{-5x}{7} > 10$ [$x < -14, x \in I$]

e) $\frac{8x}{3} \leq -5 + x$ [$x \leq -3, x \in I$]

Mental Math
1. If $m(x) = 2|x + 5|$, find

a) $m(-7)$ [4]   b) $m(25)$ [60]

c) $m\left(\frac{3}{4}\right)$ [11.5]   d) $m(-6.5)$ [3]

e) $m(200)$ [410]   f) $m(-15)$ [20]

2. Calculate.

a) 8.1×89 [720.9]   b) 53×5.7 [302.1]

c) 46×4.4 [202.4]   d) 0.65×65 [42.25]

e) 720×78 [56 160]   f) 2.9×2.1 [6.09]

Explore/Inquire Answers
Explore: Interpret the Graphs

a) $3, -7$ b) $7, -1$ c) $-3, -7$ d) $3, 9$

Inquire

1. a) by substitution
2. There are two numbers whose absolute value is the given positive number.
3. a) $17, -5$ b) $1, -19$ c) $-16, -18$ d) $11, -5$
4. 365 min, 355 min
5. b) The left side is positive or zero, while the right side is negative.

Teaching Suggestions
Read with the class the opening paragraphs on student text page 288. Review the method of evaluating absolute value expressions. Ask:

If $|x - 2| = 5$, what two equations can you write?

Lead the students to see that the expression inside the absolute value symbol and its opposite can be equated to the numerical value on the other side of the equation. If $|x - 2| = 5$, then $x - 2 = 5$, or $-(x - 2) = 5$.

Assign the Explore section and the Inquire questions to pairs of students. For Inquire question 2, point out that, because two equations can be written from an absolute value equation, then, an absolute value equation has two solutions.

Ensure that the students check all the solutions in the original absolute value equation.

Have volunteers present their results to the class. Then, review with the class teaching examples 1 to 10 on student text pages 289 to 295. Have several students work alongside the rest of the class with a graphing calculator, and demonstrate their graphs on the calculator.

Integrating Technology

Graphing Calculators
How would you use your graphing calculator to solve the absolute value equations in the Explore section on student text page 288, in teaching example 1 on student text page 289, in teaching examples 2 and 3 on student text page 290, and in teaching example 4 on student text page 291? On a TI-83, the Y= key, the Absolute Value function, and the Zero operation, or the Y= key, the Absolute Value function, and the Intersect operation are used.

The Absolute Value function is the first item under the second menu NUM when the MATH key is pressed. It is also the first item when the CATALOG (i.e., 2nd 0) key is pressed.

Press the CATALOG (i.e., 2nd 0) key and the ENTER key to select abs(.

At the abs(prompt, enter the expression and a closing bracket.

When the equation is written equal to zero, graph the function corresponding to the other side of the equation and find the x-intercepts.

Press the Y= key, clear any equations that exist, and turn off any plots that are highlighted.

Enter the left side of the equation at Y1=, using the Absolute Value function described above.

Press the ZOOM key and the 6 key to select ZStandard.

Press the CALC (i.e., 2nd TRACE) key and the 2 key to select the Zero operation.

When the equation is written with a non-zero expression on each side of the equal sign, graph the function corresponding to each side of the equation and find the intersection points.

Press the Y= key, clear any equations that exist, and turn off any plots that are highlighted.

Enter the left side of the equation at Y1=, using the Absolute Value function described above.

Enter the right side of the equation at Y2=, using the Absolute Value function described above.

Press the ZOOM key and the 6 key to select ZStandard.

Press the CALC (i.e., 2nd TRACE) key and the 5 key to select the Intersect operation.

For each equation solved in the teaching examples, solve using the other method, and check that the solutions are the same. For example, rewrite the equation in teaching example 3 as $|x + 2| = |3x - 10|$ and solve using the Intersect operation.

How would you use your graphing calculator to solve the absolute value inequalities in teaching example 5 on student text page 292, in teaching example 6 on student text page 293, and in teaching example 7 on student text page 294? On a TI-83, the Y= key, the Absolute Value function, and the Intersect operation are used. The graphing process is the same as for equations. Interpret the graphs, that is, identify the values of x for which one function is above (> 0), below (< 0), above or the same as (≥ 0), or below or the same as (≤ 0) the other.

As with equations, the Y= key, the Absolute Value function, and the Zero operation can also be used. The graphing process is the same as for equations. Interpret the graph, that is, identify the values of x for which the function is below (< 0), above (> 0), on or below (≤ 0), or on or above (≥ 0) the x-axis. For each inequality solved in the teaching examples, solve using this method and check that the solutions are the same. For example, rewrite the equation in teaching example 7 as $|x + 2| + |x - 1| - 3 > 0$.

Graph the solution to the inequality in teaching example 10 on student text 295. The standard viewing window is not useful. Create a viewing window based on the given information.

Use your graphing calculator to solve the equations and inequalities, and to graph the functions in the questions on student text pages 296 to 298.

A method for graphing the solution to an equation is presented in questions 110 and 111 on student text page 297. The equal sign is the first item under the Test menu when the TEST (i.e., 2nd MATH) key is pressed.

A method for graphing the solution to an inequality is presented in questions 112 and 113 on student text page 298. Inequality signs are under the Test menu when the TEST (i.e., 2nd MATH) key is pressed.

Enrichment

The general form of an absolute value function is $y = a|bx + c| + d$.

With a partner, experiment with different values of a, b, c, and d. Write a short essay describing the change in the graph of $y = |x|$ for different values of a, b, c, and d. Compare your results with those of another pair of students in your class.

Math Journal

Compare and contrast the graphs of $y = |x|$ and $|y| = x$. Identify the domain and the range of each graph.

Problem Levels of Difficulty

A: 1–99, 124   **B:** 100–118   **C:** 119–123

Assessing the Outcomes

Written Assignment

1. Solve.
   a) $|x + 4| = 3$
   b) $2|-x + 1| + x = 8$
   c) $|2x + 1| - |x - 3| = 1$

2. Solve.
   a) $|2x + 2| ≤ 3$
   b) $|x - 7| > |2x + 1|$
   c) $|x + 3| + |x + 1| > 2$

3. Graph $f(x) = |x + 4| - 1$ and determine the values of x for which $f(x) ≥ 0$.

4. a) Graph $y = |x^2 - 9|$.
   b) Determine the domain and the range.
   c) Determine the values of any zeros.
   d) Describe any symmetry.

5.6 Rational Functions, Equations, and Inequalities

Student Text Pages
Pp. 299–312

Materials
graphing calculators, Teacher's Resource Master 1 (0.5-cm grid paper), overhead projector

Learning Outcomes
- Define rational functions.
- Identify asymptotes.
- Find points of discontinuity of rational functions.
- Find the inverse of rational functions.
- Compare rational functions and polynomial functions.
- Solve rational equations.
- Solve rational inequalities.
- Solve problems involving rational equations.

Prerequisite Skills
1. Indicate the restrictions on the variables.

a) $y = \dfrac{1}{x+2}$ [−2] b) $y = \dfrac{3x}{x+1}$ [−1]

c) $y = \dfrac{x-1}{2x}$ [0] d) $y = \dfrac{3}{(x+6)(x-1)}$ [1, −6]

2. Evaluate $f(x)$ for the given values of x.

a) $f(x) = 3x + 2$; $x = -1, 0, 1$ [−1, 2, 5]

b) $f(x) = x^2 - 5$; $x = 2, 4, 6$ [−1, 11, 31]

c) $f(x) = \dfrac{2x}{x-1}$; $x = -3, -2, -1$ $\left[1\frac{1}{2}, \frac{4}{3}, 1\right]$

d) $f(x) = \dfrac{x+2}{x^2-5}$; $x = 0, 1, 2$ $\left[-\frac{2}{5}, -\frac{3}{4}, -4\right]$

Mental Math
1. If $h(x) = 3x^2 - x + 5$, find

a) $h(2)$ [15] b) $h(-5)$ [85]

c) $h\left(\dfrac{1}{2}\right)$ $\left[5\frac{1}{4}\right]$ d) $h(-0.2)$ [5.32]

e) $h\left(-\dfrac{1}{2}\right)$ $\left[6\frac{1}{4}\right]$ f) $h(10)$ [295]

2. Evaluate for $m = -1$ and $n = 2$.

a) $3m - n$ [−5] b) $-m + 4n$ [9]

c) $m^2 + n$ [3] d) $2m - n + 5$ [1]

e) $m^3 + n^2$ [5] f) $3m^5 + 7$ [4]

Explore/Inquire Answers
Explore: Draw a Graph

a)

x	$\frac{1}{4}$	$\frac{1}{3}$	$\frac{1}{2}$	1	2	3	4
y	4	3	2	1	$\frac{1}{2}$	$\frac{1}{3}$	$\frac{1}{4}$
x	$-\frac{1}{4}$	$-\frac{1}{3}$	$-\frac{1}{2}$	−1	−2	−3	−4
y	−4	−3	−2	−1	$-\frac{1}{2}$	$-\frac{1}{3}$	$-\frac{1}{4}$

b)

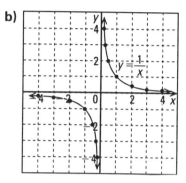

Inquire

1. The ordered pairs (x, y) on the graph have both positive coordinates or both negative coordinates.

2. the set of real numbers, $x \neq 0$

3. Table 1: 1, 0.1, 0.01, 0.001; 1, 10, 100, 1000
   Table 2: −1, −0.1, −0.01, −0.001; −1, −10, −100, −1000

4. a) decreases b) no; the value of $\frac{1}{x}$ is never 0
   c) increases d) no; the smaller the value of x becomes (i.e., as x tends to 0), the greater the value of $\frac{1}{x}$ becomes

5. a) increases b) no; the value of $\frac{1}{x}$ is never 0
   c) decreases d) no; the greater the value of x becomes, the smaller the value of $\frac{1}{x}$ becomes (i.e., $\frac{1}{x}$ tends to 0)

6. a) $d > 0, l \geq 0$ b) 4 lux c) 2 m

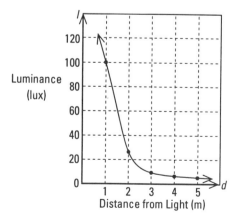

Teaching Suggestions

Method 1

(0.5-cm grid paper, overhead projector) Read with the class the opening paragraphs on student text page 299. Assign the Explore section to pairs of students. Ask:

What value of x is inadmissible for the function $y = \frac{1}{x}$? Explain.

How would you identify an extraneous solution of a rational equation?

Then, assign the Inquire questions. For question 6, ask:

What values go on the horizontal axis? the vertical axis?

Encourage the students to discuss and compare their results with those of other students in the class. Provide an overhead projector and have volunteers present their results to the class.

Review with the class the lower half of student text page 300. Ask:

What is an asymptote?

How would you find the equation of a vertical asymptote? a horizontal asymptote?

If you were given the equation of an asymptote, how would you know if it was a horizontal asymptote or a vertical asymptote?

Lead the students to see that vertical asymptotes occur for values of the variable that make the denominator equal to zero. The horizontal asymptote occurs for the value to which the rational function tends as x becomes very large and very small. Ask:

What does an asymptote represent?

Ensure that the students realize that the asymptote is not part of the graph, but is a line to which the graph comes closer and closer, but never meets. Ask:

Why is it useful to be able to identify the asymptotes without creating a table of values?

Point out that knowing the location of the asymptotes helps with the sketching of the rational function.

Review with the class teaching examples 1 to 8 on student text pages 301 to 308. Ensure that some students work with a graphing calculator and demonstrate the results to the rest of the class.

For teaching example 5, ensure that the students realize that using cross multiplication often introduces an extraneous root that would not be there if you multiplied every term of the equation by the LCM. Stress upon the students that they should always multiply both sides by the LCM of all the denominators. Ensure that the students know how to factor polynomials, as this skill is very useful in solving rational equations.

Method 2

(0.5-cm grid paper, overhead projector) Introduce the term "rational function" to the class. Explain that the form of a rational function is $f(x) = \frac{\text{polynomial in } x}{\text{polynomial in } x}$.

Write these two rational functions on the chalkboard.

$$y = \frac{1}{x + 1} \qquad y = \frac{x}{x - 3}$$

Organize the class into 6 groups, and have two groups create a table of values and graph the first function, and have two groups create a table of values and graph the second function. Have the remaining two groups use graphing calculators to graph both functions. Instruct the groups to use values of x from -10 to $+10$, and to include some fractional values. Give the groups who are working on the same function an opportunity to discuss and compare their results.

Then, ask:

What do you notice about the graph of the first function?

What do you notice about the graph of the second function?

Introduce the terms "vertical asymptote" and "horizontal asymptote."

Have volunteers present their graphs and indicate where the asymptotes occur in their graphs.

Discuss with the class the features of the graphs they constructed.

Review with the class teaching examples 1 to 8 on student text pages 301 to 308.

Logic Power Answer

no

Integrating Technology

Graphing Calculator

How would you use your graphing calculator to graph the rational functions on student text page 300, in teaching example 1 on student text page 301, and teaching examples 3 and 4 on student text page 303? On a TI-83, the Y= key is used, as with other functions. Remember to place brackets around numerators and/or denominators with more than one term. Note that in connected mode, the calculator attempts to connect all the points on a graph, resulting in a line that closely approximates vertical asymptotes.

To use the Draw instruction for teaching example 3 on student text page 303, see *Integrating Technology* in Section 5.3 on page 192 of this teacher's resource.

In teaching example 2 on student text page 302, as in division of functions, the break in the graph is not visible in the standard viewing window. To see the break in the graph, use an enlarged decimal viewing window. Press the ZOOM key and the 4 key to select Zdecimal.

Press the WINDOW key, move the cursor to the right of Ymax = 3.1, press × 2 and the GRAPH key to graph the function in the enlarged viewing window that shows the break.

To view the table showing the error where the break occurs, press the TABLE (i.e., 2nd GRAPH) key.

How would you use your graphing calculator to solve the rational equation in teaching example 5 on student text page 304? On a TI-83, the Y= key and the Intersect operation are used.
Press the Y= key, clear any equations that exist, and turn off any plots that are highlighted.
Enter the left side of the equation at Y1=.
Enter the right side of the equation at Y2=.
Press the ZOOM key and the 6 key to select ZStandard.
Press the CALC (i.e., 2nd TRACE) key and the 5 key to select the Intersect operation.

The Y= key and the Zero operation can also be used, as with other equations. When the equation is written equal to zero, graph the function corresponding to the other side of the equation and find the x-intercepts.
Press the Y= key, clear any equations that exist, and turn off any plots that are highlighted.
Enter the left side of the equation at Y1=.
Press the ZOOM key and the 6 key to select ZStandard.
Press the CALC (i.e., 2nd TRACE) key and the 2 key to select the Zero operation.

How would you use your graphing calculator to solve the rational inequalities in teaching example 7 on student text page 306? On a TI-83, the Y= key and the Intersect operation are used. The graphing process is the same as for equations. Interpret the graphs, that is, identify the values of x for which one function is above (> 0), below (< 0), above or the same as (≥ 0), or below or the same as (≤ 0) the other.

As well, the Y= key and the Zero operation can also be used. When the inequality is written with 0 on one side, graph the function corresponding to the other side of the inequality, and find the x-intercepts. Interpret the graph, that is, identify the values of x for which the function is below (< 0), above (> 0), on or below (≤ 0), or on or above (≥ 0) the x-axis.

Use your graphing calculator to graph the functions, and to solve the equations and inequalities in the questions on student text pages 309 to 312.

A method for graphing the solution to an inequality is presented in questions 124 and 125 on student text page 312. Inequality signs are under the Test menu when the TEST (i.e., 2nd MATH) key is pressed.

See *MATHPOWER™ 11, Western Edition, Blackline Masters* pages 134 to 136 for Rational Equations and Inequalities.

Extension

Find the vertical asymptotes of the rational function
$$y = \frac{(x + 2)}{x^2 + 3x - 5}.$$

Enrichment

Write the equation of a rational function that has vertical asymptotes at $x = -1$ and $x = 3$ and a horizontal asymptote at $y = 0$.

Math Journal

vertical asymptote, horizontal asymptote, point discontinuity   Write a definition for each of these terms in your journal. Include a diagram as part of your explanation.

Problem Levels of Difficulty

A: 1–98, 109, 110
B: 99–108, 111–126
C: 127–129

Assessing the Outcomes

Journal

Describe the similarities and differences between a discontinuity point and an asymptote, and how you would identify each one.

Technology

Exploring Rational Functions With a Graphing Calculator

Student Text Page
P. 313

Materials
graphing calculators

Learning Outcomes
- Graph rational functions using a graphing calculator, and determine the domain, the range, any real zeros, and any asymptotes or any point discontinuity.
- Identify transformations of rational functions.

Prerequisite Skills
Sketch the graph of a rational function with asymptotes at
a) $x = -3$ and $x = 2$
b) $x = 1$, $x = 5$, and $y = -3$

Teaching Suggestions
Discuss using a graphing calculator to graph rational functions. On a TI-83, the Y= key is used, as with other functions. Remind the students to place brackets around numerators and/or denominators with more than one term. Point out that in connected mode, the calculator attempts to connect all the points on a graph, resulting in a line that closely approximates vertical asymptotes.

When assigning Exploration 1, remind the students that they can change the viewing window to focus on any portion of the graph when the detail in the standard viewing window may not be as clear as needed.

When assigning Exploration 2, discuss how to use the VARS key in question 1 to avoid re-entering the portion of the function that is the same in each part and still have all the functions graphed together for comparison. Press the VARS key, the right arrow key, the 1 key, and the 1 key again to select Y1.

As well, discuss how to deselect functions in order to graph just the specified pairs in question 3. Move the cursor to the equal sign of the function to be deselected and press the ENTER key. Functions are reselected the same way.

Assessing the Outcomes

Journal
Write about what you have learned about the graphs of rational functions.

5.7 Radical Functions, Equations, and Inequalities

Student Text Pages
Pp. 314–327

Materials
graphing calculators, Teacher's Resource Master 1 (0.5-cm grid paper), overhead projector

Learning Outcomes
- Identify radical functions and their domain and range.
- Graph radical functions.
- Solve radical equations.
- Solve radical inequalities.
- Identify extraneous solutions of radical equations and inequalities.
- Solve problems involving radical equations.

Prerequisite Skills
1. Evaluate for each value of x. Leave answers in radical form.
   a) $\sqrt{2x - 1}$; $x = 1, 3$ $[1, \sqrt{5}]$
   b) $3\sqrt{x + 2}$; $x = -1, 2$ $[3, 6]$
   c) $-\sqrt{x^2 + 1}$; $x = -1, 0$ $[-\sqrt{2}, -1]$
   d) $-5\sqrt{2 - x}$; $x = -2, -1$ $[-10, -5\sqrt{3}]$

2. Remove the brackets in each expression.
   a) $(x + 2)^2$ $[x^2 + 4x + 4]$
   b) $-(x + 1)^2$ $[-x^2 - 2x - 1]$
   c) $2(x + 5)^2$ $[2x^2 + 20x + 50]$
   d) $-(3x + 1)^2$ $[-9x^2 - 6x - 1]$

Mental Math
1. If $p(x) = 3\sqrt{x - 2} + 9$, find
   a) $p(6)$ $[15]$ b) $p(11)$ $[18]$
   c) $p\left(\dfrac{9}{4}\right)$ $\left[10\tfrac{1}{2}\right]$ d) $p(4.25)$ $[13.5]$
   e) $p(51)$ $[30]$ f) $p(18)$ $[21]$

2. Calculate.
   a) 37×33 $[1221]$ b) 54×56 $[3024]$
   c) 92×98 $[9016]$ d) 71×79 $[5609]$
   e) 26×24 $[624]$ f) 85×85 $[7225]$

Explore/Inquire Answers
Explore: Draw a Graph

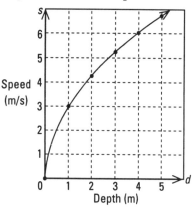

Inquire
1. $d \geq 0$; You cannot take the square root of a negative number.
2. $s \geq 0$
3. a) 30 m/s   b) 1.8 km/h
4. a) 203 m/s   b) 12 km/h

Teaching Suggestions
(0.5-cm grid paper, overhead projector) Read with the class the opening paragraph on student text page 314. Ask:

Has anyone ever heard the term "tsunami" before? In what context?

Why do you think it is useful to know the speed of a tsunami wave?

What kind of career would be involved in studying tsunami waves?

Provide pairs of students with grid paper and assign the Explore section on student text page 314. Ask:
What data should be plotted on the horizontal axis? the vertical axis?

Then, assign the Inquire questions. For question 1, ask:
What values can d not have? Explain.

For question 2, ask:
What values can s not have? Explain.

Have volunteers present their results to the class. Provide an overhead projector so that students can present their graphs to the class.

Review with the class teaching examples 1 to 9 on student text pages 314 to 322. Ensure that some students work along with the class with a graphing calculator, and give them an opportunity to show their calculator work.

Teaching example 3 demonstrates the necessity to always check the solutions to radical equations in the original equation.

For teaching example 4, remind the students that when you square each side of an equation, you cannot just square each term, but each side must be treated as you would one term, and square accordingly. If the side contains two terms, then to square the side, you effectively expand the square of a binomial.

Have volunteers present their results to the class.

Number Power Answer

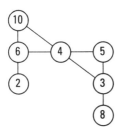

Integrating Technology

Graphing Calculators

How would you use your graphing calculator to graph the radical functions in teaching example 1 on student text pages 314 and 315? On a TI-83, the Y= key is used, as with other functions. When the square root (i.e., 2nd x^2) key is pressed, the √ (prompt appears. Enter the expression under the radical sign and a closing bracket.

How would you use your graphing calculator to solve the radical equations in teaching example 2 on student text pages 315, teaching example 3 on student text page 316, teaching examples 4 and 5 on student text pages 317, and teaching example 6 on student text page 318? On a TI-83, the Y= key and the Intersect operation are used, as with other equations. When the equation is written with a non-zero expression on each side of the equal sign, graph the function corresponding to each side of the equation and find the intersection points.

The Y= key and the Zero operation can also be used, as with other equations. When the equation is written equal to zero, graph the function corresponding to the other side of the equation and find the x-intercepts.

In teaching example 6 on student text page 318, the standard viewing window is not useful. Create a viewing window based on the given information. Neither speed nor depth can be negative. The intersection point will be on the line $y = 10$. The window shown uses an Xmin of 0, an Xmax of 15, an Xscl of 1, a Ymin of 0, a Ymax of 12, and a Yscl of 1.

How would you use your graphing calculator to solve the radical inequalities in teaching example 7 on student text page 319, teaching example 8 on student text page 321, and teaching example 9 on student text page 322?

On a TI-83, the Y= key and the Intersect operation, or the Y= key and the Zero operation are used. When the inequality is written with a non-zero expression on each side of the inequality sign, graph the function corresponding to each side of the inequality and find the intersection points. Interpret the graphs, that is, identify the values of x for which one function is above (> 0), below (< 0), above or the same as (≥ 0), or below or the same as (≤ 0) the other. When the inequality is written with 0 on one side, graph the function corresponding to the other side of the inequality and find the x-intercepts. Interpret the graph, that is, identify the values of x for which the function is below (< 0), above (> 0), on or below (≤ 0), or on or above (≥ 0) the x-axis.

Use your graphing calculator to graph the functions, and to solve the equations and inequalities in the questions on student text pages 323 to 327.

A method for graphing the solution to an inequality is presented in questions 131 and 132 on student text page 326. Inequality signs are under the Test menu when the TEST (i.e., 2nd MATH) key is pressed.

Enrichment

For an equation containing two radical expressions and a constant, construct a flow chart that lists the steps needed to solve such an equation.

Math Journal

Write a short essay describing the differences in your method of solving a radical equation containing one radical expression and a radical equation containing two radical expressions. Discuss and compare your essay with that of a classmate's and then, present your essay to the class.

Problem Levels of Difficulty

A: 1–101, 102 a), b), 103 a), b), 107
B: 102 c) – f), 103 c), d), 104–106, 108–130
C: 131–141

Assessing the Outcomes

Journal

Write a letter to a friend explaining how to solve an inequality containing a radical expression. Add your letter to a class bulletin board.

Observation

Some of the questions you might want to consider in this section include:
• Do the students understand the problems?
• Do the students show persistence?
• Do the students check their solutions in the original equations?
• Do the students show confidence when using a graphing calculator?

Connecting Math and Astronomy

Gravitational Forces

Student Text Pages
Pp. 328–329

Materials
scientific or graphing calculators

Learning Outcome
- Study the effect of gravitational forces on the weights of objects on different planets.

Prerequisite Skills
1. Write each number in scientific notation.

a) 1 005 000 000   [1.05×10^9]

b) 0.000 000 21   [2.1×10^{-7}]

c) 345   [3.45×10^2]

d) 0.000 22   [2.2×10^{-4}]

2. Calculate.

a) $(2.54 \times 10^5) \times (1.01 \times 10^{-2})$ [2.5654×10^3]

b) $(6.5 \times 10^2) \times (9.2 \times 10^7)$ [5.98×10^{10}]

Mental Math
1. If $f(x) = -2x^2 + 3x + 1$, find

a) $f(5)$ [-34]   b) $f(-10)$ [-229]

c) $f\left(\frac{2}{3}\right)$ $\left[2\frac{1}{9}\right]$ d) $f(1.1)$ [1.88]

e) $f(-2)$ [-13]   f) $f(10)$ [-169]

2. Subtract.

a) $94 - 48$ [46]   b) $83 - 67$ [16]

c) $71 - 38$ [33]   d) $63 - 25$ [38]

e) $152 - 97$ [55]   f) $385 - 129$ [256]

Teaching Suggestions
Read with the class the opening paragraphs on student text page 328. Ask:

What kind of function is Newton's law of gravitation?

Ensure the students identify it as a rational function.

Check that the students know how to multiply and divide numbers written in scientific notation, and that they can differentiate between the use of the subscript numbers and the superscript numbers in Newton's law of gravitation.

Divide the class into 4 groups of approximately equal size. Assign Investigation 1 to two of the groups and Investigation 2 to the other two groups. Give the groups that are working on the same investigation an opportunity to discuss and compare their results with each other.

For question 8 in Investigation 1, ask:

What type of function is given in question 8?

Ensure the students identify it as a radical function. Have volunteers present their results to the class.

Integrating Technology

Graphing Calculators
How would you use your calculator to evaluate expressions involving scientific notation? On a TI-83, the EE (i.e., 2nd ,) key is used. For example, to find the quotient of 7.5×10^{-7} and 1.5×10^{14}, do the following. Press (8.5.
Press the EE (i.e., 2nd ,) key.
Press the $(-)$ key and 7) ÷ 1.5.
Press the EE (i.e., 2nd ,) key.
Then, press 14 and the ENTER key.
The answer is not automatically displayed in scientific notation. The size of the number determines the display. If you want answers displayed in scientific notation each time, change the Mode setting to Sci, which is the second option in the first row when the MODE key is pressed.

Internet
Use the Internet to find more information about gravitational force, escape velocities, and black holes.

Enrichment
Research the life and works of Sir Isaac Newton. Write a short essay describing another law that he discovered.

Math Journal
Include Newton's law of gravitation in your journal, along with a diagram.

Assessing the Outcome

Journal
Write about
- the most interesting thing you found in this section.
- what else you would like to know about Newton's laws.

Review

Student Text Pages
Pp. 330–331

Materials
Teacher's Resource Master 1 (0.5-cm grid paper),
Teacher's Resource Master 2 (1-cm grid paper)

Learning Outcome
- Review the skills and concepts in Chapter 5.

Using the Review
Have the students work independently to complete the
Review. Meeting in small groups, the students can mark
and discuss the work. Groups can then share their
solutions and report any questions that caused them
difficulty. Discuss these questions with the class.

Reteaching Suggestions
For those students having difficulty with the chapter
material, form small groups and use the following
exercises.
   If you feel that the class has had particular difficulty
mastering any concept, you may wish to work through
a problem from each section as a model of excellence
of solution, which some students require just prior
to assessment.

Operations With Functions
1. For the functions $h(x) = 5x + 3$ and $f(x) = -2x$,
   the domain is the set of real numbers. Find
   a) $(h + f)(x)$ b) $(h - f)(x)$
   c) $(hf)(x)$ d) $\left(\dfrac{h}{f}\right)(x)$

2. For the functions $g(x) = 3x - 2$ and $d(x) = x + 5$,
   the domain is the set of real numbers. Find
   a) $(g + d)(2)$ b) $(g - d)(-5)$
   c) $(gd)(0)$ d) $\left(\dfrac{g}{d}\right)(10)$

3. Use the graphs of the functions $f(x) = 3x - 1$ and
   $g(x) = x - 5$ to find the graph of the sum $(f + g)(x)$.
   The domain of x is the real numbers.

4. For the functions $f(x) = x^2 + 2x - 3$ and $h(x) = x + 5$,
   the domain is the set of real numbers. Find
   a) $(f + h)(x)$ b) $(f - h)(x)$
   c) $(fh)(x)$ d) $\left(\dfrac{f}{h}\right)(x)$

5. If $g(x) = \dfrac{2x}{x + 1}$ and $h(x) = \dfrac{x}{x - 3}$, find each of the
   following functions. State any restrictions on the
   variable.
   a) $(f + g)(x)$ b) $\left(\dfrac{f}{g}\right)(x)$ c) $(fg)(x)$

6. If $f(x) = 3\sqrt{x} + 5$ and $g(x) = -\sqrt{x} - 2$, write each
   of the following in the simplest form.
   a) $(f + g)(x)$ b) $(f - g)(x)$
   c) $(fg)(x)$ d) $\left(\dfrac{f}{g}\right)(x)$

7. Given $f(x) = -x^2 - 3x + 1$ and $g(x) = 2x + 1$, find
   a) $-f(x)$ b) $2g(x) + f(x)$ c) $(gg)(x)$

Composition of Functions
1. Given $f(x) = 3x + 1$ and $g(x) = 2x^2 - 3$, find
   a) $(f \circ g)(3)$ b) $(g \circ f)(-2)$
2. If $f(x) = 2x^2 + 3$ and $g(x) = x - 4$, write
   a) $f \circ g$ b) $g \circ f$ c) $f \circ f$ d) $g \circ g$
3. Given $f(x) = \sqrt{x} + 1$ and $g(x) = x + 3$, find
   a) $(f \circ g)(x)$ and $(g \circ f)(x)$
   b) the domain and the range of f, g, $f \circ g$, and $g \circ f$
4. Given $f(x) = \sqrt{x - 2}$ and $g(x) = |2x| + 3$.
   a) Find $f \circ g$ and $g \circ f$, if they exist.
   b) Find the ranges of $f \circ g$ and $g \circ f$, if they exist.
5. Given $f(x) = \dfrac{x}{x + 3}$ and $g(x) = -5x$.
   a) Find $f \circ g$ and $g \circ f$.
   b) State any restrictions on the variable.

Inverse Functions
1. Find the inverse of each function.
   a) (2, 4), (3, 6), (4, 8), (5, 10), (6, 12)
   b) $f(x) = 7x - 4$
2. Determine if the inverses in question 1 above are
   functions.
3. Determine if each pair of functions are inverses
   of each other.
   a) $f(x) = -2x + 4$, $g(x) = -\dfrac{x}{2} + 2$
   b) $f(x) = \dfrac{3x}{x - 2}$, $g(x) = \dfrac{2x}{x + 2}$
4. a) Find the inverse of $f(x) = x^2 + 5$.
   b) Graph $f(x)$ and its inverse.
   c) Determine the domain and the range of $f(x)$ and
      its inverse.
   d) Is the inverse of $f(x)$ a function? If not, restrict the
      domain of $f(x)$ so that its inverse is a function.

5. Find each inverse.

a) $y = \dfrac{5}{x-3}$

b) $y = \dfrac{x}{2x+1}$

Polynomial Functions and Inequalities

1. Determine whether each function is a polynomial function. Justify your conclusion. Identify the degree of the polynomial functions.

a) $y = x^4 + 2x^2 - \dfrac{1}{3}x + 5$

b) $y = 3^{2x} - 9^x$

c) $y = \dfrac{5}{2x} + 4$

2. The graph of $y = f(x)$ is shown. Determine

a) the domain and range of $f(x)$

b) the real zeros of $f(x)$

c) the y-intercept

d) the intervals where $f(x) < 0$

e) the approximate coordinates of any relative maximums or relative minimums

f) any symmetry

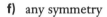

3. a) Graph $y = x^2(x^2 + 2)$.

b) Find the domain, range, any zeros, and the y-intercept.

c) Describe any symmetry.

4. Graph $f(x) = (x - 5)(x + 2)(x + 2)$. Determine

a) the real zeros of $f(x)$ **b)** the domain and range

c) the y-intercept   **d)** the intervals where $f(x) \geq 0$

e) any symmetry   **f)** the end behaviour

5. a) Graph the function $f(x) = 2x^3 + 4x^2 + 2x$.

b) Verify that the equation $f(x) = 0$ has two roots that equal -1.

6. a) Solve $x^2 - 2x \geq 15$.

b) Solve $x^3 + x^2 - 10x < -8$.

Absolute Value Functions, Equations, and Inequalities

1. Solve.

a) $|3x + 1| = 3$

b) $|x + 3| = 5x + 2$

c) $|x - 1| - |2x + 5| = 0$

d) $|x + 2| + |x - 5| = 2$

e) $|x + 6| > 2$

f) $|x - 1| > |x + 4|$

g) $|x - 5| + |x + 2| \geq 4$

2. Graph $f(x) = |x + 2| - 1$ and determine the values of x for which $f(x) > 0$.

Rational Functions, Equations, and Inequalities

1. Graph $f(x) = \dfrac{x}{x - 1}$.

2. a) Graph $f(x) = \dfrac{x^2 - 1}{x + 1}$.

b) If $g(x) = x - 1$, how does its graph differ from the graph of $f(x)$?

c) State the domain and range of $f(x)$.

3. a) Graph the inverse of $y = \dfrac{2x}{x + 1}$.

b) Determine the domain and range of the inverse.

4. a) Graph $y = x^2 - 4$ and determine the zeros.

b) Use the zeros of $y = x^2 - 4$ to determine the vertical asymptotes of $y = \dfrac{1}{x^2 - 4}$.

c) Compare the graphs of $y = x^2 - 4$ and $y = \dfrac{1}{x^2 - 4}$ with respect to the domain, range, symmetry, zeros, and asymptotes.

5. Solve and check $\dfrac{2x}{x + 1} = \dfrac{3x}{2x + 2}$.

6. Solve. Graph the solution.

a) $\dfrac{x^2 + 3x + 2}{x - 1} \leq 0$

b) $x + 2 > \dfrac{2}{x + 3}$

c) $|x + 1| \leq \dfrac{2}{x}$

Radical Functions, Equations, and Inequalities

1. Graph each function and determine the domain and range.

a) $y = \sqrt{x + 2}$

b) $y = \sqrt{x - 2}$

2. Solve and check.

a) $\sqrt{x - 2} - 1 = 8$

b) $\sqrt{x + 4} = -\sqrt{x - 5} + 9$

c) $1 + \sqrt{4x} = \sqrt{3x - 2}$

3. Find the roots of $5 - 2x + \sqrt{x + 1} = 0$. Round your answer to the nearest tenth.

4. Solve. Graph the solution.

a) $\sqrt{9 - x} \leq \sqrt{3 + x}$

b) $\sqrt{x - 2} < \sqrt{x + 2}$

5. Solve $\dfrac{x - 2}{4} \leq \dfrac{1}{\sqrt{x}}$.

Answers to Reteaching Suggestions

Operations With Functions

1. a) $3x + 3$ **b)** $7x + 3$

  c) $-10x^2 - 6x$ **d)** $\dfrac{5x + 3}{-2x}$

2. a) 11 **b)** -1 **c)** -10 **d)** $\dfrac{28}{15}$

4. a) $x^2 + 3x + 2$ **b)** $x^2 + x - 8$

  c) $x^3 + 7x^2 + 7x - 15$ **d)** $\dfrac{x^2 + 2x - 3}{x + 5}$

5. a) $\dfrac{3x^2 - 5x}{x^2 - 2x - 3}$ **b)** $\dfrac{2x - 6}{x + 1}$ **c)** $\dfrac{2x^2}{x^2 - 2x - 3}$

6. a) $2\sqrt{x} + 3$ **b)** $4\sqrt{x} + 7$

  c) $-3x - 11\sqrt{x} - 10$ **d)** $-\dfrac{3\sqrt{x} + 5}{\sqrt{x} + 2}$

7. a) $x^2 + 3x - 1$ **b)** $-x^2 + x + 3$

  c) $4x^2 + 4x + 1$

Composition of Functions

1. a) 46 **b)** 269

2. a) $2x^2 - 16x + 35$ **b)** $2x^2 - 1$

  c) $8x^4 + 24x^2 + 21$ **d)** $x - 8$

3. a) $f \circ g = \sqrt{x + 4}$, $g \circ f = \sqrt{x + 1} + 3$

  b) f: D: $x \geq -1$, $x \in R$; R: $y \geq 0$, $y \in R$

    g: D: $x \in R$; R: $y \in R$

    $f \circ g$: D: $x \geq -4$, $x \in R$; R: $y \geq 0$, $y \in R$

    $g \circ f$: D: $x \geq -1$, $x \in R$; R: $y \geq 3$, $y \in R$

4. a) $f \circ g = \sqrt{|2x| + 1}$, $g \circ f = |2\sqrt{x - 1}| + 3$

  b) $f \circ g$ D: $x \in R$; R: $y \geq 0$, $y \in R$

    $g \circ f = $ D: $x \geq 2$, $x \in R$; R: $y \geq 3$, $y \in R$

5. a) $f \circ g = \dfrac{5x}{5x - 3}$, $g \circ f = \dfrac{-5x}{x + 3}$

  b) $x \neq 3, -3$

Inverse Functions

1. a) $(4, 2), (6, 3), (8, 4), (10, 5), (12, 6)$

  b) $y = \dfrac{x + 4}{7}$

2. a) yes   **b)** yes

3. a) $f \circ g = g \circ f = x$; f and g are inverses of each other

  b) $f \circ g = \dfrac{-3x}{2}$, $g \circ f = \dfrac{6x}{5x - 4}$; f and g are not inverses of each other

4. a) $y = \sqrt{x - 5}$

  c) $f(x)$ D: $x \in R$; R: $y \geq 5$, $y \in R$

    $f^{-1}(x)$ D: $x \geq 5$, $x \in R$; R: $y \geq 0$, $y \in R$

  d) inverse is not a function; $y = \sqrt{x - 5}$, $x \geq 5$, $x \in R$ is a function and $y = -\sqrt{x - 5}$, $x \geq 5$, $x \in R$ is a function

5. a) $y = \dfrac{3x + 5}{x}$ **b)** $y = \dfrac{-x}{2x - 1}$

Polynomial Functions and Inequalities

1. a) not a polynomial function, degree 4

  b) not a polynomial function

2. a) D: $x \in R$; R: $y \in R$ **b)** $-3, -1, 1, 2$

  c) 6 **d)** $-3 < y < -1, 1 < y < 2$

  e) relative maximum $(0, 6)$; relative minimums $(-2, -12), (1.5, -2.8)$ **f)** no symmetry

3. b) D = $\{x \in R\}$; R = $\{y \mid y \geq 0, y \in R\}$, $x = 0, y = 0$

  c) y-axis

4. a) $5, -2$ **b)** D = $\{x \in R\}$; R = $\{y \in R\}$

  c) -12 **d)** $x > -5, x \in R$ **e)** none

  f) left-most y-values are negative, right-most y-values are positive

5. b) $f^{(-1)} = 0$

6. a) $x < -3, x > 5, x \in 5$ **b)** $-4 < x < 1; x > 2, x \in R$

Absolute Value Functions, Equations, and Inequalities

1. a) $x = \dfrac{2}{3}$ or $\dfrac{-4}{3}$ **b)** $x = \dfrac{1}{4}$ or $\dfrac{-5}{6}$

  c) $x = -6$ or $\dfrac{-4}{3}$ **d)** $x = \dfrac{5}{?}$ or $\dfrac{1}{?}$

  e) $x > -4$ or $x < -8$ **f)** $x \neq \dfrac{-3}{2}$

  g) $x < \dfrac{7}{2}$

2. $x < -3$

Rational Functions, Equations, and Inequalities

2. b) $f(x)$ has no value for $x = -1$, but $g(x)$ does.

  c) D: $x \neq -1, x \in R$; R: $y \in R$

3. b) $y = \dfrac{-x}{x - 2}$; D: $x \neq 2, x \in R$; R: $y \in R$

4. a) $2, -2$ **b)** $x = 2, x = -2$

  c) $y = x^2 - 4$; D: $x \in R$; R: $y \in R$, symmetric about the y-axis, zeros ± 2, no asymptotes

    $y = \dfrac{1}{x^2 - 4}$; D: $x \neq \pm 2, x \in R$; R: $y \in R$

5. $0, -1$

6. a) $x \leq -1, x \neq 1$ **b)** $x > -4, x \neq -3$

  c) $x \leq 1$ or $x > \dfrac{-1 \pm i\sqrt{7}}{2}$

Radical Functions, Equations, and Inequalities

1. a) D: $x \geq -2, x \in R$; R: $y \geq 0, y \in R$

  b) D: $x \geq 2, x \in R$; R: $y \geq 0, y \in R$

2. a) 83 **b)** $21 - 11 \pm \sqrt{112}$

3. $3.6, 1.7$

4. a) $x \geq 3, x \in R$ **b)** no solutions

5. $x \leq 4, x \in R$

Exploring Mathematics

The Game of Pong Hau K'i

(blue counters, red counters)   Provide pairs of students with red counters and blue counters, and have each player play the game of Pong Hau K'i. Give the students an opportunity to discuss and compare their strategies with other pairs of students. Have volunteers present their results to the class.

Chapter Check

Student Text Page
P. 332

Learning Outcome

• Evaluate the skills and concepts in Chapter 5.

Assessing the Outcome

Observation

If you assign the Chapter Check as a student assessment, look for the following:
• Can they find the composition of functions?
• Can they find the inverse of a function?
• Can they identify polynomial functions and solve polynomial inequalities?
• Can they manipulate absolute value functions and solve absolute value equations and inequalities?
• Can they manipulate rational functions and solve rational equations and inequalities?
• Can they manipulate radical functions and solve radical equations and inequalities?

Problem Solving

Student Text Page
P. 333

Learning Outcome
• Use problem solving strategies to solve problems.

Using the Strategies
The problems on this page allow the students to use the problem solving strategies discussed in Chapters 1 to 3. These strategies are
• Use a Diagram
• Use a Data Bank
• Solve Fermi Problems
• Solve a Simpler Problem
• Use Logic
• Look for a Pattern
• Guess and Check
• Work Backward
• Use a Table or Spreadsheet

Teaching Suggestions
Encourage the students to work in pairs or small groups. When students have completed the problems, have them share and discuss their strategies and solutions with other students.

For question 2, remind the students to use a table to organize the information. Point out that if all but one of the possibilities have been eliminated, then the remaining possibility is the required outcome.

For question 3, point out that this is a system of three equations in three unknowns. You can subtract equation 3 from equation 1 to find a value for S. This value can be substituted into either equation 1 or equation 3 to find an expression for R in terms of T. Then, substitute for S and R in equation 2.

For question 4, the three-digit number whose digits are all the same can be represented by

$$aaa = 100a + 10a + a$$
$$= a(100 + 10 + 1)$$
$$= 111a$$

The sum of the digits is $a + a + a = 3a$.

Thus, $\dfrac{aaa}{a + a + a} = \dfrac{111a}{3a} = \dfrac{111}{3} = 37$.

For a number with n digits the same, the number will

always be $\dfrac{m(11...1)}{mn}$ ◄——⌐ n ones.

$= \dfrac{(11...1)}{n}$ ◄——⌐ n ones.

which is a constant.

Have students present their results to the class.

Assessing the Outcome
As you make your problem solving assessment of each student, consider the following:
• Do they understand the problem?
• Do they consider a variety of strategies?
• Do they use an organized approach?
• Do they create and use diagrams effectively?
• Do they show persistence?

CHAPTER 5

● Student Text Answers

Chapter Opener   p. 239

1. R^3: 1.94×10^{32}, 1.26×10^{33}, 3.31×10^{33}, 1.19×10^{34}, 4.71×10^{35}, 2.92×10^{36};
T^2: 5.78×10^{13}, 3.76×10^{14}, 9.99×10^{14}, 3.53×10^{15}, 1.40×10^{17}, 8.65×10^{17};
$\frac{R^3}{T^2}$: 3.36×10^{18}, 3.35×10^{18}, 3.31×10^{18}, 3.37×10^{18}, 3.36×10^{18}, 3.38×10^{18}

2. **a)** They are all almost equal.
   b) 3.355×10^{18}

3. **a)** $T = \sqrt{\dfrac{R^3}{k}}$
   b) 2.65×10^9 s; 5.21×10^9 s

4. **a)** $R = \sqrt[3]{kT^2}$
   b) 5.90×10^{12} m

Getting Started   pp. 240–241

Designing With Functions

1. **a)** $y = x - 3$, $y = \frac{1}{2}x$, $y = x + 9$, $y = -\frac{1}{2}x + 6$, $y = \frac{1}{6}x + 2$, $y = -\frac{1}{6}x + 4$

2. **a)** $y = -x^2 + 4$, $y = -\frac{1}{4}x^2 + 4$, $y = x^2 + 4$, $y = \frac{1}{4}x^2 + 4$

3. **a)** $y = -4x^2 + 36$, $y = 4x^2$, $y = -2x^2 + 18$, $y = 2x^2 + 18$, $y = 18$, $y = 18x + 18$, $y = -18x + 18$

Warm Up

1. $5x + 1$
2. $3x^2 + 6x - 7$
3. $13x + 15$
4. $-x^2 - 3$
5. $3x^2 + x - 2$
6. $2x^3 - 7x^2 + 7x - 2$
7. $x - 2$
8. $3x - 2$
9. $4\sqrt{x} + 1$
10. $-8\sqrt{x} + 1$
11. $3x + 2\sqrt{x} - 1$
12. $-8x + 10\sqrt{x} - 3$
13. $x + 4\sqrt{x} + 4$
14. $9x - 6\sqrt{x} + 1$
15. $\dfrac{x + 2\sqrt{x} + 1}{x - 1}$
16. $\dfrac{2x - 5\sqrt{x} + 2}{x - 4}$
17. $y = \dfrac{x - 2}{3}$
18. $y = \dfrac{2}{x} - 2$
19. $y = \dfrac{3}{x + 5}$
20. $y = \dfrac{x - 5}{x - 2}$
21. 2
22. 4
23. 1
24. 0
25. 4
26. 1
27. 6
28. 9
29. 6
30. -2
31. $\frac{1}{2}$
32. -6
33. $-\frac{3}{2}$
34. 1
35. 11
36. $-\frac{1}{4}$

37. $x \neq 0$
38. $x \neq 1$
39. $x \neq -\frac{1}{2}$
40. $x \neq 0$
41. $x \neq \pm 3$
42. $x \neq -2, 3$

Mental Math

Evaluating Functions

1. **a)** -5 **b)** 1   **c)** 16
2. **a)** -2 **b)** -1 **c)** 0
3. **a)** 3   **b)** 9   **c)** 9
4. **a)** -1 **b)** $-\frac{2}{3}$ **c)** $-\frac{1}{4}$

Dividing Using Compatible Numbers

1. 24
2. 11
3. 9
4. 13
5. 9
6. 12
7. 12
8. 29
9. 18
10. 22
11. 19
12. 12
13. 1.2
14. 1.3
15. 1.9
16. 0.21
17. 0.09
18. 160
19. 220
20. 230
21. 410
22. **a)** m, m, m

Section 5.1   pp. 247–250

Practice (Section 5.1)

1. **a)** $(f + g)(x) = 4x + 2$ **b)** $(f - g)(x) = 2x - 10$
   c) $(fg)(x) = 3x^2 + 14x - 24$
   d) $\left(\dfrac{f}{g}\right)(x) = \dfrac{3x - 4}{x + 6}$, $x \neq -6$

2. **a)** $(f + g)(x) = 3x + 11$ **b)** $(f - g)(x) = -x + 5$
   c) $(fg)(x) = 2x^2 + 19x + 24$
   d) $\left(\dfrac{f}{g}\right)(x) = \dfrac{x + 8}{2x + 3}$, $x \neq -1.5$

3. **a)** $(f + g)(x) = 3x - 6$ **b)** $(f - g)(x) = -x - 4$
   c) $(fg)(x) = 2x^2 - 11x + 5$
   d) $\left(\dfrac{f}{g}\right)(x) = \dfrac{x - 5}{2x - 1}$, $x \neq 0.5$

4. **a)** $(f + g)(x) = 3x - 6$ **b)** $(f - g)(x) = x - 2$
   c) $(fg)(x) = 2x^2 - 8x + 8$
   d) $\left(\dfrac{f}{g}\right)(x) = 2$, $x \neq 2$

5. **a)** $(f + g)(x) = 10 - 5x$ **b)** $(f - g)(x) = 10 + 5x$
   c) $(fg)(x) = -50x$
   d) $\left(\dfrac{f}{g}\right)(x) = \dfrac{-2}{x}$, $x \neq 0$

6. **a)** $(f + g)(x) = -4x + 4$ **b)** $(f - g)(x) = 4x + 14$
   c) $(fg)(x) = -36x - 45$
   d) $\left(\dfrac{f}{g}\right)(x) = \dfrac{-9}{4x + 5}$, $x \neq -1.25$

7. a) $(f + g)(x) = 0$ **b)** $(f - g)(x) = 6x$

c) $(fg)(x) = -9x^2$

d) $\left(\dfrac{f}{g}\right)(x) = -1, x \neq 0$

8. a) $(f + g)(x) = 2x - 5$ **b)** $(f - g)(x) = -5$

c) $(fg)(x) = x^2 - 5x$

d) $\left(\dfrac{f}{g}\right)(x) = \dfrac{x - 5}{x}, x \neq 0$

9. a) 7   **b)** -7 **c)** -6 **d)** -2.5

10. a) 11   **b)** 3   **c)** 7   **d)** $\dfrac{1}{3}$

11. a) 17   **b)** 3   **c)** 22   **d)** 0.5

12. a) 1   **b)** 1   **c)** -6 **d)** -2

13. a) 19   **b)** 3   **c)** 36   **d)** 0

20. a) $(f + g)(x) = x^2 + x - 1$

b) $(f - g)(x) = x^2 - x + 1$

c) $(fg)(x) = x^3 - x^2$

d) $\left(\dfrac{f}{g}\right)(x) = \dfrac{x^2}{x - 1}, x \neq 1$

21. a) $(f + g)(x) = x^2 + x + 3$

b) $(f - g)(x) = x^2 - x - 5$

c) $(fg)(x) = x^3 + 4x^2 - x - 4$

d) $\left(\dfrac{f}{g}\right)(x) = \dfrac{x^2 - 1}{x + 4}, x \neq -4$

22. a) $(f + g)(x) = 2x^2 + 3x - 1$

b) $(f - g)(x) = -2x^2 + 3x - 1$

c) $(fg)(x) = 6x^3 - 2x^2$

d) $\left(\dfrac{f}{g}\right)(x) = \dfrac{3x - 1}{2x^2}, x \neq 0$

23. a) $(f + g)(x) = 2x^2 + 2x + 2$

b) $(f - g)(x) = 2x^2 - 2x - 8$

c) $(fg)(x) = 4x^3 + 10x^2 - 6x - 15$

d) $\left(\dfrac{f}{g}\right)(x) = \dfrac{2x^2 - 3}{2x + 5}, x \neq -2.5$

24. a) $(f + g)(x) = x^2 + x + 1$

b) $(f - g)(x) = -x^2 + x - 1$

c) $(fg)(x) = x^3 + x$

d) $\left(\dfrac{f}{g}\right)(x) = \dfrac{x}{x^2 + 1}$

25. a) $(f + g)(x) = 2x^2 - 2x$

b) $(f - g)(x) = 2x^2 - 6x$

c) $(fg)(x) = 4x^3 - 8x$

d) $\left(\dfrac{f}{g}\right)(x) = x - 2, x \neq 0$

26. a) $(f + g)(x) = x^2 - x$

b) $(f - g)(x) = x^2 - 3x + 2$

c) $(fg)(x) = x^3 - 3x^2 + 3x - 1$

d) $\left(\dfrac{f}{g}\right)(x) = x - 1, x \neq 1$

27. a) $(f + g)(x) = -2x^2 + 3x$

b) $(f - g)(x) = -2x^2 - 3x$

c) $(fg)(x) = -6x^3$

d) $\left(\dfrac{f}{g}\right)(x) = -\dfrac{2}{3}x, x \neq 0$

28. a) $(f + g)(x) = 2x^2 + 5x$

b) $(f - g)(x) = 2x^2 + x - 10$

c) $(fg)(x) = 4x^3 + 16x^2 + 5x - 25$

d) $\left(\dfrac{f}{g}\right)(x) = x - 1, x \neq -2.5$

29. a) $(f + g)(x) = x^2 - 3x + 14$

b) $(f - g)(x) = -x^2 + 3x + 10$

c) $(fg)(x) = 12x^2 - 36x + 24$

d) $\left(\dfrac{f}{g}\right)(x) = \dfrac{12}{x^2 - 3x + 2}, x \neq 1, 2$

30. a) $(f + g)(x) = 4x^2 + 2x - 2$

b) $(f - g)(x) = 4x^2 - 2x$

c) $(fg)(x) = 8x^3 - 4x^2 - 2x + 1$

d) $\left(\dfrac{f}{g}\right)(x) = 2x + 1, x \neq 0.5$

31. a) 0   **b)** 2   **c)** 0   **d)** 3

32. a) 1   **b)** 2   **c)** 0   **d)** $\dfrac{11}{6}$

33. a) -5 **b)** 9   **c)** 0   **d)** $-\dfrac{8}{9}$

34. a) 2   **b)** 2   **c)** 1   **d)** $\dfrac{1}{4}$

35. a) 3   **b)** 0   **c)** 0   **d)** 6

36. a) $(f + g)(x) = \dfrac{2x + 1}{x^2 + x}, x \neq 0, -1$

b) $(f - g)(x) = \dfrac{-1}{x^2 + x}, x \neq 0, -1$

c) $(fg)(x) = \dfrac{1}{x^2 + x}, x \neq 0, -1$

d) $\left(\dfrac{f}{g}\right)(x) = \dfrac{x}{x + 1}, x \neq 0, -1$

37. a) $(f + g)(x) = \dfrac{5x + 5}{(x + 3)(x - 2)}, x \neq -3, 2$

b) $(f - g)(x) = \dfrac{-x - 13}{(x + 3)(x - 2)}, x \neq -3, 2$

c) $(fg)(x) = \dfrac{6}{(x + 3)(x - 2)}, x \neq -3, 2$

d) $\left(\dfrac{f}{g}\right)(x) = \dfrac{2(x - 2)}{3(x + 3)}, x \neq -3, 2$

38. a) $(f + g)(x) = \dfrac{2x^2 - 5x}{(x - 1)(x - 4)}, x \neq 1, 4$

b) $(f - g)(x) = \dfrac{-3x}{(x - 1)(x - 4)}, x \neq 1, 4$

c) $(fg)(x) = \dfrac{x^2}{(x - 1)(x - 4)}, x \neq 1, 4$

d) $\left(\dfrac{f}{g}\right)(x) = \dfrac{x - 4}{x - 1}, x \neq 0, 1, 4$

39. a) $(f + g)(x) = \dfrac{3x^2 - 4x}{x^2 - 16}, x \neq \pm 4$

b) $(f - g)(x) = \dfrac{-x^2 + 12x}{x^2 - 16}, x \neq \pm 4$

c) $(fg)(x) = \dfrac{2x^2}{x^2 - 16}, x \neq \pm 4$

d) $\left(\dfrac{f}{g}\right)(x) = \dfrac{x + 4}{2(x - 4)}, x \neq 0, \pm 4$

40. a) $(f + g)(x) = 4\sqrt{x}, x \geq 0$
   b) $(f - g)(x) = 2\sqrt{x}, x \geq 0$
   c) $(fg)(x) = 3x, x \geq 0$
   d) $\left(\dfrac{f}{g}\right)(x) = 3, x > 0$

41. a) $(f + g)(x) = 3\sqrt{x} + 3, x \geq 0$
   b) $(f - g)(x) = -\sqrt{x} + 3, x \geq 0$
   c) $(fg)(x) = 2x + 6\sqrt{x}, x \geq 0$
   d) $\left(\dfrac{f}{g}\right)(x) = \dfrac{\sqrt{x} + 3}{2\sqrt{x}}, x > 0$

42. a) $(f + g)(x) = 2\sqrt{x}, x \geq 0$
   b) $(f - g)(x) = -4, x \geq 0$
   c) $(fg)(x) = x - 4, x \geq 0$
   d) $\left(\dfrac{f}{g}\right)(x) = \dfrac{\sqrt{x} - 2}{\sqrt{x} + 2}, x \geq 0$

43. a) $(f + g)(x) = 3\sqrt{x}, x \geq 0$
   b) $(f - g)(x) = \sqrt{x} - 2, x \geq 0$
   c) $(fg)(x) = 2x + \sqrt{x} - 1, x \geq 0$
   d) $\left(\dfrac{f}{g}\right)(x) = \dfrac{2\sqrt{x} - 1}{\sqrt{x} + 1}, x \geq 0$

44. a) $4x - 1$ **b)** $-7x + 18$
   c) $4x^2 - 12x + 9$

45. a) $-x^2 + 13$ **b)** $4x^2 + 3$
   c) $-2x^4 + 2x^2 + 12$

46. a) $4x^2 - 3x - 9$ **b)** $-8x^2 + x + 3$
   c) $x^2 + 6x + 9$

47. a) $-2x^2 + 2$ **b)** $2x^2 - 2$
   c) $2, x \neq \pm 1$

48. $7 - 3x - 4x^2$ **49.** $5x - 4$
50. $7x^2 - 9x - 9$ **51.** $9 - 4x + x^2$
52. $-2x + 4$ **53.** $-4x^2 - 5x + 2$

Applications and Problem Solving (Section 5.1)

54. a) $r(x) = 450, p(x) = 15x - 562.5$
   b) $t(x) = 15x - 112.5$
   c) $x \geq 37.5$; Joseph works at least a regular 37.5 h week every week.
   d) \$532.50

55. a) 3   **b)** -3 **c)** 40
   d) No. g is not defined at $x = 1$.

56. a) $w(x) = 2x + 1$ **b)** 11 m

57. a) $r(x) = 2x^2$ **b)** $c(x) = \dfrac{\pi x^2}{8}$
   c) $w(x) = \dfrac{(16 + \pi)x^2}{8}$

58. a) $C(x) = 3x^2 + 6x$
   b) x by $3x + 6$, $3x$ by $x + 2$

59. a) $B(x) = x^2$ **b)** $V(x) = 0.21x^3$
   c) 2 555 000 m³

60. a) $A(s) = s^2$ **b)** $P(s) = 4s$
   c) $s > 0$; The side length of a square must be positive.
   d) $r(s) = \dfrac{s}{4}$ **e)** 80 m, 400 m²

61. a) $B(r) = \pi r^2$ **b)** $h(r) = 3r$
   c) $V(r) = 3\pi r^3$ **d)** 3233 cm³

62. a) $A(r) = \pi r^2$ **b)** $B(r) = \dfrac{\pi r^2}{64}$
   c) $C(r) = \dfrac{63\pi r^2}{64}$ **d)** 111 cm²

63. Find $(m + n)(x)$, then find $(m + n)(3)$, or find $m(3)$ and $n(3)$, then find $m(3) + n(3)$.

64. a) 2, -2; -3, 3; The values in each pair are the negatives of each other.
   b) The values are both 0.
   c) $(f - g)(x)$ is the negative of $(g - f)(x)$.

65. $(fg)(x) = (gf)(x)$; Multiplication is commutative.
66. Either $f(x) = 0$, $g(x) = 0$, or both.

67. a) $\left(\dfrac{f}{g}\right)(x)$ has a restriction at $x = 0$, while $h(x)$ does not.
   b) $\left(\dfrac{f}{g}\right)(x)$ has a restriction at $x = 0$, while $h(x)$ does not.
   c) $\left(\dfrac{f}{g}\right)(x)$ has a restriction at $x = -9$, while $h(x)$ does not.

68. The graphs are reflections in the y-axis.
69. a) $f(x) = 2x + 3, g(x) = x^2 - 4$
   b) +A1^2+2*A1−1
   c) B: 5, 1, 7, -1; C: $-3, -3, 0, 0$; D: 2, $-2, 7, -1$

70. a) quadratic   **b)** quadratic
   c) quadratic   **d)** neither

71. Answers may vary. $f(x) = 3x + 5, g(x) = 2x - 7$
72. a) $(fg)(x) = x^2 - 4$ **b)** The domain is the same. The range for $f(x)$ and $g(x)$ is all real numbers. The range for $(fg)(x)$ is $y \geq -4$.

73. $h(x) = x - 1$
74. $h(x) = x^2 + x - 2$
75. Subtract values of $f(x)$ from values of $(f + g)(x)$ with equal x-coordinates.
76. $f(g(x)) = 6x - 4$
77. Answers may vary.

Section 5.2   pp. 256–259

Practice (Section 5.2)

1. 4   **2.** 2   **3.** 2   **4.** 5
5. 7   **6.** -3 **7.** 12   **8.** 0
9. a) {(5, 4), (4, 5), (3, 2), (2, 1), (1, 2)}
   b) {(12, 7), (7, 12), (2, -3), (0, -3), (-3, 0)}
10. a) {(2, 7), (1, 4), (0, -3), (-1, -4)}
   b) does not exist   **c)** does not exist
   d) does not exist

11. a) does not exist   **b)** does not exist
   c) does not exist   **d)** does not exist

12. 9   **13.** 10   **14.** 11   **15.** 14

16. -19 **17.** -28 **18.** 14   **19.** 12

20. $(f \circ g)(x) = 2x + 7$

21. $(g \circ f)(x) = 2x + 3$

22. $(f \circ g)(x) = 500 - 5x, (g \circ f)(x) = 100 - 5x$

23. $(f \circ g)(x) = 144 - 24x + x^2, (g \circ f)(x) = 12 - x^2$

24. $(f \circ g)(x) = 9, (g \circ f)(x) = 13$

25. $(f \circ g)(x) = 3x^2, (g \circ f)(x) = 9x^2$

26. $(f \circ g)(x) = x - 10, (g \circ f)(x) = x + 10$

27. $(f \circ g)(x) = x, (g \circ f)(x) = x$

28. $(f \circ g)(x) = -x^2, (g \circ f)(x) = x^2$

29. $(f \circ g)(x) = 9x^2 + 6x - 1, (g \circ f)(x) = 3x^2 - 5$

30. $(f \circ g)(x) = -2x^2 - 2, (g \circ f)(x) = 2x^2 - 4x + 5$

31. $(f \circ g)(x) = -4x^2 + 4x + 3, (g \circ f)(x) = -2x^2 + 7$

32. $(f \circ g)(x) = |3x|, (g \circ f)(x) = 3|x|$

33. $(f \circ g)(x) = |x|, (g \circ f)(x) = |x + 1| - 1$

34. $(f \circ g)(x) = \sqrt{x + 1}, (g \circ f)(x) = \sqrt{x} + 1$

35. $(f \circ g)(x) = 2\sqrt{2x} - 1, (g \circ f)(x) = \sqrt{4x - 2}$

36. a) 11   **b)** $(h \circ h)(x) = x + 6$

37. a) -25 **b)** $(g \circ g)(x) = 9x - 16$

38. a) 1   **b)** $(f \circ f)(x) = x^4$

39. a) 3   **b)** $(f \circ f)(x) = x$

40. 16   **41.** 12   **42.** 121

43. 27   **44.** 64   **45.** -18

46. $(h \circ k)(x) = 3(x - 1)^2$

47. $(k \circ h)(x) = (3x - 1)^2$

48. $(h \circ h)(x) = 9x$

49. $(k \circ k)(x) = (x^2 - 2x)^2$

50. does not exist

51. $(h \circ g)(x) = 3\sqrt{x} + 2, \text{R: } y \geq 2$

52. $(h \circ k)(x) = \sqrt{|x|} - 1, \text{R: } y \geq -1$

53. does not exist

54. $(f \circ g)(x) = 2 - |x - 1|, \text{R: } y \leq 2$

55. $(g \circ f)(x) = 2\sqrt{-x^2}, \text{R: } y \geq 0$

56. $(g \circ f)(x) = x + 1, \text{R: all real numbers}$

57. does not exist

58. $(f \circ g)(x) = \frac{-1}{x}, x \neq 0, (g \circ f)(x) = \frac{-1}{x}, x \neq 0$

59. $(f \circ g)(x) = \frac{1}{x^2}, x \neq 0, (g \circ f)(x) = -\frac{1}{x^2}, x \neq 0$

60. $(f \circ g)(x) = \frac{1}{5 - x}, x \neq 5, (g \circ f)(x) = \frac{3x + 5}{x + 2}, x \neq -2$

61. $(f \circ g)(x) = \frac{x}{x - 1}, x \neq 1, (g \circ f)(x) = \frac{2x}{x - 2}, x \neq 2$

62. a) $(f \circ g)(x) = \sqrt{3x}, (g \circ f)(x) = 3\sqrt{x}$
   b) f: $x \geq 0$, g: all real numbers,
     $f \circ g$: $x \geq 0, g \circ f$: $x \geq 0$
   c) $f \circ g$: $y \geq 0, g \circ f$: $y \geq 0$

63. a) $(h \circ k)(x) = \sqrt{x - 2}, (k \circ h)(x) = \sqrt{x} - 2$
   b) h: $x \geq 0$, k: all real numbers,
     $h \circ k$: $x \geq 2, k \circ h$: $x \geq 0$
   c) $h \circ k$: $y \geq 0, k \circ h$: $y \geq -2$

64. a) $(h \circ k)(x) = \sqrt{4x + 1}, (k \circ h)(x) = 4\sqrt{x} + 1$
   b) h: $x \geq -1$, k: all real numbers,
     $h \circ k$: $x \geq -\frac{1}{4}, k \circ h$: $x \geq 1$
   c) $h \circ k$: $y \geq 0, k \circ h$: $y \geq 0$

65. a) $(f \circ g)(x) = \sqrt{x^2 - 4}, (g \circ f)(x) = x - 4$
   b) f: $x \geq 2$, g: all real numbers,
     $f \circ g$: $x \geq 2, x \leq -2, g \circ f$: all real numbers
   c) $f \circ g$: $y \geq 0, g \circ f$: all real numbers

66. a) $(h \circ k)(x) = \frac{1}{5x}, (k \circ h)(x) = \frac{5}{x}$
   b) h: $x \neq 0$, k: all real numbers,
     $h \circ k$: $x \neq 0, k \circ h$: $x \neq 0$
   c) $h \circ k$: $y \neq 0, k \circ h$: $y \neq 0$

67. a) $(f \circ g)(x) = \frac{1}{x - 2}, (g \circ f)(x) = \frac{2 - x}{x - 1}$
   b) f: $x \neq 1$, g: all real numbers,
     $f \circ g$: $x \neq 2, g \circ f$: $x \neq 1$
   c) $f \circ g$: $y \neq 0, g \circ f$: $y \neq -1$

68. a) $(f \circ g)(x) = 2|x|, (g \circ f)(x) = |2x|$
   b) f: all real numbers, g: all real numbers,
     $f \circ g$: all real numbers, $g \circ f$: all real numbers
   c) $f \circ g$: $y \geq 0, g \circ f$: $y \geq 0$

Applications and Problem Solving (Section 5.2)

69. a) $s(d) = 8d$ **b)** 8000 schillings
   c) $d(s) = \frac{s}{8}$ **d)** \$125

70. a) $v_1(c) = 0.8c$ **b)** $v_2(v_1) = 0.9v_1$
   c) $v_3(v_2) = 0.9v_2, v_4(v_3) = 0.9v_3$
   d) $v_4(c) = 0.5832c$ **e)** \$37 908
   f) \$52 500

71. a) $l(x) = \sqrt{x}$ **b)** $r(l) = 3l$
   c) $r(x) = 3\sqrt{x}$
   d) 15 square units   **e)** 64 square units

72. a) $A(s) = s^2$ **b)** $s(d) = \frac{\sqrt{2}}{2}d$
   c) $A(d) = \frac{d^2}{2}$ **d)** 72 cm^2

73. a) $d(t) = 330t$ **b)** $A(d) = \pi d^2$
   c) $A(t) = 108\,900\pi t^2$ **d)** 3420 m^2
   e) 1.7 s

74. a) $s(x) = x - 250\,000$ **b)** $p(s) = 0.03s$
   c) $(p \circ s)(x) = 0.03(x - 250\,000)$
   d) The composition represents the bonus Connor gets for sales over \$250 000.
   e) \$3750

75. a) $s(c) = 625c$ **b)** $c(b) = \frac{b}{25}$
   c) $i(n) = \frac{n}{2}$ **d)** $s(i) = 250i$
   e) Israeli shekels: 1250; Norwegian krones: 2500; Belgian francs: 12 500; South Korean won: 312 500

76. a) $g(d) = 0.09d$
   b) Answers may vary. Use a cost of \$0.50. $c(g) = 0.5g$
   c) $c(d) = 0.045d$ **d)** \$38.25

e) $d(c) = \dfrac{200}{9c}$ **f)** 666.7 km

77. a) $s(p) = \dfrac{p}{3}$ **b)** $A(s) = \dfrac{\sqrt{3}}{4}s^2$

   c) $A(p) = \dfrac{\sqrt{3}}{36}p^2$ **d)** 43 cm²

78. a) $D = 0.75c$ **b)** less   **c)** 300%

79. $(f \circ f)(x) = \dfrac{2x + 1}{x + 1}$, $x \neq 0, -1$

Answers may vary for 80–83.

80. $f(x) = 3x$, $g(x) = x$
81. $f(x) = 2x$, $g(x) = x + 1$
82. $f(x) = \dfrac{1}{x}$, $g(x) = x - 4$
83. $f(x) = x^2 + 1$, $g(x) = x - 1$
84. $t = \dfrac{q(1 - r)}{1 - p}$
85. $x = -1$
86. $(f \circ g)(x): y \leq 0$, $(g \circ f)(x): y \geq 0$
87. a) $S = 0.7R$ **b)** $T = 1.15S$
   c) $T = 0.805R$ **d)** \$40.25
88. a) $j(r) = 0.8r$ **b)** $s(r) = 0.6r$
   c) $j(s(r)) = s(j(r)) = 0.48r$; The first composition means the sale discount is calculated before the employee discount. The second composition means the employee discount is calculated before the sale discount.
   d) No. See part c.
   e) $m(r) = r - 5$; $j(m(r)) = 0.8r - 4$; $m(j(r)) = 0.8r - 5$; Yes. The two composite functions are different.
89. a) $A = \pi r^2$ **b)** $r = \dfrac{C}{2\pi}$
   c) $A = \dfrac{C^2}{4\pi}$ **d)** 796 cm²
90. No. $f \circ g \neq g \circ f$ in general.
91. $g(x) = 1 - x$
92. a) always true   **b)** never true
   c) never true   **d)** sometimes true
93. Answers may vary. $f(x) = 2x - 1$, $g(x) = x^2$
94. Answers may vary. $f(x) = x$, $g(x) = x^2$
95. a) $(h \circ g \circ f)(x) = 3$ **b)** $(g \circ f \circ h)(x) = 24$
   c) $(f \circ g \circ h)(x) = 60$ **d)** $(f \circ f \circ f)(x) = 125x$
   e) $(f \circ g \circ f)(x) = 25x + 45$
   f) $(g \circ g \circ g)(x) = x + 27$
96. $f(x) = 1$ or $f(x) = x^2$
97. a) no   **b)** x: $-9, -4, -1, 0, 1, 4, 9$; $f \circ f$ is undefined for all values of x, except 0.
   c) The graph consists of only one point: (0, 0). This does not show on the graphing calculator.

Technology   p. 260

1 Reviewing Reflections

   2. $(-1, -2)$, $(4, -4)$, $(5, -1)$
   3. $(1, 2)$, $(-4, 4)$, $(-5, 1)$

4. a) The image point of (x, y) reflected in the x-axis is $(x, -y)$.
   b) The image point of (x, y) reflected in the y-axis is $(-x, y)$.
5. a) y-axis   **b)** x-axis

2 Exploring the Mapping $(x, y) \rightarrow (y, x)$

   3. $(4, 4)$ **4.** equal   **5.** 90°
   6. $1, -1$ **7.** yes   **8.** yes
   9. $(-1, -1)$; equal; 90°; $1, -1$; yes; yes
   10. the line $y = x$
   11. $(4, 1)$, $(5, -2)$, $(-4, -3)$

3 Problem Solving

   1. a) 2   **b)** 0 and undefined
   2. a) no   **b)** 1 and -1

Section 5.3   pp. 268–270

Practice (Section 5.3)

   1. $f^{-1} = \{(2, 0), (3, 1), (4, 2), (5, 3)\}$
   2. $g^{-1} = \{(-3, -1), (-2, 1), (4, 3), (0, 5), (1, 6)\}$
   3. $f^{-1} = \{(3, -2), (2, -1), (0, 0), (-2, 4)\}$; function
   4. $g^{-1} = \{(-2, 4), (1, 2), (3, 1), (-2, 0), (-3, -3)\}$; not a function

   5. $x = \dfrac{y - 2}{3}$ **6.** $x = \dfrac{12 - 3y}{2}$

   7. $x = \dfrac{3 - y}{4}$ **8.** $x = 4y - 3$

   9. $x = 2(y + 5)$ **10.** $x = \pm\sqrt{y - 3}$

   11. $f^{-1}(x) = x + 1$ **12.** $f^{-1}(x) = 2x$

   13. $f^{-1}(x) = x - 3$ **14.** $f^{-1}(x) = \dfrac{3}{4}x$

   15. $f^{-1}(x) = \dfrac{x - 1}{2}$ **16.** $f^{-1}(x) = 3x - 2$

   17. $g^{-1}(x) = \dfrac{2}{5}(x + 4)$ **18.** $h^{-1}(x) = 5(x - 1)$

   19. $f^{-1}(x) = x - 2$ **20.** $f^{-1}(x) = \dfrac{1}{4}x$

   21. $f^{-1}(x) = \dfrac{x + 2}{3}$ **22.** $f^{-1}(x) = x$

   23. $f^{-1}(x) = 3 - x$ **24.** $f^{-1}(x) = 3x + 2$

   25. $f^{-1}(x) = \dfrac{x + 5}{2}$; function

   26. $f^{-1}(x) = 4x - 3$; function
   27. $f^{-1}(x) = 4(x - 3)$; function
   28. $f^{-1}(x) = 5 - x$; function
   29. yes   **30.** yes   **31.** yes   **32.** no
   33. no   **34.** no   **35.** yes
   36. a) $f^{-1}(x) = \pm\sqrt{x + 3}$
     c) f: D: all real numbers, R: $y \geq -3$; f^{-1}: D: $x \geq 0$, R: all real numbers
   37. a) $f^{-1}(x) = \pm\sqrt{x - 1}$
     c) f: D: all real numbers, R: $y \geq 1$; f^{-1}: D: $x \geq 1$, R: all real numbers

38. a) $f^{-1}(x) = \pm\sqrt{-x}$
c) f: D: all real numbers, R: $y \le 0$; f^{-1}: D: $x \le 0$,
R: all real numbers

39. a) $f^{-1}(x) = \pm\sqrt{-x-1}$
c) f: D: all real numbers, R: $y \le -1$; f^{-1}: D: $x \le -1$,
R: all real numbers

40. a) $f^{-1}(x) = \pm\sqrt{x+2}$
c) f: D: all real numbers, R: $y \ge 0$; f^{-1}: D: $x \ge 0$,
R: all real numbers

41. a) $f^{-1}(x) = \pm\sqrt{x-1}$
c) f: D: all real numbers, R: $y \ge 0$; f^{-1}: D: $x \ge 0$,
R: all real numbers

48. no   **49.** no

50. $f^{-1}(x) = \dfrac{x+3}{2}$; D: all real numbers,
R: all real numbers

51. $f^{-1}(x) = \dfrac{2-x}{4}$; D: all real numbers,
R: all real numbers

52. $f^{-1}(x) = \dfrac{x}{3} + 2$; D: all real numbers,
R: all real numbers

53. $f^{-1}(x) = 2x + 6$; D: all real numbers,
R: all real numbers

54. $f^{-1}(x) = \pm\sqrt{x}$ **55.** $f^{-1}(x) = \pm\sqrt{x-2}$

56. $f^{-1}(x) = \pm\sqrt{x+4}$ **57.** $f^{-1}(x) = \pm\dfrac{\sqrt{2(x+1)}}{2}$

58. $f^{-1}(x) = \pm\sqrt{x+3}$ **59.** $f-1(x) = \pm\sqrt{x-2}$

60. a) $f^{-1}(x) = \sqrt{x}$
c) f: $x \ge 0$, $y \ge 0$; f^{-1}: $x \ge 0$, $y \ge 0$

61. a) $f^{-1}(x) = \sqrt{x+2}$
c) f: $x \ge 0$, $y \ge -2$; f^{-1}: $x \ge -2$, $y \ge 0$

62. a) $f^{-1}(x) = -\sqrt{x-4}$
c) f: $x \le 0$, $y \ge 4$; f^{-1}: $x \ge 4$, $y \le 0$

63. a) $f^{-1}(x) = \sqrt{3-x}$
c) f: $x \ge 0$, $y \le 3$; f^{-1}: $x \le 3$, $y \ge 0$

64. a) $f^{-1}(x) = \sqrt{x+4}$
c) f: $x \ge 4$, $y \ge 0$; f^{-1}: $x \ge 0$, $y \ge 4$

65. a) $f^{-1}(x) = -\sqrt{x-3}$
c) f: $x \le -3$, $y \ge 0$; f^{-1}: $x \ge 0$, $y \le -3$

66. $f^{-1}(x) = \dfrac{1}{x}$ **67.** $f^{-1}(x) = \dfrac{1}{x-2}$

68. $f^{-1}(x) = \dfrac{1}{x} - 3$ **69.** $f^{-1}(x) = \dfrac{1-2x}{x+1}$

70. $f^{-1}(x) = \dfrac{2x}{1-x}$ **71.** $f^{-1}(x) = \dfrac{1}{x-1}$

72. $f^{-1}(x) = x^2$; $x \ge 0$ **73.** $f^{-1}(x) = x^2 + 2$; $x \ge 2$

74. $f^{-1}(x) = 3 - x^2$; $x \le 3$ **75.** $f^{-1}(x) = \pm\sqrt{x^2 - 9}$

76. a) $f^{-1}(x) = \pm\sqrt{x-3}$
c) $x \ge 0$
e) f: D: all real numbers, R: $y \ge 3$; f^{-1}: D: $x \ge 3$,
R: all real numbers

77. a) $f^{-1}(x) = \pm\dfrac{\sqrt{2x}}{2}$
c) $x \ge 0$
e) f: D: all real numbers, R: $y \ge 0$; f^{-1}: D: $x \ge 0$,
R: all real numbers

78. a) $f^{-1}(x) = \pm\sqrt{x+1}$
c) $x \ge 0$
e) f: D: all real numbers, R: $y \ge -1$; f^{-1}: D: $x \ge -1$,
R: all real numbers

79. a) $f^{-1}(x) = \pm\sqrt{-x}$
c) $x \ge 0$
e) f: D: all real numbers, R: $y \le 0$; f^{-1}: D: $x \le 0$,
R: all real numbers

80. a) $f^{-1}(x) = \pm\sqrt{1-x}$
c) $x \ge 0$
e) f: D: all real numbers, R: $y \le 1$; f^{-1}: D: $x \le 1$,
R: all real numbers

81. a) $f^{-1}(x) = \pm\sqrt{x} + 2$
c) $x \ge 2$
e) f: D: all real numbers, R: $y \ge 0$; f^{-1}: D: $x \ge 0$,
R: all real numbers

82. a) $f^{-1}(x) = 4 \pm\sqrt{x}$
c) $x \ge 4$
e) f: D: all real numbers, R: $y \ge 0$; f^{-1}: D: $x \ge 0$,
R: all real numbers

83. a) $f^{-1}(x) = -5 \pm\sqrt{-x}$
c) $x \ge -5$
e) f: D: all real numbers, R: $y \le 0$; f^{-1}: $x \le 0$,
R: all real numbers

Applications and Problem Solving (Section 5.3)

84. a) $f(x) = 2\pi x$ **b)** $f^{-1}(x) = \dfrac{x}{2\pi}$ **c)** yes
d) The inverse finds the radius given the
circumference x.

85. a) $f(x) = 4\pi x^2$, $x \ge 0$ **b)** $f-1(x) = \sqrt{\dfrac{x}{4\pi}}$
c) $x \ge 0$, y all real numbers   **d)** yes
e) The inverse finds the radius given the surface
area x.

86. a) $a(d) = 50 + 0.15d$ **b)** $d(a) = \dfrac{a - 50}{0.15}$
c) The inverse finds the distance driven given
the total cost a.

87. a) $s(p) = 0.7p$ **b)** $p(s) = \dfrac{s}{0.7}$
c) The inverse finds the original price given
the sale price s.

88. a) $u(c) = 0.7c$ **b)** $c(u) = 1.43u$ **c)** \$214.50

89. $(63 \times 2 + 10) \div 8 - 6 = 11$

90. a) $T(d) = 35d + 20$ **b)** $d(T) = \dfrac{T - 20}{35}$
  c) 2 km
91. a) $E(s) = 400 + 0.05s$ **b)** $s(E) = 20(E - 400)$
  c) The inverse represents the sales given Jana's total weekly earnings E.
92. a) 128.6° **b)** $n(i) = \dfrac{360}{180 - i}$
  c) decagon
93. b) $t(h) = \sqrt{\dfrac{80 - h}{5}}$
  c) Yes. The domain of $h(t)$ is restricted to $t \geq 0$, so $t(h)$ is a function.
  d) the time of the fall given the height above the ground **e)** 3.3 s **f)** 4 s
94. a) $t \geq 0$ **b)** $t(d) = \sqrt{\dfrac{d^3}{830}}$
  c) Yes. Since the domain is restricted to $t \geq 0$, the inverse is a function. **d)** 35 h
95. No. $x \geq 0$
96. a) If a horizontal line crosses the original function at more than one point, the inverse is not a function. **b)** yes
97. Answers may vary. $y = x$, $y = -x$, $y = 2 - x$, $y = 7 - x$
98. a) yes
  b) No, because then f would not be a function.
99. 4 square units
100. a) Yes. It passes the vertical line test.
  b) The inverse of $y = k$ is $x = k$, a vertical line, which is not a function.
101. The original function. The inverse function undoes the original function. The inverse of the inverse undoes the undoing, returning the original function.

Computer Data Bank p. 271

1 The "Average" Vehicle

3. a) minivan; sport-utility vehicle; luxury car; pickup truck; large car; coupe; medium car; sports/sporty car; small car
  b) pickup truck; large car; luxury car; coupe and minivan; medium car; sport-utility vehicle; sports/sporty car; small car
  c) large car and minivan; coupe, luxury car, medium car, pickup truck, sports/sporty car, and sport-utility vehicle; small car
  d) luxury car; coupe and large car; sport-utility vehicle; medium car; pickup truck; minivan; sports/sporty car; small car
  e) small car, sports/sporty car, large car, medium car, coupe, luxury car, minivan, pickup truck, sport-utility vehicle
  f) small car, sports/sporty car, medium car, large car, coupe, luxury car, minivan, sport-utility vehicle, pickup truck

4. Answers will vary. For example: None of the orders are identical. The closest orders are highway and city fuel efficiency, with two pairs of vehicles switched. The heaviest is not the longest or widest, nor does it have the greatest power; but the lightest is the shortest and narrowest, and has the least horsepower. Small cars are always the least except in fuel efficiencies, where they are the greatest.

2 Acceleration Times

Answers may vary because of rounding.
  1. Answers will vary.
  2. 103
  3. 0 to 48 km/h: Buick Riviera, BMW 3-series, and Pontiac Sunfire; 0 to 96 km/h: BMW 3-series and Volvo S70/V70
  4. Answers will vary.
  5. Answers will vary.
  6. 77.7%
  7. 23.3%

3 Buying a Vehicle

  1. Chevrolet Malibu, Ford Contour, Nissan 200SX, Plymouth Breeze, Pontiac Grand Am, Toyota Avalon
  2. Answers will vary.
  3. Answers will vary.

Technology p. 273

1 Analyzing Functions

  1. a) 1; negative, positive; 0
    b) 1; positive, negative; 0
    c) 2; positive, positive; 1
    d) 2; negative, negative; 1
    e) 3; negative, positive; 2
    f) 3; positive, negative; 2
    g) 3; negative, positive; 0
    h) 3; positive, negative; 0
    i) 4; positive, positive; 3
    j) 4; negative, negative; 3
    k) 4; positive, positive; 1
    l) 5; negative, positive; 4
    m) 5; negative, positive; 0
    n) 5; positive, negative; 2
    o) 5; negative, positive; 4
  2. If the leading coefficients are opposite in sign, the end behaviours are opposite in sign.
  3. a) They are equal.
  4. a) They are opposite.
  5. a) 0, 1, 2, 3
    b) The maximum number of turning points is one less than the degree of the function. **c)** 6

Section 5.4   pp. 282–285

Practice (Section 5.4)

1. polynomial; degree 5
2. not polynomial
3. not polynomial
4. polynomial; degree 4
5. not polynomial
6. polynomial; degree 3
7. not polynomial
8. not polynomial
9. D: all real numbers, R: all real numbers, maximum: (1.4, 0.4), minimum: (2.6, −0.4), y-intercept: −6
10. D: all real numbers, R: all real numbers, minimum: (0, 2), maximum: (2, 6), y-intercept: 2
11. D: all real numbers, R: $y \geq -9$, minimums: (−2.3, −9), (1.3, −9), maximum: (−0.5, 1.6), y-intercept: 0
12. D: all real numbers, R: $y \leq 9.6$, maximums: (−0.3, 6), (3.8, 9.6), minimum: (1.7, −9.8), y-intercept: 5
13. zeros: −3, −1, 2; $f(x) \geq 0$: $-3 \leq x \leq -1$, $x \geq 2$; $f(x) < 0$: $-1 < x < 2$
14. zeros: −2, −1, 2, 3; $f(x) \geq 0$: $-2 \leq x \leq -1$, $2 \leq x \leq 3$, $f(x) < 0$: $-1 < x < 2$, $x > 3$
15. zeros: −2, −0.3; $f(x) \geq 0$: $x \leq -2$, $x \geq -0.3$; $f(x) < 0$: $-2 < x < -0.3$
16. zeros: −3, −2, 1.1, 2; $f(x) \geq 0$: $x \leq -3$, $-2 \leq x \leq 1.1$, $x \geq 2$; $f(x) < 0$: $-3 < x < -2$, $1.1 \leq x \leq 2$
17. **a)** D: all real numbers, R: $y \geq -4$
    b) −2, 0, 2   **c)** 0
    d) minimums: (−1.4, −4), (1.4, −4), maximum: (0, 0)
    e) symmetric about the y-axis
    f) positive, positive
18. **a)** D: all real numbers, R: all real numbers
    b) 0, 3   **c)** 0
    d) maximum: (0, 0), minimum: (2, −4)
    e) no symmetry   **f)** negative, positive
19. **a)** D: all real numbers, R: all real numbers
    b) −3, 0, 3   **c)** 0
    d) minimum: (−1.7, −10.4), maximum: (1.7, 10.4)
    e) symmetric in the origin
    f) positive, negative
20. **a)** D: all real numbers, R: $y \geq 0$
    b) 0   **c)** 0   **d)** minimum: (0, 0)
    e) symmetric about the y-axis
    f) positive, positive
21. **a)** D: all real numbers, R: all real numbers
    b) 0, 4   **c)** 0
    d) minimum: (0, 0), maximum: (2.7, 9.5)
    e) no symmetry
    f) positive, negative
22. **a)** D: all real numbers, R: all real numbers
    b) −0.6, 0, 3.6   **c)** 0
    d) maximum: (−0.3, 0.3), minimum: (2.3, −8.3)
    e) no symmetry   **f)** negative, positive

23. **a)** D: all real numbers, R: all real numbers
    b) −2, −1, 1   **c)** −2
    d) maximum: (−1.5, 0.6), minimum: (0.2, −2.1)
    e) no symmetry   **f)** negative, positive
24. **a)** D: all real numbers, R: all real numbers
    b) −1   **c)** 4   **d)** none
    e) no symmetry   **f)** negative, positive
25. **a)** D: all real numbers, R: $y \geq 5$
    b) none   **c)** 5   **d)** minimum; (0, 5)
    e) symmetric about the y-axis
    f) positive, positive
26. **a)** D: all real numbers, R: $y \leq 6$
    b) −1.6, 1.6   **c)** 6   **d)** maximum: (0, 6)
    e) symmetric about the y-axis
    f) negative, negative
27. **a)** D: all real numbers, R: all real numbers
    b) −2, 0, 2   **c)** 0
    d) maximum: (−1.5, 5.9), minimum: (1.5, −5.9)
    e) symmetric in the origin
    f) negative, positive
28. **a)** D: all real numbers, R: all real numbers
    b) 0, 1.6   **c)** 0
    d) minimum: (0, 0), maximum: (1.2, 3.2)
    e) no symmetry   **f)** positive, negative
29. **a)** D: all real numbers, R: all real numbers
    b) −2, 0, 2   **c)** 0
    d) maximum: (−1.2, 3.1), minimum: (1.2, −3.1)
    e) symmetric in the origin
    f) negative, positive
30. **a)** D: all real numbers, R: all real numbers
    b) −1, 1   **c)** −1
    d) maximum: (−1, 0), minimum: (0.3, −1.2)
    e) symmetric in the origin
    f) negative, positive
31. **a)** D: all real numbers, R: all real numbers
    b) −1, 2, 3   **c)** 6
    d) maximum: (0.1, 6.1), minimum: (2.5, −0.9)
    e) no symmetry   **f)** negative, positive
32. **a)** D: all real numbers, R: $y \geq -2.2$
    b) −2, −1, 1, 2   **c)** 4
    d) minimums: (−1.6, −2.3), (1.6, −2.3), maximum: (0, 4)
    e) symmetric about the y-axis
    f) positive, positive
33. **a)** D: all real numbers, R: all real numbers
    b) −1, 2, 4   **c)** 8
    d) $f(x) > 0$: $-1 < x < 2$, $x > 4$; $f(x) \leq 0$: $x \leq -1$, $2 \leq x \leq 4$
    e) no symmetry   **f)** negative, positive
34. **a)** D: all real numbers, R: all real numbers
    b) −3, −1, 2   **c)** 6
    d) $f(x) > 0$: $x < -3$, $-1 < x < 2$; $f(x) \leq 0$: $-3 \leq x \leq -1$, $x \geq 2$
    e) no symmetry   **f)** positive, negative

35. a) D: all real numbers, R: $y \geq -9$
  b) $-2, 0, 1, 3$ **c)** 0
  d) $f(x) > 0$: $x < -2, 0 < x < 1, x > 3$;
      $f(x) \leq 0$: $-2 \leq x \leq 0, 1 \leq x \leq 3$
  e) no symmetry   **f)** positive, positive
36. a) D: all real numbers, R: $y \leq 3.1$
  b) $-3, 0, 1$ **c)** 0
  d) $f(x) > 0$: $0 < x < 1$, $f(x) \leq 0$: $x \leq 0, x \geq 1$
  e) no symmetry   **f)** negative, positive
41. $x < -1, x > 3$ **42.** $-2 < x < 3$
43. $x \leq -1, x \geq -\dfrac{1}{3}$ **44.** $-\dfrac{3}{2} \leq x \leq \dfrac{1}{2}$
45. $x < -4, x > 3$ **46.** $-2 \leq x \leq 5$
47. $x \neq -2$ **48.** $x \leq \dfrac{1}{2}, x \geq 3$
49. $x < -2, -1 < x < 1$ **50.** $x \geq 0$
51. $-\dfrac{1}{2} < x < 0, x > 2$ **52.** $x \leq -1, \dfrac{1}{2} \leq x \leq 2$
53. $x < -3, 0 < x < 3$ **54.** $-1 \leq x \leq 1, x \geq 2$
55. $x \leq -3, -1 \leq x \leq 5$ **56.** $-\dfrac{3}{2} < x < 0, x > 2$

Applications and Problem Solving (Section 5.4)
57. a) $-2 \leq x \leq 1$ **b)** $x < -2, x > -1$
  c) $x < -3, -1 \leq x < 1$ **d)** $-3 \leq x \leq -2, x \geq -1$
58. a) $-2.3 \leq x \leq 1.3$ **b)** $x < -1.1, 1.2 < x < 3.9$
  c) $-1 \leq x \leq 0$ **d)** $-2 < x < -1.5, x > 1.5$
59. b) The zeros are the same, but the maximum is higher and the minimum is lower for the second function.
60. b) 17 m
61. a) $V = 2\pi r^3$ **c)** $r \geq 0, V \geq 0$
62. a) $A(x) = 14x^2$, $V(x) = 3x^3$ **b)** $\dfrac{14}{3}$
  c) $0 < x < \dfrac{14}{3}; x > \dfrac{14}{3}$
  d) For part b, find x to satisfy $A(x) - V(x) = 0$.
  For part c, find x to satisfy $A(x) - V(x) > 0$ and
  $A(x) - V(x) < 0$.
63. a) Answers may vary. $t \geq 0$
  b) 110 lm   **c)** 27°C
64. a) $V(w) = w(w + 5)(w - 2)$
  b) $w > 2$ **d)** 9000 m³   **e)** 28 m
65. a) $y = x$: 0; negative, positive; $y = x^2$: 0, positive, positive; $y = x^3$: 0; negative, positive; $y = x^4$: 0; positive, positive; $y = x^5$: 0; negative, positive; $y = x^6$: 0; positive, positive
  b) If n is even, $y = x^n$ looks like $y = x^2$. If n is odd, $y = x^n$ looks like $y = x^3$.
66. $w \geq 7, l \geq 12$
67. Add the y-values for corresponding x-values of $y = x^2 - 2$ and $y = x$ to find the y-values of $y = x + x^2 - 2$.
68. Subtract the y-values of $y = x^3 + 2$ from the y-values of $y = x$ for corresponding x-values to find the y-values of $y = x - (x^3 + 2)$.
69. a) $V(x) = x(11 - 2x)(9 - 2x)$ **c)** 1.6 cm
  d) 72 cm³ **e)** 0 cm $< x <$ 1.1 cm, 2.3 cm $< x <$ 6.6 cm

70. a) $V(x) = \dfrac{\sqrt{3}}{4}x^3$ **b)** $x > 0$
  d) 54 cm³   **e)** 3.6 cm
71. a) function   **b)** not a function
72. a) $-3 < x < -1, x > 1$ **b)** $x > 1$
  c) The condition $-3 < x < -2$ is discarded because it would result in negative values for the width and the height.
73. Answers may vary.
  $x^2 + 1 < 0, -x^2 - x - 1 > 0, x^2 + 4x + 5 \leq 0$
74. a) $x^2 - x - 2 \leq 0$ **b)** $2x^2 - 7x - 4 > 0$
75. $-7 \leq x < 5$
76. Answers may vary.

Technology   pp. 286–287

1 Verifying Equal Roots
1. The roots are $-\dfrac{1}{3}, \dfrac{2}{3}, \dfrac{2}{3}$.
2. The roots are $-1, 2, 2$.
3. The roots are $-\dfrac{4}{3}, \dfrac{8}{3}, \dfrac{8}{3}$.

2 Investigating Patterns
1. a) $k(c) = -\dfrac{4}{27}c^3$
  b) $k = -\dfrac{4}{27}$; The roots are $-\dfrac{2}{3}, -\dfrac{2}{3}, \dfrac{1}{3}$.
2. a) $-\dfrac{1}{3}, \dfrac{2}{3}, \dfrac{2}{3}; \dfrac{4}{3}, \dfrac{4}{3}, -\dfrac{2}{3}; -1, 2, 2; -\dfrac{4}{3}, \dfrac{8}{3}, \dfrac{8}{3};$
  The equal roots are -2 times the distinct root.
  The equal roots are positive if k is positive.
  The product of the roots is equal to k.
  b) $k = \dfrac{500}{27}$
  c) $\dfrac{10}{3}, \dfrac{10}{3}, -\dfrac{5}{3}$
  d) $f\left(\dfrac{10}{3}\right) = 0, f\left(-\dfrac{5}{3}\right) = 0$

Section 5.5   pp. 296–298
Practice (Section 5.5)

1. ±3	**2.** ±4	**3.** no solution
4. $-7, 11$	**5.** $-28, 12$	**6.** $-8, 14$
7. $0, -10$	**8.** $-17, 13$	**9.** no solution
10. no solution	**11.** $-3, 4$	**12.** $2, -\dfrac{10}{3}$
13. $-2, 5$	**14.** $-2, \dfrac{10}{3}$	**15.** no solution
16. $-3, 1$	**17.** $0, 2$	**18.** $-20, 16$
19. $\dfrac{9}{2}, -\dfrac{3}{2}$	**20.** $-8, 7$	**21.** -1
22. $\dfrac{3}{2}$	**23.** no solution	**24.** 1
25. 3	**26.** 2	**27.** no solution
28. $-\dfrac{1}{3}, 3$	**29.** $\dfrac{9}{2}, 9$	**30.** -1

31. 3

32. $0, \frac{12}{5}$

33. $4, -\frac{4}{3}$

34. $\frac{1}{6}$

35. 0

36. $-\frac{1}{2}, \frac{4}{3}$

37. $\frac{3}{2}, \frac{11}{4}$

38. $-4, 0$

39. no solution

40. $-\frac{7}{5}, 1$

41. $2, -2$

42. $-3 \le x \le 2$

43. no solution

44. $-\frac{7}{2}$

45. $m \ge -4$

46. $4, -\frac{2}{3}$

47. no solution

48. $-3 \le x \le 3$

49. $-2 < x < 2$

50. $x \le -5, x \ge 5$

51. $y < -5, y > 5$

52. no solution

53. $-5 < g < 5$

54. $x \le -2, x \ge 2$

55. $a < -5, a > 5$

56. $x < -4, x > 12$

57. all real numbers

58. all real numbers

59. $x < -2, x > 3$

60. $-2 < x < 8$

61. $-8 \le x \le 4$

62. $z < -3, z > 5$

63. $x < 2$

64. $x > 1$

65. $x \ge -7$

66. $x \le 2$

67. $x > \frac{5}{2}$

68. no solution

69. $-1 < x < 1$

70. $b \le -\frac{3}{2}, b \ge 1$

71. $-3 \le x \le 0$

72. $x < \frac{11}{3}, x > \frac{6}{5}$

73. $-3 \le x \le 3$

74. $x < -3, x > 5$

75. $a \ge -2$

76. $x < -6, x > 4$

77. all real numbers

78. $-\frac{1}{2} < x < \frac{17}{2}$

79. all real numbers

80. $-3 \le y \le \frac{1}{3}$

81. $x < \frac{1}{4}$

82. $x \le -5, x > 1$

83. a) D: all real numbers, R: $y \ge -4$
b) $-6, 2$ **c)** $x \le -6, x \ge 2$
d) symmetric about $x = -2$

84. a) D: all real numbers, R: $y \ge -5$
b) $-2, 8$ **c)** $x \le -2, x \ge 8$
d) symmetric about $x = 3$

85. a) D: all real numbers, R: $y \ge 1$
b) no zeros **c)** all real numbers
d) symmetric about $x = -2$

86. a) D: all real numbers, R: $y \le 0$
b) 5 **c)** $x = 5$
d) symmetric about $x = 5$

87. a) D: all real numbers, R: $y \le 3$
b) $-7, -1$ **c)** $-7 \le x \le -1$
d) symmetric about $x = -4$

88. a) D: all real numbers, R: $y \ge -2$
b) $-2.5, -0.5$ **c)** $x \le -2.5, x \ge -0.5$
d) symmetric about $x = -1.5$

89. a) D: all real numbers, R: $y \ge -3$
b) $0, 2$ **c)** $x \le 0, x \ge 2$
d) symmetric about $x = 1$

90. a) D: all real numbers, R: $y \le 4$
b) $-6, 10$ **c)** $-6 \le x \le 10$
d) symmetric about $x = 2$

91. a) D: all real numbers, R: $y \ge 0$
b) $-1, 1$ **c)** $x \ne \pm 1$
d) symmetric about the y-axis

92. a) D: all real numbers, R: $y \le 0$
b) ± 3 **c)** no values of x
d) symmetric about the y-axis

93. a) D: all real numbers, R: $y \ge -4$
b) $\pm 2\sqrt{2}, 0$ **c)** $x < -2\sqrt{2}, x > 2\sqrt{2}$
d) symmetric about the y-axis

94. a) D: all real numbers, R: $y \ge 0$
b) $0, 2$ **c)** $x \ne 0, 2$
d) symmetric about $x = 1$

95. a) D: all real numbers, R: $y \le 0$
b) $-6, 0$ **c)** no values of x
d) symmetric about $x = -3$

96. a) D: all real numbers, R: $y \ge 0$
b) $0, -3$ **c)** $x \ne -3, 0$
d) symmetric about $x = -1.5$

97. a) D: all real numbers, R: $y \ge -7$
b) $-4, 4$ **c)** $x < -4, x > 4$
d) symmetric about the y-axis

98. a) D: all real numbers, R: $y \ge 0$
b) $-3, 4$ **c)** $x \ne -3, 4$
d) symmetric about $x = 0.5$

Applications and Problem Solving (Section 5.5)

99. 06:40 to 07:20

100. $|x - 9| \le 1.4$

101. $0 \le d \le 30$

102. maximum: 152 million km; minimum: 147 million km

103. water

104. 8 m

105. $|s - 7| \le 5$

106. a) $5 < s < 11$
b) The third side must be less than the sum of the other two sides.
c) No. The solution is different.
d) Yes. The solution is the same.

107. The inverses are the reflections of the original functions in the line $y = x$.

108. They are the same.

109. $m \ge 0$

110. a) $-5 \le x \le 1$ **c)** Answers may vary.
d) Answers may vary. Test them.

111. a) $-2 \le x \le 3$ **b)** $-3 \le x \le 4$ **c)** $x \le -4$
d) $x \ge \frac{3}{2}$ **e)** $x \le -\frac{1}{2}$

112. a) $-3 \le x \le 5$ **c)** Answers may vary.
d) Answers may vary. Test them.

113. a) all real numbers **b)** $x < -1, x > 4$
c) $-3 < x < 3$ **d)** $-2 \le x \le 0$
e) $x \le -\frac{7}{2}, x \ge \frac{1}{2}$

114. a) The same for $x \geq -2$, reflection in the x-axis for $x < -2$.
b) The same for $x \geq \frac{1}{2}$, reflection in the x-axis for $x < \frac{1}{2}$.
c) the same
d) The same for $x \leq -1$, $x \geq 1$, reflection in the x-axis for $-1 < x < 1$.
e) The same for $f(x) \geq 0$, reflection in the x-axis for $f(x) < 0$.

115. $y = |2x| + 1$

116. a) $|x| < 2$ **b)** $|x - 2| \leq 2$
c) $|2x + 1| > 5$ **d)** $|x - 3| \geq 2$

117. No solution. A positive quantity cannot be less than a negative quantity.

118. a) $m = \pm 1$ **b)** $m < -1, m > 1$
c) $-1 < m < 1$

119. Sometimes true; If $f(x) = x^2$, the statement is true. If $f(x) = x + 2$, the statement is false.

120. a) $-1, 5$ **b)** $-1, 5$ **c)** same
d) Answers may vary.   **e)** $-2, 4$
f) $-5, -1$ **g)** $-5, -3$ **h)** $0, \frac{4}{3}$
i) $-2, 1$ **j)** $0, 3$

121. a) $x \leq -3, x \geq 3$ **b)** $x \leq -3, x \geq 3$
c) $-3 < x < 3$

122. a) $k < 1$ **b)** $k < -3$ **c)** $k < -4$

123. c) $-1 \leq x \leq 2$

124. Answers may vary.

Section 5.6   pp. 308–312

Practice (Section 5.6)

1. polynomial   **2.** rational   **3.** polynomial
4. other   **5.** rational   **6.** other
7. rational   **8.** other   **9.** rational
10. polynomial   **11.** rational   **12.** polynomial
13. a) $x = 1, y = 0$ **b)** D: $x \neq 1$, R: $y \neq 0$
14. a) $x = -1, y = 0$ **b)** D: $x \neq -1$, R: $y \neq 0$
15. a) $x = 3, y = 0$ **b)** D: $x \neq 3$, R: $y \neq 0$
16. a) $x = -4, y = 0$ **b)** D: $x \neq -4$, R: $y \neq 0$
17. a) $x = -3, y = 0$ **b)** D: $x \neq -3$, R: $y \neq 0$
18. a) $x = 2, y = 0$ **b)** D: $x \neq 2$, R: $y \neq 0$
19. a) $x = 5, y = 0$ **b)** D: $x \neq 5$, R: $y \neq 0$
20. a) $x = 2, y = 0$ **b)** D: $x \neq 2$, R: $y \neq 0$
21. a) $x = -2, y = 1$ **b)** D: $x \neq -2$, R: $y \neq 1$
22. a) $x = 1, y = 1$ **b)** D: $x \neq 1$, R: $y \neq 1$
23. a) $x = -3, y = 1$ **b)** D: $x \neq -3$, R: $y \neq 1$
24. a) $x = -1, y = 2$ **b)** D: $x \neq -1$, R: $y \neq 2$
25. a) $x = 2, y = 3$ **b)** D: $x \neq 2$, R: $y \neq 3$
26. a) $x = 2, y = -3$ **b)** D: $x \neq 2$, R: $y \neq -3$
27. D: $x \neq -2$, R: $y \neq -4$ **28.** D: $x \neq 3$, R: $y \neq -6$
29. D: $x \neq -1$, R: $y \neq 0$ **30.** D: $x \neq 2$, R: $y \neq 0$
31. D: $x \neq 3$, R: $y \neq 5$ **32.** D: $x \neq -2$, R: $y \neq -1$

33. a) $x = 0, y = 1$ **b)** D: $x \neq 0$, R: $y \neq 1$
34. a) $x = 0, y = -2$ **b)** D: $x \neq 0$, R: $y \neq -2$
35. a) $x = 1, y = 0$ **b)** D: $x \neq 1$, R: $y \neq 0$
36. a) $x = 1, y = 0$ **b)** D: $x \neq 1$, R: $y \neq 0$
37. a) $x = 1, y = 3$ **b)** D: $x \neq 1$, R: $y \neq 3$
38. a) $x = 1, y = -1$ **b)** D: $x \neq 1$, R: $y \neq -1$
39. a) $x = -1, y = 2$ **b)** D: $x \neq -1$, R: $y \neq 2$
40. a) $x = -2, y = 2$ **b)** D: $x \neq -2$, R: $y \neq 2$
41. a) $x = \frac{3}{2}, y = \frac{1}{2}$ **b)** D: $x \neq \frac{3}{2}$, R: $y \neq \frac{1}{2}$
42. a) $x = 2, y = -2$ **b)** D: $x \neq 2$, R: $y \neq -2$
43. a) -3 **b)** $x = -3$
44. a) 5 **b)** $x = 5$
45. a) ± 2 **b)** $x = \pm 2$
46. a) ± 1 **b)** $x = \pm 1$
47. a) $0, -2$ **b)** $x = 0, x = -2$
48. a) $-1, 2$ **b)** $x = -1, x = 2$
49. $-3, 2$ **50.** -1 **51.** $-2, 5$
52. 0 **53.** no solution   **54.** 0
55. ± 2 **56.** $5, 6$ **57.** 1
58. all real numbers except $n = 1$
59. $\dfrac{-1 \pm \sqrt{17}}{2}$ **60.** $\dfrac{3}{2}$ **61.** $-\dfrac{5}{3}, 2$
62. $\dfrac{2}{5}$ **63.** $-3, -1$ **64.** $-2, \dfrac{9}{2}$
65. -3 **66.** -3 **67.** -1
68. no solution   **69.** no solution
70. all real numbers except $x = -1, -\dfrac{1}{2}$
71. $-1, 2$ **72.** $-2.7, 0.7$ **73.** $-1.5, 9.5$
74. $-4.7, -1.3$ **75.** $0.2, 1.8$ **76.** $-0.1, 0.8$
77. $x > 5, x < 0$ **78.** $x > 1, x \leq -4$
79. $-5 < y < 3$ **80.** $x < 2, x \geq 7$
81. $x < -3, x > -2$ **82.** $-6 \leq m < -1$
83. $x < -1$ **84.** $x > 5$
85. $a < -3, 1 < a < 5$ **86.** $-2 < x < 1, x > 4$
87. $-4 \leq x \leq -2, x > 3$ **88.** $-1 < n \leq 6, n < -1$
89. $0 < x \leq 2$ **90.** $x < -2, -1 < x < 0$
91. $\dfrac{1}{2} < k \leq \dfrac{7}{11}, k > 1$ **92.** $-5 \leq x < 1$
93. $x > \dfrac{2}{3}$ **94.** $c > 1, -4 < c < -3$
95. $w < -1$ **96.** $x \leq -1, 2 < x \leq 4$

Applications and Problem Solving (Section 5.6)

97. a) $x = -3, x = 2, y = 0$
b) D: $x \neq -3, 2$, R: $y \neq 0$
98. a) $x = -4, x = -2, y = 0$
b) D: $x \neq -4, -2$, R: $y \neq 0$
99. a) $x = \pm \dfrac{3}{2}, y = 0$
b) D: $x \neq \pm \dfrac{3}{2}$, R: $y \neq 0$
100. a) $x = -4, x = 1, y = 0$
b) D: $x \neq -4, 1$, R: $y \neq 0$
101. a) $x = -3, y = 0$
b) D: $x \neq -3$, R: $y \neq 0$

102. a) $x = \frac{1}{2}$, $x = 3$, $y = 0$

b) D: $x \neq \frac{1}{2}$, 3, R: $y \neq 0$

103. $-4 \leq x < -1$, $-1 < x < 7$
104. $x \leq 3$, $4 \leq x < 5$, $x > 6$
105. $-8 < x < 0$, $1 < x < 4$
106. $x < -4$, $-1 < x < 0$, $x > 2$
107. $x < 0$, $x > 1$
108. $x < 0$, $x > 3$
109. 14
110. $\pm\sqrt{2}$
111. a) Laura: 75 km/h, Mariko: 80 km/h **b)** 08:00
112. Gersh: 6 km/h, Jason: 10 km/h
113. 125 g   **114.** 62 km/h
115. 6.9 km/h   **116.** 2 units
117. a) not rational   **b)** rational
118. a) $R = \dfrac{R_1 R_2}{R_1 + R_2}$ **b)** $R_1 = \dfrac{RR_2}{R_2 - R}$

c) $R_2 = \dfrac{RR_1}{R_1 - R}$ **d)** 24 Ω

119. 1, 2   **120.** Answers may vary.
121. a) $-6, -1$ **b)** $-3, -2, 1$ **c)** $\pm 1, \pm 2$
122. $x = \dfrac{y}{yz - 1}$

123. $x = \dfrac{c + d}{2}$; or if $c = d$, $x < c$ or $x > c$

124. a) $-1 < x < 3$ **b)** Answers may vary.
c) Answers may vary. Test them.
125. a) $x < -4$, $x \geq 2$ **b)** $x < 1$, $2 < x \leq 4$
c) $x < -2$, $-1 < x < 2$, $x > 4$

d) $x < \dfrac{1}{2}$

e) $x < -1$, $-\dfrac{1}{2} \leq x < 0$, $x \geq 2$

126. a) $f = \dfrac{106\,330}{343 \pm u}$

b) The $+$ sign is used when the sound is moving toward you, and the $-$ sign is used when the sound is moving away from you.
c) 298 Hz; 323 Hz
127. b) $f(x)$ is undefined at $x = -1$ and $x = -2$.
128. $m = 2$, $n = 1$
129. Answers may vary. $f(x) = \dfrac{5x}{x - 2}$

Technology p. 313

1 Exploring Rational Functions

1. asymptotes: $x = \pm 2$, $y = 1$; D: $x \neq \pm 2$,
R: $y > 1$, $y \leq 0$; zeros: 0, symmetry: about the y-axis
2. asymptotes: $x = 0$, $y = 1$; D: $x \neq 0$, R: $y < 1$;
zeros: ± 2, symmetry: about the y-axis
3. asymptotes: $x = -1$, $y = 1$; D: $x \neq -1$, R: $y \geq 0$;
zeros: 0, symmetry: none
4. asymptotes: $y = 1$; D: all real numbers,
R: $0 \leq y < 1$; zeros: 0, symmetry: about the y-axis

5. asymptotes: $x = 0$, $y = 1$; D: $x \neq 0$, R: $y > 1$;
zeros: none, symmetry: about the y-axis
6. asymptotes: $x = \pm 3$, $y = 1$; D: $x \neq \pm 3$, R: $y > 1$,
$y \leq 0$; zeros: 0, symmetry: about the y-axis
7. asymptotes: $x = 0$, $y = 1$; D: $x \neq 0$, R: $y < 1$;
zeros: ± 1, symmetry: about the y-axis
8. asymptotes: $x = \pm 1$, $y = 1$; D: $x \neq \pm 1$, R: $y > 1$,
$y \leq -1$; zeros: none, symmetry: about the y-axis
9. asymptotes: $y = 1$; D: all real numbers,
R: $-1 \leq y < 1$; zeros: ± 1, symmetry: about the
y-axis
10. asymptotes: $x = 0$, $y = 1$; D: $x \neq 0$, R: $y \geq 0$;
zeros: -2, symmetry: none
11. asymptotes: $x = 1$, $y = 1$; D: $x \neq 1$, R: $y < \dfrac{4}{3}$;
zeros: ± 2, symmetry: none
12. asymptotes: $x = 1$, $x = 3$, $y = 1$; D: $x \neq 1$, 3,
R: $y \geq 0$, $y \leq -3$; zeros: 0, symmetry: none

13. $y = \dfrac{x^2 - 1}{x^2 - 1}$ has point discontinuities at ± 1.

2 Exploring Transformations of Rational Functions

2. It moves up or down the graph.
3. a) reflection in the x-axis
b) reflection in the line $y = 2$
c) reflection in the line $y = -4$

Section 5.7 pp. 323–327

Practice (Section 5.7)

1. D: $x \geq -2$, R: $y \geq 0$ **2.** D: $x \leq 3$, R: $y \geq 0$
3. D: $x \geq -\dfrac{1}{2}$, R: $y \geq 0$ **4.** D: $x \leq \dfrac{3}{2}$, R: $y \geq 0$
5. D: $x \geq -8$, R: $y \geq 0$ **6.** D: $x \geq 0$, R: $y \geq 0$
7. D: $x \geq 1$, R: $y \geq 0$ **8.** D: $x \leq -1$, R: $y \geq 0$
9. D: $x \geq -3$, R: $y \leq 0$ **10.** D: $x \leq 2$, R: $y \leq 0$
11. D: $x \geq -3$, R: $y \geq 1$ **12.** D: $x \geq -1$, R: $y \geq -5$
13. D: $x \geq 4$, R: $y \geq -2$ **14.** D: $x \leq 2$, R: $y \geq -3$
15. D: $x \geq 0$, R: $y \geq -4$ **16.** D: $x \geq -\dfrac{5}{2}$, R: $y \geq 2$
17. D: $x \leq 1$, R: $y \geq 3$ **18.** D: $x \geq -2$, R: $y \leq 2$
19. D: $x \leq 5$, R: $y \leq 1$ **20.** D: $x \geq 0$, R: $y \leq -3$
21. D: $x \geq \dfrac{1}{2}$, R: $y \leq -1$ **22.** D: $x \geq 2$, R: $y \leq 5$

23. 25   **24.** 4   **25.** -3 **26.** 3
27. -13 **28.** no solution   **29.** 4
30. 0   **31.** no solution   **32.** 9
33. 6   **34.** no solution   **35.** 26
36. -1 **37.** no solution   **38.** 2
39. 7   **40.** -1 **41.** 2   **42.** $-\dfrac{1}{2}$
43. 5   **44.** $\dfrac{3}{2}$ **45.** 21
46. no solution   **47.** 8
48. no solution   **49.** no solution
50. 3   **51.** 2   **52.** 12   **53.** 1
54. 5   **55.** -2 **56.** 1
57. no solution

58. 9, 21   **59.** 2   **60.** 2.4

61. -1.3 **62.** -0.5 **63.** 4.6

64. 3.6   **65.** -5.5 **66.** 0.9

67. 9.8   **68.** $-1 \le x < 8$ **69.** $x \le -2$

70. $-\frac{5}{2} \le x \le 2$ **71.** $x \le \frac{4}{3}$ **72.** $0 \le x \le 3.5$

73. $1 < x \le 4$ **74.** $3 \le n \le 9$ **75.** $t \ge 2$

76. no solution   **77.** $0 \le x \le 2$ **78.** $x \le 1$

79. $x > 5$ **80.** $x < -1$ **81.** $d \le 3$

82. $\frac{1}{2} \le x < 5$ **83.** $x \ge \frac{1}{2}$ **84.** $1 < x \le 5$

85. $0 \le c < 4$ **86.** $x \ge 5$ **87.** $1 \le x < 5$

88. $0 \le x \le 1$ **89.** $0 < y < 9$ **90.** $0 \le x \le 1$

91. $0 \le x < 2, x > 4$ **92.** $0 \le n < 3, x \ge 4$

93. $0 \le x < 2$ **94.** $0 \le x < 2$

95. $x > -2$ **96.** no solution

97. $m > -1$ **98.** $-3 < x < -2$

99. $-2 < x \le -1$ **100.** $t > 2$ **101.** $x \ge 3$

Applications and Problem Solving (Section 5.7)

102. **a)** rational   **b)** rational   **c)** radical
     d) rational   **e)** radical   **f)** rational

103. **a)** $-2 \le x < 2.9$ **b)** $x < -6.8$
     c) $x \ge 4.2$ **d)** $x \ge 16.8$

104. **a)** D: $x \le -2, x \ge 2$, R: $y \ge 0$
     b) D: $x \le -2, x \ge 2$, R: $y \le 0$
     c) D: $-3 \le x \le 3$, R: $0 \le y \le 3$
     d) D: $-3 \le x \le 3$, R: $-3 \le y \le 0$

105. **a)** 9   **b)** 6   **c)** 3

106. They are reflections of each other in the x-axis.

107. **a)** 3.7 cm   **b)** 137 cm²

108. **a)** $y = x^2, x \ge 0$; function
     b) $y = x^2 - 2, x \ge 0$; function
     c) $y = (x - 2)^2 + 1, x \ge 2$; function

109. **a)** 0   **b)** 2   **c)** 0, 2

110. C(7, 13), D(1, 13) or C(7, -11), D(1, -11)

111. C(2, 11) or C(2, -5)

112. **a)** 12   **b)** 45

113. P(12, 0) or P(-12, 0)

114. P(0, 8) or P(0, -8)

115. **a)** 5 to the left, 5 to the right
     b) 3 up, 3 down
     c) 5 left, 3 up and 5 left, 3 down
     d) 5 right, 3 up and 5 right, 3 down

116. The transformations have the same effect.

117. $\frac{19}{6}$ **118.** 147

119. **a)** 1 s   **b)** 4 m

120. $\sqrt{n - 4} \ge 5, n \ge 29$

121. **a)** $A = \frac{\sqrt{3}}{4} s^2$ **b)** $s = \frac{2\sqrt{A}}{\sqrt[4]{3}}$
     c) 24 cm

122. $\sqrt{n + 2} \le 10, -2 \le n \le 98$

123. $a = b$ or $a = -b$

124. Squaring both sides of the equation or inequality can introduce extraneous solutions.

125. **a)** $d = \sqrt{L^2 - 40\ 000}$
     b) $L > 200$ **d)** 150 m; the observer is 250 m horizontally from the balloon.

126. **b)** Answers may vary. $d \ge 5$ **c)** 59 m

127. **b)** 1280 km/h   **c)** 5°C

128. **b)** Answers may vary. $0 \le a \le 20, 0 \le d \le 450$
     c) 316 km   **d)** Answers may vary.

129. 78 m

130. **a)** 3   **b)** 16

131. **a)** $1 \le x < 5$ **c)** Answers may vary.
     d) Answers may vary. Test them.

132. **a)** $x \ge -1$ **b)** $3 \le x \le 7$ **c)** $-1 \le x < 2$
     d) $x \le -3$ **e)** $-\frac{5}{4} < x < 5$ **f)** $x \ge 1$
     g) $0 \le x < 1$ **h)** $x \ge -4$
     i) $-2 \le x < 2, x \ge 3$

133. **a)** $b = \sqrt{w^2 - 2wh}$
     b) $A = \frac{1}{2}\sqrt{w^2 - 2wh}$
     c) $A = \frac{1}{2}\sqrt{100 - 2b}$
     e) $0 < b < 5, 0 < A < 9.6$ **f)** 3.3 cm
     g) 9.6 cm²

134. **a)** $\sqrt{x - 2} < 3$ **b)** $\sqrt{2 - x} < 3$

135. $-2 \le x < 1, x > 1$

136. 0.25   **137.** 10

138. **a)** Let $y = \sqrt{x}$. Rewrite the expression as $y^2 + 2y + 1$ and factor: $(y + 1)^2$. Substitute $y = \sqrt{x}$: $(\sqrt{x} + 1)^2$.
     b) 1   **c)** 4, 9
     d) 16   **e)** no solution

139. Answers may vary.

140. **a)** 5   **b)** 0
     c) $x > 1$ **d)** $x \ge -10$

141. **a)** Answers may vary.
     b) 2   **c)** 3   **d)** 3

Connecting Math and Astronomy
pp. 328–329

1 The Earth and the Moon

1. 9.8 N

2. $W = 9.8m$

3. 588 N

4. 1.6 N

5. $W = 1.6m$

6. 96 N

7. 5.1 m

8. **a)** 11 200 m/s   **b)** 40 300 km/h

9. **a)** 2400 m/s   **b)** 8500 km/h

10. It would increase.

11. 6370 km

2 Planets and the Sun

1. Mars: 3.7 N, Jupiter: 24.5 N, Saturn: 10.4 N, Pluto: 0.6 N, Sun: 274.1 N

2. a) 0.4 m   **b)** 17.4 m

3. no

4. a) 5000 m/s   **b)** 35 500 m/s

5. a) $\sqrt{\dfrac{Gm_1m_2}{F}}$ **b)** 24 800 km

6. a) $m_1 = \dfrac{Fd^2}{Gm^2}$ **b)** 3.3×10^{23} kg

7. 3.4×10^{17} N

Review pp. 330–331

1. a) $(f+g)(x) = x + 8$
   b) $(f-g)(x) = 3x + 2$
   c) $(fg)(x) = -2x^2 + x + 15$
   d) $\left(\dfrac{f}{g}\right)(x) = \dfrac{2x+5}{3-x}, x \neq 3$

2. a) $(f+g)(x) = 9x^2 + 3x - 2$
   b) $(f-g)(x) = 9x^2 - 3x$
   c) $(fg)(x) = 27x^3 - 9x^2 - 3x + 1$
   d) $\left(\dfrac{f}{g}\right)(x) = 3x + 1, x \neq \dfrac{1}{3}$

3. a) $(f+g)(x) = \dfrac{x^2 + 3x - 6}{x(x-2)}$
   b) $(f-g)(x) = \dfrac{x^2 - 3x + 6}{x(x-2)}$
   c) $(fg)(x) = \dfrac{3}{x-2}$
   d) $\left(\dfrac{f}{g}\right)(x) = \dfrac{x^2}{3(x-2)}, x \neq 0, 2$

4. a) $(f+g)(x) = 3 - \sqrt{x}, x \geq 0$
   b) $(f-g)(x) = -1 - 3\sqrt{x}, x \geq 0$
   c) $(fg)(x) = -2x - 3\sqrt{x} + 2, x \geq 0$
   d) $\left(\dfrac{f}{g}\right)(x) = \dfrac{1 - 2\sqrt{x}}{\sqrt{x} + 2}, x \geq 0$

5. a) 4   **b)** 9   **c)** -2 **d)** 0

6. a) 0   **b)** -5 **c)** 36   **d)** 6

7. a) $x^2 - 6x + 8$ **b)** $18 - 24x + 8x^2$
   c) $2x^3 - x^2 - 2x + 1$

9. $\{(-2, 0), (-4, -1), (6, 4), (8, 5)\}$

10. does not exist   **11.** does not exist

12. does not exist

13. 36   **14.** -4 **15.** 0   **16.** 16

17. $(f \circ g)(x) = 5 - 2x^2$

18. $(g \circ f)(x) = -4x^2 + 4x + 2$

19. $(f \circ f)(x) = 4x - 3$

20. $(g \circ g)(x) = -x^4 + 6x^2 - 6$

21. a) $(f \circ g)(x) = \sqrt{3x + 2}$
   b) $(g \circ f)(x) = 3\sqrt{x + 2}$
   c) f: D: $x \geq -2$, R: $y \geq 0$, g: D: all real numbers, R: all real numbers, $f \circ g$: D: $x \geq -\dfrac{2}{3}$, R: $y \geq 0$, $g \circ f$: D: $x \geq -2$, R: $y \geq 0$

22. a) $(f \circ g)(x) = 3|x| + 1$ **b)** $(g \circ f)(x) = |3x + 1|$
   c) f: D: all real numbers, R: all real numbers, g: D: all real numbers, R: $y \geq 0$, $f \circ g$: D: all real numbers, R: $y \geq 1$, $g \circ f$: D: all real numbers, R: $y \geq 0$

23. $(h \circ k)(x) = \dfrac{1}{1 - x^2}, x \neq 0, \pm 1;$
   $(k \circ h)(x) = \left(\dfrac{x-1}{x}\right)^2, x \neq 0, 1$

24. b) yes

25. $f^{-1}(x) = \dfrac{x - 2}{4}$

26. $f^{-1}(x) = \pm\sqrt{x + 5}$

27. $k^{-1}(x) = \pm\sqrt{x} - 7$

28. $g^{-1}(x) = 3 - \dfrac{2}{x}$

29. yes   **30.** no

31. a) $f^{-1}(x) = \pm\sqrt{3 - x}$ **c)** $x \geq 0$
   e) f: D: all real numbers, R: $y \leq 3$, f^{-1}: D: $x \leq 3$, R: $y \geq 0$

32. no   **33.** no   **34.** no

35. Yes, 5.

36. a) D: all real numbers, R: $y \geq -16$
   b) zeros: $\pm 1, \pm 3$, y-intercept: 9
   c) minimums: $(-2.2, -16), (2.2, -16)$, maximum: $(0, 9)$
   d) $f(x) > 0$: $x < -3, -1 < x < 1, x > 3$; $f(x) < 0$: $-3 < x < -1, 1 < x < 3$
   e) symmetric about the y-axis; positive, positive

37. a) D: all real numbers, R: all real numbers
   b) zeros: $-1.1, -1, 0.8$, y-intercept: -2
   c) maximum: $(-1.1, 0.0)$, maximum: $(0, -2)$
   d) $f(x) > 0$: $-1.1 < x < -1, x > 0.8$; $f(x) < 0$: $x < -1.1, -1 < x < 0.8$
   e) no symmetry; negative, positive

38. a) D: all real numbers, R: $y \geq -1$
   b) zeros: $0, \pm 1, 2$; y-intercept: 0
   c) minimums: $(-0.6, -1), (1.6, -1)$, maximum: $(0.5, 0.6)$
   d) $f(x) > 0$: $x < -1, 0 < x < 1, x > 2$; $f(x) < 0$: $-1 < x < 0, 1 < x < 2$
   e) symmetric about $x = 0.5$; positive, positive

39. a) D: all real numbers, R: all real numbers
   b) zeros: $-1, 1.6, -0.6$, y-intercept: 1
   c) minimum: $(-0.8, -0.1)$, maximum: $(0.8, 2.1)$
   d) $f(x) > 0$: $x < -1, -0.6 < x < 1.6$; $f(x) < 0$: $-1 < x < -0.6, x > 1.6$
   e) no symmetry; positive, negative

40. $x < -3, x > 0$

41. $x < -1$ **42.** $-3, 11$ **43.** 1

44. $\dfrac{2}{3}, 6$ **45.** 5, -3

46. $x < -4, x > 10$

47. $q \leq -\frac{10}{3}, q \geq 2$ **48.** $x > \frac{3}{2}$

49. $-2 \leq d \leq 2$

50. a) D: all real numbers, R: $y \geq -2$
b) 1, 5   **c)** $x \leq 1, x \geq 5$
d) symmetric about $x = 3$

51. a) D: all real numbers, R: $y \leq 5$
b) $-6, 4$ **c)** $-6 \leq x \leq 4$
d) symmetric about $x = -1$

52. a) D: all real numbers, R: $y \geq -3$
b) ± 2 **c)** $x \leq -2, x \geq 2$
d) symmetric about y-axis

53. a) D: all real numbers, R: $y \geq -2$
b) $\pm\sqrt{2}, \pm\sqrt{6}$
c) $x \leq -\sqrt{6}, -\sqrt{2} \leq x \leq \sqrt{2}, x \geq \sqrt{6}$
d) symmetric about the y-axis

54. a) $x = 3, y = 0$ **b)** D: $x \neq 3$, R: $y \neq 0$
55. a) $x = -4, y = 1$ **b)** D: $x \neq -4$, R: $y \neq 1$
56. a) none   **b)** D: $m \neq 3$, R: $y \neq 6$
57. a) none   **b)** D: $p \neq -2$, R: $y \neq -6$
58. $x = -1, y = 2$, D: $x \neq -1$, R: $y \neq 2$
59. a) 0, 4   **b)** $x = 0, x = 4$
60. 3   **61.** 0, 7
62. $n < -3, n \geq 8$
63. $-4 < x < 3, x > 24$
64. D: $x \geq -2$, R: $y \geq 4$
65. D: $x \geq 1$, R: $y \leq 3$
66. 3   **67.** -2 **68.** 2   **69.** $-\frac{3}{4}$
70. $d > 2$ **71.** $-1 \leq n \leq 1$
72. $x \geq 8$ **73.** $w > -2$

Exploring Math p. 331

1. b) Answers may vary.
2. Answers may vary.

Chapter Check p. 332

1. a) $(f + g)(x) = 3x + 1$
b) $(f - g)(x) = 5x - 3$
c) $(fg)(x) = -4x^2 + 9x - 2$
d) $\left(\frac{f}{g}\right)(x) = \frac{4x - 1}{2 - x}, x \neq 0$

2. a) $(f + g)(x) = x^2 + 9x + 20$
b) $(f - g)(x) = x^2 + 7x + 10$
c) $(fg)(x) = x^3 + 13x^2 + 55x + 75$
d) $\left(\frac{f}{g}\right)(x) = x + 3, x \neq -5$

3. a) $(f + g)(x) = \frac{x^2 + 4x - 2}{(x + 2)(x - 1)}, x \neq -2, 1$
b) $(f - g)(x) = \frac{-2 - x^2}{(x + 2)(x - 1)}, x \neq -2, 1$
c) $(fg)(x) = \frac{2x}{(x + 2)(x - 1)}, x \neq -2, 1$
d) $\left(\frac{f}{g}\right)(x) = \frac{2(x - 1)}{x(x + 2)}$

4. a) $(f + g)(x) = 4\sqrt{x} + 2, x \geq 0$
b) $(f - g)(x) = -2\sqrt{x} + 4, x \geq 0$
c) $(fg)(x) = 3x + 8\sqrt{x} - 3, x \geq 0$
d) $\left(\frac{f}{g}\right)(x) = \frac{3x + 10\sqrt{x} + 3}{9x - 1}, x \geq 0, x \neq \frac{1}{9}$

5. a) -5 **b)** 1   **c)** 30   **d)** $-\frac{3}{4}$
6. a) -8 **b)** 7   **c)** -36 **d)** -4
7. $65 - 2x^2 - 3x$ **8.** $\frac{5 - x}{x + 5}, x \neq \pm 5$
9. 1   **10.** -16 **11.** 225
12. $(h \circ k)(x) = 3 - x^2$
13. $(k \circ h)(x) = x^2 - 10x + 27$
14. $(h \circ h)(x) = x$
15. $(k \circ k)(x) = x^4 + 4x^2 + 6$
16. a) $(f \circ g)(x) = \sqrt{3x} - 2$
b) $(g \circ f)(x) = \sqrt{3(x - 2)}$
c) f: D: all real numbers, R: all real numbers;
g: D: $x \geq 0$, R: $y \geq 0$; $f \circ g$: D: $x \geq 0$, R: $y \geq -2$;
$g \circ f$: D: $x \geq 2$, R: $y \geq 0$
17. a) $(f \circ g)(x) = |\sqrt{x} - 1|$
b) $(g \circ f)(x) = \sqrt{|x - 1|}$
c) f: D: all real numbers, R: $y \geq 0$;
g: D: $x \geq 0$, R: $y \geq 0$; $f \circ g$: D: $x \geq 0$, R: $y \geq 0$;
$g \circ f$: D: all real numbers, R: $y \geq 0$
18. $(f \circ g)(x) = \frac{1}{x + 3}, x \neq -3$; $(g \circ f)(x) = \frac{1}{x} + 3, x \neq 0$
19. a) $f^{-1}(x) = x - \frac{2}{5}$ **b)** yes
20. a) $h^{-1}(x) = \pm\frac{\sqrt{3(x + 2)}}{3}$ **b)** no
21. no   **22.** yes
23. a) D: all real numbers, R: all real numbers
b) zeros: $-1, \frac{1}{2}, 3$, y-intercept: 3
c) maximum: $(-0.3, 3.7)$, minimum: $(2, -9)$
d) $f(x) > 0$: $-1 < x < \frac{1}{2}, x > 3$;
$f(x) < 0$: $x < -1, \frac{1}{2} < x < 3$
e) no symmetry; negative, positive
24. a) D: all real numbers, R: $y \geq 0$
b) zeros: ± 2, y-intercept: 16
c) minimums: $(-2, 0), (2, 0)$, maximum: $(0, 16)$
d) $f(x) > 0$: all real numbers except $x = \pm 2$;
$f(x) < 0$: no values of x
e) symmetric about the y-axis; positive, positive
25. $-3 \leq x \leq -\frac{3}{2}, 0 \leq x \leq 1$
26. $x < -\sqrt{3}, 0 < x < \sqrt{3}$
27. a) D: all real numbers, R: $y \leq 3$
b) 1, 7   **c)** $1 \leq x \leq 7$
d) symmetric about $x = 4$

28. a) D: all real numbers, R: $y \geq -2$

b) $\pm\sqrt{7}, \pm\sqrt{11}$

c) $x \leq -\sqrt{11}, -\sqrt{7} \leq x \leq \sqrt{7}, x \geq \sqrt{11}$

d) symmetric about the y-axis

29. a) $x = 2, y = 0$ **b)** D: $x \neq 2$, R: $y \neq 0$

30. a) none   **b)** D: $x \neq 1$, R: $y \neq 7$

31. a) -3 **b)** $x = -3$

32. 9   **33.** 1   **34.** $-\dfrac{5}{2}, \dfrac{1}{4}$ **35.** $-5, 2$

36. 4   **37.** ± 1 **38.** 7

39. 4   **40.** 0   **41.** 1

42. $b < -2, b > 8$ **43.** $-1 < g < 5$

44. $x \geq 1$ **45.** $-6 \leq e \leq -1$

46. $-3 \leq v < 3$ **47.** $-3 < b < 0, b > 2$

48. $q > 5$ **49.** $x \geq 1$

Using the Strategies   p. 333

1. Cut 4 rods into lengths of 5, 5, 3. Cut 5 rods into lengths of 4, 4, 5. Cut 3 rods into lengths of 3, 3, 3, 4.

2. Beth Baker had juice, lamb, and cheesecake. Barbara Brown had salmon.

3. $S = 4, R = -2$ or 6, $T = -6$ or 2

4. **a)** 37   **b)** Answers may vary.
   c) Yes. Answers may vary.

5. 24 km

6. 7

7. Use the initial 4 tires for 12 000 km each, label the remaining 5 tires with the letters A, B, C, D, and E. Rotate the tires as follows, using each group for 3000 km: A, B, C, D; B, C, D, E; C, D, E, A; D, E, A, B; E, A, B, C

8. 7

9. no

10. 12

Data Bank

1. Winnipeg to Regina: 95 km/h; Regina to Saskatoon: 65 km/h

CHAPTER 6

Reasoning

Chapter Introduction

Chapter Materials

graphing calculators, playing cards, straightedges, scissors, overhead projector, overhead graphing calculator

Chapter Concepts

Chapter 6 reviews or introduces
- defining and using inductive reasoning to make conjectures
- defining counterexamples and using them to show conjectures are false
- defining deductive reasoning and using it to prove conclusions
- defining compound statements and proving them true
- understanding and using Venn diagrams to decide if a compound statement is true/false
- graphing compound statements on number lines
- interpreting and drawing Venn diagrams
- understanding the concepts of conditional statements, converses, biconditional statements, and contrapositive statements
- writing conditional, converse, and contrapositive statements
- determining the truth of statements
- using reasoning to solve problems
- understanding the methods of direct proof and indirect proof
- writing the steps of an indirect proof
- defining and proving a converse of a proof

Teaching Suggestions

Read with the class the opening paragraph on student text page 335.

Ensure that the class knows how the graph is constructed. Ask:

Which age group gets the least amount of sleep? the most amount of sleep?

Have small groups of students study the graph and decide the answers to the questions. Have volunteers present their results to the class.

For question 4, remind the students that the word "or" can either be inclusive or exclusive. Sometimes "or" means "both," and sometimes "or" means "one or the other, but not both." Because of these two uses of "or" there are two possible answers for this question.

Enrichment

Take a survey of the TV viewing patterns of the students in your class and of each of your family members. Combine your results with those of the other students in your class, and make a graph similar to the one on student text page 335 for the whole class.

Make up some questions about age groups and their TV viewing habits. Present your questions to the class, and have a class discussion about some of them. Some questions might be:

During what time periods does everyone in the family watch TV together?

If you were an advertising executive, how could you use the class graph to make decisions about the types of commercials and when to show them on TV?

How could you combine the information given in the sleep patterns graph with the information given in the television viewing graph to make decisions about scheduling TV programs?

Assessing the Outcomes

Observation

You might consider some of these questions as you observe the students work.

- Do the students know how to survey?
- Do the students understand the legend of the graph?
- Do the students know how to extract information from a graph?
- Do the students work well in pairs?
- Do the students persist until they find a solution?
- Do the students attempt all the questions?

Getting Started

Student Text Pages
Pp. 336–337

Materials

playing cards

Learning Outcomes

- Develop algebraic models to find strategies for winning games.
- Use logic to solve problems.

Prerequisite Skills

1. Two sisters and two mothers leave the room. The number of people in the room was reduced by three. Explain.

   [A grandmother, a mother, and a daughter left the room. The mother is also a daughter and the grandmother is also a mother.]

2. Three cats can catch 3 mice in 3 minutes. How long will it take 100 cats to catch 100 mice? [3 minutes]

Teaching Suggestions

Patterns and Observations

(playing cards) Assign Exploration 1 to the class. Organize the class into three groups and provide each group with a deck of playing cards. Assign each group different selections of cards: Group 1 to select one of the top 11 cards in step 1 and 28 cards in step 2, Group 2 to select the top 15 cards in step 1 and 20 cards in step 2, and Group 3 to select the top 10 cards in step 1 and 14 cards in step 2.

Have each student of the group take turns trying the trick. Challenge them to explain how the trick works. Have volunteers present their results to the class.

Assign questions 1 to 3. Challenge the groups to come up with an algebraic model of the solution. It should look something like this.

3. a) $n - x$ b) $n - x + y$
   c) $n - x + y + x + 1 = n + y + 1$

Using Logical Reasoning

Assign Exploration 2 to the class. Have small groups complete each question and present their results to the class. Discuss the problem solving strategy that could be used to help solve the problem (constructing a diagram or making a table). Ask:

What is the purpose of the table?

Elicit from the students that the table helps to organize the information given in the problem. The notion is that if all the possible outcomes, except one, are false, then, the remaining outcome is true.

Finally, work through Exploration 3 as a class. Have volunteers offer their suggestions as to where a cross or a check mark should go.

Encourage the rest of the students to agree or disagree with any suggestions, but ensure that the students who agree or disagree can justify their answers.

Mental Math

Students could choose, or be assigned, certain questions from each section. Alternatively, small groups could work as teams, sharing the questions and explaining the answers to the rest of the group.

Extension

1. A box contains 20 cubes. Remove 1 to 9 cubes from the box and throw them away. Add the digits of the remaining number of cubes. Remove this number of cubes from the box. Remove another 2 cubes from the box.

   a) Try this trick several times. What is the result?

   b) Use an algebraic model to prove that this trick always gives the same result.

2. a) Make up a trick of your own similar to the one in question 1. Exchange your trick with that of another student in the class.

   b) Prove that the trick will always work.

   Remove x. Number left is $20 - x$.
   The number left is a two-digit number whose tens digit is 1. The units digit is $10 - x$.
   Sum of the digits is $1 + (10 - x) = 11 - x$.
   Remove $11 - x$ from $20 - x$. $20 - x - (11 - x)$.
   Then, remove 2. $20 - x - (11 - x) - 2$
   $= 20 - x - 11 + x - 2$
   $= 7$

Assessing the Outcomes

Observation

You may want to consider some of the following skills as the students complete this lesson.

- Do the students understand the problems?
- Do the students use algebra to find a model for the solution?
- Do the students check that their algebraic model works?
- Can the students organize the information in a table?
- Can the students draw conclusions from the given information?
- Do the students work well together or do they tend to discover the mathematics independently?

6.1 Inductive Reasoning and Conjecturing

Student Text Pages

Pp. 338–342

Materials

graphing calculators, paper, straightedges, scissors, overhead projector

Learning Outcomes

- Understand the process of inductive reasoning.
- Use inductive reasoning to make conjectures.

Prerequisite Skills

Write the next number in each sequence.

a) $1, \frac{1}{2}, \frac{1}{3}, \frac{1}{4}, ?$ $\left[\frac{1}{5}\right]$

b) $5, 12, 19, 26, ?$ $[33]$

c) $2, 8, 32, 128, ?$ $[512]$

Mental Math

1. What is the measure of the complementary angle to each of the following?

a) $49°$ $[41°]$ b) $88°$ $[2°]$

c) $61°$ $[29°]$ d) $59°$ $[31°]$

e) $1°$ $[89°]$ f) $78°$ $[12°]$

2. Divide.

a) $651 \div 21$ $[31]$ b) $594 \div 54$ $[11]$

c) $288 \div 16$ $[18]$ d) $154 \div 11$ $[14]$

e) $341 \div 31$ $[11]$ f) $352 \div 44$ $[8]$

Explore/Inquire Answers

Inquire

1. The interior angles of a triangle have a sum of 180°.

2. An exterior angle of a triangle is equal to the sum of the two interior and opposite angles.

6. The interior angles of a quadrilateral have a sum of 360°.

7. a) $a = 70$ b) $b = 25$ c) $x = 60$ d) $y = 95$

Teaching Suggestions

Method 1

(paper, straightedges, scissors) Read with the class the opening paragraphs on student text page 338. Ask:

What does the term "educated guess" mean?

When have you ever given an educated guess?

Discuss with the students how it is often impossible to prove a conjecture made as a result of inductive reasoning.

Assign the Explore section and the Inquire questions to pairs of students. Ask:

How would you describe the three angles in part d) of the Explore section?

Have volunteers present their results to the class. Provide an overhead projector for the students to use if they wish.

Review the conjectures at the top of student text page 339. Assign teaching examples 1 to 3 on student text pages 339 and 340. For teaching example 1, ask:

How many experiments do you need to conduct?

Discuss with the students the importance of conducting enough experiments or collecting enough data before making a conjecture.

For teaching example 2, ask:

Is it possible to test every pair of numbers to see if your conjecture is true? Explain.

Ensure that the students realize that because pairs of numbers are infinite, then it is impossible to show that the conjectures in teaching example 2 are true. But, if enough pairs of numbers are studied, you can say that the conjecture is likely to be true.

For teaching example 3, ask:

What is the next number of the sequence 2, 4, ...? Explain.

Encourage students to think of as many explanations as possible. Some possible explanations are: the numbers are even numbers, so the next number is 6; the next number is double the previous number, so the next number is 8; the next number is two less than three times the previous number, so the next number is 10. Ask:

How many examples do you need to be able to identify a pattern?

Ensure that the students realize that they need a minimum of 3 examples in order to justify any pattern they think they see. More than 3 examples would further justify their conjecture.

Method 2

Write the following problem on the chalkboard.

$$\frac{1}{2} - \frac{1}{3} = \frac{1}{6}$$

$$\frac{1}{3} - \frac{1}{4} = \frac{1}{12}$$

$$\frac{1}{4} - \frac{1}{5} = \frac{1}{20}$$

Ask the students:

How are the denominators of the fractions on the left side of each equation related to each other?

How are the denominators of the fractions on the left side of each equation related to the denominator of the fraction on the right side of each equation?

Have pairs of students write two more examples of each equation using the same pattern they have described. Then, have them use the variable *m* to write an equation in general terms for the preceding equations. Suggest that they compare and discuss their results with other students. Then, ask:

How would you describe in words the pattern you noticed for the given equations?

Ensure that the students notice that the denominators of the fractions on the left side of each equation are consecutive numbers, and the denominator of the fraction on the right side is the product of the denominators on the left side. So, a general equation could be written $\frac{1}{m} - \frac{1}{m+1} = \frac{1}{m(m+1)}$.

Have the students list the steps they followed in finding the general equation. Lead them to see that they first looked at several examples and studied them. Then, they identified a possible pattern, and looked at several more examples to see if the pattern held. Then, they reached a general conclusion about the examples. Explain that this is the process of inductive thinking. Draw this flowchart on the chalkboard.

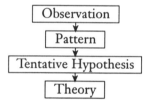

Ask:

Is it possible to prove that your theory is true for every pair of consecutive denominators?

Explain that it is impossible to prove that the theory is true, but with enough examples, it is likely to be true.

Review with the class the teaching examples on student text pages 339 and 340.

Number Power Answer

From row 1: $A + 2B + C = 20$...................................(1)
From row 2: $A + B + 2C = 21$...................................(2)
From column 4: $A + 2C + D = 23$.........................(3)
From the diagonal: $2A + C + D = 25$...................(4)
(1) − (2): $B − C = −1$
$\qquad\qquad\quad B = C − 1$...(5)
Substitute (5) into (1).
$A + 2(C − 1) + C = 20$
$\quad A + 2C + C − 2 = 20$
$\qquad\qquad A + 3C = 22$..(6)
(4) − (3): $A − C = 2$...(7)
(6) − (7): $4C = 20$
$\qquad\qquad\quad C = 5$
Substitute $C = 5$ into (7).
$A − 5 = 2$
$\quad A = 7$
Substitute $A = 7$ and $C = 5$ into (1).
$A + 2B + C = 20$
$7 + 2B + 5 = 20$
$\qquad\quad 2B = 8$
$\qquad\qquad B = 4$
Substitute $A = 7$ and $C = 5$ into (3).
$A + 2C + D = 23$
$7 + 2(5) + D = 23$
$\qquad\qquad\quad D = 6$
Thus, the sum of the second column is
$A + B + C + D = 7 + 4 + 5 + 6$
$\qquad\qquad\qquad\quad = 22$
Thus, $\square = 22$.

Integrating Technology

Internet

Use the Internet to find information about the Bermuda Triangle, Christian Goldbach, Leonard Euler, and the Fibonacci sequence.

Extension

Perform an experiment on any quadrilateral and come up with a conjecture related to the sides, angles, or diagonals. Compare your conjecture with those of other students in your class.

Math Journal

inductive thinking   Describe the method of inductive thinking.

Problem Levels of Difficulty

A: 1–12, 13 a), b), 21, 22
B: 13 c)–e), 14–18
C: 19, 20

Assessing the Outcomes

Written Assignment

1. Examine the pattern of asterisks in the following diagrams.

Diagram 1   Diagram 2   Diagram 3

a) Make a conjecture about the number of asterisks in the nth diagram.

b) Show that your conjecture is true for the seventh diagram.

2. Draw a large triangle. Draw the bisectors of two of the angles of the triangle. Mark the point of intersection of the two bisectors. Join this point of intersection and the third vertex of your triangle. Measure the two angles formed by the line joining the third vertex and the intersection point. Repeat this investigation three more times. Make a conjecture about the bisectors of the angles of a triangle.

6.2 Analyzing Conjectures Using Examples and Counterexamples

Student Text Pages
Pp. 343–346

Materials
graphing calculators

Learning Outcomes
- Understand the use of counterexamples.
- Demonstrate conjectures are false using counterexamples.

Prerequisite Skills
State whether each of the following is true (T) or false (F).
1. Points A, B, and C lie in a straight line. They are the vertices of a triangle.　[F]
2. AB and CD intersect at E. Then, $\angle AEC = \angle BED$.　[T]
3. $x + 3 = 11$. Then, $x = 5$.　[F]
4. $y^2 = 9$. Then, $y = 3$ or -3.　[T]

Mental Math
1. What is the measure of the supplementary angle to each of the following?

a)	39°	[141°]	b)	64°	[116°]
c)	179°	[1°]	d)	91°	[89°]
e)	125°	[55°]	f)	101°	[79°]

2. Divide.

a)	$20.3 \div 7$	[2.9]	b)	$3.06 \div 1.8$	[1.7]
c)	$1023 \div 33$	[31]	d)	$5670 \div 27$	[210]
e)	$210 \div 4.2$	[50]	f)	$732 \div 61$	[12]

Explore/Inquire Answers

Explore: Look for a Pattern

a) The sequence of numbers in the pattern of regions is 2, 4, 8, ...

Each term is double the previous term.

b) Prediction: 16

c) Since each term is double the previous term, then the formula involves a power of 2.

The formula is 2^{n-1}.

Inquire
1. Answers will vary. For example, you can draw diagrams and count regions for different numbers of points.

2. $2^{6-1} = 2^5 = 32$

3.

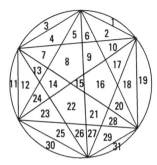

4. a) The conjecture is untrue for 6 points.

b) restricting the value of n for which the values are true

5. Answers may vary. For example,

a) Mexico is a country bordering on the United States. Mexico is not Canada.

b) A rectangle is a quadrilateral with 4 right angles. It is not a square.

c) A helicopter is a mechanically driven heavier-than-air vehicle. It is not an airplane.

d) 9 is a whole odd number less than 10, but it is not a prime number.

Teaching Suggestions

Method 1

Review the process of inductive reasoning from the previous section. Read with the class the opening paragraphs on student text page 343.

Assign the Explore section and the Inquire questions to small groups of students. If students have difficulty with counting the regions for 5 points and 6 points, suggest that the points be distributed evenly about the circumference. Caution them about locating the points immediately across from each other, of making their diagrams too small, of using pencils with thick points, and of locating the points too close to each other on the circumference. All of these actions will make the regions so small that it will be difficult to identify them and, therefore, to count.

Give the groups an opportunity to compare and discuss their results. Have volunteers present their results to the class.

For question 4, ask:

Does your formula work for 2 points? for 3 points? for 4 points? for 5 points?

For how many points does your formula not work?

Are there any other number of points for which the formula doesn't work?

Point out that it doesn't matter if the formula works for all other points except 6; this one counterexample renders the conjecture false.

Assign teaching examples 1 to 3 on student text pages 344 and 345 to the groups of students, giving them an opportunity to discuss and compare their results with other groups. Have volunteers present their results to the class.

Method 2

Write this example on the chalkboard.

Is the following conjecture true?

AB, BC, and AC are three lines. Therefore, A, B, and C are the vertices of a triangle.

Ask:

Is it possible that A, B, and C are the vertices of a triangle?

Can you think of a case in which the points A, B, and C would not form a triangle?

Review with the students the process of inductive thinking: Data is collected and studied. A pattern in the data may appear. Observations are made from this apparent pattern. More data is collected and, if the pattern still holds for the additional data, then, a conjecture is made. One example that shows the conjecture to be false is called a counterexample.

Remind the students that truth is absolute, and so, it only takes one counterexample to show that the conjecture is false.

Ask:

Why is it impossible to prove absolutely whether a conjecture is true?

Remind the students that it is impossible to test every case in nature or in the number system, and so, unless every case is tested, it is impossible to prove a conjecture.

Have small groups of students come up with a conjecture that they have arrived at from a set of facts. Each group can come up with a true or a false conjecture. Then, have a volunteer from each group present the facts and the conjecture to the class, and challenge the students to state whether the conjecture is true or false. Have the students identify any counterexamples they can provide to show that the conjecture is false.

Review with the class teaching examples 1 to 3 on student text pages 344 and 345.

Pattern Power Answer

1. In each column, the sum of the top two numbers equals the sum of the lower three numbers.

2. 13

Integrating Technology

Graphing Calculators

How would you use your graphing calculator to create the graphs in teaching example 3 on student text page 345? On a TI-83, the Y= and the ^ keys are used. Press the Y= key, and enter the right side of the first equation at the Y1 = prompt, using the ^ key to indicate the exponent.
Then, press the ZOOM key and the 6 key to select ZStandard.
To reveal some points to the left of the y-axis, press the ZOOM key, the 2 key, and the ENTER key to select Zoom In.
To reveal more points to the left of the y-axis, press the ZOOM key and the 4 key to select ZDecimal.

In question 21 on student text page 346, some ways to find a counterexample are using different viewing windows and using a table.

Computer Data Bank

Use the databases in *MATHPOWER™ 11, Western Edition, Computer Data Bank* to find information to write conjectures for which counterexamples exist. Display your conjectures and challenge classmates to find counterexamples.

Internet

Use the Internet to find information about the flat-Earth conjecture and Ferdinand Magellan.

Extension

State whether the following conjecture is true of false. If it is false, use counterexamples to show that it is false.

If ∠A and ∠B are complementary and if ∠A and ∠C are complementary, then ∠B and ∠C are complementary.

Math Journal

counterexample Write a definition of the term counterexample in your journal. Include an example of a conjecture and a counterexample that disproves the conjecture.

Problem Levels of Difficulty

A: 1–14   **B:** 15–19   **C:** 20–21

Assessing the Outcomes

Observation

You may wish to consider some of these questions as you watch the students work:

- Do the students understand the process of inductive reasoning?
- Can the students suggest conjectures from patterns they see?
- Can the students support their conjectures with counterexamples?
- Can the students express their ideas clearly?
- Do the students attempt all the questions?
- Do the students work well as a team?

6.3 Deductive Reasoning

Student Text Pages
Pp. 347–349

Learning Outcomes
- Understand the process of deductive reasoning.
- Use deductive reasoning to prove conclusions.

Prerequisite Skills

Insert the word "even" or "odd" to make a true statement.

m and n are any two numbers.

1. m is even and n is odd.

$m + n$ is _____ . [odd]

2. m is odd and n is odd.

$m + n$ is _____ . [even]

3. m is even and n is even.

$m + n$ is _____ . [even]

4. m is even and n is odd.

mn is _____ . [even]

5. m is odd and n is odd.

mn is _____ . [odd]

Mental Math

1. What is the measure of the complementary angle to each of the following?

a) 19°   [71°]   **b)** 52°   [38°]

c) 70°   [20°]   **d)** 24°   [66°]

e) 11°   [79°]   **f)** 33°   [57°]

2. Simplify.

a) $\sqrt{128}$ $[8\sqrt{2}]$ **b)** $\sqrt{162}$ $[9\sqrt{2}]$

c) $\sqrt{108}$ $[6\sqrt{3}]$ **d)** $\sqrt{99}$ $[3\sqrt{11}]$

e) $\sqrt{32}$ $[4\sqrt{2}]$ **f)** $\sqrt{150}$ $[5\sqrt{6}]$

Explore/Inquire Answers

Explore: Use Inductive and Deductive Reasoning

a) $a + b = 180°, c + b = 180°$

b) $a + b = c + b$

d) $a = c$

Inquire

1. The opposite angles formed by intersecting lines are equal.

2. No, because it is impossible to test every pair of intersecting straight lines.

4. $b + c = 180$ (given straight lines)

$d + c = 180$ (given straight lines)

Thus, $b = d$.

5. a) $a = 65, b = c = 115$

b) $x = 120, y = z = 60$

c) $p = 20, q = r = 160$

6. True statements: I will eat one of these cakes. It can't possibly make me larger.

Conjectures: It will change my size. I will become smaller.

Teaching Suggestions

Method 1

Review with the students the opening paragraphs on student text page 347. Explain that deductive reasoning begins with a specific fact and uses the fact to find other facts. It allows us to use information we accept as true to draw conclusions.

Assign the Explore section and the Inquire questions to small groups of students. Give students an opportunity to discuss and compare their results.

Review with the class teaching examples 1 to 3 on student text pages 348 and 349.

Method 2

Say to the class:

Today, all the students in the class received their mark for their math test. Jerry was in the class today. Therefore, he received his mark for his math test.

Introduce the term "deductive reasoning" and point out that this is an example of deductive reasoning. Explain that in deductive reasoning, an accepted fact is used to prove additional facts. Draw this flowchart of the process of deductive thinking on the chalkboard.

Ask:

What everyday examples can you think of that are examples of deductive reasoning?

Have them explain how deductive reasoning was used to prove the conclusion above.

Present to the class this diagram of one of the stages in a game of X's and O's.

Tell the students to assume that the players are playing by the accepted rules of the game.

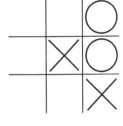

Have the students deduce which player started the game, X or O. Give the students an opportunity to discuss and compare their reasoning. Their reasoning should be something like "The winner of the game is the player who fills in three boxes in a row. The X in the third column was the last box to be filled, since it stopped the other player from winning. Since an X was the last mark in a box, and since the players take turns, then the mark before must have been an O, the mark before that an X, and, as a result, the first mark an O."

Review with the class the process of deductive reasoning used to conclude who made the last mark:

a) The assumed facts were each player takes a turn; three marks in a row is a winning game; a winning game is prevented by placing a different mark in a row with two of the same marks.

b) It was assumed that the players would play by these rules.

c) Therefore, the last mark was an X, and so the first mark was an O.

Ask:

How could the diagram be changed so that you could deduce that the first mark was an X?

Review with the class teaching examples 1 to 3 on student text pages 348 and 349.

Sample Solution

Page 349, question 18

Given $\triangle ADC$ is right.
Then, $a + b = 90$ ....(1)
Given $\triangle ABC$ is right.
Then, $a + c = 90$. ....(2)
The sum of the angles of $\triangle ABC$ is 180°.
Then, $b + d = 90$. ....(3)
Given $\triangle ABD$ is right.
Then, $c + d = 90$. ....(4)
Subtract (4) from (3).
$b + d - (c + d) = 90 - 90$
$b - c = 0$
$b = c$
Subtract (1) from (3).
$b + d - (a + b) = 90 - 90$
$d - a = 0$
$a = d$

In $\triangle ADC$, $\triangle ADB$, and $\triangle ABC$, one angle is right, one angle is a, and one angle is b. Since the angles of all three triangles are the same, then the triangles are similar.

Integrating Technology

Internet

Use the Internet to find information about Lewis Carroll and *Alice's Adventures in Wonderland*.

Enrichment

Write a short essay describing the difference between deductive and inductive reasoning. Share your essay with the class, and discuss any similarities and differences in your ideas.

Common Errors

• Students are often confused between inductive and deductive reasoning.

R_x With the use of examples, remind students that inductive reasoning begins with examples, and deductive reasoning begins with a rule.

Problem Levels of Difficulty

A: 1–8   **B:** 9–17   **C:** 18, 19

Assessing the Outcomes

Written Assignment

Make up a number trick with at least 5 steps that always results in a value of 8.

The Connecting Words *And*, *Or*, and *Not*

Student Text Pages
Pp. 350–356

Materials
graphing calculators

Learning Outcomes
- Understand the concept of compound statements.
- Identify true compound statements.
- Understand the use of Venn diagrams.
- Use Venn diagrams to help decide if a compound statement is true or false.
- Graph compound statements on number lines.
- Interpret and draw Venn diagrams.

Prerequisite Skills
Use the set of whole numbers from 1 to 30, inclusive. Give each of the following sets of numbers.

a) The numbers are even and multiples of 3.

[6, 12, 18, 24, and 30]

b) The numbers are odd but not prime.

[1, 9, 15, 21, 25, 27]

c) The numbers are less than 5 or end in a 5.

[1, 2, 3, 4, 5, 10, 15, 25]

d) The numbers are greater than or equal to 27 or multiples of 6.

[6, 12, 18, 24, 27, 28, 29, 30]

Mental Math
1. What is the measure of the complementary angle to each of the following?

a) 89°	[1°]	b) 46°	[44°]
c) 37°	[53°]	d) 12°	[78°]
e) 69°	[21°]	f) 4°	[86°]

2. If $y(x) = 3\sqrt{x+7} - 1$, find

a) $y(2)$	[8]	b) $y(-3)$	[5]
c) $y(9)$	[11]	d) $y(-6)$	[2]
e) $y(93)$	[29]	f) $y(29)$	[17]

Explore/Inquire Answers

Explore: Compound Statements With *And* and *Or*

Answers will vary.

Inquire
1. Statements: a), b), d), e), f), h);

Not statements: c) and g)

2. a) exclusive b) inclusive c) exclusive
   d) inclusive e) inclusive

Teaching Suggestions

Method 1
Read with the students the opening paragraphs on student text page 350. Ask:

What does the word "compound" mean?

Where have you heard the word "compound" used in everyday life?

Stress that a sentence that is either true or false is a statement; otherwise, it is an opinion.

Assign the Explore section and the Inquire questions to small groups of students. Give the students ample time to discuss and compare their results with other students. Have volunteers present their results to the class.

Review with the class teaching examples 1 to 7 on student text pages 351 to 354. Begin by reviewing Venn diagrams. Ask.

Why are Venn diagrams useful in organizing information and solving problems?

How are the circles used in Venn diagrams?

Where are the numbers placed in Venn diagrams?

How are totals checked?

How would you describe the part of a Venn diagram that represents a statement involving the connecting word "and"? the connecting word "or"?

How would you describe the part of a Venn diagram that represents the negation of a statement?

For teaching example 2, review the use of open dots and solid dots on the line graphs. Ask:

When do you use an open dot on a line graph? a solid dot?

Have volunteers present their results to the class.

Method 2
Write these four sentences on the chalkboard.
   A: A number is even.
   B: A number is a multiple of 5.
   C: A number is less than 4.
   D: A number is more than 15.
Tell the class that a sentence is a statement whether it is true or false; otherwise, it is an opinion. Ask:

What does the word "compound" mean?

Discuss with the class how combining statements A and B with "and" results in an inclusive compound statement.

A number is even and is a multiple of 5.

Ask:

What does the word "inclusive" mean in this case?

Elicit from the students that inclusive means the number must be both an even number and a multiple of 5 for the statement to be true. Point out that compound statements joined with "and" are always inclusive.

Next, discuss how combining statements with "or" results in a compound statement that can be either inclusive or exclusive. For example, combining statements A and B with "or" results in an inclusive compound statement.

A number is even or a multiple of 5.

In this case, the number can be even or a multiple of 5 or both. All three cases are true. But, combining statements A and C with "or" results in an exclusive compound statement.

A number is a multiple of 5 or less than 4.

Ask:

What does the word "exclusive" mean in this case?

Elicit from the students that exclusive means the number can be a multiple of 5 or it can be less than 4, but it cannot be both.

Finally, the word "not" can be used to form the negation of a statement. For example, the negation of statement A is

A number is not even.

Have small groups of students use statements A to D to write examples of compound statements that are inclusive and exclusive. Remind them to use the compound words "and" and "or." Then, have them write a negation of any of statements A to D. Challenge them to write compound statements that include the negation of any of statements A to D.

Finally, ask the groups to make up their own statements and repeat this assignment. Have volunteers present their results to the class.

Review teaching examples 1 to 7 on student text pages 351 to 354.

Word Power Answer

Answers may vary. For example,
FOOT, FOOL, POOL, POLL, POLE, VOLE,
VOTE, NOTE

Integrating Technology

Computer Data Bank

Use the databases in *MATHPOWER™ 11, Western Edition, Computer Data Bank* to find information to write problems that can be solved using Venn diagrams. Display your problems for classmates to solve.

Internet

Use the Internet to find information to represent using Venn diagrams. Display your diagrams for classmates to interpret.

Extension

Create a problem of your own using Venn diagrams. Exchange your problem with that of another student in the class, and solve the problem.

Enrichment

Write a short essay about the life and works of John Venn. Compare your notes with those of other students in the class, and display the essays on a class bulletin board.

Math Journal

Venn diagrams Describe a Venn diagram and its uses. Include an example to illustrate its uses.

Problem Levels of Difficulty

A: 1–53, 63   **B:** 54–60   **C:** 61, 62

Assessing the Outcomes

Journal

Write a few sentences describing the difference between an inclusive compound statement and an exclusive compound statement. Include an example of each type of statement for clarity.

Technology

Logic and Internet Search Engines

Student Text Page
P. 357

Materials
Internet access

Learning Outcomes
- Interpret Internet searches that use Boolean operations.
- Conduct an Internet search that uses Boolean operations.

Prerequisite Skills
Name three integers for each.
a) $x \geq -3$ and $x < 4$ [Any of $-3, -2, -1, 0, 1, 2, 3$]
b) $x + 2 < 5$ or $x + 2 > 5$ [Any integer except 3]

Teaching Suggestions
Discuss the search information presented on student text page 357.

Ask students to demonstrate searching techniques using their favourite search engines, and discuss the Boolean operations used and the relative number of hits in the searches.

Assign Explorations 1 and 2 to small groups of students to be completed over a period of time that allows adequate computer time.

Assessing the Outcomes

Observation

While students are searching on the Internet, do they
- use a favourite search engine or do they experiment with, and compare, different engines?
- apply Boolean operations?
- use quotation marks?
- avoid using upper case?

If...then Statements, the Converse, and the Contrapositive

Student Text Pages
Pp. 358–362

Learning Outcomes

- Understand the concepts of conditional statements, converses, biconditional statements, and contrapositive statements.
- Write conditional, converse, and contrapositive statements.
- Determine the truth of statements.
- Use reasoning to solve problems.

Prerequisite Skills

The proverb "Many hands make light work" can be rewritten in an *If...then* format.

If there are many hands, then the work will be light.

Rewrite each of the following proverbs in an *If...then* format.

a) A bird in the hand is worth two in the bush.

[If a bird is in the hand, then it is worth two in the bush.]

b) A rolling stone gathers no moss.

[If a stone rolls, then it gathers no moss.]

c) Absence makes the heart grow fonder.

[If you are absent, then the heart will grow fonder.]

Mental Math

1. What is the measure of the supplementary angle to each of the following?

a) $35°$ [$145°$]   **b)** $172°$ [$8°$]
c) $88°$ [$92°$]   **d)** $114°$ [$66°$]
e) $137°$ [$43°$]   **f)** $6°$ [$174°$]

2. For each inequality, write three different ordered pairs that include the given coordinate and satisfy the inequality.

[Answers may vary. For example,]

a) $x + y > 1$; ($\blacksquare$, 1)   [(2, 1), (3, 1), (4, 1)]
b) $-x - y > 5$; (2, $\blacksquare$)   [(2, −8), (2, −9), (2, −10)]
c) $y \geq 2x + 3$; (3, $\blacksquare$)   [(3, 9), (3, 10), (3, 11)]
d) $2x - y \leq 1$; ($\blacksquare$, −1)   [(0, −1), (−1, −1), (−2, −1)]

Explore/Inquire Answers

Explore: Interpret the Statement

a) $x = 2$ **b)** $x^2 = 4$ **c)** yes
d) If $x^2 = 4$, then $x = 2$.   **e)** $x^2 = 4$ **f)** $x = 2$
g) No; If $x^2 = 4$, x could be -2.

Inquire

2. If $x < 2$, then $x^2 < 4$.

3. No; It is false for negative numbers such as $-2, -3, ...$

4. If $x^2 < 4$, then $x < 2$.

5. Yes; If $x^2 < 4$, x is between -2 and 2. So, $x \leq 2$.

Teaching Suggestions

Read with the class the opening paragraphs on student text page 358. Ask:

What do the words "hypothesis" and "converse" mean?

What other word have you seen that is related to the words "hypothesis" and "converse"?

Review the format of an *If...then* statement and the converse of a statement. Point out to the students that it is important for a sentence to be written in *If...then* format before writing the converse of the statement. Have the students practise rewriting conditional statements in the *If...then* format. For example, "People who practise often become better." can be written as "If you practise often, then you will become better."

Organize the class into pairs. Have one student make up a statement and then, have the partner rewrite the statement in the *If...then* format.

Review the paragraphs on the lower half of student text page 359. Discuss the terminology "biconditional statement" and "contrapositive."

Provide some statements and have the students write the statements in the *If...then* format then, write their converse and their contrapositives. For example,

All squares have 4 equal sides.
All parallelograms have opposites parallel.
A quadrilateral with 4 right angles is a square.
Smoking is harmful to your health.
Dogs have 4 legs.
Plants need water to grow.

Have the students state whether the statements, the converses, and the contrapositives, are true, and provide a counterexample, if necessary, to justify their answers. Then, ask:

If a conditional statement is true, is its converse always true, sometimes true, or never true?

If a conditional statement is false, is its converse always false, sometimes false, or never false?

Review Examples 1 to 4 on student text pages 360 and 361.

Number Power Answer

A = 1, B = 2, C = D = E = 6, F = 4

Integrating Technology

Internet

Use the Internet to find more information about Lewis Carroll and *Alice's Adventures in Wonderland.*

Enrichment

Research the real name of Lewis Carroll, the author of *Alice in Wonderland.* Write a short essay about his life and works, and the connections to mathematics, logic, and story telling.

Math Journal

conditional statement, converse, biconditional statement, contrapositive   Write a definition for each of these terms. Include an example for clarity.

Common Errors

• Students often find it difficult to write statements in the *If...then* format.

R_x Remind the students that the format of the *If...then* statement is
   If (hypothesis), then (conclusion).
Point out that the subject of the statement usually provides the hypothesis, while the predicate of the statement usually provides the conclusion. Suggest that the students write the sentence
   If (subject), then (predicate).
It may be necessary to rewrite the sentence so that it reads better.

Problem Levels of Difficulty

A: 1–27   **B:** 28–31   **C:** 32–34

Assessing the Outcomes

Written Assignment

Write the following conditional statements in the *If...then* format. For each, write its converse and its contrapositive. State whether the statement, the converse, and the contrapositive are true or false.

1. An equilateral triangle is an acute triangle.
2. Friday follows Thursday.
3. A quadrilateral with all sides equal is a square.
4. All birds fly.
5. An angle greater than 180° is a reflex angle.

Technology

Testing *If...then* Statements Using a Graphing Calculator

Student Text Page
P. 363

Materials
graphing calculators

Learning Outcome
- Use a graphing calculator to test the truth of statements involving inequalities and their solutions.

Prerequisite Skills
1. Locate the inequality signs on your graphing calculator.
   [On a TI-83, they are under the Test menu when the TEST (i.e., 2nd MATH) key is pressed.]
2. Locate the absolute value operation on your graphing calculator.
   [On a TI-83, one place is the first item when the CATALOG (i.e., 2nd 0) key is pressed.]

Teaching Suggestions
Discuss the use of 1 and 0 to indicate true and false statements. Recall displaying solutions to linear inequalities using a graphing calculator in Chapter 2. See student text page 65. The display was compared to a number line. In this chapter, quadratic, rational, absolute value, as well as linear inequalities are graphed to test the validity of the given solutions.

Discuss how to graph the inequality and test values displayed on student text page 363. On a TI-83, the Dot mode, and the Y= and Value operations are used. Press the Y= key, and enter x^2.
Press the TEST (i.e., 2nd MATH) key and the 4 key to select $\geq$.
Enter $6x - 5$.
Press the MODE key, and use the arrow keys to reach Dot (to the right of Connected), and then, press the ENTER key.
Press the ZOOM key and the 6 key to select ZStandard.
Press the CALC (i.e., 2nd TRACE) key and the 1 key to select value.
At the X= prompt, enter the x-value to be tested, and press the ENTER key.

Assign Explorations 1 and 2.

Common Errors
- Some students enter inequalities involving fractions incorrectly.
- $\mathbf{R}_x$ Suggest that students write inequalities involving fractions using division signs instead of fraction bars, inserting brackets where needed, but only where needed. Then, they use the rewritten inequalities while entering the inequalities.

Assessing the Outcome

Written Assignment

Record the keys that must be pressed to test the truth of the following statement. Then, test the truth.

If $\dfrac{3}{x+1} < \dfrac{x}{2}$, then $-3 < x < -1$.

[False, $-3 < x < -1$ or $x > 2$]

Investigating Math

Reviewing Congruent Triangles

Student Text Pages

Pp. 364–365

Learning Outcomes

- Review the theorems for congruent triangles.
- Identify equal pairs of angles and sides of congruent triangles with common sides and points.

Prerequisite Skills

Write the parts of the triangles that are equal.

a) $\triangle ABC \cong \triangle PQR$

[AB = PQ, BC = QR, AC = PR, ∠ABC = ∠PQR, ∠BAC = ∠QPR, ∠BCA = ∠QRP]

b)

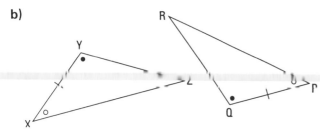

[XY = PQ, YZ = QR, XZ = PR, ∠XYZ = ∠PQR, ∠YXZ = ∠QPR, ∠YZX = ∠QRP]

Mental Math

1. Evaluate for $x = 3$ and $y = -2$.

a) $x + y$	[1]	b) $-2x + 2y$	[−10]
c) $x^2 + 5y$	[−1]	d) $x + 2y$	[−1]
e) $x^2 + y^2$	[13]	f) $3y + 4x$	[6]

2. Calculate.

a) 4.7×43 [202.1]

b) 93×9.7 [902.1]

c) 490×410 [200 900]

d) 630×67 [42 210]

e) 8.8×8.2 [72.16]

f) 0.32×3.8 [1.216]

Teaching Suggestions

Review the opening paragraphs on student text page 364. Ask:

If $\triangle ABC \cong \triangle MNP$, how can you identify which sides are equal and which pairs of angles are equal without seeing a diagram?

Remind the students that the congruence relation is written so that the labels of the corresponding angles are in corresponding positions in the congruence relation. Thus, for

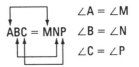

$$\angle A = \angle M$$
$$\angle B = \angle N$$
$$\angle C = \angle P$$

Then, assign Investigation 1 to small groups of students. Give the groups ample opportunity to compare and discuss their results with other groups. Have volunteers present their results to the class.

Then, assign Investigation 2 to different small groups of students. Remind the students that equal angles are opposite sides that are marked alike, i.e., with one stroke or two strokes, etc., and equal sides are opposite equal angles.

Caution students to keep this in mind, as many students can identify wrong corresponding sides if the triangles overlap.

Again have students discuss and compare their results with other groups, and have volunteers present their results to the class.

Extension

Draw a pair of triangles that have five pairs of congruent parts but are not congruent. Discuss and compare your results with other students until you have found a solution. Present your solution to the class.

[Triangles with three pairs of equal angles and two pairs of equal, but not corresponding, sides.]

Common Errors

- Students sometimes find it difficult to identify corresponding parts when the triangles are not drawn in the same position or orientation.

R_x Before attempting to identify corresponding parts, suggest that students redraw the triangles so that they have the same orientation.

Assessing the Outcomes

Journal

Write a short essay about what new information you have learned about congruent triangles.

6.6 Direct and Indirect Proof

Student Text Pages
Pp. 366–372

Materials
graphing calculators

Learning Outcomes
- Understand the methods of direct proof and indirect proof.
- Write the steps of an indirect proof.
- Define and write corollaries of theorems.
- Define a converse of a proof.
- Prove a converse of a proof.

Prerequisite Skills

1. Find the number.
- It is between 7 and 12, inclusive.
- It is a factor of 88.
- It is a prime number.   [11]

2. Find the number.
- It is a three-digit number.
- All the digits are even numbers.
- None of the digits repeats.
- No digit is greater than 6.
- The ones digit is one-third the hundreds digit.   [642]

3. Write the opposite of each of the following.

a) $\angle A = \angle B$ $[\angle A \neq \angle B]$

b) $2 > x$ $[2 < x]$

Mental Math

1. What is the measure of the supplementary angle to each of the following?

a) $163°$ $[17°]$ b) $49°$ $[131°]$

c) $86°$ $[94°]$ d) $177°$ $[3°]$

e) $25°$ $[155°]$ f) $180°$ $[0°]$

2. Complete each ordered pair so that it satisfies the given equation.

a) $x + 2y = 1$; $(2, \blacksquare)$ $\left[-\dfrac{1}{2}\right]$

b) $x - y = -2$; $(5, \blacksquare)$ $[7]$

c) $2x + y = 5$; $(\blacksquare, -5)$ $[5]$

d) $y = -x + 7$; $(5, \blacksquare)$ $[2]$

Explore/Inquire Answers

Inquire

1. AD is given as a bisector.

2. It is assumed that AD is perpendicular to BC. Thus, $\angle ADB = \angle ADC = 90°$.

3. AD is common to $\triangle ABD$ and $\triangle ADC$. Thus, since two angles and an included side of $\triangle ABD$ are equal to two corresponding angles and an included side of $\triangle ADC$, they are congruent.

4. AB and AC are the corresponding sides of congruent triangles and thus, they are equal.

5. $\triangle ABC$ is given as scalene. Thus, all sides of $\triangle ABC$ are unequal. This means AB and AC are unequal. This contradicts the statement in question 4.

6. No; because this would mean that two sides of the scalene triangles would have to be equal, which is impossible by definition.

7. Either $x^2 \neq 2$ or $x^2 = 2$. Assume $x^2 = 2$. Then, substitute $x^2 = 2$ in $x^2 = 5x$.

$$\text{L.S.} = x^2 \qquad\qquad \text{R.S.} = 5x$$
$$= (2)^2 \qquad\qquad\quad = 5(2)$$
$$= 4 \qquad\qquad\qquad = 10$$

But $4 \neq 10$. Thus, our assumption is false, and the only other possibility is true, i.e., since $x^2 = 5x$, then $x^2 \neq 2$.

8. yes

Teaching Suggestions

Review with the class the opening paragraphs on student text page 366. Discuss the terms "direct proof" and "indirect proof." Point out that the method of direct proof has a starting statement of this form: If _____, then _____ .

The method of indirect proof is to identify all possibilities, assume the given statement is false, show that the assumption is false, and therefore, the given statement is true. Remind the students that a statement is either true or false. If you show that it is not false, then it must be true. Review the list of steps required to write an indirect proof.

Assign the Explore section and the Inquire questions to small groups of students. Give the groups an opportunity to compare and discuss their results. Have volunteers present their results to the class.

Review with the class teaching examples 1 to 8 on student text pages 367 to 371. Point out the importance of knowing the definitions and properties of geometric figures and shapes and the properties of numbers in proving statements.

Number Power Answer

1 is not used.

Integrating Technology

Internet

Use the Internet to find information about Sherlock Holmes, *The Sign of Four*, the author, and other Sherlock Holmes novels.

Extension

Although each of the following statements contains an error, each result is correct.

$$\frac{1\cancel{6}}{\cancel{6}4} = \frac{1}{4} \qquad \frac{3}{4} - \frac{2}{3} = \frac{3-2}{12} = \frac{1}{12}$$

Try to make up your own error-laden statement whose result is true.

Enrichment

Research the life and works of Euclid and how his work relates to finding proofs. Write a short essay and display it on a class bulletin board.

Math Journal

converse, corollary   Write a definition for each term, and include a diagram and an example for clarity.

Write a list of steps required to write an indirect proof.

Problem Levels of Difficulty

A: 1–11   **B:** 12–19   **C:** 20

Assessing the Outcomes

Journal

Write a short essay describing the difference between direct proof and indirect proof.

Computer Data Bank

Western Parks

Microsoft Works for Windows users see *Part B, and* Microsoft Access users see *Part D*, of *MATHPOWER™ 11, Western Edition, Computer Data Bank Teacher's Resource.*

Student Text Page
P. 373

Learning Outcomes

- Display, find, sort, calculate, summarize, graph, and analyze data in a computer database.
- Apply logic when using several comparisons to find records.

Prerequisite Skills

Jenna has two part-time jobs.

Week of August 8

Hours Worked	Part-time Job
3	A
4	B
4	B
6	A
4	B
5	A

a) How many hours did Jenna work at both jobs? [26 h]

b) At which job did she work more hours? How many more? [A, 2 h]

Getting Started Blackline Masters C-1, C-2, and C-4 to C-9

Teaching Suggestions

Students unfamiliar with computer databases and ClarisWorks would benefit from working through *Getting Started* Blackline Masters C-1, C-2, and C-4 to C-9, noted in the *Prerequisite Skills*, prior to doing any of the explorations on this page. Minimally, students should have *Getting Started* Blackline Masters C-1, C-2, and C-4 to C-9 available for reference.

Each exploration in *Western Parks* is independent of the others. Some or all of the explorations can be assigned to individuals, pairs, or small groups of students, to be completed over a period of time that allows students adequate computer time. Up to 1.5 h will be needed by some students to complete all six explorations.

When assigning the explorations, inform students if you expect

- any parts of the explorations to be printed off the computer
- handwritten or word-processed answers to questions that suggest a written response
- a journal-type response about what they have learned mathematically, about using databases, and/or about the subject matter of the database

Possible parts to assign for printing are a table to show the counts from Exploration 2; the bar graph from Exploration 4; and a table to show the sum and average from Exploration 5.

Parks with only group camping are not included.

1 True or False

In each of questions 1 to 4, display the records using Full Record and use the Find feature with one comparison for *Park* park of interest, confirming or correcting the given data about it, and showing all the records between questions (*Getting Started* BLM C-5).

2 Facilities

Display the records using Full Record for questions 1 to 4.

An efficient approach to question 1 for each province is to show all the records and use the Find feature with one comparison for *Province* province of interest, noting the number of records displayed. Then, use the Find feature with two comparisons for *Fishing* Yes and *Boat Launch* No, noting the number of records displayed (*Getting Started* BLM C-5). Finally, express that number as a fraction of the number of records for the province noted earlier in the question.

In question 2, show all the records and use the Find feature with five comparisons for *Province* Manitoba, *Type* Provincial, *Campsites* >250, *Firewood* Yes, and *Showers* Yes (Getting Started BLM C-5).

In question 3, show all the records and use the Find feature with one comparison for *Park* Elk Falls, noting the area. Then, show all the records and use the Find feature with three comparisons for *Area, ha* >1087, *Day Use* Yes, and *Wheelchair* No (*Getting Started* BLM C-5).

In question 4, show all the records and use the Find feature. First, enter three comparisons for *Province* British Columbia, *Swimming* Yes, and *Fishing* Yes. Then, select New Request and enter three more comparisons for *Province* Manitoba, *Swimming* Yes, and *Fishing* Yes (*Getting Started* BLM C-5).

An efficient approach to question 5 is to show all the records and create a table displaying only the *Park, Province, Firewood, Campsites,* and *Showers* fields (*Getting Started* BLM C-2). Then, use the Find feature with three comparisons for *Firewood* Yes, *Campsites* >= 50, and *Showers* No (*Getting Started* BLM C-5). Then, count and display the number of parks in each province by doing the following. Create a summary field called *Parks by Province*, using the formula that follows. Sort by *Province*. Insert a Sub-summary section. Insert the summary field in the Sub-summary section (*Getting Started* BLM C-7). Finally, express the count for each province as a percent of the number of parks in the province from question 1, using a calculator, noting the greatest percent.

COUNT('Park')

3 Hiking Trails

An efficient approach is to show all the records, displaying them using Full Record. Then, use the Find feature with three comparisons for *Province* British Columbia, *Type* Provincial, and *Hiking Trails* Yes, noting the number of records displayed. Next, use the Find feature with one comparison for *Day Use* Yes, noting the number of records displayed (*Getting Started* BLM C-5). Finally, express that number as a fraction of the number of records noted earlier in the question.

4 Campsite Density

An efficient approach to question 1 is to show all the records and create a table displaying only the *Park*, *Province*, *Area, ha*, and *Campsites* fields (*Getting Started* BLM C-2). Then, use the Find feature with three comparisons for *Province* province of interest, *Area, ha*<> −1, and *Campsites* <>−1 (*Getting Started* BLM C-5). Next, create a calculation field called *Density, campsites/ha*, using the formula that follows, to determine the number of campsites per hectare, rounded to 3 decimal places (*Getting Started* BLM C-6). Finally, sort from greatest to least density (*Getting Started* BLM C-4).

ROUND('Campsites'/'Area, ha',3)

In question 2, copy the field values for the first six records to a new spreadsheet. Then, use the *Park* and *Density, campsites/ha* fields and the Make Chart feature (*Getting Started* BLM C-9).

5 National Parks

An efficient approach is to deselect the records from the previous question and show all the records, displaying them using Table 1. Use the Find feature. First, enter three comparisons for *Province* Alberta, *Type* National, and *Area, ha* <>−1. Then, select New Request and enter three more comparisons for *Province* British Columbia, *Type* National, and *Area, ha* <>−1 (*Getting Started* BLM C-5). Next, determine and display the sum and average, rounded to 0 decimal places, of the areas for all the displayed records by doing the following. Create two summary fields called *Total Area*,

ha and *Average Area*, *ha*, using the formulas that follow. Insert a Trailing grand summary section. Insert the summary fields in the Trailing grand summary section (*Getting Started* BLM C-7).

SUM('Area, ha')

ROUND(AVERAGE('Area, ha'),0)

6 Planning a Visit

Students' responses will vary, but in question 1b), essential information from the databases is the availability of day use.

Connecting Math and Computers

Sorting Networks

Student Text Pages
Pp. 374–375

Materials
scientific (or graphing) calculators

Learning Outcome
• Determine the output of sorting networks.

Prerequisite Skills
1. Order the numbers from least to greatest.
a) 37, 5, 18, 206, 1   [1, 5, 18, 37, 206]
b) 3.1, 4.8, 0.95, 1.6, 0.08   [0.08, 0.95, 1.6, 3.1, 4.8]
2. Order the numbers from greatest to least.
a) −11, 7, −302, 87, 6.5   [87, 7, 6.5, −11, −302]
b) −9.9, 2.6, 121.05, 300   [300, 121.05, 2.6, −9.9]

Mental Math
1. Add.

a)		b)		c)	
36	[323]	82	[271]	4.7	[39.1]
93		15		3.6	
41		72		9.9	
59		27		6.4	
28		37		5.1	
+ 66		+ 38		+ 9.4	

2. Divide.
a) 192 ÷ 8   [24]
b) 156 ÷ 13   [12]
c) 240 ÷ 15   [16]
d) 234 ÷ 26   [9]
e) 882 ÷ 42   [21]
f) 9191 ÷ 91   [101]

Teaching Suggestions
Read with the class the opening paragraphs at the top of student text page 374. Ask:

Is sorting numbers from greatest to least the only way numbers can be sorted?

In what other ways can numbers be sorted?

Is it necessary for the numbers being sorted to be different? Explain.

Why would anyone want to sort numbers?

Elicit from the students that numbers can be sorted in any organized way, for example, from least to greatest. People who have to make reports about objects may need to sort numbers. For example, objects can be given code numbers, and then these numbers can be sorted.

Assign Investigation 1 to pairs of students. Suggest that they copy and complete the diagram. Ask:

How must the numbers be sorted in order for them to be sorted properly?

How would you describe the relationship between the order of the numbers in the square nodes at the left and in the square nodes at the right in question 1? in question 2?

Assign Investigation 2 to pairs of students. Once again suggest they copy and complete each diagram at the top of student text page 375. Ask:

How could you change Network 1 in order for it to work properly?

Have student pairs present their networks to the class. Encourage the students to be as creative as possible. Have the class sort their choice of 4 numbers on some of the networks of their choice presented by the students.

Integrating Technology
Internet
Use the Internet to find information about sorting networks.

Extension
Design your own network to sort 6 numbers and 8 numbers. Test your network using 6 different numbers and 8 different numbers. Exchange your networks with those of other classmates and choose an appropriate number of numbers to test these networks.

Assessing the Outcome
Observation
Some skills to watch for in this lesson are:
• Do the students show patience for a lengthy assignment?
• Do the pairs co-operate to help make the work easier?
• Are the students willing to help other students who do not understand parts of the investigation?

Review

Student Text Pages
Pp. 376–377

Learning Outcome
• Review the skills and concepts in Chapter 6.

Using the Review
Have the students work independently to complete the Review. Meeting in small groups, the students can mark and discuss the work. Groups can then share their solutions and report any questions that caused them difficulty. Discuss these questions with the class.

Reteaching Suggestions
For those students having difficulty with the chapter material, form small groups and use the following exercises.
    If you feel that the class has had particular difficulty mastering any concept, you may wish to work through a problem from each section as a model of excellence of solution, which some students require just prior to assessment.

Inductive Reasoning and Conjecturing

1. a) Describe the pattern in the numbers.

7	9		6	1		3	26
9	11		15	10		27	50

b) Using the same pattern, complete the next two diagrams.

5	?		100	88
9	8		?	49

2. Predict the next two letters in each sequence.

a) A, Z, B, Y, C, X, ?, ?

b) A, E, F, H, ?, ?

Analyzing Conjectures Using Examples and Counterexamples
Provide one example that supports each of the following conjectures, and then give one counterexample for each conjecture.

1. Multiples of 3 are divisible by 6.

2. If points A, B, and C are collinear, then B lies between A and C.

Deductive Reasoning
Write the conclusion that can be made using each pair of statements.

1. The sides of a square are equal and all the angles are 90°.
Quadrilateral PQRS has an angle of 60°.

2. A magazine and a souvenir cost $7.55. A souvenir and a pair of socks cost $9.00.

3. Prove deductively that the sum of any two

a) consecutive numbers is odd

b) consecutive even numbers is even

c) consecutive odd numbers is even

The Connecting Words *And, Or,* and *Not*
Show the solution set for each compound statement on a number line. In each statement, n is any real number.

1. $n > 5$ and $n < 22$ **2.** $n \geq -3$ and $n \leq 4$

3. $n \leq -1$ or $n < 5$ **4.** $n > 2$ or $n \leq -5$

5. A survey of 120 students was taken.

66 students study English.

42 students study social studies.

38 students study math.

19 students study English and social studies.

18 students study English and math.

16 students study social studies and math.

8 students study English, social studies, and math.

a) Display this information in a Venn diagram.

b) How many students study English and math, but not social studies?

If...then Statements, the Converse, and the Contrapositive
Write the following conditional statements in the *If...then* format. For each, write its converse and its contrapositive. State whether the statement, the converse, and the contrapositive are true or false.

1. The base angles of an isosceles triangle are equal.

2. Congruent triangles are similar triangles.

3. A cow has four legs.

Indirect Proof

1. In △ABC, AB = AC and $x \neq y$.
Use an indirect proof to show that AD is not a median of △ABC.

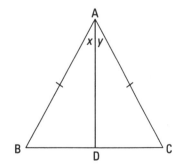

MATHPOWER™ 11, Western Edition, Teacher's Resource

Answers to Reteaching Suggestions

Inductive Reasoning and Conjecturing

1. **a)** The sums of diagonals are equal.   **b)** 4, 61
2. **a)** D, W   **b)** I, K: no curves

Analyzing Conjectures Using Examples and Counterexamples

1. 12 is a multiple of 3. 12 is divisible by 6. Counterexample: 9 is a multiple of 3. 9 is not divisible by 6.
2. The points could lie A, C, and B consecutively on the line.

Deductive Reasoning

Answers may vary.

1. Quadrilateral PQRS is not a square.
2. A magazine could cost $5, a souvenir could cost $2.55, and a pair of socks could cost $6.45.

The Connecting Words And, Or, and Not

1. {6, 7, ..., 20, 21}
2. {−3, −2, −1, ..., 3, 4}
3. {..., −1, 0, 1, 2, 3, 4}
4. {..., −7, −6, −5} or {3, 4, 5, ...}
5. **a)** see diagram   **b)** 10

If...then Statements, the Converse, and the Contrapositive

1. If the base angles of a triangle are equal, then it is isosceles. (true)

   If a triangle is isosceles, then its base angles are equal. (true)

   If the base angles of a triangle are not equal, then it is not isosceles. (true)

2. If triangles are congruent, then they are similar. (true)

   If triangles are similar, then they are congruent. (false)

   If triangles are not congruent, then they are not similar. (true)

3. If the animal is a cow, then it has 4 legs. (true)

   If the animal has 4 legs, then it is a cow. (false)

   If the animal is a not cow, then it does not have 4 legs. (false)

Exploring Mathematics

Mathematical Induction   Read with the class the steps of the process of mathematical induction. Discuss with the class how the method of mathematical induction is like lining up a row of dominoes in such a way that when the first one is knocked over, it knocks the next one, and that one knocks the next one, and so on. Ask:

What is the first step in proving a statement using mathematical induction?

What is the next step?

What is the final step?

Ensure that the students know that the first step is to verify the statement for the first value given, usually $n = 1$. Then, they should assume the statement is true for $n = k$, by rewriting the statement replacing n with k. Finally, they should verify the statement for $k = k + 1$.

Point out to the students that the first value given is not always $n = 1$. For example, the statement $2^n > 2^{n-1} + 1$ is true for all values of n greater than or equal to 2, but it is not true for $n = 1$.

Organize the class into 4 groups and have two groups complete question 1 and two groups complete question 2. When each group has completed the exploration, encourage the groups doing the same exploration to combine and discuss and compare their results. Encourage the students within the combined groups to settle on a proof and then, appoint a spokesperson to present the results to the class.

Chapter Check

Student Text Page
P. 378

Learning Outcome
- Evaluate the skills and concepts in Chapter 6.

Assessing the Outcome

If you assign the Chapter Check as a student assessment, look for the following:
- Do they understand the difference between inductive and deductive reasoning?
- Can they use inductive reasoning to make conjectures?
- Can they provide counterexamples and use them to show false conjectures?
- Can they use deductive reasoning to prove conclusions?
- Can they write compound statements and decide if they are true or false?
- Can they write conditional, contrapositive, converse, and contrapositive statements?

Problem Solving

Learning Outcome
• Use problem solving strategies to solve problems.

Using the Strategies

The problems on this page allow the students to use the problem solving strategies discussed in Chapters 1 to 3. These strategies are
• Use a Diagram
• Use a Data Bank
• Solve Fermi Problems
• Solve a Simpler Problem
• Use Logic
• Look for a Pattern
• Guess and Check
• Work Backward
• Use a Table or Spreadsheet

Teaching Suggestions

Encourage the students to work in pairs or small groups. When students have completed the problems, have them share and discuss their strategies and solutions with other students.

For question 1, suggest that the students write the two-digit prime numbers, and then identify the required pairs of digits.

Question 2 is a Fermi problem, and requires the use of educated guesses or estimates. Have volunteers suggest some questions to be answered. For example,

What would you say is an average speed of a car as it passes through an intersection during rush-hour?

What is the average length of time of one green light?

What do you think is an average distance between the front of one car and the front of the following car as the traffic travels along a road?

For question 7, suggest that the students begin by writing all the 3-digit numbers that are perfect squares.

For question 10, the diagram required to find the total area is shown.

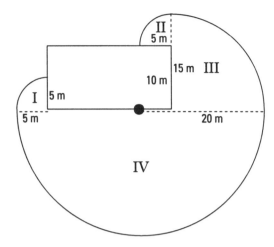

Areas I and II are quarter circles with radius 5 m. Area III is a quarter circle with radius 15 m. Area IV is a semi-circle with radius 20 m.

Sample Solution

Page 379, question 4

Let a and b be the sides of the right triangle. Then, the hypotenuse of the right triangle is $\sqrt{a^2 + b^2}$, and the area of the right triangle is $\frac{ab}{2}$.

Length of sides are a, b, and $\sqrt{a^2 + b^2}$.

$$a + b + \sqrt{a^2 + b^2} = 18 \quad\text{.............(1)}$$
$$a^2 + b^2 + a^2 + b^2 = 128$$
$$2a^2 + 2b^2 = 128$$
$$a^2 + b^2 = 64 \quad\text{.............(2)}$$
$$\sqrt{a^2 + b^2} = 8 \quad\text{.............(3)}$$

Substitute (3) into (1).
$$a + b + 8 = 18$$
$$a + b = 10$$
$$(a + b)^2 = 100$$
$$a^2 + 2ab + b^2 = 100 \quad\text{.............(4)}$$

Substitute (2) into (4).
$$2ab + 64 = 100$$
$$2ab = 32$$
$$ab = 16$$
$$\frac{ab}{2} = 8$$

Area of triangle is 8 cm².

Assessing the Outcome

Observation

As you make your problem solving assessment of each student, consider the following:
• Do they understand the problem?
• Do they consider a variety of strategies?
• Do they use an organized approach?
• Do they create and use diagrams effectively?
• Do they show persistence?

CHAPTER 6

Student Text Answers

Chapter Opener   p. 335

1. **a)** 06:30 to 20:00
   b) 19:00 to 05:00 and 14:00 to 14:30
   c) 20:00 to 22:00, 22:30 to 02:00, 02:30 to 05:00, 06:00 to 07:00
2. 22:00 to 22:30, 02:00 to 02:30, 05:00 to 06:00
3. **a)** 06:30 to 09:30, 12:00 to 13:00, 16:30 to 19:00
   b) 23:00 to 05:00
4. Selina interpreted *or* as either, or both.
   Victor interpreted *or* as either, but not both.

Getting Started   pp. 336–337

1 Patterns and Observations

1. 20th
2. $n + y + 1$
3. **a)** $n - x + 1$ **b)** $n - x + 1 + y$ **c)** $n + y + 1$

2 Using Logical Reasoning

1. Mike and Tia; Carl and Amy; Hari and Sarah
2. **a)** 1, 2, 3   **b)** 2, 5, 4
   c) Mike and Tia; Carl and Amy; Hari and Sarah

3 A Logic Challenge

Carys and Dianne are swimming. Andrew, Barb, and Erik are not swimming.

Mental Math

Complementary and Supplementary Angles

1. 30°	**2.** 70°	**3.** 45°	**4.** 75°
5. 50°	**6.** 18°	**7.** 39°	**8.** 7°
9. 66°	**10.** 86°	**11.** 57°	**12.** 22°
13. 70°	**14.** 130°	**15.** 135°	**16.** 140°
17. 65°	**18.** 105°	**19.** 75°	**20.** 85°
21. 117°	**22.** 68°	**23.** 162°	**24.** 121°

Adding a Column of Numbers

1. 150	**2.** 221	**3.** 299	**4.** 422
5. 440	**6.** 23.7	**7.** 31.3	**8.** 2390
9. 3010	**10.** 2255		

Section 6.1   pp. 340–342

Practice (Section 6.1)

1. The square of a number composed of n 1s consists of the digits 1 to n and $n - 1$ to 1 in order.
   $11\ 111^2 = 123\ 454\ 321$;
   $111\ 111^2 = 12\ 345\ 654\ 321$

2. The sum of the first n odd numbers is equal to n^2.
   $1 + 3 + 5 + 7 + 9 = 25$; $1 + 3 + 5 + 7 + 9 + 11 = 36$
3. The difference between the squares of the $(n + 1)$th and nth odd numbers is equal to $8n$.
   $11^2 - 9^2 = 40$; $13^2 - 11^2 = 48$
4. The last digit of the product of 11 and a two-digit number is the second digit of the two-digit number. The first digits are the sum of the two-digit number and the first digit of the two-digit number.
   $13 \times 11 = 143$; $99 \times 11 = 1089$
5. The sum of a two-digit number and the number consisting of the reverse of the digits of the two-digit number is 11 times the sum of the digits.
   $34 + 43 = 77$; $56 + 65 = 121$
6. The product of a number consisting of n 2s and 9 consists of 1, $(n - 1)$ 9s, and 8.
   $22\ 222 \times 9 = 199\ 998$; $222\ 222 \times 9 = 1\ 999\ 998$
7. The measures of opposite angles of intersecting lines are equal.
8. **a)** In a triangle, the longest side is opposite the largest angle.
   b) In a triangle, the shortest side is opposite the smallest angle.
9. The line segment joining the midpoints of two sides of a triangle is parallel to the third side, and one-half the length of the third side.
10. **a)** The sum of the numbers in the nth row is $(n - 1)^3 + n^3$.
    b) $26 + 27 + 28 + 29 + 30 + 31 + 32 + 33 + 34 + 35 + 36 = 341 = 5^3 + 6^3$

Applications and Problem Solving (Section 6.1)

11. The sums of the two pairs of numbers at opposite corners of a rectangular array on a calendar page are equal.
12. A figure with a diagonal made from n cross-stitches has $2n - 2$ cross-stitches.
13. **a)** 768, 3072   **b)** 45, 52   **c)** 256, 8192
    d) U, B   **e)** N, O
14. $98 = 79 + 19$
15. **a)** 6
    b) $\dfrac{n(n - 1)}{2}$ line segments are required to join every pair of points when there are n points in a plane.
16. **b)** There are $2n + 2$ hydrogen atoms for n carbon atoms in a straight-chain alkane.

17. For a pendulum length of l centimetres, the period is $\frac{\sqrt{l}}{5}$ seconds.

18. a) 7
  b) The maximum number of pieces for k cuts is $\frac{k(k+1)}{2} + 1$.

19. 7, 8, 40; The numbers are arranged first according to the number of letters in the name of the number, and then in numerical order.

20. a) 1, 1, 2, 3, 5, 8, 13, 21, 34, 55, 89, 144
  b) 4, 12, 33, 88, 143
  c) $t_2 + t_4 + t_6 + \ldots + t_{2k} = t_{2k+1} - 1$

21. a) $\angle 3$ is equal to $\angle 7$; $\angle 2$ and $\angle 6$, $\angle 1$ and $\angle 5$, $\angle 4$ and $\angle 8$; yes
  b) The sum of $\angle 3$ and $\angle 6$ is 180°; $\angle 4$ and $\angle 5$; yes

22. a) $x \triangle y$ means multiply the first number by one more than the second number.

Section 6.2 pp. 345–346

Practice (Section 6.2)

1. 8, 16; 12
2. 25 + 49 = 74, 9 + 1 = 10, 9 + 16 = 25
3. 4 − 1 = 3, 9 − 4 = 5; 25 − 16 = 9
4. $\sqrt{9} = 3$, $\sqrt{16} = 4$; $\sqrt{0.01} = 0.1$
5. $52 = 4^2 + 6^2$, $100 = 6^2 + 8^2$; $74 = 5^2 + 7^2$
6. $\sqrt{5^2} = 5$, $\sqrt{6^2} = 6$; $\sqrt{(-5)^2} = 5$
7. (2, 5), (3, 6); (2, −1)

Applications and Problem Solving (Section 6.2)

13. Prince Edward Island
14. a) penguins   **b)** Manx cats
15. a) $a = 1$, $b = 2$, $c = 3$, $d = 4$, $a = 5$, $b = 6$, $c = 7$, $d = 8$; $a = -5$, $b = 5$, $c = -7$, $d = 7$
  b) positive real numbers
16. b) rhombus
17. b) $A_1 = \frac{\pi d^2}{4}$; $A_2 = \pi d^2$
18. a) $1 + 2 = 3$, $1 + 2 + 4 = 7$; $1 + 2 + 4 + 8 = 15$
  b) $2^2 - 1 = 3$, $2^3 - 1 = 7$; $2^1 - 1 = 1$
  c) $1^2 - 1 + 41 = 41$; $2^2 - 2 + 41 = 43$; $41^2 - 41 + 41 = 41^2$
19. equilateral triangle; quadrilateral with 3 equal angles and one not equal
20. a) $2 + 7 = 9$ but $7 - 2 = 5$, $7 - 3 = 4$ but $7 + 3 = 10$; $2 + 2 = 4$, $2 - 2 = 0$
  b) This is the only counterexample.
21. a) $0 < y \leq 1.4$ **b)** $x = -1$ gives $y = -1$
  c) Answers may vary.

Section 6.3 p. 349

Practice (Section 6.3)

1. Paulette lives in Alberta.
2. All dogs have hearts.
3. Stella is taller than Annisa.
4. The sum of 11 and 12 is an odd number.
5. The diagonals of PQRS bisect each other.
6. The diagonals of KLMN intersect at right angles.
7. $\triangle ABC$ has two equal angles.
8. a) The final number is the original number.

Applications and Problem Solving (Section 6.3)

12. Their heights are also different.
13. PQRS is a kite.

Section 6.4 pp. 354–356

Practice (Section 6.4)

1. statement
2. not a statement
3. statement
4. not a statement
5. statement
6. 1, 2, 3, 6
7. 0, 2, 4, 6, 8
8. 1, 3
9. 0, 1, 4, 9, 16, 25, 36, 49
10. 2, 3, 5, 7, 11, 13, 17, 19
11. 1, 2, 3, 4, 6, 8, 9, 12, 18, 24
12. 0, 1, 2, 3, 4, 5, 6, 7, 8, 9, 12
13. 1, 2, 3, 6
14. 0, 1, 3, 5, 15
15. 1, 2, 3, 5, 6, 7, 9, 11, 18
32. $n \leq 1$ and $n \geq -4$
33. $n < 2$ and $n \geq -1$
34. $n < 3$ and $n > -1$
35. $n \leq 4$ and $n > -4$
36. $n < -2$ or $n \geq 2$
37. Answers may vary. $n > -4$ or $n > 2$
38. $n < 0$ or $n > 0$
39. $n < -1$ or $n \geq 1$
40. Paulo does not live in Edmonton.
41. The number 3 is not the smallest prime number.
42. Not all isosceles triangles have 3 acute angles.
43. Ben is not older than Katerina.
44. Deepak is not telling the truth.
45. The Canucks did not win their game last night.
47. 3, 5, 7, 11, 13, 17, 19
48. 2, 3, 4, 5, 6, 7, 8, 10, 11, 12, 13, 14, 16, 17, 18, 19
49. 1, 9, 15
50. There are no numbers that are even, odd, and prime.
51. b) 6

Applications and Problem Solving (Section 6.4)

53. $n < 4$

55. $x \geq -1$ and $x < 4$

56. a) 151   **b)** 65   **c)** 63   **d)** 13

57. b) 109   **c)** 2

58. b) 218

59. Answers may vary. $x \geq 0$ or $x < 0$

60. $x \leq 5$ and $x \geq 5$

61. $x^2 < 0$ or $-x^2 > 0$

62. a) not possible   **b)** $x < 0$ and $x > 0$

63. b) 6   **c)** 37

Technology p. 357

1 Comparing Searches

1. G or H; I

2. Logically the searches have the same meaning.

3. D

4. AND and OR are associative.

2 Making Up Searches

1. mathematics AND NOT magic OR mathematics AND NOT cards

Section 6.5 pp. 361–362

Practice (Section 6.5)

1. If angles are opposite, then they are equal.

2. If you are a Canadian at least 18 years old, then you may vote.

3. If a figure is a quadrilateral, then it is a polygon.

4. If a prime number is greater than 2, then it is odd.

5. If an angle measures 90°, then its sine is 1.

6. If a figure is a rectangle, then its diagonals bisect each other.

7. If a person lives in Moose Jaw, then the person lives in Saskatchewan.

8. If a triangle is a right triangle, then it has two acute angles.

9. A polygon is a pentagon if and only if it has exactly five sides.

10. A number is rational if and only if it can be expressed as a quotient of two integers.

11. A number is prime if and only if it has no factors other than itself and one.

12. A triangle is isosceles if and only if it has two sides of equal length.

13. A trinomial is a perfect square trinomial if and only if it can be factored as the square of a binomial.

14. If $x^2 = 36$, then $x = 6$; false, $x = -6$

15. If $|x| = 4$, then $x = -4$; false, $x = 4$

16. If $n + 1$ is an odd number, then n is an even number; true

17. If a rectangle is a square, then it has 4 equal sides; true

18. If a triangle is equilateral, then it has three equal sides; true

19. If a quadrilateral is a trapezoid, then it has one pair of opposite sides that are parallel; true

20. If the slope of a line is 3, then the equation of the line is $y = 3x + 1$; false, $y = 3x + 2$

21. true; If $x^2 = 16$, then $x = -4$, false; If $x^2 \neq 16$, then $x \neq -4$, true

22. true; If $|x| = 3$, then $x = 3$, false; If $|x| \neq 3$, then $x \neq 3$, true

23. true; If $2n + 1$ is odd, then n is even, false; If $2n + 1$ is even, then n is odd, true

24. true; If n is a multiple of 3, then n is a multiple of 6, false; If n is not a multiple of 3, then n is not a multiple of 6, true

25. true; If x is an odd number, then x^2 is an odd number, true; If x is an even number, then x^2 is an even number, true

26. true; If the diagonals of a quadrilateral are equal, it is a rectangle, false; If the diagonals of a quadrilateral are not equal, it is not a rectangle, true

27. true; If $x = 7$, then $3x - 5 = 16$, true; If $x \neq 7$, then $3x - 5 \neq 16$, true

Applications and Problem Solving (Section 6.5)

28. a) yes   **b)** If $x^2 > 0$, then $x < 0$; false
c) If $x^2 \leq 0$, then $x \leq 0$; true (for $x = 0$)

29. a) no   **b)** If $a = b$, then $a^2 = b^2$; true
c) If $a \neq b$, then $a^2 \neq b^2$; false

30. a) yes
b) If the midpoint of AB is M(5, 10), then the endpoints of AB are A(3, 8) and B(7, 12); false; A(5, 5) and B(5, 15) have a midpoint of M(5, 10).

31. a) that if you have good taste, you will eat at their restaurant
b) People with good taste eat at other restaurants.

32. a) If p is a factor of c, then $x - p$ is a factor of $x^2 + bx + c$; $x - 3$ is not a factor of $x^2 + 6x + 9$, but 3 is a factor of 9
b) If p is not a factor of c, then $x - p$ is not a factor of $x^2 + bx + c$.

33. Answers may vary.

34. The contrapositive must be true.

Technology p. 363

1 Testing If ... then Statements

1. false   **2.** true   **3.** true   **4.** false
5. false   **6.** false   **7.** true   **8.** true
9. true   **10.** true   **11.** true   **12.** false

2 Solving Inequalities

1. If $12 - 3x \geq 23 - 14x$, then $x \geq 1$.

2. If $4x - 13 \leq -3x + 8$, then $x \leq 3$.

3. If $x^2 < x - 20$, then x is not a real number.

4. If $x^2 > -3x + 18$, then $x < -6$ or $x > 3$.

5. If $\dfrac{8}{x-3} > 4$, then $x > 3$ and $x < 5$.

6. If $\dfrac{5}{x+4} \leq 2$, then $x < -4$ or $x \geq -\dfrac{3}{2}$.

Investigating Math pp. 364–365

1 Congruent Triangles

1. a) AB = PQ, BC = QR, ∠ABC = ∠PQR
   b) SAS
   c) AC = PR, ∠BAC = ∠QPR, ∠BCA = ∠QRP
2. a) ∠EDF = ∠KJL, DF = JL, ∠DFE = ∠JLK
   b) ASA
   c) ∠DEF = ∠JKL, DE = JK, EF = KL
3. a) ZX = TR, ∠ZXY = ∠TRS, XY = RS
   b) SAS
   c) ∠XYZ = ∠RST, YZ = ST, ∠YZX = ∠STR
4. a) PQ = UW, QR = WV, RP = VU
   b) SSS
   c) ∠PQR = ∠UWV, ∠QRP = ∠WVU, ∠RAQ = ∠VUW

2 Triangles with Common Points and Sides

1. a) AB = CD, BC = DA, AC = CA
   b) SSS
   c) ∠ABC = ∠CDA, ∠BCA = ∠DAC, ∠CAB = ∠ACD
2. a) PR = TR, ∠PRQ = ∠TRS, RQ = RS
   b) SAS
   c) ∠RQP = ∠RST, QP = ST, ∠QPR = ∠STR
3. a) WZ = YZ, ∠WZX = ∠YZX, ZX = ZX
   b) SAS
   c) ∠ZXW = ∠ZXY, XW = XY, ∠XWZ = ∠XYZ
4. a) ∠EDF = ∠GHR, DF = HF, ∠DFE = ∠HFG
   b) ASA
   c) FE = FG, ∠FED = ∠FGH, ED = GH
5. a) ∠DAC = ∠BCA, AC = CA, ∠DCA = ∠BAC
   b) ASA
   c) AD = CB, ∠ADC = ∠CBA, DC = BA
6. a) UT = WT, TV = TV, VU = VW
   b) SSS
   c) ∠UTV = ∠WTV, ∠TVU = ∠TVW, ∠VUT = ∠VWT
7. a) JM = LM, ∠JMK = ∠LMK, MK = MK
   b) SAS
   c) ∠MKJ = ∠MKL, KJ = KL, ∠KJM = ∠KLM
8. a) ∠XYW = ∠ZYW, YW = YW, ∠YWX = ∠YWZ   **b)** ASA
   c) WX = WZ, ∠WXY = ∠WZY, XY = ZY
9. a) KL = NM, ∠KLM = ∠NML, LM = ML
   b) SAS
   c) ∠LMK = ∠MLN, MK = LN, ∠MKL = ∠LNM

10. a) ∠BAD = ∠CDA, AD = DA, ∠BDA = ∠CAD
   b) ASA
   c) AB = DC, ∠ABD = ∠DCA, BD = CA

Section 6.6 p. 372

Practice (Section 6.6)

1. Less than 2 people were born in the same month.
2. There is a greatest whole number.
3. The sum of two odd integers is an odd integer.
4. Suspect A is guilty of the crime.

Computer Data Bank p. 373

1 True or False

1. true
2. false, change 60 campsites to 30
3. true
4. false, change national to provincial

2 Facilities

1. Alberta $\dfrac{8}{51}$; British Columbia $\dfrac{87}{191}$, Manitoba $\dfrac{1}{33}$; Saskatchewan $\dfrac{3}{23}$
2. Birds Hill, Grand Beach, Spruce Woods, and Whiteshell
3. 27
4. 161
5. Alberta

3 Hiking Trails

$\dfrac{92}{103}$

4 Campsite Density

1. Answers will vary.
2. Answers will vary.

5 National Parks

47 087 662 ha, 5 231 962 ha

6 Planning a Visit

1. Answers will vary.
2. Answers will vary.

Connecting Math and Computers
pp. 374–375

1 Determining the Output

1. a) 2 and 7 **b)** 7 and 18 **c)** 2 and 18 **d)** yes
2. a) x, y **b)** x, z **c)** y, z **d)** yes

2 More Complicated Sorting Networks

1. a) 5 and 22 **b)** 29 and 51 **c)** 5 and 51
   d) 22 and 51 **e)** 5 and 29
2. no **3.** yes

1. **a)** 8, 188, 2888, 38 888   **b)** 8 888 888 888
2. 144
3. **a)** 95, 191   **b)** 244, 730
   c) 6561, 1 594 323   **d)** 44, 47
4. $(-4, -7); (4, -7)$
5. $8 \div 4 = 2; 6 \div 4 = 1.5$
7. 1; 0
9. 96 is divisible by 6.
10. $\angle R$ is a reflex angle.
11. Miko will go swimming tomorrow.
12. In $\triangle KLM$, each of the three angles measures 60°.
13. **a)** The result is the original number.
23. **b)** 12
24. **b)** 30   **c)** 51%   **d)** 68
25. true; If a prime number is odd, then it is greater than 2, true; If a prime number is even, then it is less than or equal to 2, true
26. true; If a polygon is a triangle, then it has three sides, true; If a polygon is not a triangle, then it does not have three sides, true
27. true; If $\triangle XYZ$ is obtuse, then $\angle X + \angle Y < 90°$, false; If $\triangle XYZ$ is not obtuse, then $\angle X + \angle Y \geq 90°$, true
28. false; If $x > 0$, then $x^2 > 0$, true; If $x \leq 0$, then $x^2 \leq 0$, false

Chapter Check p. 378

1. **a)** $6 + 12\ 345 \times 9 = 111\ 111$,
      $7 + 123\ 456 \times 9 = 1\ 111\ 111$
2. **a)** 6, 10
   b) The number of angles formed by n rays is $\dfrac{n^2 - n}{2}$.
3. January; February
4. 3; 2
5. $-1, 2, -3; 1, 2, 3$
9. Marcel is likely to get a speeding ticket.
10. Sonya is a teenager.
11. The point P is in the third quadrant.
12. 1, 2
13. 2, 4, 6, 12
14. 1, 2, 3, 4, 5, 6, 7, 9, 11, 12
15. 0, 1, 2, 3, 4, 6, 8, 9, 12, 15, 18, 24
16. true; If $a + b$ is an odd number, then a and b are consecutive natural numbers, false; If $a + b$ is an even number, then a and b are not consecutive natural numbers, true
17. true; If $\triangle ABC$ contains two acute angles, then it is a right triangle, false; If $\triangle ABC$ does not contain two acute angles, then it is not a right triangle, true
18. false; If $x = 5$, then $x^2 = 25$, true; If $x \neq 5$, then $x^2 \neq 25$, false
19. $\angle x + \angle y = 180°$

Using the Strategies p. 379

1. 3
3. 6 km/h
4. 9 square units
5. D
6. 1982
7. 12
8. 25
9. 13
10. 825 m²
11. 35

Data Bank

1. 7.2 m
2. Answers may vary.
3. Answers may vary.

CHAPTER 7

The Circle

Chapter Introduction

Chapter Materials

graphing calculators, Teacher's Resource Master 1 (0.5-cm grid paper), overhead projector, overhead graphing calculator, compasses, rulers, Miras, protractors, straightedges, string, coloured pencils, geometry software

Chapter Concepts

Chapter 7 reviews or introduces
- proving geometric theorems using the formal two-column, the flow-chart, and the informal paragraph methods of proof
- developing the chord properties of a circle
- developing the properties of the angles in a circle
- developing the theorems of the angles of a cyclic quadrilateral
- developing the theorems of the tangents of a circle
- developing the formula for finding the arc length and the area of a sector of a circle

Teaching Suggestions

Method 1

(compasses, straightedges, overhead projector) Read with the class the opening paragraphs on student text page 381. Assign the assignment to small groups of students. Point out to the students that they are to deal with one circle that is to touch three other circles. Encourage them to be organized by asking:

If any or all of the 3 fixed circles can be placed either inside or outside the large circle, how many combinations are possible?

Lead the students to see that

1. the smallest fixed circle can be inside and the other 2 outside
2. the middle fixed circle can be inside and the other 2 outside
3. the largest fixed circle can be inside and the other 2 outside
4. the smallest and the middle fixed circles can be inside and the largest outside
5. the smallest and the largest fixed circles can be inside and the middle outside
6. the middle and the largest fixed circles can be inside and the smallest outside
7. all 3 fixed circles can be inside
8. all 3 fixed circles can be outside

Ask:

Which solutions are given on the student text page?

Challenge the groups to sketch the remaining 6 solutions, and then, have each group choose 2 of the solutions to draw accurately. Ensure that all the solutions are evenly chosen.

Have volunteers present their results to the class. Provide an overhead projector for the students' use. The following are the 6 remaining solutions.

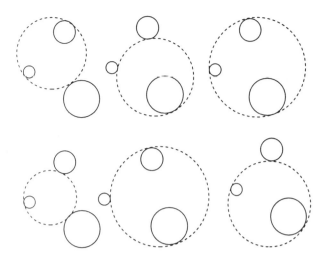

Method 2

(compasses, straightedges)   Have small groups of students construct circles congruent to the 4 given circles on student text page 389. Have the students colour the moveable circle one colour and the 3 fixed circles a second colour. Then, have them label the 3 fixed circles small, medium, and large.

Suggest that the groups move the circles around on a table top until a suitable solution has been found.

Have volunteers present their results to the class. Provide an overhead projector for the students' use. Ensure that the remaining 6 solutions are found.

Integrating Technology

Internet

Use the Internet to find information about The Great Geometer, Apollonius of Perga and circles in architecture.

Enrichment

Make a poster of Apollonius' problem. Include some information about his life, works, and peers. Display your poster on a class bulletin board.

Assessing the Outcomes

Observation

You might consider some of these questions as you observe the students work.
- Do they know how to use the compasses and straightedges?
- Do they know how to organize the information?
- Do they work well in pairs or groups?
- Do they persist until they find a solution?
- Do they attempt all the questions?
- Do they use a variety of problem solving strategies?

Getting Started

Student Text Pages
Pp. 382–383

Materials
overhead projector

Learning Outcomes
- Develop angle relationships.
- Review congruent triangles theorems.

Prerequisite Skills
Solve.

a) $2x + 5 = 75$ [35]

b) $4x - 2 = 3x + 50$ [52]

c) $3x + 2x + 10 + 5x - 30 = 180$ [20]

d) $5x + 3x - 15 = 89$ [13]

e) $90 - (3x - 5) = 2x$ [19]

f) $180 - (2x + 50) = 20$ [55]

Teaching Suggestions

Angle Relationships

(overhead projector) Review with the class the terms "complementary angles" and "supplementary angles," and the theorems developed in Chapter 6 of *MATHPOWER™ 11, Western Edition*. These theorems include the Triangle Angle Sum Theorem, the Exterior Angle Theorem, the Opposite Angle Theorem, and the Transversal Parallel Lines Theorem and its converse.

Have volunteers present a theorem to the class. Encourage them to draw diagrams on the chalkboard, or to prepare diagrams in advance and present them on an overhead projector.

Organize the class into 4 groups and assign 4 questions of Investigation 1 to each group. Ensure that all the questions in Investigation 1 are assigned.

Have volunteers present their results to the class. Provide an overhead projector, if necessary.

Congruent Triangles

Review with the class the theorems explored in *Investigating Math, Reviewing Congruent Triangles*, in *MATHPOWER™ 11, Western Edition*, on student text pages 364 and 365. Have volunteers present their theorems, along with appropriate diagrams to the class. Provide an overhead projector, if necessary.

Show the students an example of ASS—where you have both an obtuse and an acute possibility from the given information. Explain to the students that this is an example of the ambiguous case.

Assign one question to pairs of students, ensuring that all the questions are assigned. Have volunteers present their results to the class.

Mental Math
Students could choose, or be assigned, certain questions from each section. Alternatively, small groups could work as teams, sharing the questions and explaining the answers to the rest of the group.

Assessing the Outcomes
Observation
You may want to consider some of the following skills as the students complete this lesson.
- Do the students remember the theorems they previously developed?
- Do the students use algebra to find the required values for the variables?
- Do the students check their algebraic work?
- Do the students work well together or do they tend to work independently?

Investigating Math

Using the Equality Properties of Real Numbers

Student Text Page
P. 384

Learning Outcomes
- Review the equality properties of real numbers.
- Write reasons to explain the truth of statements.
- Give reasons for each step of the solution of an equation.

Mental Math
1. Evaluate for $x = 1$ and $y = -5$.

a) $2x + 2y$ $[-8]$ b) $-x + 3y$ $[-16]$

c) $x^2 - y^2$ $[-24]$ d) $x^2 + 2y$ $[-9]$

e) $3x^2 + y^2$ $[28]$ f) $5y + x$ $[-24]$

2. Calculate.

a) 9.7×92 $[802.4]$ b) 47×43 $[2021]$

c) 61×0.63 $[38.43]$ d) 32×48 $[1536]$

e) 4.9×4.1 $[20.09]$ f) 8.2×89 $[729.8]$

Teaching Suggestions

Review the table of properties given at the top of student text page 384. Challenge volunteers to present to the class a numerical example for each property. Remind the students that the variables can represent fractions and decimals.

Arrange the class into 5 groups of approximately the same size, and assign Investigation 1. Have group 1 complete statements 1 to 3, group 2 complete statements 4 to 6, etc. Have volunteers present their results to the class.

Assign Investigation 2. Have each group choose an equation, ensuring that all the equations are chosen, and complete the investigation. Have volunteers present their results to the class.

Extension
Write three statements like those in Investigation 1. Exchange your statements with those of another student, and identify which property your classmate used in the statements. Discuss and compare your statements with your classmate.

Math Journal
real number properties   Copy the table of properties of real numbers into your journal. Include a numerical example of each property for clarity.

Common Errors
- Students sometimes find it difficult to differentiate between the transitive property and the substitution property.

$\mathbf{R_x}$ Point out to the students that with the transitive property, one whole side is replaced by another expression, but with the substitution property, only the variable is replaced by a number or expression.

    Also, the transitive property involves three expressions, while the substitution property involves two.

Assessing the Outcomes
Journal

Write a short essay about a property of a number that you did not know before completing this section.

    Select one property that you think is the most significant, and defend you choice in a short essay.

Written Assignment

Identify the property used to write each statement.

1. If $2x + 1 = 0$, then $2x = -1$.
2. If $5x = 15$, then $x = 3$.
3. If $5y - 2 = 11$, then $5y = 13$.
4. If $\frac{x}{2} = -1$, then $x = -2$.
5. If $3x + 6 = 2y + 6$, then $3x = 2y$.
6. If $2x = 9$ and $3y = 9$, then $2x = 3y$.
7. If $2x = 3y$, then $2xy = 3y^2$.

7.1 Geometric Proofs

Student Text Pages
Pp. 385–392

Learning Outcomes

- Understand the process of writing two-column geometric proofs.
- Understand the process of writing flow-chart geometric proofs.
- Understand the process of writing paragraph or informal geometric proofs.

Prerequisite Skills

Give a reason why each statement is true.

1.
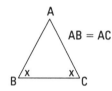

$AB = AC$

[The sides opposite the equal angles of an isosceles triangle are equal.]

2.
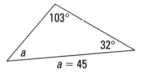

$a = 45$

[The sum of the angles of a triangle is 180°.]

3.
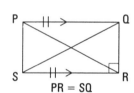

$PR = SQ$

[The diagonals of a rectangle are equal.]

4.
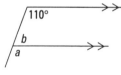

$a = 110, b = 70$

[The corresponding angles made by parallel lines cut by a transversal are equal. Angles that form a straight line are supplementary.]

Mental Math

1. Find the value of each variable.

a)   b)
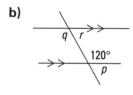

[44]   [$q = 120, r = p = 60$]

2. Evaluate each expression for the given values of x.
   a) $x + 2$; $x = -1, 0, 1, 2$ [1, 2, 3, 4]
   b) $3x - 5$; $x = 0, 1, 1.5, 2$ [−5, −2, −0.5, 1]
   c) $x^2 - 1$; $x = -2, -1, 0, 1$ [3, 0, −1, 0]
   d) $-2x - 9$; $x = 2, 4, 6, 8$ [−13, −17, −21, −27]
   e) $3x - x + 1$; $x = 0, 1, 2, 3$ [1, 3, 5, 7]
   f) $-x^2 + x$; $x = \frac{1}{2}, 1, \frac{3}{2}, 2$ $\left[\frac{1}{4}, 0, -\frac{3}{4}, -2\right]$

Explore/Inquire Answers

Explore: Complete the Proof

a) given b) given c) Opposite Angles Theorem
d) SAS e) congruent triangles f) Transversal Parallel Lines Theorem (alternate angles)

Inquire

1. From lines a) and c), we know that point A corresponds to point C, since point E corresponds to point F. Thus, the angles at A and C are equal.
2. $\angle ADE = \angle CBE$

Teaching Suggestions

Read with the class the opening paragraphs on student text page 385. Ask:

What examples can you give of the use of the word "proof" in every day life?

What type of reasoning do you use to prove theorems?

What type of reasoning do you use when stating postulates?

Review the properties of numbers from *Investigating Math* on student text page 384, and then, assign the Explore section and the Inquire questions to pairs of students.

Have each pair of students work through Inquire question 3, and discuss and compare their results with other students. Have volunteers present their results to the class.

Discuss the three formats of writing a proof given in teaching examples 1 to 3 on student text pages 386 to 387. Point out that the starting point of the two-column proof is the given facts and the end point is the statement that has to be proven. The steps in between are to be completed as necessary.

Try to write the steps in the order of the congruency theorem you plan to use. That is, if you are using SAS, start with a side, then an angle, and then a side.

Review with the students the methods used in teaching examples 4 to 6 on student text pages 388 and 389. Challenge some students to rewrite a proof using a different method. Have volunteers present their results to the class.

Integrating Technology

Internet

Use the Internet to find information about Sherlock Holmes, *The Five Orange Pips*, Sir Arthur Conan Doyle, and Euclid.

Enrichment

Research a career that uses proof to establish facts. Present your career to the class.

Math Journal

Write a short essay describing which method of proof you prefer and why. Exchange your essay with that of a classmate's and read his or her essay. If the other student prefers a method of proof other than your preferred method, engage in constructive debate about the merits of your choice.

Common Errors

- Students often become confused about the different theorems and postulates as more of them are introduced.

R_x Ensure that the students keep a list of the theorems and postulates as they are introduced in the text. The students can use this list as an easy reference whenever necessary.

Problem Levels of Difficulty

A: 1–14   **B:** 15–30   **C:** 31–34

Assessing the Outcomes

Journal

Describe each method of proof: formal two-column, flow-chart, and informal paragraph. Explain a strength and a weakness of each one.

Written Assignment

1. Use the diagram to write a two-column proof to show that ∠EKB = ∠AJM.

2. Use the diagram to write a flow-chart proof to show that ∠EKJ and ∠KJG are supplementary.

3. Use the diagram to write a paragraph proof to show that ∠EKB + ∠DLF + ∠HMC + ∠AJG = 360°.

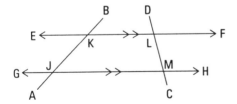

Computer Data Bank

Terrestrial Craters

Microsoft Works for Windows users see *Part B*, and Microsoft Access users see *Part D*, of *MATHPOWER*™ 11, *Western Edition, Computer Data Bank Teacher's Resource*.

Student Text Page

P. 393

Learning Outcomes

- Display, find, sort, calculate, and analyze data in a computer database.
- Interpret quadratic functions.
- Model using quadratic functions.

Prerequisite Skills

Write a quadratic equation for the parabola with vertex $(5, -1)$, passing through $(10, 0)$.

$$\left[y = \frac{1}{25}(x - 5)^2 - 1 \right]$$

Getting Started Blackline Masters C-1, C-2, C-4 to C-6, and C-8

Teaching Suggestions

Students unfamiliar with computer databases and ClarisWorks would benefit from working through *Getting Started* Blackline Masters C-1, C-2, C-4 to C-6, and C-8, noted in the Prerequisite Skills, prior to doing any of the explorations on this page. Minimally, students should have *Getting Started* Blackline Masters C-1, C-2, C-4 to C-6, and C-8 available for reference.

Exploration 1 must be completed before the other explorations, all of which are independent of one another, can be attempted. Some or all of the explorations can be assigned to individuals, pairs, or small groups of students, to be completed over a period of time that allows students adequate computer time. Up to 1.5 h will be needed by some students to complete all four explorations.

Terrestrial Craters is an opportunity for cross-curricular learning.

When assigning the explorations, inform students if you expect

- any parts of the explorations to be printed off the computer
- handwritten or word-processed answers to questions that suggest a written response
- a journal-type response about what they have learned mathematically, about using databases, and/or about the subject matter of the database

Possible parts to assign for printing are a table to show the simple craters with the calculation fields and the values of *a* sorted from Exploration 2; tables to justify

answers from Exploration 3; and tables to justify answers from Exploration 4.

The craters in the database are the known terrestrial craters.

1 Simple and Complex Craters

If a crater has at least one of the two central peak dimensions, it must be complex. If a crater has neither of the central peak dimensions, there is a good chance that it is a simple crater. However, it could just be that the central peak dimensions are not available.

An efficient approach to question 2 is to display the records using Table 2 and use the Find feature with two comparisons for *Central Peak Height, km* -1 and *Central Peak Diameter, km* -1, to find the simple craters, noting the number of records displayed. Then, subtract that number from the total number of records to find the number of complex craters, because all the other craters have at least one of the two central peak dimensions.

2 Simple Craters

In question 1, show all the records, displaying them using Full Record. Then, use the Find feature with three comparisons for *Country* Canada, *Diameter, km* 2.44, and *Apparent Depth, km* 0.34 (*Getting Started* BLM C-5).

In question 2, some students will sketch the parabolic shape symmetrically about the positive vertical axis; others will sketch it symmetrically about the negative vertical axis; others will sketch it in the first quadrant, starting at the positive vertical axis; others will sketch it in the fourth quadrant, starting at the origin. The responses that follow are for the last situation.

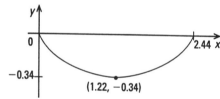

In question 3, p is half of the diameter, and q is the opposite of the apparent depth.

In question 4, the value of a is found by substituting the values of p and q found in question 3 and values for x and y using a point on the parabola, such as $(0, 0)$ or $(2.44, 0)$, into $y = a(x - p)^2 + q$, and solving.

An efficient approach to question 5 is to analyze the equation solved for a in question 4.

$$y = a(x - p)^2 + q, \qquad \text{where } y = 0,\ x = 0,$$
$$0 = a(0 - 1.22)^2 - 0.34 \quad p = 1.22,\ \text{and}\ q = -0.34$$
$$\frac{0.34}{(1.22)^2} = a$$
$$\text{i.e., } \frac{-q}{p^2} = a$$

Then, show all the records and use the Find feature with four comparisons for *Central Peak Height, km* -1, *Central Peak Diameter, km* -1, *Diameter, km* $<>-1$, and *Apparent Depth, km* $<>-1$ (*Getting Started*

BLM C-5). Next, create a table displaying only the *Name*, *Diameter, km*, and *Apparent Depth, km* fields (*Getting Started* BLM C-2). Then, create three calculation fields called *p*, *q*, and *a*, using the formulas that follow, with *a* rounded to 3 decimal places (*Getting Started* BLM C-6). Finally, for each displayed record, the values for *p*, *q*, and *a* can be substituted into $y = a(x - p)^2 + q$ to model the shape of the crater.

'Diameter, km'/2

−'Apparent Depth, km'

ROUND(−'q'/'p'^2,3)

In question 7, sort from least to greatest value of *a* (*Getting Started* BLM C-4).

3 Simple Crater Characteristics

An efficient approach to question 1 is to deal with each generalization separately. Show all the records, displaying them using Full Record. Then, use the Find feature with four comparisons for *Central Peak Height, km* −1, *Central Peak Diameter, km* −1, *Diameter, km* <>−1, and *True Depth, km* <>−1, noting the number of records displayed (*Getting Started* BLM C-5). Next, create a table displaying only the *Name*, *Diameter*, and *True Depth, km* fields (*Getting Started* BLM C-2). Then, create a calculation field called *True Depth as a Percent of Diameter*, using the formula that follows, to express the true depth as a percent of the diameter, rounded to 2 decimal places (*Getting Started* BLM C-6). Next, sort the calculation field (*Getting Started* BLM C-4). It is useful to print the sorted table to use in question 2. Then, identify how many records have a true depth as a percent of diameter that is close to 20%, for example, between 16% and 24%. Next, express that number of records as a percent of the number of records displayed, using a calculator.

ROUND('True Depth, km'/'Diameter, km'*100,2)

Then, show all the records, displaying them using Full Record. Next, use the Find feature with four comparisons for *Central Peak Height, km* −1, *Central Peak Diameter, km* −1, *Diameter, km* <>−1, and *Rim Height, km* <>−1 (*Getting Started* BLM C-5). Then, create a table displaying only the *Name*, *Diameter*, and *Rim Height, km* fields (*Getting Started* BLM C-2). Next, create a calculation field called *Rim Height as a Percent of Diameter*, using the formula that follows, to express the rim height as a percent of the diameter, rounded to 2 decimal places (*Getting Started* BLM C-6). Then, sort the calculation field (*Getting Started* BLM C-4). It is useful to print the sorted table to use in question 2. Next, identify how many records have a rim height as a percent of diameter that is close to 4%, for example, between 3% and 5%. Then, express that number of records as a percent of the number of records displayed, using a calculator. Finally, decide if the generalizations are validated by these records.

ROUND('Rim Height, km'/'Diameter, km'*100,2)

In question 2, use the printed tables of the sorted records from question 1 to locate a crater that is close to both percents of interest.

4 Complex Crater Characteristics

An efficient approach to question 1 is similar to the approach to Exploration 3, dealing with each generalization separately. Show all the records, displaying them using Full Record. Then, use the Find feature with two comparisons for *Diameter, km* <>−1 and *Central Peak Diameter, km* <>−1, noting the number of records displayed (*Getting Started* BLM C-5). Next, create a table displaying only the *Name*, *Diameter*, and *Central Peak Diameter, km* fields (*Getting Started* BLM C-2). Then, create a calculation field called *Central Peak Diameter as a Percent of Diameter*, using the formula that follows, to express the central peak diameter as a percent of the diameter, rounded to 2 decimal places (*Getting Started* BLM C-6). Next, sort the calculation field (*Getting Started* BLM C-4). It is useful to print the sorted table to use in question 2. Then, identify how many records have a central peak diameter as a percent of diameter that is close to 22%, for example, between 18% and 26%. Next, express that number of records as a percent of the number of records displayed, using a calculator.

ROUND('Central Peak Diameter, km'/'Diameter, km'*100,2)

Then, show all the records, displaying them using Full Record. Next, use the Find feature with two comparisons for *Diameter, km* <>−1 and *Central Peak Height, km* <>−1, noting the number of records displayed (*Getting Started* BLM C-5). Then, create a table displaying only the *Name*, *Diameter*, and *Central Peak Height, km* fields (*Getting Started* BLM C-2). Next, create a calculation field called *Central Peak Height as a Percent of Diameter*, using the formula that follows, to express the central peak height as a percent of the diameter, rounded to 2 decimal places (*Getting Started* BLM C-6). Then, sort the calculation field (*Getting Started* BLM C-4). It is useful to print the sorted table to use in question 2. Next, identify how many records have a central peak height as a percent of diameter that is close to 8%, for example, between 6% and 10%. Then, express that number of records as a percent of the number of records displayed, using a calculator. Finally, decide if these generalizations are validated by these records.

ROUND('Central Peak Height, km'/'Diameter, km'*100,2)

In question 2, use the printed tables of sorted records to decide which are more valid — these generalizations or those in Exploration 3.

Technology

Exploring Chord Properties With Geometry Software

Student Text Page
P. 394

Materials

geometry software

Learning Outcomes

- Explore the perpendicular bisector of a chord passing through the centre of the circle.
- Explore the perpendicular from the centre of a circle to a chord bisecting the chord.
- Explore the line segment from the centre of a circle to the midpoint of a chord and perpendicular to the chord.

Prerequisite Skills

1. Explain the difference between line segment A that is perpendicular to line segment B, and line segment C that is the perpendicular bisector of line segment D.
   [In the latter, the intersection forming 90° angles is at the midpoint of line segment D.]

2. With geometry software, construct a circle using the circle tool at the left of the screen.

Teaching Suggestions

Points are not named to avoid the extra, time-consuming work that would be required by students to label their constructions to match.

When using Geometer's Sketchpad,
- always select the object or objects needed before selecting the menu item that you want to apply
- return the cursor to a pointer by clicking the pointer tool at the left of the screen
- select more than one object at a time by pressing the Shift key while clicking all the objects after the first one
  Before assigning the explorations, discuss constructing circles and chords using geometry software. With Geometer's Sketchpad, one method uses the circle tool at the left of the screen and the Segment construction.
Click the circle tool at the left of the screen.
Move the cursor to near the centre of the sketch area.
Click and drag until a circle appears.
Click Point On Object from the Construct menu while the circle is still selected.
Click the pointer tool at the left side of the screen to return the cursor to a pointer.

While pressing the Shift key, click the first point on the circle to select it while the second point just constructed on the circle is still selected.
Click Segment from the Construct menu.
  Continue the constructions in Exploration 1.
Click Point At Midpoint from the Construct menu.
While pressing the Shift key, click the chord to select it while the midpoint just constructed is still selected.
Click Perpendicular Line from the Construct menu.
Click and drag the endpoint of the chord that was the second point on the circle to move it around the circumference.
  Discuss the findings in Exploration 1, and assign Exploration 2.
Click New Sketch from the File menu.
Repeat the steps described earlier to construct a circle and a chord.
While pressing the Shift key, click the centre of the circle to select it while the chord just constructed is still selected.
Click Perpendicular Line from the Construct menu.
While pressing the Shift key, click the chord to select it while the perpendicular line just constructed is still selected.
Click Point At Intersection from the Construct menu.
While pressing the Shift key, click one endpoint of the chord to select it while the intersection point just constructed is still selected.
Click Distance from the Measure menu.
Click the other endpoint of the chord, and while pressing the Shift key, click the intersection point.
Click Distance from the Measure menu.
Click and drag the endpoint of the chord that was the second point on the circle to move it around the circumference.
  Discuss the findings in Exploration 2, and assign Exploration 3.
Click New Sketch from the File menu.
Repeat the steps described earlier to construct a circle and a chord.
Click Point at Midpoint from the Construct menu.
While pressing the Shift key, click the centre of the circle to select it while the midpoint just constructed is still selected.
Click Segment from the Construct menu.
Click the centre of the circle, and while pressing the Shift key, click the midpoint and one endpoint of the chord, ensuring that the three points are selected with the midpoint (vertex) in the middle.
Click Angle from the Measure menu.
Click the other endpoint of the chord, and while pressing the Shift key, click the midpoint and the centre of the circle, ensuring that the three points are selected with the midpoint (vertex) in the middle.
Click Angle from the Measure menu.
  Discuss the findings in Exploration 3.

Common Errors

- Students often forget to select the object or objects necessary for a construction, resulting in the construction they want not being available.

R_x Suggest that students print the Construction Help, noting the constructions being used in this section. Then, before each construction, they check what is needed.

Assessing the Outcomes

Journal

Write about what you like best about using geometry software, what you like least, and what you could do so that what you like least isn't as unlikeable.

Investigating Math

Exploring Chord Properties

Student Text Page
P. 395

Materials
graphing calculators, compasses, rulers, Miras, protractors

Learning Outcomes
- Determine that the perpendicular bisector of a chord passes through the centre of the circle.
- Determine that the perpendicular from the centre of a circle to a chord bisects the chord.
- Determine that the line segment from the centre of a circle to the midpoint of a chord is perpendicular to the chord.

Prerequisite Skills
1. Draw a line and construct the perpendicular bisector of your line.
2. Draw a line and construct a perpendicular from a point not on the line to a point on the line.

Mental Math
1. Calculate.

a) $1 + 2 + 3 + ... + 32$ [528]

b) $1 + 2 + 3 + ... + 27$ [378]

c) $2 + 4 + 6 + ... + 18$ [90]

d) $2 + 4 + 6 + ... + 26$ [182]

e) $1 + 3 + 5 + ... + 41$ [441]

f) $1 + 3 + 5 + ... + 23$ [144]

2. Evaluate for $x = 1$ and $y = -1$.

a) $x - y$ [2]   b) $2x + 2y$ [0]

c) $x + 4y - 1$ [−4]   d) $x + 2y^2$ [3]

e) $x^2 - y^2$ [0]   f) $-3y - 4x$ [1]

Teaching Suggestions
(compasses, rulers, Miras, protractors)   Review the skills required to complete the Prerequisite Skills section on this teacher's resource page. Encourage the students to use different methods to complete the exercise, such as those suggested in the opening paragraph on student text page 395. Have volunteers demonstrate the use of the manipulatives required to complete the exercise.

Arrange the class into 6 groups of approximately equal size. Assign Investigation 1 to two groups, Investigation 2 to two groups, and Investigation 3 to two groups.

Have each group complete its own investigation. Then, have the groups who are completing the same investigation discuss and compare their results.

Encourage the groups working on the same investigation to use different materials to arrive at the same final statement. For example, for Investigation 1, one group could use compasses and a ruler, while the other group uses a Mira to construct the perpendicular bisector.

Have volunteers from the combined groups present their results to the class. Suggest that each combined group demonstrate both methods used to complete the investigation.

Extension
Develop an experiment to discover
- the relationship between the distance from the centre of chords that are equal in length.
- the relationship between the length of chords that are equidistant from the centre.

Math Journal
Write a statement about the relation between
- the centre of a circle and the perpendicular bisector of a chord of the circle.
- a perpendicular line segment from the centre of a circle to a chord and the point of intersection of the line segment with the chord.
- a line segment from the centre of a circle to the midpoint of a chord of the circle and the angle made by the line segment.

Assessing the Outcomes
Observation

The following are some questions you might consider as you observe the students in this investigation.
- Do the students know how to do the constructions required?
- Do the students use a variety of manipulatives for the same investigation?
- Do the students work in a neat and organized manner?
- Are the students able to describe their results?
- When using computer software, do the students guess a result, test it, and then, make it visible on the screen?

Student Text Pages
Pp. 396–401

Materials

graphing calculators, compasses, rulers, protractors

Learning Outcomes

• Define the parts of a circle.
• Develop the properties of the chords of a circle.
• Solve problems involving the chords of a circle.

Prerequisite Skills

(compasses, straightedges)
1. a) Draw a line 6 cm in length. Construct the perpendicular bisector of the line.

b) Draw a line 6 cm in length. Mark a point above the line. Draw the perpendicular from the point to the line.

c) Draw a line 6 cm in length. Mark a point on the line. Draw the perpendicular to the point on the line.

2. Find the length of AC. Round your answer to the nearest tenth of a unit.

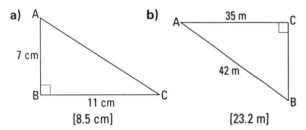

a)

7 cm

11 cm

[8.5 cm]

b)

35 m

42 m

[23.2 m]

Mental Math

1. Find the measures of the indicated angles.

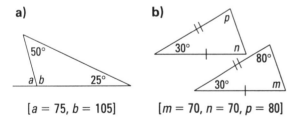

a)

50°

25°

[a = 75, b = 105]

b)

30°

80°

30°

[m = 70, n = 70, p = 80]

2. Multiply.
a) 0.023×120 [2.76]   **b)** 3.1×0.5 [1.55]
c) 9×4.9 [44.1]   **d)** 6.2×0.19 [1.178]
e) 85×99 [8415]   **f)** 510×28 [14 280]

Explore/Inquire Answers

Explore: Use a Diagram

Inquire

1. right
2. Pythagorean Theorem
3. OA = 1.285, OP = 0.595,
   $PA = \sqrt{1.285^2 - 0.595^2} = 1.138\ 946\ 8$ m
4. 2.28 m

Teaching Suggestions

Method 1

(rulers, compasses, protractors) Review with the class the terms "diameter," "secant," and "chord."
   Provide pairs of students with rulers, compasses, and protractors. Assign the Explore section and the Inquire questions to pairs of students. Have volunteers present their results to the class.
   Review with the class teaching examples 1 to 3 on student text pages 397 and 398. Ask:
What method of proof is used in each example? Explain.
   Challenge the students to rewrite teaching examples 1 to 3 using a different method of proof. Have volunteers present their results to the class.
   Review with the class teaching examples 4 and 5 on student text pages 398 and 399. Again, challenge the students to use a different method of proof. Have volunteers present their results to the class.

Method 2

(compasses, rulers, protractors, overhead projector) Review with the class the terms "diameter," "secant," and "chord." Have the students who have no difficulty remembering the constructions in the Prerequisite Skills section on this teacher's resource page help those students who do have difficulty remembering.
   Organize the class into 6 groups of approximately equal size, and have each group complete one of the following investigations. Ensure that two groups do each investigation.
   Let each student complete his or her own investigation, and then, combine his or her results with those of the other students in the group.
   Have the groups who are completing the same investigation combine into one group, and discuss, compare, and combine their results.

Suggest that 2 volunteers from each combined group present the results of their investigation to the class. One student could display the diagrams on an overhead projector, while the other describes the investigation undertaken, and the conclusions reached by the group.

Investigation 1
Draw a circle of any radius and mark the centre O. Draw any chord of the circle. Construct the perpendicular bisector of the chord.

Repeat this investigation 6 more times.

What do the perpendicular bisectors of the chords have in common?

Investigation 2
Draw a circle of any radius and mark the centre O. Draw any chord PQ of the circle. Construct the perpendicular line from the centre of the circle to meet the chord PQ at X. Measure PX and QX.

Repeat this investigation 5 more times.

What do you notice?

Circle	Radius	Measure of PX	Measure of QX
1			
2			
3			
4			
5			
6			

Investigation 3
Draw a circle of any radius and mark the centre O. Draw any chord PQ of the circle. Construct the line from the centre of the circle to the midpoint Y of chord PQ. Measure $\angle$PYO and $\angle$QYO.

Repeat this investigation 5 more times.

What relationship, if any, exists between $\angle$PYO and $\angle$QYO?

Circle	Measure of $\angle$PYO	Measure of $\angle$QYO
1		
2		
3		
4		
5		
6		

Ensure that all the students in the class understand the results of each investigation. Ask:

What do you know about a line from the centre of a circle, that is perpendicular to a chord?

What do you know about a line from the centre of a circle to the midpoint of a chord?

What do you know about a line that is a perpendicular bisector of a chord of a circle, as it relates to the centre of the circle?

Review with the class teaching examples 1 to 5 on student text pages 397 to 399.

Sample Solution

Page 401, question 33

The greatest straight line distance between any two points on the perimeter of a square is the diagonal. If a square is to fit into a circle, the diagonal of the square must be less than or equal to the diameter of the square.

Side length of the square is 15 cm.

The length of the diagonal of the square is

$$\sqrt{15^2 + 15^2} = \sqrt{225 + 225}$$
$$= \sqrt{450}$$
$$= 21.2 \text{ (to 1 decimal place)}$$

Radius of circle is 10 cm.

Thus, diameter of circle is 20 cm.

Since the length of the diagonal of the square is greater than the diameter of the circle, it will not fit.

Extension

A circumcircle is the circle drawn outside a triangle and through its vertices. The centre of a circumcircle is the circumcentre and the point of intersection of the perpendicular bisectors of the sides of the triangle. Explain why the point of intersection of the perpendicular bisectors of the sides of a triangle is the centre of the circumcircle of a triangle. Demonstrate using a triangle with sides 11 cm, 8 cm, and 3 cm. What is the radius of the circumcircle of such a triangle?

An incircle is the circle drawn inside a triangle and touching each side of the triangle once. The centre of an incircle is the incentre and the point of intersection of the bisectors of the angles of the triangle. Explain why the point of intersection of the bisectors of the angles of a triangle is the centre of the incircle of a triangle. Demonstrate using a triangle with sides 11 cm, 8 cm, and 3 cm.

Enrichment

Research the meaning of the word "circumcircle."

Make a list of the steps required to construct the circumcircle of any regular polygon.

Math Journal

chord perpendicular bisector theorem   Rewrite the theorems in the chord perpendicular bisector theorem as If...then statements. Include in your journal diagrams and examples for clarity.

Cross-Discipline

Building Construction   Carpenters and other tradespeople often need to find the centre of a circle in order to draw a secant of the circle.

In order to insulate a stained glass window, a carpenter needs to cut a piece of plain glass to completely cover it. A diagram of the window is shown.

Scale 1:25

Use your construction techniques and your knowledge of chords of a circle to find the centre of the circle.

Use the given scale to find an approximate measure of the radius of the circle, to the nearest whole centimetre.

Problem Levels of Difficulty

A: 1–20   **B:** 21–32   **C:** 33–36

Assessing the Outcomes

Written Assignment

1. Copy these 3 points. Construct the circle that passes through them.

    • A

          • B

    • C

2. The distance from the centre of a circle to a chord is 14 cm. The length of the chord is 9 cm. Calculate the radius of the circle to 1 decimal place.

Technology

Exploring Properties of Angles in a Circle Using Geometry Software

Student Text Pages

Pp. 402–405

Materials

geometry software

Learning Outcomes

- Explore central angles subtended by equal arcs.
- Explore inscribed angles subtended by the same arc.
- Determine that inscribed angles subtended by equal arcs are equal.
- Explore angles inscribed in a semicircle.
- Explore the central angle subtended by the same arc as an inscribed.
- Explore opposite angles in a cyclic quadrilateral.

Prerequisite Skills

With geometry software, construct a circle using the Circle By Centre And Point construction. Change the size of the circle. Change the location of the circle.

Teaching Suggestions

Most points are not named to avoid the extra, time-consuming work that would be required by students to label their constructions to match.

When using Geometer's Sketchpad,
- always select the object or objects needed before selecting the menu item that you want to apply
- return the cursor to a pointer by clicking the pointer tool at the left of the screen
- select more than one object at a time by pressing the Shift key while clicking all the objects after the first one
  Before assigning the explorations, discuss constructing circles and arcs using geometry software. With Geometer's Sketchpad, one method uses the Circle By Centre And Point and the Arc On A Circle constructions.

Click the point tool at the left of the screen.
Move the cursor to near the centre of the sketch area and click.
Move the cursor away from the point just constructed and click.
Click the pointer tool at the left side of the screen to return the cursor to a pointer.
While pressing the Shift key, click the first point constructed while the last point just constructed is still selected.

Click Circle By Centre And Point from the Construct menu.
Click the point on the circle.
Click Show Label from the Display menu.
Click the circle.
Click Point On Object from the Construct menu.
Click the circle.
Click Point On Object from the Construct menu a second time.
While pressing the Shift key, click the first point constructed on the circle and the circle to select them while the last point just constructed is still selected.
Click Arc On A Circle from the Construct menu, constructing an arc in a counterclockwise direction, which may be a major or minor arc.
Click Arc Length from the Measure menu.

Continue with Exploration 1, constructing and measuring a second arc using the same process as for the first, remembering to click the circle because the first arc, not the circle, is selected now.
Click the endpoint of one arc and drag it until its measurement matches that of the other arc exactly.
While pressing the Shift key, click the centre of the circle to select it while one endpoint is still selected.
Click Segment from the Construct menu.
Click the other endpoint, and while pressing the Shift key, click the centre of the circle.
Click Segment from the Construct menu.
Click one endpoint of the arc, and while pressing the Shift key, click the centre of the circle and the other endpoint of the arc, ensuring that the three points are selected with the centre (vertex) in the middle.
Click Angle from the Measure menu.

Continue with Exploration 1, constructing and measuring the central angle subtended by the other arc using the same process as for the first.

Discuss the findings in Exploration 1, and assign Exploration 2.
Click New Sketch from the File menu.
Construct a circle and one arc using the same processes as in Exploration 1.

Continue with Exploration 2, constructing a vertex and then, an inscribed angle.
Click the circle.
Click Point On Object from the Construct menu.
If the point is on the arc, click and drag it off.
While pressing the Shift key, click one endpoint of the arc to select it while the new point for the vertex is still selected.
Click Segment from the Construct menu.
Click the point for the vertex, and while pressing the Shift key, click the other endpoint of the arc.
Click Segment from the Construct menu.
Click one endpoint of the arc, and while pressing the Shift key, click the point for the vertex and the other

endpoint of the arc, ensuring that the three points are selected with the vertex in the middle.
Click Angle from the Measure menu.

Continue with questions 5 to 8 in Exploration 2.
Click the vertex and drag it around the part of the circumference that is not on the arc.
Click the centre or the labelled point used to construct the circle and drag it to change the size of the circle. Then, click the vertex and drag it around the part of the circumference that is not on the arc.
Click one endpoint of the arc and drag is around the circumference. Then, click the vertex and drag it around the part of the circumference that is not on the arc. Next, click the centre or the labelled point used to construct the circle and drag it to change the size of the circle. Finally, click the vertex and drag it around the part of the circumference that is not on the arc.

Discuss the findings in Exploration 2, and assign Explorations 3 to 7.
Click New Sketch from the File menu.
Construct circles, arcs, and angles; measure the angles; and apply the dynamic properties of the software using the processes from the previous explorations.

Discuss and compare the findings of each exploration.

Common Errors

- Some students have difficulty selecting more than one object at a time when needed.

R_x Remind students to press the Shift key while clicking all the objects after the first one. Frequently, the last object constructed is one of the objects needed next. In that case, the Shift key is pressed before any other objects are selected. When the last object constructed is not one of the objects needed next, the first object is selected, and then the Shift key is pressed before any other objects are selected.

- Sometimes students think the circle is selected when only an arc is, and vice versa.

R_x Point out to students that when a circle is selected, the selection markings go around the entire circumference. If they do not, click another location on the circumference. When an arc is selected, the selection markings are only on the arc. If they are not, click another location on the arc.

Assessing the Outcomes

Written Assignment

Summarize the properties of angles in a circle in terms of both arcs and chords.

Investigating Math

Exploring Properties of Angles in a Circle

Student Text Pages
Pp. 406–407

Materials
graphing calculators, compasses, rulers, protractors

Learning Outcomes
- Determine that central angles subtended by equal arcs are equal.
- Determine that inscribed angles subtended by the same arc are equal.
- Determine that inscribed angles subtended by equal arcs are equal.
- Determine that angles inscribed in a semicircle are right angles.
- Determine that the central angle subtended by the same arc as an inscribed is double the inscribed angle.
- Determine that opposite angles in a cyclic quadrilateral are supplementary.

Mental Math
1. What is the measure of the supplementary angle to each of the following?

   a) 55°   [125°]   b) 177°   [3°]
   c) 78°   [102°]   d) 144°   [36°]
   e) 107°   [73°]   f) 2°   [178°]

2. For each inequality, write three different ordered pairs that include the given coordinate and satisfy the inequality.   [Answers may vary. For example,]

   a) $x + y > 2$; ($\blacksquare$, 1)   [(3, 1), (4, 1), (5, 1)]
   b) $x - y \leq -1$; (2, $\blacksquare$)   [(2, 3), (2, 4), (2, 5)]
   c) $y < -x - 1$; (3, $\blacksquare$)   [(3, −5), (3, −6), (3, −7)]
   d) $x - 2y \geq 2$; ($\blacksquare$, −1)   [(0, −1), (1, −1), (2, −1)]

Teaching Suggestions
(compasses, rulers, protractors)   Review with the class the vocabulary associated with the circle: diameter, radius, sector, chord, major arc, minor arc, central angle, inscribed angle, etc.

Organize the class into 6 groups of approximately equal size. Assign Explorations 1 to 3 to three of the groups, and Explorations 4 to 6 to the other three groups. Have the groups complete their explorations. Encourage the groups completing the same explorations to discuss and compare their results,

ensuring that they all reach a consensus of opinion.

When the groups have completed their explorations, have each group present the results of one of the explorations to the class. Ensure that all the explorations are presented to the class.

Finally, have all the groups complete Exploration 7, and have volunteers present their results to the class. Part of the explanation by the students to question 1 might be: considering the chords instead of the arcs does not affect the measures of the angles, and so the results apply equally as well to chords as to arcs.

Math Journal
Include in your journal, along with diagrams and examples, your conclusions from the following explorations on circles.
- angles subtended by equal arcs
- angles subtended by the same arc
- inscribed angles subtended by equal arcs
- central and inscribed angles subtended by the same arc
- angles inscribed in a semicircle
- opposite angles of a cyclic quadrilateral

Assessing the Outcomes
Journal

Write a short essay about the new information you have learned about the properties of the angles in a circle.

7.3 Angles in a Circle

Student Text Pages
Pp. 408–414

Materials
graphing calculators, compasses, rulers, protractors, overhead projector

Learning Outcomes
- Develop the properties of the angles in a circle.
- Use the properties of the angles of a circle to find angle measures.

Mental Math

1. Find the measures of the indicated angles.

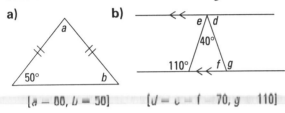

a)   b)

$[a = 80, b = 50]$ $[d = e = f = 70, g = 110]$

2. What is the measure of the complementary angle to each of the following?

a) $59°$	[31°]	b) $58°$	[32°]
c) $81°$	[9°]	d) $89°$	[1°]
e) $3°$	[87°]	f) $18°$	[72°]

Explore/Inquire Answers

Inquire

1. They are equal.
2. a) Move players inside the circle.
b) Move players outside the circle.

Teaching Suggestions

Method 1
(compasses, rulers, protractors, overhead projector) Review with the class the terms "inscribed angle," "central angle," and "subtended." Ask:

What examples can you find of the use of the word or parts of the word "inscribed" in real life?

How are these examples and the meaning of "inscribed angle" related?

Assign the Explore section and the Inquire questions to pairs of students. Have students discuss and compare their results with those of other students. Have volunteers present their results to the class. Provide an overhead projector, if necessary.

Review with the class teaching examples 1 to 5 on student text pages 409 to 412. As you go along, have the students identify the method of proof used in each teaching example. Ask:

How would you identify the method of proof of the alternative proof in teaching example 1?

Lead the students to identify the method of proof in teaching examples 1 and 2 as the two-column formal method, and the alternate method of proof as an algebraic method.

When theorems and corollaries are developed, have the students immediately enter them, along with diagrams and examples, into their math journals. Ensure that the students include in their journals the different cases for any theorem.

Method 2
(compasses, rulers, protractors) Review with the class the terms "subtended," "central angle," and "inscribed angle."

Organize the class into small groups. Have the groups complete the following investigation.

Investigation
- Draw a large circle. Mark the centre O.
- Mark points A, B, C, and D on the circumference of the circle.
- Join AB, BC, CD, AD, BD, and AC.
- Join AO, BO, CO, and DO.
- Name inscribed angles on the same side of a chord.
- Name pairs of central angles and inscribed angles on the same side of the chord.
- Copy and complete the table.

Circle	1	2	3	4
Measure of ∠ACB				
Measure of ∠ADB				
.				
.				
.				
Measure of ∠AOB				
.				
.				
.				

- Measure the inscribed angles. Record the measures in the table.
- Measure the central angles. Record the measures in the table.
- Repeat the investigation for about 4 more circles.

What conclusion can you make about the measures of the inscribed angles on the same side of the same chord?

What conclusion can you make about the measures of the inscribed angle and the central angle subtended on the same chord and on the same side of the chord?

When the groups are finished, have them discuss and compare their results with other groups. Have volunteers present their results to the class. Provide an overhead projector, if necessary.

Review with the class teaching examples 1 to 5 on student text pages 409 to 412.

Number Power Answer

The number of days in the months of the year is either 28 (not a leap year), 30, or 31. The total number of days in a year (not a leap year) is 365.
In a non-leap year, one month has exactly 28 days, 4 months have exactly 30 days, and 7 months have exactly 31 days.
Thus, $28x + 30y + 31z = 28(1) + 30(4) + 31(7)$
$$= 28 + 120 + 217$$
$$= 365$$
Thus, $x = 1$, $y = 4$, and $z = 7$.

Extension

A circle with an inscribed angle is drawn.
How would you describe the measure of an angle subtended on the same side of the same chord as the given inscribed angle, but whose vertex
• lies inside the circle?
• lies outside the circle?

Enrichment

1. Draw a circle. Draw diagrams to help you describe how you could use a set square to find the centre of a circle.

2. Draw a rectangle. Draw diagrams to help you describe how to draw a circumscribed circle of the rectangle.

Math Journal

Write a short essay about what you have learned in this lesson.

Common Errors

• Students often have trouble determining the arc that subtends a given angle.

$\mathbf{R}_x$ Have the student read the angle aloud, say ∠ABC. The first letter and the last letter of the angle form the arc that subtends ∠ABC, i.e., arc AC.

• In complex drawings, students often cannot find another angle (either inscribed or central) subtended by the same arc.

$\mathbf{R}_x$ For a subtended angle, have the students place fingers on the two points on the circumference of the circle and trace along the arms of the angle to the vertex. Then, have them try to trace a different angle from the same two points. If another vertex is on the circumference, then it is an inscribed angle; if the other vertex is at the centre of the circle, then, it is a central angle.

Problem Levels of Difficulty

A: 1–28   **B:** 29–37   **C:** 38–40

Assessing the Outcomes

Written Assignment

Points K, L, M, and N lie in order on a circle.
If ∠KLM = 75°, ∠LMK = 56°, and ∠NKL = 80°, find ∠LNK, ∠MKL, ∠LNM, and ∠MNK.

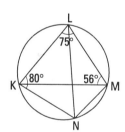

7.4 Cyclic Quadrilaterals

Student Text Pages
Pp. 415–421

Materials
graphing calculators, compasses, rulers, protractors, overhead projector

Learning Outcomes
- Define "cyclic polygon" and "concyclic points."
- Develop the properties of cyclic quadrilaterals.
- Prove points are concyclic.

Prerequisite Skills
Find the missing variable.

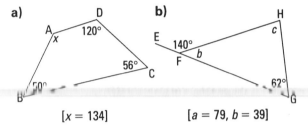

a)
D 120° A x 56° C B 50°

[$x = 134$]

b)
H c E 140° F b 62° G

[$a = 79, b = 39$]

Mental Math
1. Calculate.
a) $1 + 2 + 3 + \ldots + 40$ [820]
b) $1 + 2 + 3 + \ldots + 65$ [2145]
c) $2 + 4 + 6 + \ldots + 56$ [812]
d) $2 + 4 + 6 + \ldots + 70$ [1260]
e) $1 + 3 + 5 + \ldots + 39$ [400]
f) $1 + 3 + 5 + \ldots + 59$ [900]

2. Divide.
a) $65.1 \div 2.1$ [31]   b) $59.4 \div 5.4$ [11]
c) $28.8 \div 1.6$ [18]   d) $154 \div 11$ [14]
e) $3.52 \div 44$ [0.08]   f) $3.41 \div 0.31$ [11]

Explore/Inquire Answers

Explore: Use a Diagram
a) $2x$ b) $2y$

Inquire
1. $2x + 2y$ 2. 360°   3. 180°   4. 180°
5. Join AO and CO. Repeat the steps in parts a) and b) of the Explore section and Inquire questions 1 to 4 above.
6. The sum of the measures of the opposite angles of a cyclic quadrilateral is 180°.

7. a) $x = 95, y = 57$ **b)** $a = 86, b = 67, c = 113$
c) $d = 53, e = 127, f = 104, g = 76$

8. Each side of a cyclic quadrilateral is a chord of a circle that subtends an arc of a circle. Each arc in Escher's drawing is subtended by a chord.

Teaching Suggestions

Method 1
(compasses, rulers, protractors, overhead projector) Read with the class the opening paragraphs on student text page 415. Ask:

Have you ever seen Escher art?

What other examples of Escher's work have you seen?

Review the terms "cyclic" and "concyclic." Ask:

What does the word "cyclic" mean?

What other words do you know that contain part of the word "cyclic?"

Assign the Explore section and the Inquire questions to pairs of students. Provide them with compasses, rulers, and protractors. Ask:

How do you draw a cyclic quadrilateral?

For Inquire question 4, suggest that the students write the sum of $\angle$A and $\angle$C in terms of x and y, and then, find the value of the sum in degrees.

Have pairs discuss and compare their results with other students. Have volunteers present their results to the class. Provide an overhead projector, if necessary.

Review with the class the meaning of the terms "converse" and "corollary."

Have pairs of students work through teaching examples 1 to 5 on student text pages 416 to 419. Give the students plenty of opportunity to discuss and compare their results with those of other students in the class.

Suggest that as the students go along, they add each new theorem, corollary, and converse to a list in their math journal.

Method 2
(compasses, rulers, protractors, overhead projector) Review with the class the terms "cyclic" and "concyclic."

Organize the class into 8 groups equal in size, and have each group complete one of the investigations below. Ensure that 4 groups do each investigation.

When each group has completed its own investigation, have the groups doing the same investigation combine their results.

Suggest that 2 volunteers from each combined group present their results to the class. One student could display the diagrams on an overhead projector, while the other describes the investigation undertaken, and the conclusions reached by the group.

Investigation 1

Draw a circle of any radius and mark the centre O. Mark any four points, A, B, C, and D, on the circumference of the circle, and join them in order to form a quadrilateral. Find the measure of ∠A, ∠B, ∠C, and ∠D.

Repeat this investigation 5 more times.
Copy and complete the table.

Circle	Measure of				Measure of	Measure of
	∠A	∠B	∠C	∠D	∠A + ∠C	∠B + ∠D
1						
2						
3						
4						
5						
6						

Investigation 2

Draw a circle of any radius and mark the centre O. Mark any four points, A, B, C, and D, on the circumference of the circle, and join them in order to form a quadrilateral. Extend each side of the quadrilateral in one direction to form an exterior angle at each vertex. Find the measure of interior ∠A, ∠B, ∠C, and ∠D, and of exterior ∠A, ∠B, ∠C, and ∠D.

Repeat this investigation 5 more times.
Copy and complete the table.

Circle	Measure of Interior				Measure of Exterior			
	∠A	∠B	∠C	∠D	∠A	∠B	∠C	∠D
1								
2								
3								
4								
5								
6								

Ensure that all the students understand the results of each investigation. Ask:

What do you know about the measures of the opposite angles of a cyclic quadrilateral?

What do you know about the measure of the external angle of a cyclic quadrilateral and the corresponding interior opposite angle?

Review with the class teaching examples 1 to 5 on student text pages 416 to 419. Review with the class the meaning of the terms "converse" and "corollary." Ensure that the differences in their meanings are fully understood by the students.

Sample Solution

Page 421, Question 26

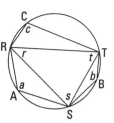

In ΔRST,
∠r + ∠s + ∠t = 180°.
In quadrilateral RAST,
∠a = 180° − ∠t.........(1)
In quadrilateral ASBT,
∠b = 180° − ∠r.........(2)
In quadrilateral RCTS,
∠c = 180° − ∠s.........(3)
Add (1), (2), and (3).
∠a + ∠b + ∠c
= 180° − ∠t + (180° − ∠r) + (180° − ∠s)
= 180° + 180° + 180° − (∠t + ∠r + ∠s)
= 540° − 180°
= 360°

Pattern Power Answer

The product of the first two numbers in each row is half the product of the last two numbers in each row. Let the missing number be x.

$$10 \times 3 = \frac{1}{2} \times x \times 4$$
$$60 = 4x$$
$$x = 15$$

The missing number is 15.

Enrichment

Brahmagupta's Formula is used to find the area A, of a cyclic quadrilateral with side lengths a, b, c, and d.

$A = \sqrt{(s-a)(s-b)(s-c)(s-d)}$, where
$s = \frac{a+b+c+d}{2}$

Construct a cyclic quadrilateral and measure each side. Use your measures to find the area of your quadrilateral. Round your answer to 1 decimal place.

Create a formula similar to Brahmagupta's Formula, only for a polygon of any number of sides.

Construct any polygon and check to see if this formula also works for your polygon. Present your results to the class.

Math Journal

Write a few sentences describing a cyclic quadrilateral. Include diagrams and examples for clarity.

Problem Levels of Difficulty

A: 1–17   **B:** 18–25   **C:** 26, 27

Assessing the Outcomes

Written Assignment

Find the measures of the variables in each diagram.

1.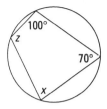

2.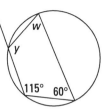

3. In △ABC, AB = AC, and the bisectors of ∠ABC and ∠ACB meet AC and AB at X and Y, respectively.

a) Draw a diagram for the given information.

b) Prove that B, C, X, and Y are concyclic.

Technology

Exploring Tangent Properties Using Geometry Software

Student Text Pages

Pp. 422–423

Materials

geometry software

Learning Outcomes

- Explore the perpendicular to a radius at its outer endpoint.
- Explore the tangent and the radius at the point of tangency.
- Explore tangent segments from the same external point to a circle.
- Explore the angle between a tangent and a chord.

Prerequisite Skills

With geometry software, construct a circle using the circle tool at the left of the screen.

Teaching Suggestions

Points are not named to avoid the extra, time-consuming work that would be required by students to label their constructions to match.

When using Geometer's Sketchpad,

- always select the object or objects needed before selecting the menu item that you want to apply
- change from segment to line and vice versa as needed by clicking the tool at the left of the screen to display the options
- return the cursor to a pointer by clicking the pointer tool at the left of the screen
- select more than one object at a time by pressing the Shift key while clicking all the objects after the first one
  Before assigning the explorations, discuss
constructing circles and radii using geometry software.
With Geometer's Sketchpad, one method uses the circle tool at the left of the screen and the Segment construction.
Click the circle tool at the left of the screen.
Move the cursor to near the centre of the sketch area.
Click and drag until a circle appears.
Click the pointer tool at the left side of the screen to return the cursor to a pointer.
Click the point on the circle, and while pressing the Shift key, click the centre of the circle.
Click Segment from the Construct menu.

Continue with Exploration 1, constructing the perpendicular and the intersection point.
While pressing the Shift key, click the outer endpoint of the radius to select it while the radius is still selected.
Click Perpendicular Line from the Construct menu.
While pressing the Shift key, click the radius to select it while the perpendicular is still selected.
Click Point At Intersection from the Construct menu.
Click the outer endpoint of the radius and drag it around the circumference.

Discuss the findings in Exploration 1, and assign Exploration 2.
Click New Sketch from the File menu.
Click the circle tool at the left of the screen.
Move the cursor to near the centre of the sketch area.
Click and drag until a circle appears.
Click the point tool at the left side of the screen.
Move the cursor to a location outside the circle so that a line passing through it and the point on the circle would be nearly tangent to the circle, and click.
Click the pointer tool at the left side of the screen to return the cursor to a pointer.
While pressing the Shift key, click the point on the circle to select it while the point outside the circle is still selected.
Click the segment tool at the left of the screen to display the options, and drag to the line tool.
Click Line from the Construct menu.

Continue with Exploration 2.
Click the pointer tool at the left side of the screen to return the cursor to a pointer.
While pressing the Shift key, click the circle to select it while the line just constructed is still selected.
Click Point At Intersection from the Construct menu.
Unless the intersection point and the original point on the circle are the same, click the point outside the circle and move it until the two points are the same.
Click the point of intersection/original point on the circle, and while pressing the Shift key, click the centre of the circle.
Click the line tool at the left of the screen to display the options, and drag to the segment tool.
Click Segment from the Construct menu.
Click the pointer tool at the left side of the screen to return the cursor to a pointer.
Click the centre of the circle, and while pressing the Shift key, click the point of intersection/original point on the circle and the point outside the circle, ensuring that the three points are selected with the point of intersection/original point on the circle (vertex) in the middle.
Click Angle from the Measure menu.

Discuss the findings in Exploration 2, and assign Exploration 3.
Click New Sketch from the File menu.

Construct a circle, a radius, and a line perpendicular to the outer endpoint of the radius (a tangent), using the process from Exploration 1.

Then, repeat the construction of a radius and tangent by first constructing another point on the circle.

Continue with questions 5 to 8 in Exploration 3. While pressing the Shift key, click the first tangent to select it while the second tangent is still selected.

Click Point At Intersection from the Construct menu. While pressing the Shift key, click the outer endpoint of one radius to select it while the intersection point is still selected.

Click Distance from the Measure menu. Click the outer endpoint of the other radius, and while pressing the Shift key, click the intersection point.

Click Distance from the Measure menu.

Click the outer endpoint of the other radius and drag it to change the lengths of the tangent segments.

Discuss the findings in Exploration 3, and assign Exploration 4.

Click New Sketch from the File menu.

Click the circle tool at the left of the screen.

Move the cursor to near the centre of the sketch area.

Click and drag until a circle appears.

Click Point On Object from the Construct menu while the circle is still selected.

Click the pointer tool at the left side of the screen to return the cursor to a pointer.

While pressing the Shift key, click the first point on the circle to select it while the second point just constructed on the circle is still selected.

Click Segment from the Construct menu.

Continue the constructions in Exploration 4.

Click one endpoint of the chord, and while pressing the Shift key, click the centre of the circle.

Click Segment from the Construct menu.

While pressing the Shift key, click the outer end point of the radius to select it while the radius is still selected.

Click Perpendicular Line from the Construct menu.

To measure the angle, a point is needed on the tangent.

Click Point On Object from the Construct menu while the tangent is selected.

While pressing the Shift key, click the outer endpoint of the radius/end of chord and the other end of the chord while the point just constructed is still selected, ensuring that the three points are selected with the outer endpoint of the radius/end of chord (vertex) in the middle.

Click Angle from the Measure menu.

Click the circle.

Click Point On Object from the Construct menu. If the point is not on the opposite side of the chord from the angle just measured, click and drag it there.

While pressing the Shift key, click the outer endpoint of the radius/end of chord while the new point is still selected.

Click Segment from the Construct menu.

Click the other endpoint of the chord, and while pressing the Shift key, click the new point.

Click Segment from the Construct menu.

Click one endpoint of the chord, and while pressing the Shift key, click the new point and the other endpoint of the chord, ensuring that the three points are selected with the new point (vertex) in the middle.

Click Angle from the Measure menu.

Click anywhere on the sketch area to deselect the three points.

Click the outer endpoint of the radius/end of chord and drag it.

Discuss the findings in Exploration 4.

Common Errors

- Sometimes students think they can find the distance between points once the points are evident from a construction, such as when an intersection point is evident from the construction of a line that passes through another, but the Distance measure will not be available until the point itself is actually constructed (and shows as an open dot).

R_x Remind students to follow all the steps in an exploration. They direct you to construct such points before measuring a distance.

Assessing the Outcomes

Journal

Summarize the tangent properties.

Investigating Math

Exploring Tangent Properties

Student Text Pages
Pp. 424–425

Materials
graphing calculators, compasses, rulers, protractors

Learning Outcomes
- Determine that the perpendicular to a radius at its outer endpoint is tangent to the circle.
- Determine that the tangent and the radius at the point of tangency are perpendicular.
- Determine that tangent segments from the same external point to a circle are the same length.
- Determine that the angle between a tangent and a chord is equal to the inscribed angle on the opposite side of the chord.

Prerequisite Skills
Draw a line. Construct a perpendicular at one end of the line.

Mental Math
1. Calculate.

a) $1 + 2 + 3 + ... + 50$ [1275]

b) $1 + 2 + 3 + ... + 85$ [3655]

c) $2 + 4 + 6 + ... + 64$ [1056]

d) $2 + 4 + 6 + ... + 96$ [2352]

e) $1 + 3 + 5 + ... + 79$ [1600]

f) $1 + 3 + 5 + ... + 121$ [3721]

2. Simplify.

a) $\sqrt{125}$ $[5\sqrt{5}]$ b) $\sqrt{363}$ $[11\sqrt{3}]$

c) $\sqrt{162}$ $[9\sqrt{2}]$ d) $\sqrt{32}$ $[4\sqrt{2}]$

e) $\sqrt{288}$ $[12\sqrt{2}]$ f) $\sqrt{300}$ $[10\sqrt{3}]$

Teaching Suggestions
(compasses, rulers, protractors, overhead projector)
Review with the class the terms "tangent" and "point of tangency."

Organize the class into 8 small groups and assign 2 groups to each exploration.

When each group has completed its exploration, have the groups who are completing the same exploration combine, and discuss and compare their results.

Have a volunteer from each combined group present their results to the class. Provide an overhead projector, if necessary.

Assessing the Outcomes

Journal

Write a short essay about the new information you have learned about the properties of tangents to circles.

7.5 Tangents to a Circle

Student Text Pages
Pp. 426–432

Materials
graphing calculators, compasses, rulers, protractors, overhead projector

Learning Outcomes
- Define the terms "tangent" and "point of tangency."
- Develop the theorems of the tangents to a circle and their converses.
- Use the theorems of tangents to circles to find lengths and angle measures.

Prerequisite Skills
Identify pairs of equal sides.

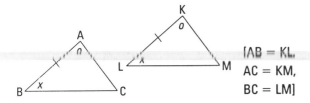

[AB = KL,
AC = KM,
BC = LM]

Mental Math
1. Calculate.
a) $1 + 2 + 3 + ... + 100$ [5050]
b) $1 + 2 + 3 + ... + 75$ [2850]
c) $2 + 4 + 6 + ... + 66$ [1122]
d) $2 + 4 + 6 + ... + 40$ [420]
e) $1 + 3 + 5 + ... + 33$ [289]
f) $1 + 3 + 5 + ... + 49$ [525]

2. Multiply.
a) 61×11 [671]   **b)** 9×89 [801]
c) 39×16 [624]   **d)** 52×12 [624]
e) 41×29 [1189]   **f)** 91×0.9 [81.9]

Explore/Inquire Answers

Inquire
1. a) 0   **b)** 90°   **c)** 90°
2. a) 0   **b)** approaches 0
c) The line is a tangent to the circle.
3. The angle is a right angle.

Teaching Suggestions

Method 1
Read with the class the opening paragraphs on student text page 426. Review the terms "tangent," "secant," and "point of tangency." Ask:

How are a secant and a tangent similar? different?

What examples of tangents have you seen in real life?

Assign the Explore section to pairs of students. Suggest that one student complete Investigation 1, while the other completes Investigation 2. When the students have completed their investigations, have them discuss and compare their results.

Then, assign the Inquire questions, suggesting that the students match the questions they complete with the investigation they did in the Explore section. Review the meaning of the term "conjecture," and ask:

What type of reasoning is used to find the results of Investigations 1 and 2 in the Explore section?

Have volunteers present their results to the class.

Review with the class teaching examples 1 to 7 on student text pages 427 to 430. Review the term "converse," and discuss how to write the converse of a statement. Remind the students that not all converse statements are true. Have the students identify the method used to write the proof in teaching examples 1, 2, 3, 4, and 6.

Method 2
(compasses, rulers, protractors) Organize the class into 8 small groups of equal size, and have each group complete one of the investigations below. Ensure that 2 groups complete each of the investigations. Suggest that the students complete the investigation as a group.

Have the groups who completed the same investigation combine, and discuss, compare, and combine their results.

Suggest that 2 volunteers from each combined group present their results to the class. One student could display the diagrams on an overhead projector, while the other describes the investigation undertaken, and the conclusions reached by the group.

Investigation 1
Draw any circle and mark the centre.

From a point outside the circle, draw a tangent to the circle. Mark the point of tangency.

Join the centre of the circle and the point of tangency.

Measure the angle between the radius of the circle and the tangent of the circle at the point of tangency.

Repeat this investigation 5 more times.

What is the measure of the angle between a radius and a tangent of the circle at the point of tangency?

Investigation 2

Draw any circle and mark the centre. Draw a radius of the circle. Construct a secant perpendicular to the radius at the point at which the radius touches the circle. Mark the points at which the secant cuts the circle.

Investigation 3

Draw any circle and mark the centre.

From a point outside the circle, draw two tangents to the circle. Mark the points of tangency.

Measure the length of each tangent.

Repeat this investigation 5 more times.

How are the tangents drawn from an exterior point of a circle related to each other?

Investigation 4

Draw any circle and mark the centre. Draw a tangent to the circle and mark the point of tangency. Draw a chord of the circle that has one end point, the point of tangency. Mark the other end point of the chord.

On the opposite side of the chord from the tangent, draw an angle subtended at the circumference by the drawn chord. Measure the angle between the chord and the tangent.

Measure the angle subtended at the circumference by the chord on the side of the chord opposite the tangent.

Repeat this investigation 5 more times.

Copy and complete the table.

Circle	Measure of angle between tangent and chord	Measure of angle subtended at the circumference on the opposite side of the chord
1		
2		
:		
.		
6		

How is the measure of the angle between the tangent and the chord related to the measure of the angle subtended at the circumference on the opposite side of the chord?

Sample Solution

Page 432, question 31

CY and DY are radii of a circle.
AC and AD are tangents to the circles.
Thus, AC = AD.
From the tangent theorem,
∠ACY = ∠ADY = 90°
In ΔACY and ΔADY,
∠ACY = ∠ADY
  AC = AD
  AY = AY
Thus,
ΔACY ≅ ΔADY (HS)
Thus, ∠CAY = ∠DAY.
Since ∠CAD = 60°, then ∠YAD = 30°.
In ΔXAE, from the tangent theorem,
  ∠XEA = 90°
  ∠XAE = 30°
    XE = 8 cm (given)
Thus, $\sin 30° = \dfrac{XE}{AX}$

$\dfrac{1}{2} = \dfrac{8}{AX}$

  AX = 16
Thus, AX is 16 cm.
AZ = AX + XZ
   = 16 + 8
   = 24
AZ is 24 cm.
AY = AZ + y
   = 24 + y
In ΔYAD, $\sin 30° = \dfrac{YD}{AY}$

$\dfrac{1}{2} = \dfrac{y}{24 + y}$

24 + y = 2y
    24 = y
The radius of the larger circle is 24 cm.

Extension

How many tangents can be drawn
- at a point on the circle?
- from a point outside the circle?
- through a point inside the circle?

Draw diagrams to illustrate the possible cases.
Is it possible for a pair of circles to have
- no common tangents?
- one common tangent?
- 2 common tangents?
- 3 common tangents?
- 4 common tangents?
- 5 common tangents?

Math Journal

tangent theorem, tangent theorem converse, tangent chord theorem, tangent chord theorem converse
Write these theorems and converses in your journal.
Include diagrams for each theorem for clarity.

Problem Levels of Difficulty

A: 1–17   **B:** 18–28   **C:** 29–32

Assessing the Outcomes

Written Assignment

In the diagrams below, tangents have been drawn from point P. Find the values of the variables.

1.

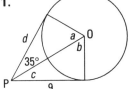

2.

7.6 Arc Length and Sector Area

Student Text Pages
Pp. 433–437

Materials

graphing calculators or scientific calculators, Teacher's Resource Master 1 (0.5 cm grid paper), compasses, rulers, protractors, string, overhead projector

Learning Outcomes

- Define "sector" and "sector angle."
- Develop a method of finding the area of a sector.
- Develop a method of finding the length of an arc.
- Solve problems involving the lengths of arcs and the areas of sectors.

Prerequisite Skills

1. Evaluate each formula for the given values of the variables. Round your answers to 1 decimal place, if necessary.

   a) $P = 2l + 2w$; $l = 3$, $w = 1.5$ [9]

   b) $A = \pi r^2$; $r = 4.5$ [63.6]

   c) $A = \frac{h}{2}(a + b)$; $a = 5$, $b = 9$, $h = 6$ [42]

   d) $V = lwh$; $l = 2$, $w = 1.5$, $h = 10$ [30]

2. Find the area of each circle. Round your answers to 1 decimal place, if necessary.

   a) radius 5 cm   [78.5 cm²]

   b) diameter 22 m   [379.9 m²]

3. Find the circumference of each circle. Round your answers to 1 decimal place, if necessary.

   a) diameter 11.5 cm   [36.1 cm]

   b) radius 52 cm   [326.6 cm]

Mental Math

1. Calculate.

   a) $1 + 2 + 3 + ... + 20$ [210]

   b) $1 + 2 + 3 + ... + 25$ [325]

   c) $2 + 4 + 6 + ... + 44$ [506]

   d) $2 + 4 + 6 + ... + 36$ [342]

   e) $1 + 3 + 5 + ... + 19$ [120]

   f) $1 + 3 + 5 + ... + 31$ [256]

2. Simplify.

   a) $\sqrt{68}$ [$2\sqrt{17}$]   b) $\sqrt{192}$ [$8\sqrt{3}$]

   c) $\sqrt{75}$ [$5\sqrt{3}$]   d) $\sqrt{242}$ [$11\sqrt{2}$]

   e) $\sqrt{288}$ [$12\sqrt{2}$]   f) $\sqrt{200}$ [$2\sqrt{10}$]

Explore/Inquire Answers

Explore: Interpret the Information

1. a) 50 ha   b) 13 ha, 2 ha, 38 ha

   c) 2510 m   d) 628 m, 314 m, 942 m

Inquire

1. a) $\frac{1}{6}$ b) $\frac{1}{12}$ c) $\frac{1}{3}$ 2. $A = \frac{m}{360}(\pi r^2)$

3. a) $\frac{1}{18}$ b) $\frac{5}{18}$ c) $\frac{5}{6}$ 4. $l = \frac{m}{360}(2\pi r)$

5. a) $A \doteq 35$ cm², $l \doteq 7$ cm

   b) $A \doteq 314$ cm², $l \doteq 42$ cm

   c) $A \doteq 4909$ cm², $l \doteq 196$ cm

   d) $A \doteq 4189$ cm², $l \doteq 209$ cm

Teaching Suggestions

Method 1

Read with the class the opening paragraph on student text page 433. Review the meaning of the terms "sector" and "sector angle." Ask:

What real-life examples can you think of of the use of the word "sector?"

How is this real-life example related to a sector of a circle?

Assign the Explore section to pairs of students. For part a), ask:

What is the formula for the area of a circle?

How can you use this formula to find the area of the field?

For part b), ask:

What fraction of a complete rotation is a rotation of 90°? 180°? 270°?

How can you use these fractions to find the area of the sectors with these central angles?

For part c), ask:

What is the formula for the circumference of a circle?

For part d), ask:

What fraction of a complete rotation is a rotation of 90°? 45°? 135°?

How can you use these fractions to find the arc lengths with these central angles?

Have volunteers present their results to the class. Then, assign the Inquire questions to pairs of students. For Inquire question 2, ask:

How is the area of a circle related to the area of a sector of that circle?

How is the circumference of a circle related to the arc length of a sector of that circle?

Give pairs of students an opportunity to discuss and compare their results with other pairs of students. Encourage them to come to a consensus about a solution. Have volunteers present their results to the class.

Review with the class teaching examples 1 and 2 on student text pages 434 and 435.

Encourage some students to work along with the rest of the class with a graphing calculator. Have volunteers present their results to the class.

Method 2

(compasses, rulers, protractors, 0.5-cm grid paper, string)
Discuss the terms "minor arc," "major arc," and "sector." Organize the class into 4 groups of equal size, and assign 2 groups to each of the following investigations. Encourage the groups who are completing the same investigation to discuss and compare their results. Encourage them to come to a consensus about the final outcome.

Ask 2 volunteers from each combined group to present their results to the class. Provide an overhead projector, and have one student display the diagram on the chalkboard, while the other describes the results.

Investigation 1

Draw a circle and mark the centre O. On the circle, mark two points, A and B, that are not opposite each other. Join OA and OB. Measure ∠AOB. Use 0.5-cm grid paper to estimate the area of sector AOB.

Repeat the investigation 4 more times.

Copy and complete the table.

Circle	1	2	3	4
Radius				
Area				
Measure of ∠AOB				
Area of sector AOB				
$\frac{\angle AOB}{360°}$				
area of AOB / area of circle				

Study the results and describe how you would find the area of a sector of a circle.

Devise a formula for the area of a sector of a circle.

Investigation 2

Draw a circle and mark the centre, O. On the circle, mark two points, A and B, that are not opposite each other. Join OA and OB. Measure ∠AOB. Find the length of minor arc AB, by carefully laying a piece of string along the minor arc AB, and then, measuring the length of this string.

Repeat this investigation 4 more times.

Copy and complete the table.

Circle	1	2	3	4
Radius				
Circumference				
Measure of ∠AOB				
Length of minor arc AB				
$\frac{\angle AOB}{360°}$				
Length of minor arc AB / Circumference of circle				

Study the results and describe how you would find the length of an arc of a circle.

Devise a formula for the length of an arc of a circle.

Review with the class teaching examples 1 and 2 on student text pages 434 and 435.

Sample Solution

Page 437, question 42

Since the triangle is equilateral, then its angles are 60°. The length of the arc of a circle subtended on a 60° central angle is

$$l = \frac{60}{360}(2\pi r), \text{ or } \frac{\pi r}{3}$$

The rotor is made up of three arcs.

The perimeter of the rotor is $3 \times \frac{\pi r}{3} = \pi r$.

Word Power Answer

a, an, ran, rant, train, rating, parting

Integrating Technology

Graphing Calculators

How would you use your graphing calculator to determine the measure of ∠TOP in teaching example 2 on student text page 435? On a TI-83, the cos⁻¹ (i.e., 2nd cos) key is used.
Press 6, the ÷ key, 88.8, and the ENTER key to determine what cos ∠TOP equals.
Then, press the cos⁻¹ (i.e., 2nd cos) key, the ANS (i.e., 2nd (−)) key, the) key, and the ENTER key.

Use your calculator to find lengths and angle measures as needed in the questions on student text pages 435 to 437.

See *MATHPOWER™ 11, Western Edition, Blackline Masters* pages 184 to 186 for Trigonometry.

Extension

1. Show how the length of an arc of a circle changes when the radius of the circle is doubled in length.
2. Show how the area of a sector of a circle changes when the radius of the circle is doubled in length.
3. A semicircle and a quarter circle are equal in perimeter. Show that the area of the quarter circle is greater than the area of the semicircle.

Enrichment

Find the area of the shaded region of the diagram shown below.

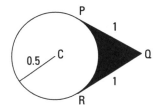

[Find area of PQRC. $\left(2 \times \dfrac{1 \times 0.5}{2} = \dfrac{1}{2}\right)$

Find the measure of $\angle$PCR. $\tan \angle$PCQ $= \dfrac{1}{0.5} = 2$

Find the area of sector PCR. Subtract area of sector PCR from area PQRC.]

Math Journal

area of a sector of a circle, arc length of a circle
Write the formula for finding the area of a sector of a circle, and the formula for the arc length of a circle. Include diagrams and examples for clarity.

Problem Levels of Difficulty

A: 1–34   **B:** 35–40   **C:** 41–43

Assessing the Outcomes

Journal

Describe in words, without the use of variables, how you would find the length of an arc and the area of a sector.

Written Assignment

Calculate the area of the shaded region and the length of arc ABC in each diagram. Round your answers to 1 decimal place, if necessary.

1.
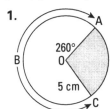

2.
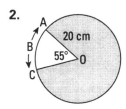

Technology

Exploring the Sums of the Interior Angles in Polygons

Student Text Page
P. 438

Materials
geometry software, spreadsheet software

Learning Outcome
- Determine the sum of interior angles in terms of right angles.

Prerequisite Skills
Could three angles measuring 50°, 65°, and 70° be the interior angles of a triangle? Explain.

[No, their sum is 185°; the sum of the interior angles in a triangle is always 180°.]

Teaching Suggestions
Before assigning Exploration 1, discuss how to construct polygons and diagonals using geometry software. With Geometer's Sketchpad, one method uses the point tool at the left of the screen and the Segment construction.

To construct, for example, a pentagon and its diagonals, do the following:
Click the point tool at the left of the screen.
Move the cursor into the sketch area and click.
Move the cursor to four other locations, clicking at each.
Click the pointer tool at the left side of the screen to return the cursor to a pointer.
While pressing the Shift key, click each of the other points in clockwise or counterclockwise order while the last point constructed is still selected.
Click Segment from the Construct menu.
Click one vertex, and while pressing the Shift key, click a non-adjacent vertex.
Click Segment from the Construct menu.
Click the vertex at one end of the diagonal, and while pressing the Shift key, click the other non-adjacent vertex.
Click Segment from the Construct menu.

Discuss the relationship, and then, assign Exploration 2. Relate the formulas to the relationship from Exploration 1. In column A, the formula and the Fill Down feature give the numbers of sides in the polygons from 3 to 10. In column B, the formula and the Fill Down feature give the numbers of triangles in the polygon, which are two less than the numbers of sides.

In column C, the formula and the Fill Down feature give the sums of the interior angles in multiples of 180°, which are the numbers of triangles in the polygon. In column D, the formula and the Fill Down feature give the sums of the interior angles in multiples of 90°, which are twice the sums of the interior angles in multiples of 180°.

Assessing the Outcome

Journal

Write about why you might be interested in expressing the sum of interior angles in terms of right angles.

7.7 Angles and Polygons

Student Text Pages
Pp. 439–443

Materials
graphing calculators, overhead projector

Learning Outcomes
- Define "concave" and "convex" polygons.
- Develop the interior angle sum theorem for polygons and its corollary.
- Develop the exterior angle sum theorem for polygons and its corollary.
- Determine angle measures of polygons.

Prerequisite Skills
1. Simplify.
a) $2x + 3y - 5x + 4 + 7y - 1$ $[-3x + 10y + 3]$
b) $z^2 + 2z - 5 - 2z^2 - 6z + 11$ $[-z^2 - 4z + 6]$
c) $2(x + 5) + 3(2x - 1) + 6x$ $[14x + 7]$
d) $-3(x + 1) + 3y + 2x + 5(y - 4)$ $[-x + 8y - 23]$
2. How many right angles are in each angle measure?
a) $270°$ [3]   b) $540°$ [6]   c) $1080°$ [12]
3. Evaluate each expression for the given value of the variable.
a) $2(x + 5) + 3x; x = 4$ [30]
b) $-5(2x + 3) + (x + 1); x = 7$ [−77]
c) $15(x + 1) + 3x; x = 20$ [375]

Mental Math
1. Find the measure of the indicated angles.
a)

b)
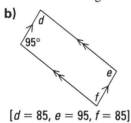

$[c = 60]$ $[d = 85, e = 95, f = 85]$

2. Calculate.
a) $1 + 2 + 3 + ... + 61$ [1830]
b) $1 + 2 + 3 + ... + 44$ [990]
c) $2 + 4 + 6 + ... + 38$ [380]
d) $2 + 4 + 6 + ... + 96$ [2450]
e) $1 + 3 + 5 + ... + 51$ [676]
f) $1 + 3 + 5 + ... + 45$ [529]

Explore/Inquire Answers
Explore: Look for a Pattern

Polygon	Number of Sides	Number of Triangles	Sum of Interior Angle Measures (degrees)	Sum of Interior Angle Measures (in Right Angles)
triangle	3	1	180	2
quadrilateral	4	2	360	4
pentagon	5	3	540	6
hexagon	6	4	720	8
heptagon	7	5	900	10
octagon	8	6	1080	12
nonagon	9	7	1260	14
decagon	10	8	1440	16

Inquire
1. The number of triangles is 2 less than the number of sides.
2. a) 18   b) 3240°, 36 right angles
3. a) $n - 2$ b) $(n - 2)180°$ c) $2(n - 2)$
4. a) 135°   b) 15 right angles

Teaching Suggestions

Method 1
(overhead projector)   Review with the class the opening paragraphs on student text page 439. Review the terms "concave polygon," "convex polygon," "interior angle," and "exterior angle." Ask:

Where have you heard the words "concave" and "convex" used in everyday life?

Assign the Explore section and the Inquire questions to pairs of students. Have volunteers present their results to the class. Provide an overhead projector, if necessary.

Review with the class teaching examples 1 and 2 on student text pages 440 and 441.

After teaching example 2, ask:

Do you think this theorem is true for concave polygons? Explain.

Encourage students to use diagrams to justify the answers to your question. Ensure that the students conclude that the exterior angle sum for polygons applies only to convex polygons.

Method 2
(overhead projector)   Organize the class into 4 groups of equal size, and assign 2 groups to each of the following investigations. Encourage the groups who are

completing the same investigation to discuss and compare their results. Encourage them to come to a consensus about the final outcome.

Have the groups doing the same investigation combine and discuss their results. Have 2 volunteers from each combined group present their results to the class. Provide an overhead projector, and have one student display the diagram on the chalkboard, while the other describes the results.

Investigation 1

Draw any polygon. Choose any vertex of the polygon. Draw lines from that vertex to the other non-adjacent vertices. Count the number of triangles into which the polygon has been divided.

Repeat this investigation with 5 more polygons with different numbers of sides.

Study your results to determine how the number of triangles is related to the number of sides of the polygon.

Devise a formula for the sum of the interior angles of a polygon.

Investigation 2

Draw a convex heptagon. Extend each side of the heptagon in one direction, to form an external angle at each vertex of the heptagon. Determine the answers to these questions:

What is the sum of the measures of the interior angles of the heptagon?

What is the sum of the measures of the exterior angle and the interior angle at each vertex of the heptagon?

What is the sum of the measures of the exterior angles and the interior angles of the heptagon?

What is the sum of the measures of the exterior angles of the heptagon?

Repeat this investigation for a convex hexagon, a convex septagon, a convex octagon, a convex nonagon, and a convex decagon.

Write a conclusion about the sum of the exterior angles of a convex polygon.

Sample Solution

Page 443, question 36

a) $\angle 1, \angle 2, \angle 3, \angle 4,$ and $\angle 5$ are the vertically opposite angles of the interior angles of the polygon.

Thus, $\angle 1 + \angle 2 + \angle 3 + \angle 4 + \angle 5$
= sum of the interior angles of the polygon
= $3 \times 180°$, or $540°$
In the diagram containing $\angle a$,
$\angle a = \angle 1 - \angle x$
$\angle x = 180° - \angle 5$
$\angle a = \angle 1 - (180° - \angle 5)$
     $= \angle 1 + \angle 5 - 180°$

Similarly, $\angle b = \angle 1 + \angle 2 - 180°$
$\angle c = \angle 2 + \angle 3 - 180°$
$\angle d = \angle 3 + \angle 4 - 180°$
$\angle e = \angle 4 + \angle 5 - 180°$
$\angle a + \angle b + \angle c + \angle d + \angle e$
$= 2\angle 1 + 2\angle 2 + 2\angle 3 + 2\angle 4 + 2\angle 5 - 5(180°)$
$= 2(\angle 1 + \angle 2 + \angle 3 + \angle 4 + \angle 5) - 5(180°)$
Since $\angle 1 + \angle 2 + \angle 3 + \angle 4 + \angle 5 = 540°$, then,
$\angle a + \angle b + \angle c + \angle d + \angle e = 2(540°) - 5(180°)$
$= 1080° - 900°$
$= 180°$

Logic Power Answer

The next figure is a blank.
A model of an electronic digit is shown at the right. Each digit is created by removing different line segments.
The electronic digits from 0 to 8 are shown below.

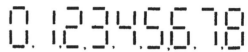

The logic power problem gives the line segments that are not required for the electronic digits from 0 to 7.

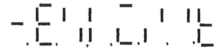

The electronic digit 8 uses every line segment possible. Zero line segments are not required. Thus, a blank is the next figure in the sequence.

Extension

Write an equation and solve it to find the number of sides of a convex polygon with the following interior angle sums.
a) $4500°$ b) $35\ 640°$ c) $77\ 580°$
Confer with a classmate to check that your answers are correct.

Math Journal

interior angle sum theorem, exterior angle sum theorem Write a few sentences explaining the interior angle sum for a polygon and its converse, and the exterior angle sum theorem and its converse. Include diagrams and examples for clarity.

Common Errors

- Students often confuse the exterior angle sum (360°) with the interior angle sum [$180°(n-2)$]. They often calculate $360° \div n$ as the measure of the interior angle instead of the exterior angle of a regular polygon with n sides.

$\mathbf{R}_x$ Remind the students that the sum of the interior angles depends on the number of triangles into which a polygon can be divided, but the exterior angle sum is always 360°. Thus, the measure of the interior angles of a regular polygon with n sides is $\dfrac{180°(n-2)}{n}$, while the measure of the exterior angles of a regular polygon with n sides is $\dfrac{360°}{n}$.

Problem Levels of Difficulty

A: 1–33   **B:** 34–37   **C:** 38, 39

Assessing the Outcomes

Self-Evaluation Assignment

Make up a problem about the interior and exterior angles of a convex polygon. Solve your problem. Discuss how confident you are about your answers.

Connecting Math and Biology

Honeybees

Student Text Pages
Pp. 444–445

Materials
scientific (or graphing) calculators

Learning Outcomes
- Determine the volume of wax in honeybee cells.
- Examine how honeybees determine distances to food sources.
- Examine how honeybees signal food source locations.

Prerequisite Skills
1. Calculate the volume of each solid.

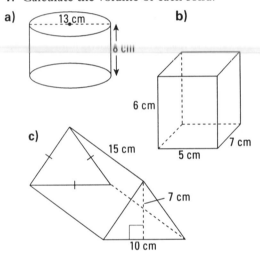

a) 13 cm, 8 cm
b) 6 cm, 5 cm, 7 cm
c) 15 cm, 7 cm, 10 cm

[a) 2197 cm³ b) 210 cm³ c) 525 cm³]

2. This diagram represents a rotation of 180° clockwise.

180°

Draw a diagram to represent each rotation.

a) 270° counterclockwise **b)** 90° clockwise

c) 180° counterclockwise **d)** 270° clockwise

Mental Math

1. Add.

a)		b)		c)	
45	[441]	95	[284]	4.7	[27.0]
82		33		5.2	
77		89		8.1	
49		15		0.9	
22		7		3.7	
+ 166		+ 45		+ 4.4	

2. Divide.
a) 189 ÷ 9   [21]   **b)** 156 ÷ 12   [13]
c) 3040 ÷ 16   [190]   **d)** 108 ÷ 36   [3]
e) 882 ÷ 42   [21]   **f)** 1820 ÷ 91   [20]

Teaching Suggestions
Read with the class the opening paragraphs on student text page **444**.

Review with the class the names of the solids and the formulas for the volumes of solid prisms.

Before assigning Exploration 1 to pairs of students, ask:
What is a tile?
What does it mean when you say a polygon tiles a plane?
Do all polygons tile planes?

Ensure that students know that a tile is a polygon that is used to cover a plane, and tiling a plane means covering the plane with the tile, so that the tiles do not overlap and there is no space between the tiles. Point out that not all polygon tiles tile a plane surface. Ask:
What is the general formula for the volume of a prism?

Look for an answer from the students such as: the volume of a prism is the product of the area of the base and the height. For question 4, lead the students to see that any regular polygon can have a circle inscribed in it. Thus, a regular octagon can enclose a cell cylinder. Have volunteers present their results to the class.

Read with the class the first column of Exploration 2 on student text page 445 before assigning the questions to pairs of students.

Integrating Technology
Internet
Use the Internet to find more information about honeybees, honeycomb cells, and signalling distance and directions to food.

Extension
Research how other insects, birds, or animals use movement to communicate information. Choose one of these life forms and write a short description of the movement and what information is communicated. Present your results to the class.

Assessing the Outcomes
Observation
Some skills to watch for in this lesson are:
- Do the students remember their formulas for volumes of solids?
- Do the students know how to apply the formulas?
- Do the students show patience for a lengthy assignment?
- Do the pairs co-operate to help make the work easier?
- Are the students willing to help other students who do not understand parts of the exploration?

Review

Student Text Pages
Pp. 446–447

Materials
compasses, rulers

Learning Outcome
• Review the skills and concepts in Chapter 7.

Using the Review
Have the students work independently to complete the Review. Meeting in small groups, the students can mark and discuss the work. Groups can then share their solutions and report any questions that caused them difficulty. Discuss these questions with the class.

Reteaching Suggestions
For those students having difficulty with the chapter material, form small groups and use the following exercises.

If you feel that the class has had particular difficulty mastering any concept, you may wish to work through a problem from each section as a model of excellence of solution, which some students require just prior to assessment.

Geometric Proofs
1. In quadrilateral KLMN, ∠KNL = ∠MLN, and ∠KLN = ∠MNL. Write a two-paragraph proof to show that MN = KL.

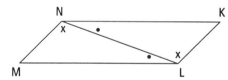

2. In the diagram, AC = AD and ED = BC. Write a flow-chart proof to show that ∠EAD = ∠BAC.

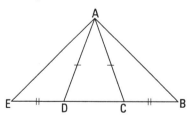

3. In the diagram, QR = SR and ∠QRP = ∠SRP. Write a paragraph proof to show that RP bisects ∠QPS.

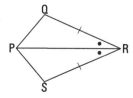

Chord Properties
1. Prove that two chords that are equidistant from the centre are congruent.
2. A circle with a radius of 5 cm has a chord 3 cm from the centre. How long is the chord?
3. The perpendicular bisector of a chord meets the chord at point X. The radius of the circle is 9 cm and the distance the chord is from the centre of the circle is 5 cm. What is the length of the chord? Round your answer to 1 decimal place.

Angles in a Circle
1. Find the values of the indicated variables.

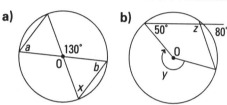

2. Points A, B, C, and D lie, in order, on a circle with centre O. BD is a diameter and ∠CAB = ∠CAD. Write a two-column proof to show that BD and OC are perpendicular.

3. Write a flow-chart proof to show that BD = BA.

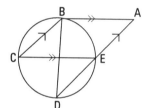

Cyclic Quadrilaterals
1. Name the cyclic quadrilaterals in the diagram.

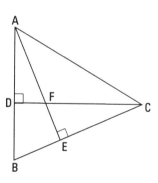

2. Find the values of the variables.

3. In ΔABC, AB = AC and the bisectors of ∠ABC and ∠ACB meet at X and Y, respectively. Prove that B, C, X, and Y are concyclic points.

Tangents to a Circle

1. In the following diagrams, tangents have been drawn to circles. Find the values of the variables.

a)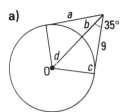

b)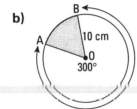

2. Two tangents from external point X meet the circle at M and N. Prove ∠XMN = ∠XNM.

Arc Length and Sector Area

1. Calculate the length of each arc and the area of each shaded sector. Use $\pi = 3.14$. Round your answers to 1 decimal place.

a)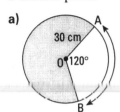

b)

2. A circle has a radius of 25 cm. Calculate the length of the arc that subtends an angle of 52°. Round your answer to the nearest tenth of a centimetre.

3. Calculate the area of the segment. Round your answer to the nearest tenth of a centimetre.

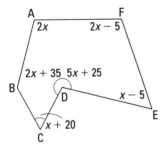

Angles and Polygons

1. Determine the measures of the angles of the polygon.

2. What is the sum of the measures of the interior angles of an octagon?

3. The sum of the interior angles of a polygon is 900°. How many sides does the polygon have?

4. The measure of the exterior angles of a regular polygon is 40°. How many sides does the polygon have?

Answers to Reteaching Suggestions

Chord Properties

2. 8 cm

3. 7.5 cm

Angles in a Circle

1. a) $a = b = x = 65$

   b) $z = 100, y = 200$

Cyclic Quadrilaterals

1. ADEC and DFEB

2. $x = 75, y = 95$

Tangents to a Circle

1. a) $a = 9, b = 35, c = 90, d = 55$

   b) $x = 105, z = 45, y = 75$

Arc Length and Sector Area

1. a) 125.7 cm, 1885.0 cm² b) 10.5 cm, 52.4 cm²

2. 22.7 cm

3. 28.5 cm²

Angles and Polygons

1. ∠A = 100°, ∠B = 135°, ∠C = 70°, ∠D = 275°, ∠E = 45°, ∠F = 95°

2. 1080°   3. 7   4. 9

Exploring Mathematics

Investigating Inscribed Circles

(compasses, rulers)   Review with the class the constructions for bisecting an angle and for drawing a perpendicular from a point not on a line to a line. For question 1, elicit from the students that since the radius of the circle meets the side at one point, then the sides are tangents to the circle.

For question 2, ask:

What type of triangle has side measures 5 cm, 12 cm, and 13 cm?

How could you use this information to find the measures of the angles of the triangle?

Lead the students to see that the triangle is a right triangle, and trigonometry could be used to find the measures of the angles. The following solution lacks reasons for many statements. Have the students provide them.

In $\triangle ABC$,
$AB^2 + BC^2 = AC^2$.
Thus, $\triangle ABC$ is right
and $\angle B = 90°$.
BE and DC are
bisectors of $\angle B$ and
$\angle C$, respectively.
Thus, Y is the incentre.

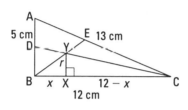

YX is a perpendicular from the incentre to the side of the triangle. Thus, YX is the radius of the incircle.

In $\triangle ACB$, $\tan C = \dfrac{5}{12}$.

Thus, $\angle C = 22.6°$ and $\angle XCY = 11.3°$.
In $\triangle YBX$, $\angle YBX = 45°$ and $\angle YXB = 90°$.
Thus, $\angle BYX = 45°$ and BX = XY.
Thus, $x = r$.

In $\triangle YXC$, $\tan XCY = \dfrac{r}{12 - x}$

$$\tan 11.3° = \frac{r}{12 - x}$$

$$0.2 = \frac{r}{12 - r}$$

$$0.2(12 - r) = r$$
$$2(12 - r) = 10r$$
$$24 - 2r = 10r$$
$$24 = 12r$$
$$r = 2$$

Thus, the radius of the incircle is 2 cm.

For question 3, ask:

If the perimeter of an equilateral triangle is 30 cm, what is the measure of each length of the sides of the triangle?

What is the measure of each angle of the triangle?

The following is a partial solution to question 3. Have the students justify the information in the diagram and each statement in the solution.

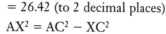

In $\triangle YXC$,
$$\tan 30° = \frac{r}{5}$$
$$r = 5 \tan 30°$$
$$= 2.9$$
Area of incircle
$= \pi r^2$
$= 3.14 \times (2.9)^2$
$= 26.42$ (to 2 decimal places)
$AX^2 = AC^2 - XC^2$
$AX = \sqrt{75}$
Area of $\triangle ABC = XC \times XA$
$= 5 \times 5\sqrt{3}$
$= 43.30$ (to 2 decimal places)
Fraction that the area of the incircle is of the area

of the triangle $= \dfrac{26.42}{43.30}$

$= 0.610$ (to 3 decimal places)
Percent that the area of the incircle is of the area of the triangle is 61%, to the nearest percent.

For question 4, ask:

What does the term "regular polygon" mean?

What information do you know about the hexagon if it is described as regular?

Have the students justify the information in the diagram and the statements in the following solution.

In $\triangle ABX$,
$$\tan 30° = \frac{5}{r}$$
$$r = 5 \tan 30°$$
$$= 2.89 \text{ (to 2}$$
$$\text{decimal places)}$$
Area of $\triangle ABX$
$= \dfrac{1}{2} \times 5 \times 2.89$
Area of hexagon $= 12 \times \dfrac{1}{2} \times 5 \times 2.89$
$= 30 \times 2.89$
Area of incircle $= \pi(2.89)^2$
Fraction that the area of the incircle is of the area

of the hexagon $= \dfrac{\pi(2.89)^2}{30 \times 2.89}$

$= 0.302$ (to 3 decimal places)
The area of the incircle is 30% of the area of the hexagon, to the nearest percent.

For question 5, ask:

When a circle is inscribed in a square, how is the radius of the circle related to the sides of the square?

Have the students justify the information in the diagram and each statement in the following solution.

Let the radius of the smaller circle be x.

Then, $OB = x$.

$AB = OB$

$\angle OBA = 90°$

$OA^2 = AB^2 + BO^2$

$\quad\quad = 2BO^2$

$\quad\quad = 2x^2$

$OA = \sqrt{2}x$

$AD = DC$

$\angle ADC = 90°$

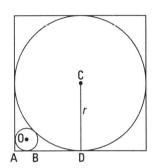

$AC^2 = AD^2 + DC^2$

$\quad\quad = r^2 + r^2$

$\quad\quad = 2r^2$

$AC = \sqrt{2}r$

$AC = OA + OC$

$\sqrt{2}r = \sqrt{2}x + x + r$

$\sqrt{2}r - r = \sqrt{2}x + x$

$r(\sqrt{2} - 1) = x(\sqrt{2} + 1)$

$x = \dfrac{r\sqrt{2} - 1}{\sqrt{2} + 1}$

$\quad = \dfrac{r\sqrt{2} - 1}{\sqrt{2} + 1} \times \dfrac{\sqrt{2} - 1}{\sqrt{2} - 1}$

$\quad = (3 - 2\sqrt{2})r$

Chapter Check

Student Text Page
P. 448

Learning Outcome

- Evaluate the skills and concepts in Chapter 7.

Assessing the Outcome

Observation

If you assign the Chapter Check as a student assessment, look for the following.

- Can they write a two-column, a flow-chart, and a paragraph proof?
- Do they know the properties of the chords of a circle?
- Do they know the properties of the angles of a circle?
- Do they understand the properties of cyclic quadrilaterals and concyclic points?
- Can they find the equation of a tangent to a circle at the point of tangency and the length of the tangent?
- Can they find the arc length and the area of a sector of a circle?
- Can they find the number of sides of a polygon from the sum of the interior angles?
- Can they find the measure of the interior angles of a regular polygon from the number of sides of the polygon?

Problem Solving

Student Text Page
P. 449

Materials
Teacher's Resource Master 1 (0.5-cm grid paper)

Learning Outcome
- Use problem solving strategies to solve problems.

Using the Strategies
The problems on this page allow the students to use the problem solving strategies discussed in Chapters 1 to 3. These strategies are
- Use a Diagram
- Use a Data Bank
- Solve Fermi Problems
- Solve a Simpler Problem
- Use Logic
- Look for a Pattern
- Guess and Check
- Work Backward
- Use a Table or Spreadsheet

Teaching Suggestions
(0.5-cm grid paper) Encourage the students to work in pairs or small groups. When students have completed the problems, have them share and discuss their strategies and solutions with other students.

For question 1, ask:

What is the difference between a natural number, a whole number, and an integer?

For question 2, a Venn diagram can be drawn. Ask:

What is the significance of the words "at least" in the problem?

Lead the students to see that "at least" means that more than one subject can be taken. This means that the intersection of the circle is included in the number taking the courses.

For question 6, ask:

What is the difference between a graph and a sketch?

Remind them that a sketch is a general graph that does not require scales and grids and particular values.

For question 7, ask:

What is a reciprocal?

The students might find it helpful to remember that $(A + B)^2 = A^2 + 2AB + B^2$.

For question 8, ask:

What type of triangle is $\triangle QPO$?

Provide students with grid paper, and suggest they draw a diagram.

Sample Solution

Page 449, question 4 a)

$$9x + 24 = A[X + B(X + C)]$$
$$= A[X + BX + BC]$$
$$= AX + ABX + ABC$$
$$= X(A + AB) + ABC$$

Equate the coefficients of like terms.

$$A + AB = 9$$
$$A(1 + B) = 9 \quad \text{.........................(1)}$$
$$ABC = 24$$
$$C = \frac{24}{AB} \quad \text{.....................(2)}$$

In (1), since A and B are integers, then we can ask: What two integers have a product of 9? The possibilities are 1 and 9; 3 and 3; -3 and -3; and -1 and -9.

Suppose $A = 1$. Then, $1 + B = 9$ and $B = 8$.
Suppose $A = -1$. Then, $1 + B = -9$ and $B = -10$.
Suppose $A = 3$. Then, $1 + B = 3$ and $B = 2$.
Suppose $A = -3$. Then, $1 + B = -3$ and $B = -4$.
Suppose $A = 9$. Then, $1 + B = 1$ and $B = 0$.
Suppose $A = -9$. Then, $1 + B = -1$ and $B = -2$.
Substitute the corresponding values of A and B in (2).

A	B	$C = \dfrac{24}{AB}$	
1	8	$\dfrac{24}{8} = 3$	valid answer
-1	-10	$\dfrac{24}{-10}$	not an integer
3	2	$\dfrac{24}{6} = 4$	valid answer
-3	-4	$\dfrac{24}{12} = 2$	valid answer
9	0	undefined	inadmissible value of B
-9	-2	$\dfrac{24}{18}$	not an integer

Possible values for A and B are $A = 1$, $B = 8$; $A = 3$, $B = 2$; and $A = -3$, $B = -4$.

Assessing the Outcome

Observation

As you make your problem solving assessment of each student, consider the following:
- Do they understand the problem?
- Do they consider a variety of strategies?
- Do they use an organized approach?
- Do they create and use diagrams effectively?
- Do they show persistence?

Student Text Answers

Getting Started pp. 382–383

1 Angle Relationships

  1. $w = 37°, x = 52°, y = 91°, z = 52°$
  2. $x = 72°$
  3. $a = 67°, b = 65°, c = 48°$
  4. $w = 33°, x = 37°, y = 33°, z = 110°$
  5. $a = 54°, b = 54°, c = 126°, d = 126°, e = 54°$
  6. $d = 51°, e = 58°, f = 71°, g = 122°, h = 58°$
  7. $w = 50°, x = 92°, y = 38°, z = 50°$
  8. $a = 55°, b = 55°, c = 40°, d = 55°, e = 125°,$
  $f = 95°, g = 85°, h = 85°$
  9. $40°$ **10.** $30°$
  11. $31°$ **12.** $44°$
  13. $22°$ **14.** $11°$
  15. $37°$ **16.** $35°$

2 Congruent Triangles

Some answers may vary.
  1. a) AB = AD, BC = DC, CA = CA (SSS)
    b) ∠ABC = ∠ADC, ∠BCA = ∠DCA,
    ∠CAB = ∠CAD
  2. a) GI = GJ, ∠GHI = ∠GKJ,
    ∠GIH = ∠GIK (AAS)
    b) GH = GK, IH = JK, ∠IGH = ∠JGK
  3. a) ∠FDE = ∠FHG, ∠FED = ∠FGH,
    DE = HG (ASA)
    b) DF = HF, EF = GF, ∠DFE = ∠HFG
  4. a) PQ = RS, ∠QPR = ∠SRP, PR = RP (SAS)
    b) QR = SP, ∠PRQ = ∠RPS, ∠RQP = ∠PSR
  5. a) ∠ADB = ∠CBD, DB = BD,
    ∠ABD = ∠CDB (ASA)
    b) AD = CB, AB = CD, ∠DAB = ∠BCD
  6. a) ∠RTS = ∠UST, TS = ST,
    ∠SRT = ∠TUS (AAS)
    b) ∠RST = ∠UTS, RS = UT, RT = US

Mental Math

Angle Measures

  1. $a = 30°, b = 75°$
  2. $a = 55°, b = 75°, c = 50°$
  3. $p = 70°, q = 110°, r = 70°, s = 110°$
  4. $a = 30°, b = 70°, c = 70°$

Adding the First n Whole, Even, or Odd Numbers

  1. 66   **2.** 1225   **3.** 5050
  4. 500 500   **5.** Multiply n by $n + 1$.
  6. 56   **7.** 110
  8. 650   **9.** 2550

  10. a) 4   **b)** 9   **c)** 16   **d)** 25
  11. Multiply n by itself.
  12. 81   **13.** 2500

Investigating Math p. 384

1 Writing Reasons

  1. addition property   **2.** transitive property
  3. subtraction property   **4.** division property
  5. multiplication property
  6. distributive property   **7.** transitive property
  8. reflexive property   **9.** transitive property
  10. symmetric property
  11. symmetric property, transitive property
  12. addition property
  13. subtraction property, symmetric property,
    transitive property
  14. substitution property, division property
  15. substitution property, addition property

2 Solving Equations

  1. 11   **2.** 8   **3.** 3
  4. $\frac{3}{2}$ **5.** $-\frac{1}{3}$

Section 7.1 pp. 389–392

Practice (Section 7.1)

  1. BD = CD; Definition of perpendicular;
    Reflexive property; SAS; ∠B = ∠C
  2. Given; ∠DBC = ∠DCB; Given; Addition
    property; Isosceles Triangle Theorem
  3. Given; ∠PTQ = ∠RTS; Transversal Parallel Lines
    Theorem; ΔPTQ ≅ ΔRST; Congruent triangles
  4. Given; OC = OC; Radii of a circle; HS;
    Congruent triangles

Applications and Problem Solving (Section 7.1)

  15. a) yes (ASA)   **b)** yes (HS)
    c) yes (SAS)   **d)** no
    e) yes (AAS)   **f)** yes (SSS)
  22. BEC is a straight angle and EC = BE;
    AED is a straight angle and AE = ED.
  25. ΔPQR ≅ ΔCBA
  26. no
  27. a) $x = 40°$ **b)** ∠A = 75°, ∠B = 65°,
    ∠C = 40°, ∠D = 75°, ∠E = 65°, ∠F = 40°
  29. no   **30.** $\frac{13}{20}$ or 65%

Computer Data Bank   p. 393

1 Simple and Complex Craters

1. If a crater has at least one of the two central peak dimensions, it must be complex.
2. 76 simple, 80 complex

2 Simple Craters

1. West Hawk
2. Answers will vary.
3. For the parabola opening up in the fourth quadrant, $p = 1.22$, $q = -0.34$
4. a) Substitute values for all the variables except a into $y = a(x - p)^2 + q$, and solve for a.
   b) 0.228
5. Answers will vary.
7. For the parabola opening up, from most flat to least flat

3 Simple Crater Characteristics

1. Answers will vary.
2. Macha

4 Complex Crater Characteristics

1. Answers will vary.
2. simple

Technology   p. 394

1 Perpendicular Bisector of a Chord

4. It passes through the centre of the circle.
5. It passes through the centre of the circle.
6. The perpendicular bisector of a chord of a circle passes through the centre of the circle.

2 Perpendicular From the Centre of a Circle to a Chord

5. They are equal.   6. They are equal.
7. The perpendicular from the centre of a circle to a chord in the circle bisects the chord.

3 Line Segment From the Centre of a Circle to the Midpoint of a Chord

5. They are equal to 90°.
6. They are equal to 90°.
7. The line segment from the centre of a circle to the midpoint of a chord in the circle is perpendicular to the chord.

Investigating Math   p. 395

1 Perpendicular Bisector of a Chord

4. It passes through the centre of the circle.
5. It passes through the centre of the circle.
7. The perpendicular bisector of a chord of a circle passes through the centre of the circle.

2 Perpendicular From the Centre of a Circle to a Chord

5. They are equal.   6. They are equal.
8. The perpendicular from the centre of a circle to a chord in the circle bisects the chord.

3 Line Segment From the Centre of a Circle to the Midpoint of a Chord

6. They are equal to 90°.
7. They are equal to 90°.
9. The line segment from the centre of a circle to the midpoint of a chord in the circle is perpendicular to the chord.

Section 7.2   pp. 400–401

Practice (Section 7.2)

1. true   2. true
3. false   4. false
5. a) 5.8 cm   b) 10 cm
6. 41.4 cm
7. a) 1 cm   b) 5.3 cm
8. a) 10.8 cm   b) 14.8 cm
9. a) 14.2 cm   b) 22 cm
10. a) 0.5 cm   b) 17.0 cm
11. a) 5.2 cm   b) 10.4 cm
12. a) 6.4 cm   b) 2.4 cm
13. 6.2 cm
14. a) 4.0 cm   b) 4.5 cm
15. 29°
16. a) 48°   b) 49°

Applications and Problem Solving (Section 7.2)

17. 13 cm   18. 12 cm   19. 5.3 cm
22. Construct two chords using the points. The perpendicular bisectors of the chords intersect at the centre of the circle.
23. 7.4 cm   24. 3.6 cm
25. 8.09 m   26. 41.6 cm
27. 26.2 cm   28. longer chord
29. 52 cm   30. 10 cm
33. No; The diameter of the hole is 20 cm, but the diagonal of the square is 21.2 cm.
34. two, one on each side of the diameter
36. 8.9 cm

Technology   pp. 402–405

1 Central Angles Subtended by Equal Arcs

7. equal   8. equal
9. Central angles subtended by equal arcs are equal.

2 Inscribed Angles Subtended by the Same Arc

5. It stays the same.
6. It stays the same.
7. It stays the same.

8. Inscribed angles subtended by the same arc are equal.

3 Inscribed Angles Subtended by Equal Arcs

9. equal **10.** equal **11.** equal

12. Inscribed angles subtended by equal arcs are equal.

4 Inscribed Angles in a Semicircle

4. 90° **5.** 90° **6.** 90° **7.** 90°

8. Inscribed angles subtended in a semicircle are equal to 90°.

5 Central and Inscribed Angles Subtended by the Same Arc

5. The central angle is twice the inscribed angle.

6. The central angle is twice the inscribed angle.

7. The central angle is twice the inscribed angle.

8. The central angle is twice the inscribed angle subtended by the same arc.

6 Opposite Angles of a Cyclic Quadrilateral

4. supplementary

5. supplementary

6. supplementary

7. The opposite angles of a cyclic quadrilateral are supplementary.

7 Applying to Chords

1. yes

Investigating Math pp. 406–407

1 Central Angles Subtended by Equal Arcs

4. equal

7. Central angles subtended by equal arcs are equal.

2 Inscribed Angles Subtended by the Same Arc

4. equal

7. Inscribed angles subtended by the same arc are equal.

3 Inscribed Angles Subtended by Equal Arcs

4. equal

7. Inscribed angles subtended by equal arcs are equal.

4 Inscribed Angles in a Semicircle

4. They are equal to 90°.

7. Inscribed angles subtended in a semicircle are equal to 90°.

5 Central and Inscribed Angles Subtended by the Same Arc

5. The central angle is twice the inscribed angle.

8. The central angle is twice the inscribed angle subtended by the same arc.

6 Opposite Angles of a Cyclic Quadrilateral

4. They are supplementary.

7. The opposite angles of a cyclic quadrilateral are supplementary.

7 Applying to Chords

1. yes

Section 7.3 pp. 412–414

Practice (Section 7.3)

1. $\angle BAC$, $\angle BDC$

2. $\angle BAC$, $\angle BDC$, $\angle BFC$

3. a) $\angle ADB$, $\angle AOB$, $\angle ACB$
   b) $\angle CBD$, $\angle CAD$

4. a) $\angle ADB$, $\angle AOB$, $\angle ACB$
   b) $\angle CBD$, $\angle CAD$, $\angle COD$

5. 40° **6.** 60°

7. 35° **8.** 90°

9. 120° **10.** 86°

11. $a = 50°$, $b = 100°$

12. $a = 20°$, $b = 140°$, $c = 80°$

13. $a = 48°$, $b - 42°$, $c = 90°$

14. $x = 110°$

15. $a = 40°$, $b = 40°$

16. $a = 99°$, $b = 57°$

17. $a = 61°$, $b = 29°$, $c = 29°$

18. $a = 40°$, $b = 40°$

19. $a = 56°$, $b = 112°$, $c = 68°$, $d = 34°$

20. $t = 20°$, $x = 50°$, $y = 70°$, $z = 70°$

21. $x = 40°$, $y = 25°$, $z = 60°$

22. $x = 45°$, $y = 35°$, $z = 45°$

23. $a = 40°$, $b = 30°$, $c = 70°$, $d = 40°$, $e = 40°$, $f = 70°$

24. $w = 40°$, $x = 80°$, $y = 40°$, $z = 50°$

Applications and Problem Solving (Section 7.3)

32. a) Use the sheet of paper to draw two chords and to find the perpendicular bisector of the chords. The intersection point of the perpendicular bisectors is the centre of the circle.
   b) Use the carpenter's square to construct two right angles on the circle. Extend the arms of the angles to intersect the circle. The 4 intersection points form 2 diameters. The point of intersection of the diameters is the centre of the circle.

33. a) The cameras are on a circle with the scene as a chord. They all have the same filming angle.
   b) no

34. b) $\dfrac{AC}{DB} = \dfrac{CE}{BE}$, $\dfrac{AC}{DB} = \dfrac{AE}{DE}$, $\dfrac{CE}{BE} = \dfrac{AE}{DE}$
   c) 3.3 cm

35. $\angle XSY < 50°$

38. $\dfrac{(\pi - \sqrt{3})r^2}{2}$

40. No. Only a square has opposite angles supplementary.

Section 7.4 pp. 419–421

Practice (Section 7.4)

1. $\angle 1 = 84°, \angle 2 = 73°$
2. $\angle 1 = 87°, \angle 2 = 105°, \angle 3 = 93°$
3. $\angle 1 = 95°, \angle 2 = 95°, \angle 3 = 85°$
4. $\angle 1 = 40°, \angle 2 = 70°, \angle 3 = 70°$
5. $\angle 1 = 43°, \angle 2 = 47°, \angle 3 = 26°$
6. $\angle 1 = 160°, \angle 2 = 100°$
7. $\angle 1 = 130°, \angle 2 = 115°, \angle 3 = 60°$
8. $\angle 1 = 74°, \angle 2 = 106°, \angle 3 = 37°, \angle 4 = 37°,$
   $\angle 5 = 143°$
9. $\angle 1 = 80°, \angle 2 = 55°, \angle 3 = 100°$
10. $\angle 1 = 80°, \angle 2 = 80°, \angle 3 = 35°, \angle 4 = 30°,$
    $\angle 5 = 30°$
11. FDCE, ABED
12. PTRQ   **13.** JKMN
14. GFCE, GFAD, GDBE, ABEF, BCFD, ACED

Applications and Problem Solving (Section 7.4)

15. 82°
16. $\angle 1 = 86°, \angle 2 = 67°, \angle 3 = 113°, \angle 4 = 67°,$
    $\angle 5 = 94°$
23. b) $14°$

Technology pp. 422–423

1 Perpendicular to a Radius at its Outer Endpoint

4. no   **5.** no
6. The line perpendicular to a radius through the outer endpoint of the radius is a tangent to the circle.

2 Tangent and Radius at Point of Tangency

7. The angles are equal to 90°.
8. The tangent and the radius at the point of tangency are perpendicular.

3 Lengths of Tangent Segments

6. equal   **7.** equal
8. The lengths of the tangent segments from an external point are equal.

4 Angle Between a Tangent and a Chord

6. equal   **7.** equal
8. The angle between a tangent and a chord, and the inscribed angle on the opposite side of the chord are equal.

Investigating Math pp. 424–425

1 Perpendicular to a Radius at its Outer Endpoint

3. no
6. The line perpendicular to a radius through the outer endpoint of the radius is a tangent to the circle.

2 Tangent and Radius at Point of Tangency

4. The angles are equal to 90°.
7. The tangent and the radius at the point of tangency are perpendicular.

3 Lengths of Tangent Segments

5. equal
8. The lengths of the tangent segments from an external point are equal.

4 Angle Between a Tangent and a Chord

5. equal
8. The angle between a tangent and a chord, and the inscribed angle on the opposite side of the chord are equal.

Section 7.5 pp. 431–433

Practice (Section 7.5)

1. $x = 5$
2. $w = 20°, x = 70°, y = 9, z = 20°$
3. $x = 5\sqrt{5}$ **4.** $x = 13, y = 13$
5. $x = \sqrt{106} - 5$ **6.** $x = 140°$
7. $\angle 1 = 64°, \angle 2 = 71°$
8. $\angle 1 = 18°, \angle 2 = 81°$
9. $\angle 1 = 30°, \angle 2 = 75°$
10. $\angle 1 = 65°, \angle 2 = 65°$
11. $\angle 1 = 49°, \angle 2 = 61°, \angle 3 = 70°, \angle 4 = 61°,$
    $\angle 5 = 40°$
12. $\angle 1 = 51°, \angle 2 = 39°, \angle 3 = 39°$
13. $\angle 1 = 77°, \angle 2 = 37°, \angle 3 = 73°, \angle 4 = 106°$
14. $\angle 1 = 66°, \angle 2 = 66°, \angle 3 = 66°, \angle 4 = 57°,$
    $\angle 5 = 48°$

Applications and Problem Solving (Section 7.5)

16. 44°, 50°, 86°
18. a) 5.7 cm   b) 27.5 cm^2
19. 41.1 cm   **20.** 10 cm
23. 1806 km
25. a) 40 cm   b) 20 cm
26. 18 cm, 18 cm, 26 cm
27. AD = 33.5, AF = 55.5, CE = 18.5
28. OA = 19.3, CD = 29.2
29. a) 36 cm   b) 3 cm
30. 180°   **31.** 16.3 cm

Section 7.6 pp. 435–437

Practice (Section 7.6)

1. 12.9 cm	**2.** 63.4 cm
3. 65.0 cm	**4.** 261.5 cm
5. 1312.5 cm²	**6.** 349.1 cm²
7. 7259.5 cm²	**8.** 4241.2 cm²
9. 87°	**10.** 108°
11. 36°	**12.** 320°
13. 224°	**14.** 16°
15. 32.7 cm	**16.** 60.2 cm
17. 11.0 cm	**18.** 23.4 cm
19. 4.5 cm	**20.** 80.6 cm
21. 306°	**22.** 140°
23. 89°	**24.** 32°
25. 194°	**26.** 301°
27. 15.3 cm²	**28.** 21.8 cm²
29. 7.0 cm²	**30.** 32.1 cm²
31. 44.7 cm²	**32.** 27.1 cm²

Applications and Problem Solving (Section 7.6)

33. sector; 37 cm²   **34.** 2657 cm²

35. 199 cm   **36.** 133 cm

37. $\dfrac{(\pi - 2)r^2}{4}$

38. a) 120°   **b)** 123 cm

39. 8 cm, 24.5 cm

40. a) 162°   **b)** 18 096 km   **c)** 166°   **d)** no

41. Perimeter: $\dfrac{\pi a}{2}$; Area: $\dfrac{(2\sqrt{3} - \pi)a^2}{8}$

42. Perimeter = πr **43.** 1200 km

Technology p. 438

1 Number of Triangles in a Polygon

1. 180°

2. quadrilateral: 4, 2; pentagon: 5, 3; hexagon: 6, 4; heptagon: 7, 5; octagon: 8, 6; nonagon: 9, 7; decagon: 10, 8

3. The number of triangles is 2 less than the number of sides.

2 Sum of the Interior Angles in a Polygon in Terms of Right Angles

1. =A3+1 adds 1 to the number in cell A3; =A3−2 subtracts 2 from the number in cell A3; =B3 copies the number in cell B3; =2*C3 multiplies the number in cell C3 by 2

3. The number of right angles in an *n*-sided polygon is 2*n* − 4.

Section 7.7 pp. 442–443

Practice (Section 7.7)

1. ∠1 = 137°

2. ∠1 = 90°, ∠2 = 120°, ∠3 = 60°

3. ∠1 = 120°

4. ∠1 = 126°, ∠2 = 75°, ∠3 = 118°

5. 1620°, 18   **6.** 3780°, 42

7. 14 040°, 156   **8.** 6300°, 70

9. 180°(y − 2), 2y − 4

10. 180°(3t − 2), 6t − 4

11. 11	**12.** 15
13. 23	**14.** 10
15. 15	**16.** 18
17. 90	**18.** 16

19. $\dfrac{360}{180 - m}$ **20.** 24

21. 36	**22.** 12
23. 20	**24.** 25

25. $\dfrac{360}{m}$ **26.** 171°, 9°

27. 157.5°, 22.5°   **28.** 165.6°, 14.4°

29. 167.59°, 12.41°

30. $180° - \dfrac{120°}{t}, \dfrac{120°}{t}$

31. $\dfrac{180°(x + y - 2)}{x + y}, \dfrac{360°}{x + y}$

Applications and Problem Solving (Section 7.7)

32. ∠A = 120°, ∠B = 83°, ∠C = 85°, ∠D = 112°, ∠E = 140°

33. ∠P = 145°, ∠Q = 95°, ∠R = 140°, ∠S = 110°, ∠T = 130°, ∠U = 100°

34. a) ∠1 = 215°
     b) ∠1 = 220°, ∠2 = 110°
     c) ∠2 = 130°, ∠3 = 250°
     d) ∠1 = 98°, ∠2 = 75°, ∠3 = 15°

35. a) 30°   **b)** 90°

36. a) 540°   **b)** 180°

37. 160°; 20°; 18

38. No, because the vertices with reflex angles do not have exterior angles in the usual sense.

39. 112.5°, 112.5°, 67.5°, 67.5°

Connecting Math and Biology
pp. 444–445

1 Honeycomb Cells

1. a) 113.10 mm²
     b) 124.71 mm²
     c) 11.61 mm²

2. 30.90 mm²

3. 73.96 mm²

4. No, because a regular octagon does not tile the plane.

2 Signalling the Distance to Food

2. Answers may vary. 2000 m
3. Answers may vary. 750 m

3 Signalling the Direction of Food

1. a) directly away from the sun
   b) 45° clockwise from the direction of the sun
   c) 135° counterclockwise from the direction of the sun

Review   pp. 446–447

3. a) 35°   b) 110°
4. 6.7 cm   5. 38.7 cm
6. $x = 125°$ 7. $x = 70°, y = 35°$
8. $m = 35°, s = 35°, t = 65°, x = 45°, y = 35°, z = 35°$
9. $a = 80°, b = 50°, c = 50°$
11. $a = 50°, b = 155°$
12. $a = 115°, y = 90°$
14. $a = 144°, b = 216°$
15. $m = 55°, x = 55°, y = 60°, z = 65°$
16. 10.2 cm   17. 5.7 cm
19. a) 10.5 cm   b) 63 cm^2
20. a) 91.6 cm   b) 1145 cm^2
21. 37°, 37 4 cm²
22. $\angle 1 = 40°, \angle 2 = 60°, \angle 3 = 120°, \angle 4 = 140°$
23. $\angle 1 = 115°, \angle 2 = 125°, \angle 3 = 106°, \angle 4 = 142°$
24. a) 4140°   b) 46
25. a) 6840°   b) 171
26. a) $(360m - 360)°$ b) $4m - 4$
27. a) 5   b) 108°
28. a) 12   b) 150
29. a) 16   b) 157.5°
30. 135°

Exploring Math   p. 447

1. Any point on an angle bisector is equidistant from the two arms of the angle. The intersection of two bisectors is therefore equidistant from all three sides.
2. 2 cm   3. 60%
4. 91%   5. $(3 - 2\sqrt{2})r$

Chapter Check   p. 448

3. 16.1 cm
5. $a = 15°, b = 30°$
6. $w = 31°, x = 59°, y = 59°, z = 31°$
7. $x = 70°, y = 140°, z = 70°$
8. $a = 115°, b = 25°$
10. PWSQ
11. $a = 10$ cm, $b = 75°, c = 15°, d = 15°$
12. $u = 40°, v = 40°, w = 40°, y = 70°, z = 100°$
14. 25°
15. a) 52 cm   b) 524 cm^2
16. a) 4.2 cm   b) 16.8 cm^2
17. 8   18. 16   19. 19
20. $\angle D = 157°, \angle E = 36°, \angle F = 109°, \angle G = 133°,$
    $\angle H = 105°$

Using the Strategies   p. 449

1. 1, 1, 1, 2, 5; 1, 1, 2, 2, 2; 1, 1, 1, 3, 3
2. 62
4. a) (3, 2, 4), (1, 8, 3), (−3, −4, 2)
   b) (1, −5, −8), (4, −2, −5), (−2, 1, −20)
5. Divide the coins into groups of three, and weigh one group against another. If they balance, the third group contains the counterfeit; if they do not, the lighter group contains the counterfeit. From the identified group, weigh one coin against another. If one is lighter, it is counterfeit. If they balance, the one not weighed is counterfeit.
7. a) 1 and 2   b) 1.5
8. 16π cm^2 9. 60

Data Bank

1. 58°
2. a) 81.2%
   b) Assume a driving speed of 80 km/h and a flying speed of 800 km/h; 8.12%

CHAPTER 8

Coordinate Geometry and Trigonometry

Chapter Introduction

Chapter Materials

scientific or graphing calculators, geometry software, Teacher's Resource Master 1 (0.5-cm grid paper), Teacher's Resource Master 2 (1-cm grid paper), overhead projector, compasses, rulers, protractors, measuring tapes, lined paper, plain paper, Miras, string, pins

Chapter Concepts

Chapter 8 reviews or introduces
• finding the division of a line segment
• finding the distance between points and lines

• developing the concept of locus
• developing the equation of a circle
• developing the solutions of systems representing intersections of lines and circles
• reviewing trigonometry
• developing the law of sines for the ambiguous case

Teaching Suggestions

Read with the class the opening paragraph of student text page 451. Ask:

Has anyone in the class heard of the Anik E-2?

What is the purpose of a satellite?

What is the purpose of a teleport?

Have the students use a map to find the town nearest to the longitude of 107.3°.

Assign the questions to pairs of students. For question 1, ask:

How far is Anik E-2 above the Earth?

What is the radius of the Earth?

About which point is Anik E-2 revolving?

What is the radius of the circle in which Anik E-2 is travelling?

What formula can you use to find the length of the path travelled by Anik E-2 in one day?

For question 2, ask:

What is another name for velocity?

What formula can you use to calculate velocity?

Elicit from the students that another name for velocity is speed, and the formula, $\text{speed} = \dfrac{\text{distance}}{\text{time}}$, can be used. Ensure that the students convert the distance into metres and the time into seconds.

For question 5, ask:

How would you find the value of r?

Ensure that the students understand that the satellite data is for *Anik E-2*.

Finally, have volunteers present their results to the class.

Integrating Technology

Internet

Use the Internet to find information about geostationary orbits, *Anik* satellites, and other communication satellites.

Enrichment

Suppose the *Anik E-2* satellite had been launched around the moon in a geostationary orbit of radius 35 880 km. Answer questions 1 to 5 on student text page 451, substituting moon data for Earth data. Write a few sentences to describe how the value of *g* changes as the location of *Anik E-2* changes.

Assessing the Outcomes

Observation

You may want to consider some of these questions as you observe the students work.

- Do the students know how to research the required data?
- Are the students able to rewrite the equation for the velocity in terms of g?
- Do the students know how to organize the information?
- Do the students work well in pairs or groups?
- Do they persist until they find a solution?
- Do the students attempt all the questions?

Getting Started

Student Text Pages
Pp. 452–453

Materials

Teacher's Resource Master 2 (1-cm grid paper), overhead projector

Learning Outcomes

• Recall the formula for the slope of a line given two points on the line.
• Recall the formula for finding the midpoint of a line.
• Recall the method for finding the distance between two points.

Prerequisite Skills

1. Find the slope of the line passing through these points.

a) A(5, 7), B(7, −13) $\qquad$ [−10]

b) C(−2, −4), D(−6, −9) $\qquad$ $\left[\frac{5}{4}\right]$

c) E(3, 11), F(−6, −1) $\qquad$ $\left[\frac{4}{3}\right]$

2. Find the distance between each pair of points.

a) G(2, −5), H(−4, −7) $\qquad$ $[2\sqrt{10}]$

b) J(5, 10), K(7, 14) $\qquad$ $[2\sqrt{5}]$

3. Find the coordinates of the midpoint of the line joining each pair of endpoints.

a) L(8, 9), M(16, 25) $\qquad$ [(12, 17)]

b) N(−6, −13), P(−2, −3) $\qquad$ [(−4, −8)]

c) Q(9, −5), R(−1, 0) $\qquad$ $\left[\left(4, -2\frac{1}{2}\right)\right]$

4. Write the equation of each line.

a) passing through (4, 5) and (−3, 8)

$\qquad$ [3x + 7y = 47]

b) with slope $\frac{1}{2}$ and y-intercept −2 $\quad$ $\left[y = \frac{1}{2}x - 2\right]$

c) with slope $-\frac{3}{4}$ and passing through (0, 2)

$\qquad$ $\left[y = -\frac{3}{4}x + 2\right]$

Teaching Suggestions

Slopes

(1-cm grid paper, overhead projector) Review with the class the method for finding the slope of a line. Ask:

What information is needed to find the slope of a line?

Elicit from the students that the coordinates of two points on the line are needed to find the slope of the line.

Provide pairs of students with grid paper and suggest that they copy each parallelogram from question 1 onto the grid paper. For question 1, ask:

What property of the opposite sides of a parallelogram do you know?

For question 2, ask:

What property of the diagonals of a square do you know?

Of what type of quadrilaterals is the quilt made?

Are these quadrilaterals concave or convex? Explain.

Have volunteers present their results to the class. Provide an overhead projector, if necessary.
Finally, ask:

How are the slopes of parallel lines related?

How are the slopes of perpendicular lines related?

Midpoints

Provide pairs of students with grid paper, and have them draw each type of quadrilateral and label the vertices with the coordinates. Ask:

How would you describe the diagonals of a parallelogram? a rectangle? a square?

Have volunteers present their results to the class. Provide an overhead projector, if necessary.

Distances

Have the students use the diagrams they drew for the midpoint assignment above. Ask:

How would you describe a parallelogram, a rectangle, and a square in terms of the lengths of its sides?

How would you describe the lengths of the diagonals of a parallelogram, a rectangle, and a square?

Have volunteers present their results to the class. Provide an overhead projector, if necessary.

Equations

Ask:

What information do you require to write the equation of a line?

Elicit from the students that you need the coordinates of two points, or the coordinates of one point and the slope, or the slope and the y-intercept.
For question 2, ask:

How are the slopes of the diagonals of a parallelogram related? of a rectangle? of a square?

Have volunteers present their results to the class. Provide an overhead projector, if necessary.

Warm Up

Assign some or all of the questions as individual or group work. Students could record their answers in their notebooks, or take turns asking questions orally with a partner.

When the students have finished, have them discuss the methods they used to answer the questions.

Mental Math

Students could choose, or be assigned, certain questions from each section. Alternatively, small groups could work as teams, sharing the questions and explaining the answers to the rest of the group.

Integrating Technology

Geometry Software

Complete the explorations using geometry software. With Geometer's Sketchpad, use Show Grid and Plot Points from the Graph menu to plot the vertices. Construct segments for the sides. Use the Slope and Angle measurements in Exploration 1. Use the Point At Midpoint construction in Exploration 2. Use the Distance or Length measurements in Exploration 3. Use the Equation measurement with lines, not segments, in Exploration 4.

Internet

Use the Internet to find information about quilts and the geometric proportion of their patterns.

Enrichment

On grid paper, create a design for a block of a quilt, using quadrilaterals. Exchange your design with that of a classmate, and ask your classmate to identify the slopes of the sides and the diagonals of the quadrilaterals of your quilt block.

Assessing the Outcomes

Observation

You may want to consider some of the following skills as the students complete this lesson.
- Do the students know how to apply the formulas for the slope, the midpoint of a line, and the length of a line?
- Do the students know their properties of quadrilaterals?
- Do the students work well together or do they tend to work independently?

Technology

Exploring Geometric Properties Using Geometry Software

Student Text Page
P. 454

Materials
geometry software

Learning Outcomes
- Determine that the midsegment of a triangle is parallel to, and half the length of, the third side.
- Determine that the quadrilateral constructed with vertices at the midpoints of any quadrilateral is a parallelogram.
- Determine that the diagonals of a parallelogram bisect each other.
- Determine that the midpoint of the hypotenuse of a right triangle is equidistant to all the vertices.

Prerequisite Skills
Construct a parallelogram and a right triangle using geometry software.

Teaching Suggestions
Points are not named to avoid the extra, time-consuming work that would be required by students to label their constructions to match.

Before assigning Explorations 1 and 2, discuss constructing polygons, and measuring angles and lengths using geometry software. With Geometer's Sketchpad, one method to complete Exploration 1 is as follows:
Click the point tool at the left of the screen.
Move the cursor into the sketch area and click.
Move the cursor to two other locations, clicking at each.
Click the pointer tool at the left side of the screen to return the cursor to a pointer.
While pressing the Shift key, click each of the other points in clockwise or counterclockwise order while the last point constructed is still selected.
Click Segment from the Construct menu.
Click Point At Midpoint from the Construct menu while all three sides are still selected.
Click anywhere on the sketch area to deselect the midpoints.
Click one midpoint, and while pressing the Shift key, click a second midpoint.
Click Segment from the Construct menu.

Continue Exploration 1, predicting the relationships. While pressing the Shift key, click the third side to select it while the midsegment is still selected. Click Length from the Measure menu to measure both lengths.
Click three points that define one interior angle of the triangle that is at one end of the third side, pressing the Shift key while pressing the second and third points, ensuring that the three points are selected with the vertex in the middle.
Click Angle from the Measure menu.
Click three points that define the corresponding angle at the midsegment, pressing the Shift key while pressing the second and third points, ensuring that the three points are selected with the vertex in the middle.
Click Angle from the Measure menu.
Click and drag different vertices and midpoints to change the size and shape of the triangle.

With Geometer's Sketchpad, one method to complete Exploration 2 is as follows:
Click New Sketch from the File menu.
Construct a quadrilateral, applying the same method as for constructing a triangle, but using a fourth point.
Click Point At Midpoint from the Construct menu while all four sides are still selected.
Click Segment from the Construct menu while all four midpoints are still selected.
After making a conjecture, click Length from the Measure menu while all four sides of the inner quadrilateral are still selected.
Click three points that define an interior angle of the inner quadrilateral, pressing the Shift key while pressing the second and third points, ensuring that the three points are selected with the vertex in the middle.
Click Angle from the Measure menu.
Select and measure each of the other three interior angles of the inner quadrilateral.
Click and drag different vertices and midpoints to change the size and shape of the quadrilaterals.

Discuss how to construct a parallelogram before assigning Exploration 3. Using Geometer's Sketchpad, one method is as follows:
Click New Sketch from the File menu.
Click the point tool at the left of the screen.
Move the cursor into the sketch area and click.
While pressing the Shift key, move the cursor to another location and click.
Click Segment from the Construct menu.
Move the cursor to one side of the segment and click.
Click the pointer tool at the left side of the screen to return the cursor to a pointer.
While pressing the Shift key, click the segment while the point just constructed is still selected.
Click Parallel Line from the Construct menu.

Click the point on the parallel line, and while pressing the Shift key, click the closest endpoint of the segment. Click Segment from the Construct menu.

While pressing the Shift key, press the other endpoint of the first segment while the segment just constructed is still selected.

Click Parallel Line from the Construct menu.

While pressing the Shift key, press the other parallel line while the one just constructed is still selected.

Click Point At Intersection from the Construct menu.

To show just the parallelogram, while pressing the Shift key, click the endpoint of either segment through which one of the parallel lines was constructed, while the intersection point of the parallel lines is still selected, and then, click Segment from the Construct menu. Next, click elsewhere on that parallel line to select it, and click Hide Line from the Display menu. Repeat for the fourth side.

Continue Exploration 3, constructing the diagonals. Click one vertex.

While pressing the Shift key, click the opposite vertex.

Click Segment from the Construct menu.

Click one of the other vertices.

While pressing the Shift key, click the opposite vertex. Click Segment from the Construct menu.

While pressing the Shift key, click the first diagonal while the second one is still selected.

Click Point At Intersection.

After predicting the relationship, measure the distances between each vertex and the intersection point.

While pressing the Shift key, click one vertex while the intersection point is still selected.

Click Distance from the Measure menu.

Select and measure the distance between the point of intersection and each of the other vertices.

Click and drag any vertex, except the one that was dragged to make the sides equal in length, to change the size and shape of the parallelogram.

Discuss how to construct a right triangle before assigning Exploration 4. Using Geometer's Sketchpad, one method is as follows:

Click New Sketch from the File menu.

Click the point tool at the left of the screen.

Move the cursor into the sketch area and click.

Move the cursor to another location and click.

Click the pointer tool at the left side of the screen to return the cursor to a pointer.

While pressing the Shift key, click the first point constructed while the second one is still selected.

Click Segment from the Construct menu.

While pressing the Shift key, click one endpoint of the segment while the segment is still selected.

Click Perpendicular Line from the Construct menu.

Click Point On Object from the Construct menu while the perpendicular line is still selected.

If the point is very close to the endpoint of the segment, click and drag it away.

While pressing the Shift key, click that endpoint of the segment to select it while the other point on the perpendicular line is selected.

Click Segment from the Construct menu.

Click elsewhere on the perpendicular line.

Click Hide Line from the Display menu.

Click the endpoint of one segment that is only on that segment.

While pressing the Shift key, click the endpoint of the other segment that is only on that segment.

Click Segment from the Construct menu to construct the hypotenuse.

Click Point At Midpoint from the Construct menu while the hypotenuse is still selected.

After making a conjecture, measure the distance from the midpoint to each vertex.

Click and drag any vertex to change the size and shape of the right triangle.

Common Errors

- Students are sometimes confused as to whether they should use the Distance measure or the Length measure.

R$_x$ Remind students that if a segment has been constructed between two points, they can either select the points and measure the distance between them, or select the segment and measure its length. But if a segment has not been constructed between two points, i.e., the points lie on a line or larger segment, there is no constructed segment to select, so students must select the two points and measure the distance between them.

Assessing the Outcomes

Written Assignment

Summarize the geometric properties investigated.

8.1 Connecting Coordinate Geometry and Plane Geometry

Student Text Pages
Pp. 455–461

Materials
graphing calculators, Teacher's Resource Master 2 (1-cm grid paper), overhead projector

Learning Outcomes
- Review the slopes of perpendicular lines.
- Review the method for finding the midpoint of a line.
- Review the method for finding the length of a line.
- Use coordinates to verify a right triangle.
- Use coordinates to verify the properties of plane figures.
- Develop the triangle midsegment theorem using coordinates.

Prerequisite Skills
1. Which of the following statements are always true (T), sometimes true (S), or never true (N)?

a) A square is a rectangle. [T]

b) A triangle can be equilateral and obtuse. [N]

c) A parallelogram is a square. [S]

d) A right triangle has an angle of 55° and an angle of 50°. [N]

e) A quadrilateral with four equal sides is a square. [S]

f) The sum of the angles of a trapezium is 360°. [T]

2. Find the distance between each pair of points.

a) A(5, 7), B(11, 15) [10 units]

b) C(-5, 6), D(10, 18) [$3\sqrt{41}$ units]

3. Find the value of x. Give an exact answer, and then round your answer to 1 decimal place.

a) $x^2 = 7^2 + 11^2$ [$\sqrt{170}$, 13.0]

b) $25^2 = x^2 + 9^2$ [$4\sqrt{34}$, 23.3]

Mental Math
1. Find the measures of the indicated angles.

a)   b)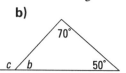

c) 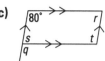   [$a = 60$, $b = 60$, $c = 120$, $q = 80$, $r = 100$, $s = 100$, $t = 80$]

2. Divide.

a) $10.4 \div 4$ [2.6]   b) $21.6 \div 12$ [1.8]

c) $96 \div 80$ [1.4]   d) $126 \div 60$ [2.1]

e) $4.41 \div 21$ [0.21]   f) $273 \div 13$ [21]

Explore/Inquire Answers

Explore: Use the Diagram
a) (0, 0), (27.4, 0), (27.4, 27.4), (0, 27.4)

b) horizontal sides: slope is 0; vertical sides: slope is undefined; diagonals: slopes are 1 and -1

Inquire
1. a) Their product, when defined, is -1.

  b) yes   c) yes

2. a) (13.7, 13.7)   b) yes

3. 19.4 m   4. no

Teaching Suggestions

Method 1
Read with the class the opening paragraphs on student text page 455. Ask:

Why is a baseball field called a baseball diamond?

What type of polygon is a diamond?

What other name could you give to the shape of a baseball diamond?

Elicit from the students that a diamond is a polygon with 4 equal sides. From the point of view of the player at home base, the field is diamond-shaped. A baseball diamond could also be called a square.

Assign the Explore section. Ask:

What one coordinate of any point on the x-axis can you name?

What one coordinate of any point on the y-axis can you name?

How does this help you to name the coordinates of first base? of third base?

How does knowing that the shape of a baseball diamond is a square help you to name the coordinates of second base?

Assign the Inquire questions to pairs of students.

Ask:

What is the equation of any line parallel to the x-axis? the y-axis?

Is the position of home plate in the diagram on the student text page the best position for batting home runs? Explain.

When the students have completed the Inquire questions, have volunteers present their results to the class. Provide an overhead projector, if necessary.

Review with the class teaching examples 1 to 4 on student text pages 456 to 460.

Method 2

(1-cm grid paper) Display the following diagrams on an overhead projector. Provide grid paper to pairs of students and have them copy the diagrams from the chalkboard onto the grid paper. Suggest that they use the distance formula to find the lengths of the sides of the triangles.

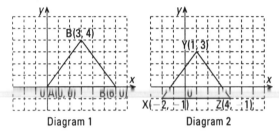

Diagram 1   Diagram 2

Give the students ample opportunity to discuss and compare their results with other students in the class. Ask:

What type of triangle is in each diagram?

When the students have finished, have volunteers present their results to the class. One student could display the diagrams on an overhead projector, while the other explains the process they used to show that each triangle is isosceles.

As a class, discuss the process of using coordinates to prove theorems. Ask:

Which triangle was easier to show that it is isosceles? Explain.

Lead the students to see that $\triangle ABC$ is easier to show that it is isosceles because some of the values of the coordinates of the vertices are zero. These zero values simplify the calculations required to find the lengths of the sides.

Challenge the students to come up with some rules that would make the use of coordinates for the purpose of proving theorems easier. These rules should include:
- Use the origin as one of the vertices.
- Place at least one side of the figure along an axis.
- Place the figure in the first quadrant.
- Use coordinates that simplify the computations.

Have the students justify each of the rules they make up.

Review teaching examples 1 to 4 on student text pages 456 to 460.

Sample Solution

Page 461, question 21

Slope of AC
$$= \frac{y_1 - y_2}{x_1 - x_2}$$
$$= \frac{-(y_2 - y_1)}{x_1 - x_2}$$

Slope of BD $= \dfrac{y_2 - y_1}{x_1 - x_2}$

Slope of AC $\times$ Slope of BD

$$= \frac{-(y_2 - y_1)}{x_1 - x_2} \times \frac{y_2 - y_1}{x_1 - x_2} \quad \text{------(1)}$$

Length of AB $= x_2 - x_1$
Length of AD $= y_2 - y_1$

Since AB and AD are the sides of a square, then, the length of AB equals the length of AD.

So, $x_2 - x_1 = y_2 - y_1$.

Substitute $x_2 - x_1 = y_2 - y_1$ in (1).

Slope of AC $\times$ Slope of BD

$$= \frac{-(y_2 - y_1)}{x_1 - x_2} \times \frac{y_2 - y_1}{x_1 - x_2}$$
$$= \frac{-(x_2 - x_1)}{x_1 - x_2} \times \frac{x_2 - x_1}{x_1 - x_2}$$
$$= \frac{-(x_2 - x_1)}{-(x_2 - x_1)} \times \frac{x_2 - x_1}{-(x_2 - x_1)}$$
$$= 1 \times -1$$
$$= -1$$

Since the product of the slopes of AC and BD is -1, then AC is perpendicular to BD. Thus, the diagonals of any square are perpendicular.

Integrating Technology

Internet

Use the Internet to find the dimensions of other playing fields and surfaces.

Extension

Position a regular hexagon on a coordinate plane. Label the vertices with variables such as x_1, y_1, x_2, y_2, etc. Use as few variables as possible.

Repeat the assignment above for each polygon.

a) an isosceles triangle

b) a rectangle

c) a right triangle

Compare your results with those of your classmates. Discuss the method of labelling each polygon that results in less work when proving theorems.

Enrichment

Use coordinates to prove that the angle in a semicircle is a right angle.

Math Journal

Make a list of the rules you would use to make proving theorems with coordinates easier. Include in your list of rules diagrams and examples for clarity.

Common Errors

- Sometimes when students are placing diagrams on the coordinate grid they draw diagrams that imply more information than is given. For example, they may draw a diagram that is a rectangle when they need to draw a diagram for any quadrilateral.

R_x Remind the students that diagrams that include all possible cases must be drawn.

Problem Levels of Difficulty

A: 1–15, 30   **B:** 16–25   **C:** 26–29

Assessing the Outcomes

Journal

Write a short essay describing what you have learned about using coordinates to prove theorems.

Written Assignment

Use coordinates to prove
a) that the diagonals of a rhombus are perpendicular.
b) that the point of intersection of the diagonals is the midpoint of each diagonal.

Investigating Math

Exploring the Division of Line Segments

Student Text Pages
Pp. 462–463

Materials
Teacher's Resource Master 1 (0.5-cm grid paper), overhead projector

Learning Outcomes
- Explore the division of horizontal line segments.
- Explore the division of vertical line segments.
- Explore the division of sloping line segments.

Mental Math
1. Calculate.

a) $1 + 2 + 3 + \ldots + 32$ [528]

b) $1 + 2 + 3 + \ldots + 27$ [378]

c) $2 + 4 + 6 + \ldots + 18$ [90]

d) $2 + 4 + 6 + \ldots + 26$ [182]

e) $1 + 3 + 5 + \ldots + 41$ [441]

f) $1 + 3 + 5 + \ldots + 23$ [144]

2. Evaluate for $x = 1$ and $y = -1$.

a) $x - y$ [2]   b) $2x + 2y$ [0]

c) $x + 4y - 1$ [−4]   d) $x + 2y^2$ [3]

e) $x^2 - y^2$ [0]   f) $-3y - 4x$ [−1]

Teaching Suggestions

Division of Horizontal Line Segments
(0.5-cm grid paper, overhead projector)   Ask:

How would you describe a horizontal line segment?

Provide pairs of students with grid paper, and have them complete this exploration. Then, have volunteers present their results to the class. Provide an overhead projector, if necessary.

Ensure that the students find this rule:

The number of units between each point of division is $\dfrac{x_1 + x_2 + \ldots + x_n}{n}$. Begin at one endpoint and add the number of units to find each successive point of division.

Then, ask:

What other method could you use to divide the horizontal line segment into 4 equal parts?

Elicit from the students that the midpoint of the whole line segment could be found using $\dfrac{x_1 + x_2}{2}$.

Then, this midpoint could be used to find the midpoint between each endpoint and the midpoint of the whole line segment. Ask:

For what number of equal parts can this method be used?

Division of Vertical Line Segments
(0.5-cm grid paper, overhead projector)   Ask:

How would you describe a vertical line segment?

Provide pairs of students with grid paper, and have them complete this exploration. Then, have volunteers present their results to the class. Provide an overhead projector, if necessary.

Ensure that the students find this rule:

The number of units between each point of division is $\dfrac{y_1 + y_2 + \ldots + y_n}{n}$. Begin at one endpoint and add the number of units to find each successive point of division.

Then, ask:

What other method could you use to divide the vertical line segment into 4 equal parts?

Elicit from the students that the midpoint of the whole line segment could be found using $\dfrac{y_1 + y_2}{2}$.

Then, this midpoint could be used to find the midpoint between each endpoint and the midpoint of the whole line segment. Ask:

For what number of equal parts can this method be used?

Division of Sloping Line Segments
(0.5-cm grid paper, overhead projector)   Ask:

What is the difference between a line segment and a line?

How would you describe a sloping line segment?

Provide pairs of students with grid paper, and have them complete this exploration. Then, have volunteers present their results to the class. Provide an overhead projector, if necessary.

Ensure that the students find this rule:

The number of horizontal units between each point of division is $\dfrac{y_1 + y_2 + \ldots + y_n}{n}$. The number of vertical units between each point of division is $\dfrac{y_1 + y_2 + \ldots + y_n}{n}$.

To find the coordinates of each point of division, begin at one endpoint and add the number of horizontal units to the x-coordinate and the number of vertical units to the y-coordinate.

Then, ask:

What other method could you use to divide the sloping line segment into 4 equal parts?

Elicit from the students that the midpoint of the whole line segment could be found using $\left(\dfrac{x_1 + x_2}{2}, \dfrac{y_1 + y_2}{2} \right)$, where (x_1, y_1) and (x_2, y_2) are the coordinates of the endpoints of the whole line segment. Then, this midpoint can be used to find the midpoint between each endpoint and the midpoint of the whole line segment. Ask:

For what number of equal parts can this method be used?

Extension

The line segment AB has endpoints A(-5, -10) and B(10, 15).

1. Point X divides AB in the ratio AX:XB = 2:3. What are the coordinates of point X?

2. Point Y divides AB in the ratio AY:YB = 5:3. What are the coordinates of point Y?

Math Journal

Write a few sentences describing how you would find the coordinates of the points that divide a line segment into equal parts.

Assessing the Outcomes

Written Assignment

1. The endpoints of a line segment are (-3, 5) and (7, 20). Find the coordinates of the points that divide the line segment into 5 equal parts.

2. A line segment has been divided into 4 equal parts. One endpoint has coordinates (2, 4) and the coordinates of the midpoint of the line segment are (8, 12). Find the coordinates of the other endpoint and the other points of division.

8.2 Division of a Line Segment

Student Text Pages
Pp. 464–469

Materials
graphing calculators

Learning Outcomes
- Review the midpoint formula.
- Divide a line segment into congruent parts.
- Solve problems involving the division of a line segment.

Prerequisite Skills

1. Evaluate.

a) $|-2|$ [2] b) $|2-5|$ [3]

c) $-|5^2-2|$ [-23] d) $|(2-3)+(4-2)|$ [1]

e) $\frac{1}{2}|-6|$ [3] f) $-2|-7+9|$ [-4]

2. Find the distance between the points. Give an exact answer and an answer rounded to 1 decimal place.

a) P(5, 4), Q(7, 11) $[\sqrt{53}, 7.3]$

b) X(-2, -5), Y(6, 9) $[2\sqrt{65}, 16.1]$

Mental Math

1. Calculate.

a) 0.32^2 [0.1024] b) 520^2 [270 400]

c) 7.1^2 [50.41] d) 82^2 [6724]

e) 0.021^2 [0.000 441] f) 61^2 [3721]

2. Multiply.

a) 0.023×120 [2.76] b) 3.1×0.5 [1.55]

c) 9×4.9 [44.1] d) 6.2×0.19 [1.178]

e) 85×99 [8415] f) 510×28 [14 280]

Explore/Inquire Answers

Explore: Look for a Pattern

4, 2.4; 2, 1.2; $\frac{4}{3}$, 0.8; 1, 0.6; $\frac{4}{n}$, $\frac{2.4}{n}$

Inquire

1. a) 0.4 m **b)** 0.24 m

2. a) 16 **b)** 15 cm

3. a) 28 cm, 20 cm **b)** 3

c) (84, 60); (28, 20), (56, 40)

d) (21, 15), (42, 30), (63, 45)

Teaching Suggestions
Read with the class the opening paragraphs on student text page 464. Point out to the students that they can assume that the risers are all equal in height and the treads are all equal in length, but the risers are not necessarily equal in length to the treads.

Tell the students to find a staircase in the school, and measure the riser and tread. Ask:

How can you find the height of the room from knowing the riser length, the tread length, and the number of steps in the staircase?

Assign the Explore section and the Inquire questions to pairs of students. Have volunteers present their results to the class.

Review with the class teaching examples 1 and 2 on student text pages 466 and 467.

Word Power Answer
Naming (0, 5) as S gives SLOVENIA for a). Naming (0, 0) as P gives SPAIN for b). In c), the letters are S, A, O, and L giving LAOS.

Integrating Technology

Internet

Use the Internet to find information about Arthur Erickson, stramps, and Canadian architecture.

Enrichment
The formula for the coordinates of the midpoint of line segment AB with endpoints $A(x_1, y_1)$ and $B(x_2, y_2)$ is

$$\left(\frac{|x_2-x_1|}{2}, \frac{|y_2-y_1|}{2}\right).$$

Develop a formula for the point of division, C, of a line segment with endpoints $A(x_1, y_1)$ and $B(x_2, y_2)$, and divides the line segment into the ratio AC:CB = m:n.

Math Journal
Describe how you would find the coordinates of the point of division, if a line segment is divided in the ratio a:b.

Cross-Discipline

Construction   When constructing stairs, certain minimum requirements must be met for safety regulations. These requirements are called code requirements. One code requirement for stairs is that the sum of the tread and the riser must be between 43 cm and 46 cm.

1. What are some possible measures of the dimensions of the tread and the riser of a staircase, to meet the required code?

2. A carpenter calculated that a staircase needed 12 steps in order to meet the required code. Construct a grid and draw a diagram of a staircase, with the bottom of the first riser at the origin, and the back edge of the final tread at (300, 240).

a) If you assume that all the risers are equal and all the treads are equal, find the coordinates of the points where the back edges of the treads meet the bases of the risers.

b) Does this staircase meet code requirements? Explain.

Problem Levels of Difficulty

A: 1–25, 36   **B:** 26–32   **C:** 33–35

Assessing the Outcomes

Written Assignment

Determine the coordinates of the points that divide the line segment with endpoints X(−3, 2) and Y(3, −3) into 5 equal parts.

8.3 Distances Between Points and Lines

Student Text Pages
Pp. 470–476

Materials
graphing calculators, measuring tapes, rulers, overhead projector, lined paper, plain paper, pins

Learning Outcomes
- Find the distance from a point to a line.
- Find the distance between parallel lines.
- Solve problems involving distances between points and lines.

Prerequisite Skills

1. The scale of a diagram of a car is 1:50.

a) The actual measure of the length of the car is 5 m. What is the measure of the length of the car on the diagram? **[10 cm]**

b) The height of the highest point on the car in the diagram is 1.5 m. What is the actual height of this highest point? **[3 cm]**

2. What is the slope of the line perpendicular to a line with each slope?

a) 2 $\left[-\dfrac{1}{2}\right]$ b) $-\dfrac{2}{3}$ $\left[\dfrac{3}{2}\right]$

c) 1 $[-1]$ d) 0 [undefined]

3. Calculate the distance between each pair of points. Leave your answer in radical form.

a) $(3, 7), (5, 12)$ $[\sqrt{29}]$

b) $(-8, -2), (-20, -14)$ $[12\sqrt{2}]$

c) $(0, 9), (7, -1)$ $[\sqrt{149}]$

Mental Math

1. Calculate the exact answer.

a) $\sqrt{(3 + 1)^2 + (5 - 7)^2}$ $[2\sqrt{5}]$

b) $\sqrt{(-4 - 2)^2 + (7 + 3)^2}$ $[2\sqrt{34}]$

c) $\sqrt{(0 - 5)^2 + (2 - 11)^2}$ $[\sqrt{106}]$

2. Calculate.

a) 32^2 [1024]   b) 8.2^2 [67.24]

c) 0.21^2 [0.0441]   d) 510^2 [260 100]

Explore/Inquire Answers

Explore: Use the Diagram
a) 1:500 000

Inquire
1. a) 15 km   b) 7.5 km   c) 5 km
2. 90°
3. a) parallel   b) 10 km
4. 90°

Teaching Suggestions

Method 1
(measuring tapes, rulers, overhead projector) Have small groups of students choose a line in the classroom and a point not on that line. Have each student in each group measure the distance between the point and the line. Have volunteers present their answers. Ask:

Does everyone in the group have the same answer? Explain.

Which length is the correct length?

Discuss the importance of defining the distance between a point not on a line and a line.

Review with the class the opening paragraphs on student text page 470. Ask:

Where have you seen examples of a radar screen being used?

Assign the Explore section and the Inquire questions to small groups of students. Ask:

How would you describe the course of a ship?

If you are sitting in your seat and facing the front, how would you describe a course of 180°? 90°? 270°? 0°?

Ensure that the students understand that courses in real life are amounts of rotation, in degrees, in a clockwise direction beginning at North. Encourage the students to use the classroom walls to describe the courses. For example, for a student sitting in a chair and facing the front, a course of 180° would be one moving toward the back wall of the classroom, a course of 90° would be one moving toward the wall on the right, etc.

When the students have completed the Inquire questions, have volunteers present their results to the class. Provide an overhead projector, if necessary.

Review with the class the definition of the distance from a point not on the line to a line. This distance is represented by the length of a line segment from the point not on the line, perpendicular to the line. The distance between one line to a second line is represented by the length of a perpendicular line segment from one point on the first line to the final line. Point out that the perpendicular line segment from the first line need not be a perpendicular to the first line.

For example, the distance from point W to line CD is represented by the line WZ.

The distance from point Y to line AB is represented by the line XY.

Note that the distance from any point not on the line to the line may be different for every point on the line, with the exception of one case. Ask:

How would you describe two lines in which the distance from each point on one line to the other line is always the same?

Ensure the students realize that such lines are parallel lines.

Review with the class teaching examples 1 to 4 on student text pages 470 to 474.

Method 2

(lined paper, plain paper, pins) Organize the class into pairs and have them complete the following assignment.

Step 1: Cut a strip of paper from lined note paper, and number the lines.

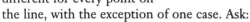

Step 2: On a sheet of plain paper, draw a line and mark a point not on the line.

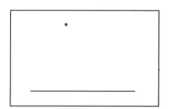

Step 3: Attach the paper strip to the point with a pin, so that it pivots freely about the point, and does not touch the line.

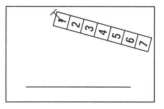

Step 4: Turn the paper strip until it touches the line.
Use the numbers on the line to mark the distance from the point to the line.

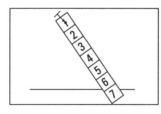

Step 5: Continue turning the strip and measuring the distance from the point to the line. Stop when the strip is over on the left side and once again, not touching the line.

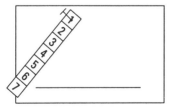

Step 6: Study the measurements and note the least measurement. Return the strip to this measurement, and decide if there is a position that would give a shorter distance between the point and the line. Record this shorter distance.

Step 7: Repeat step 6 until the shortest distance between the point and the line is found. Mark this point on the line. Join the point on the line to the other point on the paper. Measure the angle between the line joining the points and the original line.

Have the students discuss and compare their results with other pairs of students. Then, have volunteers present their results to the class. Ask:

What did you notice about the angle you measured?

How would you define the distance between a point and a line?

Ensure that the students come to a consensus—the angle measured is 90°. Lead the students to a definition of the distance between a line and a point not on the line, i.e., the perpendicular distance between the point and the line.

Review with the class teaching examples 1 to 4 on student text pages 470 to 474.

Integrating Technology

Graphing Calculators

How would you use your graphing calculator to find the coordinates of intersection points like in teaching examples 2, 3, and 4 on student text pages 472, 473, and 474? On a TI-83, the Y = key and the Intersect operation are used.

Press the Y= key. Clear any equations. If Plot1 is highlighted, move the cursor to it and turn it off by pressing the ENTER key.

Enter the right side of the first equation at Y1 = and the right side of the second equation at Y2 =. Press the ZOOM key and the 5 key to select ZStandard.

Press the CALC (i.e., 2nd TRACE) key and the 5 key to select intersect.

Press the right or left arrow key to move the cursor onto the intersection.

Press the ENTER key three times to define the First curve, the Second curve, and your Guess.

If, as in teaching example 2, the intersection is not visible in the standard viewing window, change the viewing window.

On a TI-83, find the square root using the $\sqrt{}$ (i.e., 2nd x^2) key, remembering to enter a closing bracket.

Use your graphing calculator to find coordinates of points of intersection and to evaluate square roots in the questions on student text pages 475 and 476, where appropriate.

See *MATHPOWER™ 11, Western Edition, Blackline Masters* pages 21 to 23 for Solving Linear Systems

Graphically. See *MATHPOWER*™ 11, *Western Edition*, *Blackline Masters* pages 27 to 29 for Setting Viewing Window.

Enrichment

The distance, d, between a line, $Ax + By + C = 0$, and a point not on the line, $P(x_1, y_1)$, can be determined using this formula:

$$d = \frac{|Ax_1 + By_1 + C|}{\sqrt{A^2 + B^2}}$$

Use the formula to find the distance between each point and line.

1. line $x + y + 2 = 0$, point $(-1, 3)$

2. line $2x - 3y - 3 = 0$, point $(6, -2)$

3. line $3x + 2y + 4 = 0$, point $(2.5, 3.5)$

Math Journal

distance from a line to a point not on the line
Write a definition for the distance from a line to a point not on the line. Include a diagram and examples for clarity.

Problem Levels of Difficulty

A: 1–49, 60, 61   **B:** 50–55   **C:** 56–59

Assessing the Outcomes

Written Assignment
Find the shortest distance from $(1, 3)$ to the line $y = -\frac{1}{2}x + 3$.

Observation
You may want to consider some of these questions as you observe students working.
- Does the student understand the concept of distance between a point and a line?
- Is the student able to explain his or her method of solution?
- Does the student help the others to understand the concept being studied?

Investigating Math

Exploring the Concept of a Locus

Student Text Page
P. 477

Materials
Teacher's Resource Master 2 (1-cm grid paper), overhead projector

Learning Outcomes
- Understand the concept of a locus.
- Write equations to describe loci.

Prerequisite Skills
1. Write the equation of each line.

a) parallel to the x-axis and passing through the point (5, 3) $[y = 3]$

b) parallel to the y-axis and passing through the point (−2, −4) $[x = -2]$

c) parallel to the x-axis and passing through the point (0, −5) $[y = -5]$

d) parallel to the y-axis and passing through the point (15, −4) $[x = 15]$

2. Which of the following lines are parallel? perpendicular?

A: $y = 2x + 5$ B: $y = -3x - 2$

C: $y = 2x - 50$ D: $y = -x - 2$

E: $y = \frac{1}{3}x + 7$ F: $y = -2x - 4$

[parallel: A and C; perpendicular: B and E]

Mental Math
1. What is the measure of the complementary angle to each of the following?

a) 50°   [40°]   b) 77°   [13°]

c) 18°   [72°]   d) 64°   [26°]

e) 47°   [43°]   f) 3°   [87°]

2. Calculate the mean of each pair of numbers.

a) 2.5, 3.7   [3.1]   b) −1.3, −1.1   [−1.2]

c) −5.2, 4.6   [−0.3]   d) 215, 255   [235]

e) −66, −98   [−82]   f) 0.25, 0.83   [0.54]

Teaching Suggestions
(1-cm grid paper, overhead projector) Review with the class the term "locus." Include in your review the plural form of the word, loci. Ask:

What word do you know that begins with all or part of the word "locus"?

What real-life examples of loci can you think of?

Have the students justify their examples. Some loci presented by the students might be a dog on a leash, a person on a swing, a person swinging a baseball bat, etc.

Provide pairs of students with grid paper and assign the questions on student text page 477. For question 1, ask:

How would you describe the x-axis, horizontal or vertical?

How would you describe a line that is always the same distance from another line?

How many lines, parallel to another line, can you draw?

How many lines, 6 units from the x-axis, can you draw?

Elicit from the students that a line that is always the same distance from another line is parallel to the line, that an infinite number of lines can be drawn parallel to another line, and that 2 lines, 6 units from the x-axis, can be drawn, one above the x-axis and one below.

Point out to the students that the equation of the locus can consist of more than one equation of a line, and that all points, lines, or planes that are part of the locus must be defined when identifying the locus.

For question 3, ask:

What are the slopes of the lines in part (a)?

What does this tell you about the lines?

What points are equidistant from y = x + 5?

What points are equidistant from y = x − 7?

Which points are common to both sets of points that are equidistant from y = x + 5 and y = x − 7?

For question 4, ask:

On what line do the points that are equidistant from the arms of an angle lie?

Elicit from the students that the points on the bisector of an angle are equidistant from the arms of the angle. Point out that if each quadrant is taken in turn, then, the problem becomes one of finding the points equidistant from the arms of each right angle that occurs at the origin, where the axes intersect. This results in two lines whose points are equidistant from the axes. Ask:

How are the slopes of the lines of the locus related?

Elicit from the students that since the product of the slopes is −1, the lines are perpendicular to each other.

For question 6, ask:

What are the properties of a rectangle?

What are the properties of the diagonals of a rectangle?

Elicit from the students that the diagonals of a rectangle are equal and bisect each other. This means that the point of bisection of the diagonals is equidistant from each vertex of the rectangle. Thus, the locus is the point of intersection of the diagonals. Ask:

How is the point of intersection related to each diagonal?
What formula can you use to find this point of intersection?

Elicit that since the point of intersection is equidistant from the vertices, then, the formula for the midpoint of a line segment can be used.

When the students have completed the questions, have volunteers present their results to the class. Provide an overhead projector, if necessary.

Integrating Technology

Geometry Software

Investigate the Locus construction in geometry software.

Math Journal

locus Define the term "locus" and include the plural form of the word in your definition.

Write a short essay about what new information you have learned about loci.

Assessing the Outcomes

Journal

Think of a locus you see in everyday life and write a short essay describing it.

8.4 The Equation of a Circle

Student Text Pages
Pp. 478–482

Materials
graphing calculators, Teacher's Resource Master 2 (1-cm grid paper), compasses, rulers, string, pins, overhead projector

Learning Outcomes
- Develop the general equation of a circle with centre at the origin.
- Develop the general equation of a circle with centre at any point other than the origin.
- Find the general equations of circles.
- Solve problems involving the general equation of a circle.

Prerequisite Skills
1. Find the exact distance between each pair of points.

a) $(3, 5)$, $(7, 11)$ $[2\sqrt{13}]$

b) $(-2, -6)$, $(-12, -10)$ $[4\sqrt{29}]$

c) $(7, -8)$, $(-3, 0)$ $[2\sqrt{41}]$

d) $(8, 8)$, $(-2, -4)$ $[4\sqrt{61}]$

2. Solve for x.

a) $5^2 + 10^2 = x^2$ $[\pm5\sqrt{5}]$

b) $x^2 + 6^2 = 9^2$ $[\pm3\sqrt{5}]$

Mental Math
1. Calculate.

a) $1 + 2 + 3 + \ldots + 50$ [1275]

b) $1 + 2 + 3 + \ldots + 77$ [3003]

c) $2 + 4 + 6 + \ldots + 46$ [552]

d) $2 + 4 + 6 + \ldots + 60$ [930]

e) $1 + 3 + 5 + \ldots + 89$ [2025]

f) $1 + 3 + 5 + \ldots + 67$ [1156]

2. Divide.

a) $0.651 \div 21$ [0.031]   **b)** $594 \div 54$ [11]

c) $288 \div 16$ [18]   **d)** $154 \div 11$ [14]

e) $352 \div 4.4$ [80]   **f)** $341 \div 3.1$ [110]

Explore/Inquire Answers

Explore: Draw a Graph
a) $(5, 0)$, $(-5, 0)$, $(0, 5)$, $(0, -5)$, $(3, 4)$, $(3, -4)$, $(-3, 4)$, $(-3, -4)$, $(4, 3)$, $(4, -3)$, $(-4, 3)$, $(-4, -3)$

Inquire
1. no; it does not pass the vertical line test

2. $(0, 0)$ **3.** 5 **4. b)** $(0, 0)$, 3

5. a) $(0, 0)$, 4 **6.** $(0, 0)$, r

7. a) centre of Saturn   **b)** 67 million metres

Teaching Suggestions

Method 1
(1-cm grid paper, compasses, rulers, overhead projector)
Read with the class the opening paragraph on student text page 478. Ask:

What real-life examples can you think of in which an object moves about another fixed object, making circles?

What careers or activities require making circles?

Some careers or activities that students might suggest are carpentry, making stained-glass windows, and farming (irrigating fields).

Review the meaning of the term "locus." Assign the Explore section and the Inquire questions to pairs of students. For inquire question 1, ask:

What is a function?

How would you recognize a function by looking at its graph?

Have volunteers present their results to the class. Provide an overhead projector, if necessary.

Review the equation of a circle, shown at the bottom of student text page 478. Point out to the students that the form of the equation of a circle given here is for circles whose centre is the origin.

Work through teaching example 1 on student text page 479. Discuss how the form of the equation of the circle changes, when the centre is no longer the origin. Ask:

How are the coordinates of the origin related to the equation of a circle with centre not the origin?

Provide the following examples of equations of circles whose centres are not at the origin. Have the students identify the centre of each circle and its radius.

1. $(x - 5)^2 + (y - 2)^2 = 25$

2. $(x - 3)^2 + (y + 1)^2 = 16$

3. $(x + 1)^2 + (y - 4)^2 = 36$

4. $(x + 2)^2 + (y + 7)^2 = 400$

Stress that the equation of the circle must be written or envisioned in the form $(x - h)^2 + (y - k)^2 = r^2$, so that the values of the centre and the radius can be identified. Thus, the equation $(x + 2)^2 + (y + 7)^2 = 400$ must be rewritten as $[x - (-2)]^2 + [y - (-7)]^2 = 20^2$. Then, the centre can be identified as $(-2, -7)$, and the radius is 20.

Point out to the students that when the equation of the circle is required, there is no need to simplify the equation by removing the brackets.

Assign teaching examples 3 and 4 on student text page 480 to pairs of students.

Method 2

(1-cm grid paper, compasses, rulers, string, pins, overhead projector)   Provide pairs of students with grid paper, string, and pins. Ask:

What instrument is used to draw circles?

How does a set of compasses work?

How can you use the method by which a set of compasses draws a circle to define a circle?

Have each pair of students complete the following investigation.

Investigation

Step 1: Construct a set of labelled axes on grid paper.

Step 2: Pin one end of a piece of string to the origin of the axes.

Step 3: Pull the string tight along the positive x-axis and tie a pencil at $(0, 5)$ so that when the pencil is in a vertical position, its point is 5 units from the origin.

Step 4: With the string pulled tight and the pencil held in a vertical position, rotate the string and the pencil in a complete turn around the origin, marking a line on the grid paper.

Step 5: Mark the coordinates of the points of intersection on the grid lines through which the point of your pencil has passed.

Step 6: Use the distance formula to find the distance between the origin and each of these points on your circle. Describe what you notice about these distances. What is the radius of the circle?

Step 7: Suppose the coordinates of a general point on the circle are (x, y). What is the distance between (x, y) and the origin? Write an equation involving the coordinates (x, y), the origin, and the radius.

Step 8: Repeat this investigation for a pencil at point $(0, 13)$.

Step 9: Suppose the pencil begins at $(0, r)$. Write an equation involving the coordinates (x, y), the origin, and the radius, r.

Give the students an opportunity to discuss and compare their results with those of other pairs of students in the class. Have them write an equation for a circle with centre the origin and radius r. Have volunteers present their results to the class. Provide an overhead projector for students who wish to use their diagrams as part of their results.

Challenge the students to repeat the investigation, but with a centre not the origin. Have volunteers present their results to the class.

Review teaching examples 1 to 4 on student text pages 479 and 480.

Sample Solution

Page 482, question 55

In order to show that an equation represents the equation of a circle, it must be rewritten in the form $(x - h)^2 + (y - k)^2 = r^2$.

$$x^2 + y^2 - 10x + 12y - 3 = 0$$
$$(x^2 - 10x) + (y^2 + 12y) - 3 = 0$$
$$(x^2 - 10x + 25 - 25) + (y^2 + 12y + 36 - 36) - 3 = 0$$
$$(x^2 - 10x + 25) - 25 + (y^2 + 12y + 36) - 36 - 3 = 0$$
$$(x - 5)^2 - 25 + (y + 6)^2 - 36 - 3 = 0$$
$$(x - 5)^2 + (y + 6)^2 - 36 - 3 - 25 = 0$$
$$(x - 5)^2 + (y + 6)^2 - 64 = 0$$
$$(x - 5)^2 + (y + 6)^2 = 64$$

This final equation is of the form $(x - h)^2 + (y - k)^2 = r^2$, where $h = 5$, $k = -6$, and $r^2 = 64$. Thus, $x^2 + y^2 - 10x + 12y - 3 = 0$ is the equation of a circle with centre $(5, -6)$ and radius 8.

Integrating Technology

Internet

Use the Internet to find information about other circles in sports, in astronomy, and in other fields to create problems that involve equations of circles. Display your problems for classmates to solve.

Extension

Find the circumference and the area of each circle. Leave you answer in exact form.

1. $x^2 + y^2 = 21$

2. $(x - 2)^2 + (y - 5)^2 = 90$

3. $(x + 3)^2 + (y - 11)^2 = 45$

Enrichment

A piece of rope is wrapped around the equator of the Earth so that there is no overlap and it fits snugly. One metre is added to the length of the rope, and the rope is placed around the Earth so that it is equally above the Earth at every point from the equator. Assuming the Earth is a perfect sphere and its centre is the origin, what is the equation of the circle formed by the rope?

Math Journal

equation of a circle   Write the equation of a circle given the centre (a, b) and radius r. Include diagrams and examples for clarity.

Problem Levels of Difficulty

A: 1–39, 56   **B:** 40–51   **C:** 52–55

Assessing the Outcomes

Journal

Make up a problem involving the equation of a circle and the circumference or the area of the circle. Exchange your problem with a classmate's and solve it.

Written Assignment

1. Write the equation of a circle with centre $(-1, 3)$ and radius 4.

2. The endpoints of the diameter of a circle are $(3, 0)$ and $(3, 6)$.

a) Find the circumference of the circle.

b) Find the area of the circle.

8.5 Intersections of Lines and Circles

Student Text Pages
Pp. 483–491

Materials

graphing calculators, Teacher's Resource Master 1 (0.5-cm grid paper), overhead projector

Learning Outcomes

- Find the points of intersection of a line and a circle.
- Find the equation of a tangent to a circle.
- Find the length of a tangent to a circle from a point not on the circle.
- Solve problems involving lines, circles, and tangents.

Prerequisite Skills

1. Find the values of the variable. Round your answer to 1 decimal place, if necessary.

a) $5^2 + 12^2 = r^2$ [±13]

b) $2.5^2 + 6.5^2 = x^2$ [±7.0]

c) $9^2 + z^2 = 13^2$ [±9.4]

d) $w^2 + 7^2 = 10^2$ [±7.1]

2. Graph each line.

a) $y = -5x$ b) $y = 2x + 3$

c) $x + 2y = -1$ d) $3x - y + 4 = 0$

e) $x = 5$ f) $y = -2$

3. Find the slope of a line passing through each set of points.

a) A(2, 7), P(5, 10)   [1]

b) X(−5, 6), D(3, −2)   [−1]

c) W(−6, −2), V(−1, −5) $\left[-\dfrac{3}{5}\right]$

d) R(9, 8), Q(11, 10)   [1]

e) M(7, −1), N(10, 4) $\left[\dfrac{5}{3}\right]$

4. Identify which lines in question 3 are

a) perpendicular   [AP and XD; XD and RQ; WV and MN]

b) parallel   [AP and RQ]

Mental Math

1. Calculate the mean of each pair of numbers.

a) 7, −9   [−1]   b) 22, 20   [21]

c) 35, 33   [34]   d) 41, 43   [42]

e) −16, −18   [−17]   f) 50, −52   [−1]

2. Multiply.

a) 51 × 9   [459]   b) 11 × 98   [1078]

c) 29 × 15   [435]   d) 22 × 41   [902]

e) 31 × 31   [961]   f) 19 × 2.9   [55.1]

Explore/Inquire Answers

Explore: Draw a Graph

a) $x + y = 20.25$

b)

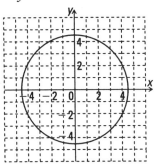

Inquire

1. a) (3.2, 3.2), (−3.2, −3.2)

b) no intersection points

c) (4.5, 0)

2. a) 2   b) 0

3. a) 0   b) 1   c) 2   d) 2

Teaching Suggestions

Method 1

(0.5-cm grid paper)   Read with the class the opening paragraph on student text page 483. Ask:

In how many points does the line cut the centre circle?

What name can be given to a line that intersects a circle in two points?

What name can be given to a line that intersects a circle in one point?

Elicit from the students that a line that cuts a circle in two points is a secant, and a line that cuts a circle in one point is a tangent.

Provide pairs of students with grid paper, and assign the Explore section and the Inquire questions. For question 3, ask:

Any line whose distance from the centre is greater than 4.5 units will not intersect the circle. Explain.

Review with the class teaching examples 1 to 3 on student text pages 484 to 487.

Then, ask:

What information do you need to find the equation of a line?

How could this information be used to find the equation of a tangent?

Elicit from the students that two points on the line, or one point and the slope, or the slope and the y-intercept are required to find the equation of a line. Since a tangent is a line, then the slope of a tangent and the point at which the tangent touches the circle gives the equation of the tangent. If the slope is not directly given, then, it can often be found from other information. Remind the students that the point of tangency is also a point on the circumference of the circle. Thus, the coordinates of this point and of the centre of the circle can be used to find the slope of the radius of the circle. Ask:

How can the slope of the radius of the circle, at the point of tangency, be used to find the slope of the tangent to the circle?

How can you use this slope of the tangent and the coordinates of the point of tangency to find the equation of the tangent?

Assign teaching example 4 on student text page 487 to pairs of students. Have volunteers present their results to the class. Review with the class teaching example 5 on student text page 488. Point out that this example demonstrates with coordinate geometry how tangents from the same point to a circle are equal in length.

Method 2

(0.5-cm grid paper, overhead projector) Write the following equations on the chalkboard.
$x - y = -1$
$x^2 + y^2 = 25$

Provide pairs of students with grid paper and have them sketch the graph of each equation. Ask:

Describe the graphs of the equations in your diagram.

In how many points do the graphs intersect?

What are the coordinates of the points of intersection of the line and the circle?

Then, have the students find the points of intersection of the two equations by isolating one of the variables of equation (1) on one side and substituting into equation (2). Ask:

How do the coordinates of the points of intersection of the line and the circle in your diagrams compare to the solutions to the system of equations?

Then, solve the system of equations algebraically. Ask:

How do the solutions to the system of equations and the coordinates of the points of intersection compare?

How could you find the length of the radius of the circle you graphed?

Review with the class the properties of tangents and circles. Ask:

How many tangents can be drawn from a point outside the circle to the circle?

How are the tangents from a point outside the circle to the circle related to each other?

How many tangents can be drawn to a point on the circle?

How is a tangent related to the radius of a circle?

How is the slope of a tangent and the slope of the radius to the point of tangency related?

How can you use this information to find the equation of a tangent at the point of tangency?

How can you use this information to find the length of a tangent from a point outside the circle to the point of tangency?

Review with the class teaching examples 1 to 5 on student text pages 484 to 488.

Sample Solution

Page 491, question 97

a) Draw a radius from the centre of the larger circle, X, to its point of contact with the x-axis, W. Draw a line from Y, the centre of the smaller circle, perpendicular to XW to meet XW at Z.

XW = 8 units (radius of the larger circle)
YP = 2 units (radius of the smaller circle)
YP = ZW = 2 units
XZ = XW − ZW
    = 8 − 2
    = 6
XZ = 6 units
XY is the sum of the radii of the circles.
XY = 10 units

In $\triangle$XZY, $\angle$XZY = 90°.
Using Pythagoras' theorem,
$XY^2 = XZ^2 + ZY^2$
$10^2 = 6^2 + ZY^2$
$ZY^2 = 10^2 - 6^2$
    = 100 − 36
    = 64
ZY = 8
ZY = WP
OP = OW + WP
OW is the length of the radius of the larger circle.
OP = 8 + 8
    = 16
OP is 16 units.

b) Since OP is 16 units, then the coordinates of the centre of the smaller circle are (16, 2). The radius of the smaller circle is 2 units. The equation of the smaller circle is
$(x - h)^2 + (y - k)^2 = r^2$, where $(h, k) = (16, 2)$
$(x - 16)^2 + (y - 2)^2 = 4$ and $r = 2$.

Integrating Technology

How would you use your graphing calculator to determine the intersection of a circle and a line as in teaching examples 1 and 2 on student text pages 484 and 485? On a TI-83, the equation of the circle is changed to two equations in the form $y =$, and the Y= key and the Intersect operation are used.

Press the Y= key. Clear any equations. If Plot1 is highlighted, move the cursor to it and turn it off by pressing the ENTER key.

Enter the right side of the equation with the positive square root at Y1=, the right side of the equation with the negative square root at Y2=, and the right side of the linear equation at Y3=.

Press the ZOOM key and the 5 key to select Zsquare to display the graph with the circle appearing round.

Press the CALC (i.e., 2nd TRACE) key and the 5 key to select intersect.

Press the right arrow key to move the cursor to the intersection of the upper curve and the line. Press the ENTER key. The cursor jumps to the other curve of the circle (Y2) rather than the line (Y3).

Press the up arrow key twice to move to the line and press the ENTER key.

Press the ENTER key to define your Guess.

If, as in teaching example 2, the graph is not visible using Zsquare, change the viewing window, and then, press the ZOOM key and the 5 key to select Zsquare.

When solving the quadratic formula as in teaching example 2 on student text page 485 using a TI-83, rather than re-entering the expression with the negative square root term, press the ENTRY (i.e., 2nd ENTER) key, and use the arrow keys to move to the + sign and replace it with a − sign.

Use your graphing calculator to find coordinates of points of intersection, to evaluate square roots, and to solve the quadratic formula in the questions on student text pages 488 to 491, where appropriate.

See *MATHPOWER*™ *11, Western Edition, Blackline Masters* pages 27 to 29 for Setting Viewing Window.

Math Journal

Describe a method for finding the equation of a tangent to a circle and the length of a tangent to a circle. Include a list of the information you need.

Problem Levels of Difficulty

A: 1–73, 98   **B:** 74–91   **C:** 92–97

Assessing the Outcomes

1. Write an equation for the tangent at the point $(2, -7)$ on the circle $(x - 3)^2 + (y + 2)^2 = 26$.
2. Find the length of the tangent from the point $(-2, 2)$ to the circle $(x - 1)^2 + (y + 4)^2 = 5$.

Computer Data Bank

Air Travel

Microsoft Works for Windows users see *Part B*, and Microsoft Access users see *Part D*, of *MATHPOWER™ 11, Western Edition, Computer Data Bank Teacher's Resource*.

Student Text Page
P. 492

Learning Outcomes

- Display, find, sort, calculate, summarize, and analyze data in a computer database.
- Solve systems of linear/quadratic equations.
- Calculate the distance between points.

Prerequisite Skills

1. Solve $y = -x - 4$ and $(x + 3)^2 + (y + 2)^2 = 13$.
   [(5, 0), (0, −4)]

2. Find the distance between the points in question 1, rounded to one decimal place.   [7.1 units]

Getting Started Blackline Masters C-1 to C-8

Teaching Suggestions

Students unfamiliar with computer databases and ClarisWorks would benefit from working through *Getting Started* Blackline Masters C-1 to C-8, noted in the Prerequisite Skills, prior to doing any of the explorations on this page. Minimally, students should have the *Getting Started* Blackline Masters C-1 to C-8 available for reference.

The explorations in *Air Travel* use two databases. Exploration 1 uses both *Aircraft* and *Airports*. Exploration 2 uses *Airports*. The remaining explorations use *Aircraft*.

Each exploration in *Air Travel* is independent of the others. Some or all of the explorations can be assigned to individuals, pairs, or small groups of students, to be completed over a period of time that allows students adequate computer time. Up to 1.5 h will be needed by some students to complete all five explorations.

When assigning the explorations, inform students if you expect

- any parts of the explorations to be printed off the computer
- handwritten or word-processed answers to questions that suggest a written response
- a journal-type response about what they have learned mathematically, about using databases, and/or about the subject matter of the databases

Possible parts to assign for printing are a table to show the average of the increases in runway length

from landing to takeoff as percents of the landing runway lengths from Exploration 1, and a table to show the average dimensions from Exploration 3.

Point out that in *Maximum Speed, km/h or Mach* and *Cruise Speed, km/h or Mach*, the numbers in the hundreds are in kilometres per hour, and the others are Mach numbers, and that although a Mach number is not a unit of speed, Mach numbers are often used when referring to aircraft speeds. See the Exploration 4 notes.

1 Takeoff and Landing

An efficient approach to question 1 is to use the *Airports* database, displaying the records using Full Record. For parts a) to g), use the Find feature with one comparison for *Name* airport of interest, noting the length of the longest runway and showing all the records between parts (*Getting Started* BLM C-5). For part h), show all the records and sort the lengths of longest runways from least to greatest (*Getting Started* BLM C-4). Then, use the *Aircraft* database, displaying the records using Table 2. Use the Match feature with the following formula, deselecting the records from the previous part and showing all the records between parts (*Getting Started* BLM C-5).

AND('Takeoff Runway Length, m'<>−1,'Landing Runway Length, m'<>−1,'Takeoff Runway Length, m'<=x,'Landing Runway Length, m'<=x), where x is the number of metres just found for each part

An efficient approach to question 2a) is to deselect the records from the previous question and use the Match feature with the formula that follows, noting the number of records selected (*Getting Started* BLM C-5). Most aircraft require a greater takeoff runway length than landing runway length to allow for the possibility of aborted takeoffs. After a certain distance, when the length of runway remaining is not enough for a safe landing, a takeoff cannot be safely aborted.

AND('Takeoff Runway Length, m'<>−1,'Landing Runway Length, m'<>−1,'Takeoff Runway Length'>'Landing Runway Length, m')

An efficient approach to question 3a) is to hide the unselected records and deselect the records from the previous question. Then, create a calculation field called *Percent Increase*, using the formula that follows, to determine the increase in runway length from landing to takeoff as a percent of the landing runway length, rounded to 2 decimal places (*Getting Started* BLM C-6).

ROUND(('Takeoff Runway Length, m'−'Landing Runway Length, m')/'Landing Runway Length, m'*100,2)

In part b), determine and display the average of the percent increases, rounded to 2 decimal places, for all the displayed records by doing the following. Create a summary field called *Average Percent Increase in Runway Length*, using the formula that follows. Insert a Trailing grand summary section. Insert the summary field in the Trailing grand summary section (*Getting Started* BLM C-7).

ROUND(AVERAGE('Percent Increase'),2)

2 Airport Categories

In question 1, show all the records in the *Airports* database and sort the categories (*Getting Started* BLM C-4). Examine the records, noting that the airports with the greater longest runways tend to have higher category numbers and the international airports have the highest numbers.

The category numbers describe the level of Emergency Response Services (ERS) coverage provided at airports in Canada. For example, category 9 airports are equipped with 24 500 L of water for foam production and 450 kg of dry chemical. They are the only airports equipped to handle aircraft that are 61 m or longer.

3 Comparing Aircraft

In question 1, show all the records in the *Aircraft* database, displaying them in Table 1. Then, use the Find feature with one comparison for *Passengers* >300, noting the number of records displayed (*Getting Started* BLM C-5). Repeat for *Passengers* >400 and *Passengers* >500. Finally, express each number as a percent of the total number of aircraft, using a calculator.

An efficient approach to question 2 is to show all the records. Then, use the Find feature with four comparisons for *Wing Span, m* <>−1, *Length, m* <>−1, *Height, m* <>−1, and *Mass, t* <>−1 (*Getting Started* BLM C-5). Because all four measurements are available for all the records, the four average summary fields can be created for all the records. Next, count and display the number of models, and determine and display the average of each of the dimensions, with the numbers of metres rounded to 1 decimal place and the number of tonnes rounded to 0 decimal places, in each type by doing the following. Create five summary fields called *Number of Models by Type*, *Average Wing Span by Type, m*, *Average Length by Type, m*, *Average Height by Type, m*, and *Average Mass by Type, t*, using the formulas that follow. Sort by *Type*. Insert a Sub-summary section. Insert the summary fields in the Sub-summary section (*Getting Started* BLM C-7).

COUNT('Model')

ROUND(AVERAGE('Wing Span, m'),1)

ROUND(AVERAGE('Length, m'),1)

ROUND(AVERAGE('Height, m'),1)

ROUND(AVERAGE('Mass, t'),0)

In question 3, create a calculation field called *Ratio*, using the formula that follows, to determine the ratio of length to wing span, rounded to 2 decimal places (*Getting Started* BLM C-6). Then, use the Find feature with one comparison for *Ratio* <=1 (*Getting Started* BLM C-5).

ROUND('Length, m'/'Wing Span, m',2)

4 Mach Numbers

In question 1, show all the records, displaying them using Table 2. Then, sort the maximum speeds, noting the maximum speed that is the greatest number not in the hundreds, and its aircraft model (*Getting Started* BLM C-4).

In question 2, use the Match feature with the following formula, noting the number of records displayed (*Getting Started* BLM C-5).

AND('Maximum Speed, km/h or Mach'<>−1, 'Maximum Speed, km/h or Mach'<=2, 'Cruise Speed, km/h or Mach'<>−1,'Cruise Speed, km/h or Mach'<=2')

An efficient approach to question 3 is to hide the unselected records and deselect the records from the previous question. Then, create a calculation field called *Difference* using the following formula, to subtract the cruise speed from the maximum speed (*Getting Started* BLM C-6).

'Maximum Speed, km/h or Mach' − 'Cruise Speed, km/h or Mach'

A Mach number is the ratio of the speed of the aircraft to the speed of sound—actually, the ratio of the speed of any object to the speed of sound in the same medium. The speed of sound in the air at sea level is 1229 km/h, reducing with temperature to 1062 km/h at 11 000 m, where the temperature is −56.46°C. The variation in speed of sound in air is a key factor in aircraft design and operation. Mach 1 is sonic, below Mach 1 is subsonic, above Mach 1 is supersonic, and Mach numbers between 5 and 10, depending on the altitude and temperature, are hypersonic.

5 Flight Path

An efficient approach to question 1 is to show all the records and create a table displaying only the *Model* and *Maximum Speed, km/h or Mach* fields (*Getting Started* BLM C-2). Then, use the Find feature with one comparison for *Maximum Speed* >2 (*Getting Started* BLM C-5). Next, solve the system of linear/quadratic equations graphically or algebraically to find intersection points of (40, 40) and (50, 50). Then, determine the distance between the two points of intersection, rounded to 2 decimal places, either manually or by creating a calculation field called *Distance, km*, using the first formula that follows (*Getting Started* BLM C-6). Next, create a calculation field called *Time, min*, using the second formula that follows if the distance was determined using a calculated field or the third formula that follows if the distance was determined manually, to determine the time spent travelling that distance, rounded to 1 decimal place (*Getting Started* BLM C-6).

ROUND(SQRT((50(40)^2+(50(40)^2),2)

ROUND('Distance, km'/'Maximum Speed, km/h or Mach'*60,1)

ROUND(14.14/'Maximum Speed, km/h or Mach'*60,1)

In question 2, sort the times (*Getting Started* BLM C-4).

Student Text Pages
Pp. 493–499

Materials
graphing calculators, overhead projector

Learning Outcomes
- Review the primary trigonometric ratios.
- Solve right triangles.
- Review the law of sines and the law of cosines.
- Solve problems using trigonometry.

Prerequisite Skills

1. Find the value of x.

a) $\sin 35° = x$ [0.5736]

b) $\cos 66° = x$ [0.4067]

c) $\tan 14° = x$ [0.2493]

d) $\cos 160° = x$ [−0.9397]

e) $\tan 125° = x$ [−1.4281]

f) $\sin 105° = x$ [0.9659]

2. Find the value of θ.

a) $\sin \theta = 0.6691$ [42°]

b) $\cos \theta = 0.8192$ [35°]

c) $\tan \theta = -7.1154$ [98° or −82°]

d) $\cos \theta = -0.4695$ [118°]

e) $\tan \theta = 3.7321$ [75°]

f) $\sin \theta = 0.7880$ [52° or 128°]

Mental Math

1. Calculate the mean of each pair of numbers.

a) 36, 38   [37]   b) 120, 122   [121]

c) −64, −66   [−65]   d) 368, 366   [367]

e) 5.2, 5.4   [5.3]   f) −13.9, −13.7   [−13.8]

2. Evaluate for $x = 5$ and $y = -10$.

a) $7x + y$ [25]   b) $x + 10y$ [−95]

c) $-x^2 - 5y$ [25]   d) $-x - 6y$ [55]

e) $x^2 - 2y^2$ [−175]   f) $y - 4x + 1$ [−29]

Explore/Inquire Answers

Explore: Use a Diagram

a) height of the lighthouse

b) height of the foot of the lighthouse above sea level

Inquire

1. a) BC = AB tan 4.3°   b) 75.2 m

2. a) BD = AB tan 4.9   b) 85.7 m

3. 10.5 m

4. cosine, law of sines   **5.** 4.9°

Teaching Suggestions

Method 1

(overhead projector)   Review with the class the opening paragraph on student text page 493. Discuss the terms "angle of elevation" and "angle of depression." Invite students to identify examples of angles of elevation and depression in the classroom.

     Assign the Explore section and the Inquire questions to pairs of students. Ask:

What kind of triangle is $\triangle ABC$? $\triangle ABD$?

Why is this important in finding the length of BC and AB?

     For Inquire question 5, ask:

How are the angle of elevation and the angle of depression between two points related to each other?

     Elicit from the students that the angle of elevation from point X to point Y and the angle of depression from point Y to point X are the same.

     Assign teaching examples 1 to 4 on student text pages 494 to 496 to pairs of students. For teaching example 1, ask:

What does it mean to solve a triangle?

     Ensure that the students know that solving a triangle means finding the unknown measures of the sides and angles of the triangle.

     Then, ask:

What does "contained angle" mean?

How do you know when you need to use the law of sines or the law of cosines to solve a triangle?

     Elicit from the students that if three sides, or two sides and a contained angle are given, then the law of cosines should be used; if two sides and a non-contained angle, or two angles and any side are given, then the law of sines should be used.

     Have volunteers present their results to the class. Provide an overhead projector, if necessary.

Method 2

Review with the students the trigonometric ratios. Draw the following diagram on the chalkboard.

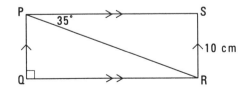

Ask:

What kind of triangle is △PQR?

How would you find the measures of the sides of △PQR?

What does it mean to solve a triangle?

Have the students find the unknown measures. Then, have them identify an angle of elevation and an angle of depression. Ask:

How are the angles of elevation and depression in the given diagram related to each other? Explain.

What examples of angles of elevation and depression can you see in the classroom?

Review with the class the two forms of the law of sines and the three forms of the law of cosines. Then, draw the following diagrams on the chalkboard.

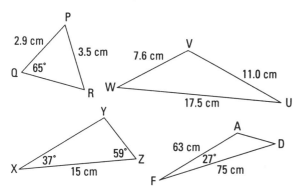

Have the students identify which law to use, the law of sines or the law of cosines, to find the measures of the unknown sides and angles in each triangle. Then, have pairs of students copy the diagrams and find the values of the sides and angles not given in each triangle. Have volunteers present their results to the class. Provide an overhead projector, if necessary.

As a class, work through teaching examples 1 to 4 on student text pages 494 to 496.

Sample Solution

Page 499, question 53

The area of △XYZ

$= \frac{1}{2} \times$ height $\times$ base.

From X, draw a perpendicular to meet base ZY at W.

In △XYZ, using the law of cosines,

$$\cos \angle XZY = \frac{XZ^2 + ZY^2 - XY^2}{2(XZ)(ZY)}$$

$$= \frac{10.2^2 + 9.5^2 - 6.8^2}{2(10.2)(9.5)}$$

$$= 0.7639 \text{ (to 4 decimal places)}$$

$\angle XZY = 40.2°$ (to the nearest tenth of a degree)

In △XZW, $\angle XWZ = 90°$.

$$\sin 40.2° = \frac{XW}{XZ}$$

$$XW = XZ \sin 40.2°$$

$$= 10.2 \times 0.6455$$

$$= 6.6$$

(to 1 decimal place)

Area △XYZ $= \frac{1}{2} \times XW \times ZY$

$$= \frac{1}{2} \times 6.6 \times 9.5$$

$$= 31.35$$

Area of △XYZ is 31.3 m², to the nearest tenth of a square metre.

Integrating Technology

Graphing Calculators

How would you use your graphing calculator to solve equations using sine, cosine, or tangent as in teaching examples 1, 2, and 3 on student text pages 494 to 496? On a TI-83, the Mode is set to Degree, and the sin, cos, and tan keys are used. When the sine, cosine, or tangent of an angle is known, the sin⁻¹ (i.e., 2nd sin), cos⁻¹ (i.e., 2nd cos), or tan⁻¹ (i.e., 2nd tan) keys are used to determine the angle. Remember to enter a closing bracket at the appropriate place when an opening bracket is provided, and to enter dividends and divisors in brackets, when necessary.

Use your graphing calculator to find unknown measures in the questions on student text pages 497 to 499, where appropriate.

See *MATHPOWER™ 11, Western Edition, Blackline Masters* pages 184 to 186 for Trigonometry.

Extension

Show that the law of sines and the law of cosines is also true for a right triangle.

Enrichment

Create a question, using the law of sines or the law of cosines. Exchange your question for that of a classmate's and solve it. Compare your answers and discuss any similarities or differences in your solutions.

Math Journal

law of sines, law of cosines   Write the two forms of the law of sines and the three forms of the law of cosines in your journal. Include diagrams and examples for clarity.

Problem Levels of Difficulty

A: 1–45   **B:** 46–50   **C:** 51–54

Assessing the Outcomes

Journal

Write a short essay describing how you decide whether
to use the law of sines or the law of cosines when
finding the measures of angles or sides in a triangle.

Written Assignment

Solve each of the following triangles.

1. $\triangle ABC$, $a = 26$ cm, $\angle B = 53.5°$, $c = 19$ cm
2. $\triangle DEF$, $\angle E = 90°$, $\angle F = 57°$, $f = 13.5$ cm
3. $\triangle PQR$, $r = 50$ cm, $p = 60$ cm, $q = 70$ cm
4. $\triangle KLM$, $m = 11$ cm, $\angle K = 37.3°$, $l = 14$ cm

Investigating Math

Constructing Triangles Using Side-Side-Angle (SSA)

Student Text Pages
Pp. 500–501

Materials
graphing calculators, protractors, rulers, compasses, overhead projector

Learning Outcomes
- Review the ambiguous case of the law of cosines.
- Write the conditions on the values of a, b, and sin A that result in 0, 1, or 2 triangles.
- Apply the conditions on the values of a, b, and sin A.

Prerequisite Skills
Find the value of x.

a) $\cos x = 0.5878$ [54°]

b) $\cos x = 0.9903$ [8°]

c) $\cos x = 0.1564$ [81°]

d) $\cos 25° = x$ [0.9063]

e) $\cos 72° = x$ [0.3090]

f) $\cos 39° = x$ [0.7771]

Mental Math
1. Evaluate for $x = 1.5$ and $y = -0.5$.

a) $2x + 2y$ [2]   b) $-x - 3y$ [0]

c) $x^2 - y^2$ [2]   d) $-x^2 + 2y$ [-3.25]

e) $x^2 + y^2$ [2.5]   f) $5y + x$ [-1]

2. If $h(x) = 3x^2 - 2$, find

a) $h(0)$ [-2]   b) $h(-5)$ [73]

c) $h(2)$ [10]   d) $2h(1)$ [2]

e) $-h(6)$ [-106]   f) $3h(-1) + 1$ [4]

Teaching Suggestions
(protractors, rulers, compasses, overhead projector) Read with the class the opening paragraphs on student text page 500.

Provide pairs of students with protractors, rulers, and compasses, and assign the investigations. As each investigation is completed by the class, have volunteers present their results to the class. Provide an overhead projector, if necessary.

Math Journal
Write a short essay describing how the values of a, b, and sin A of $\triangle ABC$ determine whether 0, 1, or 2 triangles are possible. Include diagrams for clarity.

Assessing the Outcomes

Written Assignment

Determine whether each set of data defines no triangle, one triangle, or two possible triangles.

a) In $\triangle XYZ$, X = 40°, $\angle XZ$ = 8 cm, and YZ = 5 cm

b) In $\triangle KLM$, $\angle K$ = 76°, KM = 10 cm, LM = 12 cm

c) In $\triangle PQR$, P = 36°, PR = 10.5 cm, and QR = 3.5 cm

Student Text Pages
Pp. 502–512

Materials

graphing calculators, protractors, rulers, overhead projector

Learning Outcomes

- Understand the concept of ambiguous cases in solving triangles.
- Use the law of sines to solve triangles involving ambiguous cases.
- Use the law of sines to solve problems involving ambiguous cases.

Prerequisite Skills

1. The centre of a circle has coordinates $(5, 2)$. The radius of the circle is 5 units. Write an equation for the circle.

$$[(x - 5)^2 + (y - 2)^2 = 25]$$

2. The centre of a circle has coordinates $(-7, 3)$. The radius of the circle is 10 units. Write an equation for the circle.

$$[(x + 7)^2 + (y - 3)^2 = 100]$$

3. Find the value for x.

a) $\sin x = 0.6946$ [44° or 136°]

b) $\sin x = 0.9848$ [80° or 100°]

c) $\sin x = 0.1045$ [6° or 174°]

d) $\sin 160° = x$ [0.3420]

e) $\sin 113° = x$ [0.9205]

f) $\sin 91° = x$ [0.9998]

Mental Math

1. Calculate.

a) 52^2 [2704]   b) 3.2^2 [10.24]

c) 0.92^2 [0.8464]   d) 11.1^2 [123.21]

e) 81^2 [6561]   f) 710^2 [504 100]

2. Calculate the exact answer.

a) $\sqrt{(6 - 1)^2 + (9 - 7)^2}$ $[\sqrt{29}]$

b) $\sqrt{(7 + 1)^2 + (1 + 3)^2}$ $[4\sqrt{5}]$

c) $\sqrt{(-2 + 4)^2 + (5 - (-2))^2}$ $[\sqrt{53}]$

d) $\sqrt{(-5 - 1)^2 + (-3 - 6)^2}$ $[3\sqrt{13}]$

Explore/Inquire Answers

Explore: Draw a Diagram

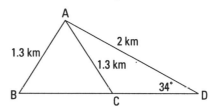

Inquire

1. $\sin ABD = \dfrac{2 \sin ADB}{AB}$

2. $\sin ACD = \dfrac{2 \sin ADB}{AC}$

3. a) equal   b) equal

4. a) acute   b) obtuse   c) no   d) both

Teaching Suggestions

(protractors, rulers, overhead projector) Review with the class the opening paragraphs on student text page 502. Ask:

What does the word "ambiguous" mean?

Where have you seen this word used in real life?

Assign the Explore section and the Inquire questions to pairs of students. Ask:

Why are the right sides in Inquire questions 1 and 2 equal?

Elicit from the students that since AB = AC, then, the right side of each equation is the same. Have volunteers present their results to the class. Provide an overhead projector, if necessary. Review the minimum information needed about a triangle in order to use the law of sines.

Provide pairs of students with protractors and rulers, and have them draw the triangles possible when two sides and a non-contained angle are given. Give the students ample opportunity to compare and discuss the results shown on student text page 503.

Review with the class teaching examples 1 to 4 on student text pages 504 to 509.

Sample Solution

Page 512, question 38

Draw a perpendicular line from C to side AB, meeting AB at X.

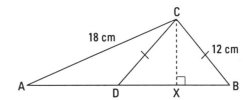

Area $\triangle ACD$ = Area $\triangle ACX$ − Area $\triangle CDX$

Area $\triangle ACX$ = $\frac{1}{2}CX \times AX$

Area $\triangle CDX$ = $\frac{1}{2}CX \times DX$

Area $\triangle ACD$ = $\frac{1}{2}CX \times AX - \frac{1}{2}CX \times DX$

$\qquad\quad = \frac{1}{2}CX(AX - DX)$

$\qquad\quad = \frac{1}{2}CX \times AD$

Area $\triangle ACB$ = $\frac{1}{2}CX \times AB$

$\dfrac{\text{Area } \triangle ACD}{\text{Area} \triangle ACB} = \dfrac{\frac{1}{2}CX \times AD}{\frac{1}{2}CX \times AB} = \dfrac{AD}{AB}$

In $\triangle ACD$, $\dfrac{AD}{\sin ACD} = \dfrac{CD}{\sin CAD}$.

In $\triangle ACB$, $\dfrac{AB}{\sin ACB} = \dfrac{CB}{\sin CAB}$.

But, $\qquad\qquad CD = CB.$

Then, $\qquad \dfrac{CD}{\sin CAD} = \dfrac{CB}{\sin CAB}$

$\qquad\qquad \dfrac{AD}{AB} = \dfrac{\sin ACD}{\sin ACB}$

Logic Power Answer

If both ends of a fuse are lit simultaneously, the fuse will take 30 s to burn.

Paula simultaneously lights one piece of fuse at both ends and one piece of fuse at one end. When the fuse with the two lit ends is burned, the other fuse will be half-burned. She then lights the end of the half-burned fuse, which will take 15 s to finish burning.

Integrating Technology

Graphing Calculators

How would you use your graphing calculator to solve equations using sine, cosine, or tangent as in teaching examples 1, 2, and 4 on student text pages 504, 505, 508, and 509? On a TI-83, the Mode is set to Degree, and the sin, cos, and tan keys are used. When the sine, cosine, or tangent of an angle is known, the $\sin^{-1}$ (i.e., 2nd sin), $\cos^{-1}$ (i.e., 2nd cos), or $\tan^{-1}$ (i.e., 2nd tan) keys are used to determine the angle. Remember to enter a closing bracket at the appropriate place when an opening bracket is provided, and to enter dividends and divisors in brackets, when necessary.

When solving the quadratic formula as in teaching example 3 on student text page 507 using a TI-83, rather than re-entering the expression with the negative square root term, press the ENTRY (i.e., 2nd ENTER)

key, and use the arrow keys to move to the + sign and replace it with a − sign.

How would you use your graphing calculator to determine the intersection of a circle and a line as in teaching example 3 on student text page 507? On a TI-83, the equation of the circle is changed to two equations in the form $y =$, and the Y= key and the Intersect operation are used.

Press the Y= key. Clear any equations. If Plot1 is highlighted, move the cursor to it and turn it off by pressing the ENTER key.

Enter the right side of the equation with the positive square root at Y1=, the right side of the equation with the negative square root at Y2=, and the right side of the linear equation at Y3=.

Press the ZOOM key and the 5 key to select Zsquare to display the graph with the circle appearing round.

Press the CALC (i.e., 2nd TRACE) key and the 5 key to select intersect.

Press the up and down keys to select the correct curve of the circle and the line as Curve 1 and Curve 2.

Press the right and left arrow keys to move the cursor to the intersection of the curve and the line.

Press the ENTER key to define your Guess.

Use your graphing calculator to answer the questions on student text pages 510 to 512, where appropriate.

See *MATHPOWER™ 11, Western Edition, Blackline Masters* pages 184 to 186 for Trigonometry.

Extension

Which of the following statements are true?
The law of sines can be used if

1. 3 sides of a triangle are given.
2. 2 sides and a non-contained angle are given.
3. 2 sides and a contained angle are given.
4. 3 angles are given.
5. 2 angles and a contained side are given.
6. 2 angles and a non-contained side are given.

For which of the statements above is it possible to have more than one solution? Explain.

Enrichment

Create a question, using an ambiguous case of the law of sines. Exchange questions with that of a classmate's and solve it. Compare your answers and discuss any similarities or differences in your solutions.

Math Journal

law of sines (ambiguous case) Make a list of the possible triangles for values of a, b, and c of $\triangle ABC$, and under what conditions there is 1 possible triangle, two possible triangles, or no possible triangles. Include diagrams and examples for clarity.

Common Errors

- Students often make errors when performing calculations involving the law of sines.

$\mathbf{R}_x$ Encourage students to estimate their answers and check them. For example, the shortest side is opposite the smallest angle in a triangle or the sum of two of the sides of a triangle must be greater than the third side.

Problem Levels of Difficulty

A: 1–33   **B:** 34–38   **C:** 39–41

Assessing the Outcomes

Journal

Write a short essay describing the ambiguous case of the law of sines. Include diagrams illustrating your explanation.

Investigating Math

The Ambiguous Case and the Law of Cosines

Student Text Page
P. 513

Materials

graphing calculators, compasses, rulers, protractors, overhead projector

Learning Outcomes

- Understand the ambiguous case of the law of cosines.
- Find the third side of a triangle given two sides and a non-contained angle of the triangle.
- Determine whether a set of measurements for a triangle will give one triangle, two triangles, or no triangles.
- Solve triangles using the law of cosines.

Prerequisite Skills

1. Solve each equation.

a) $x^2 - 4x + 4 = 0$	[±2]
b) $x^2 - 5x + 6 = 0$	[2, 3]
c) $x^2 + 2x - 3 = 0$	[1, −3]
d) $x^2 + 7x + 10 = 0$	[−2, −5]

2. Find the value of x.

a) $\cos 67° = x$	[0.3907]
b) $\cos 100° = x$	[−0.1736]
c) $\cos 19° = x$	[0.9455]
d) $\cos x = 0.0872$	[85°]
e) $\cos x = 0.9976$	[4°]
f) $\cos x = -0.6427$	[130°]

Mental Math

1. Calculate.

a) $1 + 2 + \ldots + 27$	[378]
b) $1 + 2 + \ldots + 15$	[120]
c) $2 + 4 + 6 + \ldots + 20$	[110]
d) $2 + 4 + 6 + \ldots + 52$	[702]
e) $1 + 3 + \ldots + 39$	[400]
f) $1 + 3 + \ldots + 59$	[900]

2. Simplify.

a) $3x + 2x$	[5x]
b) $-2y + y + 2z + z$	[−y + 3z]
c) $x^2 + 2x - 3x^2 - 11x$	[−2x² − 9x]
d) $xy + 2x - y + 3xy + 5x$	[4xy + 7x − y]

Teaching Suggestions

(compasses, rulers, protractors, overhead projector) Read with the class the opening paragraphs on student text page 513. Review the three forms of the law of cosines.

Encourage the students to draw diagrams to help with the problem solving process of the questions.

Have a spokesperson from each combined group present the results to the class. Provide an overhead projector, if necessary.

Integrating Technology

Graphing Calculators

Use your graphing calculator to find unknown measures in the questions on student text page 513, where appropriate.

See *MATHPOWER™ 11, Western Edition, Blackline Masters* pages 184 to 186 for Trigonometry.

Extension

Show that the Pythagorean theorem for a right triangle is a special case of the law of cosines.

Enrichment

Describe the law of cosines in words without the use of letters or numbers.

Assessing the Outcomes

Journal

Write a short essay about what new information you have learned about the ambiguous case and the law of cosines.

Connecting Math and Fashion

Styles of Tying Shoelaces

Student Text Pages
Pp. 514–515

Materials
scientific (or graphing) calculators

Learning Outcome
- Determine the formulas for determining the lengths of shoelaces for different styles of shoes.

Prerequisite Skills
1. Find the value of x.

a) $x^2 = 3^2 + 9^2$ [$3\sqrt{10}$]

b) $5^2 + 7^2 = x^2$ [$\sqrt{74}$]

c) $11^2 + x^2 = 15^2$ [$2\sqrt{26}$]

d) $x^2 + 8^2 = 20^2$ [$4\sqrt{21}$]

2. Evaluate each expression for the given values of the variables.

a) $2x + 3y - z^2; x = 2, y = -1, z = 5$ [-24]

b) $3p^3 - q + 7; p = -3, q = 10$ [-84]

c) $-5a + b^2 + 3c; a = -2, b = 5, c = \dfrac{2}{3}$ [37]

Mental Math
1. Calculate the mean of each pair of numbers.

a) $-7, 11$ [2]   b) $55, 35$ [45]

c) $0, -22$ [-11]   d) $15.4, -13.2$ [1.1]

e) $122, 222$ [172]   f) $-0.3, -0.9$ [-0.6]

2. Calculate.

a) 51^2 [2601]   b) 2.2^2 [4.84]

c) 10.2^2 [104.04]   d) 0.71^2 [0.5041]

e) $(-52)^2$ [2704]   f) -3.1^2 [-9.61]

Teaching Suggestions
Read with the class the opening paragraphs on student text page 514. Ask:

How many students have shoes with eyelets?

How many eyelets?

Which method do you use to lace your shoelaces?

Assign the explorations to small groups of students. Encourage the groups to discuss and compare their results with those of other groups. Have volunteers present their results to the class.

Invite students to bring in their shoes with eyelets. Have them mark where their lace begins and ends in their shoe, and then remove the lace and measure the length used to lace the shoe.

Survey the class to see what number of students use each method of tying shoelaces.

Integrating Technology

Internet

Use the Internet to find more information about styles of lacing shoe laces.

Extension
Make up a method of your own for tying shoelaces. Draw a diagram of your method and find a formula for the length of lace required for your method.

Present your method to the class, and compare your method with those of other students. Discuss any similarities and differences in the methods.

Display diagrams and formulas for interesting methods of shoelace tying.

Assessing the Outcome

Observation

Some skills to watch for in this lesson are:
- Do the students have difficulty with creating formulas?
- Do the students know how to substitute into the formulas?
- Do the students know how to apply the Pythagorean theorem?
- Do the pairs cooperate to help make the work easier?
- Do the students persevere until they have found a formula, or do they give up and let others do the work?

Review

Student Text Pages
Pp. 516–517

Materials

scientific or graphing calculators, Teacher's Resource Master 2 (1-cm grid paper)

Learning Outcome

• Review the skills and concepts in Chapter 8.

Using the Review

Have the students work independently to complete the Review. Meeting in small groups, the students can mark and discuss the work. Groups can then share their solutions and report any questions that caused them difficulty. Discuss these questions with the class.

Reteaching Suggestions

For those students having difficulty with the chapter material, form small groups and use the following exercises.

If you feel that the class has had particular difficulty mastering any concept, you may wish to work through a problem from each section as a model of excellence of solution, which some students require just prior to assessment.

Connecting Coordinate Geometry and Plane Geometry

1. Quadrilateral ABCD have vertices A(-1, 2), B(3, 2), C(3, -2), and D(-1, -2).
a) Prove ABCD is a square.
b) Prove AC = BD.
c) Prove AC is perpendicular to BD.

Division of a Line Segment

1. Determine the coordinates of the points that divide the line segment with endpoints A(2, 4) and B(8, -2) into 3 equal parts.
2. Find the point P(x, y) that divides the line segment joining points A(-2, -2) and B(8, 3) internally in the ratio of AP:PB = 1:4.

Distances Between Points and Lines

1. Find the shortest distance from (-1, 2) to the line $y = 2x - 1$.
2. A perpendicular from point (4, 2) meets the line $y = \frac{1}{2}x + 3$.

a) At what point does the perpendicular from (4, 2) meet the line?
b) What is the shortest distance from the point to the line. Round your answer to 1 decimal place.

The Equation of a Circle

1. Write the equation of a circle with centre (1, 2) and radius 5.
2. The equation of a circle is $(x - 1)^2 + (y + 3)^2 = 36$.
a) Find the length of the diameter of the circle.
b) Find the circumference of the circle to 1 decimal place.
c) Find the area of the circle to 1 decimal place.

Intersections of Lines and Circles

1. Write an equation of the tangent at the point (2, 2) on the circle $x^2 + y^2 = 8$.
2. The line $y = \frac{2}{5}x$ intersects the circle $(x - 3)^2 + (y - 2)^2 = 4$ at points A and B. Find the length of AB to 1 decimal place.
3. The line $5x - 4y + 11 = 0$ intersects the circle $(x + 3)^2 + (y + 1)^2 = 41$ at points M and N. Show that MN is a diameter of the circle.
4. Find the length of the tangent from the point (-4, -4) to the circle $(x - 1)^2 + (y - 1)^2 = 4$.

Reviewing Trigonometry

1. In $\triangle$ABC, c = 52.7 cm, $\angle$C = 90°, and a = 34.6 cm. Solve the triangle. Round your lengths to 1 decimal place and the angles to the nearest whole degree, if necessary.
2. In $\triangle$MNP, n = 3.2 cm, m = 2.7 cm, and $\angle$P = 121.4°. Find p. Round your answer to 1 decimal place.
3. In $\triangle$PQR, PQ = 4.2 cm, QR = 5.1 cm, and $\angle$PQR = 39°. Solve the triangle. Round your lengths to 1 decimal place and the angles to the nearest whole degree, if necessary.

The Law of Sines: The Ambiguous Case

For each triangle, decide whether there is no solution, one solution, or two solutions. Solve each triangle. Round lengths to 1 decimal place and angle measures to the nearest whole degree.

1. In $\triangle$PQR, P = $\angle$52°, QR = 3 cm, and PR = 7 cm.
2. In $\triangle$LMN, MN = 12 m, LN = 8.3 m, and $\angle$L = 72°.
3. In $\triangle$XYZ, YZ = 15.0 cm, $\angle$X = 27°, and XZ = 33.0 cm.
4. In $\triangle$DEF, EF = 3.7 cm, DF = 5.2 cm, and $\angle$D = 19°.

Answers to Reteaching Suggestions

Division of a Line Segment

1. (4, 2), (6, 0)   **2.** (0, −1)

Distances Between Points and Lines

1. $\sqrt{5}$ **2. a)** (2.8, 4.4)   **b)** 2.7 units

The Equation of a Circle

1. $(x - 1)^2 + (y - 2)^2 = 25$
2. a) 12 units   **b)** 37.7 units   **c)** 113.1 square units

Intersections of Lines and Circles

1. $x + y - 4 = 0$ **2.** 3.7 units
3. M(−7, −6), N(1, −4); MN = $2\sqrt{41}$ = twice
 the radius
4. $\sqrt{46}$ units

Reviewing Trigonometry

1. $b = 39.8$, $\angle A = 41°$, $\angle B = 49°$
2. 5.2 cm
3. $q = 3.2$ cm, $\angle R = 56°$, $\angle P = 85°$

The Law of Sines: The Ambiguous Case

1. no solution
2. one solution; LM = 11.6 m, N = $\angle 67°$, M = $\angle 41°$
3. two solutions; $\angle Y = 87°$, $\angle Z = 66°$, XY = 30.2 cm,
 or, $\angle Y = 93°$, XY = 30.2 cm, $\angle Z = 60°$
4. two solutions; $\angle E = 27°$, $\angle F = 134°$, DE = 8.2 cm,
 or, $\angle E = 153°$, $\angle F = 8°$, DE = 1.6 cm

Exploring Mathematics

Tetrominoes

(1-cm grid paper)   Provide pairs of students with grid
paper and assign the exploration. Give the students
ample opportunity to discuss and compare their results
with those of other students in the class.

 Have volunteers present their results to the class.
Ensure that diagrams similar to these are presented
as the results.

1.   **2.**

3.   **4.**

Chapter Check

Student Text Page
P. 518

Learning Outcome
• Evaluate the skills and concepts in Chapter 8.

Assessing the Outcome
If you assign the Chapter Check as a student
assessment, look for the following:
• Can they use coordinates to prove properties of lines
 and planes?
• Can they find the points of division of a line segment?
• Can they find the distance between a point and a
 line?
• Can they write the equation of a circle given the
 radius and the centre?
• Can they find the points of intersection of a line and
 a circle?
• Can they find the equation of a tangent?
• Can they find the length of a tangent to a circle from
 a point outside the circle?
• Can they use trigonometry to solve right triangles?
• Can they use the law of sines and the law of cosines
 to solve oblique triangles?
• Can they identify the number of triangles possible
 for the ambiguous case of the law of sines?

Problem Solving

Student Text Page
P. 519

Materials

graphing or scientific calculator, Teacher's Resource Master 1 (0.5-cm grid paper), overhead projector

Learning Outcome

• Use problem solving strategies to solve problems.

Using the Strategies

The problems on this page allow the students to use the problem solving strategies discussed in Chapters 1 to 3. These strategies are
• Use a Diagram
• Use a Data Bank
• Solve Fermi Problems
• Solve a Simpler Problem
• Use Logic
• Look for a Pattern
• Guess and Check
• Work Backward
• Use a Table or Spreadsheet

Teaching Suggestions

(0.5-cm grid paper, overhead projector)   Encourage the students to work in pairs or small groups. When students have completed the problems, have them share and discuss their strategies and solutions with other students.

For question 1, ask:

How can you use an average mark to find the total marks on the tests?

If the highest mark on one test is 95%, what is the total on the other 5 tests?

What is the next highest mark that Kelly could achieve?

If you assume that Kelly achieved this next highest mark on 4 of the tests, what would the mark on the fifth test have to be?

For question 5, ask:

How are a regular hexagon and an equilateral triangle related?

Have volunteers present their results to the class. Provide an overhead projector, if necessary.

Sample Solution
Page 519, question 3

Let the area of the overlapping part of the circles be P.
Area of circle, radius 4 cm = 16π cm^2
Area of circle, radius 3 cm = 9π cm^2
Area of non-overlapping part of circle,
radius 4 cm = $(16\pi - P)$ cm^2
Area of non-overlapping part of circle,
radius 3 cm = $(9\pi - P)$ cm^2
Difference in areas of non-overlapping parts of circles
$= 16\pi - P - (9\pi - P)$
$= 16\pi - P - 9\pi + P$
$= 16\pi - 9\pi$
$= 7\pi$
Difference in areas is 7π cm^2.

Page 519, question 11

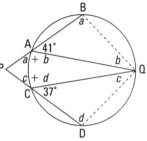

Join BQ and DQ.
$\angle$PAQ is an external angle of $\triangle$ABQ.
$\angle$PAQ
$= \angle$ABQ + $\angle$AQB
$= a + b$
$\angle$PCQ is an external angle of $\triangle$CDQ.
$\angle$PCQ = $\angle$CDQ + $\angle$CQD
$\quad\quad = d + c$
The sum of the angles of $\triangle$ABQ and $\triangle$CDQ is 360°. Thus,
$a + b + c + d + 41 + 37 = 360$ ----------------------(1)
In quadrilateral PAQC, the sum of the angles is 360°. Thus,
$a + b + c + d + \angle P + \angle AQD = 360$ ----------------(2)
Subtract (2) from (1).
$41 + 37 - (\angle P + \angle AQD) = 0$
$41 + 37 = \angle P + \angle AQD$
$78 = \angle P + \angle AQD$
Thus, the sum of $\angle P$ and $\angle AQD$ is 78°.

Assessing the Outcome

Observations

As you make your problem solving assessment of each student, consider the following:
• Do they understand the problem?
• Do they consider a variety of strategies?
• Do they use an organized approach?
• Do they create and use diagrams effectively?
• Do they show persistence?

Cumulative Review, Chapters 5-8

Student Text Pages
Pp. 520–521

Learning Outcome
• Review skills and concepts in Chapters 5 to 8.

Teaching Suggestions

Method 1
The review of these four chapters can take several days.

Divide the class into groups of four. Each group is to decide which chapter each student will review. The students who are assigned the same chapter are to then form expert groups.

They are to decide on strategies for reviewing the questions and solutions with their home groups. They are also to be the discussion leaders for the questions in these groups, ensuring that all of the group members can complete each question and explain each solution.

Each student from the expert group is to then return to his or her home group and lead a review of the chapter he or she was assigned.

Method 2
Have pairs of students choose one question from every section in each of the chapter reviews. The partner may correct the answers.

If a student is having difficulty with any particular type of question, reteach the concepts to the student, and assign other similar questions for reinforcement.

Reteaching Suggestions

Chapter 5   Functions

1. $f(x) = 2x^2 - x$ and $g(x) = 1 - 2x$. Find
   a) $f + g$ b) $f - g$ c) fg
   d) $\dfrac{f}{g}$ e) ff f) $2g + f$

2. If $f(x) = r(x)$ and $g(x) = x^2 + 9$, find
   a) $(f \circ g)(x)$ b) $(g \circ f)(x)$
   c) $(f \circ g)(-2)$ d) $(g \circ f)(3)$

3. a) Find the inverse of the function $f(x) = x^2 + 3$.
   b) Is the inverse of $f(x)$ a function?
   c) State the domain and the range of $f(x)$ and its inverse.

4. Find the inverse of $y = \dfrac{x + 1}{2x - 3}$.

5. Determine whether each function is a polynomial function. State the degree of each polynomial function.
   a) $y = 2x^3 + 3x$ b) $y = 5 - 2^x$
   c) $y = -x^2 + 3x + 2\sqrt{2}$ d) $y = 3x - \dfrac{3}{2x}$

Graph each function and determine
a) *the equation of any asymptotes*
b) *the domain and the range*

6. $y = \dfrac{x}{x^2 - 1}$ 7. $y = \dfrac{3x}{x + 7}$

Solve and check.

8. $\dfrac{x - 5}{3} = \dfrac{2}{x}$ 9. $\dfrac{x}{6x + 1} = \dfrac{x}{7x + 3}$

Solve. Graph the solution.

10. $|x + 5| < 4$ 11. $|x - 1| > |x + 3|$

Graph each function and determine the domain and the range.

12. $f(x) = |x + 2| - 1$ 13. $f(x) = |x^2 - 9| + 2$

Solve and check.

14. $\sqrt{x - 3} - 2 = 5$ 15. $\sqrt{n - 2} = \sqrt{1 - 2n}$

Solve. Graph the solution.

16. $\sqrt{m - 3} \le \sqrt{3 - 2m}$ 17. $\sqrt{3x} > \dfrac{2x}{3}$

Chapter 6   Reasoning

1. Study the figures below.

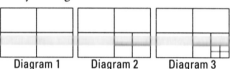

Diagram 1   Diagram 2   Diagram 3

   a) Make a conjecture about the number of rectangles in diagram n.
   b) Show that your conjecture is true for diagram 7.

2. Provide one example that supports each of the following conjectures, and then, give one counterexample for each conjecture.
   a) All birds fly.
   b) If a is any integer, and $b > 3$, then, $a + b > 8$.

3. Prove that the sum of the first n whole numbers is given by the expression $\dfrac{n(n + 1)}{2}$.

4. Phil, Bill, and Jill each have one of a dime, a nickel, and a quarter. Bill has the quarter. Jill does not have the quarter. Phil does not have the dime. Which coin does Jill have?

5. Use a number line to indicate the numbers $x \ge -5$ and $x < 3$.

6. A group of 85 students were surveyed about the numbers of videos, CDs, and tapes they possess.
   18 own CDs only
   3 own videos only
   12 own all three — CDs, videos, and tapes
   23 own videos and CDs
   16 own videos and tapes
   14 own CDs and tapes
   a) Display this data on a Venn diagram.
   b) How many students own only tapes?

c) How many student own videos and CDs, but no tapes?

7. Write each statement as a biconditional statement.

a) Two points are awarded for every win.

b) Winter begins officially on December 22.

8. Write the converse and the contrapositive of each conditional statement. Decide whether each of the statements is true, and provide a counterexample for any statement that is not true.

a) If a quadrilateral has diagonals that are perpendicular to each other, then it is a square.

b) Even numbers always have a factor of 2.

9. In scalene triangle ABC, D is the midpoint of BC. Use the method of indirect proof to show that AC is not perpendicular to BC.

Chapter 7   The Circle

1. $\triangle$PQR and $\triangle$SQR are on the same side of the line QR. $\angle$PQR = $\angle$SRQ and $\angle$SQR = $\angle$PRQ. Write a two-column proof to show that PQ = SR.

2. The length of a chord of a circle is 10 cm. If the chord is 5 cm from the centre of the circle, what is the radius of the circle?

3. Points X, Y, and Z lie on a circle with centre O, and $\angle$XYZ = 45°. Write a flow-chart proof to show that XO is perpendicular to ZO.

4. Find the values of the variables.

5. ABCD is a cyclic quadrilateral and X and Y are points on AB and CD, respectively, such that XY $\parallel$ BC. Prove that AXYD is a cyclic quadrilateral.

6. In the following diagrams, tangents have been drawn to circles. Find the values of the variables.

a)

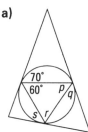

b)

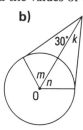

7. Calculate the length of arc ABC and the area of the sector ABCO. Round your answers to 1 decimal place.

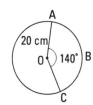

8. What is the sum of the measures of the interior angles of a polygon with 15 sides?

9. The sum of the interior angles of a polygon is 540°. How many sides does the polygon have?

10. The measure of the exterior angles of a regular polygon is 24°. How many sides does the polygon have?

Chapter 8   Coordinate Geometry and Trigonometry

1. The coordinates of quadrilateral PQRS are P(−1, 4), Q(2, 1), R(1, −3), and S(−5, 3).

a) Prove that quadrilateral PQRS is a trapezium.

b) Prove that the non-parallel sides of quadrilateral PQRS are equal in length.

2. Determine the coordinates of the points that divide the line segment with end points M(−3, −3) and N(5, 1) into 4 equal parts.

3. Find the shortest distance from (2, −3) to the line $y = -x + 2$. Give an exact answer.

4. Write the equation of a circle with centre (3, −1) and radius 10.

5. The diameter of a circle is 7 units, and the centre of the circle is (−2, −10). Write the equation of the circle.

6. Write an equation of the tangent at the point $(4, -3 + \sqrt{7})$ on the circle $(x - 1)^2 + (y + 3)^2 = 16$.

7. Find the length of the tangent from the point (7, 5) to the circle $(x - 3)^2 + (y - 2)^2 = 9$.

Answers to Reteaching Suggestions

Chapter 5

1. a) $2x^2 - 3x + 1$ **b)** $2x^2 + x - 1$
c) $-4x^3 + 4x^2 - x$ **d)** $-x$
e) $4x^4 - 4x^3 + x^2$ **f)** $2x^2 - 5x + 2$

2. a) $\sqrt{x^2 + 9}$ **b)** $x + 9$
c) $\sqrt{13}$ **d)** 12

3. a) $y = \pm\sqrt{x - 3}$ **b)** no
c) $f(x)$ domain $x \in R$; range $y \geq 3, y \in R$; inverse domain $x \geq 3, x \in R$; range $y \geq 0, y \in R$

4. $y = \dfrac{3x + 1}{2x - 1}$

5. a) function; 3 **b)** not a function
c) function; 2 **d)** not a function

6. $x = 1, -1$; domain: $x \neq \pm1, x \in R$; range: $y \in R$

7. $x = -7$; domain: $x \neq -7, x \in R$; range: $y \in R$

8. 6, −1 **9.** 0, −2

10. $-9 < x < -1$ [number line from −10 to 0]

11. $-3 \leq x < -1, x \in R$ [number line from −4 to 1]

12. domain: $x \in R$; range: $f(x) \geq -1, y \in R$

13. domain: $x \in R$; range: $f(x) \geq 2, y \in R$

14. 52   **15.** 1   **16.** $m \geq 3$ **17.** $0 < x < \frac{27}{4}$

Chapter 6

4. nickel

5.

6. a)

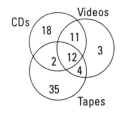

   b) 35   **c)** 11

7. a) If you win, then you are awarded 2 points.

   b) If it is December 22, then winter begins.

8. a) converse: if a quadrilateral is a square, then its diagonals are perpendicular to each other, contrapositive: If a quadrilateral has diagonals that are not perpendicular to each other, then it is not a square. false; a rhombus has diagonals that are perpendicular to each other; not all rhombi are squares

   b) converse: Numbers that have a factor of 2 are even; contrapositive: If a number is not even, then, it does not have a factor of 2. true

Chapter 7

2. $5\sqrt{2}$ units

4. $b = z = 70, a = 110$

6. a) $r = 70, p = s = 50, q = 60$

   b) $m = n = 60, k = 30$

7. length 48.9 cm, area 488.7 cm²

8. 2340°   **9.** 5   **10.** 15

Chapter 8

2. $(-1, -2), (1, -1), (3, 0)$

3. $\dfrac{3}{\sqrt{2}}$

4. $(x - 3)^2 + (y + 1)^2 = 100$

5. $(x + 2)^2 + (y + 10)^2 = \dfrac{9}{4}$ or $4(x + 2)^2 + 4(y + 10)^2 = 9$

6. $x + y - 4 = 0$

7. 4 units

CHAPTER 8

Student Text Answers

Chapter Opener p. 451

1. 265 465 km **2.** 3073 m/s
3. 463 m/s **4.** 6.6 times
5. a) $g = \dfrac{v^2}{r}$ **b)** 0.22 m/s^2 **c)** 44 times

Getting Started pp. 452–453

1 Slopes

1. a) A: 1 and undefined; C: 0 and -1
  b) equal **c)** yes **d)** 0; undefined
2. a) 1, -1 **b)** negative reciprocals
  c) 90° **d)** no

2 Midpoints

1. a) (12, 10), (12, 10) **b)** equal **c)** yes

3 Distances

1. a) $2\sqrt{2}, 6\sqrt{2}, 2\sqrt{2}, 6\sqrt{2}$
  b) equal **c)** yes
2. a) $4\sqrt{2}, 4\sqrt{2}$ **b)** equal **c)** no

4 Equations

1. a) $y = 12$ **b)** $x = 4$
2. a) $y = -x + 16$ **b)** $y = 2x - 8$

Warm Up

1. 3 **2.** -1 **3.** 1.4
4. -5 **5.** -2 **6.** 3
7. $\dfrac{1}{2}$ **8.** -2 **9.** $-\dfrac{1}{2}$
10. $\dfrac{1}{3}$ **11.** 2 **12.** $-\dfrac{3}{2}$
13. -1 **14.** $\dfrac{4}{3}$ **15.** $-\dfrac{2}{5}$
16. -5 **17.** $y = x + 4$ **18.** $y = -x + 3$
19. $y = \dfrac{1}{2}x - 2$ **20.** $y = -2x - 5$ **21.** 2; 6
22. $-5; \dfrac{5}{2}$ **23.** $-6; 4$ **24.** $-4; -8$
25. $-\dfrac{3}{5}$; no y-intercept
26. no x-intercept; 6
27. (1, 2) **28.** $(-1, 1)$ **29.** (2, 5)
30. $(-3, -7)$

Mental Math

Order of Operations

1. 8 **2.** -1 **3.** 3
4. -5 **5.** 5.5 **6.** -4.5
7. -3.5 **8.** -4.5 **9.** 5
10. 10 **11.** $\sqrt{58}$ **12.** 13
13. $\sqrt{85}$

Squaring Numbers Ending in One or Two

1. 441 **2.** 1681 **3.** 8281
4. 10 201 **5.** 26.01 **6.** 50.41
7. 656 100 **8.** 372 100 **9.** 484
10. 2704 **11.** 6724 **12.** 10 404
13. 84.64 **14.** 38.44 **15.** 176 400
16. 518 400
17. A number ending in 1 is $10n + 1$. $10n(10n + 2) + 1$ $= 100n^2 + 20n + 1 = (10n + 1)^2$; A number ending in 2 is $10n + 2$. $10n(10n + 4) + 4 = 100n^2 + 40n + 4 = (10n + 2)^2$
18. Multiply the numbers that are 3 above and 3 below the number. Then add 9.
19. Use the rule for numbers ending in 1 for numbers ending in 9. Use the rule for numbers ending in 2 for numbers ending in 8.

Technology p. 454

1 Midsegment of a Triangle

4. trapezoid; The midsegment is parallel to and one-half the length of the third side.

2 Midpoints of the Sides of a Quadrilateral

4. parallelogram

3 Diagonals of a Parallelogram

3. The diagonals bisect each other.

4 Midpoint of the Hypotenuse of a Right Triangle

3. The midpoint of the hypotenuse of a right triangle is equidistant from the vertices of the triangle.

Section 8.1 pp. 460–461

Applications and Problem Solving (Section 8.1)

15. a) R$(a + c, b)$
16. a) $y = 0, x = 4, y = -x + 4$ **17.** $\left(\dfrac{8}{3}, \dfrac{8}{3}\right)$
25. b) Yes; the diagonals of a square are perpendicular.

Investigating Math   pp. 462–463

1 Division of Horizontal Line Segments

1. a) (3, 0), (4, 0)   **b)** (3, 3), (5, 3)
   c) (1, 2), (5, 2)   **d)** (−7, −4), (−4, −4)
3. a) (2, 0), (3, 0), (4, 0)
   b) (2, 2), (4, 2), (6, 2)
   c) (−1, 1), (2, 1), (5, 1)
   d) (−4, −2), (0, −2), (4, −2)
5. a) (4, 0), (5, 0), (6, 0), (7, 0)
   b) (3, 5), (5, 5), (7, 5), (9, 5)
   c) (−2, 2), (1, 2), (4, 2), (7, 2)
   d) (−8, −6), (−4, −6), (0, −6), (4, −6)

8. a) $\left(\frac{a}{3}, 0\right)$, $\left(\frac{2a}{3}, 0\right)$
   b) $\left(\frac{a}{4}, 0\right)$, $\left(\frac{a}{2}, 0\right)$, $\left(\frac{3a}{4}, 0\right)$
   c) $\left(\frac{a}{5}, 0\right)$, $\left(\frac{2a}{5}, 0\right)$, $\left(\frac{3a}{5}, 0\right)$, $\left(\frac{4a}{5}, 0\right)$
   d) $\left(\frac{a}{6}, 0\right)$, $\left(\frac{a}{3}, 0\right)$, $\left(\frac{a}{2}, 0\right)$, $\left(\frac{2a}{3}, 0\right)$, $\left(\frac{5a}{6}, 0\right)$
   e) $\left(\frac{a}{8}, 0\right)$, $\left(\frac{a}{4}, 0\right)$, $\left(\frac{3a}{8}, 0\right)$, $\left(\frac{a}{2}, 0\right)$, $\left(\frac{5a}{8}, 0\right)$, $\left(\frac{3a}{4}, 0\right)$, $\left(\frac{7a}{8}, 0\right)$

2 Division of Vertical Line Segments

1. a) (0, 2), (0, 3)   **b)** (2, 4), (2, 6)
   c) (3, −2), (3, 1)   **d)** (−1, −8), (−1, −4)
3. a) (0, 3), (0, 4), (0, 5)
   b) (1, 6), (1, 8), (1, 10)
   c) (2, −3), (2, 0), (2, 3)
   d) (−3, −5), (−3, −1), (−3, 3)
5. a) (0, 1), (0, 2), (0, 3), (0, 4)
   b) (−1, 4), (−1, 6), (−1, 8), (−1, 10)
   c) (−2, −3), (−2, 0), (−2, 3), (−2, 6)
   d) (3, −5), (3, −1), (3, 3), (3, 7)

8. a) $\left(0, \frac{b}{3}\right)$, $\left(0, \frac{2b}{3}\right)$
   b) $\left(0, \frac{b}{4}\right)$, $\left(0, \frac{b}{2}\right)$, $\left(0, \frac{3b}{4}\right)$
   c) $\left(0, \frac{b}{5}\right)$, $\left(0, \frac{2b}{5}\right)$, $\left(0, \frac{3b}{5}\right)$, $\left(0, \frac{4b}{5}\right)$
   d) $\left(0, \frac{b}{7}\right)$, $\left(0, \frac{2b}{7}\right)$, $\left(0, \frac{3b}{7}\right)$, $\left(0, \frac{4b}{7}\right)$, $\left(0, \frac{5b}{7}\right)$, $\left(0, \frac{6b}{7}\right)$
   e) $\left(0, \frac{b}{10}\right)$, $\left(0, \frac{b}{5}\right)$, $\left(0, \frac{3b}{10}\right)$, $\left(0, \frac{2b}{5}\right)$, $\left(0, \frac{b}{2}\right)$, $\left(0, \frac{3b}{5}\right)$, $\left(0, \frac{7b}{10}\right)$, $\left(0, \frac{4b}{5}\right)$, $\left(0, \frac{9b}{10}\right)$

3 Division of Sloping Line Segments

1. f) (3, 3), (5, 4)
2. a) (1, 2), (3, 0)   **b)** (0, −1), (−3, −5)
3. a) (−3, 0), (−2, −1), (−1, −2)
   b) (0, 0), (−2, −3), (−4, −6)

4. a) (1, 4), (2, 3), (3, 2), (4, 1)
   b) (2, 7), (0, 4), (−2, 1), (−4, −2)
6. a) $\left(\frac{a}{3}, \frac{b}{3}\right)$, $\left(\frac{2a}{3}, \frac{2b}{3}\right)$
   b) $\left(\frac{a}{4}, \frac{b}{4}\right)$, $\left(\frac{a}{2}, \frac{b}{2}\right)$, $\left(\frac{3a}{4}, \frac{3b}{4}\right)$
   c) $\left(\frac{a}{5}, \frac{b}{5}\right)$, $\left(\frac{2a}{5}, \frac{2b}{5}\right)$, $\left(\frac{3a}{5}, \frac{3b}{5}\right)$, $\left(\frac{4a}{5}, \frac{4b}{5}\right)$
   d) $\left(\frac{a}{6}, \frac{b}{6}\right)$, $\left(\frac{a}{3}, \frac{b}{3}\right)$, $\left(\frac{a}{2}, \frac{b}{2}\right)$, $\left(\frac{2a}{3}, \frac{2b}{3}\right)$, $\left(\frac{5a}{6}, \frac{5b}{6}\right)$
   e) $\left(\frac{a}{n}, \frac{b}{n}\right)$, $\left(\frac{2a}{n}, \frac{2b}{n}\right)$, $\left(\frac{3a}{n}, \frac{3b}{n}\right)$, ..., $\left(\frac{(n-1)a}{n}, \frac{(n-1)b}{n}\right)$

Section 8.2   pp. 467–469

Practice (Section 8.2)

1. (0, 5)
2. (5, 0), (7, 0)
3. (−3, 2), (−5, 2), (−7, 2)
4. (−4, 0), (−4, −2)
5. (4.5, −1)
6. $\left(-3, -\frac{8}{5}\right)$, $\left(-3, -\frac{6}{5}\right)$, $\left(-3, -\frac{4}{5}\right)$, $\left(-3, -\frac{2}{5}\right)$
7. (0, 11)
8. (6, 8), (8, 11), (10, 14)
9. (1, 2), (2, 5)
10. (−2, 8), (−4, 6), (−6, 4), (−8, 2)
11. (−2, −6), (−1, −4), (0, −2), (1, 0), (2, 2)
12. $\left(\frac{1}{2}, \frac{9}{2}\right)$
13. $\left(7, \frac{5}{3}\right)$, $\left(6, \frac{4}{3}\right)$
14. $\left(\frac{4}{5}, 5\right)$, $\left(\frac{8}{5}, 6\right)$, $\left(\frac{12}{5}, 7\right)$, $\left(\frac{16}{5}, 8\right)$
15. $\left(-\frac{1}{3}, 3\right)$, $\left(\frac{4}{3}, 5\right)$
16. $\left(-\frac{19}{2}, -\frac{15}{2}\right)$, $\left(-7, -7\right)$, $\left(-\frac{9}{2}, -\frac{13}{2}\right)$
17. $\left(\frac{7}{2}, -1\right)$, $\left(5, -6\right)$, $\left(\frac{13}{2}, -11\right)$
18. $\left(-\frac{19}{2}, -\frac{1}{3}\right)$, $\left(-7, -\frac{14}{3}\right)$, $\left(-\frac{9}{2}, -9\right)$, $\left(-2, -\frac{40}{3}\right)$, $\left(\frac{1}{2}, -\frac{53}{3}\right)$
19. (6, 10)
20. (3, −5)
21. (44, 70)
22. $\left(-\frac{11}{2}, -\frac{7}{2}\right)$

Applications and Problem Solving (Section 8.2)

23. $\left(-2\sqrt{2}, \frac{22\sqrt{5}}{5}\right)$
24. (9, 13)

25. a) (−2, 15), (0, 11), (2, 7), (4, 3)
   b) −4, −2, 0, 2, 4, 6
   c) 19, 15, 11, 7, 3, −1
   d) arithmetic
26. A(7, 8), B(−5, 10)
27. 27 m
28. a) (3, 5), (4, 7), (5, 9); (−5, 7), (−4, 5), (−3, 3),
   (−2, 1), (−1, −1), (0, −3), (1, −5)   **b)** no
29. a) (500, 100)
   b) (100, 20), (200, 40), (300, 60), (400, 80)
   c) 102 m   **d)** 117 m
30. (261.8, 21.3), (523.6, 42.6)
31. a) 2060 m   **b)** 1950 m
   c) Assume the support towers are equally spaced;
   (1200, 400)
32. a) 3.5 m   **b)** (2, 1.4)
33. a) (14, 30)   **b)** (10, 22)
34. a) 1.5   **b)** 19
35. a) (3, −5)   **b)** (4, 3)   **c)** (7, −3)
   d) $\left(-2 + \dfrac{15m}{m+n}, 15 - \dfrac{30m}{m+n}\right)$

Section 8.3 pp. 475–476

Practice (Section 8.3)

1. $-\dfrac{1}{4}$ **2.** $\dfrac{1}{3}$ **3.** −2

4. $\dfrac{2}{5}$ **5.** 1   **6.** $-\dfrac{3}{2}$

7. $\dfrac{1}{3}$ **8.** $-\dfrac{1}{2}$ **9.** $y = x + 1$

10. $y = -2x + 5$ **11.** $2x - 3y - 8 = 0$
12. $x + 2y + 11 = 0$
13. $4x + 3y + 2 = 0$

14. $y = \dfrac{6}{5}x$ **15.** $2\sqrt{2}$ **16.** $3\sqrt{2}$

17. $\dfrac{9\sqrt{10}}{10}$ **18.** $\sqrt{5}$ **19.** 2

20. 3   **21.** $3\sqrt{13}$ **22.** $2\sqrt{5}$
23. 2.1   **24.** 1.4   **25.** 1.8
26. 1.2   **27.** 0.5   **28.** 1.8
29. 2.5   **30.** 2.2   **31.** 0.7
32. 6.7   **33.** 4.2   **34.** 4.9
35. 4.5   **36.** 1.9   **37.** 0.2
38. 0.9   **39.** 7; 7; 4.95   **40.** 5; 2.5; 2.24
41. 14; 28; 12.52   **42.** 6; 2; 1.90   **43.** 6; 12; 5.37
44. 7; 2.33; 2.21   **45.** 2.6; 6.5; 2.41
46. 1.71; 1.09; 0.92

Applications and Problem Solving (Section 8.3)

47. 6.01
48. 6.7
49. 0; The point is on the line.
50. a) 3.94, 5.58, 3.78   **b)** 11.5
51. a) 0.38   **b)** 0.14
52. a) rectangle   **b)** 40

53. 60
54. yes
55. a) $y = \dfrac{7}{12x} - 20$ **c)** $y = 1.42x - 220.5$
   e) yes
56. a) 1.9 m   **b)** 2.375 m   **c)** no
57. a) 2.8   **b)** 1.8
   c) 6.4   **d)** 1.7
58. $99x - 77y - 121 = 0$
59. $\left(\dfrac{32}{3}, 0\right), \left(-\dfrac{8}{3}, 0\right)$
60. Answers may vary.
61. It is $\dfrac{\sqrt{3}}{2}$ times the *x*-intercept.

Investigating Math p. 477

1. c) $y = 2, y = -2$
2. b) $x = 3$
3. a) parallel   **c)** $y = x - 1$
4. b) $y = x, y = -x$

6. a) No; only the centre of the rectangle is
   equidistant from the vertices.
   b) $\left(\dfrac{3}{2}, 2\right)$

Section 8.4 pp. 481–482

Practice (Section 8.4)

1. $x^2 + y^2 = 25$
2. $x^2 + y^2 = 81$
3. $x^2 + y^2 = 6.25$
4. $x^2 + y^2 = 3$
5. $x^2 + y^2 = 20$
6. $x^2 + y^2 = d^2$
7. $x^2 + (y - 2)^2 = 25$
8. $(x - 2)^2 + (y - 4)^2 = 9$
9. $(x + 2)^2 + (y - 3)^2 = 64$
10. $(x - 5)^2 + (y + 2)^2 = 16$
11. $x^2 + y^2 = 2$
12. $(x + 3)^2 + (y + 8)^2 = 100$
13. $(x + 4)^2 + y^2 = 32$
14. $(x - a)^2 + (y + b)^2 = c^2$
15. $x^2 + y^2 = 100$
16. $x^2 + y^2 = 20$
17. $x^2 + y^2 = 18$
18. $x^2 + y^2 = 26$
19. $x^2 + y^2 = 36$
20. $x^2 + y^2 = 25$
21. $(x - 1)^2 + y^2 = 25$
22. $(x + 1)^2 + (y + 2)^2 = 25$
23. $x^2 + (y - 1)^2 = 10$
24. $(x - 2)^2 + (y - 5)^2 = 36$
25. $(x + 3)^2 + (y - 4)^2 = 13$
26. $(x - 11)^2 + (y + 9)^2 = 625$

27. $(0, 0), 7$

28. $(0, 7), 3$

29. $(-5, 0), 1$

30. $(3, 4), 5$

31. $(-1, 2), 2$

32. $(0, 0), 0.1$

33. $(-0.3, 0.2), 0.5$

34. $(312, -458), 80$

35. $(2, -1), 4$

36. $(a, b), c$

Applications and Problem Solving (Section 8.4)

37. a) yes   b) yes   c) no   d) yes

38. $2 \pm \sqrt{11}$

39. a) $x^2 + y^2 = 81$
    b) $(x - 50)^2 + (y - 30)^2 = 81$
    c) $(x + 30)^2 + (y + 50)^2 = 81$

40. a) $(x - 2)^2 + y^2 = 25$
    b) $(x - 1)^2 + (y + 1)^2 = 29$

41. $x^2 + y^2 = 20$

42. $x^2 + y^2 = 1\,440\,000; x^2 + y^2 = 12\,250\,000;$
    $x^2 + y^2 = 40\,960\,000$

43. $x^2 + y^2 = 1\,785\,062\,500$

44. $(5, 19), (5, -7)$

45. b) $y = -x + 1$

46. a) 34.4 b) 94.2

47. a) $x^2 + y^2 = a^2 + b^2$
    b) $(x - 1)^2 + (y - 2)^2 = (a - 1)^2 + (b - 2)^2$

48. a) at the centre of the ring
    b) at the closest point on the backboard
    c) at the top of the ring

49. a) $(-13, 0), (13, 0)$

50. a) $[1, 2]$ b) $[-3, -4]$ c) $[0, 1]$
    d) $[-2, 0]$ e) $[h, k]$

51. $x^2 + (y + 3)^2 = 34$

52. $x^2 + y^2 = 200$

53. $(x + 2)^2 + (y + 1)^2 = 25$

54. $(x - h)^2 + (y - h)^2 = 2h^2 + 6h + 9$

55. radius: 8; centre: $(5, -6)$

Section 8.5   pp. 488–491

Practice (Section 8.5)

1. $(3, 3), (-3, -3)$ 2. $(0, -5), (3, 4)$

3. $(-2, -6), (6, 2)$

4. no points of intersection

5. $(12, -5), (-12, -5)$

6. no points of intersection

7. $(3, 4)$ 8. $(3, -9), (-9, -3)$

9. $(-1, -1), (6, 6)$ 10. $(2, 4), (-3, -1)$

11. no points of intersection

12. $(0.2, 0.4), (-1, -2)$ 13. $(0, 0), (-1, 1)$

14. no points of intersection

15. $(0, -2.7), (0, -9.3)$ 16. $(3.8, 2), (8.2, 2)$

17. $(0.5, 4.0), (-4.1, -5.2)$

18. $(0.7, -4.4), (-13.5, 2.8)$

19. $(1, 6), (-8, 5)$

20. $(-9.0, 9.2), (10.9, 4.3)$

21. 8.94 22. 4

23. 4.9 24. 5.7

25. 6.8 26. 6.9

27. $y = 5, y = -5$ 28. $y = 7, y = -7$

29. $y = 1, y = -1$ 30. $y = 30, y = -30$

31. $y = -\dfrac{3}{4}, y = \dfrac{3}{4}$ 32. $y = 1.2, y = -1.2$

33. $x = 2, x = -2$ 34. $x = 8, x = -8$

35. $x = 15, x = -15$ 36. $x = 90, x = -90$

37. $x = 0.5, x = -0.5$ 38. $x = 4\sqrt{2}, x = -4\sqrt{2}$

39. $y = -x + 2$ 40. $y = x + 10$

41. $x - 3y + 10 = 0$

42. $2x + 5y - 29 = 0$

43. $2x + 3y - 13 = 0$

44. $5x + 7y + 74 = 0$

45. $x - 2y - 10 = 0$

46. $5x - 3y + 34 = 0$

47. a) $(2, 3)$ b) $x + 2y - 18 = 0$

48. b) $3x - 4y = 0$ 49. $x + 4y = 0$

50. $x + 5y - 12 = 0$ 51. $2x + 3y - 18 = 0$

52. $3x - y - 30 = 0$ 53. $3x + 7y - 13 = 0$

54. $2x + y + 4 = 0$ 55. 8

56. 4 57. $3\sqrt{10}$

58. $\sqrt{10}$ 59. $5\sqrt{3}$

60. $\sqrt{114}$ 61. 6

62. 4 63. $\sqrt{37}$

64. 1 65. $2\sqrt{5}$

66. $2\sqrt{33}$

Applications and Problem Solving (Section 8.5)

68. a) $(5, 0), (2, 1)$

70. a) $\sqrt{106}$ b) 5.1

71. $x = 1$

72. $y = -1$

73. $\sqrt{10}$

74. equal

75. $y = x, y = -x$

76. a) $x^2 + y^2 = 2500$ b) 33 min

77. $3x + 4y - 51 = 0$

78. $8x + 15y - 289 = 0$

79. a) 14.4 m   b) $4.1x - 5.9y + 51.62 = 0$

80. 23 km/h

81. a) $x - \sqrt{3}y + 2 = 0$ b) $4x - 2y - 5\sqrt{2} = 0$

82. $x^2 + y^2 = 49$

83. $(x + 1)^2 + (y - 3)^2 = 81$

84. a) $y = k + r, y = k - r$ b) $x = h + r, x = h - r$

85. a) $5x + 12y - 169 = 0$
    b) $5x + 12y + 169 = 0$

86. $x_1 x + y_1 y = x_1^2 + y_1^2$

87. $(x - \sqrt{10})^2 + (y - \sqrt{10})^2 = 10$; $(x + \sqrt{10})^2 + (y - \sqrt{10})^2 = 10$; $(x + \sqrt{10})^2 + (y + \sqrt{10})^2 = 10$; $(x - \sqrt{10})^2 + (y + \sqrt{10})^2 = 10$

88. $(x - 1)^2 + (y - 5)^2 = 25$

89. a) $(x - 5\sqrt{2})^2 + (y - 5\sqrt{2})^2 = 25$; $(x + 5\sqrt{2})^2 + (y + 5\sqrt{2})^2 = 25$
b) 9.4 m

90. $x^2 + y^2 = 20$

91. a) ± 8
b) $3x + 4y = 50$; $3x - 4y = 50$

92. a) $y = \dfrac{a + b}{a - bx}$

93. a) $\left(\dfrac{p + q}{2}, \dfrac{-p + q}{2}\right)$ **b)** $\dfrac{-p + q}{p + q}$
c) $\dfrac{-p - q}{q - p}$

94. a) $OT = r$, $OP = \sqrt{a^2 + b^2}$
b) $PT = \sqrt{a^2 + b^2 - r^2}$

95. a) $\dfrac{b}{a}$ **b)** $-\dfrac{a}{b}$
c) $ax + by = a^2 + b^2$

96. b) The distance is equal to the sum of their radii.
c) $(x - 3)^2 + (y + 1)^2 = 9$; $(x + 3)^2 + (y + 1)^2 = 9$. Yes; there are two possible answers.

97. a) 16
b) $(x - 16)^2 + (y - 2)^2 = 4$

98. 0, 1, 2, 3, or 4

Computer Data Bank p. 492

1 Takeoff and Landing
1. a) 36 **b)** 120 **c)** 36
d) 60 **e)** 92 **f)** 69
g) 109 **h)** 1
2. a) 114
3. b) 49.93%

2 Airport Categories
1. Answers will vary.

3 Comparing Aircraft
Some answers may vary due to rounding.
1. 19.5%, 8.1%, 0.8%
2. 93 turbofans, average wing span 42.0 m, average length 49.0 m, average height 13.7 m, average mass 161 t; 30 turboprops, average wing span 23.2 m, average length 23.0 m, average height 7.0 m, average mass 19 t
3. 22

4 Mach Numbers
1. British Aerospace Concorde, Mach 2.00
2. 12
3. 7 at 0.03, 5 at 0.04

5 Flight Path
1. Answers will vary.
2. 0.8 min, 2.0 min

Section 8.6 pp. 497–499

Practice (Section 8.6)
1. 22.2 **2.** 2.8 **3.** 8.0 **4.** 25.7
5. 111.2 **6.** 12.9 **7.** 44.7° **8.** 43.3°
9. 38.1° **10.** 49.7° **11.** 11.2 **12.** 12.4
13. 2.4 **14.** 11.6 **15.** 73.1 **16.** 16.5
17. 73.7° **18.** 44.1° **19.** 68.0° **20.** 25.3°
21. 110.2° **22.** 36.1°
23. $y = 8.5$ cm, $\angle Y = 63.8°$, $\angle Z = 26.2°$
24. $\angle L = 53°$, $l = 9.8$ cm, $k = 7.4$ cm
25. $\angle C = 34.9°$, $a = 5.9$ m, $c = 3.3$ m
26. $\angle D = 50.7°$, $\angle F = 39.3°$, $e = 23.5$ cm
27. $\angle B = 56°$, $b = 4.7$ m, $c = 3.6$ m
28. $\angle P = 52.0°$, $\angle Q = 99.5°$, $q = 13.0$ cm
29. $\angle L = 81.2°$, $\angle K = 36.8°$, $k = 10.2$ m
30. $\angle U = 33.9°$, $u = 40.6$ km, $w = 60.4$ km
31. $x = 4.3$ cm, $\angle Y = 46.6°$, $\angle Z = 41.1°$
32. $\angle F = 115.9°$, $\angle G = 37.4°$, $\angle H = 26.7°$
33. 66.8 **34.** 4.9 **35.** 31.0 **36.** 5.7
37. 6.0 **38.** 7.1 **39.** 9.7° **40.** 39.0°
41. 104.3° **42.** 37.8°

Applications and Problem Solving (Section 8.6)
43. 85.9 m **44.** 10.4° **45.** 30 964 km
46. 728 m **47.** 23 m **48.** 73 m
49. 13 m **50.** 20.8 mm
51. a) 15.6 **b)** 15.6 **c)** since sin 90° = 1
52. a) 9.0 **b)** 9.0 **c)** since cos 90° = 0
53. 31.3 m²

Investigating Math pp. 500–501

1 Exploring the SSA Case
1. a) 2 **b)** 2 **c)** 67°, 113°
2. a) 4.6 cm **b)** 90°
3. a) none **b)** 1
4. a) CB ≤ 6 **b)** CB > 6 **c)** no

2 Making Generalizations
1. a) 90° **b)** $a = b \sin A$
2. a) supplementary **b)** $\dfrac{a}{\sin A} = \dfrac{b}{\sin B}$
c) $b \sin A < a < b$
3. a) $a > b$ **b)** $a \le b$

3 Applying the Concepts

1. two **2.** one **3.** none
4. one **5.** none **6.** one
7. two **8.** none **9.** two
10. one

Section 8.7 pp. 510–512

Practice (Section 8.7)

1. $x = 46.7°$, $y = 133.3°$
2. $x = 130.1°$, $y = 49.9°$
3. $x = 39.3°$, $y = 140.7°$
4. $x = 46.0°$, $y = 134.0°$
5. $x = 56.9°$, $y = 123.1°$
6. $x = 120.0°$, $y = 60.0°$
7. one; $\angle B = 33.9°$, $\angle C = 104.1°$
8. two; $\angle C = 33.0°$, $\angle A = 120°$; or $\angle C = 147.0°$, $\angle A = 6.0°$
9. one; $\angle Q = 90°$, $\angle R = 30°$
10. two; $\angle L = 39.9°$, $\angle K = 102.8°$; or $\angle L = 140.1°$, $\angle K = 2.6°$
11. none
12. two; $\angle C = 66.9°$, $\angle A = 65.1°$; or $\angle C = 113.1°$, $\angle A = 18.9°$
13. one; $\angle Z = 25.7°$, $\angle Y = 34.3°$
14. none
15. $\angle B = 34.4°$, $\angle C = 100.6°$, $c = 41.7$ cm
16. $\angle X = 14.5°$, $\angle Z = 132.8°$, $z = 73.3$ cm
17. $\angle Q = 48.1°$, $\angle P = 91.6°$, $p = 54.4$ cm; or $\angle Q = 131.9°$, $\angle P = 7.8°$, $p = 7.4$ cm
18. $\angle F = 33.7°$, $\angle H = 41.3°$, $b = 4.2$ cm
19. no triangle
20. $\angle F = 76.5°$, $\angle D = 32.3°$, $d = 16.7$ cm; or $\angle F = 103.5°$, $\angle D = 5.3°$, $d = 2.9$ cm
21. no triangle
22. $\angle N = 52.7°$, $\angle M = 84.5°$, $m = 23.1$ cm; or $\angle N = 127.3°$, $\angle M = 9.9°$, $m = 4.0$ cm
23. a) $\angle BCD = 54.3°$, $\angle BDA = 125.7°$ **b)** 18.7 cm
24. 6.0 m
25. 5.3 cm
26. a) (0, 12) **b)** (0, 18.24) or (0, 5.74)
  c) not possible **d)** (0, 26.15)
27. a) 6
28. 24.78
29. 14.64

Applications and Problem Solving (Section 8.7)

30. $AB = 4\sqrt{2}$, $AC = 2\sqrt{5}$, $BC = 6$, $\angle ABC = 45°$, $\angle ACB = 63.43°$, $\angle CAB = 71.57°$; $AB = 4\sqrt{2}$, $BD = 2$, $DA = 2\sqrt{5}$, $\angle ABD = 45°$, $\angle ADB = 116.57°$, $\angle DAB = 18.43°$
31. 9 km or 4 km
32. a) 8 **b)** 8
33. 1.5 m **34.** 365 m **35.** 20.4 m

36. 3.6 h **37.** 0.004 s
39. a) 12.0 m **b)** 4.5 m **c)** 2.2 m
  d) 6.0 m **e)** 6.6 m
40. $AB = \sqrt{65}$, $BC = 7$, $CA = \sqrt{2}$, $\angle B = 7.1°$, $\angle A = 37.9°$, $\angle C = 135°$; $AB = \sqrt{65}$, $BC = 7$, $CA = 8\sqrt{2}$, $\angle A = 37.9°$, $\angle B = 97.1°$, $\angle C = 45°$
41. 286°, 14°

Investigating Math p. 513

1 Finding the Third Side

1. a) $c = 5$ **b)** one; there is one solution to the quadratic equation.
2. a) $c = 2.6$ or 7.4 **b)** two; there are two solutions to the quadratic equation.
3. a) $c = 13.3$ **b)** one; there is one positive solution to the quadratic equation.
4. a) no solution **b)** zero; there is no solution to the quadratic equation.

2 Solving Triangles

1. a) two triangles
  b) $b = 5.0$ cm, $\angle B = 89.6°$, $\angle C = 53.4°$; or $b = 1.4$ cm, $\angle B = 10.4°$, $\angle C = 126.6°$
2. a) no triangle
3. a) one triangle
  b) $r = 5.4$ cm, $\angle R = 58.5°$, $\angle T = 51.5°$
4. a) no triangle
5. a) two triangles
  b) $l = 3.9$ cm, $\angle L = 23.2°$, $\angle N = 115.6°$; or $l = 9.5$ cm, $\angle L = 74.4°$, $\angle N = 64.4°$
6. a) one triangle
  b) $c = 9.9$ cm, $\angle C = 60°$, $\angle B = 90°$
7. a) one triangle
  b) $p = 2.8$ cm, $\angle P = 9.4°$, $\angle Q = 20.6°$
8. a) no triangle

Connecting Math and Fashion
pp. 514–515

1 Developing a Formula

1. a) $l = g + 12\sqrt{d^2 + g^2}$
  b) $l = 6g + 2\sqrt{d^2 + g^2} + 5\sqrt{4d^2 + g^2}$
  c) $l = 6g + 6\sqrt{d^2 + g^2} + \sqrt{36d^2 + g^2}$
2. a) North American **b)** shoe store
3. Answers may vary.

2 Developing a More General Formula

1. a) $l = g + 2(n - 1)\sqrt{d^2 + g^2}$
  b) $l = (n - 1)g + 2\sqrt{d^2 + g^2} + (n - 2)\sqrt{4d^2 + g^2}$
  c) $l = (n - 1)g + (n - 1)\sqrt{d^2 + g^2} + \sqrt{(n - 1)2d^2 + g^2}$

2. a) North American   **b)** shoe store
3. a) North American
     b) European and shoe store
4. The lengths are all equal.
5. When $n = 2$, the formulas all simplify to the same formula: $l = g + 2\sqrt{d^2 + g^2}$.

3 Comparing With Other Styles
1. a) $l = (n - 1)(2d + g)$; $l = (n - 1)(2d + g)$
     b) equal
2. The length is less than all three other methods.
3. Answers may vary.

Review   pp. 516–517
6. $(0, 2)$
7. $(0, 1)$, $(3, 3)$
8. $(2, 2)$, $(1, -1)$, $(0, -4)$, $(-1, -7)$
9. $(1, -5.5)$
10. $(8.5, 1.5)$, $(4, 0)$, $(-0.5, -1.5)$
11. $\left(-\frac{4}{3}, 3\right)$, $\left(\frac{4}{3}, 0\right)$
12. $(7, 0)$, $(0, 14)$ **13.** $\frac{5\sqrt{2}}{2}$
14. $\frac{\sqrt{5}}{5}$ **15.** $\frac{6\sqrt{10}}{5}$
16. $4\sqrt{2}$ **17.** $2\sqrt{5}$
18. $\frac{2\sqrt{5}}{5}$ **19.** 5.7
20. 4.5 **21.** 6.0
22. 6; 2; 1.90 **23.** 7; 28; 6.79
24. 6; 12; 5.37 **25.** $x^2 + y^2 = 9$
26. $(x - 3)^2 + (y - 7)^2 = 49$
27. $(x + 7)^2 + (y + 3)^2 = 36$
28. $(x - 6)^2 + (y + 3)^2 = 144$
29. $(x + 4)^2 + (y - 5)^2 = 5$
30. $(x - 11)^2 + (y + 12)^2 = 27$
31. $(0, 0)$, 11
32. $(1, 0)$, 0.5
33. $(-3, 4)$, 9
34. $(3.5, -6.5)$, 8
35. $x^2 + y^2 = 100$
36. $x^2 + y^2 = 81$
37. $(x - 2)^2 + (y - 1)^2 = 9$
38. $(x + 1)^2 + (y - 3)^2 = 100$
39. $(x - 4)^2 + (y + 1)^2 = 65$
40. $(x + 5)^2 + (y + 5)^2 = 72$
41. a) $(-2.6, 2.3)$, $(-3.4, -0.3)$ **b)** 2.8
42. a) $(1, -3)$
43. a) $(3, -2)$
44. a) $(-5, 1)$, $(0, -4)$ **b)** 7.1
45. a) $(-3, 1)$
46. $x = \pm 20$, $y = \pm 20$
47. $x = \pm 15$, $y = \pm 15$
48. $x + 4y - 17 = 0$

49. $3x - 2y + 24 = 0$
50. $2\sqrt{34}$
51. $2\sqrt{17}$
52. $\angle F = 65°$, $e = 2.2$ cm, $d = 5.3$ cm
53. $m = 8.7$ cm, $\angle L = 45.2°$, $\angle M = 44.8°$
54. $\angle Y = 12.3°$, $\angle Z = 41.9°$, $z = 25.8$ m
55. $\angle S = 37.6°$, $\angle T = 112.2°$, $\angle U = 30.2°$
56. $\angle P = 73.2°$
57. 70 m
58. two triangles; $\angle H = 58.8°$, $\angle I = 101.2°$;
     or $\angle H = 121.2°$, $\angle I = 38.8°$
59. no triangle
60. one triangle; $\angle C = 20.4°$, $\angle A = 55.6°$
61. two triangles; $\angle M = 42.7°$, $\angle K = 111.3°$;
     or $\angle M = 137.3°$, $\angle K = 16.7°$
62. $\angle QRS = 62.7°$, $\angle QSP = 117.3°$, RS $= 3.6$ cm

Exploring Math   p. 517
1. 40 **2.** 33 **3.** 33 **4.** 27

Chapter Check   p. 518
4. $(-2, -3)$, $(1, -1)$, $(4, 1)$
5. $(-1, 3)$
6. $(0, 1)$, $(5, -2)$
7. $(0, -5.2)$, $(-1, -2.4)$, $(-2, 0.4)$, $(-3, 3.2)$
8. $(1.5, -2.5)$ **9.** $\left(\frac{2}{3}, 0\right)$, $\left(-\frac{2}{3}, 5\right)$
10. $\frac{3\sqrt{2}}{2}$ **11.** $\frac{6\sqrt{5}}{5}$
12. $\frac{7\sqrt{5}}{5}$ **13.** $\frac{9\sqrt{10}}{10}$
14. 3.8 **15.** 3.6
16. 3; 0.75; 0.73 **17.** 5; 15; 4.74
18. 3; 2; 1.66 **19.** $x^2 + y^2 = 64$
20. $(x + 2)^2 + (y - 7)^2 = 81$
21. $(x - 4)^2 + (y + 8)^2 = 10$
22. $(5, 0)$, 13
23. $(-6, 4.5)$, 4
24. $x^2 + y^2 = 64$
25. $x^2 + y^2 = 25$
26. $(x - 4)^2 + (y + 2)^2 = 25$
27. $(x + 2)^2 + (y + 3)^2 = 29$
28. a) $(2, 6)$, $(6, -2)$ **b)** 8.9
29. a) $(0.8, 3.4)$, $(-0.8, 4.6)$ **b)** 2
30. a) $(-1, -2)$, $(2, 1)$ **b)** 4.2
31. $3x - 5y + 34 = 0$
32. $x + 3y + 10 = 0$
33. $\sqrt{57}$
34. $b = 2.4$ m, $\angle B = 71.3°$, $\angle C = 18.7°$
35. $\angle Y = 61.3°$, $z = 27.5$ cm, $x = 57.2$ cm
36. $\angle P = 118.7°$, $\angle Q = 35.1°$, $\angle R = 26.2°$
37. $\angle H = 44.8°$, $\angle I = 46.4°$, $i = 30.9$ cm
38. no triangle

39. two triangles; $\angle T = 56.2°$, $\angle U = 94.8°$;
or $\angle T = 123.8°$, $\angle U = 27.2°$
40. one triangle; $\angle Y = 18.6°$, $\angle Z = 65.4°$
41. two triangles; $\angle H = 64.4°$, $\angle F = 74.6°$;
or $\angle H = 115.6°$, $\angle F = 23.4°$
42. AC = 38 m or AC = 52 m

Using the Strategies   p. 519

1. 51%   **2.** 150   **3.** 7π
4. A = 12, B = 20, C = 64, D = 4

5. $\dfrac{2}{3}$ **6.** 6   **7.** 17

8. 5   **10.** 2   **11.** 78°

Data Bank

2. 5.6 h

Cumulative Review, Chapters 5–8
pp. 520–521

Chapter 5

1. a) $(f + g)(x) = x^2 + 3x - 4$
   b) $(f - g)(x) = x^2 + x - 2$
   c) $(fg)(x) = x^3 + x^2 - 5x + 3$
   d) $\left(\dfrac{f}{g}\right)(x) = x + 3, x \neq 1$
   e) $f(x) + 2g(x) = x^2 + 4x - 5$
   f) $2(gg)(x) - f(x) = x^2 - 6x + 5$
2. a) $(f \circ g)(x) = -x^2$; $(g \circ f)(x) = x^2$
   b) f: domain: all real numbers, range: $y \leq 0$;
   g: domain: all real numbers, R: $y \geq 0$; $f \circ g$: domain:
   all real numbers, R: $y \leq 0$; $g \circ f$: domain: all real
   numbers, R: $y \geq 0$
3. $y = -3x - 6$
4. yes
5. a) domain: all real numbers, range: all real numbers
   b) $-2, 1, 3; 6$
   c) maximum: $(-0.8, 8.2)$, minimum: $(2.1, -4.1)$
   d) $f(x) > 0$: $-2 < x < 1, x > 3$;
      $f(x) < 0$: $x < -2, 1 < x < 3$
   e) no symmetry; negative, positive
6. a) domain: all real numbers, range: $y \geq 0$
   b) 1, 5   **c)** $f(x) \geq 0$: all values of x
   d) symmetric about $x = 3$
7. a) $x = -3, y = 1$
   b) domain: $x \neq 3$, range: $y \neq 1$
8. domain: $x \geq -3$, range: $y \geq 0$
9. no solution
10. 1.5
11. $-2 \leq m < 2$
12. $-3 \leq w \leq 1$

Chapter 6

1. a) 10, 12   **b)** $2n + 2$ people can be seated at n
   square tables joined in a row.
2. -1 is the opposite of 1. 0 has no opposite.
5. 16, 20, 24, 28, 32, 36, 40, 44, 48
6. 1, 2, 3, 4, 5, 6, 7, 8, 9, 11, 12, 13, 15, 17, 19
7. b) 13
8. a) true
   b) If the diagonals of a quadrilateral are
   perpendicular, with the longer one bisecting the
   shorter one, then the quadrilateral is a kite; true
   c) If the diagonals of a quadrilateral are not
   perpendicular, and the longer one does not
   bisect the shorter one, then the quadrilateral
   is not a kite; true

Chapter 7

2. 2.2 m
4. $x = 230°$
5. $a = 40°$, $b = 35°$, $c = 35°$, $d = 15°$, $e = 15°$
6. $a = 75°$
7. $x = 45°$, $y = 45°$, $z = 45°$
9. $x = 14.5$ cm, $y = 14.5$ cm
10. $a = 8$ cm, $b = 8.5$ cm, $c = 3$ cm
11. 11.8 cm, 53.0 cm²
12. 160°, 20°

Chapter 8

2. $(0, -2), (3, 1)$
3. $(-1, 4), (0, 1), (1, -2), (2, -5)$
4. $(2.5, 0), (5, -1), (7.5, -2)$
5. 2.8
6. 2.7
7. $x^2 + y^2 = 9$
8. $(x + 1)^2 + (y - 5)^2 = 16$
9. $x^2 + y^2 = 25$
10. $(x - 4)^2 + (y - 2)^2 = 20$
11. a) $(0, 5)$
12. a) $(4.0, -1.2), (5.0, -5.8)$ **b)** 4.7
13. $2\sqrt{5}$
14. $y = 3.3$ m, $\angle Y = 69.9°$, $\angle Z = 20.1°$
15. $\angle J = 34°$, $j = 12.5$ cm, $k = 18.3$ cm
16. 0.7 m or 2.6 m

CHAPTER 9

Personal Finance

Chapter Introduction

Chapter Materials

scientific or graphing calculators, Teacher's Resource Master 8 (budget sheet), business sections of newspapers, overhead projector, spreadsheet software

Chapter Concepts

Chapter 9 reviews or introduces
- calculating total earnings
- calculating net earnings
- calculating interest and annuities
- calculating the effective annual rate of interest
- calculating debt generated from credit cards distributed by stores
- calculating mortgages and total costs of housing
- balancing and adjusting a budget

Teaching Suggestions

Read with the class the opening paragraph of student text page 523. Discuss the characteristics of the graph. Ask:

What is the meaning of the wavy line in the lower part of the vertical axis?

Give pairs of students an opportunity to research the answers to the questions. Have volunteers present their results to the class.

For question 5, ask:

How can you tell from the graph when the Canadian dollar is worth more than the US dollar? less than the US dollar? the same as the US dollar?

Integrating Technology

Internet

Use the Internet to find more information about the value of the Canadian dollar in US dollars and reasons for the fluctuations.

Enrichment

Think of today's price of an item or the cost of attending an event. Use the graph given on student text page 523 to find the corresponding price of that item or event in a previous year of your choice. Then, research the actual price of that item or event in the year of your choice. Are the two prices you found the same? Explain any differences in price.

Present your examples to the class and discuss your explanation with your classmates.

Assessing the Outcomes

Observation

You might consider some of these questions as you observe the students work.
- Do the students know how to research the required data?
- Are the students able to read data from the graph?
- Do the students persist until they find a solution?
- Do the students attempt all the questions?

Getting Started

Student Text Pages
Pp. 524–525

Learning Outcomes
* Calculate unit prices.
* Use unit price to determine the better buy.

Teaching Suggestions

Comparing Unit Prices

Assign this exploration to pairs of students. For question 2, ask:

Is the unit price always the best way to determine the best deal?

Lead the students in a discussion about how people choose the best buy. For example, if the best buy requires the purchase of a very large quantity of an item, and the person purchasing the item lives alone, or is part of a very small family, so that the item will spoil before being used, then the lowest unit price is not always the best buy.

For question 3, ask:

What is a trend?

Have volunteers present their results to the class.

Buying at a Supermarket

Assign this exploration to pairs of students and have volunteers present their results to the class.

Warm Up

Assign some or all of the questions as individual or group work. Students could record their answers in their notebooks, or take turns asking questions orally with a partner.

When the students have finished, have them discuss the methods they used to answer the questions.

Mental Math

Students could choose, or be assigned, certain questions from each section. Alternatively, small groups could work as teams, sharing the questions and explaining the answers to the rest of the group.

Assessing the Outcomes

Observation

You may want to consider some of the following skills as the students complete this lesson.
* Do the students appear to be able to solve the Mental Math questions?
* Do the students understand the process of finding the unit price?
* Do the students provide reasons for their answers?
* Do the students work well together or do they tend to work independently?

Investigating Math

Foreign Exchange

Student Text Page
P. 526

Materials

graphing calculators, business sections of newspapers

Learning Outcomes

- Use exchange rates to convert from one currency to another.
- Use exchange rates to convert from one currency to a second and then, from the second currency to a third.
- Calculate the cost of buying one currency using another.
- Calculate the cost of selling one currency using another.

Mental Math

1. Express each as a percent.

a) $8.00 out of $400	[2%]	
b) $55 out of $2000	[2.75%]	
c) $1.50 out of $60	[2.5%]	
d) $200 out of $400	[50%]	
e) $2.50 out of $10	[25%]	
f) $4 out of $2	[200%]	

2. Calculate the mean of each pair of numbers.

a) 7, 15	[11]		**b)** $-12, -30$	[-21]	
c) 22, -10	[6]		**d)** 150, 162	[156]	
e) 3.2, 5.6	[4.4]		**f)** 25, 245	[135]	

Teaching Suggestions

(graphing calculators, business sections of newspapers)
Discuss with the students the different currencies of the world. Invite the students to bring to class any samples of foreign coins they may have at home. Make a class display of the different currencies along with the name of the currency, the country of origin, and the current exchange rate. Ask:

How many of you have ever exchanged one foreign currency for another?

Where did this exchange take place?

Provide the business section of a national newspaper so that the students can find the exchange rates. Assign the investigations to pairs of students. Have volunteers present their results to the class.

Integrating Technology

Internet
Use the Internet to find current exchange rates and then, use them to answer the questions on student text page 526.

Enrichment

Write a few sentences describing how a change in the rate of exchange of a currency of a country can affect the imports and exports of that country. Discuss and compare your essay with other students and present your results to the class.

Math Journal

Research the careers that involve the exchange of foreign currencies. Write a short essay describing one of the careers.

Assessing the Outcomes

Observation

- Does the student understand how to convert from one currency to another?
- Does the student understand why the exchange rate of a currency is different depending on whether you are buying or selling the currency?
- Is the student able to explain his or her method of solution?
- Does the student help others to understand the concept being studied?

9.1 Earning Income

Student Text Pages
Pp. 527–531

Materials
graphing calculators, spreadsheet software

Learning Outcomes
- Define the term "gross income."
- Calculate gross income from earning an hourly rate.
- Calculate gross income from earning gratuities.
- Calculate gross income from commissions.
- Calculate gross income from earning by piecework.

Prerequisite Skills
1. Calculate.

a) 25% of $2050   [$512.50]

b) 1.2% of $35 490   [$425.88]

c) 3% of $2500 + 4.5% of $20 000   [$975.00]

d) 7% of $36.55 + 24% of $99   [$26.32]

2. What percent is the first amount of the second amount?

a) $20, $500   [4%]

b) $21.36, $213.60   [10%]

c) $849.60, $35 400   [2.4%]

d) $1095, $7300   [15%]

Mental Math
Calculate.

a) 25×35 [875]

b) 0.75×65 [48.75]

c) 1.5×25 [37.5]

d) 35×4.5 [157.5]

e) 11.5×1.25 [14.375]

f) 550×45 [24 750]

Explore/Inquire Answers

Explore: Interpret the Graph
a) Newfoundland, Ontario

b) Ontario, Alberta, British Columbia

Inquire
1. Answers will vary.

2. Some lower income areas have lower costs, which at least has a counter effect, so that the lower income may not indicate a much lower standard of living.

3. Answers will vary.

Teaching Suggestions
Introduce the term "gross income," and ask students to explain what the term means. Ask:

How many have a part-time job?

How do you calculate your gross income?

Why is it important to be able to calculate gross income?

Read with the class the opening paragraph on student text page 527. Assign the Explore section and the Inquire questions to pairs of students. Have volunteers present their results to the class. Ask:

How is the average Canadian household cash income calculated?

What factors could affect the average Canadian household cash income?

Review with the class teaching example 1 on student text page 528. Ask:

What types of jobs use the hourly rate as a method of payment?

Does anyone in the class calculate income using the hourly rate method?

Review with the class teaching example 2 on student text page 528. Ask:

Do you think it is fair to give part of a tip to employees who do not earn in tips directly?

What other jobs besides waiting tables generate tips?

Review with the class teaching example 3 on student text page 529. Ask:

What type of jobs use commissions as a method of payment?

Why do you think commissions are used as a method of payment?

Review with the class teaching example 4 on student text page 530. Ask:

What type of jobs use piecework as a method of payment?

Do you think this is a fair method of payment? Explain.

Sample Solution

Page 531, question 28

a) $3000 = $2000 + $1000

Gross earnings for first month

= $2000 + 6.5% of $1000

= $2000 + $65

= $2065

$2885 = $2000 + $885

Gross earnings for second month

= $2000 + 6.5% of $885

= $2000 + $57.53

= $2057.53

$5088 = $2000 + $3088

Gross earnings for third month
= $2000 + 6.5% of $3088
= $2000 + $200.72
= $2200.72
$5227 = $2000 + $3227

Gross earnings for fourth month
= $2000 + 6.5% of $3227
= $2000 + $209.76
= $2209.76

His gross monthly earnings for the four previous months were $2065, $2057.53, $2200.72, and $2209.76.

b)

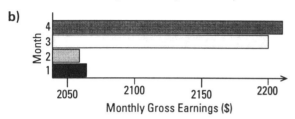

Monthly Gross Earnings ($)

Integrating Technology

Computer Spreadsheets

Use spreadsheet software to construct the graph in Inquire question 3 on student text page 527.

Internet

Use the Internet to find the average cash income for Canadian households by province to answer Inquire question 3 on student text page 527.

Enrichment

Write a short essay about the different methods of payment for employment, and which method you prefer. Justify your choice.

Math Journal

gross income Write a definition of gross income, and list the different methods used to calculate the gross income of employees.

Problem Levels of Difficulty

A: 1–19, 29   **B:** 20–26   **C:** 27, 28

Assessing the Outcomes

Written Assignment

Calculate the gross income for each employee.

a) Andre is paid $14.50/h. One week he works 35 h.

b) Simone works in a coffee shop and is paid $7/h plus tips. She is required to give 20% of her tips to the kitchen staff. One week she works 39 h.

c) Miranda is paid 3% on her first $10 000 of sales plus 4.5% on sales over $10 000. One week her sales were $22 559.

d) Tony makes birdhouses for an environmental supplies store. He is paid $19 per birdhouse. One week he provides the store with 23 birdhouses.

9.2 Net Income

Student Text Pages
Pp. 532–537

Materials
graphing calculators

Learning Outcomes
• Calculate Canada Pension Plan contributions and Employment Insurance premiums.
• Calculate net annual income.

Prerequisite Skills
1. Calculate 3.2% of each amount.
a) $23 501   [$752.03]
b) $15 770   [$504.64]
c) $42 500   [$1360.00]
d) $4006   [$128.19]
2. Calculate 2.7% of each amount in question 1.
[a) $634.53   b) $425.79   c) $1147.50   d) $108.16]

Mental Math
1. Calculate.
a) 15×0.25 [3.75]
b) 45×350 [15 750]
c) 65×75 [4875]
d) 5.5×4.5 [24.75]
e) 250×350 [87 500]
f) 9.5×8.5 [80.75]
2. Calculate.
a) 34×36 [1224]   b) 5.7×5.3 [30.21]
c) 710×79 [56 090]   d) 98×920 [90 160]
e) 1.6×14 [22.4]   f) 66×640 [42 240]

Explore/Inquire Answers

Explore: Use a Table
a) British Columbia   b) Answers will vary.

Inquire
1. 44.4%; 49.3%   2. June 25
3. Answers will vary.

Teaching Suggestions
Read with the class the opening paragraph on student text page 532. Assign the Explore section and the Inquire questions. Have volunteers present their results to the class.

Review with the class the paragraphs immediately preceding teaching example 1 on student text page 532. Ask:
How many pay Canada Pension Plan contributions?
Review teaching example 2 on student text pages 534 and 535.

Logic Power Answer
1. This is a standard graphing problem, and the diagram is a network with 14 odd vertices and 43 edges. Any network with more than 2 odd vertices cannot be walked around without crossing some edges more than once. An edge with a single arrowhead represents a walk in the direction of the arrowhead. An edge with a double arrowhead represents a walk in one direction and then the return direction.
   In order to change odd vertices into even vertices, odd vertices are paired with an edge containing a double arrowhead. Except for two of the odd vertices (unpaired vertices), pair the odd vertices with an edge containing a double arrowhead, ensuring that each odd vertex is paired only once. Begin the walk at one of the odd unpaired vertices, and end at the other odd unpaired vertex. The diagram at the right is one example of this arrangement of paired odd vertices.

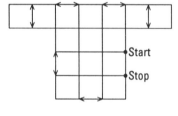

The diagram at the right is one example of Tabitha's completed route. There are many others.

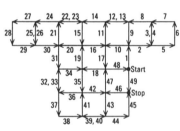

The numbers represent the order of the edges taken.
2. Since the network has 43 edges and 6 of the edges are repeated, the minimum distance is 43 + 6 = 49.

Integrating Technology

Internet

Use the Internet to find
• current Tax Freedom Day data to answer Inquire question 3 on student text page 532
• current rates for CPP, EI, and income tax to answer the questions on student text pages 536 and 537

- tables used by payroll departments to answer question 36 on student text page 537
- how to collect employment insurance benefits to answer question 37 on student text page 537

Enrichment

Research the meaning of the term "long-term disability," and write a few sentences about whether you think it should be compulsory for an employee to purchase it. Present your results to the class, and have a class debate about the pros and cons of long-term disability.

Math Journal

Write a few sentences describing how CPP contributions, EI premiums, and net income are calculated.

Problem Levels of Difficulty

A: 1–30. 37, 38   **B:** 31–34   **C:** 35, 36

Assessing the Outcomes

Written Assignment

Rachel is a sales representative in a toy store. Her gross weekly earnings are $400. Her basic personal tax credit is $6456 and she pays a monthly contribution of $100 to an RRSP.

a) Calculate her annual deductions for CPP and EI.

b) Calculate her annual taxes.

c) Calculate her net annual income.

9.3 Interest and Annuities

Student Text Pages
Pp. 538–543

Materials
scientific or graphing calculators, spreadsheet software

Learning Outcomes
• Calculate compound interest.
• Compare amounts with different compounding periods.
• Compare registered retirement savings investments.
• Calculate the amount of an annuity.

Prerequisite Skills

1. Calculate each amount.

a) 6% of $500 [$30]

b) 3.5% of $25 [$0.88]

c) 1.5% of $2500 [$37.50]

d) 0.75% of $500 000 [$3750]

2. Evaluate each formula for the value of the given variables. Round your answer to the nearest tenth, if necessary.

a) $P = 2l + 2w$, $l = 10$, $w = 3$ [26]

b) $A = \pi r^2$, $r = 3.5$, $\pi = 3.14$ [38.5]

c) $D = \dfrac{M}{V}$; $M = 30$, $V = 48$ [0.63]

Mental Math

1. Calculate.

a) 45×35 [1575]   b) 75×650 [48 750]

c) 65×55 [3575]   d) 105×9.5 [997.5]

e) 2.5×150 [375]   f) 3.5×0.25 [0.875]

2. Copy and complete each ordered pair so that it satisfies the given equation.

a) $x + y = -1$; ($\blacksquare$, 2) [−3]

b) $2x - y = 3$; (-1, $\blacksquare$) [−5]

c) $y = \dfrac{1}{2}x + 7$; ($\blacksquare$, 12) [10]

d) $3x + y - 6 = 0$; ($\blacksquare$, -3) [3]

e) $-x + 4y = 12$; (4, $\blacksquare$) [4]

f) $y = 5x - 2$; (-3, $\blacksquare$) [−17]

Explore/Inquire Answers

Explore: Use a Table

Year	Principal ($) (at the beginning of the year)	Interest Rate (%)	Amount ($) (at the end of the year)
1	1000.00	5.5	1055.00
2	1055.00	5.5	1113.03
3	1113.03	5.5	1174.25
4	1174.25	5.5	1238.83
5	1238.83	5.5	1306.97
6	1306.97	5.5	1378.85

Inquire

1. $378.85   **2.** $330.00

3. Answers may vary.

4. a) $200   **b)** $506.25

Teaching Suggestions

Read with the class the opening paragraphs on student text page 538. Review the formula for calculating simple interest and compound interest. Ask.

Where do you see examples of simple interest?

Where do you see examples of compound interest?

Assign the Explore section and the Inquire questions to pairs of students. Ask:

What formula is used to calculate each line in the table in the Explore section?

How do you find the amount?

Ensure that the students use the simple interest formula, and that the amount is the sum of the principal and the interest.

Have volunteers present their results to the class.

Review with the class the information presented on student text page 539. Ask:

Does anyone have a Canada Savings Bond?

Work through teaching examples 1 to 4 on student text pages 540 to 542.

Integrating Technology

Graphing Calculators

How would you use your graphing calculator to perform the interest calculations in teaching examples 1 and 2 on student text page 540? On a TI-83, in each solution shown, i is evaluated and the ANS (i.e., 2nd (−)) key is used to substitute i into the expression for A. The calculations could be performed in one step by placing brackets around the division required for i.

Use a graphing calculator to perform the calculations required in the questions on student text page 543.

Computer Spreadsheets

How would you use a spreadsheet as in solution 2 of teaching example 4 on student text page 542? Set 2 as a fixed number of decimal places for the cells with monetary values. Enter the headings, the first column, the initial principal, and the formulas =B2*.05*.5 in cell C2, =B2+C2 in cell C3, and =750+D2 in cell B3. Then, use the Fill Down feature to complete the columns.

Use spreadsheet software to determine some of the amounts in the questions on student text page 543.

Internet

Use the Internet to find more information about the history of paying interest on borrowed money.

Extension

Write a few sentences describing the advantages and disadvantages of each type of Canada Savings Bond.

Enrichment

When investing in GICs, Canada Savings Bonds, and other financial vehicles, time is considered to be the most important factor in generating the best return on an investment. Research the meaning of this statement, and write a few sentences justifying it.

Math Journal

simple interest, compound interest, annuity   Write the definition of each of these terms in your journal. Include formulas and examples for clarity.

Common Errors

- Students often have difficulty distinguishing between simple interest and compound interest.

R_x Explain to the students that simple interest uses the original principal amount, whereas compound interest adds the interest earned at the end of one compound time period to the principal at the beginning of the compound period. This total amount then becomes the principal at the beginning of the next compound period.

Problem Levels of Difficulty

A: 1–32, 37   **B:** 33–35   **C:** 36

Assessing the Outcomes

Written Assignment

1. Ryan borrows $2000 for 2 years at 9.5% per annum, compounded semi-annually. How much does Ryan need to repay the loan?

2. Siva is paid on the 30th of each month. On the first day of each month she deposits $200 into a savings account that pays 4.5% per annum, compounded monthly. What will Siva's savings amount to at the end of the month after she has made three deposits?

Observation

- Does the student understand simple interest, compound interest, and annuities?
- Is the student able to perform the algebra required to make the calculations?
- Does the student help others to understand the concept being studied?
- Does the student persevere in finding the correct answer?

Technology

Financial Calculations Using A Graphing Calculator

Student Text Pages
Pp. 544–545

Materials
graphing calculator with capability to perform financial calculations

Learning Outcome
• Determine number of payment periods, annual interest rate, present value, payment, or future value, given the others, using a graphing calculator.

Prerequisite Skills
Interpret the following problem to enter the known and unknown values in the table below.

An annuity of $50 000 earning 6.75% per annum, compounded monthly, pays $750 monthly. What is the value of the annuity after 3 years?

Number of payment periods	[12 × 3]
Annual interest rate, %	[6.75]
Present value, $	[50 000]
Payment, $	[750]
Future value, $	[unknown]
Payments per year	[12]
Compounding periods in a year	[12]

Teaching Suggestions

Discuss how to use a graphing calculator to perform financial calculations, as shown on student text pages 544 to 545, using the introductory paragraphs on student text page 544. On a TI-83, the TMV Solver, which is the first item under the CALC menu when the FINANCE (i.e., 2nd x^{-1}) key is pressed, is used. Point out that TMV stands for Time Value of Money.

Using the problem in *Prerequisite Skills* above, work through the steps with the class. Interpret the problem and determine the six values to be entered and the one to be calculated, as done in the *Prerequisite Skills*. Discuss whether present value or payment should be negative—one must be. From the investor's point of view, $50 000 has been paid out and $750 will be received each month. So, the values would be −50 000 and 750. Or, from the financial institution's point of view, $50 000 has come in and $750 per month must be paid out. So, the values would be 50 000 and −750.

Have some students perform the calculation from the investor's point of view and others from the financial institution's point of view.

Press the MODE key, move the cursor to 2 in the second line, and press the ENTER key to select two decimal places.
Press the FINANCE (i.e., 2nd x^{-1}) key and the 1 key to select TMV Solver.
Enter each value in order, followed by the ENTER key. N can be entered as 12 × 3.
At FV, press the down arrow key, leaving whatever value was there last.
END is selected by default, indicating that payments are made at the end of each period.
Press the up arrow key to move the cursor to FV.
Press the SOLVE (i.e., ALPHA ENTER) key.

Discuss how to interpret the results from each point of view. When PV is entered as a negative value and PMT as a positive value, i.e., from the investor's point of view, FV is $31 352.87, which indicates that there is still $31 352.87 to come to the investor. When PV is entered as a positive value and PMT as a negative value, i.e., from the financial institution's point of view, FV is −$31 352.87, which indicates that the financial institution must still pay $31 352.87. Either way, the value of the annuity is $31 352.87.

Discuss the effect of payments being made versus no payments being made. Assign each exploration, encouraging students to record the values that must be entered before actually entering them, and to discuss each problem to facilitate interpretation of their results.

See *MATHPOWER™ 11, Western Edition, Blackline Masters* pages 204 to 206 for Financial Calculations.

Common Errors
• Some students have difficulty entering the correct values for N, P/Y, and C/Y.

R_x Remind students to first record the values to be entered, and to refer to the examples on student text pages 544 and 545 to help them.

• Many students forget to enter negative monetary values and, therefore, obtain incorrect results.

R_x Suggest that students perform each calculation from both the lender's and borrower's points of view.

Assessing the Outcome

Journal

Write about the importance of understanding the values being entered in financial calculations in order to interpret the results.

Technology

Calculating Annuities Using a Spreadsheet

Student Text Page
P. 546

Materials
spreadsheet software

Learning Outcomes
- Determine the amount remaining in an annuity using spreadsheet software.
- Determine the equal monthly payments of an annuity using spreadsheet software.

Prerequisite Skills
1. What is the interest per quarter when the interest rate is 8.75% per annum, compounded quarterly?
$$\left[\frac{0.0875}{4}\right]$$

2. What is the interest for one month when the interest rate is 6.5% per annum, compounded monthly?
$$\left[\frac{0.065}{12}\right]$$

Teaching Suggestions
Discuss the spreadsheet shown on student text page 546. Discuss why the interest calculation has B2 multiplied by $\frac{0.11}{12}$, and why the closing balance is B2 plus C2 less D2.

Assign the explorations. Remind students to set 2 as a fixed number of decimal places for the cells with monetary values.

To use the Fill Down feature, select a cell with a formula and the cells in the column below it that are to be completed. Columns A and B can be completed at the same time because they start at the same row. Then, columns C, D, and E can be completed at the same time because they too start at the same row. As successive columns are completed, the entries in the previous columns will change, and are only accurate when the last column has been completed.

Discuss how to determine suitable starting points for finding the equal monthly payments based on, for example, starting a bit higher than the amount it would be if the principal was simply divided into the set number of equal payments, and results of previous questions. After the value of the payment is changed in the first row, the other cells in the column do not automatically change. They can be changed using the Fill Down feature.

Extension
Answer the questions on student text page 546 using a graphing calculator with financial calculation capabilities.

Common Errors
- Some students do not recognize the power of the spreadsheet software, and think they should complete a row at a time.

$\mathbf{R}_x$ Have students determine the initial values and all the formulas to be entered before entering anything, as done on student text page 546, and then, have them use the Fill Down feature to see how all the values change as the software applies each formula to its column.

Assessing the Outcomes

Written Assignment
Compare and contrast using a graphing calculator and using spreadsheet software to perform financial calculations. What are some advantages of each?

9.4 Effective Annual Rate of Interest

Student Text Pages
Pp. 547–550

Materials
scientific or graphing calculators

Learning Outcomes
- Calculate the effective annual interest rate.
- Use effective annual interest rates to determine the better investment.

Prerequisite Skills
1. Calculate.
a) 10% of $250   [$25]
b) 13% of $500   [$65]
c) 0.5% of $5000   [$25]
d) 150% of $600   [$900]

2. Calculate the simple interest earned on each amount.
a) $200 at 5% per annum for 3 months   [$2.50]
b) $3000 at 2.5% per annum for 2 years   [$150]
c) $60 at 10% per annum for 6 months   [$3]

Mental Math
1. Calculate.
a) 15×0.05 [0.75]
b) 3.5×45 [157.5]
c) 0.55×450 [247.5]
d) 7.5×65 [487.5]
e) 950×850 [807 500]
f) 11.5×10.5 [120.75]

2. Evaluate each expression for the given values of x.
a) $-x + 5$; $x = 1, 2, 3, 4$ [4, 3, 2, 1]
b) $2x - 4$; $x = -2, -4, -6, -8$ [−8, −12, −16, −20]
c) $x^2 + 7$; $x = 0, 1, 3, 5$ [7, 8, 16, 32]
d) $-2x^3$; $x = -2, -1, 0, 1, 2$ [16, 2, 0, −2, −16]
e) $(x - 2)^2$; $x = 1, 2, 3, 4$ [1, 0, 1, 4]
f) $-(x + 1)^2 + 3$; $x = -3, -2, -1, 0$ [−4, −1, 0, −1]

Explore/Inquire Answers
Explore: Use a Table

	Principal ($)	Nominal Annual Interest Rate (%)	Compound Period	Amount ($)
A	$100	4	semi-annually	$104.04
B	$100	5	quarterly	$105.10
C	$100	9.76	semi-annually	$115.12
D	$100	9.65	quarterly	$110.00

Inquire
1. $4.04, $5.10, $15.12, $10
2. 4.04%, 5.1%, 15.12%, 10%
3. yes
4. a) $576   b) 576%
5. a) $9125   b) 9125%

Teaching Suggestions
Read with the class the opening paragraphs on student text page 547. Review the terms "nominal interest rate" and "effective interest rate." Review the formulas for simple interest and compound interest. Assign the Explore section and the Inquire questions to small groups of students. Give the students an opportunity to discuss and compare their results. Have volunteers present their results to the class. Work through teaching examples 1 and 2 on student text pages 548 to 549.

Sample Solution
Page 550, question 18, parts a) and b)

For 1 compound period per year, nominal interest rate is 12%.

For 2 compound periods per year, nominal interest rate for each period is 6%:

For an investment of $1, $A = (1 + 0.06)^2$
$$= 1.1236$$
Interest earned is $1.1236 − $1 = $0.1236
This is equivalent to 12.36% per annum.

For 3 compound periods per year, nominal interest rate for each period is 4%:

For an investment of $1, $A = (1 + 0.04)^3$
$$= 1.1249$$
Interest earned is $1.1249 − $1 = $0.1249
This is equivalent to 12.49% per annum.

For 4 compound periods per year, nominal interest rate for each period is 3%:

For an investment of $1, $A = (1 + 0.03)^4$
$$= 1.1255$$
Interest earned is $1.1255 − $1 = $0.1255
This is equivalent to 12.55% per annum.

For 6 compound periods per year, nominal interest rate for each period is 2%:

For an investment of $1, $A = (1 + 0.02)^6$
$$= 1.1262$$
Interest earned is $1.1262 − $1 = $0.1262
This is equivalent to 12.62% per annum.

For 12 compound periods per year, nominal interest rate for each period is 1%:

For an investment of $1, $A = (1 + 0.01)^{12}$
$$= 1.1268$$
Interest earned is $1.1268 − $1 = $0.1268
This is equivalent to 12.68% per annum.

For 24 compound periods per year, nominal interest rate for each period is 0.5%:

For an investment of $1, $A = (1 + 0.005)^{24}$
$$= 1.1272$$
Interest earned is $1.1272 − $1 = $0.1272
This is equivalent to 12.72% per annum.

For 52 compound periods per year, nominal interest rate for each period is 0.2308%:

For an investment of $1, $A = (1 + 0.002\ 308)^{52}$
$$= 1.1274$$
Interest earned is $1.1274 − $1 = $0.1274
This is equivalent to 12.74% per annum.

b)

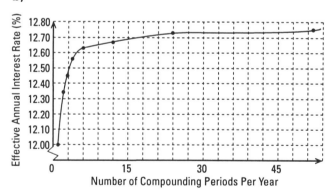

Word Power Answer

a, at, rat, rate, tamer, stream, mastery

Integrating Technology

Graphing Calculators

How would you use your graphing calculator to perform the calculations in teaching examples 1 and 2 on student text page 548? On a TI-83, in each solution shown, *i* is evaluated and the ANS (i.e., 2nd (−) key is used to substitute *i* into the expression for *A*. The calculations could be performed in one step by placing brackets around the division required for *i*.

How would you use your graphing calculator to answer question 19 on student text page 550? On a TI-83, the effective annual interest rate is option C under the CALC menu when the FINANCE (i.e., 2nd x^{-1}) key is pressed. (Use the down arrow key to see the last items.)

Use a graphing calculator to perform the calculations required in the questions on student text pages 549 and 550.

Enrichment

Write a short essay describing the use of finding the effective interest rate.

Math Journal

nominal interest rate, effective interest rate   Include in your journal the definition of each of these terms.

Problem Levels of Difficulty

A: 1–12   **B:** 13–17, 19   **C:** 18, 20

Assessing the Outcomes

Written Assignment

Which is the better investment?
A: $5000 invested at 5.2% per annum, compounded quarterly

B: $4500 invested at 6.5% per annum, compounded monthly

9.5 Consumer Credit

Student Text Pages
Pp. 551–556

Materials
graphing calculators, spreadsheet software

Learning Outcomes
- Calculate the instalment cost.
- Calculate the interest on a retail charge account.
- Calculate the interest on a bank credit card.

Prerequisite Skills
Calculate the simple interest earned on each amount.
a) $100 at 6% per annum for 30 days   [$0.49]
b) $1500 at 8.5% per annum for 60 days   [$20.96]
c) $240 at 15% per annum for 3 months   [$9.00]

Mental Math
1. Evaluate.
a) 5% of $50   [$2.50]
b) 1.2% of $250   [$3.00]
c) 10% of $135   [$13.50]
d) 50% of $95   [$47.50]
e) 2.5% of $2500   [$62.50]
f) 6% of $45 000   [$2700]
2. Simplify.
a) $\sqrt{32}$ $[4\sqrt{2}]$
b) $-\sqrt{108}$ $[-6\sqrt{3}]$
c) $\sqrt{18} + \sqrt{8}$ $[5\sqrt{2}]$
d) $\sqrt{12} - \sqrt{27} + 3$ $[3 - \sqrt{3}]$
e) $-\sqrt{50} + 5\sqrt{2}$ $[0]$
f) $-(3\sqrt{7})^2 + 40$ $[-23]$

Explore/Inquire Answers

Explore: Interpret the Information
a) $658.80   b) $59.80

Inquire
1. The store makes money, either directly from finance charges, or indirectly by selling the instalment contract to a finance company for more than the price of the item.
2. The store added 10% to the cost, then divided by 12.
3. Answers may vary.

Teaching Suggestions
Discuss with the class the term "consumer credit." Ask:
What is a consumer?
What is consumer credit?
How does a person obtain consumer credit?
How many of you have credit cards?

Read with the class the opening paragraphs on student text page 551. Ask:
Why do you think the assessment for a credit rating is partly based on past record of debt paying? character? assets? present ability to repay?

Assign the Explore section and the Inquire questions to small groups of students. Remind the students that the down payment must be included in the total instalment cost of the item. Have volunteers present their results to the class.

Review with the class teaching examples 1 to 3 on student text pages 551 to 555.

Integrating Technology

Graphing Calculators

Use a calculator to perform the calculations required in the questions on student text pages 555 and 556.

Computer Spreadsheets

Use spreadsheet software to complete the table in question 28 on student text page 556.

Enrichment
Write a short essay explaining why a poor credit rating can cause problems in your every day life.

Math Journal
credit rating   Write a definition of credit rating, including how a credit rating is assessed.

Problem Levels of Difficulty
A: 1–26, 32   **B:** 27–29   **C:** 30, 31

Assessing the Outcomes

Written Assignment

The selling price of a refrigerator is $890, including taxes. You make a down payment of $100 and agree to pay $55.75 per month for 18 months.

a) Calculate the instalment price of the refrigerator.

b) Calculate the interest charges on the instalment price.

9.6 Housing Costs

Student Text Pages
Pp. 557–561

Materials
graphing calculators

Learning Outcomes
- Calculate monthly mortgage payments.
- Calculate property taxes.
- Calculate housing costs.

Prerequisite Skills

1. Calculate.

a) 2% of $300   [$6.00]

b) 1.75% of $5000   [$87.50]

c) 3.5% of $60 000   [$2100]

2. Calculate what percent the first amount is of the second amount. Round your answers to 1 decimal place, if necessary.

a) $41.25, $550   [7.5%]

b) $675.00, $4500   [15%]

c) $18 750, $150 000   [12.5%]

Mental Math

1. Evaluate.

a) 6% of $40   [$2.40]

b) 3.5% of $500   [$17.50]

c) 20% of $65   [$13]

d) 75% of $600   [$450]

e) 15% of $5000   [$750]

f) 200% of $8.50   [$17]

2. If $f(x) = 3x^2 + 2x + 6$, find

a) $f(0)$ [6]   **b)** $f(-2)$ [14]

c) $f(5)$ [91]   **d)** $2f(-10)$ [572]

e) $-f(1) + 3$ [-8]   **f)** $xf(-1)$ [-7]

Explore/Inquire Answers

Explore: Use a Table

a) $1071.60   **b)** $840.00

Inquire

1. 6.5%   **2.** $71   **3.** B

4. Shorter amortization period means less interest is charged.

Teaching Suggestions

Read with the class the opening paragraphs on student text page 557. Discuss the terms "mortgagor" and "mortgagee." Ask:

What is the meaning of the prefix "mort"?

What other words do you know that have the prefix "mort"?

Ensure that the students recognize that the mortgagor is the person to whom the banks, or the mortgagees, give the mortgage.

Assign the Explore section and the Inquire questions to small groups of students. Have students discuss and compare their results. Have volunteers present their results to the class.

Review with the class teaching example 1 on student text page 558. Ask:

What is the difference between a personal loan from the bank and a mortgage?

Lead the students to see that a mortgage is secured with the property being purchased. Ask:

What does it mean to use the property as security for the mortgage?

Review the term "property tax." Ask:

How many students have family members who pay property taxes?

Do people who live in apartment buildings pay property taxes?

What are property taxes used for?

Who collects property taxes? Why?

Review with the class teaching examples 2 and 3 on student text page 559. For teaching example 3, ask:

What other costs are there in owning a home besides the monthly housing costs?

Is it less expensive to rent a home? Explain.

Number Power Answer

94 people each won $7000

Integrating Technology

Graphing Calculators

How would you use your graphing calculator to perform the mortgage calculation in method 2 of teaching example 1 on student text page 558? On a TI-83, the TMV Solver, which is the first item under the CALC menu when the FINANCE (i.e., 2nd x^{-1}) key is pressed, is used. See *Technology: Financial Calculations Using a Graphing Calculator* on page 368 of this teacher's resource for more information about the TMV Solver.

Use a graphing calculator to perform mortgage calculations in the questions on student text pages 560 and 561.

See *MATHPOWER*™ *11, Western Edition, Blackline Masters* pages 204 to 206 for Financial Calculations.

Internet

Use the Internet to find
- information about different types of mortgages and use it to answer question 37 on student text page 561
- information about equity in homes and use it to answer question 39 on student text page 561
- mill rates for your community and then, use them to answer question 40 on student text page 561

Extension

Research and write a few sentences about the origin of the word "mortgage" and explain the difference between a mortgage and a personal loan. Present your description to the class.

Enrichment

Write a short essay describing the advantages and disadvantages of owning a home compared to renting a home. Compare and discuss your point of view with those of some of your classmates. Add any advantages or disadvantages you learn from your classmates.

Math Journal

amortizing a mortgage   Describe the process of amortizing a mortgage. Include in your description terms and definitions associated with the process.

Problem Levels of Difficulty

A: 1–27, 40   **B:** 28–37   **C:** 38, 39

Assessing the Outcomes

Written Assignment

Romero bought a house for $225 000, with a 25% down payment. He arranged a 5-year mortgage at 6.5% per annum amortized over 25 years. The assessed value of his house, for the purposes of property taxes, is $195 000, and the mill rate for the house is 14.667.

a) Calculate Romero's monthly mortgage payment.

b) Calculate Romero's annual property taxes.

c) Calculate Romero's monthly housing costs.

9.7 Balancing a Budget

Student Text Pages
Pp. 562–566

Materials

graphing calculators, Teacher's Resource Master 8 (budget sheet), overhead projector, spreadsheet software

Learning Outcomes

- Complete a personal budget.
- Revise a budget.

Mental Math

1. Evaluate.

a) 35% of $30   [$10.50]

b) 80% of $2500   [$2000]

c) 1% of $35 750   [$357.50]

d) 0.5% of $80   [$0.40]

e) 12.5% of $2400   [$300]

f) 150% of $460   [$690]

2. Find the measure of the complementary angle to each of the following.

a) 42°   [48°]   **b)** 37°   [53°]

c) 1°   [89°]   **d)** 86°   [4°]

3. Find the measure of the supplementary angle to each of the following.

a) 65°   [115°]   **b)** 7°   [173°]

c) 21°   [159°]   **d)** 126°   [54°]

Explore/Inquire Answers

Explore: Interpret the Graph

a) elderly benefits   **b)** crown corporations

Inquire

1. a) $17.1 billion   **b)** $10.9 billion

2. Answers may vary. For example: for a provincial budget, health and education; for a municipal budget, snow removal and public transportation

3. taxes and transfer payments from the level of government above

4. Answers may vary. The only means of paying for services is by levying taxes on Canadians. It is useful to know where the money goes and how much is spent on each category.

5. A circle graph is useful to show into what categories a whole amount is divided.

Teaching Suggestions

(budget sheets) Read with the students the opening paragraph on student text page 562, and assign the Explore section and the Inquire questions to small groups of students. Have volunteers present their results to the class.

Review with the class the process of constructing a circle graph. Ask:

Under what circumstances do you think a person might complete a budget sheet?

Provide pairs of students with budget sheets, and have them complete their own budget sheet for their weekly expenditures. Have volunteers present their budgets to the class. Provide an overhead projector, if necessary.

Review with the class teaching examples 1 and 2 on student text pages 562 to 564.

Provide budget sheets for the students' use in the Applications and Problem Solving section.

Integrating Technology

Graphing Calculators

Use a calculator to perform the calculations required in the questions on student text pages 565 and 566.

Computer Spreadsheets

Use spreadsheet software to construct the graphs required in question 21 on student text page 565 and question 25 on student text page 566.

Extension

Create a personal weekly budget. Think of something special that you would like to buy, or an event that you would like to attend. Try to adjust your weekly budget so that you can pay for the item or the event yourself. Discuss and compare budgets with your classmates.

Enrichment

Research the meaning of the term "cash flow." Write a few sentences describing how you could use a personal budget to adjust your cash flow.

Problem Levels of Difficulty

A: 1–21, 27–29   **B:** 22–24   **C:** 25, 26

Assessing the Outcomes

Written Assignment

Marci has a monthly income of $1150, and she wants to share an apartment with Francine. The apartment rental is $950 per month, and the monthly utilities are as follows: hydro $52.50, telephone $35, cable $27.50.

Marci has the following monthly personal expenses: clothing $100, personal hygiene $25, food $75, transportation $80, entertainment $200.

a) Draw up a monthly budget for Marci. How much money does Marci have left for savings?

b) Marci would like to buy a used car. The monthly expenses for the car would be car loan $170 and running expenses $140. Make up a new budget to accommodate Marci's desire to buy the car. Make any necessary adjustments to her variable expenses in order to balance the budget.

Investigating Math

Financial Statements

Student Text Pages
Pp. 567–569

Materials
scientific or graphing calculators, overhead projector

Learning Outcomes
• Understand a bank statement.
• Reconcile a bank statement with a personal transaction record.
• Understand a small business account records.

Mental Math
1. Express each as a percent.

a) $7.00 out of $28   [25%]

b) $1.50 out of $150   [10%]

c) $1.75 out of $3500   [0.05%]

d) $2 out of $10   [20%]

e) $0.50 out of $8   [6.25%]

f) $10 out of $200   [5%]

2. Calculate.

a) 41^2 [1681]   b) 7.1^2 [50.41]

c) 0.91^2 [0.8281]   d) 3.1^2 [9.61]

e) 51^2 [2601]   f) 110^2 [12 100]

Teaching Suggestions
Review the terms "reconcile" and "personal transaction record." Ask:

How many of you have a direct debit bank card?

How many of you have a bank account?

Do you keep an up-to-date personal transaction record?

How often do you reconcile your bank statement?

What are the service charges on your bank account?

Organize the students into small groups. Have all the groups complete Investigation 1. Have volunteers present their results to the class. Provide an overhead projector, if necessary.

Review the terms "debit" and "credit."

Assign Investigation 2 to half of the groups and Investigation 3 to the other half of the groups. Give the groups completing the same investigation an opportunity to discuss and compare their results. Have volunteers present their results to the class. Provide an overhead projector, if necessary.

When the students have completed all the investigations, ask:

How many of you have ever kept a small business account record? Explain.

How many of you have ever read a financial statement other than a personal financial statement? Explain.

Enrichment
Write a short essay about service charges and whether you think they are too high. Include as many different instances in which you have been charged a financial charge.

Math Journal
debit, credit, reconcile, personal transaction record, service charge   Write a definition of each of these terms in your journal.

Assessing the Outcomes

Observation

• Does the student understand the concept of reconciling a bank statement?
• Does the student know the terminology associated with financial statements?
• Does the student persevere when looking for errors?
• Does the student help others understand the concept being studied?

Connecting Math and Transportation

So You Want to Buy a Car!

Student Text Pages
Pp. 570–571

Materials
graphing calculators

Learning Outcomes
- Make decisions about purchasing a car.
- Understand how to finance a car purchase.
- Understand the operating costs of a car?

Mental Math
1. Evaluate.

a)	$1\frac{1}{2}$% of $80	[$1.20]
b)	70% of $80	[$56]
c)	300% of $900	[$2700]
d)	90% of $295	[$265.50]
e)	15% of $550	[$82.50]
f)	4% of $45 000	[$1800]

2. Calculate.

a)	$1 + 2 + 3 + ... + 25$	[325]
b)	$1 + 2 + 3 + ... + 57$	[1653]
c)	$2 + 4 + 6 + ... + 28$	[210]
d)	$2 + 4 + 6 + ... + 36$	[342]
e)	$1 + 3 + 5 + ... + 31$	[256]
f)	$1 + 3 + 5 + ... + 63$	[1024]

Teaching Suggestions
Organize the class into 6 groups and assign each exploration to two groups. Ensure that all the explorations are assigned. Give the groups who are completing the same exploration ample time to discuss and compare their results. When the groups have completed the exploration have volunteers present their results to the class.

Integrating Technology

Internet
Use the Internet to find information in order to
- determine the actual price of the same car from two different retailers
- compare car dealership and bank financing costs
- determine the advantages and disadvantages of leasing a car
- estimate the cost of insuring a car and use the information to answer the questions on student text pages 570 and 571.

Math Journal
Write two advantages and two disadvantages of leasing a car over buying a new car.

Write two advantages and two disadvantages of buying a used car over buying a new car.

Assessing the Outcomes

Observation
- Does the student know the costs of buying a new car?
- Is the student able to assess the value of a used car?
- Does the student know the advantages and disadvantages of buying a new car over a used car?
- Does the student know the advantages and disadvantages of buying a new car over leasing a car?

Review

Student Text Pages
Pp. 572–573

Materials
scientific or graphing calculators

Learning Outcome
- Review the skills and concepts in Chapter 9.

Using the Review
Have the students work independently to complete the Review. Meeting in small groups, the students can mark and discuss the work. Groups can then share their solutions and report any questions that caused them difficulty. Discuss these questions with the class.

Reteaching Suggestions
For those students having difficulty with the chapter material, form small groups and use the following exercises.

If you feel that the class has had particular difficulty mastering any concept, you may wish to work through a problem from each section as a model of excellence of solution, which some students require just prior to assessment.

Earning Income
1. Marci earns $12.50/h plus time and a half for hours worked over 35 h each week. Last week she worked 42 h. What was her gross weekly earnings?
2. Margo is a clerk in an insurance company. She is paid $11.55/h, time and a half for hours in excess of 35 h, and double time for hours in excess of 42 h. One week she worked 45 h. What was her gross income for that week?
3. Remi is a retail salesman in a sports equipment store. Each week he earns $250 plus 5% commission on all sales. One week his total sales were $10 625. What were his gross earnings for that week?
4. The average daily tips for an evening shift at the Sports Cafe is $75 and for a day shift is $27. Each shift is 8 h in length and pays $7.75/h. One week Marco worked 3 day shifts and 2 evening shifts. Estimate his gross earnings for that week.
5. Jon charges $3.50 per page for word processing documents. One project was to input 275 pages of final copy. What did he charge for the project?

Net Income
1. Use the tax tables on student text page 534 to calculate the federal tax and the provincial tax on these annual taxable incomes.
   a) $42 500
   b) $26 345
2. Sula works in Victoria, British Columbia, and her annual salary is $47 880. Her personal tax credit is $6456 and she has $300 deducted each month for an RRSP.
   a) Calculate her annual deductions for CPP and EI.
   b) Calculate her net annual income.

Interest and Annuities
1. Find the amount of a $4500 Canada Savings Bond after 2 years, with interest at 4.25% per annum, compounded annually.
2. What amount is required to repay a loan of $5000 for 3 years with interest at 6.8% per annum, compounded semi-annually?
3. Jamil deposited $250 in a savings account one March 1. He deposited $250 on the first day of each of the next 3 months. The account paid interest of 3.2% per annum, compounded semi-annually.
   a) What amount was in his account at the end of one year?
   b) How much interest did he earn on his savings?

Effective Annual Rate of Interest
1. What is the effective annual interest rate on an investment that earns 4.5% per annum, compounded quarterly? Round your answer to 1 decimal place.
2. Which is the better investment, A or B?
   A: $1000 invested at 6.6% per annum, compounded quarterly for 2 years
   B: $1000 invested at 7% per annum, compounded semi-annually for 18 months

Consumer Credit
1. A racing bicycle sells for $785, including taxes. With a down payment of $100, the monthly payments are $121.20 for 6 months.
   a) What is the instalment plan price?
   b) What is the finance charge?
2. Rona's balance owing on a retail store's charge card is $685. If the credit charge is 1.9% per month, what is Rona's balance owing on her next month's statement? Assume Rona made no additional transactions.

Housing Costs

1. Salvatore bought a house for $135 000. He paid 30% down and obtained a 5-year mortgage at 6.5% amortized over 25 years.

a) Use the monthly amortization table on student text page 590 to calculate his monthly mortgage payment.

b) If you assume that the terms of the mortgage continue for the balance of the 25 years, how much would Salvatore pay for the house?

2. The assessment value of a house is $205 000. If the residential mill rate is 13.266, what is the annual property tax on the house?

Balancing a Budget

1. This year, Gwen has a net annual income of $24 650 plus $1500 in earned interest from investments. Her annual expenses are: accommodation $11 400, food $3500, utilities $495, telephone and cable $635, house insurance $290, car licence $90, car insurance $855, gasoline $760, car repairs $500, clothing $1500 entertainment $2890, and personal care products $375. She saves the balance of her income.

a) Complete an annual budget statement.

b) Her goal is to save at least 10% of her annual income each year? Will she meet her goal for this year if she sticks to her budget? Explain.

c) What percent of her annual income did she save this year?

Answers to Reteaching Suggestions

Earning Income

1. $568.75   2. $594.83   3. $781.25
4. $589.00   5. $962.50

Net Income

1. a) Federal: $8386.90, Provincial: B.C. $4235.38, Alta $3816.04, Sask $4193.45, Man $4361
   b) Federal: $4478.65, Provincial: B.C. $2261.72, Alta $2037.79, Sask $2239.33, Man $2328.90
2. a) CPP $1180.80, EI $1053
   b) $27 680.43

Interest and Annuities

1. $4890.63
2. $6110.73
3. a) $1080.57   b) $330.57

Effective Annual Rate of Interest

1. 4.6%
2. A $1139.88, B $1108.72, A is better.

Consumer Credit

1. a) $827.20   b) $42.20
2. $698.02

Housing Costs

1. a) $633.15   b) $230 445
2. $2719.53

Balancing a Budget

1. b) Her expenses amount to $23 290. She would like to save at least $2329 this year.
   c) $2860

Exploring Mathematics

Perfect, Abundant, Deficient, and Amicable Numbers

Begin by reviewing with the class the terms "perfect," "abundant," "deficient," and "amicable." Ask:

What does perfect mean?

What does abundant mean?

What does deficient mean?

What does amicable mean?

Why do you think each of these numbers was named as such?

Which divisor of a number is not a proper divisor?

Is it possible for a number to be both abundant and deficient? abundant and perfect? deficient and perfect? Explain.

Assign the exploration to pairs of students. When they have completed the questions, have volunteers present their results to the class.

Chapter Check

Learning Outcome
- Evaluate the skills and concepts in Chapter 9.

Assessing the Outcome
If you assign the Chapter Check as a student assessment, look for the following.
- Can they calculate their gross income and net income?
- Can they calculate the interest earned from simple interest and compound interest?
- Can they compare different investments?
- Can they calculate the amount of an annuity?
- Can they calculate the effective annual rate of interest?
- Can they use effective annual rates of interest to decide which investment is better?
- Can they calculate the interest on a retail charge account and on a bank credit card?
- Can they calculate the total instalment cost of an item?
- Can they calculate the monthly payment for a mortgage?
- Can they calculate the property taxes for a house?
- Can they calculate the monthly housing costs of a property?
- Can they complete a personal budget?
- Can they revise a personal budget?

Problem Solving

Materials
scientific or graphing calculator, overhead projector

Learning Outcome
- Use problem solving strategies to solve problems.

Using the Strategies
The problems on this page allow the students to use the problem solving strategies discussed in Chapters 1 to 3. These strategies are
- Use a Diagram
- Use a Data Bank
- Solve Fermi Problems
- Solve a Simpler Problem
- Use Logic
- Look for a Pattern
- Guess and Check
- Work Backward
- Use a Table or Spreadsheet

Teaching Suggestions
Encourage the students to work in pairs or small groups.

For question 2, have the students draw $\angle ABC$, mark point E inside the angle, and join B and E.

Then, have the students mark point D between A and E, and join BD. Thus, $\angle ABC = \angle ABD + \angle DBE + \angle EBC$. Next, have the students relocate point D between E and C and join BD. Now, $\angle ABC \neq \angle ABD + \angle DBE + \angle EBC$ because $\angle DBE$ is part of $\angle ABD$ and so it is included twice. Thus, this one counterexample, disproves the statement.

For question 4, point out that, another way of approaching the question is to ask:
How many three-digit whole numbers contain the digits 0, 3, and 7?

Have the students explain this question. Thus, the problem to be solved is now:
In how many ways can a three-digit whole number be formed from the digits 0, 3, and 7?

For question 6, suggest that the students take a very quick informal survey of the number of people wearing apparel with professional sports team logos. Remind the students that a survey of the students in the school is biased, as young people are more likely to wear such an article of clothing. A survey of a group of people on the street is more accurate.

For question 10, ask:

What type of expression is $x^2 + 10x$?

Help the students see that $y = x^2 + 10x$ is a quadratic function that opens upward. Thus, the value of the expression at the turning point is a minimum. Suggest that the students find the vertex of the quadratic function $y = x^2 + 10x$ and read the value of x that corresponds to the minimum value of the function.

$$y = x^2 + 10x$$
$$= (x + 5)^2 - 25$$

The vertex is $(-5, -25)$. So, the minimum value is -25, and occurs when $x = -5$.

When students have completed the problems, have them share and discuss their strategies and solutions with other students. Have volunteers present their results to the class. Provide an overhead projector, if necessary.

The sum of the digits in the hundreds column plus the one carried is E, or 4. Thus, the sum of the digits in the hundreds column is 3. Thus, D is 1.

The digits are D = 1, E = 4, F = 8.

Assessing the Outcome

Observation

As you make your problem solving assessment of each student, consider the following:
- Do they understand the problem?
- Do they consider a variety of strategies?
- Do they use an organized approach?
- Do they create and use diagrams effectively?
- Do they show persistence?

Sample Solution

Page 575, question 8

Since E is the first digit of the answer, it cannot equal 0. If F = 1, 2, or 3, then no amount is carried to the next column. If you carry 0, then you have to answer the question for the digits in the tens column:

What digit, when you multiply it by 3 gives a number whose final digit is the original digit? No digit gives this result.

If F = 4, 5, or 6, then 1 is carried to the next column. If you carry 1, then you have to answer the question for the digits in the tens column:

What digit, when you multiply it by 3 and then add 1 to the result, gives a number whose final digit is the original digit. No digit gives this result.

If F = 7, 8, or 9, then 2 is carried to the next column. If you carry 2, then you have to answer the question for the digits in the tens column:

What digit, when you multiply it by 3 and then add 2 to the result, results in a number whose final digit is the original digit?

For example, $3 \times 4 + 2 = 14$.

Thus, E could be 4.

If E is 4, then, the sum of the digits in the units column must end in 4 and have a tens digit of 2. Thus, $3 \times 8 = 24$, F = 8.

Cumulative Review, Chapters 1–9

Learning Outcome

- Review skills and concepts in chapters 1 to 9.

Teaching Suggestions

Method 1

The review of these four chapters can take several days.

Divide the class into groups of four. Each group is to decide which chapter each student will review. The students who are assigned the same chapter are to then form expert groups. They are to decide on strategies for reviewing the questions and solutions with their home groups. They are also to be the discussion leaders for the questions in these groups, ensuring that all of the group members can complete each question and explain each solution.

Each student from the expert group is to then return to his or her home group and lead a review of the chapter he or she was assigned.

Method 2

Have pairs of students choose one question from every section in each of the chapter reviews, The partner may correct the answers. If a student is having difficulty with any particular type of question, reteach the concepts to the student, and assign other similar questions for reinforcement.

Reteaching Suggestions

Without solving, determine whether each system has no solution, one solution, or infinitely many solutions. Then, solve the systems with one solution graphically.

1. $3x - y = 7$
$x - 2y = 4$

2. $5x - y + 4 = 0$
$5x - y - 2 = 0$

3. $y = \frac{1}{2}x + 3$
$2y = x + 6$

4. $10x - y = -7$
$x - y - 2 = 0$

Solve each system by substitution. Check each solution.

5. $3x + y = 7$
$-7x + y = -3$

6. $y = -\frac{1}{2}x - 3$
$y = 3x + 4$

Solve each system by elimination. Check each solution.

7. $2x - y = 5$
$5x + y = -5$

8. $y = 5x + 7$
$3y - 5x = 1$

9. $x - 2y = 27$
$2x + y = -1$

10. $3x - 2y = -7$
$6x - 5y = -19$

Which method would you use to solve each system of equations? Explain. Then, solve and check each system.

11. $y = 4x - 2$
$y = -11x - 2$

12. $x + y = 7$
$2x - 3y = -16$

13. $2x + 5y = 20$
$-x + 5y = 5$

14. $-5x + 3y = 35$
$3x + 4y = -21$

Solve each system of equations. Check each solution.

15. $m + n - p = -\frac{1}{2}$
$3m + n = 1$
$n = -2$

16. $a + 2b - c = -5$
$-3a + 4b + c = 24$
$2a + b + 2c = -2.5$

17. Numbers The sum of two numbers is 160. Three times the larger number plus four times the smaller number is 549. What are the numbers?

18. Birds Twice the average mass of the emu is 5 kg more than three times the average mass of the greater rhea. The average mass of the greater rhea plus half the average mass of the emu is 45 kg. What is the average mass of each bird?

Solve and check.

19. $m + 3 < -2$

20. $3a - 2 \geq 7$

21. $5(n + 1) \leq -20$

22. $4x + 10 < -x - 5$

23. $3(f + 2) - 1 > 2(f - 3) + 2$

24. $\frac{y}{4} - 2 \leq 1$

25. $\frac{2}{3}z + 2 > 4$

26. $\frac{n + 2}{3} < \frac{5 + n}{2}$

27. $\frac{k - 1}{4} \geq \frac{2k + 5}{3} - \frac{3}{2}$

Which of the given ordered pairs are solutions to the inequality?

28. $5m + 2n > -2$ $(0, 0), (-2, -3), (1, 7), (0, -1)$

Graph each inequality.

29. $y < x + 2$

30. $x - y \geq 5$

31. $2x + y > -3$

32. $2x - 3y + 1 \leq 3x$

33. $y \geq \frac{2}{3}x - 5$

34. $\frac{x}{2} + \frac{3}{4}y < -1$

Solve each system of inequalities by graphing.

35. $x + y \geq 5$
$x - y < -5$

36. $y < -2$
$x + 2y \leq 1$

37. $y \geq 2x + 1$
$3x < 2y - 10$

38. $x + 2y \leq 5$
$\frac{3}{5}x + y > 0$

39. $3x + 7y > 0$
$-x - y \leq -3$

40. $5x + y - 4 < 0$
$-3x + 6y \geq 1$

41. Grace has dimes and quarters in her pocket that total at least $20.

  a) Write an inequality that represents the numbers of dimes and quarters in her pocket.

  b) State any restrictions on the variables.

  c) Graph the inequality.

Without sketching each parabola, state

a) *the direction of the opening*

b) *the coordinates of the vertex*

c) *the equations of the axis of symmetry*

d) *the domain and range*

e) *the maximum or minimum value*

42. $y = -3x^2$

43. $f(x) = x^2 - 2$

44. $y = (x - 3)^2 + 2$

45. $f(x) = -2(x + 5)^2$

46. $y = 4(x - 1)^2 - 2$

47. $y = -\frac{1}{3}(x + 5)^2 + 6$

Write an equation that defines each parabola.

48. vertex $(0, -1)$; passing through $(2, 1)$

49. congruent to $y = x^2$, opens down; vertex $(0, -2)$

50. vertex $(3, 5)$; passing through $(-1, -1)$

51. vertex $(-2, -3)$; y-intercept 3

Find the coordinates of the vertex.

52. $y = x^2 - 2x - 2$

53. $y = x^2 + 10x + 24$

54. $y = \frac{2}{3}x^2 + 12x$

55. $y = 2x^2 - 16x + 21$

56. The height of a rocket fired down a practice range, h, in metres, after t seconds, is given by $h = -\frac{1}{4}t^2 + 3t + 45$.

a) What is the maximum height of the rocket?

b) How long did it take the rocket to reach its maximum height?

c) What was the initial height of the rocket?

57. A rectangular field is to be enclosed with 600 m of fencing. What dimensions will produce a maximum area?

Solve by graphing.

58. $x^2 + 2x = 3$

59. $x^2 + 7x = -10$

Solve. Express radical solutions in simplest radical form.

60. $n^2 = -2n + 5$

61. $2m^2 - 3m - 6 = 0$

62. $x^2 + 11 = 90$

63. $-5x^2 = -x - 3$

64. $3b^2 + 4b + 1 = 0$

65. $m^2 - m = 15$

66. $6x^2 + 5x = 2$

67. $-5 = -2x^4 + 3x^2$

Determine the nature of the roots.

68. $2x^2 - 5x + 3 = 0$

69. $x^2 - 6x + 9 = 0$

Solve. Round your answers to the nearest hundredth, if necessary.

70. $x^2 - 3x + 1 = 0$

71. $x^2 - 11x = 3$

72. Write a quadratic equation with roots 4 and $-\frac{3}{4}$.

73. Determine the values of k that will give two distinct real roots for $3x^2 + 10x - k = 0$.

74. Factor $z^3 + 2z^2 - z - 2$ completely.

Find the exact roots.

75. $z^3 + 2z^2 - 2z - 1 = 0$

76. $2m^3 = 5m^2 + 13m + 5$

77. For $f(x) = x^2 + 2$ and $g(x) = 3x + 1$, find

a) $(f + g)(x)$

b) $(f - g)(x)$

c) $(fg)(x)$

d) $\left(\dfrac{f}{g}\right)(x)$

e) $-f(x) + 4g(x)$

f) $(ff)(x) + (gg)(x)$

78. For $(f)(x) = 3x + 1$ and $(g)(x) = 2\sqrt{x}$, find

a) $(f \circ g)(x)$ and $(g \circ f)(x)$, if each exists

b) the domain and range of f, g, $f \circ g$, and $g \circ f$

Find the inverse of each relation.

79. $y = 1 + \dfrac{1}{x}$

80. $y = \dfrac{4x - 3}{3x + 2}$

81. Graph $y = x^3 + x^2 - x - 1$ and determine

a) the domain and range

b) any real zeros and the y-intercept

c) the coordinates of any relative maximums or relative minimums

d) the intervals where $f(x) > 0$ and $f(x) < 0$

e) any symmetry and the end behaviour

82. Graph $f(x) = |x^2 - 3|$ and

a) determine the domain and the range

b) determine the values of any real zeros

c) describe any symmetry

83. Graph $y = \dfrac{2x}{x^2 - 9}$ and determine

a) the equations of any asymptotes

b) the domain and range

84. Graph $y = \sqrt{x + 3} - 7$ and determine the domain and the range.

Solve and check.

85. $|3x + 2| = -2x$

86. $|x - 3| = -3x - 5$

Solve. Graph each solution.

87. $|x + 1| = |2x - 7|$

88. $|x + 3| \le 2$

89. $|x + 2| < |x - 1|$

Show each solution set on a number line.

90. $m < 5$ and $m > -3$

91. $n \ge 2$ or $n < -1$

92. $p < 3$ and $p \le -2$

93. $k > -1$ or $k > 2$

94. Guests at a party chose from a buffet containing potato salad, lasagne, and mixed vegetables.
25 guests chose potato salad
20 guests chose lasagne
32 guests chose vegetables
10 guests chose lasagne and vegetables
8 guests chose potato salad and lasagne
15 guests chose potato salad and vegetables

4 guests chose potato salad, lasagne, and vegetables

6 guests chose neither potato salad, lasagne, nor vegetables

   a) Show the data on a Venn diagram.

   b) How many guests were at the party?

   c) How many guests chose only lasagne?

   d) How many guests chose potato salad but not vegetables?

95. VW and XY intersect at D, the midpoint of VW and XY. Write a flow-chart proof to show that VX∥YW.

96. A circle with centre O has a radius of 8 cm. The distance from O to a chord is 4.5 cm. Find the length of the chord. Round your answer to 1 decimal place.

Find the values of the variables.

97.

98.

99. Find the measure of ∠NMK and ∠NKM.

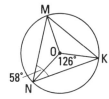

100. AB is the diameter of a circle and C is another point on the circle. F lies on AC, G lies on chord BC, and FH is perpendicular to AB. Prove that H, F, C, and B are concyclic points.

101. In the following diagrams, tangents have been drawn to circles. Find the values of the variables.

   a)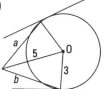

   b)

102. PL and PK are tangents from an external point P that meet the circle with centre O at L and K. LOM is a diameter and ∠PKL = 53°. Find ∠KOM.

103. Calculate the length of arc ABC and the area of the sector ABCO. Round answers to 1 decimal place.

104. What is the sum of the measures of the interior angles of a decagon?

105. The sum of the interior angles of a polygon is 1800°. How many sides does the polygon have?

106. The measure of the exterior angles of a regular polygon is 36°. How many sides does the polygon have?

107. The coordinates of the vertices of △XYZ are X(−1, 1), Y(3, 4), and Z(3, −2).

   a) Prove that △XYZ is isosceles.

   b) Find the coordinates of the midpoints of the sides of △XYZ.

   c) Join the midpoints of △XYZ and prove that the resulting triangle is also isosceles.

108. Determine the coordinates of the points that divide the line segment with endpoints D(9, −5) and E(−3, 1) into 6 equal parts.

109. Write the equation of a circle with centre (−4, −1) and radius $\frac{1}{2}$.

110. Find the shortest distance from (−4, −5) to the line $y = 3x + 1$. Round your answer to 1 decimal place.

111. Write an equation of the tangent at the point (−2, −4) on the circle $(x + 1)^2 + (y + 1)^2 = 10$.

112. Stevie works as a groomer on a horse farm and is paid $10.50/h. One week he works 38.5 h. What is his gross income for that week?

113. Jose earns straight commission of 3.5% on sales of investments. Over a 2-week period his sales totalled $126 600. What was his gross earnings for that 2-week period?

114. Sabrina sells educational toys at private home parties. Her monthly income is 5% of the first $5000 of sales plus 7% of sales in excess of $5000. In December Sabrina's sales totalled $25 632. What was her gross monthly income for that month?

115. Joko is a tour guide for a bus company and earns $11.75/h. He has to give 20% of any tips he receives to the bus driver. One bus trip takes 6 h and he receives an average of $150 in tips per trip. One week he completed 4 bus tours. What was his gross weekly earnings for that week?

116. Ariadne is a tailor and charges $210 to sew a dress. One month she sewed 13 dresses. What was her gross income for that month?

117. Brandon works in Medicine Hat. His gross monthly income is $3950 and his personal tax credit is $6456. His monthly deductions are $45 for disability insurance, $27 for union dues, and $150 for an RRSP. Calculate

   a) his gross annual salary.

   b) his annual deductions for EI and CPP.

   c) his total annual taxes.

   d) his annual net income.

118. Find the value of a $10\ 000 Canada Savings Bond after 4 years with interest at 3.75% per annum, compounded annually.

119. Brandon borrows $6500 at 9.5% per annum, compounded semi-annually. What interest does he pay on the loan after 2 years?

120. What is the effective annual interest rate on an investment that earns 5.75% per annum, compounded monthly?

121. A stereo system sells for $305, including taxes. With a down payment of $50, the monthly payments are $22.98 for 12 months.
  a) What is the instalment plan price?
  b) What is the finance charge?

122. Noreen bought a house for $209 000. She paid 25% down and obtained a 7-year mortgage at 7% per annum, amortized over 20 years. Use the monthly amortization table on student text page 590 to calculate her monthly mortgage payment.

123. The assessment value of a house is $169 000. If the residential mill rate is 17.299, what is the annual property tax on the house?

124. Jamil has a net monthly income of $1050. He wants to rent an apartment. The monthly expenses for the apartment are: rent $800, utilities $120, telephone $35, and cable $24.50. His estimates for other monthly expenses are: food $275, clothing $100, transportation $90, entertainment $300, and personal items $40.
  a) Make up a monthly budget for Jamil's expenses.
  b) If Jamil stayed true to his budget, how much could he save each month?
  c) Next year, he wants to take a trip. The total cost of the trip would be $900. How much would Jamil have to add to his trip fund each month?
  d) Can he afford to go? Explain.
  e) How could he adjust his monthly budget so that he would be able to take the trip?

Reteaching Suggestions
Student Answers

1. one; $(2, -1)$　　**2.** none

3. infinitely many; Answers may vary, for example, $(4, 5)$

4. one; $(-1, -3)$　　**5.** $(1, 4)$　　**6.** $(-2, -2)$

7. $(0, -5)$　　**8.** $(-2, -3)$　　**9.** $(5, -11)$

10. $(1, 5)$　　**11.** $(0, -2)$　　**12.** $(1, 6)$

13. $(5, 2)$　　**14.** $(-7, 0)$

15. $m = 1, n = -2, p = \frac{1}{2}$

16. $a = -5, b = 1.5, c = 3$

17. 91, 69

18. emu 40 kg, greater rhea 25 kg

19. $m < -5$　　**20.** $a \geq 3$　　**21.** $n \leq -5$

22. $x < -3$　　**23.** $f > -9$　　**24.** $y \leq 12$

25. $z > 3$　　**26.** $n > -11$　　**27.** $k \leq -1$

28. $(0, 0), (1, 7)$

41. a) $10x + 25y \geq 2000$　**b)** $x \geq 0, y \geq 0, x, y \in W$

42. a) downward　**b)** $(0, 0)$　　**c)** $x = 0$
  d) domain: $x \in R$; range: $y \leq 0, y \in R$
  e) maximum 0

43. a) upward　**b)** $(0, -2)$　　**c)** $x = 0$
  d) domain: $x \in R$; range: $y \geq -2, y \in R$
  e) minimum -2

44. a) upward　**b)** $(3, 2)$　　**c)** $x = 3$
  d) domain: $x \in R$; range: $y \geq 2, y \in R$
  e) minimum 2

45. a) downward　**b)** $(-5, 0)$　　**c)** $x = -5$
  d) domain: $x \in R$; range: $y \leq 0, y \in R$
  e) maximum 0

46. a) upward　**b)** $(1, -2)$　　**c)** $x = 1$
  d) domain: $x \in R$; range: $y \geq -2, y \in R$
  e) minimum -2

47. a) downward　**b)** $(-5, 6)$　　**c)** $x = -5$
  d) domain: $x \in R$; range: $y \leq 6, y \in R$
  e) maximum 6

48. $y = \frac{1}{2}x^2 - 1$　　**49.** $y = -x^2 - 2$

50. $y = -\frac{3}{8}(x - 3)^2 + 5$　　**51.** $y = \frac{3}{2}(x + 2)^2 - 3$

52. $(1, -3)$　　**53.** $(-5, -1)$　　**54.** $(-9, -54)$

55. $(4, -11)$

56. a) 54 m　　**b)** 6 s　　**c)** 45 m

57. 150 m $\times$ 150 m　**58.** $x = 1, -3$

59. $x = -2, -5$

60. $-1 \pm \sqrt{6}$　　**61.** $\dfrac{3 \pm \sqrt{57}}{4}$

62. $\pm\sqrt{79}$　　**63.** $\dfrac{1 \pm \sqrt{61}}{10}$

64. $-\dfrac{1}{3}, -1$　　**65.** $\dfrac{1 \pm \sqrt{61}}{2}$

66. $\dfrac{-5 \pm \sqrt{73}}{12}$　　**67.** $\pm\sqrt{\dfrac{5}{2}}, \pm i$

68. real, unequal　　**69.** real, equal

70. 2.62, 0.38　　**71.** 11.27, -0.27

72. $4x^2 - 13x - 12 = 0$　　**73.** $k > -\dfrac{25}{3}, k \in R$

74. $(z - 1)(z + 1)(z + 2)$　　**75.** 1, $\dfrac{-3 \pm \sqrt{5}}{2}$

76. $-\dfrac{1}{2}, \dfrac{3 \pm \sqrt{29}}{2}$

77. a) $x^2 + 3x + 3$

    b) $x^2 - 3x + 1$

    c) $3x^3 + x^2 + 6x + 2$

    d) $\dfrac{x^2 + 2}{3x + 1}$

    e) $-x^2 + 12x + 2$

    f) $x^4 + 13x^2 + 6x + 5$

78. a) $f \circ g = 6\sqrt{x} + 1$, $g \circ f = 2\sqrt{3x + 1}$

    b) f: domain: $x \in R$; range: $y \in R$

    g: domain: $x \geq 0$, $x \in R$; range: $y \geq 0$, $y \in R$

    $f \circ g$: domain: $x \geq 0$, $x \in R$; range: $y \geq 1$, $y \in R$

    $g \circ f$: domain: $x \geq -\dfrac{1}{3}$, $x \in R$; range: $y \geq 0$, $y \in R$

79. $y = \dfrac{1}{x - 1}$

80. $y = \dfrac{-2x - 3}{3x - 4}$

81. a) domain: $x \in R$; range: $y \in R$

    b) zeros ± 1; y-intercept -1

    c) relative maximum $(-1, 0)$,

    relative minimum $\left(\dfrac{1}{3}, \dfrac{-32}{27}\right)$

    d) $f(x) > 0$ for $-\dfrac{3}{2} < x < 1$; $f(x) < 0$ for $1 < x < 2$

    e) no symmetry; the left-hand most values are negative, the right-hand most values are positive

82. a) domain: $x \in R$; range: $y \geq 0$, $y \in R$

    b) $\pm\sqrt{3}$

    c) symmetry about the y-axis

83. a) $x = \pm 3$

    b) domain: $x \neq \pm 3$, $x \in R$; range: $y \in R$

84. domain: $x \geq -3$, $x \in R$; range: $y \geq -7$, $y \in R$

85. $-\dfrac{2}{5}, -2$

86. -4

87. $2, 8$

88. $-5 \leq x \leq -1$

89. $x < -\dfrac{1}{2}$

90.

91.

92.

93.

94. a) 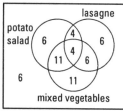   **b)** 54 **c)** 6 **d)** 10

96. 13.2 cm

97. $a = 35$, $x = 90$, $y = 50$

98. $m = 50$, $b = n = z = 40$

99. $\angle NMK = 63°$, $\angle NKM = 59°$

101. a) $a = b = 4$ **b)** $y = z = 30$, $x = 60$

102. $74°$

103. 104.7 cm, 2618.0 cm²

104. $1440°$

105. 12

106. 10

107. b) $(1, 2.5), (3, 1), (1, -0.5)$

108. $(-1, 0), (1, -1), (3, -2), (5, -3), (7, -4)$

109. $(x + 4)^2 + (y + 1)^2 = \dfrac{1}{4}$

110. 1.9 units

111. $x + 3y + 14 = 0$

112. \$404.25

113. \$4431

114. \$1694.24

115. \$762

116. \$2730

117. a) \$47 400   **b)** EI \$1053, CPP \$1180.80

    c) \$10 712.51   **d)** \$31 789.69

118. \$11 586.50

119. \$1325.81

120. 5.9%

121. a) \$325.76   **b)** \$20.76

122. \$1205.41

123. \$2923.53

124. b) \$65.50   **c)** \$75

    d) No; he does not have enough left over to add \$75 to his trip fund each month.

    e) Answers will vary.

CHAPTER 9

Student Text Answers

Chapter Opener p. 523
1. US Civil War
2. World War I
3. The Great Depression
4. World War II
5. a) 30%   b) 30%   c) 40%

Getting Started pp. 524–525
1 Comparing Unit Prices
1. a) the price of a specified unit of a product
   b) olive oil: $0.0144/mL, $0.0120/mL;
   tomato ketchup: $0.0053/mL, $0.0036/mL;
   orange juice: $0.0020/mL, $0.0017/mL; bleach:
   $0.0014/mL, $0.0009/mL
   c) Answers may vary.
2. olive oil: 500 mL; tomato ketchup: 1.25 L;
   orange juice: 1.89 L; bleach: 1.8 L
3. a) The larger size has a lower unit price.
   b) Answers may vary.
4. Answers may vary. The person may not need the
   larger size, or may not have enough storage space.

2 Buying at a Supermarket
1. bagels: Foodmart; oranges: EconoFoods;
   detergent: EconoFoods; cream cheese: Foodmart
2. Answers may vary. You assume quality is the same,
   and in products such as bagels and oranges, you
   assume size is the same.
3. Answers may vary. quality
4. Answers may vary. quality, location, selection

3 Warm Up
Estimates may vary for 1–7.

1. $39	2. $93	3. $4
4. $26	5. $360	6. $1.10
7. $630	8. $22.40	9. $327.82
10. $4.563	11. $84.60	12. $448
13. $15 620	14. $23.65	15. $425.21
16. 0.3, 30%	17. 0.25, 25%	18. 0.5, 50%
19. 0.17, 17%	20. 0.8, 80%	21. 0.32, 32%
22. 0.55, 55%	23. 1.25, 125%	24. 0.75
25. 0.07	26. 0.045	27. 0.0275
28. 1.25	29. 0.005	

Estimates may vary for 30–37.

30. 60	31. 2400	32. $500	33. $3
34. $1	35. $5200	36. $800	37. $17
38. $4852.80	39. $234	40. $690	41. $36

42. $0.44	43. $0.27

44. $3 out of $10
45. $8 out of $40
46. $18 out of $192

Mental Math

1. $8.75	2. $0.25	3. $0.60	4. $0.48
5. $48	6. $130	7. $1.50	8. $60
9. $15	10. $0.18	11. 5.5%	12. 16%
13. 13%	14. 5%	15. 0.1%	16. 1%
17. 0.5%	18. 0.25%		

Multiplying Numbers That Differ by 10 and End in 5

1. 375	2. 2475	3. 9975	4. 16 875
5. 357 500	6. 637 500	7. 15.75	8. 80.75

9. The numbers are $10x + 5$ and $10x - 5$. Their
   product is $(10x + 5)(10x - 5) = 100x^2 - 25$.
10. a) Drop the 5 from the larger, and add to the
    smaller, multiply and subtract 75.
    b) The numbers are $10x - 5$ and $10(x + 1) + 5$.
    Their product is $100x^2 + 100x - 75$, or
    $100x(x + 1) - 75$.

Investigating Math p. 526
1 Converting Currencies
1. a) drachma, krona, krone, peseta
   b) 196 078 drachma; 5200 krona; 4331 krone;
   96 154 peseta
2. $524.35
3. $38 142.50
4. a) $63 792.50   b) 243 390 francs
5. $152.57
6. No. The exchange rate may change in four years.
7. a) 38 462 bolivar; 65 pesos   b) 6 pesos

2 Buying and Selling
1. The bank pays less if you are selling than they
   charge if you are buying. This is how they
   make money.
2. 71% represents a Canadian dollar worth US71¢.
   132% represents a US dollar worth $1.32 Canadian.
3. a) increased   b) decreased

Section 9.1 pp. 530–531
Practice (Section 9.1)

1. 15	2. 9	3. 22.5	4. 28.5
5. 5.25	6. 18.75		

7. a) $3640 **b)** $840 **c)** $24/h
8. $495 **9.** $560 **10.** $384 **11.** $521.25
12. $814.13 **13.** $5570 **14.** $1960.10 **15.** $360
16. a) the 40-h week **b)** $52
17. $2211 **18.** $15 600 **19.** $1239.75

Applications and Problem Solving (Section 9.1)
20. $42 **21.** $524.10 **22.** $422.50
23. $588 **24.** $3038.50
25. a) piecework **b)** $470 **c)** tips
26. 15%
27. a) He would earn $87 more for Option B.
  b) Answers may vary. Option A: pays less,
  but Anton can improve his keyboarding;
  Option B: pays more, but no room for improvement
28. a) $2195, $2187.53, $2330.72, $2339.76
29. a) A: $2625; B: $3000; C: $3125
  c) $15 000

Section 9.2 pp. 536–537

Practice (Section 9.2)
1. 52 **2.** 12 **3.** 26
4. 24 **5.** $17.09 **6.** $16.60
7. $63.21 **8.** $55.08 **9.** $11.53
10. $40.67 **11.** $11.02 **12.** $29.75
13. $58.73 **14.** $43.88 **15.** $18.47
16. $37.87 **17.** $4556 **18.** $3111.85
19. $5692.78 **20.** $9874.10 **21.** $14 457.90
22. $1647.33 **23.** $1421.66 **24.** $2551.83
25. $1507.95 **26.** $904.34
27. CPP: $1068.80; EI: $1053; taxable income:
  $39 294; basic federal tax: $6095.11
28. CPP: $844.80; EI: $807.30; taxable income:
  $29 900; basic federal tax: $3332.51

Applications and Problem Solving (Section 9.2)
29. a) CPP: $896; EI: $850.50 **b)** $6219.38
30. a) CPP: $1068.80; EI: $1053 **b)** $11 861.03
  c) $31 881.17
31. $35 389.06
32. $27 485.41
33. a) $2980 **b)** $26 881.28
34. a) the employer's earnings
  b) Answers may vary. **c)** Answers may vary.
35. a) $582.75 **b)** Answers may vary.
36. Net claim code is a category on which the amount
  of tax deduction is based.
  b) Codes are based on the personal tax credit an
  employee expects to have.
37. Answers may vary.
38. Answers may vary.

Section 9.3 pp. 542–543

Practice (Section 9.3)
1. 4% **2.** 2% **3.** 0.667%
4. 0.022% **5.** 6 **6.** 8
7. 5 **8.** 48 **9.** 6
10. 6 **11.** 31 **12.** 61
13. 1.5%; 12 **14.** 3%; 12 **15.** 6%; 10
16. 0.5%; 12 **17.** 0.016%; 30 **18.** $2604.52
19. $2389.66 **20.** $3077.25 **21.** $2029.81
22. $97.42 **23.** $34.85 **24.** $59.18
25. $2.78 **26.** $3738.55 **27.** $2089.36
28. $2813.77

Applications and Problem Solving (Section 9.3)
29. $2567.36 **30.** $20 805.70
31. $1210.54 **32.** $13 589.85
33. a) Option C **b)** $2.18
34. a) $2122.35 **b)** $122.35
35. a) $108, $116, $124, $132, $140, $148, $156, $164,
  $172, $180, $188, $196; $108.24, $117.17, $126.82,
  $137.28, $148.59, $160.84, $174.10, $188.45,
  $203.99, $220.80, $239.01, $258.71 **c)** Yes.
  There is only one y-value for each x-value.
  d) Simple interest gives a straight line. The amount
  of interest is the slope, and it does not change.
  Compound interest gives a curve. Since the
  interest is increasing, the slope is increasing.
36. $3653.45
37. about 18 years

Technology pp. 544–545

1 No Payments Made
1. $5378.54
2. 5.25 years
3. 7.86%
4. 7% compounded annually

2 Monthly Payments Made
1. Yes. $3139.27 must still be paid.
2. −$8261; The annuity has run out.
3. 6.87%
4. $462.32
5. a) $306 837.52 **b)** 10.84% **c)** $329.52
  d) Yes. The earlier you start, the more interest
  you earn.

Technology p. 546

1 Annuity Remaining
1. Answers may vary.
2. $4254.52
3. after 3 years
4. a) $34 371.59 **b)** $56 394.89 **c)** $18 938.81

2 Annuity Payments

1. a) $701.33 **b)** $424.94 **c)** $1267.43 **d)** $113.55

Section 9.4 pp. 549–550

Practice (Section 9.4)

1. 8.16%	**2.** 8.24%	**3.** 8.30%
4. 12.55%	**5.** 6.09%	**6.** 8.57%
7. 5.06%	**8.** 7.71%	**9.** 5.97%
10. 4.33%		

Applications and Problem Solving (Section 9.4)

11. 5.25% compounded semi-annually; $1.92
12. a) A **b)** A: 8.77%; B: 8.30%
13. the bank loan
14. 7.12%
15. a) The annual rate is the daily rate times 365.
b) 1.53% **c)** 20.03%
16. 19.56%
17. a) Option A: 7.02%; Option B: 7.2%
b) Answers may vary. She may think the interest rate will go down.
18. a) 12%, 12.36%, 12.49%, 12.55%, 12.62%, 12.68%, 12.72%, 12.73%
c) 12.75% **d)** 12.75%
19. a) 7.71% **b)** 10.67% **c)** 9.65% **d)** 6.40%
20. 6.4%

Section 9.5 pp. 555–556

Practice (Section 9.5)

1. a) $375.12 **b)** $46.12
2. a) $1700 **b)** $220 **c)** $2420

3. $9.55	**4.** $4.24	**5.** $0.83
6. $10.25	**7.** $5.88; $397.88	
8. $0.95; $64.40	**9.** $0.72; $48.97	
10. $1.24; $83.75	**11.** $4.43	**12.** $0.81
13. $3.82	**14.** $5.94	**15.** $5.42
16. $0.44	**17.** $0.98	**18.** $0.13
19. $2.82	**20.** $3.11	**21.** $114.40
22. $217.69	**23.** $500.94	**24.** $437.75
25. $601.71		

Applications and Problem Solving (Section 9.5)

26. a) $554.85 **b)** $419.85 **c)** $4118.85
27. Answers may vary.
28. $298.51
29. a) $7.01 **b)** $483 **c)** $93.55
d) $3 **e)** $93.07
30. a) The store's offer is less expensive.
b) Answers may vary.

Section 9.6 pp. 560–561

Practice (Section 9.6)

1. $50 000	**2.** $7375	**3.** $4995
4. $20 625	**5.** $822.03	**6.** $1513.53
7. $1138.29	**8.** $1174.68	**9.** $745.20
10. $1074.00	**11.** $1264.36	**12.** $3492.72
13. $2140.45	**14.** $2533.25	**15.** $4899.76
16. $7535.63	**17.** $8176.96	**18.** $13 676.36
19. $2093.94	**20.** $177 895.83	**21.** $40 073.82
22. $1 155 167.75	**23.** $34 445	**24.** $64 353.35
25. $443 164.36		

Applications and Problem Solving (Section 9.6)

26. a) $669.82 **b)** $200 946 **c)** $100 946
27. a) $144 900 **b)** $1157.17
28. a) $126 000 **b)** $882.52
c) $313 756 **d)** $138 756
29. $19 449.16
30. a) $1638.11 **b)** $766.64
31. $1333.84
32. a) $1135.32 **b)** $996.30
33. $1218.41
34. $4806.86
35. a) $307.42 **b)** Answers may vary.
36. 6.6599
38. a) $152 188 **b)** $1293.60 **c)** $4784

Section 9.7 pp. 565–566

Practice (Section 9.7)

1. education/reading
2. gifts
3. shelter
4. utilities
5. personal care
6. food
7. entertainment
8. gifts
9. food
10. clothing or personal care
11. charitable donations
12. personal care
13. home furnishings
14. clothing
15. balanced
16. surplus of 6.5%
17. deficit
18. surplus of 7.6%
19. $48.50
20. b) $780

Applications and Problem Solving (Section 9.7)

21. a) $675

22. a) Hydro: $76.92, $25.64; Gas: $80.75, $26.92;
Food: $410.17, $136.72; TV: $22, $7.33;
Phone: $35, $11.67   **c)** $510.83

24. a) 34.8%, 18.6%, 9.3%, 7.1%, 7.0%, 23.2%
c) −$26.41, +$37.50, −$61.69, +$5.60, $0, +$45

Investigating Math   pp. 567–569

1 Understanding a Bank Statement

1. a) $1807   **b)** Debit is an amount subtracted
from an account, and credit is an amount added
to an account.

2. a) Direct debit is the use of your bank card in a
store or a bill payment is taken directly from your
account; instant teller withdrawal is withdrawal of
money from a bank machine.

3. It was cashed first.

4. Yes, if the bank allows overdrafts.

5. Option A

2 Reconciling a Bank Statement with a Personal Transaction Record

1. Answers may vary.

2. Answers may vary.

3. a) The error was writing $88.95 instead of $88.59
for cheque 003.

Connecting Math and Transportation
pp. 570–571

1 Which Car to Buy?

1. freight and dealer preparation, taxes, licence,
possibly dealer options

4. "Black book" value is the average retail price of the
given model, with stated options, in good condition.

2 Financing a Car Purchase

1. a) $1880   **b)** $493   **c)** the bank

3 Operating Costs

1. fixed: depreciation, insurance, licence;
variable: gas, maintenance

3. $20 480

Review   pp. 572–573

1. $435.63   **2.** $239.25   **3.** $3240
4. $90.80   **5.** $3548.41   **6.** $2566.23
7. $5528.81   **8.** $4672.10   **9.** $1159.58
10. $998.30   **11.** $1565.49
12. a) CPP: $1068.80; EI: $1053   **b)** $9613.01
c) $28 165.19
13. $5705.83   **14.** $309.08

15. a) $2838.51   **b)** $338.51
16. a) $2704.43   **b)** $204.43
17. 4.59%   **18.** Option A
19. $5\frac{1}{4}$% compounded semi-annually
20. a) $300.98   **b)** $11.98
21. $8.97; $607.22
22. $1.63; $110.13
23. $13.90; $940.68
24. $15.83; $1071.13
25. a) $0.29   **b)** $0.54   **c)** $0.68
26. $441.86   **27.** $58.89   **28.** $2366.25

Exploring Math   pp. 573

1. deficient   **2.** deficient   **3.** perfect
4. deficient   **5.** abundant   **6.** deficient
7. deficient   **8.** abundant   **9.** perfect
10. abundant   **11.** deficient   **12.** abundant
13. sum of proper factors of 220: 284; sum of proper
factors of 284: 220
14. sum of proper factors of 1184: 1210; sum of proper
factors of 1210: 1184
15. No. Since the proper factors of any perfect number
add to the number itself, they cannot add to any
other number.

Chapter Check   p. 574

1. a) $682.50   **b)** $435   **c)** $483.75
d) $1347.50
2. $1300   **3.** $309
4. a) $86.67   **b)** $81   **c)** $6503.62
5. $358.24   **6.** $2045.42   **7.** 9.2%
8. a) $518.18   **b)** $88.87   **c)** 20.7%
9. $254 579.50
10. a) $0.98   **b)** $1.31   **c)** $0.98   **d)** $4.42
11. $1144.28
12. $1281.30
13. a) $2866.26   **b)** $786.26

Using the Strategies   p. 575

1. 10
3. no
4. 18
5. 785 m
7. $x = 2y − z$
8. D = 1, E = 4, F = 8
9. 441, 1444
10. −25
11. 343
12. a) 219, 438, 657
b) 327, 654, 981 and 273, 546, 819

1. a) increase   **b)** $55+$ years

Cumulative Review, Chapters 1–9
pp. 576–579

1. one solution; $(-2, 2)$
2. no solution
3. one solution; $(-4, -4)$
4. infinitely many solutions
5. $(2, -1)$ **6.** $(-\frac{1}{2}, 2)$ **7.** $(-1, 0)$
8. $(2, 1)$ **9.** $(2, -1)$ **10.** $(-3, 2)$
11. $(-2, 0)$ **12.** $(1, -3)$ **13.** $(2, -\frac{1}{2})$
14. $(2, -2)$ **15.** $(3, 2, 1)$ **16.** $(-1, 1, 0)$
17. length: 563 km, breadth: 257 km
18. bachelor: 48; 1-bedroom: 60; 2-bedroom: 60
19. $p < -7$ **20.** $b > 3$ **21.** $f \geq 4$
22. $n \leq 12$ **23.** $g \leq 2$ **24.** $y > -12$
25. $x \leq 12$ **26.** $m > 11$ **27.** $d < \frac{7}{3}$
28. $(1, 6), (-5, 1), (-2, -2)$
41. a) $5x + 8y \leq 40$ **b)** $x \geq 0, y \geq 0$
42. a) down   **b)** $(0, 0)$ **c)** $x = 0$
    d) domain: all real numbers, range: $y \leq 0$
    e) maximum: 0
43. a) up   **b)** $(0, 5)$ **c)** $x = 0$
    d) domain: all real numbers, range: $y \geq 5$
    e) minimum: 5
44. a) down   **b)** $(1, -3)$ **c)** $x = 1$
    d) domain: all real numbers, range: $y \leq -3$
    e) maximum: -3
45. a) up   **b)** $(5, 0)$ **c)** $x = 5$
    d) domain: all real numbers, range: $y \geq 0$
    e) minimum: 0
46. a) up   **b)** $(-3, -4)$ **c)** $x = -3$
    d) domain: all real numbers, range: $y \geq -4$
    e) minimum: -4
47. a) down   **b)** $(-7, 2)$ **c)** $x = -7$
    d) domain: all real numbers, range: $y \leq 2$
    e) maximum: 2
48. $y = 4x^2 + 3$ **49.** $y = -(x + 2)^2 - 3$
50. $y = \frac{1}{2}(x + 2)^2 + 5$ **51.** $y = (x + 3)^2 - 3$
52. $(5, -13)$ **53.** $(-4, 15)$
54. $(3, -3)$ **55.** $(1, 1)$
56. a) 8 m   **b)** 10 m   **c)** 1 m
    d) 1.7 m   **e)** 20.7 m
57. a) 200 m by 200 m   **b)** 40 000 m²
58. $-4, 3$ **59.** $3, 5$
60. $-1, 9$ **61.** $-2, \frac{1}{3}$
62. ± 11 **63.** $\dfrac{-9 \pm \sqrt{69}}{2}$

64. $\dfrac{5 \pm \sqrt{33}}{4}$ **65.** $-1, -2$
66. $-\frac{1}{5}, -1$ **67.** $\pm\dfrac{1}{\sqrt{3}}$
68. no real roots   **69.** real, equal
70. $1, 2$ **71.** $-7.14, 0.14$
72. $3x^2 + 13x - 10 = 0$ **73.** $k < \dfrac{25}{8}$
74. $(2p - 1)(p + 1)(p - 1)$ **75.** $3, \pm 1$
76. $-\frac{1}{2}, 1, 2$
77. Yes. 180 cm by 90 cm   **78.** 0.75 m
79. a) $(f + g)(x) = 4x^2 + 2x - 12$
    b) $(f - g)(x) = 4x^2 - 2x - 6$
    c) $(fg)(x) = 8x^3 - 12x^2 - 18x + 27$
    d) $\left(\dfrac{f}{g}\right)(x) = 2x + 3, x \neq \dfrac{3}{2}$
    e) $f(x) + 3g(x) = 4x^2 + 6x - 18$
    f) $(gg)(x) + f(x) = 8x^2 - 12x$
80. a) $(f \circ g)(x) = \sqrt{5x + 3}, (g \circ f)(x) = 5\sqrt{x + 3}$
    b) f: domain: $x \geq -3$, range: $y \geq 0$;
    g: domain: all real numbers, range: all real numbers;
    $f \circ g$: domain: $x \geq -\dfrac{3}{5}$, range: $y \geq 0$;
    $g \circ f$: domain: $x \geq -3$, range: $y \geq 0$
82. a) domain: all real numbers, range: all real numbers
    b) $-1, 5; -5$
    c) maximum: $(-1, 0)$; minimum: $(3, -32)$
    d) $f(x) > 0$: $x > 5$; $f(x) < 0$: $x < -1, -1 < x < 5$
    e) no symmetry; negative, positive
83. a) domain: all real numbers, range: $y \geq -5$
    b) $-3, 3$ **c)** $x \leq -3, x \geq 3$
    d) symmetric about the y-axis
84. a) $x = 0, y = x$
    b) domain: $x \geq 0$, range: all real numbers
85. domain: $x \geq 2$, range: $y \geq 3$
86. $\dfrac{4}{5}$ **87.** 2   **88.** $w < 8$ **89.** $g \geq 2$
90. b) $\dfrac{n(n + 1)}{2}$ cubes make n steps.
92. 4 has square roots -2 and $+2$; 0 has only one square root of 0
93. a) The result is one greater than the original number.
98. b) 45
99. a) false
    b) If a whole number is a factor of 12, then it is a factor of 24; true
    c) If a whole number is not a factor of 12, then it is not a factor of 24; false
102. 6.0 m
104. $x = 50°, y = 25°$
105. $a = 90°, b = 15°$
106. $a = 110°, b = 110°, c = 70°$
107. $p = 85°, q = 75°, r = 105°, s = 85°, t = 95°,$
    $u = 105°$

109. $a = 60°$, $b = 60°$, $c = 60°$

110. $x = 12$ cm, $y = 14$ cm, $z = 15$ cm

111. 64.8 cm^2

112. 9

113. 30

114. 18

115. PQ $= \sqrt{73}$, QR $= \sqrt{73}$; Thus, PQ $=$ QR and $\triangle$PQR is isosceles.

116. $(-5, -3)$, $(-3, 0)$, $(-1, 3)$

117. $\left(1, \dfrac{7}{3}\right)$, $\left(4, \dfrac{11}{3}\right)$

118. 3; 12; 2.91

119. 7; 3.5; 3.13

120. $(-3, 6)$, 6

121. $(4, 0)$, $\sqrt{10}$

122. a) $(2, -3)$, $(3, 2)$ **b)** 5.1

123. a) no points of intersection

124. $3x - 2y + 1 = 0$

125. 99.1°

126. 13.07

127. $468.75

128. $812.50

129. $650

130. $583

131. $518

132. CPP: $80.27; EI: $75.60

133. $830.62

134. 5.64%

135. $205

136. $960.06

Teacher's Resource Master 2
1-cm Grid Paper

x^2-tiles

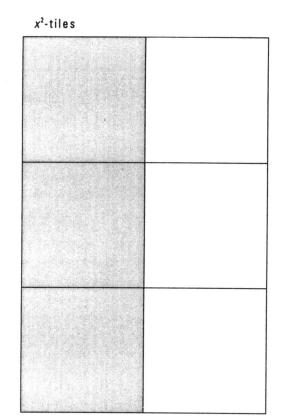

x-tiles

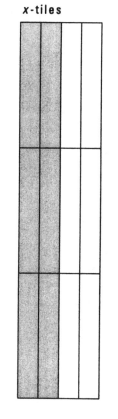

1-tiles

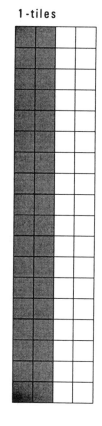

xy-tiles

y^2-tiles

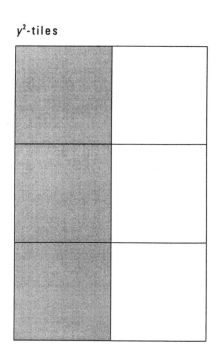

y-tiles

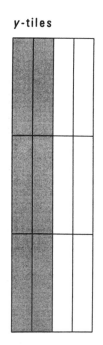

$-xy$-tiles

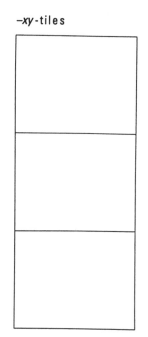

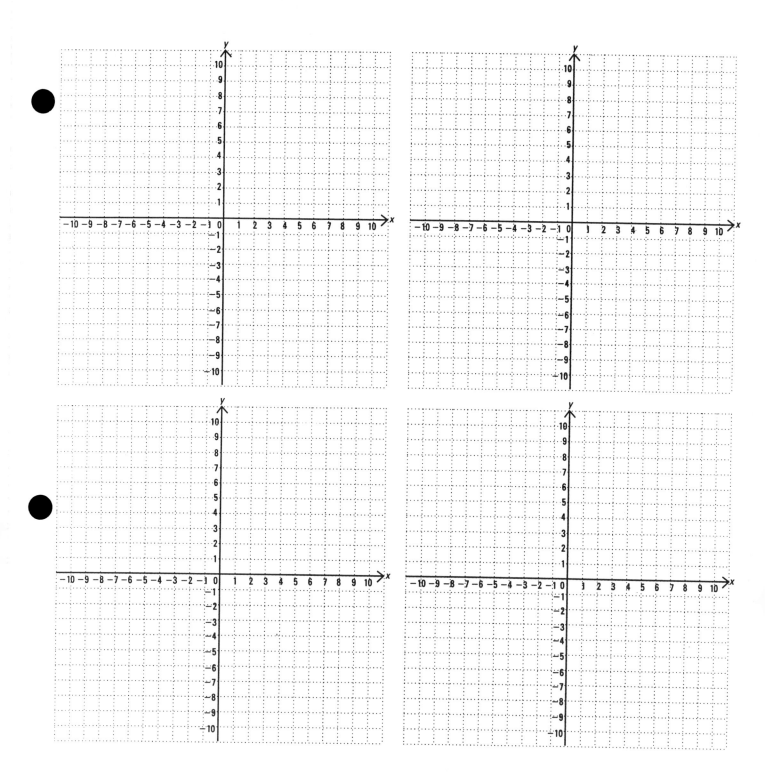

Teacher's Resource Master 6
2-cm Grid Paper

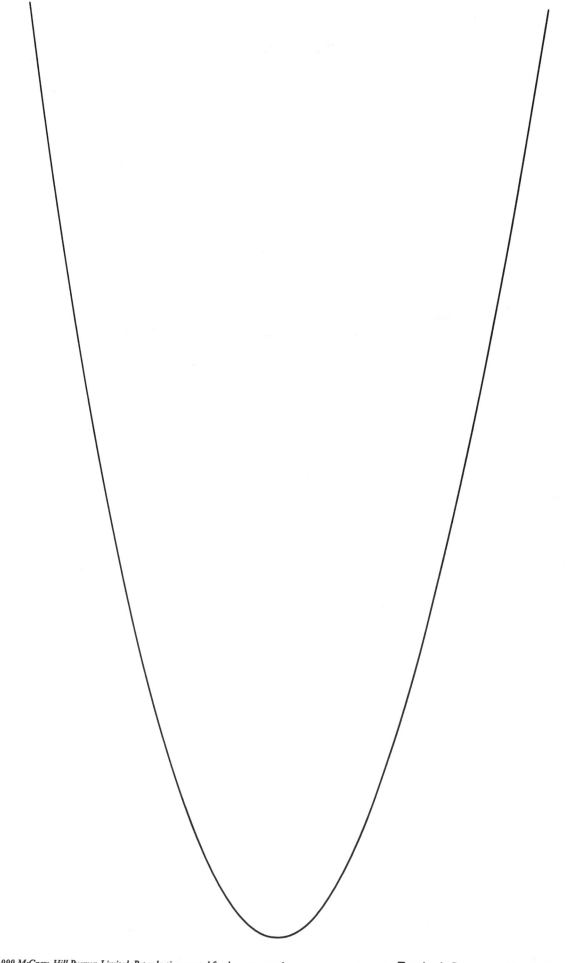

Budget Statement

Income

Item	
Net Employment Income	
Investments	
Gifts	
Other	
Total	

Expenditures

Fixed Expenses		Variable Expenses		Occasional Expenses	
Item	*Amount*	*Item*	*Amount*	*Item*	*Amount*
Shelter		Food		Home Repairs	
Utilities		Clothing		Home Furnishings	
Car Licence		Gasoline		Charitable Donations	
Car Insurance		Entertainment		Gifts	
Home Insurance		Education/Reading		Travel	
Cable TV		Personal Care		Personal Business	
Other		Telephone		Car Repairs	
Other		Other		Other	
Total		Total		Total	

Total Expenditures =

Balance = Total Income − Total Expenditures

    =

    =

Observation Checklist

Class: _____   Date(s): _____

Name										

Assessing Students and Mathematics

Name: _____   **Date:** _____ ⬤

Topic: _____

What did you like about this topic?

_____

_____

_____

How is this topic based on other mathematics you have learned?

_____

_____

_____

What did you find surprising about the mathematics in this topic?

_____

_____ ⬤

_____

What do you think is important to you about this topic?

_____

_____

_____

What would you like to know more about in this topic?

_____

_____

_____

What would you like to see changed about the mathematics in this topic?

_____

_____

_____

⬤

Attitudes Assessment

Name: _____ **Date:** _____

	Rarely	Sometimes	Frequently
Perseveres at tasks.	☐	☐	☐
Asks questions when it is necessary.	☐	☐	☐
Completes tasks.	☐	☐	☐
Shows confidence with mathematical ideas.	☐	☐	☐
Tries another method when the first method does not work.	☐	☐	☐
Works well individually.	☐	☐	☐
Works well in a pair.	☐	☐	☐
Works well in a group.	☐	☐	☐
Shows independent thinking.	☐	☐	☐
Appreciates the value of mathematics.	☐	☐	☐
Enjoys the challenge of the unknown.	☐	☐	☐
Is willing to take risks.	☐	☐	☐
Is curious about mathematics.	☐	☐	☐

Problem Solving Checklist

Name: _____   Date: _____

	Rarely	Sometimes	Frequently
Understands the problem.	☐	☐	☐
Thinks of a plan.	☐	☐	☐
Carries out the plan.	☐	☐	☐
Looks back.	☐	☐	☐
Uses a variety of strategies.	☐	☐	☐
Combines strategies when appropriate.	☐	☐	☐
Develops and applies own strategies.	☐	☐	☐
Understands that different strategies can solve a problem.	☐	☐	☐

Comments: _____

_____

_____

_____

_____

_____

_____

_____

_____

Individual Observations

Name: _____   Date(s): _____

Observation Notes: _____

_____

_____

_____

_____

_____

_____

_____

Action Required: _____

_____

_____

_____

_____

_____

_____

Action Taken: _____

_____

_____

_____

_____

Interview

Name: _____   Date(s): _____

Interview Topic: _____

_____

_____

Interview Procedure: _____

_____

_____

Interview Results: _____

_____

_____

_____

Action Required: _____

_____

_____

_____

_____

Action Taken: _____

_____

_____

_____

_____

Group Work Assessment

Group Members: _____

Assignment: _____

Date(s): _____

	Rarely	Sometimes	Frequently
Makes a plan for the task before acting.	☐	☐	☐
Revises a plan when appropriate.	☐	☐	☐
Clearly and confidently presents and explains ideas.	☐	☐	☐
Takes an active role in the group.	☐	☐	☐
Supports arguments with evidence.	☐	☐	☐
Listens to and considers the arguments of others.	☐	☐	☐
Becomes involved in the task.	☐	☐	☐
Offers assistance to others.	☐	☐	☐
Organizes and interprets data.	☐	☐	☐
Uses time in a productive way.	☐	☐	☐
Explains relationships.	☐	☐	☐
Uses manipulatives when appropriate.	☐	☐	☐
Uses needed tools effectively.	☐	☐	☐
Completes the task.	☐	☐	☐
Records the results.	☐	☐	☐
Reviews the process and the results.	☐	☐	☐
Synthesizes and summarizes the results.	☐	☐	☐

Group Self-Assessment

Group Members: _____   **Date:** _____

_____

Assignment: _____

The purpose of this assignment was _____

_____

We completed this assignment by _____

_____

_____

_____

_____

We found that _____

_____

_____

_____

_____

As a group, we were good at _____

_____

As a group, we were not good at _____

_____

We could improve our group work by _____

_____

Assessing Working in a Group

Name: _____ **Date:** _____

Group Members: _____

When I agree with the people in my group, I _____

_____

When I disagree with the people in my group, I _____

_____

When I disagree with the people in my group, my group _____

_____

When I understand what the people in my group are saying, I _____

_____

When I do not understand what the people in my group are saying, I _____

_____

_____

When someone else in my group does not understand what the people in my group are saying, I _____

_____

_____

When I do not understand the mathematics, I _____

_____

_____

When I find a different way to solve a problem my group is working on, I _____

_____

When I find a different way to solve a problem my group is working on, my group _____

_____

_____

Self-Assessment

Name: _____ Date: _____

Place a check mark in the appropriate box, or complete the sentence.

	Yes	No	Unsure
I can solve most mathematics problems with little difficulty.	☐	☐	☐
Often, I do not know how to begin a problem.	☐	☐	☐

When the problem is too difficult, I _____

_____

The most important thing in mathematics is _____

_____

I would use the mathematics in this section/chapter in my life to _____

_____

	Yes	No	Unsure
I like the parts of mathematics that can be memorized.	☐	☐	☐
I like the parts of mathematics I need to work out for myself.	☐	☐	☐

The problems I like best are _____

_____

	Yes	No	Unsure
There is only one way to solve each problem in mathematics.	☐	☐	☐
There are often several ways to solve a mathematical problem.	☐	☐	☐

I really enjoy _____ in mathematics.

I could do better in mathematics if _____

MATHPOWER™ 11, Western Edition, Teacher's Resource Credits